APPLIED
SOCIAL
PSYCHOLOGY

APPLIED SOCIAL PSYCHOLOGY

Second Edition

Stuart Oskamp
Claremont Graduate University

P. Wesley Schultz
California State University, San Marcos

Prentice Hall, Upper Saddle River, New Jersey 07458

Library of Congress Cataloging-in-Publication Data

Oskamp, Stuart.
  Applied social psychology / Stuart Oskamp, P. Wesley Schultz. —
2nd ed.
    p.   cm.
  Includes bibliographical references and index.
  ISBN 0–13–533837–9
  1. Social psychology.   I. Schultz, P. Wesley.   II. Title.
HM251.075   1998
302—dc21   97–15004
                                                CIP

Editorial director: Charlyce Jones Owen
Editor-in-chief: Nancy Roberts
Executive editor: Bill Webber
Assistant editor: Jennifer Hood
Managing editor: Bonnie Biller
Project manager: Fran Russello
Editorial/production supervision and interior design: Mary McDonald/P.M. Gordon Associates
Prepress and manufacturing buyer: Lynn Pearlman
Cover design: Kiwi Design
Marketing manager: Michael Alread
Copy editor: David Watt

This book was set in 10/12 Times Roman by The Composing Room of Michigan, Inc.
and was printed and bound by RR Donnelley & Sons Company.
The cover was printed by Phoenix Color Corp.

 © 1998, 1984 by Prentice-Hall, Inc.
Simon & Schuster/A Viacom Company
Upper Saddle River, New Jersey 07458

Printed in the United States of America
10   9   8   7   6   5   4   3   2   1

ISBN 0-13-533837-9

Prentice-Hall International (UK) Limited, *London*
Prentice-Hall of Australia Pty. Limited, *Sydney*
Prentice-Hall Canada, Inc., *Toronto*
Prentice-Hall Hispanoamericana, S.A., *Mexico*
Prentice-Hall of India Private Limited, *New Delhi*
Prentice-Hall of Japan, Inc., *Tokyo*
Simon & Schuster Asia Pte. Ltd., *Singapore*
Editora Prentice-Hall do Brasil, Ltda., *Rio de Janeiro*

To Catherine and Lori,
for all your love, support, time, sacrifices,
compromises, discussions, critiques, and confidence.

Contents

Preface

Applied social psychology is "where the rubber hits the road." That is, it can provide crucial tests of the validity and strength of our psychological theories. It is an exciting area, where psychological methods and findings are brought to bear on problems of society and on policies to combat them. Applied social psychologists can make a difference to the functioning of individuals, groups, and organizations, and we hope this volume conveys much of the excitement of this growing and important field.

The first edition of this book was hailed by some reviewers as a classic that helped to define the young field of applied social psychology. Like its predecessor, this second edition aims at being (a) rigorous in presenting well-founded empirical science with thorough detail and references, (b) broad and comprehensive in its coverage of topics, (c) intensive rather than superficial, by exploring key topics in depth, (d) clear in its writing and organization, (e) interesting in its selection of topics that are important as well as motivating to readers, and (f) effective pedagogically, by including learning aids such as chapter outlines, summaries, key terms shown in boldface and defined, and suggestions for further reading.

Because of its breadth and coverage of interdisciplinary research, this book should be appropriate as a text for courses on applied social research, social problems, or policy issues in departments of psychology, sociology, public policy, political science, and communications. It is designed for upper division and graduate students who have completed basic courses in some social science and who have some understanding of social research methods and how to interpret research findings and data tables.

The volume has four main sections. The first section presents an introduction and overview of the field's scope, concepts, and theories. The second section contains five chapters that summarize key aspects of the field's main research methods. Each of these chapters contains an extended illustration of studies that have used the research methods on important topics (e.g., effects of television, drug prevention programs). The third section has eight chapters covering the eight most heavily researched areas of the field. Each of these chapters presents a brief summary of the varied types of research in that area, including references that students and instructors can use for further reading and background; each chapter then focuses in depth on a full discussion of one central subtopic (e.g., gender and ethnic diversity, job satisfaction, environmental conservation, or consumer advertising). Finally, the fourth section discusses the crucial but rarely presented topic of achieving social change, with chapters on social activism and influencing public policy.

In addition to retaining the strengths of the first edition, this edition has expanded its coverage to include newly developing areas of the field. Two entirely new chapters cover gender and ethnic diversity, and consumer advertising. Other new sections of chapters include work on drug prevention programs, sexual behavior, education methods for a multicultural society, ecological sustainability, health promotion programs, eyewitness accuracy, and welfare reform. All topics have been thoroughly updated, with many references from the last few years. The learning aids of key terms highlighted in boldface and defined, chapter outlines, summaries, and suggested readings for further exploration should help students' comprehension and professors' use of the book's material.

We have many people to thank for their part in making this a successful volume. First, the psychology department at Claremont Graduate School, which has been an academic home for both of us, and second, our wives and families, for making our other home a source of love and support. The library staff and computer facilities at St. Lawrence University aided in the background research. Our colleagues Allan Wicker, Stewart Donaldson, Cherry Granrose, Cathy Crosby-Currie, Tom Greene, and Kim Mooney have offered help and constructive advice. Reviewers who read the manuscript and made suggestions for additions include Thomas Pettigrew of the University of California at Santa Cruz, Linden Nelson and Shawn Burn of California State Polytechnic University at San Luis Obispo, Marti Gonzalez of the University of Minnesota, and Kellina Craig of the University of Illinois. Students Maria Arrigo, Sara Austin, Larry Daniels, and Dan Gray helped to provide ideas and library materi-

als, as did Jane Eaton and Barbara Joyce. Departmental secretaries Jane Gray, Gloria Leffer, Kathy Lenz, and B. J. Reich expedited much correspondence and copying, and our word processors saved much secretarial labor. At Prentice Hall, Heidi Freund, Nancy Roberts, Emsal Hasan, and Bill Webber were helpful in many phases of the book's development, and Mary McDonald served as the production editor. We thank them all for their assistance.

We hope that this edition will meet with as much approval as the first one did, and that readers will find its material as fascinating as we do.

Stuart Oskamp
Claremont, California

P. Wesley Schultz
San Marcos, California

CHAPTER 1

Applying Social Psychology—Typical Features, Roles, and Problems

All science must be applied science, the goal of which is to lighten the toil of everyday life.

—Galileo

Social psychology, briefly defined, is the scientific study of relationships between people. It develops systematic knowledge about people's beliefs, feelings, and behavior concerning their social environment, and the effects of their social environment on them. Despite the goal stated in Galileo's quotation above, much of psychology (like other sciences) is not applied.

Applied social psychology, again stated very simply, takes some aspect of the knowledge base of social psychology and applies it systematically for some social purpose. The purposes for which social psychological knowledge is used, however, are not scientifically governed and can be extremely varied—from advancing world peace to selling iceboxes to Eskimos. We will return to a fuller consideration of these definitions shortly. In recent years applied social psychology has been expanding rapidly on many different fronts, so let's begin with some examples of its variety.

One well-known social psychologist, Edwin Hollander, summarized his own participation in a fascinating variety of projects. Topics of his work have included attitudes toward the uses of atomic power, opinions about various political leaders, prediction of long-term job performance, and advice on how to maintain effective group functioning on lengthy space flights. His atomic power study was sponsored by UNESCO in order to compare the attitudes of young people in several different countries, while his report on interpersonal factors in space flight was of crucial interest to the U.S. authorities in NASA (Hollander, 1979).

Similarly, a French applied psychologist, Claude Levy-Leboyer (1988), has described several of her applied projects. They included helping to design TV presentations on alcoholism prevention, analyzing reasons for high versus low turnover of nursing personnel in wards of Parisian hospitals, finding and correcting reasons for vandalism to public phone booths, and determining acceptable schedules for weekend night work shifts for heavy machine operators in an automobile factory.

Another social psychologist, Judith Rodin, gave testimony to a U.S. congressional committee in hearings about the budget of the National Science Foundation. She began by stating, "We stand at the threshold of an era where the burdens of modern society can, in large part, be attributed to problems of behavior." As examples, she cited problems of energy use, overcrowding of cities, poverty, and crime, as well as her own research on the causes and consequences of obesity in humans. She concluded that solutions to these problems "rely heavily on the scientific study of human behavior" (Lowman, 1980, p. 160).

Social psychologists can attack social problems on several different levels. For instance, on an *individual* level, the widespread problem of personal shyness was studied by social psychologist Philip Zimbardo and his colleagues. Their research culminated in a popular book offering scientifically based advice on how to overcome shyness (Zimbardo, 1977).

At the level of *group interactions*, the social problems of prejudice and racism have concerned social psychologists for most of this century. Over 40 years ago social psychological research was cited in the Supreme Court's decision outlawing racial segregation in schools in the case of *Brown v. Board of Education* (Cook, 1979). In subsequent years, many social psychologists have worked toward improving interracial relations in desegregated schools, for example by introducing theory-based systems of small-group cooperative learning. We will discuss educational issues of this sort in Chapter 8.

Social psychologists have also been active at the level of complex organizations. Notable examples include "team-building" approaches to foster cooperative work-team efforts toward common goals; innovative organizational procedures such as "quality circles," participative management, and employee ownership; and emphasis on humanizing the work environment and improving the "quality of working life." A critical issue in recent years is how to handle increasing ethnic, cultural, and gender diversity among organizational members (cf. Chemers, Oskamp, & Costanzo, 1995). We will discuss some of these applications of social psychology in organizational settings in both Chapters 9 and 10.

Finally, in the area of government policy and programs, there has been a wide range of social science research. There are notable examples concerning programs to fight poverty, such as the famous negative income tax experiment sponsored by the Office of Economic Opportunity, programs to improve health care, and educational innovations such as Head Start (cf. Zigler & Muenchow, 1992). Some of these are described in more detail in Chapter 17.

A DEFINITION OF APPLIED SOCIAL PSYCHOLOGY

After these examples, let us consider definitional issues more carefully. Defining any intellectual discipline or field of knowledge is a nebulous endeavor because discipline boundaries often shift as trends and emphases in the field change. For this reason the most complete, though not elegant, definitions are ones stated in terms of what topics are being worked on— for example, defining "psychology" as "what psychologists do"—because such definitions are the only ones likely to capture the full range of a field.

For a more systematic approach, however, we suggest defining **applied social psychology** as *applications of social psychological methods, theories, principles, or research findings to understanding or solution of social problems.* In adopting this definition, we should realize that applied work in turn can contribute fruitfully to fundamental psychological theories, principles, and methods (cf. Leventhal, 1980). Thus the direction of influence is reciprocal—from basic psychology to applied work, and from applied psychology back to basic knowledge.

The above definition of applied social psychology aims at being inclusive but also focused. Note that it specifies a problem orientation: Applied work begins with a group or societal problem, not just with scientific curiosity about some phenomenon. The definition also implies heavy concentration on field settings—

that is, natural settings where social problems are manifested—though it does not prevent the use of laboratory experiments when they can help to solve problems. Furthermore, it suggests serious attention to encouraging social change through the solution of social problems—a much more activist stance than social psychologists have traditionally taken. The phrase "solution of social problems" should be interpreted broadly to include helping groups of people and organizations, as well as attempting to influence public policy. Finally, the definition includes the use of social psychological methods, not just theories or research findings—an important additional aspect of applied work that has often been overlooked or excluded by more restrictive definitions.

Some authors would not define applied social psychology so broadly, particularly in reference to its use of methods. It is clear that many of the methods used by social psychologists are not unique to them but are also used by sociologists, political scientists, economists, or members of other social science disciplines (for instance, this is true of survey research, of evaluation research, and of many statistical techniques such as multiple regression analysis). In fact, social psychology is a field shared and contributed to by sociologists as well as psychologists. Thus, some of the methods and the findings discussed in this book can be referred to more broadly as "applied social science," and some of the work cited here has been done by researchers from other social science disciplines, not just by people who would call themselves "psychologists."

Nevertheless, where social psychologists have worked productively in a research area, and where they have used social psychological concepts, principles, and theories to explain their findings, it seems legitimate to refer to the whole area as "applied social psychology" and to include the work of other social scientists in the discussion of findings. Certainly there are enough applied problems for all of us to work on, so we should not need to fight over the turf; and it is important to realize that each social science discipline has some unique contributions to offer to an interdisciplinary problem-solving approach.

Much of what is said in this book would apply equally well to applications in other social science fields, such as applied sociology (see Lazarsfeld & Reitz, 1975). However, psychologists can be differentiated from other disciplines by typical aspects of their approach, which include rigorous experimental research methods and emphasis on psychological processes and concepts as explanations of obtained findings. A little later in this chapter we will discuss some of the other typical features of the field.

Divisions of the Field

One way to divide a discipline is by content areas or topics. Thus applied social psychology might be divided into content areas such as the environment, mass media, health and health care, consumer issues, crime and the law, and so on. Though such divisions may overlook newly emerging areas of the field, they are usually quite satisfactory as organizational headings, and the third section of this book has been organized according to such major content areas. An alternative way to partition a field is by its major types of research methods. Because use of social psychological research methods is such an important portion of the field's applications, we have organized the second section of this book according to that scheme, emphasizing the strengths and weaknesses of each of five main research approaches.

Another common way to divide an applied discipline is a three-part one, using the categories of theory, research, and practice. For instance, Ronald J. Fisher (1982) organized his description of applied social psychology in that way. Moreover, he held that every applied social psychologist needed to possess skills in all three categories in order to work effectively on any given type of problem, and that applied psychologists should not be solely researchers nor solely practitioners. In keeping with this view, major theories and principles used in applied social psychology are summarized in Chapter 2 and at many places throughout this volume. Similarly, examples of practice in creating social change are presented in many chapters and particularly in the fourth section of the book.

A different model of applied social psychology was offered by Clara Mayo and Marianne La France (1980), who stated the goal of the field as improving the *quality of life*. This stress on improving the quality of life as the goal of applied efforts is incorporated in several chapters of this volume.

TYPICAL FEATURES OF APPLIED SOCIAL PSYCHOLOGY

How does applied social psychology differ from other fields of psychology? Starting from the definition of applied social psychology given above, let's look at some of its typical features.

A Problem Orientation

Our definition stated the aim of the field as "understanding or solution of social problems." This highlights one of the key features of the field: the fact that it typically begins by focusing on some kind of problem in society. For example, an applied social psychologist might start with a concern about violence in our society. From there, he or she might: (a) design a study to learn more about the phenomenon, or (b) analyze the already available research knowledge and use it to plan an intervention or social program that would try to reduce some aspect of violence. In either case, the focus would be on the problem—violence.

In contrast, the approach of traditional "basic" science would choose a topic for study because of its relevance to some theory in the field, and would focus on finding evidence to support or refute the theory in question. A traditional basic scientist who chose to study a topic like violence would typically consider it as a special case of a theoretical concept—for instance, as an example of aggression within the frustration-aggression theory. Basic scientists would be less likely to plan an intervention to reduce societal violence, but if they did do so, it would be mainly for the purpose of providing support for the theory that they were using.

Thus there may be considerable overlap between the activities of basic and applied scientists. Both may plan studies to gather new information. Both may stress theories as ways of understanding a social phenomenon, though that is more apt to be the central focus of interest of a basic scientist. Both may carry out interventions designed to change some social phenomenon, but that is more likely to be the main goal of an applied scientist. The key difference is in the scientists' goals rather than their activities—are they interested primarily in developing, supporting, or refuting a theory; or are they hoping to contribute toward solving a social problem?

Of course, many studies and many scientists are both basic and applied. The same woman or man can switch back and forth between the two types of scientific work. And some studies—often the most valuable ones of all—seem quite clearly to be both theory-oriented and problem-oriented. Such dual-purpose studies provide good examples of applied research on social problems at the same time that they contribute new theoretical knowledge about the world we live in. Further aspects of theory-oriented versus problem-oriented research are discussed in a very useful chapter by Morton Deutsch (1980).

A Value Orientation

The claim that conventional science is value-free—seeking "knowledge for its own sake"—has often been challenged (for instance, in the famous appendix on values in Myrdal's 1944 book, *An American Dilemma*; also by Ring, 1967). However, there is no controversy about the status of applied science—it definitely is *not* value-free. The definition of some topic as a social "problem" obviously requires a negative value judgment, which is, in the final analysis, always a personal one by the investigator. In some societies and historical periods, killing another person has not been considered a serious offense, whereas in our society murder is strongly condemned. Even in our society, some people see the more than 20,000 murders committed in the United States every year as a social problem requiring strenuous action, such as handgun registration and control, whereas other people see them merely as "a price we pay for freedom" (a quote from congressional testimony by an official of the National Rifle Association).

The above example illustrates an important point about value orientations. Our complex, pluralistic society contains many groups, each of which may have its own typical value system, and these varying systems are often at least partially incompatible. Similarly, as individuals, we often find ourselves in situations where two positive values are in conflict and we have

to choose between them (Smith, 1978). The freedom to bear arms versus the desire to reduce murders; the value of better medical care for developing nations versus the wisdom of investing those same funds in birth control assistance to reduce overpopulation or in emergency food supplies to prevent widespread famine—these are value conflicts where no general consensus is likely. Yet applied social scientists who want to work on such problem areas must start with a value position that will help them determine for themselves what circumstances constitute a social problem that needs solving. A number of social psychologists have offered such guidelines for desirable value positions for researchers (e.g., Kelman & Warwick, 1978; Opotow, 1990; Smith, 1975, 1976). It is also possible that applied research findings can influence people's values, as we have seen in the last several decades in changing American attitudes toward gender equality (cf. Chapter 9).

As mentioned above, one suggested value standard is improvement of people's quality of life (Mayo & La France, 1980). This approach embodies a positive and proactive stance of actively fostering people's overall well-being rather than merely reacting to the negative aspects of life, which we term social problems. It also requires applied social scientists to adopt an explicit value commitment as a basis for their work.

Social Utility

Implicit in the two features discussed above is the assumption that the knowledge and methods of social psychology will be *useful* in achieving social goals. This was a cardinal principle of Kurt Lewin (1948), one of the most important figures in American social psychology. Lewin proposed the concept of **action research** to denote scientific work firmly grounded in theory but at the same time directed toward "resolving social conflicts."

The theme of social psychology's usefulness was extended by Michael Saks (1978), who advocated a "high-impact applied social psychology." He proposed that applied scientists should focus their efforts on the specific aspects of a social problem where they would have the most impact in resolving it. For example, an applied researcher might concentrate on trying to pre-

Photograph courtesy of M.I.T. Museum and Historical Collections. Reprinted by permission.

Box 1-1

KURT LEWIN, PROPONENT OF A USEFUL PSYCHOLOGY

One of the most influential founders of modern social psychology, Kurt Lewin was born in Prussia in 1890. He studied at Freiburg and Munich and earned his Ph.D. at the University of Berlin in 1914. After serving in the German Army in World War I, he returned to teach at the University of Berlin. There he became a noted member of Berlin's famous school of Gestalt psychology and later developed his own theoretical approach, termed field theory. After some international teaching and travels, he left Germany to escape Nazism in 1932 and taught briefly at Stanford and Cornell before settling at the University of Iowa. In 1944 he moved to M.I.T. to found the Research Center for Group Dynamics, which was transferred to the University of Michigan after Lewin's untimely death in 1947.

Lewin preeminently combined applied and basic scientific interests and activities. He was noted as a theorist for his development of psychological field theory. Yet he strongly emphasized the value of applied work on social problems, and he originated the concept of "action research," combining basic theoretical research and social action in a coordinated program. He became famous for studies of democratic and autocratic group leadership methods, group discussion and decision processes, and group participation methods in organizational management. He also worked on practical projects to lessen prejudice and reduce public attitude problems during World War II. His concepts of "group dynamic" processes were instrumental both in the scientific study of human groups and in the founding of the National Training Laboratory at Bethel, Maine, where the "T-group method" was developed as a means of improving group effectiveness and personal social adjustment.

vent crime rather than to rehabilitate criminals or to console victims of crime. This general principle can be applied to the choice of problems to study, the selection of variables to concentrate on within a given problem, the question of whether to treat a problem's consequences or try to prevent them from occurring in the first place, and the decision about what kind of interventions to use in attacking the problem.

Another aspect of social utility is that social scientists' work, no matter how important, must be *understandable* to others before it will be readily adopted and used. In order to be seen as relevant and useful, we must simplify all unnecessary complexity in describing our work, and express it in plain English rather than technical jargon. In addition, we should try to communicate to the general public through nontechnical journals, the mass media, and popular lectures or workshops (Posavac, 1992).

A Focus on Social Situations

A characteristic that both basic and applied social psychology share is emphasis on the power of social situations to affect people's beliefs, feelings, and behavior. This emphasis on the power of situations is in contrast to some other areas of psychology, which tend to stress the importance of physiological factors or personality characteristics. For instance, a prominent concept in social psychology is the **fundamental attributional error**—the common tendency to underestimate the situational causes of other people's behavior and exaggerate the dispositional or personality causes (see Chapter 2 for more details). In short, social psychologists usually think of situational factors as the most important ones in influencing behavior.

A Broad Approach

To be as useful as possible, applied social psychology needs to be comprehensive and inclusive in its approach to social problems. This means, for instance, considering the whole range of variables that might influence a particular area of concern. This may also be referred to as a macro rather than micro level of analysis. In studying a topic such as expression of racial prejudice, for example, we need to know not only individual attitudes and experiences and immediate stimulus events, but also the social norms and expectations people have learned during their lives, and the characteristics of the overall social system within which they live (Lott & Maluso, 1995; see Chapter 9). Often such considerations will lead to an interdisciplinary approach, in which sociological, economic, and political factors are considered in addition to psychological ones.

Field Settings

It is clear that applied social psychologists are more inclined than most psychologists to do research in **field settings**—that is, natural settings where people live, work, or play, and consequently feel comfortable and behave in their usual ways. This naturalness is in marked contrast to the artificial atmosphere of most laboratory experiments.

In traditional social psychology the well-controlled laboratory experiment has been the research method of choice. As we will see in Chapter 4, this approach allows a few variables to be selected for study out of the multitude of factors that may influence a phenomenon of interest, and these variables can then be carefully controlled or manipulated, and their effects can be precisely measured. In contrast to controlled experiments, another common research tradition in social psychology has been the use of nonmanipulative or correlational methods, which will be discussed in Chapter 5. Though correlational studies can be conducted in field settings, they are most often done in classroom settings, using undergraduates as the research subjects (Sears, 1986).

Thus, in typical social psychological research the use of field settings, though often advocated, has been largely absent. During the 1960s and 1970s, studies done in field settings constituted no more than 10% of the articles appearing in the major social psychological journals (Fried, Gumpper, & Allen, 1973; Helmreich, 1975; Mark, Cook, & Diamond, 1976). Even the *Journal of Applied Social Psychology* gave only about 25% of its space to field studies at that time. These patterns have continued, only slightly abated, in the mainline social psychological journals. However, by the 1990s, the balance of articles in the *Journal of Applied Social Psychology* had shifted to about 60% field studies (Schultz & Butler, 1996).

In addition, many of the field studies of applied social psychologists are published, not in general social psychological journals, but in more specialized journals. These journals may focus solely on evaluation research or on particular content areas, such as criminal justice, health care, the environment, the mass media, educational research, consumer psychology, or organizational research. Each of these areas of research will be taken up at length in later chapters of this book.

Practical Considerations

Applied social psychology, much more than traditional social science disciplines, has to pay attention to practical considerations. To start with, much applied research is done in response to the needs or formal requests of a client or sponsoring agency. As a result, it must often be conducted under severe time constraints in order to be useful to the client or sponsor. These characteristics are quite different from the typical course of basic research in academic settings, in which investigators have relatively complete freedom to choose the topic, method, and pace of their work.

For research results to be applicable in solving social problems, they must first be strong enough to have practical importance. Second, it is important for them to generalize to other situations—that is, to different tasks, measuring instruments, research subjects, organizations, and subcultures. We will return to these issues near the end of this chapter.

Another practical consideration that has received increasing attention is cost-benefit comparisons. Even if research results are strong and broadly generalizable, they may be too expensive to implement in a practical social program. For instance, the U.S. national 55 mph speed limit, initiated during the energy shortages of the 1970s, was shown to have saved many lives and much gasoline, yet many truckers and motorists strenuously objected to it because they felt its benefits did not compensate for its personal costs to them. As a result, the national 55 mph limit was finally terminated in 1996. In recent years the computation of benefit-to-cost ratios has become common in decision making about governmental programs and industrial and commercial investments. This approach requires applied social scientists to develop quantitative estimates about both the costs and the expected benefits of social programs that they hope to implement. Since program benefits are often previously unquantified concepts like job satisfaction or improved mental health, workers in the field have had to develop and test new techniques for estimating their dollar value. An interesting example is the

calculation that every dollar spent on high-quality preschool programs would save the nation seven dollars in later costs for special education, school dropouts, welfare, delinquency, and other social problems (Barnett, 1992).

A final practical factor that applied scientists must consider is the political feasibility of programs. For example, every year in the U.S., handguns are used in approximately 15,000 of the nation's 20,000 murders and in half a million other crimes. Research results have shown that major handgun registration and control laws could decrease these totals significantly (e.g., Podell & Archer, 1994). For decades, a large majority of the U.S. population, even including gun owners, has been in favor of stricter handgun control laws (Moore & Newport, 1994). Yet, with the exception of Massachusetts, New York, and Washington, D.C., most states and cities found it politically impossible to pass handgun control laws until very recently. The reason is that very powerful lobbying organizations, such as the National Rifle Association, have shot down all other previous attempts to pass gun restriction or gun control laws (Kleck, 1991; Schumer, 1993). Other kinds of social programs may also be politically unfeasible at a given time because of strongly entrenched opposition by powerful political groups or individuals.

Basic Versus Applied Science

The above distinctions between "basic" and applied scientific approaches, as well as other related points, have been summarized in a shorthand form by Bickman (1981—see Table 1–1). As the table shows, the differences in purposes and activities between applied and basic science also produce differences in their context, methodologies, and participants.

USES OF THEORY IN APPLIED WORK

In view of all the practical considerations of applied work, what good are theories to the applied social scientist? Isn't applied scientific work often described as nontheoretical? Aren't theories often contrasted with practical reality, and theorists referred to as impractical dreamers? Yes, but these criticisms overlook the

TABLE 1-1   Comparisons Between Basic and Applied Research

Aspect	Basic	Applied
Purposes	Gaining knowledge Relationships between variables Determining causes	Solving problems Large effects Prediction
Activities	Theory development Theory testing	Program development Program evaluation
Context	University Laboratory Not time bound Short duration study Long duration program Initiated by researcher Low cost consciousness Flexible procedures and scope Stable topics of research Unidisciplinary Autonomous structure	Industrial or business Field Real time constraints Long duration study Short duration program Initiated by sponsor High cost consciousness Inflexible procedures Unstable topics Multidisciplinary Hierarchical organization
Methodologies	Experimental High precision Behavioral emphasis Single method Single level of analysis Emphasis on causes Internal validity	Quasi-experimental Low precision Self-reports used more often Multiple methods Multiple levels of analysis Emphasis on effects External validity
Participants	Specialists Solitary Peer orientation Medium compensation High prestige Evaluation by publications Average social skills required	Generalists Team orientation Client orientation High compensation Medium prestige Evaluation by experience Special social skills

Source: Reprinted and compiled from Leonard Bickman, Some distinctions between basic and applied approaches, pp. 23–44 in Leonard Bickman, ed., *Applied Social Psychology Annual 2,* © 1981 Society for the Psychological Study of Social Issues, Inc., with permission of Sage Publications.

very real value of theories in everyday life as well as in science.

"Practical" people operate, whether they know it or not, on the basis of principles that were first suggested and later verified by theorists. The "simple" act of driving a car, for example, involves the use of many scientific principles, including gravity, centrifugal force, rolling friction, inertia, peripheral vision, human reaction time, and size constancy of objects. Even though

we may not think about the concepts themselves, we still depend on our essential understanding of them to get us safely home.

In science, theories have several important functions:

1. Theories provide the ideas that guide our steps in research.
2. Like the map of an unfamiliar city, theories help us understand the findings of research. They provide a con-

text into which we can place demonstrated facts, see how and why they fit together, and note where they are inconsistent and need further exploration.

3. Theories give us a basis for predicting what will happen in the future under a given set of conditions. In turn, such predictions provide one of the best tests of a theory's adequacy.
4. Valid theories help us control events. They specify the variables or conditions we must control or manipulate to develop programs or interventions that will be likely to reach our goals.

Just as in basic scientific research, valid theories are also useful in solving social problems. Fifty years ago Kurt Lewin stressed this point in a famous quotation:

> Many psychologists working today in an applied field are keenly aware of the need for close cooperation between theoretical and applied psychology. . . .There is nothing so practical as a good theory. (1944/1951, p. 169)

Scientific theories vary widely in their scope or range of applicability. A few, such as the theory of relativity in physics, are broad, encompassing a tremendous range of phenomena. Psychological theories don't have such a broad scope; psychoanalysis may come closest to this extreme. At the other extreme are mini-theories dealing with a very limited set of events and circumstances. One example in social psychology is Latane and Darley's (1970) theory of diffusion of responsibility among bystanders in emergency situations. Between the broad, general theories and the mini-theories are many midrange psychological theories with varying degrees of scope—for instance, cognitive dissonance, learned helplessness, or social exchange theories. Any or all of these diverse theories can be useful to the applied social scientist who is trying to solve a practical problem, such as group morale, juvenile delinquency, or public health. In the following chapter we will present more extensive illustrations of social psychological theories and concepts that can be used in dealing with applied problems.

ROLES AND ACTIVITIES

Turning from the use of theories and other typical features of applied social psychology, let's consider the possible roles of people working in this field. We'll discuss them roughly in the order from traditional to newly developing roles and activities.

Research

The traditional role of scientists has been to do research. In applied social psychology, at least as much as in other scientific fields, many unanswered questions still require investigation. In addition to the collection of empirical data, there are several other aspects of the research role. Scientific scholarship often involves searching through many scattered sources in the literature in order to find relevant facts and hypotheses. It may also involve culling these facts, integrating conflicting information, and building theories about the topic. An occasional aspect of the research role is serving as an expert witness before courts or legislative committees. All of these aspects of research will continue to be a key function of applied social psychologists.

Evaluation

Evaluation is another aspect of research, but it has been growing by leaps and bounds, and it merits separate discussion. Like other scientists, evaluation researchers frequently state hypotheses and collect and analyze systematic data to support or reject them. However, they have specialized topics of study—the success or failure of particular experimental interventions or social programs.

In the last 25 years, the laws or regulations initiating many government programs have mandated an evaluation research component to help determine the program's success or failure. There has also been an increasing demand for evaluation of other kinds of programs, such as businesses' capital investment decisions. In these activities, there are important roles both for outside evaluators and for employees of the organization who function as inside evaluators. We will describe evaluation research in detail in Chapter 7.

Consultation and Change Agentry

Another kind of role for applied social psychologists is consultation with organizations, aimed at accomplishing desired changes in their operational methods or results. Often these organizations are businesses, or they may be civic organizations or government agencies. Such organizations hire many different kinds of consultants—lawyers, financial advisors, and advertising agents—as well as applied social scientists, who can help them apply the theories and findings of psychology and sociology to their organizational goals and problems. Social science consultants operate under many different names: organization development (OD) specialists; management consultants; marketing, communications, public relations, job training, and personnel selection experts. If they try to apply social science principles, we will refer to them as social science consultants.

In a useful classificatory scheme, Hornstein (1975) described several types of consultants. Among the factors considered in his scheme were the kind of service the change agent provides to the client organization, the level in the organization at which the consultant works, and the kinds of targets the consultant tries to change (external relationships, internal organizational processes, or the personal functioning of individuals). In addition to a first type of change agent (the "outside pressure" type), which we will discuss shortly, Hornstein distinguished the following basic types:

> (2) the people change (PC) technology type who works to change individual functioning in organizations through such techniques as sensitivity training, behavior modification and need achievement training;
> (3) the organization development (OD) type who works to improve a system's problem-solving capabilities by changing the norms and values regulating behavior;
> (4) the analysis for the top (AFT) type who works primarily with business and government units to improve efficiency and output and employs analytic procedures to develop expert advice. (1975, pp. 218–219)

Policy Advice

Another role for applied social psychologists is to provide policy advice. The recipients may be either public, governmental agencies, or civic or business organizations of many different types. Hornstein's type-4 change agent actually fits best under the heading of a policy advisor. That is, such a person simply gives advice to organizational managers, rather than working in or on the organization to bring about change. Of

course, policy advice must be based on a study of the particular organization or agency, as well as on application of general scientific principles and findings. But it does not involve direct attempts to change the organization's processes or personnel.

Policy science has become a popular term for the attempt to make findings from all the social sciences relevant to governmental and organizational policymaking. An influential book on this subject (Weiss, 1977b) gave examples of social science research bearing on policies for the public schools, judicial procedures, health care, congressional decisions, and State Department diplomacy. A particularly fascinating example of policy advice was a study in which Hammond and Adelman (1976), using research on human judgment, public opinion measurement techniques, and analysis of expert ballistic information, helped the city council of Denver decide what kind of bullets their police officers should be authorized to use.

In Chapter 17 of this book we will consider at length how successful social scientists have been in offering policy advice, how they can be more successful in the future, and what pitfalls and dangers there are for social scientists in giving policy advice.

Management of Organizations

Usually a social scientist's most influential role is offering advice to organizational managers. Occasionally, however, applied scientists become managers themselves. Particularly in this era of limited academic job possibilities, many more social scientists are taking jobs in business organizations or in government agencies, where they may eventually assume management responsibilities. In such situations, of course, they do not shed all their scientific knowledge and skills, and one hopes that they use their scientific background to perform relevant aspects of their job better than they could without that training.

Thus, though it is an unusual activity for social scientists, management is a legitimate role for them. A few examples of psychologists who attained high government positions are: John Gardner, Secretary of Health, Education, and Welfare under President Johnson; Richard Atkinson, head of the National Science

Foundation under President Carter and more recently president of the 9-campus University of California system; and clinical psychologist Leonard Haber, who was elected mayor of Miami Beach. Numerous social scientists have reached high positions in business and educational organizations, such as Judith Rodin, president of the University of Pennsylvania. A particularly unusual example was Pat Carrigan, who became the first woman and the first psycholo-

gist to manage a General Motors auto assembly plant (Cordes, 1982b).

Social Activism

Whereas managers work on the inside of organizations, social activists typically try to influence them from outside. Though some social activists attempt to work from the inside to change organizations, that is

◇◇◇

Photograph courtesy of Judith Rodin. Reprinted by permission.

Box 1-2

JUDITH RODIN, AN APPLIED PSYCHOLOGIST

The first woman to be named president of an ivy league university, Judith Rodin has headed the University of Pennsylvania since 1994. She earned her B.A. at that university and her Ph.D. in social psychology at Columbia under Stanley Schachter. She taught briefly at New York University before moving in 1972 to Yale, where she served successively as a psychology faculty member, department chair, dean, and provost.

Rodin's early research focused on the topic of obesity, and later expanded to many aspects of human health and behav-

ior. She has headed an international research network studying health and behavior and written over 200 articles and ten books, including the chapter on applied social psychology in the *Handbook of Social Psychology* and *Body Traps,* which examines the role of physical appearance in women's psychological health. She has been honored by election to the American Academy of Arts and Sciences and the National Academy of Sciences, and has served on President Clinton's Committee of Advisors on Science and Technology.

◇◇◇

usually a difficult (and often short-lived) position. A more typical kind of social activist is Hornstein's (1975) first type of change agent:

(1) the outside pressure (OP) type who works to change systems from the outside through the application of pressure using such tactics as mass demonstration, civil disobedience, and violence. (p. 218)

There are also social activists who apply outside pressure through less extreme techniques such as legislative lobbying, media publicity, legal suits, grassroots organizing, and effective marshaling of research evidence to get organizations and government agencies to change their ways. An outstanding example of this sort is Ralph Nader, whose organization called Public Citizen has spawned other social action groups in the fields of consumer affairs, environmental protection, and health care. Nader himself, like many other activist group organizers, is a lawyer, but many of the staff members who work in his several organizations are applied scientists—some in research roles, and some in social activist roles. In Chapter 16 we will discuss the role of the social activist at length.

IS SOCIAL PSYCHOLOGY REALLY APPLICABLE?

In view of the impressive breadth of social psychological applications cited above, it may astonish you to learn that there has been controversy about whether social psychology *can be* or *should be* applied. We will sketch a few of the key issues and responses here.

Has Social Psychology Been Applied?

One aspect of the challenge to social psychology's applicability is the question of how much it has in fact been applied. This question was examined in an early paper by Leo Meltzer (1972). At that time he noted that, though there was much potentially applicable research, relatively little of it had been used to design specific programs aimed at changing real-world problems. In order to include such programs in his list of successful applications, he also required that they had to be based on both well-established social psychological theory and clear empirical findings, and that their

results must have been carefully evaluated. These were such stringent criteria that he found few studies which qualified. However, he concluded:

Much of the literature of traditional social psychology . . . is not only applicable to effecting changes in the real world, but has actually been effectively applied. The point is that there is a huge depository in our discipline's literature of applicable findings. The discipline has power. (Meltzer, 1972, p. 18)

Since that time, many more social psychological findings have moved from the potentially applicable status to actually being applied. Other authors have pointed out the wide range of areas in which social science knowledge has been effectively applied by businesses and government (e.g., Tornatzky et al., 1982).

The Applied Versus Theoretical Conflict

There seems to be something of an identity problem within the field, for relatively few psychologists identify themselves primarily as applied psychologists, even if they are mainly doing applied work. In part, this may be due to the lower prestige which is often attached to applied work within the field, as compared to "basic" or theoretical work. In addition, it undoubtedly stems from divisions between the separate content areas of the field, for many applied psychologists identify themselves by the topic area in which they work—for example, as organizational, educational, consumer, or health psychologists.

The split between applied social psychology and basic or theoretical social psychology has received much attention. Morton Deutsch (1975) traced the split back to a conflict between two groups of Kurt Lewin's followers that erupted shortly before Lewin's death in 1947. The practitioners among Lewin's disciples concentrated on propagating new techniques for working with groups—called *T group methods,* or *sensitivity training*—and they deemphasized empirical data collection. In contrast, the post-Lewinian researchers tended to retire to their laboratories and to give up work on important social problems. Though there were offsetting events, such as the 1936 founding of the Society for the Psychological Study of Social Issues (SPSSI) by socially involved researchers, including

Lewin himself, the split between applied and research-oriented social psychologists widened during the 1950s and 1960s.

This applied-theoretical split in social psychology has been lamented by many authors (e.g., Helmreich, 1975). More recently, there are some signs of greater integration of these two aspects of the field, for instance in large-scale multivariate research that captures more of the complexity of the natural world, and in the tendency for major researchers to work in both theoretical and applied areas.

Should Social Psychology Be Experimental?

As mentioned earlier, the dominant research approach in American social psychology, at least since the 1940s, was the laboratory experiment. Surveys of the literature in the 1960s and 1970s showed that between 70% and 90% of the studies published in major social psychological journals were laboratory experiments (Fried et al., 1973; Helmreich, 1975; Higbee & Wells, 1972). Applied social psychology research also included many experiments, though not as high a proportion. By the 1990s, only 35% of articles appearing in the *Journal of Applied Social Psychology* were laboratory experiments (Schultz & Butler, 1996). Alongside their advantages of precise measurement and control of variables, laboratory experiments have the serious disadvantages of artificiality, weak effects, and considering only a few variables at a time. These disadvantages have led some social psychologists to call for their deemphasis as a tool of our field, or even their abandonment.

Suggestions for how to replace the laboratory experiment have taken several forms. The first suggestion was to move out of the laboratory into the field, where theory-oriented experimental research could be conducted in "real-world" settings (e.g., Bickman & Henchy, 1972). Others recommended placing more reliance on large-scale, multivariate, correlational studies in place of experimental research (e.g., McGuire, 1973).

The most extreme suggestion has been to almost entirely abandon the experimental method (e.g., Silver-

man, 1977; Wallach & Wallach, 1994). Beyond the common criticisms of artificiality and triviality in laboratory experiments, these critics have pointed out serious problems in the kind of naturalistic field experiments that have been advocated by many social psychologists. Even in real-life situations, Silverman argued, for ethical reasons we can use only weak manipulations, for brief periods of time, and thus can study only trivial questions. He concluded that, from such studies:

> attempts to generalize to the issues that spawned the research are folly. The ongoing molar phenomena of social development and behaviour are as unreachable for the psychologist by the experimental method as the movements of the planets are for the astronomer. And social psychology can only begin to grow into an authentic discipline when we abandon the experiment as a modus operandi. (Silverman, 1977, p. 356)

Certainly this is an extreme view, going further in its criticisms than would most social psychologists. Despite the admitted limitations of experiments, many psychologists still consider them the research method of choice, or at least a key part of the researcher's tool kit.

In this debate about the usefulness of experimental methods, this text adopts a middle position. The critics are correct in saying that laboratory experiments are often trivial and may not generalize to real-world situations, but the careful control and crucial comparisons of randomized experiments still provide the most dependable answers to scientific questions. Even "trivial and artificial" experiments can help to establish scientific principles of social behavior (Calder, Phillips, & Tybout, 1981; Schaller et al., 1995). And, particularly when they are large in scale and conducted in natural situations, experiments can overcome some of their usual limitations and give us useful and generalizable knowledge about real-world behavior. Yet experiments alone are not enough, for they are often impossible for practical or ethical reasons. Therefore, other research methods, such as quasi-experiments, correlational methods, descriptive observation, and archival data analysis, are also important scientific tools. We will consider examples of all of these techniques, together with their strengths and limitations, in Chapters 3 through 7.

Can Social Science Influence Public Policy?

A final question about social psychology's applicability is whether it can or does affect policy decisions, even in situations where it has relevant knowledge to offer. Or, on the other hand, do personal, practical, political, or ethical considerations prevent the use of established social science knowledge in forming public policy, and if so, where and why? This important question should be kept in mind, but it would be premature to try to answer it at this point. We will consider it in detail in Chapter 17.

Other Responses Concerning Applicability

In addition to the above discussion of social psychology's applicability, let us look at some other viewpoints supporting the effort to make social psychology relevant to important social issues. An early proponent of this view was George Miller (1969) who, as president of the American Psychological Association, called for its members to "give psychology away" to all who could benefit from its knowledge and methods. Shortly thereafter, a large-scale survey of psychologists clearly demonstrated their beliefs that psychology could be applied constructively to the social problems of our society, but that too little had yet been done to achieve relevance (Lipsey, 1974). A recent survey of members and leaders of the American Psychological Association confirmed that applications of psychology are still considered to be among the most important issues for the profession (Oakland, 1994).

Another type of answer is to reverse the applicability challenge and assert that social psychology cannot *not* be applied. This answer highlights the universal tendency for social decision-makers, like all human beings, to act on what they think they know about human behavior. Though individuals' supposed knowledge may be incorrect or incomplete, they will use it in making decisions about policies or programs, hiring employees, planning social gatherings, or whatever. The resulting social actions are largely based on the "knowledge" of the time (for instance, that the world is flat, or that frustration leads to aggression). As one

example, the U.S. Supreme Court explicitly cited social science knowledge in its 1954 decision requiring desegregation of public schools, but in 1896 it had also relied on the purported "knowledge" of the time—that Black Americans were socially inferior to Whites—in its separate-but-equal-facilities decision in the case of *Plessy v. Ferguson*.

The point of this argument is that, whether social psychologists try to apply their science or not, many of their findings will inevitably be disseminated (perhaps in distorted forms) by the popular media and used in one way or another by people who have heard of them. Many social psychologists have concluded that, since research knowledge will often be used in some form by social planners and practitioners, social scientists should take an active part in disseminating their findings and trying to direct their application in relevant areas of social life (e.g., Shippee, 1979).

Though the major journals in social psychology continue to publish mostly theoretically oriented laboratory research, many other journals feature applied research in their special fields, such as community psychology, law and criminal justice, or health psychology. Also, the traditional federal agencies that provide research funds have become more receptive to applied research projects, and many single-mission agencies such as the National Institute of Justice (NIJ) have been established, which provide support for a wide variety of applied social research. Finally, a number of graduate schools have developed programs that emphasize applied aspects of social psychology, and their graduates are increasingly finding jobs in nontraditional positions in community agencies, contract-research firms, industrial companies, or government organizations.

PROBLEMS FOR APPLIED SOCIAL PSYCHOLOGY

Many problems are implicit in the typical features and roles of applied social psychology. Here we will discuss the following major areas of potential problems in the field: the research evidence, the generalizability of the evidence, unintended consequences, and ethical questions.

What Is the Evidence?

A key problem in applying any science is to assess the available scientific knowledge. It is not enough to have theories, for there must be firm supportive evidence that the theories are correct before we can feel safe in using them to build a bridge or design a social program. We need to ask: What studies have been done? What did they show? How were the data obtained? Unfortunately, methods used in the social sciences sometimes are not appropriate to support the conclusions drawn, and in other cases the methods are appropriate but not powerful enough to produce an effect. If the methods are acceptable, we should ask: How strong are the results? Are the effects large enough to be of practical importance as well as being statistically significant? If so, we have satisfied the criterion of **internal validity** of the research (Campbell & Stanley, 1966; Cook & Shadish, 1994).

Is the Evidence Generalizable?

The next question, and a major problem for applied social science, is the **external validity** or **generalizability** of the research findings. If research findings are to be applied, we must know under what circumstances the findings will hold true and what other circumstances will produce different results. In this regard the extremely artificial conditions in many laboratory experiments may limit the generalizability of their findings to other situations (though the extent to which they do is an empirical question).

In engineering, the physical principles that apply to building a bridge in one nation apply equally to building a bridge somewhere else. But this is often not the case in social science. Some social psychological principles are applicable in most nations or cultures, but other findings are limited to the culture, subculture, or setting in which they were obtained (Heller, 1990). For instance, the effect of an absent father on children's development may be very different in a cultural milieu featuring strong extended family networks (such as many Black and Hispanic groups) than in subcultures where the nuclear family has no such support networks. Clearly, a social program to compensate for absent fathers would have different implications and chances of success in these two cultural settings.

In addition to cultural patterns, individual personal characteristics and task demands often produce research findings that are not broadly generalizable. A prominent example is in research on jury decision making. Much of this research has used "mock juries" composed of college students, who had about half an hour to read a written summary of a trial transcript and then gave their individual vote on the defendant's guilt or innocence, without any group discussion or deliberation. Obviously, there are so many differences between this situation and the typical courtroom trial that there is no way of knowing whether such research results will apply to real-life trial situations or not. Fortunately, some investigators have been sensitive to these limitations and have devised various methods to increase or at least check the generality of their jury research findings. We will discuss this topic at greater length in Chapter 15, which deals with legal issues.

Unintended Consequences

Even if research is internally valid and is applicable to the social situation in which intervention is planned, unintended consequences of the intervention may arise. One notable case of this sort was a study in which aged residents of retirement homes were visited on various schedules by college students. After the study was completed and the visits ceased, the groups of oldsters who had initially benefited from the visits exhibited "precipitous declines" in their mental and physical health (Schulz & Hanusa, 1978).

Another example of unintended consequences stemming from social programs is seen in various crime-control programs which have been successful in decreasing crime rates in one locality, while apparently raising crime rates in surrounding communities by driving many criminals there. On the other hand, the *intended* consequences of interventions are not always evident without careful research. For example, some crime-control or educational-improvement programs may seem to have little success, whereas comparison of their results with appropriate control groups would show that the apparent small improvement was distinctly better than the worsening conditions in other communities (cf. Lipsey & Wilson, 1993).

Photograph courtesy of Herbert Kelman. Reprinted by permission.

Box 1-3

HERBERT KELMAN, SOCIAL PSYCHOLOGY'S CONSCIENCE

Born in Vienna, Austria, in 1927, Herbert Kelman fled there with his family in 1939 to escape Nazi persecution. After a year as a refugee in Belgium, he arrived in the United States, and by 1947 he had earned two bachelor's degrees. He completed his Ph.D. in social psychology at Yale in 1951 and then did full-time research for several years. After five years on the Harvard University faculty, he moved to the University of Michigan, but returned to Harvard in 1968 as the holder of an endowed chair in social ethics.

The major themes of Kelman's research and writing have been international relations, conflict resolution and peace research, and ethics in social science research. He helped found the *Journal of Conflict Resolution,* edited a research volume on *International Behavior,* and has been intensely involved in programs of action research applying conflict resolution principles to workshops bringing together Arab and Israeli intellectual and governmental leaders. In the area of ethics, he has written or coauthored several volumes on human values and social research, obedience to authority, and *The Ethics of Social Intervention.* Among his many honors, Kelman has been elected president of two divisions of the American Psychological Association (APA), and six other psychological organizations, including the Peace Science Society, the Interamerican Society of Psychology, and the International Society of Political Psychology. He has also received the Kurt Lewin Award, the APA award for Psychology in the Public Interest, and the Socio-Psychological Prize of the American Association for the Advancement of Science.

The problem of unintended consequences often goes unnoticed because, if evaluation research is done at all, it is usually limited to the research participants or, at most, to the community in which the research was carried out. This fact highlights the importance, not only of appropriate control groups and research designs, but also of an even broader *systems approach* to understanding the effects of social programs. Social interventions are not discrete, isolated programs; they are embedded in a whole social system of related events and processes. As such, they are bound to have some consequences beyond their stated goals and target populations, and applied social scientists need to recognize and consider these possible unplanned effects.

Ethical Issues

The unintended consequences of social programs or research activities raise ethical issues. But beyond the problem of unintended consequences, many ethical issues can arise in applied social science, and applied scientists need to be constantly alert to avoid them if possible or, if not, at least to minimize their impact. Unfortunately, the solutions to ethical issues are usually not clear-cut because they often involve conflicting values and differing perceptions—for instance, what social situations are serious enough to constitute a "social problem"?

A fundamental question at the outset of any applied project is whether or not to intervene in the given social situation. The issue is not just a pragmatic one of whether we have useful methods or knowledge, but also an ethical one of whether they *should* be used. If we decide to participate in the project, then we will have to be ready for a later decision about when and how to terminate the intervention. "Intervention entails both taking responsibility and letting go of it" (Mayo & La France, 1980, p. 91).

There are many different ways to intervene in a social system, and they have differing ethical implications. Kelman and Warwick (1978) suggested a useful typology of kinds of interventions, based on the amount of power or control left in the hands of the people affected by the proposed social program. Its categories range from coercion, through manipulation and persuasion, to facilitation of others' own goals.

It is important to consider the ethics of intervention in each specific social situation that arises. A thoughtful volume on this topic, edited by Bermant, Kelman, and Warwick (1978), discussed ethics in a wide range of social interventions, including behavior modification, encounter groups, organization development programs, community education programs, community disputes, income maintenance experiments, federally funded housing programs, and family planning programs. Other papers or books have suggested ethical

standards for human research in general (Kimmel, 1988; Sieber, 1992), for organizational research (Mirvis & Seashore, 1979), evaluation research (Newman & Brown, 1996; Shadish et al., 1995), community research with street people (Sieber & Sorensen, 1992), and psychological intervention in the criminal justice system (Monahan, 1980).

Though many of the above areas are relatively new ones, general ethical guidelines can be applied. The American Psychological Association has had a strong ethical code ever since 1953, and it has been updated every few years to include new concerns and developing areas of research and practice. For applicable formulations, see publications by the American Psychological Association (1982, 1992) and Box 1-4. A volume edited by Bersoff (1995) has elaborated on many specific topics of ethical concern. However, there are still numerous unresolved ethical issues in applied scientific work, especially in the newly developing field of policy science, which we will discuss in Chapter 17.

Starting in the mid-1960s, various branches of the federal government adopted ethical regulations to control research and experimental treatment programs with human participants (e.g., U.S. Department of Health, Education, and Welfare, 1971). These regulations were proposed and adopted mainly because of concerns over *biomedical* research done without adequate safeguards to protect research subjects from possible harmful effects—for example, injection of senile patients with live cancer cells for research purposes, without their understanding what was being done. Though the government ethical regulations also apply to psychological research, in most cases the potential risks of such studies are minimal compared to medical research with new drugs and unproved procedures. That fact was officially recognized in 1981, when the federal regulations governing psychological research were greatly simplified and redirected toward the few studies that do carry potential risks for the participants (Fields, 1981).

Regardless of what the federal regulations may be, applied scientists should feel ethically accountable for their activities. That means that there must be some basic ultimate standard for deciding what activities are

Box 1-4

EXAMPLES OF ETHICAL GUIDELINES FOR PSYCHOLOGISTS

The following are very brief extracts from the latest revision of the *Ethical Principles of Psychologists* (American Psychological Association, 1992). In the complete document each of these general principles is elaborated, and they are followed by eight sections on ethical standards, including over 100 subsections stating specific ethical responsibilities (e.g., avoiding harm, explaining assessment results, avoiding false statements, avoiding sexual intimacies, maintaining confidentiality, accuracy in teaching, compliance with law, reporting ethical violations).

Preamble. Psychologists work to develop a valid and reliable body of scientific knowledge based on research. . . .and, where appropriate, to apply it pragmatically to improve the condition of both the individual and society. . . .Psychologists respect and protect human and civil rights and do not knowingly participate in or condone unfair discriminatory practices.

A. Competence. Psychologists strive to maintain high standards of competence in their work. They recognize the boundaries of their particular competencies and the limitations of their expertise. They provide only those services and use only those techniques for which they are qualified by education, training, or experience.

B. Integrity. Psychologists seek to promote integrity in the science, teaching, and practice of psychology. . . .In describing or reporting their qualifications, services, products, fees, research, or teaching, they do not make statements that are false, misleading, or deceptive. . . .Psychologists avoid improper and potentially harmful dual relationships.

C. Professional and Scientific Responsibility. Psycholo-gists uphold professional and scientific standards of conduct, clarify their professional roles and obligations, accept appropriate responsibility for their behavior, and adapt their methods to the needs of different populations.

D. Respect for People's Rights and Dignity. Psychologists accord appropriate respect to the fundamental rights, dignity, and worth of all people. They respect the rights of people to privacy, confidentiality, self-determination, and autonomy. . . .

E. Concern for Others' Welfare. Psychologists seek to contribute to the welfare of those with whom they interact professionally. In their professional actions, psychologists weigh the welfare and rights of their patients or clients, students, supervisees, human research participants, and other affected persons, and the welfare of animal subjects of research. . . .they do not exploit or mislead other people during or after professional relationships.

F. Social Responsibility. Psychologists are aware of their professional and scientific responsibilities to the community and the society in which they work and live. They apply and make public their knowledge of psychology in order to contribute to human welfare. Psychologists are concerned about and work to mitigate the causes of human suffering. When undertaking research, they strive to advance human welfare and the science of psychology. Psychologists try to avoid misuse of their work.

Source: American Psychological Association, 1992. *Ethical Principles of Psychologists and Code of Conduct.* Copyright © 1992 by the American Psychological Association. Reprinted with permission.

acceptable. What might such an ethical guideline be? One common suggestion has been the welfare of the client (individuals or groups). But is that a sufficient guideline? Questions such as the following have been raised about it (Deutsch, 1975, p. 10):

- Does a social psychologist have any moral responsibilities with respect to how a client uses research information the psychologist has collected?
- Should a psychologist allow a client's public distortion of research findings to go unchallenged?

- Should a client be allowed to use research information to influence third parties without their consent (e.g., to influence voters, consumers, or employees)?

Similar questions have been raised about how to handle situations when organizations misuse information or resist social interventions (Ballard, Brosz, & Parker, 1980). Deutsch (1975) has answered these questions by proposing that the ultimate standard should not be the welfare of the client (though that is important), but *the general well-being of humankind.*

That seems an excellent standard to keep in mind, though of course applying it may be a complex and difficult process.

Unfortunately, in many cases applied social science has failed to follow the guideline of the welfare of humankind. For example, we tend to define social problems in terms of the behavior of individual people, rather than focusing on the environmental situations that help to produce and maintain that behavior. This person-centered approach often leads us to "blame the victims" (e.g., of racism or poverty) for their own misfortunes (Dressel, Carter, & Balachandran, 1995; Herbert & Dunkel-Schetter, 1992).

Specific Ethical Precepts. The various ethical codes that have been developed are in relative agreement on a number of specific precepts that applied social scientists should observe. There is not enough space here to discuss them, but we will list the major points, together with useful references for further reading.

- Social scientists should avoid *harmful consequences* to research participants or clients (Warwick, 1982).
- All research participants should be told enough about the research and its likely impact on them so that they can give meaningful *informed consent* to participate (Murray, 1982).
- Clients and research subjects should not undergo any unusual *invasion of privacy* (Kelman, 1977; Murray, 1982).
- Any proposed *deception* of clients or research participants should be strictly reviewed by ethics committees before it is carried out, and it should be limited to cases where it is essential to the accomplishment of a highly desirable goal (Christensen, 1988; Elms, 1982).
- Research participants should be *debriefed* soon after the research is completed in order to remove any deception, inform them about the research, and allay any remaining anxieties (cf. Christensen, 1988; Aronson, Brewer, & Carlsmith, 1985).

In later chapters on specific content areas, we will consider further the ethical issues that are prominent in each area.

SUMMARY

The many fascinating examples of the application of social psychology to practical problems range from individual concerns, such as conquering shyness, through group and organizational problems, to issues of governmental policy. A suggested broad-gauge definition of applied social psychology is: applications of social psychological methods, theories, principles, or research findings to understanding or solution of social problems. Applied work can contribute usefully to fundamental psychological theories, principles, and methods, as well as the other way around. This text organizes its coverage of the field of applied social psychology into various content areas, such as the environment, health, and legal issues; and it also emphasizes the important uses and the limitations of the major types of social psychological research methods.

Applied social psychology differs from other fields of psychology in several key ways. It typically starts with a concern for a particular social problem, and this starting point makes explicit its value orientation toward improving people's quality of life. It aims to have social utility and to adopt a broad, comprehensive approach to social problems. Most of its work is done in natural field settings, and it has to be especially concerned about the strength and generality of its findings as well as considerations of benefit-to-cost ratios and political feasibility. Theories are useful in applied work, just as in basic science, to help explain, predict, and influence the events and variables of interest.

Six different roles can be performed by various individuals working as applied social psychologists. The most traditional is the role of researcher. Recently developing roles are evaluator of social programs, organizational consultant or change agent, and policy advisor to administrators or legislators. Rarer social scientist roles include organizational manager and social activist.

Debates over the applicability of social psychology to resolving social problems largely stem from the unfortunate split between the applied and theoretical sides of the field, and also from the limitations of tightly controlled laboratory experiments. In one sense it is impossible for individuals and groups *not* to apply whatever social science "knowledge" (either correct or incorrect) they possess. However, many social psychologists favor more active efforts to apply their discipline and increase its relevance to society.

Among the major potential problem areas in this field are: the adequacy of research methods and findings, the generalizability of the evidence to other settings and individuals, and the unintended consequences of social interventions. There are also ethical issues involving the exercise of power over other people and decisions about when and how to intervene in social situations and when and how to stop. Though our goal should be the well-being of humankind in general, there are unfortunate examples where some applied social scientists have failed to follow that standard or to adhere to the commonly accepted ethical precepts of the field.

SUGGESTED READINGS

Bermant, G., Kelman, H. C., & Warwick, D. P. (Eds.). (1978). *The ethics of social intervention*. Washington, DC: Hemisphere.—An excellent discussion of ethics in many different areas, including behavior modification, organization development, and income maintenance experiments.

Helmreich, R. (1975). Applied social psychology: The unfulfilled promise. *Personality and Social Psychology Bulletin, 1,* 548–560.—An influential article that raised several crucial questions about the field.

Levy-Leboyer, C. (1988). Success and failure in applying psychology. *American Psychologist, 43,* 779–785.—Good examples of the work of an applied social psychologist.

Sieber, J. E. (1992). *Planning ethically responsible research: A guide for students and internal review boards*. Newbury Park, CA: Sage.—Practically oriented advice for avoiding ethical problems in all aspects of research.

Weiss, C. H. (Ed.). (1977). *Using social research in public policy making*. Lexington, MA: Lexington.—Focuses on the policy advice role of applied social scientists, in areas as varied as health care, school desegregation, the judicial system, and foreign policy.

CHAPTER 2

Theories in Applied Social Psychology

There is nothing so practical as a good theory.
—Kurt Lewin (1944/1951, p. 169)

In this chapter we examine a variety of social psychological theories and principles. Recall that in the previous chapter, we defined applied social psychology as *applications of social psychological methods, theories, principles, or research findings to understanding or solution of social problems*. In that chapter we did not distinguish between the terms *principle* and *theory*, but here we need to do so. A psychological **principle** is a statement of an underlying cause for a psychological event. Psychological principles describe the basic processes by which humans think, feel, and act. In contrast, a **theory** is an integrated set of principles that describes, explains, and predicts observed events. Thus, principles are smaller in scope than theories. A principle describes some process that leads to certain types of behavior, whereas a theory integrates this process with other processes. This chapter presents a broad but by no means exhaustive overview of many of the key principles and theories of social psychology. In later chapters we will examine the methods and specific applications of social psychology, and also present more details about certain theories that have been used in particular areas of application.

This chapter frequently cites the ideas and work of Kurt Lewin and Jacobo Varela. Both of these men were pioneers in using the principles of social psychology to solve practical problems in their work as consultants to businesses, groups, and public agencies. Both Lewin and Varela stressed that valid theories can be *useful* in solving a wide range of social problems. And that is the purpose of this chapter—to suggest principles and theories that have been useful or should be useful in the work of applied social psychologists. We will not try to develop the concepts in detail, for that would take a whole volume (e.g., Higgins & Kruglanski, 1996; Shaw & Costanzo, 1982). Rather, we will start by describing a selective list of useful psychological constructs, and then we will present brief highlights of many theoretical approaches and indicate some ways in which they can be used in applied scientific work.

USEFUL PERSONALITY AND SOCIAL PSYCHOLOGICAL CONSTRUCTS

Psychometric Measurement of Abilities

One of the oldest and best established areas of psychology is psychometric measurement of various individual characteristics. The mental testing movement began in the early 1900s with various scales to measure intelligence. In the following decades it greatly improved these instruments and expanded in many other directions as well, developing scales of specialized aptitudes, vocational interest inventories, school achievement tests, personality inventories, and so on.

Many of these instruments can be used to good effect by applied social psychologists. Varela (1971) described his use of Thurstone's test of "primary mental abilities" (based on a factor analysis of different aspects of intelligence) to classify people's abilities and try to fit them to a job where their skills would be needed:

> Salesmen, for example, had to be high in verbal comprehension and word fluency; whereas a cost accountant could be low in these abilities but should be high in numerical ability and speed of perception. Each can do an excellent job if he has the required abilities for the tasks he must perform. If, however, these two individuals were to exchange jobs, the results for both would probably be very poor. (p. 21)

In addition to intellectual abilities, many other kinds of competence are important in jobs and in personal life. A prime example is social skills in interacting with others. Slaby and Guerra (1988) showed that adolescents imprisoned for antisocial violence were much less skilled than typical high school students in solving social problems, and were higher in beliefs supporting aggression. Importantly, when given a cognitive intervention aimed at teaching social skills and decreasing aggressive beliefs, the violent youths displayed increased social problem-solving skills and less aggressive beliefs and behaviors (Guerra & Slaby, 1990).

Photograph courtesy of Jacobo Varela. Reprinted by permission.

Box 2-1

JACOBO VARELA, A SOCIAL TECHNOLOGIST

Jacobo Varela is a native of Uruguay who graduated from Princeton University with a degree in civil engineering. Returning to Uruguay, he worked on engineering problems in various industrial organizations. There he observed that most people seemed dissatisfied with their work and that many industrial problems stemmed from human interactions rather than from faulty engineering. Consequently he began to use psychological tests to match workers' characteristics and job assignments.

Reading further in social science, Varela eventually left engineering completely to work on solving problems of human relations. He found concepts such as positive reinforce-

ment, approach-avoidance conflict, cognitive dissonance, and reactance motivation particularly relevant to human conflict situations. After years of using such concepts in his consulting work, he described his approach in a book titled *Psychological Solutions to Social Problems: An Introduction to Social Technology*. During periods spent in the U.S. and Canada, he taught his approach to social technology at several universities, including Columbia and the University of British Columbia. He has applied a systems approach, using principles derived from many different areas of social science research, to consulting in fields ranging from alcohol abuse, drug addiction, crime and recidivism, to family strife, strikes, and sports.

There is plentiful evidence of the value of reliable and valid tests and measurement techniques in personnel selection and assessment. For example, one study showed that widespread adoption of a valid test for selecting computer programmers could result in increased productivity worth hundreds of millions of dollars to employers (Schmidt et al., 1979). We will ex-

amine the issue of personnel selection in more detail in Chapter 10.

Interests, Values, and Motives

Vocational Interests. An aspect of individual characteristics which has been thoroughly studied by psychologists is vocational interests. For instance, E. K.

Strong, Jr. spent a lifetime doing research on the relation of interests to vocational choice and achievement, and the Strong Vocational Interest Blank has been widely used in vocational counseling and personnel selection (Hansen, 1990, 1994). Many studies have shown that people who are high in a given type of interest are more likely than others to go into a related occupational field, and also more likely to be successful once they have entered it (Landy, Shankster, & Kohler, 1994).

Values have been conceptualized as important life-goals or desired societal conditions, which serve as guiding principles for one's life (Rokeach, 1973). Most values are broad abstract concepts such as freedom, equality, and happiness, but some are more concrete, such as wealth. In either case, they are central concepts in a person's system of beliefs and attitudes, and they are expected to influence a person's behavior (Olson & Zanna, 1993). Building on Rokeach's theory of values, Schwartz (1994) has conducted several large-scale cross-cultural studies and identified two bipolar value dimensions that he considers to be universal across all people. The first dimension is self-enhancement (values such as success, wealth, and social power) versus self-transcendence (values such as inner harmony, equality, and world peace). The second crosscutting dimension is openness (e.g., creativity, daringness, variety in life) versus conservation (e.g., conformity, traditionalism, security).

Human motives are usually conceptualized as an aspect of personality, and psychologists have devoted much attention to personality measurement. Two main measurement techniques have been used: self-report inventories and projective tests. Self-report personality inventories are easy to give and are objectively scored, but they suffer from the possibility that respondents can fake a particular personality pattern if they want to and are knowledgeable enough. Projective personality tests, such as the T.A.T. or Rorschach, are much less easily faked but harder to administer and score, and they generally have not demonstrated adequate validity or reliability in many of their applications (e.g., Wood, Nezworski, & Stejskal, 1996). Nevertheless, both types of personality measures have been widely used, and with proper precautions they may prove

helpful in applied social psychology. Some of the most promising measures of personal motives are listed below, together with brief descriptions of their use in applied work.

Need for Approval. This motive was suggested as an important dimension by Crowne and Marlowe (1964), who developed and validated an inventory to measure the concept. Subsequent research has found that people high in the need for approval tend to be more compliant, easier to persuade, and more conforming in social situations than people low in need for approval (e.g., Grams & Rogers, 1990). Varela (1971) used this knowledge in designing persuasion situations that depend in part on the high-need-for-approval person's susceptibility to praise and to social pressure from others. Of course, such an approach is manipulative, and it raises ethical questions such as we discussed in Chapter 1 about the goals of the persuasion and the motives of the social scientists who use it.

Authoritarianism. Authoritarianism is another personality characteristic that has been widely studied ever since the classic research by Adorno et al. (1950). A recent review of the topic by Stone (1993) noted the wide variety of approaches to authoritarianism taken by researchers since 1950, including varying emphases on psychodynamics, cognitive processes, and group processes. In recent years, Altemeyer's (1988) scale of right-wing authoritarianism has become one of the most widely used measures. A traditional description of an authoritarian person is:

> a personality type characterized by very severe and punitive attitudes toward certain minorities, coupled with subservience to a higher authority. The authoritarian also tends to be intolerant of ambiguity . . . sees everything in terms of black and white, good or bad . . . sees relations among people more in terms of status and hierarchy than in terms of friendship . . . tends to be intolerant of other people's ideas . . . is often pathologically concerned with sexual matters but frequently represses such interests. (Varela, 1971, p. 289)

Varela has shown how a consultant can use an assessment of the degree of authoritarianism of target individuals in designing persuasion situations—for example, a rational presentation for a nonauthoritarian target person, and a high-status authority presentation for an authoritarian target. Again, the question of the social goal for which the persuasion is designed becomes an important ethical issue. However, in forming ethical judgments, one should realize that persuasive communicators will use techniques of shaping the message to fit the recipient with or without the benefit of social research findings.

Achievement Motivation. This concept was first studied 40 years ago with a projective measure and research done on college students, but since then it has expanded in many directions (Atkinson, 1977; McClelland & Franz, 1992; McClelland, Koestner, & Weinberger, 1989). Though early studies of the achievement motive investigated its effects on academic performance, McClelland later became convinced that it was most closely related to success in business enterprises. At the individual level, achievement motivation has been found to be a strong predictor of job success (McClelland, 1993). At the societal level, cross-cultural research has indicated that the typical levels of achievement motivation in a nation are predictive of its subsequent amount of economic development in the following generation (McClelland, 1961, 1971). These research findings have great importance for social scientists and policy makers, but even more intriguing to applied scientists have been attempts to use research-based understanding of human motivation to teach business and community leaders how to increase their levels of achievement motivation (McClelland & Winter, 1969). The lengthy history of this research program shows how theoretical, laboratory-based research can lead to many unexpected areas of application. McClelland (1978) summarized a wide variety of findings that show how

> advances in motivational technology have contributed to raising the standards of living for the poor, facilitated compensatory education, provided a means of assessing the contribution of higher education, helped control serious diseases, and made management of complex enterprises more effective. (p. 201)

Consistency Motives. Another useful motivational construct is the need for consistency. Social psychologists have long been interested in personal consistency,

and many of their ideas about it are reflected in attribution theory, equity theory, and cognitive dissonance theory, which are discussed below. Recently, several instruments have been developed to measure individual differences in the degree to which people consider consistency between thoughts, attitudes, and behaviors to be important. Measures of *personal need for structure* (Neuberg & Newsom, 1993; Thompson, Naccarato, & Parker, 1989), *preference for consistency* (Cialdini, Trost, & Newsom, 1995), and *certainty motivation* (Sorrentino et al., 1988) are examples of this motive.

Other potentially useful personality variables include introversion-extroversion (Eysenck, 1990), internal versus external locus of control (Strickland, 1977), explanatory styles of optimism or pessimism (Peterson, Buchanan, & Seligman, 1995; Seligman 1991), and psychological differentiation or field independence (Karp, 1977).

SOCIAL PSYCHOLOGICAL PRINCIPLES

There are many potentially useful social psychological principles which describe important social processes. For a thorough analysis of many social psychological principles, see Higgins and Kruglanski (1996). For our purposes here, we will focus on just a few of them.

Approach-Avoidance Conflict

First discussed by Lewin (1935), **approach-avoidance conflict** is defined as a situation where there are both positive and negative aspects about some goal-object that a person is thinking of pursuing. For instance, if the goal were to get a date with a new acquaintance, positive aspects might include "I like her style," and "We seem to have mutual interests," while negative aspects might be "Maybe she's already going steady," and "Maybe she'll turn me down and I'll feel foolish and rejected." None of these considerations seem very major when the goal is far away (for instance, when you're out of town and just idly thinking about future plans). However, as you approach the goal (perhaps getting ready to phone and ask for a date), both the approach motivation and the avoidance motivation be-

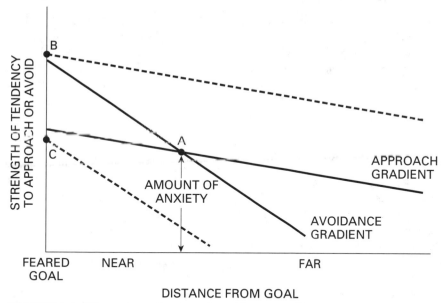

FIGURE 2-1 **The nature of approach-avoidance conflict.** (Source: Adapted from Dollard & Miller, 1950, pp. 356, 358, 361. Reprinted by permission.)

come stronger. If either one is much stronger than the other, it will prevail, and there will be relatively little feeling of conflict and tension. If the two motives are roughly equal in strength, however, a strange thing often happens (see Figure 2-1).

Many research studies, with animals as well as people, have shown that as the goal is approached, the strength of the avoidance tendency increases faster than the strength of the approach tendency. Thus you may jump up from your chair with firm resolve, but as you pick up the phone book or begin to dial, second thoughts may suddenly stop you from carrying through ("Maybe it's too late to call tonight," or "She's probably busy with that term paper this week"). That's the classic case of approach-avoidance conflict leading to indecision, and it has probably happened to everyone at some time. When the approach gradient and the avoidance gradient are about equally strong, as shown in Figure 2-1, the normal outcome is that the person gets "hung up" near point A and oscillates there, neither completely reaching the goal nor completely retreating.

Of course this state of conflict and tension doesn't last forever. Usually something happens to push one of the gradients up or down so that a decision is reached. (Perhaps you gather your courage and make the call, or you decide that it's too late to ask about a date for this weekend's dance, so you'll have to go out with the guys instead.)

One way in which this concept of conflict can be applied was suggested by Dollard and Miller (1950). They pointed out that if the conflict is resolved by raising the approach gradient (e.g., by going without dates so many weekends that you get desperate), this solution nevertheless leads to increased tension and anxiety (indicated by the longer distance of point B from the baseline, the point of minimal tension). On the other hand, anxiety can be reduced by the kind of resolution that lowers the avoidance gradient to point C in the figure (for instance, by analyzing your fears and asking yourself why it would be so bad to have your request for a date turned down). This kind of intervention is often used in psychotherapy to reduce anxiety and encourage adaptive behavior, and similar methods have proved useful for social psychologists in handling conflict in organizational settings.

Approach-avoidance conflicts in work situations may lead to serious symptoms, including absenteeism, illness, drinking, and psychological defense mechanisms like rationalization or displacement of anger onto other individuals (cf. Chapter 10). Since such reactions can be disruptive to organizational functioning, it is essential for consultants to be able to recognize and deal with conflict situations (Varela, 1971). Of course, organizational problems such as absenteeism, drinking, and poor morale often stem largely from conditions within the organization, not just from individual conflicts and maladjustment; so it is also important for consultants to be able to diagnose and prescribe ways of correcting institutional disorders rather than mistakenly blaming the victims of those organizational conditions for their negative personal consequences.

Foot-in-the-Door and Door-in-the-Face

The **foot-in-the-door technique** is a procedure of making small initial requests to which almost everyone will agree (the "foot-in-the-door"), followed within a short period (one day to two weeks) by a large related request. Generally, many more people will comply with the large request if they have previously agreed to the small request than if they had not been asked to do so. In the classic study by Freedman and Fraser (1966), 76% of homeowners agreed to put a large, poorly lettered sign stating DRIVE CAREFULLY in their front yard, after having agreed two weeks earlier to display a small three-inch-square sign on their window. However, among homeowners who had not been asked to display the three-inch sign, only 17% agreed to put the large, unsightly sign in their front yard.

This technique has been used successfully to gain support for many social causes, such as charitable fund drives, campaigns for blood donations, or to recruit volunteers to help in political campaigns (Cialdini, 1993; Lipsitz et al., 1989). The principle has also been applied to marketing and sales, where a small initial commitment like returning a card for more information, listening to an investment presentation, or accepting a free gift can often lead to a large commitment

later on (and big profits for the salesperson—Cialdini, 1993). The usual theoretical explanation of the phenomenon is a self-perception one: Persons who grant the small request come to view themselves as more helpful individuals and more involved in that particular cause (DeJong, 1979; Zuckerman, Lazzaro, & Waldgeir, 1979).

Nearly opposite to the foot-in-the-door approach is the less well-named **door-in-the-face technique**, which might better be called "rejection-then-retreat" (Cialdini et al., 1975; Cialdini, 1993). In it, a solicitor for a good cause makes a large initial request, which most people are expected to refuse, and the refusal is followed immediately by a moderate-sized request. The usual result is that many more people comply with the moderate request than if they have not been first "softened up" by being exposed to the large request (e.g., Weyant, 1994). This technique is similar to procedures that frequently occur in bargaining and negotiation, and it depends on the theoretical principle of reciprocal concessions. Though it is often very successful, there are some limiting conditions which can negate it, such as initial requests that are perceived as illegitimate or completely unreasonable. When the technique does not work, it may even boomerang and produce less compliance (Schwarzwald, Raz, & Zvibel, 1979).

Public Commitment

Another very useful technique is **public commitment**, a procedure in which people are encouraged to make a public statement that they intend to take a particular action. Study of this concept again goes back to some of Lewin's early research (Bennett, 1955; Lewin, 1947), and commitment has also been spotlighted as a key variable in dissonance theory (Brehm & Cohen, 1962). It has frequently been used in social psychology experiments to increase the amount of behavior change in persuasion situations. For example, Pallak and Cummings (1976) found that a public commitment condition where people expected to have their names listed in the city newspaper as participants in an energy conservation program produced greater energy savings than other experimental approaches (see Chapter 11).

Expectations

People's **expectations** are important factors in determining their behavior. Our expectations (or expectancies) are personal predictions about how other people will behave and what will happen in specific social situations, and we usually have some expectations about any person or social situation. They are a subset of a broader category of beliefs called *schemas*, which organize our knowledge about people or events and thus help us to understand our social world and to interact with other people more smoothly. Our expectations come from a variety of sources: our own past experiences, second-hand information from others, and from stereotypes. Once we establish an expectation for another person's behavior, research shows that we often conduct a biased search for further information that will confirm our beliefs (e.g., Snyder & Swann, 1978). Examples of expectancies that have had a great deal of research study are learned helplessness versus learned optimism about life (cf. Seligman, 1991) and **self-efficacy**—the belief that one has some control over life events and can achieve one's goals (cf. Bandura, 1997).

Sometimes our expectations can become **self-fulfilling prophecies**—situations in which our expectations about another person not only shape our own behavior, but also lead that person to behave in ways that confirm our initial beliefs (Jussim, 1986; Snyder, 1993). That is, we are likely to interact with others in ways that subtly produce the behaviors we expect to find. For example, imagine that you have the false belief that women who belong to sororities are flighty and unintelligent. You then meet one of the members of a sorority on your campus. During your conversation, you may ask simple, routine questions, keep the conversation focused on concrete topics, and converse humorously. Through these subtle means, you are likely to elicit responses from your new acquaintance that confirm your initial beliefs. As a result, you leave the conversation thinking "just like a sorority woman—flighty and unintelligent."

Expectations are central to many topics in this volume. For instance, in Chapter 4, experimenters' expectancies are shown to influence the behavior of research participants. Similarly, in Chapter 8 we will examine the effects of self-fulfilling prophecies on student achievement, an area where research indicates that students' academic performance is partially determined by teacher expectations.

THEORIES OF SOCIAL INFLUENCE

We turn next to several types of social psychological theories that can be useful in applied work. Social psychology can be defined as the scientific study of relationships between people—that is, the ways in which people think, feel, act toward, and influence others. As we pointed out in the previous chapter, the field of social psychology has many theories with different degrees of scope and different levels of analysis, ranging from the individual level, through small groups, to organizations, and to whole communities. As applied social psychologists, we are interested in using these theories to help understand and solve social problems. Theories are useful in applied work because they can help us understand why people act as they do. If we can understand the behavior that leads to or constitutes a social problem, we have a basis on which to develop interventions to change the behavior. For example, if we can understand the factors that lead children to begin using drugs, or the reasons that adults smoke cigarettes, or why ethnic discrimination occurs, then we can develop interventions to promote changes.

Our overview of social psychological theories will examine three broad types: theories of social influence, social cognition, and social relations. **Social influence** is the area of social psychology devoted to understanding the ways in which people affect or change the thoughts, feelings, and behaviors of others. Useful theories of social influence include theories of learning, persuasion, cognitive dissonance, reactance, and normative influence.

Learning Theories

Historically, much of the scientific study of human behavior has centered on processes of learning. Though there are many varieties of learning theory, we do not need to be concerned here with their subtle differences (for a comparative treatment, see Domjan, 1993).

The principle of **reinforcement** is fundamental to much of modern learning theory. Simply stated, it says that behavior that is followed by positive reinforcement (reward) will tend to be strengthened and to occur more often in the future. Even before 1920 the famous behaviorist, John B. Watson, was already applying reinforcement principles to his work for a New York advertising agency. Ever since then, reinforcement theory has been one of the dominant orientations in U.S. psychology (though much less so in Europe), and learning principles have been incorporated in every conceivable field of applied psychology. They have obvious relevance in education, where some of their fruits can be seen in computerized learning programs. In psychotherapy, Dollard and Miller (1950) built a system around reinforcement principles, and suggested learning-theory underpinnings for many Freudian and Rogerian therapeutic practices. Much of consumer psychology is aimed at getting people to learn new information, attitudes, and behaviors toward advertised products.

In social psychology also, there have been many outgrowths of learning theory. Several different theorists have built on reinforcement principles to propose **exchange theories**, dealing with the exchange of rewards and costs in human social interaction (e.g., Kelley & Thibaut, 1978). Though Bandura's (1977) theory of social learning put less emphasis on reinforcement and more on **vicarious observational learning** (by imitation without the necessity of reinforcement), he still maintained an important place in the theory for reinforcement as a facilitator of performance.

On a practical level in social interaction situations, many authors have emphasized the importance of clearly and immediately reinforcing instances of the kind of behavior that you want a person to exhibit more often in the future. Conversely, **punishment** of instances of undesirable behavior, though it may temporarily reduce their frequency, usually produces no long-term improvement unless the punishment or threat of it is continued indefinitely; and punishment has the serious undesirable side effects of creating approach-avoidance conflict, dissonance, and reactance, which we will discuss presently.

Bandura (1977) gave the example of helping a nursery school boy overcome his extreme withdrawal. Close analysis showed that the teachers were giving him much attention and consolation when he was off in a corner by himself, but were paying him no special attention when he happened to join other children. When this pattern was realized, the teachers changed their behavior and took no notice when the boy remained alone, but whenever he interacted with other children a teacher reinforced his behavior by joining the group and giving them attention and support. The result was a speedy change in his behavior from 80% seclusiveness to 60% interactive play.

Much of human behavior is maintained by **anticipated rewards** rather than by immediate reinforcement. This is the case, for example, with the athlete practicing basic skills or the employee working toward a better job despite lack of appreciation from the boss. In addition to the important role of reinforcement, new behavior patterns can also be learned through observation and imitation of others (termed **social modeling**), as in the process of learning to drive a car. In the course of such observation, one may see others receive rewards for certain behaviors and consequently may later tend to behave in similar ways oneself (the process of **vicarious reinforcement**). Another important process is learning norms of socially valued behavior that serve as standards for one's own **self-reinforcement**. In other words, people respond to their own actions in self-rewarding or self-punishing ways (Bandura, 1977).

In giving reinforcement to others, a common principle is the use of **successive approximations**. To "shape up" a desired response, one does *not* wait for it to occur in a perfect form. Rather, one rewards responses that clearly move in the desired direction. Subsequent rewards are given for closer approximations of the ultimately desired response, and eventually rewards are given only for the complete response (e.g., Taub et al., 1994). This approach is extensively used to teach children new athletic or musical skills. Another useful principle is **partial reinforcement**, or rewarding the desired response only a small percentage of the time. After the child is performing the basic skill fairly well, a good coach would gradually decrease or "fade out" the frequency of rewards for that behavior, but continue to reinforce it occasionally, on a "variable schedule." Much research has shown that such partial reinforcement will make a desired response much stronger and more resistant to extinction than will continuous reinforcement every time the response occurs (Domjan, 1993; Skinner, 1957).

A final aspect of current learning theory is that it allows a major place for *cognitive aspects of motivation,* unlike the learning theory of the 1950s and 1960s. Social learning theorists like Bandura (1977, 1995) recognize that people think and plan and hope, and that these cognitive processes interact with external factors such as reward and punishment to determine their actions. One example is that people's intrinsic motivation for an activity (that is, their internal feeling that they enjoy doing it) can sometimes be *reduced* rather than increased by applying external reinforcements that are inappropriate, unnecessary, or overly large. For instance, paying children to play baseball when they already enjoy it may decrease their enjoyment and desire to play, particularly if the rewards are later discontinued (Deci & Ryan, 1980).

Theories of Persuasion

Learning theory has been a major ingredient in theories of persuasion, but they have also drawn principles from cognitive theory, psychoanalytic theory, and research on the communication process. The communication process is often summarized as "who says what to whom, how, and with what effect?" Put more formally, the key variables in communication are: the *source* of communication, the *message,* the *medium* by which the message is transmitted, the *audience,* and the *effects*. Essentially, this is a process of social interaction, and all the variables in the model have social psychological aspects.

Early research on persuasion was conducted during and after World War II by an influential group of investigators at Yale University headed by Carl Hovland. Their analytical approach came to be known as the **Yale model of persuasive communication** (Hovland,

Janis, & Kelley, 1953). It posited that the process of persuasion has six major sequential steps: exposure to a persuasive message, attention to it, comprehension of it, acceptance, retention, and finally, action relevant to the message. A more detailed description of this theory and some of its applications is presented in Chapter 14.

Another influential theory of persuasion is the **theory of reasoned action**, developed by Fishbein and Ajzen (1975). As its name implies, it holds that people normally take actions that are reasonable in terms of their information and beliefs, though it does not imply that their reasoning is necessarily strictly logical. The theory proposes that the only important determinant of volitional behavior is one's *intentions* to take a particular action at a particular time. Two main components predict intentions: one's *attitude* toward the behavior, and one's *subjective norm* about what relevant other people think one should do. In turn, each of these components is a compound of one's salient beliefs and one's evaluations (e.g., about various specific consequences of acting in a particular way).

A later revision of the theory of reasoned action is Ajzen's (1991) **theory of planned behavior**. It adds one other element—*perceived behavioral control*—as a third factor that helps to determine whether individuals will act in accordance with their attitudes and subjective normative pressures. That is, if you don't think your behavior has a chance of accomplishing a desired goal, you are not likely even to try to reach it. More details about both the theory of reasoned action and the theory of planned behavior are also presented in Chapter 14.

One limitation of the above theories of persuasion is that the recipient is viewed as a passive target for the appeal. To counteract this assumption, Petty and Cacioppo (1986) developed a theory of persuasion that views the audience as an active processor of the persuasive appeal. Their theory is termed a **cognitive response theory** because it holds that the major determinant of persuasion is *self-persuasion* by the thoughts that one generates in response to a persuasive message. Their **elaboration likelihood model** also proposes that persuasion can occur through two distinct processes—a central route or a peripheral route. **Central route** processing involves thoughtful consideration of information—for example, the person receiving the persuasive appeal thinks about the information, elaborates on the message, and assimilates it with his or her current knowledge and beliefs. If the message fits with the person's beliefs and is accepted, then attitudes are changed toward consistency with the message. In contrast, **peripheral route** persuasion occurs without elaboration or analytical thinking. Instead, the listener relies on peripheral cues or heuristics that have little or nothing to do with the content of the message. For instance, the person may be influenced by the attractiveness or likability of the source, the way in which the message is stated, their own mood at the time of hearing the message, or other cues irrelevant to the message itself. More details concerning this theory are presented in Chapter 14.

One useful source for material on persuasion, attitude change, and social influence strategies is a readable book entitled *Influence: Science and Practice* (Cialdini, 1993). The book describes the "weapons of influence" that can be used by people who want to be effective agents of persuasion. It summarizes research on six key techniques commonly used to produce compliance: reciprocation, commitment, social proof, liking, authority, and scarcity. In addition, the book provides suggestions for resisting these influence strategies.

Cognitive Dissonance Theory

Most students of social psychology are familiar with cognitive dissonance theory, which was developed by Leon Festinger (1957) and became the most studied topic in social psychology during the 1960s. In essence, it states that **cognitive dissonance** is an unpleasant state of tension generated when a person has two or more cognitions that are inconsistent or do not "fit together." The theory holds that people will try to reduce dissonance by changing one or more of the inconsistent cognitions, by looking for additional evidence to bolster one side or the other, or by derogating the source of one of the cognitions. The greater the dissonance, the stronger the attempts to reduce it. From this brief description you can see that dissonance is one

example of the popular group of theories dealing with the central concept of **cognitive consistency**.

One great virtue of cognitive dissonance theory is that it is stated in a broad and general way, which makes it applicable to many different situations in social life—particularly ones involving attitude change or behavior change. For instance, it has been applied to understanding: (a) people's feelings of regret and changes of attitude after making a decision, (b) their patterns of exposing themselves to and searching for new information, (c) reasons that people seek social support for their beliefs, (d) attitude change in situations where a person has said or done something contrary to their customary beliefs or practice, and to numerous other topics.

Among the many applications of dissonance theory, Varela (1971) provided some stimulating illustrations. For instance, if a persuasion situation is designed to move target individuals toward a new viewpoint or action in successive steps, it is important for these individuals to resolve their dissonance after every step of the process. This can be done in various ways: by stating reasons in support of the new attitude position, by public commitment through stating the new viewpoint to another person, by seeking out other people who share the new view, or by some other action in support of the new attitude. In order to avoid **postdecision regret**, resulting in loss or reduction of the new viewpoint, Varela recommended **overpersuasion** (getting the target person to make multiple commitments on several different aspects of the new attitude), or introducing weak arguments on the other side in order to **inoculate** the target against later counterpersuasion, or having another meeting a day or two later to secure the person's **recommitment** to the new attitude.

As an unintended and unwanted organizational phenomenon, dissonance is often generated in employees by such mistakes as lack of recognition for work they have done, intentional or accidental exclusion of someone from a committee meeting, derogation of employees' importance, salary inequities, failure to provide expected benefits or perquisites, or layoffs and other unstable personnel practices. The usual reaction to such dissonance is to seek social support for one's diminished attitude toward the organization, and this can

Photograph courtesy of Robert Cialdini. Reprinted by permission.

Box 2-2

ROBERT CIALDINI, RESEARCHER ON SOCIAL INFLUENCE

Robert Cialdini did his undergraduate work at the University of Wisconsin and earned his Ph.D. at the University of North Carolina in 1970. After a year of postdoctoral study, he took a faculty position at Arizona State University, where he rose through the ranks and now holds the title of Regents' Professor. For variety, he has held visiting scholar positions at five other major universities from Ohio State to Stanford.

The author of nearly 100 articles, Cialdini is best known for his book *Influence: Science and Practice,* which has appeared in several editions and seven languages. Built on his own field research studying the influence techniques of com-

pliance professionals such as car salesmen, it describes basic psychological principles which people use to gain compliance from others. Cialdini has also used his knowledge in community programs to help consumers resist unwanted compliance pressures, and to help organizations achieve worthwhile goals such as increasing blood donations and reducing public littering. In recognition of his research contributions, he has been named to many journal editorial boards and elected president of the APA Division of Personality and Social Psychology.

quickly develop into a wave of worker unrest, obstructionism, unreasonable demands, or employee resignations. In contrast, Varela (1971) has designed ways of using dissonance concepts to resolve conflicts within organizations by persuading major participants to be less rigid in their viewpoints and more cooperative in seeking solutions to organizational problems. When this is accomplished, individuals may accept a new

proposal that differs from their earlier rigid position, and then dissonance reduction will cause them to seek social support from people in any faction and thus allow movement toward genuine agreement.

Dissonance theory has been applied to many other areas, including encouraging weight loss, reducing phobias, increasing assertiveness, and helping problem drinkers (Cialdini, Petty, & Cacioppo, 1981).

Photograph courtesy of Leon Festinger. Reprinted by permission.

Box 2-3

LEON FESTINGER, ARTISTIC THEORIST AND EXPERIMENTALIST

Called "social psychology's Picasso" in an obituary in the *American Psychologist,* Leon Festinger was the preeminent experimentalist and theorist of his era in social psychology. One of the many famous psychologists who studied under Kurt Lewin, he was born in New York in 1919, graduated from City College, and completed his Ph.D. with Lewin at the University of Iowa in 1942. After teaching briefly at the University of Rochester, he joined Lewin's new Research Center for Group Dynamics at M.I.T. Following Lewin's untimely death, he moved with the Center to the University of Michigan, until he was appointed a full professor by the University of Minnesota at the age of 32. In 1955 he moved to Stanford University, and in 1968 he returned to New York to teach at the New School for Social Research.

Festinger's 1957 book, *A Theory of Cognitive Dissonance,* became the most controversial topic of that era and stimulated a tremendous flow of creative research on attitude change. He also published widely cited theories of social communication and social comparison processes, and he was famous as a role model for many productive students. In addition to major theories and elegant laboratory research, his contributions include field and observational research studies and statistical writings. He received the APA's Distinguished Scientific Contribution Award and was elected to the National Academy of Sciences. In the early 1960s, he left social psychology to concentrate his research on the field of perception, but before his death in 1989 he wrote his retrospective thoughts about social psychology.

Reactance Theory

In many ways a relative of dissonance theory, reactance theory was developed by Jack Brehm (1966). Its basic principle is that when people receive messages that seem to limit their freedom of action, **reactance** will motivate them to oppose the idea of the message. For example, if you are told that you should be more prompt in coming to work, you will tend to defensively think of many arguments why that is difficult or unreasonable, and you are likely to continue or increase your tardiness. Even if you are pressured to do something you normally like to do (for example, "You should finish up this ice cream for dessert"), you will often tend to be resistant and feel that this time you'd rather do something different (such as having cake instead). If there is a threat of punishment involved in an order, such as a reprimand for being late to work, the re actance may take the form of substituting some other undesirable behavior or encouraging others to break the prohibition rather than running the risk of breaking it oneself. The unfortunate applications of this principle are all too clear in work situations, where reactance-provoking orders are often given to subordinates.

Varela (1971) suggested positive ways in which reactance can be used to accomplish desired ends. One point is not to issue orders or regulations from above without genuine consultation with subordinates. Second, in group problem-solving and conflict-resolution situations, it is best to avoid or soften the statement of extreme views which other group members may be motivated to contradict. Any criticism of another person's ideas tends to produce a win-lose conflict, provoking that person to defend them even more vigorously than before. Third, in persuasion situations, pressures toward compliance produce reactance motivation, so target individuals must be given the feeling that they are voluntarily and freely reaching their own decision. If the persuader states that "It is obvious that. . . ." the target person will probably react, "Not to me, it isn't."

Theories of Normative Influence

Other people play an important role in determining how we act. Our beliefs about how other people act, or should act, often strongly determine our own behavior. A **norm** is an unwritten social rule about the appropriate behavior in a given situation (Campbell & Fairey, 1989). Conformity to the normative pressures of a group often occurs because of our desire to be liked and accepted by others. Classic studies by Asch (1958) and Sherif (1936) demonstrated the power of groups in producing conformity. For instance, in Asch's study, an unsuspecting participant was faced with a group of individuals who all agreed on some judgmental decision.

In such situations, even though the target person may initially perceive the situation differently, he or she will frequently "go along" with the group consensus and then look for reasons to explain why the group was right (Bond & Smith, 1996). For example, when faced with a group unanimously stating an opinion that differs from one's own, one might generate cognitions like "they had a better angle to see the situation than I did" or "they had some prior information that I didn't have."

From an applied perspective, social norms provide an important target for interventions that are designed to change behavior. If we change a person's beliefs about what other people are doing, or beliefs about what other people should do, then we can change the behaviors that are associated with these beliefs. Consequently, social norms are one of the key elements in Fishbein and Ajzen's (1975) theory of reasoned action. We will examine interventions aimed at social norms in Chapters 7, 11, and 12.

In contrast to normative influence, **informational social influence** occurs when persons change their behavior in response to information about reality. This type of change occurs, not because of our desire to be liked and accepted, but because of our desire to be accurate in our beliefs. We use information from various sources as a test for the validity of our own beliefs (Campbell & Fairey, 1989). Changing behavior through informational influence involves providing information. For example, if we wanted to reduce smoking among adolescents, a typical informational intervention would be to provide facts about the harmful effects of smoking—a technique which is not usually very effective, as we will see in Chapter 12.

Resisting Social Influence. If we can understand the forces that lead people to act in certain ways, then perhaps we can also develop techniques by which to block these effects if they are unwanted. Such techniques would be particularly useful in eliminating certain undesirable types of attitudes or behaviors or keeping them from forming. For example, some of the candidates for this type of intervention include preventing drug and alcohol use among adolescents, reducing smoking rates, producing safer sexual behaviors in order to prevent the spread of the AIDS virus, reducing violence and intergroup conflict, mitigating the potential effect of violent television on children, and preventing drunk driving. All of these are instances where we want to prevent an attitude or behavior from occurring. A variety of techniques have been developed to accomplish this goal, and they are discussed in chapters throughout this book.

THEORIES OF SOCIAL COGNITION

Social cognition is the area of social psychology devoted to studying how people think about each other. Among the topics included within social cognition are attitudes, stereotypes, adaptation level, social comparison, social judgment, and attribution. For a comprehensive overview of social cognition, see Wyer and Srull (1994).

Attitudes

The concept of attitudes is one of the oldest and most important in the field of social psychology. **Attitudes** are mental states of readiness for some type of behavior; they are "predisposition[s] to respond in a particular way to an attitude object" (Oskamp, 1991, p. 7). One common view of attitudes is that they have a cognitive, an affective, and a behavioral component. The cognitive dimension of an attitude involves ideas and beliefs about the attitude object, which may be a person, a group, an object, or an abstract concept such as capital punishment. The affective dimension of an attitude refers to the feelings and emotions evoked by the attitude object. Finally, the behavioral component consists of readiness to respond in specific ways to the object. One of the central issues for attitude researchers is the relationship between attitudes and behaviors. Most research on the issue indicates that general attitudes are related to behavior, though often rather weakly. A variety of situational and personal factors help to determine whether the relationship will be strong or weak (e.g., Schultz & Oskamp, 1996).

Among the most prominent theories about attitudes and their relationship to behavior are the theory of reasoned action, the theory of planned behavior, and the elaboration likelihood model, all of which were men-

tioned above and are described at greater length in Chapter 14.

Stereotypes

Stereotypes are overgeneralized sets of beliefs about the characteristics or attributes of a group (Hilton & von Hipple, 1996; Stangor & Lange, 1994). These beliefs can be either positive or negative, although we most commonly think of stereotypes as being negative and prejudiced beliefs. Stereotypes are the result of the natural human tendency to categorize information, and in many ways they help us to organize and function effectively in a complex and information-loaded social world (Judd & Park, 1993). However, when our stereotypes contain biased or inaccurate negative beliefs, they become **prejudice**, and acting on these prejudiced beliefs is termed **discrimination**. Because both prejudice and discrimination can have many harmful effects, we have devoted Chapter 9 to an extensive discussion of the issues of gender and ethnic prejudice and discrimination.

Adaptation-Level Theory

A theory that is highly relevant to attitudes is adaptation-level theory (Helson, 1964). A person's **adaptation level** on any given dimension (e.g., temperature) is a level of stimulation that has become neutral through preceding exposure, and serves as a reference point for judgments on that dimension. For instance, if you leave a warm house to take a walk on a brisk day, your body will first feel the outside air as cool. But soon it will adapt so that the outside air feels normal, and when you return to the house, its air may feel too hot to you for awhile until your temperature receptors adapt again.

Helson (1964) argued that all aspects of human thought and behavior—for example, our attitudes and expectations about social interaction—are influenced by the adaptation level produced by our prior experiences. In social judgment, we tend to view our own attitudes or behavior as moderate and use them as a reference point for evaluating others' positions as "reasonable" or "too extreme" in one direction or another. However, repeated exposure to a person with a markedly different viewpoint may cause us to change our adaptation level toward that person's position. Our adaptation level on any given topic serves as a norm that has important implications for our social judgments, perceptions of equity and fairness, and expectations and emotions regarding social behavior (Kahneman & Miller, 1986).

Social Comparison Theory

Another closely related theory is **social comparison theory** (Festinger, 1954), which concerns how people evaluate their own beliefs, attitudes, and abilities. It postulates that people have a drive to make these self-evaluations and that they steadily seek out information for that purpose. Whenever possible they base their self-evaluations on objective criteria (e.g., number of seconds taken to run 100 yards). But what happens when there is no objective information, as in the case of attitudes and many beliefs? The theory proposes that in situations where there is no objective standard, we compare ourselves with the beliefs or behaviors of others. Moreover, we are most inclined to make such comparisons with others who are similar to ourselves on important dimensions, such as our friends or coworkers.

Adaptation-level theory, social comparison theory, and social judgment theory (discussed next) are all examples of social evaluation theories, which hold that people evaluate themselves and other people largely on the basis of interpersonal comparisons (Pettigrew, 1967). This principle is also incorporated in the concept of relative deprivation, which is discussed below together with equity theory.

Social Judgment Theory

Another early social cognitive theory was Sherif and Hovland's (1961) social judgment theory. An especially useful aspect of the theory concerns the concepts of latitude of acceptance and latitude of rejection of attitude statements. To illustrate these concepts, consider attitudes toward capital punishment for certain crimes. If presented with a large number of attitude statements toward this topic, arranged along a favorable-to-unfavorable continuum, almost everyone will find more

than one of the positions acceptable, though one may be most acceptable; these positions are within the person's **latitude of acceptance**. Similarly, several of the positions will probably be unacceptable, and these are within the person's **latitude of rejection**.

These concepts mesh neatly with the learning-theory principle of successive approximation, mentioned above. Varela has developed the procedure of designing a persuasive argument in a series of small steps, each step so planned as to shift the target individual from rejecting to accepting a previously least-strongly-rejected position. After a series of such steps, the individual's overall attitude on the topic in question will have shifted from, let us say, moderately unfavorable to somewhat favorable. To fully appreciate the ingenuity of this approach, read Varela's (1971) original account of the procedure.

Attribution Theory

In the 1970s, attribution theory succeeded dissonance theory as the most popular research topic of social psychologists (Jones et al., 1989; Kelley & Michela, 1980). However, the term "theory" here is something of a misnomer, for even its main proponents admit that it is: "an amorphous collection of observations . . . [without] a firm grasp of interrelated deductive principles" (Jones et al., 1971, p. x). In fact, it has several parallel and partly overlapping strands, each stemming from one of the individuals or groups that have made major research contributions, particularly Jones and Davis (1965) and Kelley (1967). Whatever its status as theory, its general subject matter is clear—it studies the process of **attribution**: how people make judgments about the reasons or causes behind social behavior (cf. Gilbert & Malone, 1995; Jones et al., 1989).

Attribution theorists see people as "naive scientists" who are trying to understand the reasons for the interpersonal events that they observe or experience. For instance, you might ask yourself, "I wonder why that person smiled at me?" Starting with such an observed event, people reason backward to the possible intentions behind it (friendliness? nervousness? scorn?) and beyond that to the personal dispositions indicated by such intentions and behavior (a friendly person? an anxious person? a cruel person?). At each inferential step people look for clues to support one attributional conclusion over other possible ones. The results of such interpersonal detective work are obviously of great practical importance in our everyday lives, for most of us are constantly in the process of sizing up other people and their behavior.

Attributions can be either internal or external. **Internal attributions** ascribe the event in question to a personal disposition ("she succeeded because she is bright"), whereas **external attributions** ascribe it to a factor outside the person, that is, something in the situation ("he was just lucky," or "she succeeded because it was such an easy task"). One of the major research findings is that participants in interpersonal settings tend to attribute the reasons for their own behavior to situational factors (including the behavior of other participants), while outside observers tend to ascribe the same behavior to the personal characteristics of the participant. This tendency of observers to exaggerate the dispositional causes of behavior and underestimate its situational causes has been called the **fundamental attributional error** (Jones, 1979; Ross, 1977).

With its emphasis on everyday judgment about people and situations, attribution theory has countless potential applications, and some of them have been systematically explored. Attribution theory and findings have been applied to understanding help-giving situations, conflicts of young couples, parole decision processes, reactions to loneliness, behavior of battered wives, consumer responses to the quality of products, factors affecting physical and emotional health, and education and training programs (Amirkhan, 1990; Frieze, Bar-Tal, & Carroll, 1979; Metalsky et al., 1995; Weiner, 1990).

THEORIES OF SOCIAL RELATIONS

In discussing social psychological principles and theories so far, we have focused primarily on the level of the individual. Our next three sets of theories move from this intra-individual level to an interpersonal one, involving a progressively broader focus on groups, organizations, and communities.

Social relations is the area of social psychology devoted to how we interact with other people. Why are we attracted to some people and not others? Why do we fall in love? What forces lead to satisfaction in our relationships? What leads to conflict in a relationship and how is it best handled? Three useful theories of social relations are equity theory, role theory, and group process theories.

Equity Theory

Equity theory has progressed toward becoming a general theory of social behavior by incorporating elements from other theoretical approaches, including reinforcement, exchange, cognitive consistency, and psychoanalytic theories. The central issue of **equity theory** is how people decide that they are being treated justly or unjustly and how they react to such treatment.

Equity in a relationship is defined as a situation where all participants' outcomes (rewards minus costs) are proportional to their inputs or contributions to the relationship (Hatfield et al., 1985; Walster, Berscheid, & Walster, 1973). Though individuals generally try to maximize their outcomes, groups typically try to maintain social stability by developing systems of equity for their members and rewarding members who treat others equitably. When individuals find themselves inequitably treated, they feel distress, and they try to restore equity—either actually, by modifying the participants' inputs or outcomes, or psychologically, by distorting their perception of the inputs or outcomes. The feeling of resentment and injustice resulting from perceived inequity is often termed **relative deprivation,** and a substantial body of theory has been developed about the kind of groups with which people will choose to compare themselves and the circumstances under which they will feel relatively deprived (Crosby, 1976; Olson, Herman, & Zanna, 1986).

It is clear that equity theory is applicable to many areas of social life. Applications can be found in business interactions, helping relationships, and romantic and intimate relationships (e.g., Buunk & Van Yperen, 1991; Clark & Mills, 1993; Walster, Walster, & Berscheid, 1978). Research on equity principles has covered such potent topics as victimization, retaliation, restitution for harmful actions, exchange of gifts or favors, romantic love, and marital satisfaction.

Role Theory

Role theory has had surprisingly little attention within psychology, though it is a popular orientation among sociologists. Many different versions of role theory have been proposed by different authors, but "because role theory never generated an integrative theoretical statement, disagreement has appeared on the boundaries and assumptions of the field" (Biddle, 1979, pp. ix–x). Despite such disagreements, role theory is important because of the prominence of role concepts in group and organizational settings.

A **role** is a patterned set of behaviors that are generally expected of a particular category of people in a society—that is, people who share the same **social position**. Positions may be based on family relationships, occupations, recreational, political, or social characteristics. For instance, they include mother, husband, farmer, physician, quarterback, soprano, citizen, friend, and juvenile gang member. Each category of people is generally expected to display certain behaviors—their roles. All people occupy many positions during their lives, some of them at the same time (for example, mother, businesswoman, and club president). Thus arises the possibility of **role conflict**, when the expected behavior for one position is incompatible with that for another position (for example, going to your child's school play versus entertaining a business client).

Social groups and complex organizations often have organization charts that specify positions within the group and some of the expected role behaviors. In other cases role behaviors are not written down but nevertheless may be rigidly recognized and understood (for example: a mother should care for her children's needs, at least while the children are young). There may also be **role confusion** or controversy. (For instance, does "caring for her children's needs" mean that a mother of young children should not also hold a paid job?)

The above description illustrates how applicable role theory concepts are to many aspects of social life. As Biddle has pointed out, they have been used in "studies of small groups, families, communities, classrooms, kinship systems, formal organizations, and counseling. . . . in education as well as in the clinical and helping professions" (1979, p. ix).

Group Process Theories

Group process theories are a heterogeneous collection, but all of them deal with the processes operating in groups when the members are in face-to-face interaction with each other. One major branch of these theories began with Kurt Lewin's concept of **group dynamics**. Out of this developed the laboratory training movement, also called T-groups or sensitivity training, and later the more freewheeling encounter group movement and its many variants (Back, 1972; Johnson, 1988). Many theories in this area are highly speculative because they are based on experiences in groups with atypical membership and activities (for instance, group therapy in mental hospitals, or nude marathon sessions).

Another outgrowth of Lewin's group dynamic movement has been empirical, relatively rigorous research on group processes, much of it conducted in academic or in business settings. Summaries of some of this work have been published in a volume edited by Wheelan, Pepitone, and Abt (1990).

One example of a practical and useful theory based on this kind of careful empirical research is Fiedler's (1967, 1993) contingency theory of leadership effectiveness (see Chapter 5). The common notion that leadership effectiveness is due to certain traits of the leader (such as intelligence, or "charisma," or supportiveness toward coworkers) has been generally discredited by empirical research. Instead, Fiedler posited that leader traits would *interact* with situational variables in producing successful or unsuccessful group performance. The research evidence has largely supported this *contingency* concept, and the theory is relevant to all kinds of real-world group settings, from sports teams to army squads to executive committees (e.g., Fiedler & House, 1988, 1994).

THEORIES OF ORGANIZATIONAL BEHAVIOR

In our progression toward ever broader theories, organizational theories represent another step upward in complexity. At the organizational level, one widely used approach is **systems theory** (Katz & Kahn, 1978). A systems view of organizations starts with the postulate that an organization is an **open system**—that is, it is a set of interacting processes, which are influenced by the external environment and in turn influence the environment. Like all open systems, organizations have a cyclic nature in which inputs affect throughput activities, which produce outputs, which provide new sources of inputs. Systems aim to maintain a steady state or equilibrium, but to do so they have to import more energy than they export (a situation termed **negative entropy**). Finally, systems have information control mechanisms, which use feedback to modify their functioning, and they exhibit role differentiation and specialization, particularly as their size increases. Thus, organizational theories typically include aspects of narrower or more fundamental theories, such as role theory, exchange theory, and group process theory. The systems viewpoint can be useful in analyzing business corporations or government bureaucracies, as well as smaller organizations like schools, social clubs, or civic groups.

Another systems approach is the sociotechnical theory of organizations (Cherns, 1987; Pasmore et al., 1982). Like Katz and Kahn's open system theory, **sociotechnical theory** views organizations as dynamic and reactive. Its unique contribution is to study organizations in terms of the interrelationship between *technology,* social groups, and the organizational environment (e.g., Trist & Bamforth, 1951). Applied work in this area has examined how changing technology within an organization changes the way that people interact, or changes the social environment of the organization (Wall, Jackson, & Davids, 1992; Winterton, 1994). A key question from the sociotechnical perspective is how to *optimize* the fit between technological and social systems in the organizational setting (Wall et al., 1990). The level of optimization has been found to affect many aspects of organizational behavior, including productivity, costs, employee withdrawal, employee attitudes, safety, grievances, and perceptions about the quality of working life (Guzzo, Jette, & Katzell, 1985; Pasmore et al., 1982).

THEORIES ABOUT COMMUNITIES

As a final level of generality we will consider viewpoints about communities. Psychology's interest in community life is a relatively new one, growing out of the mental health movement of the 1950s and 1960s, and there are as yet no full-fledged theories of community functioning and change (Heller, 1990). On one hand, organizational theories could be applied to communities, for communities certainly possess the characteristics of open systems. However, communities are usually more nebulous and more comprehensive than organizations, since they usually contain many organizations and parts of organizations. The new field of community psychology is divided between several different approaches to working with community problems: a quasi-clinical one dealing with mental health and related problems, a social-organizational one working with community organizations, and a social-action one attempting to modify community power structures (Goodstein & Sandler, 1978).

Several theorists from different camps have written about communities from their own particular perspectives. For instance, B. F. Skinner's (1948) novel, *Walden Two,* described an ideal community as conceived of by a reinforcement theorist. In a different vein, Saul Alinsky's (1946) book, *Reveille for Radicals,* advocated community organization as a conflict-oriented social action process (see Chapter 16).

The most thorough empirical study of communities by psychologists has been conducted by Roger Barker and his colleagues, using a broad-gauge ecological perspective (Barker, 1987, 1989; also see Chapter 11). For 40 years they carried on intensive study of one small town in Kansas, as well as briefer research in other communities. Wicker (1979, 1987) has written interesting accounts of the results of this research, summarizing some of the main conclusions as follows:

Behavior settings such as supermarkets, machine shops, psychology classes, basketball games, and bridge-club meetings should be thought of as active, organized, self-regulating systems and not merely as passive backdrops where people carry out actions that they have freely chosen. According to the ecological viewpoint, people are but one component of the larger behavior-setting system, which restricts the range of their behavior by promoting and sometimes demanding certain actions and by discouraging or prohibiting others. (1979, p. 4)

Wicker also described applications of Barker's ecological theory to role behavior in large and small organizations, to understaffed or overstaffed settings, and to management of the effects of behavior settings on oneself and others.

SUMMARY

This chapter has provided an overview of the different types and levels of theories and principles often used in applied social psychology. Lewin's dictum that theories are useful has been extended by Varela with his emphasis on social technology—combining theories, techniques, and findings from a wide variety of areas to accomplish a specific social goal. Among the psychological techniques that have proven useful are psychometric measurement of people's abilities, interests, and personal motives, such as authoritarianism and needs for approval, achievement, or consistency. Valuable social psychology principles include approach-avoidance conflicts, foot-in-the-door and door-in-the-face techniques, public commitment, and self-fulfilling prophecies.

Useful social psychological theories can be classified as dealing with social influence, social cognition, or social relations. Learning theory's reinforcement principles are constantly used in applied work, including the procedures of successive approximation and partial reinforcement. Traditional learning theory has also given rise to related approaches such as exchange theory and social learning theory, including the principles of observational learning through modeling, vicarious reinforcement, and self-reinforcement. Another group of theories, concerning adaptation levels, social

comparisons, and social judgment, all rely on the central principle that people evaluate themselves and other individuals by making interpersonal comparisons. The concepts of social judgment theory, such as latitudes of acceptance and rejection, and many principles from cognitive dissonance theory and reactance theory, can be combined in designing persuasion techniques. Theories of persuasion and of normative and informational influence can be used in interventions to change attitudes, stereotypes, or behavior, or to help people resist undesirable social pressures.

Attribution theory, the study of how people explain the reasons behind social behavior, has many applications in areas such as health care, the judicial system, education, and consumer psychology. Both equity theory and role theory have clear applications in business settings, as well as in families and in helping relationships of many kinds. Theories of group processes have been used in group therapy and sensitivity training and, more scientifically, in studies of group leadership. Finally, theories of organizational behavior and community processes, based on a systems viewpoint, are the broadest theories that have been used in applied social psychology.

SUGGESTED READINGS

Cialdini, R. (1993). *Influence: Science and practice* (3rd ed.). New York: HarperCollins.—A very readable book containing a systematic summary of influence tactics used to get people to buy, say, sign, or do what the influence agents desire.

Graham, S., & Folkes, V. S. (Eds.). (1990). *Attribution theory: Applications to achievement, mental health, and interpersonal conflict*. Hillsdale, NJ: Erlbaum.—An excellent collection of articles on applications of attribution theory.

Higgins, E. T., & Kruglanski, A. (Eds.) (1996). *Social psychology: Handbook of basic principles*. New York: Guilford.—An up-to-date reference work covering the concepts, theories, and research areas of social psychology.

Varela, J. A. (1977). Social technology. *American Psychologist, 32,* 914–923.—This brief paper gives some excellent examples of Varela's intriguing use of a wide variety of social psychological theories and concepts to solve social problems in creative and novel ways.

CHAPTER 3

Survey Research— The Quality of Life, and Sexuality

Society needs to be well-informed about itself in order that it may function more wisely.

—Campbell, Converse, & Rodgers (1976, p. 5)

How many people in this country today are satisfied with their lives? Which aspects of life are the sources of people's greatest satisfaction, and which aspects cause the most dissatisfaction? Are people in cities happier than people in rural areas, or less happy? Are old folks more or less satisfied with life than young adults or the middle-aged? Has happiness in this country increased or decreased over the years?

Questions such as these are usually answered by means of survey research, which is probably the most common and widespread of all forms of social research. Almost every day you can see in your newspaper or newsmagazine an account of the findings of some survey study. The Gallup Poll and the Harris Survey are just the best-known of countless survey organizations that are constantly charting the public's political opinions, consumer preferences, recreational activities, and changing moods. The results of survey research are extensively used to aid decision making in business and government. As far back as 1978, about $4 *billion* per year was spent to conduct surveys in the United States, and much more is spent on them today. A government report concluded that the technique of survey research is "indispensable in the public and private sectors" (Cordes, 1982a, p. 40).

What is a **survey**? Essentially, it is a study in which people are asked questions about some topic of interest to the investigator. The people selected as **respondents** may be any group the researcher chooses. However, the characteristics of the sample of respondents and the way in which they were chosen are vital factors in determining the adequacy of the survey. The questions may be asked orally in an **interview** or in writing on a **questionnaire**. The subject matter of the questions may vary widely, covering knowledge, attitudes, behavior, personal characteristics, or environmental situations. The format of the questions may also vary from **open-end** (questions that allow a free response) to **closed-end**—questions that have a limited set of answers to choose from (e.g., multiple choice

items, or several-point scales). Surveys may be entirely descriptive in nature, but they are apt to be designed to test various hypotheses or theories.

Survey studies vary widely in quality, so it is important to know what to look for in deciding how much credence to put in their results. In this chapter, we will discuss the important indicators of the adequacy of survey studies, and we will illustrate them with studies on two main topics. The first study we will examine has a double importance because its topic was the *quality of life,* a crucial goal in the work of applied social scientists (see Chapter 1). Later we will discuss a recent and highly publicized survey of sexuality in America.

AN EXAMPLE OF SURVEY METHODOLOGY—THE QUALITY OF LIFE

For many years economists have had quantitative measures, such as the gross national product or the consumer price index, by which they assessed the economic side of national life. In contrast, without measures of the subjective, personal side of life, we have not been able to tell whether the *quality* of people's lives has been improving or falling or holding steady. For instance, were "the good old days" really better than today or not? Today we have urban smog and traffic congestion, but 100 years ago we had slum tenements and unpaved roads covered with horse manure. Today we have hectic lives and high divorce rates, but in the last century we had poor medical care and a high death rate from disease. Which time period produced greater personal satisfaction and happiness? There is no way of answering this question without reliable, objective measures of the quality of people's lives.

The study that we will analyze was designed to gain an understanding of what standards Americans use in evaluating the quality of their lives. It was conducted by Angus Campbell, Philip Converse, and Willard

Rodgers (1976), key staff members at the Survey Research Center of the University of Michigan. In addition to studying the quality of life of Americans, the research was designed to construct a series of **social indicators**—objective measures that could be used in future studies to trace changes and trends in the subjective, psychological aspects of American life.

Background and Theory

First the investigators had to decide what they wanted to measure and to design an instrument that would accomplish their goals. Naturally, they started from the theory and findings already available in this field, though both were limited. Theorizing in the area had generally defined a good society as one that most fully satisfies the individual needs of its citizens, and this line of thought led the investigators to select *general satisfaction with life* as the most basic concept of their study. In contrast to the concept of happiness, which implies an experience of affect (emotions or feelings), "satisfaction implies a judgmental or cognitive experience [and it] can be precisely defined as the perceived discrepancy between aspiration and achievement, ranging from the perception of fulfillment to that of deprivation" (Campbell et al., 1976, p. 8).

In order to get a fuller understanding of the rise and fall of people's life satisfaction over time, the authors also wanted to break down the concept of general satisfaction into a set of more specific elements. Based on past research and on public policy relevance, they decided to use a list of 12–15 domains of life that are important for most or all people (e.g., health, family life, work, etc.). These domains are listed later in Table 3-1.

The authors then developed a model of the factors involved in a person's expressed satisfaction with any given domain of life and the way in which overall satisfaction with life is determined. In logical sequence, the model proposed that a person's *objective situation* in any given domain, such as health, is a factor in his or her *perception* of the domain, but the perception may be quite different from the objective situation due to *idiosyncratic personal characteristics*. Next, the perceived situation combines with the person's *stan-

dards of comparison* to determine his or her evaluation of that domain. Again, personal characteristics enter, combining with the person's evaluation to determine *satisfaction* with the domain. Finally, levels of satisfaction in all of the many domains of life combine to produce a person's overall life satisfaction.

The Measuring Instrument

Given this theoretical model, the authors proceeded to construct a measuring instrument that would cover its important dimensions. Some items were taken from past research, and many were constructed specially for this study. The process involved many steps: planning the wording carefully, then trying it out on pilot respondents, rewriting items and instructions to eliminate problems, and further pretesting. The authors also decided to use face-to-face household interviews as the method of collecting the data in order to allow the respondents considerable freedom in expressing themselves and to ensure a relatively high response rate.

The resulting interview schedule included 42 typed pages of questions for the interviewer to ask, plus 4 pages of items for the interviewer to fill in about the respondent, the dwelling, and the neighborhood. Such an interview would normally take an hour or more to complete, depending on how talkative the respondent was. The interview used both open-end questions to get general reactions to a topic and closed-end ones to get specific answers that could be compared from one respondent to another. The schedule frequently used a **funnel sequence,** starting with open questions and gradually moving to more precise closed-end ones on a particular topic. Here are examples of an open-end and a closed-end question:

C1. Now I have some questions on how you feel about life in this country as a whole. Do you think that there are some ways in which life in the United States is getting worse? [Space follows for recording answers.]

C4. People sometimes tell us that public officials in this country don't always treat them as fairly as they ought to. How about you—would you say that in general public officials treat you *very* fairly, fairly enough, not very fairly, or not fairly at all? [Boxes follow for recording answers.] (pp. 526–527)

The interview schedule mainly concentrated on the specific domains of life identified by the authors. It also contained questions about the respondent's background and some personality and attitude scales measuring feelings of stress, anxiety, and personal competence. Finally, it included a number of scales that allowed comparison of this study with the results of other studies (alternative measures of happiness, an index of affect, a composite measure of general well-being, and so on).

Extensive statistical work was done to show the characteristics of these indices and the relationships among them. In particular, it was important to determine their **reliability**—that is, the consistency of their measurements. Two kinds of reliability are commonly used: **internal consistency** measures, showing the amount of agreement among different items intended to assess the same concept; and **stability** measures, indicating the consistency of scores on the same scale at two different points in time. Both kinds are normally reported in terms of correlation coefficients, so a score of 0 would represent no relationship and +1.00 would represent perfect consistency.

Results for the reliability computations showed that the 8-item index of general affect had an internal consistency coefficient (Cronbach's alpha) of .89—a high level. Another indication of internal consistency was that a combination of the separate domain satisfaction scores correlated .74 with the overall life satisfaction index. A repeat interview with a subsample of respondents eight months later showed quite a high stability correlation (.76) for a composite index made up of 14 individual domain satisfaction scores. However, there were lower stability correlations for the overall satisfaction measure (.43) and for the index of affect (.56)—both undoubtedly partially due to real changes in the lives of some respondents over the 8-month period.

The Sample of Respondents

The goal of the sampling process in this study was to achieve a national **representative sample** of American adults—that is, a sample closely comparable in its characteristics to the total national population. The only way to achieve a truly representative sample is to use the process of **probability sampling**, in which every person in the population has a known probability of being selected into the sample. In this study, the complex procedure used to accomplish this goal was a multi-stage stratified random sample of dwellings in the 48 contiguous states. In such a multi-stage national sample, the first stage involves choosing a representative sample of geographic areas of the country, such as counties. Within each primary area, the second stage involves choosing a random sample of smaller areas, such as census tracts. Then, within each selected census tract, a few blocks are randomly chosen, all of their dwellings are listed, and a random selection is made of a few dwellings within each block. When all that is done and checked by the sampling staff, interviewers are sent to the specified dwellings with instructions to interview a particular individual, such as the youngest adult woman in the household. Such a sample inevitably omits transients and people living in prisons, dormitories, hospitals, and military barracks; but in other respects it should almost perfectly reflect the population of the whole country.

By procedures such as these the authors of the study chose a representative probability sample of 2720 occupied dwellings, and they designated for interview one resident age 18 or older in each dwelling. Interviewers were directed to make several visits if necessary in order to complete the interview. In the end, after repeated not-at-homes and interview refusals were subtracted, 2164 respondents were actually interviewed—a response rate of 80%, which is a very good figure for careful household interview studies.

Detailed comparisons were made between the characteristics of the sample and the national population as shown in the 1970 census. On most dimensions such as age, ethnic group, and education the distribution of the sample was close to that of the population (less than 3% different on any given category, such as percentage of high school graduates). However, as often happens in household interviews, the percentage of men in the sample was noticeably smaller (7% less) than their percentage in the population. This discrepancy was offset by the statistical procedure of *weighting* the scores of men by a factor of 1.25, thus giving them approximately their appropriate representation in comparison with women. The overall result was a sample that closely matched the characteristics of the national population.

In the final stage of their study, Campbell and his colleagues reinterviewed a portion of the original respondents about eight months later, in order to check the reliability of data and determine changes in people's satisfaction over time. The sampling procedure systematically selected one-sixth of the original respondents in every area of the country. Of the 346 selected for the reinterview sample, 285 were reinterviewed, a response rate of 82%.

Photograph courtesy of Survey Research Center, Institute for Social Research. Reprinted by permission.

Box 3-1

ANGUS CAMPBELL, "MR. SURVEY RESEARCH"

A pioneer in the field of survey research, Angus Campbell was director of the Survey Research Center at the University of Michigan for over 20 years and later head of its parent organization, the Institute for Social Research. He earned his B.A. and M.A. at the University of Oregon and his Ph.D. in experimental psychology at Stanford in 1936. He taught for a few years at Northwestern, and then received a postdoctoral fellowship, on which he conducted his first survey study.

In 1942 Campbell moved to the Division of Program Surveys of the U.S. Department of Agriculture, where he helped direct its many survey studies during World War II. Following the war, much of the division staff moved to the University of Michigan to found the Survey Research Center, which established new standards of excellence in conducting na-

tionwide surveys. Campbell remained there as a highly productive researcher until his death in 1980.

This chapter describes some of Campbell's important work in developing social indicators of the quality of American life. He also did notable studies of racial attitudes, and he was most widely known for his research on political attitudes and voting patterns, based on nationwide studies of every American election since 1948. These studies were summarized in the influential volumes *The Voter Decides, The American Voter,* and *Elections and the Political Order.* Campbell's outstanding research earned him the Distingished Contribution Awards from both the APA and the American Association of Public Opinion Research, as well as election to the National Academy of Sciences.

Interviewing, Coding, and Data Analysis

After the instrument construction and sampling are completed, there are still many time-consuming steps in a study such as this. In localities all around the country, hundreds of interviewers (who have previously been trained to a high standard of competence) have to find their assigned respondents at home and complete their interviews, a process that takes several weeks or months. Field supervisors oversee this stage of the work and check over the written interview protocols for completeness and clarity. Back in the home office, **coders** take the written answers and convert them to numerical codes, using elaborate codebooks of detailed instructions made up especially for the study. The completed coding sheets are **check-coded** for accuracy and then given to **data-entry clerks**, who type the numbers into computer files. The data files are analyzed by high-speed computers, using a wide variety of statistical programs, and the results are printed out on many reams of computer paper. Finally, after much study and further statistical analyses necessitated by the earlier results, the authors write a report summarizing their procedures and conclusions.

KEY CHARACTERISTICS OF SURVEY RESEARCH

Instrument Construction

From this fairly detailed description of the quality-of-life study, you can see most of the typical features of survey research. Following the abstract phase of theoretical conceptualization, the first hands-on activity is instrument construction. In this phase past research is invariably consulted for useful measures, and many new items and scales are usually developed as well. This process requires very careful attention to many considerations: the order of topics and questions, question format, the vocabulary used, avoiding biased or emotionally loaded wording, maximizing clarity, and ensuring both completeness and conciseness. A full treatment of these points is contained in *The Art of Asking Questions,* a useful little book by Payne (1951), and in more recent larger volumes (Fowler, 1993; Sudman & Bradburn, 1982; Sudman, Bradburn, & Schwarz,

1996). These factors can be crucial because sometimes quite subtle differences in the wording and context of items can cause large differences in respondents' answers to them (Schuman & Presser, 1981).

Instrument construction involves many steps of reviewing the wording for understandability, precision, and lack of bias; having expert colleagues check over the items and instructions for possible problems; **pretesting** the items and instructions on some appropriate respondents and noting any difficulties that arise; rewriting them for greater clarity; and further **pilot studies** with respondents similar to the ones who will be contacted in the actual study.

A final important aspect of this phase is determining the measuring instruments' reliability—either internal consistency or stability or both. In many studies, as in the Campbell et al. research, there are some single-item measures in addition to longer scales. Since internal consistency coefficients cannot be obtained for single-item measures, their reliability can only be determined by readministering them to the same respondents at a later date, as these authors took pains to do.

Sample Selection

The next major phase of a survey is selection of the respondents. All surveys are aimed at reaching some conclusions about a **population** of respondents—that is, the total group of individuals having specified features in common. For instance, the population of interest might be all American adults, or it could be as small a group as all the students in one college. Unless the population in question is a very small one, researchers usually decide to contact only a **sample**—that is, a subset of the total population. The size of the sample to be selected is determined by a tradeoff of two factors: A larger sample yields greater precision of measurement, but data collection may cost a great deal more than for a smaller sample.

The *representativeness* of the sample is a major key to the quality of the resulting data. If a sample is biased or unrepresentative, no matter how large it is, it will not accurately reflect the population. But if it is carefully drawn, even a relatively small sample (such as a few hundred individuals) should quite closely resemble its underlying population. This fact accounts for the great advantage of **probability samples**. As mentioned above, they are defined as ones where the probability of selection of every member of the population is known, and as a consequence they have a relatively small and known amount of **sampling error**—the expected degree of discrepancy between the sample data and the actual population parameter. Another advantage of probability samples is that they allow investigators to **oversample** small population subgroups—that is, to assign their members any desired higher probability of being selected into the sample, in order to get enough cases to reach dependable conclusions about them. When this is done, the resulting data are later adjusted by **weighting** the subgroups differentially to give a correct estimate of the total population, as was done for men and women respondents in the quality-of-life survey.

Because the respondents in the Campbell et al. study were selected by strict probability sampling methods, it is possible to compute the expected amount of sampling error in the resulting data. (This is not technically possible with other less rigorous techniques of sample selection, including the **quota sampling** method, which is used in the final stages of respondent selection by most commercial polls such as Gallup and Harris.) For Campbell's whole sample of 2000-plus respondents, the scores stated in percentages should have no more than a ±2½% margin of error due to sampling. However, for subsamples such as men, non-Whites, or college graduates, the sampling error of scores will be substantially larger than for the whole sample, with the smallest subsamples having the largest sampling error (for example, a subsample of 100 will have an expected error of ±10%). The authors presented tables for the expected sampling error of different subsample sizes in an appendix.

Since the size of the sampling error varies inversely with the size of the sample or subsample providing the data, a careful research report will always indicate the expected size of sampling error for each portion of the data presentation. In addition, even with a probability sample, it is important to compare the sample's characteristics with known facts about the underlying population, as Campbell et al. did. In contrast with the

sampling error, whose size can be estimated accurately for a probability sample, it is not possible to specify the size of likely errors due to nonsampling factors, such as the nonresponse rate of intended sample members, problems in question wording, or mistakes in data collection or coding. However, such errors are always present to some degree and may frequently be larger than the sampling error.

Data Collection Issues

Many problems can occur in the data collection phase of survey research. Though there are ways to minimize or compensate for every type of problem, survey researchers must be constantly alert to these threats to the validity of their data.

Interviewer Effects. Interviewer effects are distortions in the data caused by the behavior or characteristics of the interviewer. In the area of the interviewer's behavior, a common problem is inadequate training, which can cause undesirable variations in the supposedly standardized interview procedure. The interviewer's first task is quickly to build *rapport* with the respondents in order to gain their confidence and cooperation. Poorly trained interviewers may do this awkwardly or inadequately; similarly, they may not follow the specified rules for standard question wording or for the use of optional follow-up questions (**probes**). Further behavioral problems can include improperly reinforcing or discouraging the respondent's answers, giving unintentional indications of what the interviewer expects the respondent to say, and even incorrect recording of answers. Helpful guidelines for training interviewers to avoid these lapses are given by Fowler and Mangione (1990).

Though the interviewers' behavior can be modified by further training, many of their characteristics cannot. Interviewers' ethnic group, gender, age, and social class (as shown by vocabulary and accent) have all been found to affect respondents' answers in some research studies (Hatchett & Schuman, 1975; Kane & Macaulay, 1993; Schuman & Hatchett, 1974). Such effects on answers usually occur only when the interviewer and respondent differ on one of these features (such as ethnicity) *and* the topic of the questions is controversial and relevant to the differing characteristic (e.g., B. Campbell, 1981). For instance, Black and White interviewers might get somewhat different answers to questions about attitudes toward affirmative action programs. The typical effect is that some respondents tend to be "polite" and avoid stating views that might offend the interviewer. Fortunately, careful research has shown that, in published survey studies as they are actually conducted, it is rare for the data to show any appreciable differences due to interviewer effects, from either behavior or characteristics (Sudman & Bradburn, 1974; Weeks & Moore, 1981).

Response Sets. Response sets are systematic ways of answering that are not directly related to the content of the questions but may be typical of certain respondents. Probably the most common and troublesome of these is the **social desirability** response set. As the name implies, it is a tendency to answer questions in the socially desirable direction, rather than being completely truthful. It occurs most often when the topic involves aspects of social norms or "proper" behavior. Useful techniques for guarding against the social desirability set are: building good rapport and listening respectfully, assuring the respondents that there are no right or wrong answers and that their own ideas and opinions will be accepted, wording questions so that the less-common response appears acceptable, and offering alternative choices that are about equal in social desirability. Another response set is **acquiescence**, or the tendency to agree with interview questions regardless of their content. This can normally be overcome by wording questions with at least two alternatives (for example, "Do you tend to favor or oppose the proposed law?").

Reactivity. A pervasive problem of survey research is the fact that much social measurement is **reactive** in nature—that is, the act of measuring something can change what you are trying to measure. For instance, asking people "What do you think of the proposed law about _____?" may suggest that they should have some opinion about it, may remind them of some fact that influences their answer, or may stimulate them to learn more about the subject—none of which might have occurred if you hadn't asked the question. A dramatic illustration of this effect was seen in a study where people who were interviewed briefly on local political issues were more than twice as likely to vote in a subsequent primary election as were those not interviewed (Kraut & McConahay, 1973). This kind of reactivity in social viewpoints is inevitable, but its effects on survey data can be minimized by some of the same techniques used to combat social desirability response sets. Also, it is wise to assess respondents' level of information on the topic in question and to discount the opinions of uninformed respondents.

Validity. The most crucial question in any research is: Are the data really correct or **valid** indicators of what one is trying to study? Interviewer effects, response sets, and reactivity are all conditions that can lower the validity of the survey data. Even if their effect is minimized, it is often difficult to assess the validity of the data; so ideally, one would like to have an outside criterion against which to check the survey data.

Occasionally, for factual or behavioral questions, it is possible to compare *individual-level* responses with official records or behavioral observations. Wentland and Smith (1993) have presented a thorough review of such items, collected over a 40-year period. Through a meta-analysis (see Chapter 7 for an explanation of this technique), they showed that the most important feature promoting the validity of answers was the *accessibility* of the requested information to the respondent's recall. Concerning the important issue of *social desirability,* they found, surprisingly, that reports about socially *un*desirable behavior were apt to be *more* accurate than reports about socially desirable behavior. Their results suggest various techniques that can be used to increase response validity. One example is that children's self-reports of smoking were found to be more valid after saliva samples were taken and the children were shown how their saliva could be analyzed for nicotine content (Evans, Hansen, & Mittelmark, 1977).

Sometimes the validity of *aggregate-level* survey data can also be verified, as in the case of election results validating survey studies of voting intentions. For instance, in the 16 congressional and presidential elections from 1952 through 1994, the Gallup Poll's average error in predicting the result has been only 1.6%, a figure considerably smaller than the poll's expected sampling error (*Gallup Poll Monthly,* November 1994). Another worthwhile procedure is to validate measures of social attitudes by using a *criterion-groups approach.* For example, on a measure of liberalism-conservatism, there should be a marked difference between the mean score of members of Americans for Democratic Action and the mean for members of the Christian Coalition.

Two validity problems in the survey interview that are related to *time* have been discussed by Angus Campbell (1981). The first is that in only an hour or so the interviewer may not be able to plumb the deeper levels of the respondent's true feelings. The other is that the interview gives a static picture of how the respondent felt at only one point, with little information on fluctuations over time. This limitation can be partially overcome by repeated studies, either with the same respondents (a **panel study**), or with successive cross-sectional samples.

Costs. One of the practical factors in survey research is that household interviewing has become exceedingly expensive in recent years—lengthy studies can cost as much as several hundred dollars per completed interview for data collection alone. Also, refusal rates have been increasing, especially in central city areas where both interviewers and potential respondents are often fearful of contacts with strangers (Schuman & Kalton, 1985).

Three ways around these problems have gained considerable acceptance recently. One is *interviewing by telephone,* which is safe for the interviewer, is easy and relatively less expensive for the researcher, and allows closer supervision to ensure standard procedures. The problem of unlisted numbers, which may be as numerous as 40% or more in urban areas (Frey, 1989), can be completely avoided by the use of **random digit dialing**—choosing phone numbers randomly from among all possible numbers. Though telephone surveys usually have nonresponse rates that are somewhat higher than face-to-face interviews, their costs may average only half as much per respondent (Frey, 1989). Also, studies have shown that telephone interviewing can

obtain quite complete and unbiased data, even regarding socially sensitive topics; and once started, respondents are generally willing to continue talking, even up to an hour (Frey, 1989; Rogers, 1976). Furthermore, with the modern technique of **computer-assisted telephone interviewing** (CATI), a computer program can select the order of questions, which the telephone interviewer can read to the respondent directly from the computer monitor screen; and the answers can be punched directly into the computer's memory, thus saving several steps in data coding and entry. As a result of all these advantages, telephone interviewing has become the dominant method of survey research in the U.S. today (Groves, 1990). However, it has also been used extensively in recent years by solicitors and telemarketers, and as a result many people have become resistant to responding to legitimate telephone surveys.

A second technique that is sometimes substituted for household interviews is *content analysis* of published materials, such as magazine articles or newspaper editorials. This is also a survey method, but it uses written materials instead of live respondents. Where there has been sufficient media coverage of a given topic, this approach can assess the views of a representative cross-section of media writers, who are often important opinion leaders in our society. And it can often do it more quickly, cheaply, and easily than interviews (cf. Weber, 1990). A third possible substitute for household interviews is using *written questionnaires,* which are mailed to potential respondents. Dillman (1978, 1991) has summarized research findings and presented helpful techniques for increasing the typical low response rate of mail surveys—the problem that is generally their Achilles' heel.

RESULTS OF THE QUALITY-OF-LIFE SURVEY

Overall Satisfaction and Other Global Indices

To complete our discussion of the quality-of-life survey, we will present a few of its major findings here. The first major finding of the Campbell et al. (1976) study was that most Americans expressed general satisfaction with their life as a whole: 22% said they were "completely satisfied," 60% more stated other levels of satisfaction, 11% said they were "neutral," and only 7% expressed any degree of dissatisfaction. This surprisingly high degree of contentment is consistent with many other studies of people's satisfaction in various spheres, such as job satisfaction (see Chapter 10), and also with more recent data (Myers & Diener, 1995).

Of course, the absolute level of these self-reports may be influenced by a social desirability response bias, but the relative degree of overall satisfaction is still a crucial factor in comparing different individuals. For example, one of the strongest correlates of overall satisfaction was found to be marital status: Separated and divorced individuals were, on the average, much the lowest in overall satisfaction, single people were also low, widows and widowers were slightly below average, and married people averaged well above the population mean.

Comparing the cognitive measure of overall satisfaction with an affective index of general happiness, the authors found support for their view that the two indices would measure somewhat different aspects of life. For instance, Americans below age 35 were found to be the happiest age group, and people 75 and older were the least happy group. However, on satisfaction, just the opposite relationship held: The 65- to 74-year-olds were the most satisfied subgroup, with the 75-and-older group close behind, while the under-35 groups were below average in satisfaction. These differences make good sense when one considers that young adults, though generally happy, may not have achieved their aspirations and expectations yet, so they may feel somewhat less than satisfied with life. In contrast, the elderly, though less happy on the average than younger adults, often find their later years better than they had anticipated, so they may feel generally satisfied with life.

The authors also constructed a composite measure of "well-being" including *both* the affective aspects typical of happiness ratings and the more cognitive evaluation of life inherent in the satisfaction measure. This composite index of well-being had interesting relationships with various demographic variables. For instance, it showed a strong negative relationship to size of city, with the lowest group being people living in the country's 12 largest cities. In each category of increasingly smaller residential locations, feelings of well-being increased, so that rural dwellers had the highest average score of all the locations. It should be understood, however, that these patterns are correlational in nature; thus they may not indicate a causal relationship (see Chapter 5 for further discussion of this point).

Domain Satisfaction Measures

Another important aspect of the study was analysis of satisfaction in the separate domains of life. Interesting results of this analysis are presented in Table 3-1. Of these domains, marriage had the highest satisfaction rating, with only 3% of married respondents expressing any degree of dissatisfaction; and family life was next, with only 6% dissatisfied. Close to these in level of contentment were the areas of health, neighborhood, friendships, and housework or job. At the other end of the continuum, the area of financial savings caused the most dissatisfaction (36%), while amount of education was next (28% dissatisfied), and standard of living was third from the bottom (14% dissatisfied). Again, we might question the absolute level of these figures (for instance, in view of the fact that the percent of people who say that they are dissatisfied with their marriages is only about twice as high as the *annual* divorce rate). However, other survey studies in the United States and in other industrialized nations have also reported similar very high levels of satisfaction with marriage and family life (Caplow, 1982; Myers & Diener, 1995). But in any case, even if these high reported levels of satisfaction are actually somewhat exaggerated, comparing the scores for different domains can still give us clear indications of *relative* levels of satisfaction.

Which of these domains of life are most important to people? The last column of Table 3-1 displays correlations indicating how much the level of satisfaction on the domain measures contributed to the overall life satisfaction score. All of the domains were positively related to general satisfaction to a moderate degree, but satisfaction with family life, standard of living, and marriage were the most central elements in overall satisfaction with life.

TABLE 3-1   **Satisfaction in Various Domains of Life: Means and Distributions, and Correlations with Satisfaction with Life in General**

Domain	% Dissatisfied (scores of 1–3)	% Neutral (4)	% Satisfied (scores of 5–7)	Mean (on 1–7 scale)	r with life satisfaction
Marriage[a]	3%	7%	90%	6.27	.38
Family life	6	7	87	5.92	.50
Health	10	9	81	5.78	.26
Neighborhood	9	11	80	5.76	.23
Friendships	6	12	82	5.74	.32
Housework[b]	9	15	76	5.71	.34
Job[c]	8	13	79	5.67	.36
Life in United States	8	13	79	5.61	.24
City or county	9	16	75	5.60	.28
Nonwork	9	13	78	5.59	—
Housing	10	13	77	5.57	.30
Usefulness of education	12	15	73	5.53	—
Standard of living	14	14	72	5.31	.45
Amount of education[d]	28	16	56	4.69	.28
Savings	36	15	49	4.27	.36

[a]Asked only of married respondents.

[b]Asked only of women, excluding those who said they were students or retired.

[c]Asked only of those who said they worked for pay.

[d]Not asked of students.

Source: Adapted from *The Quality of American Life: Perceptions, Evaluations, and Satisfactions,* by Angus Campbell, Philip E. Converse, and William L. Rodgers. Copyright © 1976 by Russell Sage Foundation. Reprinted by permission of the publisher.

Turning from these personal domains of life satisfaction to more public aspects of American life, the authors focused attention on three key questions. These questions asked whether respondents felt they had been unfairly treated by public officials, did not feel "free enough to live the kind of life" they wanted, and felt dissatisfaction with "life in the United States today." On these three questions, the percentage of respondents expressing some degree of dissatisfaction was 22%, 11%, and 8% respectively (p. 285). Combining these three items to form an index of political alienation, the authors found that only 2% of the sample were dissatisfied on all three.

Limitations of the Study

One limitation of this study was inherent in its nature as a pioneering attempt to construct social indicators. It is unfortunate that we have relatively little good data from social indicators before 1970, for we would be intensely interested in studying time trends in people's satisfaction with life, as well as the effects of historical events such as wars, recessions, or elections on measures of satisfaction.

Another limitation of the study was that its data were actually collected in the summer of 1971, though it was finally published in 1976. The limitation here was not due to the age of the data, but to the particular events of 1971. The United States was still involved in the Vietnam War, and campus protest against the war and general public disaffection and malaise were high. The urban riots and turmoil of the late 1960s and the killing of students at Kent State University by troops of the National Guard in 1970 were recent memories. With these events as background, it is understandable why many Americans might be dubious about the national quality of life, and these factors were probably particularly strong in influencing the findings regarding political alienation reported above. Thus, to understand and evaluate the findings from this possibly atypical year of 1971, it becomes even more important to have comparative data from other years.

FOLLOW-UP STUDIES OF THE QUALITY OF LIFE

Though one of the great advantages of using social indicator measures is the possibility of making comparisons across time periods, there have been fewer follow-up studies than would be desired. In part this may be due to the high cost of conducting repeated national sample surveys. However, the General Social Survey, which is conducted regularly by the National Opinion Research Center (NORC), has repeated items on many different social issues (Niemi, Mueller, & Smith, 1989), and commercial polls such as Gallup and Harris often repeat items on a more irregular schedule.

In the quality-of-life area, there have been several important follow-up studies in the U.S. In 1978, Campbell and Converse conducted a major follow-up study with a national probability sample of almost 3700 respondents. Results of that study were reported by Campbell (1981) in a book entitled *The Sense of Well-Being in America.* Other baseline national surveys, using somewhat different items and response scales, were conducted in 1972 (Andrews & Withey, 1976), and a 16-year follow-up was reported by Andrews (1991). Later volumes on the quality of life include collections of research reports edited by Andrews (1986) and by Strack, Argyle, and Schwarz (1991), and a complex multinational study by Slottje et al. (1991). Studies on various aspects of subjective well-being continue to appear regularly in the journal, *Social Indicators Research.*

In the U.S., indices of general satisfaction with life showed essentially no change from 1971 to 1978. In both years, 22% of the respondents said they were "completely satisfied," and 60% expressed other degrees of satisfaction, while only 7% expressed any degree of dissatisfaction. Thus it appears likely that, in terms of people's general satisfaction with their lives, 1971 was not an atypical year, and the results of the Campbell et al. (1976) study have a good deal of generalizability to other time periods (Campbell, 1981).

However, on the more affective measure of happiness, there was an increase of about 6% in the percent-

age of people saying that they were "very happy" from 1972 to 1976, the period during which the Vietnam War ended. Campbell (1981) pointed out that this rise in national happiness occurred during the severe recession of 1974–1975 and the subsequent period of unemployment, inflation, and economic stagnation. Thus, there is strong evidence that affective indices of national well-being are not just determined by economic factors, and in fact can move in opposition to economic conditions. Similarly, many studies have shown that individual differences in wealth, age, gender, ethnicity, and even physical disability have very weak relationships to happiness (e.g., Andrews, 1991). "Satisfaction is less a matter of getting what you want than wanting what you have" (Myers & Diener, 1995, p. 13).

The longer-term 1972–1988 follow-up by Andrews (1991) showed that those years of economic prosperity and relative social stability in the U.S. brought with them moderate increases in people's subjective well-being in a number of domains. Specifically, across the whole sample, satisfaction ratings with life as a whole, and with the domains of self-efficacy, health, social interactions, standard of living, and how the government was handling the economy all were significantly higher in 1988, and only job satisfaction declined somewhat. Moreover, the pattern of changes in global well-being were similar for men and women, for all age cohorts, for all SES categories except the lowest one, and for Blacks and Whites—across the board, a somewhat more favorable view of life in general, though population subgroups did show some differential changes on particular domains.

A striking finding that has been replicated in many national surveys by other polling organizations is a huge difference between people's very high satisfaction with private life and their general dissatisfaction with public events (Caplow, 1982). For instance, in 1992 only 21% of respondents were satisfied with "the way things are going in the United States," whereas 79% of people said they were satisfied with things in their personal life (*Gallup Poll Monthly,* March 1992).

In comparing the results of different studies on social indicators, the studies' comparability in measures, procedures, and general content is crucial in order to be sure that apparent time trends indicate real changes rather than methodological artifacts (Turner & Krauss, 1977). In Chapter 17 we describe additional applications of survey research to issues of public policy.

Cross-National Comparisons

Many individuals and organizations have done research to compare the quality of life across countries. In terms of *subjective* well-being, data show that the average level of happiness or satisfaction in almost every country studied is on the positive side of neutral (Diener & Diener, 1996). Across nations, the correlation of average subjective well-being and national affluence is above +.6 (Inglehart, 1990), but it is clear that the single measure of per capita gross national product (GNP) is much too simple to capture the many dimensions involved in people's quality of life.

To obtain a more *objective* measure of quality of life, various systems have used anywhere from 3 to 20 or more different dimensions of comparison (e.g., Morris, 1979; Slottje et al., 1991). The United Nations has invested substantial effort in such studies, reporting a series of comparisons of the quality of life in 171 nations (e.g., United Nations, 1993). Its Human Development Index uses three key dimensions: individual purchasing power (per capita GNP adjusted for the local cost of living), life expectancy at birth, and educational standards (a combination of adult literacy and mean years of schooling). The index is scaled from 0 to 1.00, and Table 3-2 shows the 1993 standings of the top 12 industrialized nations and a diverse cross-section of 12 developing nations.

SURVEYS OF SEXUALITY

Rather than presenting more follow-up data from quality-of-life surveys, we will switch to describing an important study on a different topic, which illustrates some other aspects of large-scale surveys. Surely, sex is one of the most publicized topics in our society—pictured in films and television, written about in magazines and books, sensationally described in talk shows and scandal sheets, used as a lure in advertising. But how much do we really know about sexuality in America?

When people think of research on sexual behavior, they probably think of the work of Alfred Kinsey and his colleagues (1948, 1953), or Masters and Johnson (1966), or more recently Shere Hite (1976) or the Januses (1993). Yet, famous as these studies are, none of them was even close to being a scientific probability survey. Here we will briefly summarize their major problems. Kinsey and his colleagues were very industrious and eventually conducted face-to-face interviews with nearly 18,000 people. They approached groups, such as fraternities, PTAs, boarders in a rooming house, even hitchhikers going through town; and for greater scope, they often tried to get 100% of the group members to be interviewed. Thus, their respondents were clearly a *convenience sample,* and many of them were volunteers. Many studies have shown that people who volunteer for research, particularly on a sensitive topic such as sexuality, are systematically different than people who don't volunteer (Bradburn & Sudman, 1988). Consequently, though Kinsey's studies gained deserved fame for opening up a formerly tabooed topic, his findings could not safely be generalized to all Americans.

The same basic problem, plus some additional ones, plagued the other sex reports listed above. Masters and Johnson used a medical approach, and paid participants to perform sex acts in their laboratory so that they could observe and analyze them clinically. They made no attempt to obtain a representative sample. Hite obtained her data from questionnaires, sending out about 100,000 and getting only 3000 back—a 3% response rate. Moreover, she recruited her respondents from quite atypical groups, including chapters of the National Association for Women, university women's centers, abortion rights groups, readers of the *Village Voice,* and members of various churches. Finally, Janus and Janus also used written questionnaires, but like Kinsey, they went to particular locations, such as college classes or sex clinics, and recruited volunteers to answer their survey. By so doing, they got over a 60% response rate, and they recruited people from demographic categories that would approximate the U.S. population on variables such as age, marital status, and religion—a crude kind of *quota sample.* However, despite this feature, their re-

TABLE 3-2 **1993 Standings of 24 Nations on the UN's Human Development Index**

Country	Human development index	Human development rank	GNP per capita rank	Mean years of schooling
Industrialized nations				
Japan	.983	1	3	10.7
Canada	.982	2	11	12.1
Norway	.978	3	6	11.6
Switzerland	.978	4	1	11.1
Sweden	.977	5	5	11.1
United States	.976	6	10	12.3
Australia	.972	7	20	11.5
France	.971	8	13	11.6
Netherlands	.970	9	17	10.6
Britain	.964	10	21	11.5
Iceland	.960	11	9	8.9
Germany	.957	12	8	11.1
Developing nations				
Hong Kong	.913	24	24	7.0
South Korea	.872	33	37	8.8
Costa Rica	.852	42	76	5.7
Mexico	.805	53	60	4.7
Brazil	.730	70	53	3.9
Saudi Arabia	.688	84	31	3.7
China	.566	101	142	4.8
Kenya	.369	127	144	2.3
India	.309	134	146	2.4
Cambodia	.186	148	168	2.0
Angola	.143	160	126	1.5
Afghanistan	.066	171	169	0.8

Source: Adapted from Lewis, P. (1993, May 23). New U.N. index measures nations' quality of life. *New York Times,* p. L14.

spondents were still all volunteers and highly atypical ones at that.

Thus, these studies' lack of representative probability samples meant that their findings could not be generalized to the American population—that is, they had no **external validity** (see Chapter 4 for a fuller definition). Here is one bit of data as an example: Janus and Janus (1993) reported that over 70% of Americans age 65 and older have sex once a week, whereas a national probability survey that asked that question found that only 7% do (Michael et al., 1994, p. 24). So, despite all the titillating findings of these reports, the American public was still largely in the dark about typical American sexual patterns (Smith, 1990).

A Better Study—And Its Travails

Enter the National Health and Social Life Survey (NHSLS—Laumann et al., 1994; Michael et al., 1994). For years the U.S. scientific community had realized the need for a truly scientific study of American sexual behavior, and the onset of the AIDS epidemic in the early 1980s made that need even more imperative. In 1987, federal research agencies issued a request for proposals for a major study of general adult sexual attitudes and behavior, not just those of high-risk groups such as homosexuals. Eminent researchers at the National Opinion Research Center (NORC) responded and won the contract to design the study, which was projected to have 20,000 respondents (so that relatively small population subgroups such as homosexuals could be analyzed separately) and cost close to $20 million. They began a year of pilot work to develop questions, test interview procedures, and design the sample. During and after this period they were subjected to unremitting pressure from government funding agencies and political officials to compromise the goal and ask only about AIDS-related behaviors (e.g., avoid asking about masturbation, or terminate interviews with people who reported they were monogamous). In the end, the proposed study attracted so much criticism, particularly from religious right-wing groups, that Senator Jesse Helms was able to persuade the U.S. Senate in 1991 specifically to prohibit any such study from receiving government funds (Michael et al., 1994). (Very much the same sequence and outcome occurred with a sexual survey in Britain about two years earlier—Miller, 1995.)

It appeared that the study was dead, but the NORC researchers displayed remarkable persistence and tenacity, and eventually set a standard for effective survey research in the face of multiple adversities, as the British researchers did likewise (Miller, 1995). The NORC team appealed to private sources for funding and eventually received financial support from eight major national foundations.

Instead of interviewing the projected 20,000 respondents, they conducted what was to have been the pretest for the eventual study, with a "mere" 3432 respondents. They chose a multi-stage stratified random sample of households, with some oversampling of Blacks and Hispanics so that those groups could be analyzed separately. In each household, they randomly selected one resident who was age 18–59 and spoke English. The interviews were conducted in the respondents' homes; they used a survey booklet that was over 120 pages long and took an average of an hour and a half to administer. The interviewing period continued for seven months in 1992, and the interviewers made multiple call-backs to contact and persuade not-at-home or busy sample members to participate. The study achieved a very good response rate of 79%, and with all of the work involved in interviewer training, data collection, and data entry, the

cost per interview averaged $450 (Michael et al., 1994).

Several major problems had to be surmounted in planning and conducting the NHSLS study. First, it was crucial to ask about sexual behavior in ways that the respondents could understand and would not find offensive, so much care was taken in planning and testing the wording of questions (e.g., words like "vaginal intercourse" had to be explained). Second, 220 experienced interviewers were assembled from all over the nation and given special training for the complexities and sensitivities of this topic. Third, consistency checks on the validity of respondents' answers were included in the interview schedule, and their answers were also compared to data collected in other national probability surveys that had included a few items about sexuality. Though there is always some doubt about the validity of self-reports on sensitive topics, the interviewers reported that the respondents took the task seriously and often found it rewarding and illuminating to talk about their sexual history in a nonjudgmental way. Finally, the demographic characteristics of the 3432 respondents were compared to national census data, and the sample was found to be closely representative of the U.S. population. The largest discrepancies were about a 5% underrepresentation of men and of married people, and these figures were very similar to other carefully conducted national probability surveys (Michael et al., 1994). In the data analyses, these discrepancies were offset by weighting men and married people slightly more heavily so that they would represent their proper share of the population (Laumann et al., 1994).

A Few Findings

Some of the most important findings of the NHSLS study are ones that contrast with the sensational reports of the earlier unscientific, popularized sex surveys. For instance, based on this nationally representative sample, the typical frequency with which Americans have sex was found to be far less than the earlier reports had trumpeted. The key data are displayed in Table 3-3. It shows, for instance, that only about one-third of Americans aged 18 to 59 had sex with a partner as often as twice a week. Another third had sex a few times per

TABLE 3-3   Frequency of Sex in the Past Twelve Months

Social characteristics	Not at all	A few times per year	A few times per month	2 or 3 times a week	4 or more times a week
Gender					
Men	14%	16%	37%	26%	8%
Women	10	18	36	30	7
Age					
Men					
18–24	15	21	24	28	12
25–29	7	15	31	36	11
30–39	8	15	37	33	6
40–49	9	18	40	27	6
50–59	11	22	43	20	3
Women					
18–24	11	16	32	29	12
25–29	5	10	38	37	10
30–39	9	16	36	33	6
40–49	15	16	44	20	5
50–59	30	22	35	12	2
Marital/Residential Status					
Men					
Noncohabiting	23	25	26	19	7
Cohabiting	0	8	36	40	16
Married	1	13	43	36	7
Women					
Noncohabiting	32	23	24	15	5
Cohabiting	1	8	35	42	14
Married	3	12	47	32	7

Note: Percentages in rows total 100%.

Source: From *Sex in America: A Definitive Survey* (p. 16) by Michael et al. Copyright © 1994 by CSG Enterprises, Inc., Edward O. Laumann, Robert T. Michael, & Gina Kolata. By permission of Little, Brown and Company.

month, and the remaining third did so a few times a year or not at all. In this table, only three variables had much effect on the frequency of sexual contact. First, more people who were cohabiting but unmarried had sex relatively frequently—56% said at least twice a week, compared with about 40% of married people, and only 20%–26% of noncohabiting individuals. Second, age made a difference, with more people aged 25 to 29 having relatively frequent sex, and fewer of those in their 40s and 50s doing so. Third, though men and women were not different overall, in their 40s and 50s considerably more women than men decreased in their frequency of sexual contact. Other data showed that education and religion had no effect on frequency of sexual contact, and ethnicity had very little, though Hispanic men and women had sex slightly more frequently than Whites and Blacks (Michael et al., 1994, chap. 6).

If the sexual frequency of Americans is so much less than had earlier been publicized, does that mean that Americans are frustrated and unhappy about their sex lives? No, not according to the NHSLS study. Huge majorities (over 80%) of both men and women reported being very satisfied or extremely satisfied with their sex lives (over 40% extremely so), both in terms of physical pleasure and of emotional satisfaction. This was true even though the much-vaunted rate of orgasm was considerably below 100%—75% of men and 29% of women reported that they always had orgasms. Interestingly, both physical and emotional satisfaction were markedly lower for people who reported having two or more sexual partners in the last 12 months. In particular, of the multiple-partner group who were non-cohabiting (the supposedly "swinging singles"), less than 65% said they were very or extremely physically pleased with their relationship, and less than 45% said they were very or extremely emotionally satisfied.

How many Americans do have multiple sexual partners during a given time period? Again the NHSLS results painted a very different picture from the tabloids and the popular magazines (see Table 3-4).

During the last 12 months, only 23% of men and 12% of women said they had two or more partners. Again, age was a crucial variable, with one-third of 18- to 24-year-olds having multiple partners and the percentage declining quite regularly in each successive age group. Similarly, marital status was important, with only 5% of married individuals reporting multiple partners compared with 18%–37% for individuals who were divorced or never married. In every age group and almost every other demographic category, a majority of respondents reported having only one sexual partner in the last year.

The NHSLS study had many other fascinating and valuable findings, which you may want to read in more detail (Laumann et al., 1994; Michael et al., 1994). Its

TABLE 3-4   Number of Sex Partners in Past Twelve Months

Social characteristics	Number of sex partners			
	0	*1*	*2 to 4*	*5 or more*
Total	12%	71%	14%	3%
Gender				
Men	10	67	18	5
Women	14	75	10	2
Age				
18–24	11	57	24	9
25–29	6	72	17	6
30–34	9	73	16	2
35–39	10	77	11	2
40–44	11	75	13	1
45–49	15	75	9	1
50–54	15	79	5	0
55–59	32	65	4	0
Marital Status				
Never married, noncohabiting	25	38	28	9
Never married, cohabiting	1	75	20	5
Married	2	94	4	1
Divorced, separated widowed, noncohabiting	31	41	26	3
Divorced, separated, widowed, cohabiting	1	80	15	3

Note: Percentages in rows total 100%.

Source: From *Sex in America: A Definitive Survey* (p. 102) by Michael et al. Copyright © 1994 by CSG Enterprises, Inc., Edward O. Laumann, Robert T. Michael, & Gina Kolata. By permission of Little, Brown and Company.

main lessons for survey researchers seem to be four: (a) that with careful survey procedures, valid responses can be obtained even on highly sensitive topics such as sexual behavior, (b) the crucial importance of probability sampling to obtain a representative sample, and of (c) persistence in data collection to obtain a high response rate, and (d) the likelihood that when those procedures are used, the findings are apt to be markedly different from careless or nonscientific samples of convenience.

SUMMARY

In survey research, the most widespread social research method, a sample of respondents is asked questions, either orally or in writing. Survey studies of the quality of life exemplify the movement to develop social indicators measuring the subjective, psychological side of people's lives, in order to counterbalance the past overemphasis on economic indicators of national life.

A good survey study begins with a question of theoretical or practical interest and proceeds to careful construction and pretesting of instruments in order to ensure reliable measurement. The sample of respondents should be representative of some population, and the expected amount of sampling error should be specified. Interviewing must be carefully planned and skillfully carried out to prevent problems of interviewer effects, response sets, and reactive measurement from threatening the validity of the data. Coding and data analysis are also crucial steps in the research process.

The Campbell, Converse, and Rodgers (1976) survey of Americans' quality of life showed that most people express general satisfaction with their lives, but that indices of happiness (affective) and satisfaction (cognitive) can show different patterns of results. Satisfaction in various domains of life was highest for marriage and family life and lowest for financial savings, amount of education, and standard of living.

The National Health and Social Life Survey was a landmark study that gave the first scientifically valid picture of the general sexual behavior of the American public. Despite numerous political obstacles in carrying it out, the authors obtained a representative national sample and a high response rate, even on this sensitive topic. The results showed that American sexual behavior in the 1990s was much more similar to traditional normative patterns than had been reported by earlier popularized but unscientific surveys.

SUGGESTED READINGS

Bradburn, N. M., & Sudman, S. (1988). *Polls and surveys: Understanding what they tell us*. San Francisco: Jossey-Bass.—A readable, nontechnical overview of all aspects of polling: its history, polling organizations, how surveys are conducted, and cautions about interpreting their results.

Campbell, A. (1981). *The sense of well-being in America: Recent patterns and trends*. New York: McGraw-Hill.—Written in a popular style with few tables, this book summarizes trends found in quality-of-life studies.

Fowler, F. J., Jr. (1993). *Survey research methods* (2nd ed.). Thousand Oaks, CA: Sage.—This short volume gives a helpful summary of desirable practices in conducting survey research.

Michael, R. T., Gagnon, J. H., Laumann, E. O., & Kolata, G. (1994). *Sex in America: A definitive study*. Boston: Little, Brown.—A clearly written account of findings of the only major probability study of sexual behavior in the general American population.

Payne, S. L. (1951). *The art of asking questions*. Princeton, NJ: Princeton University Press.—A still-useful little book with how-to information on planning and constructing interview schedules and questionnaires.

CHAPTER 4

Experiments— Soliciting Donations

It is the major objective of an experiment—lab or field—to have the greatest possible impact on a subject within the limits of ethical considerations and requirements of control.

—Aronson, Brewer, & Carlsmith (1985, p. 482)

Suppose that you are going door-to-door, soliciting donations for the Heart Association or the Cancer Society. In order to collect the maximum amount for your organization, you want to make the best possible opening statement when people come to the door. What should you say? Should you emphasize that their neighbors have given? Or request a set amount of money as a goal? Or ask for any contribution, no matter how small? Or what?

Most people handle such situations by following their hunches, or using a rule-of-thumb handed down by some more experienced collector. However, to get a really valid answer to such questions, the best method would be to conduct an experiment, trying out several different solicitation approaches under controlled conditions. In this chapter we will describe in some detail one such experiment on soliciting donations, using it as a springboard for analyzing the characteristic strengths and weaknesses of social psychology experiments.

There are many recent experiments having important social applications. In this respect the situation has changed markedly since Meltzer (1972) lamented the lack of high-quality applied social research. Here are some examples of interesting experiments on a wide variety of important topics:

- Effects of erotic and violent films on viewers' aggressiveness (Sinclair, Lee, & Johnson, 1995)
- Effects of a product labeling system on environmentally conscious buying by supermarket shoppers (Linn, Vining, & Feeley, 1994)
- Increasing drivers' use of seat belts (Jonah, Dawson, & Smith, 1982)
- Reducing HIV risk behaviors among injection drug users over a 2-year period (Latkin et al., 1996)
- Improving the reading and mathematics performance of poor elementary school children over several years (Bushell, 1978)
- Effects of beer commercials on drinking expectations among 3rd, 5th, and 8th grade children (Lipsitz et al., 1993)
- Reducing the amount of welfare payments by giving recipients job training and assistance in job searches (Friedlander & Burtless, 1995)
- Increasing blood donations among high school students (Sarason et al., 1992)
- Increasing long-term energy conservation (Pallak, Cook, & Sullivan, 1980)
- Increasing the amount of money contributed to charities (Aune & Basil, 1994; Cialdini & Schroeder, 1976)

We will focus our analysis on the last of these topics.

Historically, experiments have been the most frequent research method used by social psychologists—and also the one with the highest prestige. To summarize their key characteristics, **experiments** are studies in which there is a high degree of planned manipulation of conditions by the investigator, and research participants (often termed *subjects*) are randomly assigned to groups. **Random assignment** is essential to an experiment because it creates separate groups of research participants that should be nearly identical on any variable: height, weight, self-esteem, intelligence, aggressiveness, and so on.

In an experiment the researcher **manipulates** (regulates the levels of) one or more variables, controls or holds constant other variables that might otherwise have an effect, and measures or observes the levels of one or more variables that are expected to be affected by the manipulation. The manipulated variables are called **independent variables**, and the variables expected to be influenced by the manipulation are called **dependent variables**. If random assignment produces identical groups to start with, and other procedures are conducted carefully, we can conclude that any difference between the groups on the dependent variable must be *caused* by the manipulation. Experiments typically exceed all other research methods in their degree of *control* of conditions and in the *precision* of measurement possible. As a result, experiments are better than other methods for *determining the direction of causal relationships*. Because the researcher establishes and controls all the experimental conditions, the obtained results are more likely to be due to them than to some unknown or uncontrolled factor.

On the other hand, experiments rarely attempt to simulate real-world conditions in any detail; instead they aim at *isolating* one or a few factors that may be important causes of some effect from the multitude of other factors and conditions with which they are inextricably mixed in real life. As a result, two major disadvantages of experiments for the study of social behavior are *artificiality* (in the sense that the conditions do not occur outside the laboratory) and doubt about the *generalizability* of results. A detailed look at a carefully done social psychological experiment will reveal other common characteristics.

AN ILLUSTRATIVE SOCIAL PSYCHOLOGY EXPERIMENT

A study by Cialdini and Schroeder (1976) was aimed at testing some techniques that might increase the contributions that charities could collect in door-to-door campaigns. From their own personal experience with solicitors for charities, the authors realized that requests which allowed and encouraged even small donations were particularly hard to turn down (Cialdini, 1980). This phenomenon is related to the foot-in-the-door effect (see Chapter 2), in which small initial requests often produce greater compliance to later larger requests (Dillard, 1991; Freedman & Fraser, 1966). However, a request for small donations might succeed in increasing the number of donors but fail to increase the total amount of money collected because most of the contributions would be small ones. Most charitable organizations would not view such an outcome as a success.

Theory

The authors theorized that a solicitation strategy which *legitimized minimal contributions* but did not directly request them might increase the number of donors without reducing the size of the average donation. If so, that would clearly produce a greater total collection.

Accordingly, the experimenters designed a solicitation approach featuring the key words, "Even a penny will help," at the end of the standard request format. This was a small change, but one with great theoretical importance, since it should make it harder for people to refuse to donate. An initial experiment compared this approach with the standard appeal format in a door-to-door solicitation for donations to the American Cancer Society. Results showed that the "even a penny" approach was highly successful.

However, other experimental conditions were needed in order to investigate other possible explanations of the hypothesized effect. In order to test whether the legitimization of *minimal* contributions was crucial, a third condition substituted the statement, "Even a dollar will help." A dollar was *not* a minimal amount, since it had been the median amount given by those who did contribute in the initial experiment, and therefore this condition was expected to make it easier for people to refuse to donate. A fourth condition tested whether the key factor might be the apparent *need* of the charitable organization. That is, the statement "Even a penny will help" might not just legitimate small donations, but it might also suggest that the American Cancer Society was currently very hard up for funds. To avoid that connotation while retaining the legitimization of small donations, the fourth condition gave information that people could view as a model for their own behavior, using the wording, "We've already received contributions ranging from a penny on up." These four conditions comprised the key theoretical manipulations in the experiment.

Procedure

Through the cooperation of the local branch of the American Cancer Society, the solicitors were provided with official identification badges, information pamphlets, and donation envelopes. The solicitors were four pairs of college-age research assistants, a male and a female in each pair, who were unaware of the hypotheses of the research. They went to a middle-income suburban housing area that had not been recently canvassed by the Cancer Society, at times when both men and women were likely to be home (late afternoons, evenings, and weekends). When the first adult came to the door, the solicitor of the same sex as the householder gave the appeal for funds, using one of the four prescribed formats, recited verbatim. The four pairs of solicitors contacted 123 subjects, 30 or 31 in each condition. In each case they recorded whether the subject made a contribution and, if so, the size of the contribution.

Results

Table 4-1 displays the results of the experiment for frequency and amount of donations. The gender of the target subjects was also considered as a factor, but no significant differences were found, so results for men and women were combined.

The pattern of findings in Table 4-1 was exactly as expected: the even-a-penny and social legitimization conditions were markedly higher, both in percentage of donors and in total donations. To verify the statistical significance of this pattern, three orthogonal comparisons were conducted on both dependent variables (the frequency and total amount of donations). For both variables there was no significant difference between the first two conditions, control and even-a-dollar, nor between the last two conditions, social legitimization and even-a-penny. But, as predicted, for both variables the last two conditions combined were significantly higher than the first two conditions combined ($p < .02$ and $p < .05$, respectively). Also as predicted, there was no significant difference in the size of the *average* donation actually given in the four conditions.

The practical implications of these results are clearcut. The two conditions that legitimized paltry contributions yielded 55% more donors and 50% greater total donations than the other two conditions. Any charity would certainly be overjoyed to be able to increase their revenues by that amount. However, even that difference may be somewhat of an underestimate, for the control condition had one freak contribution of $10, which was $8 more than the second-highest contribution and accounted for nearly half the total revenues in that condition. If this atypical donation were removed, and the highest donation in each of the other conditions were similarly removed as being possibly unrepresentative, the average donations in the four conditions would be almost identical, but the number of contributions would still be very different. By such a procedure the last two conditions would be estimated to produce 66% larger total revenues than the first two conditions.

One other feature of the results might be mentioned. An additional 46 subjects were contacted during the same time period and in the same area, but instead of being requested to contribute, they were asked to answer a survey question about a charitable organization's apparent need for money. Each subject was read one of the four standard appeals used by the solicitors in this experiment and asked to rate the charity's apparent "need for money" on a 7-point scale. Though the even-a-penny condition displayed the highest mean score, as expected, the four conditions did not differ significantly, and this finding cast doubt on the hypothesis that the charity's need was an important basis for people's contributions.

Remaining Questions

Though this experiment was carefully done, not everything in the report is crystal clear. One ambiguity con-

TABLE 4-1 **Frequency and Amount of Donations in Response to Four Different Solicitation Appeals**

Treatment	N	Frequency of donations		Amount of donations	
		N	%	Total	Mean
Control	31	10	32.2	$20.74	$2.07
Even-a-dollar	30	14	46.7	19.35	1.38
Social legitimization	31	20	64.5	28.61	1.43
Even-a-penny	31	18	58.1	31.30	1.74

Source: Cialdini, R. B., & Schroeder, D. A. Increasing compliance by legitimizing paltry contributions: When even a penny helps. *Journal of Personality and Social Psychology,* 1976, 34, 599–604. Copyright © by the American Psychological Association. Adapted by permission of the authors.

cerns the four pairs of solicitors and the four conditions. Did each pair use only one of the four appeals, or did each pair use all four appeals in a preselected order? The former procedure would be somewhat simpler in making arrangements and in training the solicitors, but it would be undesirable because it would *confound* the four conditions with the characteristics of the solicitors. Thus, if one pair of solicitors was more attractive or better dressed or more persuasive or added other ideas to their appeal for funds, the results would be mistaken for an effect due to the superiority of one of the standard appeals. By contrast, if each pair of solicitors used all four appeals, preferably in a preselected random order, any differences between the solicitors would be spread across all four appeals and would not contribute to any differences between the appeals. Presumably, this was what was actually done in the experiment, but the report does not mention it, so we can't be sure.

Another set of questions has to do with the generality of the findings. There is certainly no question that they apply to real-life situations, since they were obtained in an actual door-to-door solicitation procedure. There might be some doubt about geographical and social-class generalizability. Probably these results, obtained in an Arizona middle-income suburb, would be applicable to other U.S. communities like a Chicago suburb or an inner-city neighborhood in Los Angeles—even though the absolute level of giving might be different. In fact, several subsequent studies have replicated the basic finding in U.S. suburban neighborhoods (Weyant & Smith, 1987). There would, however, be more concern about the generality of these results in other countries—a topic that would take much research to verify.

A related question is the extent to which the results found by Cialdini and Schroeder would apply to other situations—for example, a campaign seeking large contributions from local businesses or rich citizens. If the results did generalize, what would be the best minimal contribution to mention? Probably not a penny, and perhaps not a dollar; some larger amount, such as $10, might be minimal for well-to-do donors. Similarly, would the technique apply to solicitations by telephone or by mail? The only way to know would be to try it out under these various circumstances. In fact, Weyant and Smith (1987) did so in a mail solicitation for the Cancer Society to a high income neighborhood, using $5, $10, and $25 as the "small" options suggested to one group of residents, and $50, $100, and $250 as the "large" options suggested to another group. Consistent with the basic principle of the even-a-penny experiment, these authors found that the "small" suggested donations yielded well over twice as many donors without decreasing the average size of donations (which was around $12)—a very useful generalization of the earlier study's findings.

We can also raise more abstract questions about the nature of the process that produced the results of the even-a-penny study. Does the legitimization of tiny contributions work by eliminating people's excuses for not complying with the solicitor's request, or by pressuring them to avoid establishing a public image as someone who is especially unhelpful, or both? Which of these processes is more important, or are there some situations where one is dominant and some where the other one is primary? Although recent studies have begun to examine some of these questions, more experimental research is needed in order to fully explicate the conditions under which various solicitation procedures will effectively produce compliance, and the types of people who are likely to comply.

Would the same effect reported above be found if the study were conducted in Germany, France, China, or Mexico? Although a cross-national replication of the study described above has not been conducted, cross-national research on the related foot-in-the-door technique suggests that the findings may have limited generality. Kilbourne (1989) conducted experimental studies on compliance in Paris, Frankfurt, and Amsterdam, and found a different pattern of results in each country.

KEY CONSIDERATIONS IN EXPERIMENTS

Planning

All experiments require a great deal of preparation and planning, most of which is usually not apparent in the final research report. Just as with surveys, *pretesting* of every phase of the procedure is essential in order to avoid problems that could invalidate the obtained results. False starts and revisions of procedures are frequent, and practical problems of scheduling and logistics always occur. For instance, in the Cialdini and Schroeder experiment, weather, transportation, and scheduling problems must have occurred, though they are not mentioned in the report. A thorough and helpful guide for novice investigators on how to plan and conduct an experiment has been provided by Aronson, Brewer, and Carlsmith (1985).

Laboratory Versus Field Experiments

Laboratory experiments are apt to be considerably more convenient for the investigator because they are conducted on home ground, where the necessary equipment and subjects are often readily available. They frequently allow more control over conditions, more isolation of variables, and greater precision of measurement than field experiments. However, they generally have the offsetting disadvantage of being more artificial situations, and that can produce a number of undesirable *artifacts* which are discussed later in this chapter. A related problem is that both practical and ethical limitations often prevent the use of strong manipulations (for example, of fear, happiness, or anger) in laboratory studies, and consequently the effects that are obtained are apt to be rather weak as well. When nonsignificant findings result, they leave doubt about whether the experimental hypothesis was wrong or the manipulations were merely too weak to have a significant effect.

The laboratory experiment's frequent artificiality has been termed lack of **mundane realism** by Aronson et al. (1985)—that is, a lack of similarity to any situation in the world outside the laboratory, as in giving subjects electric shocks. Despite being artificial in this sense, experiments can nevertheless have strong **experimental realism**—that is, convincingness and impact on the subject. Though this is a controversial issue, Aronson et al. (1985) argued that experimental realism is a more important consideration than mundane realism. As they pointed out,

> The fact that an event is similar to events that occur in the real world does not endow it with importance. Many

events that occur in the real world are boring and unimportant in the lives of the actors or observers. Thus, it is possible to put a subject to sleep if an experimental event is high on mundane realism but remains low on experimental realism. (p. 482)

Most authorities agree, however, that because of laboratory experiments' typical artificiality and frequently weak effects, their results should be taken back to the field and checked against the results of other types of research in real-world situations. Another reason for this procedure is the likelihood of *interaction effects* between variables studied in the laboratory and other variables that were not included. (Interaction effects are discussed in more detail later in this chapter.)

In any case, many experiments in applied social psychology, like the even-a-penny experiment, are **field experiments**—that is, ones conducted in a setting that is natural for the participants. Such experiments are likely to have mundane realism, and if well-designed, they can have high experimental realism as well. In many field experiments the participants are not even aware that they are subjects in an experiment, since an event such as a solicitor coming to their door seems completely natural to them. However, field experiments pose their own unique problems for the investigators, such as finding an appropriate setting and getting permission to conduct research from the relevant authorities such as the police or an employer; in this case the researchers had to obtain the cooperation of the American Cancer Society.

Instructions

Instructions are often used to manipulate one or more of the independent variables in an experiment. In the charity solicitation experiment, the four standard appeals were the main experimental manipulations. They were simple, but very effective. Even here the instructions had to be pretested, while in more complex studies they must be carefully checked for clarity and believability. In this experiment there was no deception of the participants, but in some studies, to conceal the real point of the research, the instructions have to include a false but convincing "cover story" about why the study is being done and what its topic area and purposes are.

Photograph courtesy of Elliot Aronson. Reprinted by permission.

Box 4-1

ELLIOT ARONSON, SOCIAL EXPERIMENTALIST

Famous as a social researcher, and also as a writer and teacher, Elliot Aronson was born in 1932 in Massachusetts. He was attracted to psychology by Abraham Maslow at Brandeis, where he received his B.A. Subsequently, he earned an M.A. under David McClelland at Wesleyan University and a Ph.D. in social psychology under Leon Festinger at Stanford in 1959. After brief periods on the faculty at Harvard and at the University of Minnesota, in 1965 he was appointed Professor and Director of the Social Psychology Program at the University of Texas at Austin. In 1974 he moved to the University of California at Santa Cruz, where he remains.

Aronson is widely known for his laboratory research on dissonance theory, attitude change, interpersonal attractiveness, group interaction, and social influence. His applied research on intergroup relations began when the public schools in Austin, Texas, were suddenly desegregated amidst rioting

and turmoil. The resulting program of action research, focused on fostering cooperative relationships and decreasing prejudice among elementary school students, is described in Chapter 8. More recently Aronson has also conducted applied social psychological research aimed at persuading people to conserve energy and to protect themselves from AIDS and other sexually transmitted diseases.

Among his many honors, Aronson has received the American Association for the Advancement of Science's Prize for Creative Research, the APA's National Media Award for writing, and its Distinguished Teaching Award. He served as co-editor of the massive *Handbook of Social Psychology* in 1968–1969 and in 1985, and he has authored texts on social psychology and on experimental research. Among his other well-known volumes are *The Jigsaw Classroom* and *Burnout*.

Aronson et al. (1985) advocate that, wherever possible, instead of using instructions, experimental conditions should be manipulated by an "event," because it is likely to have much more impact than instructions do. For example, in the famous study by Asch (1958), sub-

jects who underwent the personal experience of having several other subjects disagree with them about the length of some lines would be much more affected by this event than if the experimenter had merely *told* them that several other people disagreed with their judgments.

Research Participants

The choice and assignment of participants are important steps in an experiment. An unfortunate fact is that most social psychological research has been conducted with college students, in academic laboratories, and frequently using materials that require a high level of educational background (Sears, 1986). Because college students differ from the overall human population on many dimensions, there are undoubtedly many instances where the generality of these results is limited. For instance, compared to older adults, college students tend to be more willing to comply with authority, to have less structured attitudes, and to have less formulated notions of self. It is possible that these qualities have contributed to the common social psychological view of people as inconsistent and easily influenced (Sears, 1986). In addition, a large majority of college students are White, and it is often unclear how generalizable results would be from White college students to non-White college students, even within the same age cohort. Usually, generalizability of findings is increased by having a diverse sample of research participants.

As we pointed out earlier in this chapter, **randomization** in the assignment of participants to experimental conditions is the greatest advantage of an experiment over other research methods, because it equates the conditions by balancing all the personal characteristics (the subjects' sex, education, race, religion, personality, and so forth) that might affect the dependent variable. Even characteristics not yet suggested as important, and therefore uncontrollable in any other way, will be evenly spread across the experimental conditions by randomization.

In addition to random assignment of subjects, important personal characteristics are sometimes controlled by systematic choice of participants. For instance, for some purposes, only women may be chosen as subjects, or only college graduates. This procedure reduces the error variance within experimental conditions which results from the diversity of participants, but as noted above, it decreases the generality of findings. (These concepts are discussed at greater length below in the section on *internal validity and external validity*.) An excellent, though complex, way to combine the advantages of diversity of participants with control of participant characteristics is a **randomized blocks design**. In such a design, each block of people with a given level of one characteristic (for example, college graduates, high school graduates, and other educational levels) is randomly assigned across several experimental conditions, so that there are equal numbers of the given level in each condition. These various ways of equating experimental groups all help to minimize the error variance in the measures of the dependent variables.

In the charity solicitation study, the characteristics of participants were controlled in two ways. First, a homogeneous middle-income housing area was chosen as the scene of the study. This was a reasonable procedure since such areas are often targeted for door-to-door solicitation by the Cancer Society, and it certainly made the results more relevant than if only college students had been the subjects. Second, though the report did not specify it, presumably each successive household was randomly assigned to one of the four experimental appeals.

Control of Conditions

In an experiment, the investigator first determines and arranges all the aspects of the independent variable manipulation: using instructions, events, equipment, the help of research confederates, or other appropriate techniques. Also, the experimenter decides what kinds of behavior will constitute the dependent variable and exactly how it will be measured and recorded. In this regard, Aronson et al. (1985) argue strongly for more use of *behavioral* measures of the dependent variable, rather than self-report measures such as attitude scales or questionnaire answers, which quite often have dubious reliability and validity. Third, the experimenter decides what other aspects of the situation need to be held constant or explicitly controlled in some other way so that the measurements will reflect the true variables of interest and not some accidental effects of the situation. This often includes arranging circumstances to block the occurrence of certain kinds of behavior and encourage other kinds.

Cialdini and Schroeder's experiment controlled conditions in several ways. The time of day was specified so that both men and women would be at home. Solicitors worked in male-female pairs, which allowed the important control of always having the appeal made by the experimenter of the same sex as the person who came to the door. Since the sex of the solicitor can influence the respondent's degree of identification and compliance with the request, this was a very wise procedure. Using four pairs of solicitors made the findings more broadly generalizable than if only one pair of especially persuasive (or especially inept) experimenters had been used. Having each pair of solicitors use all four appeals, in random order, would be necessary in order not to confound the success of one appeal with the characteristics of one pair of solicitors.

One important type of control is to have all the experimenters dress and behave in the same ways, particularly across the various experimental conditions. This precept includes the direction of their gaze, their degree of enthusiasm or friendliness, their inflection when speaking instructions, their equipment and clothing, and all other aspects of their behavior. For instance, other charity solicitation experiments have found that donations were greater when the solicitor gazed directly at the potential donor's eyes rather than at the collection box, and when a simple identification poster was carried rather than a more complex and distracting poster with a photograph of a handicapped child (Bull & Gibson-Robinson, 1981; Isen & Noonberg, 1979).

Experimental Procedures

In the charity solicitation experiment, the dependent variables were objective behavioral measures (donation of money and amount donated), so the authors did not have to be concerned with the problems of self-report measures, or the reliability and validity issues of rating scales. Similarly, because the independent variable was a simple phrase in the appeal, there was no need for a **manipulation check**—an essential procedure with complex manipulations, in order to see whether the experimental conditions actually affected the subjects in the expected ways. Likewise, though many attitude-change experiments use both a pretest and a posttest measurement, there was no need for a premeasure in this posttest-only design. Since no complex experimental script was used to vary the conditions, there was also no need for the frequently used postexperimental questionnaire to check on the subjects' perception of the situation. As in many field experiments, there was no deception, so there was no **debriefing** session at the end of the experiment to explain the purpose of the study and the need for deception.

One especially important precaution was observed: the solicitors were "blind to" (unaware of) the hypotheses of the study. This was essential because otherwise they might have subtly changed their verbal inflection, enthusiasm, or general approach in a way favoring the hypothesized best experimental condition, thus spuriously supporting the hypothesis. In experiments where the investigators cannot be blind to the hypotheses, Aronson et al. (1985) strongly recommend that they be unaware of which experimental condition each subject is in. If necessary, this can be accomplished by using teams of researchers who each handle a different phase of the experiment. In the solicitation study, of course, the solicitors could not be kept ignorant of the conditions since they delivered the appeal orally, so their ignorance of the hypotheses of the study was essential.

However, there is some question whether the investigators' ignorance of the hypotheses was sufficient. In a replication of Cialdini and Schroeder's study, Weyant (1984) found evidence that even though the pairs of student researchers did not know the research hypotheses, their *expectations* influenced the results. Weyant's researchers conducted door-to-door solicitations for the American Cancer Society in a middle-class neighborhood. They randomly assigned each of 360 households to one of five experimental conditions, and as expected, the results showed that more people contributed, and more money was collected, in the even-a-penny condition than in any of the other four—a very useful replication. However, 68 of the householders interrupted the researchers to respond before the key sentence constituting the experimental manipulation was delivered. Of these, the percentage of participants who donated money in each of the conditions was 0%, 7%, 10%, and 23%, compared to 28% in the even-a-penny condition. Because there were no differences in the manipulation delivered to these households, the only other possibility is that the student researchers had developed their own hypotheses about the condition manipulations, and were subtly acting in such a way as to confirm their expectations. It is unclear how the expectations of the solicitors affected the results obtained by Cialdini and Schroeder, but that issue is certainly important in determining the reason for their findings.

A problem that does not apply to the solicitation study, but is common in research where new procedures are being tried out on established groups of people, is the **Hawthorne effect**. Named for the Hawthorne plant of the Western Electric Company, where it was first noticed by Mayo (1933) and Roethlisberger and Dickson (1939), this effect is an augmented response of participants due to their enthusiasm for being in a new or experimental program and the resulting attention they receive. Such an increase in production levels, or in attitude scores, can easily be mistaken for the effect of the experimental manipulation (for example, changes in work lighting in the Hawthorne studies) rather than being recognized as an experimental artifact. A typical safeguard against this effect is a **reversal design**, in which the independent variable is first added and later removed, or first increased and later decreased. If the dependent variable measure does not revert to an earlier level when the independent variable is reversed, this may indicate a Hawthorne effect, though it could also indicate a long-lasting effect of the independent variable if such a carry-over effect seemed possible.

Sometimes experiments cannot use a reversal design (for instance, when people have been given some benefit, such as pay raises or better health care, that cannot be taken away, for either practical or ethical reasons). In such cases a **multiple baseline design** is very helpful. In this design, several different independent variables (IVs) are introduced at different points in time. Each IV is expected to change its own dependent variable (DV), but if *other* DVs change when one IV is introduced, something like a Hawthorne effect may be at work. An excellent example of a multiple baseline design is seen in a study by Pierce and Risley (1974) on reducing disruptions in a youth recreation center.

When rules against several different kinds of disruptions were made and consistently enforced at several different points in time, the researchers found, as predicted, that each enforced rule largely eliminated its own kind of disruption but did not appreciably reduce other types of unruly behavior.

Experimental Artifacts

Unreliability of measures may be a problem in some experiments, depending on the types of measuring instruments that are used. It is less of a problem where the measures are **objective**—that is, ones on which all observers would agree—such as the monetary donations in the Cialdini and Schroeder experiment. However, it is always an issue when measures are subjective, such as judgmental rating scales or self-report measures. In such situations, investigators should try to determine and report reliability coefficients for their measures (either internal consistency, or stability measures, or both). If dependent variable measures are low in reliability, the results obtained using those measures may be experimental artifacts, which would not be obtained again if the study were repeated. Of course, this potential problem applies just as much, if not more, to nonexperimental studies.

Demand characteristics are present in any situation, not just in experiments. They are the perceptual cues, both explicit and implicit, that communicate what kind of behavior is expected there (Orne, 1969). For example, the demand characteristics in a library encourage one to sit and read, to speak and walk softly, and so on. In an experiment, demand characteristics that are too obvious can produce experimental artifacts by signaling to subjects the kinds of results the experimenter wants or expects. In such cases subjects who are so inclined can either be overcooperative and display the expected behavior without a genuine basis, or be negativistic and do just the opposite. That is why experimenters often go to great lengths to conceal the true purpose of the experiment, or even use deception, so that subjects cannot guess the purpose and subsequently follow or oppose the research hypothesis. Demand characteristics in an experiment can never be wholly eliminated, but they can be minimized, and useful suggestions on how to do so have been offered by Aronson et al. (1985) and by Orne (1969). Fortunately, most research has shown that relatively few subjects are inclined to be either overcooperative or negativistic (Weber & Cook, 1972). In the charity solicitation experiment, the demand characteristics seem to be about equal in all four conditions, and thus not a problem in interpreting the findings.

Experimenter effects are distortions in the results of an experiment produced by the behavior or characteristics of an experimenter (Rosenthal, 1976). They are similar to interviewer effects in surveys, and many of the same safeguards can be applied to minimize their operation. The type of experimenter effect that has been most thoroughly studied is the impact of the experimenter's *expectations* on the behavior of subjects. There is considerable research evidence that this artifact can sometimes distort experimental results (Rosenthal, 1969; Seaver, 1973), and many recommendations have been made about how to combat or minimize its effects (Aronson et al., 1985). Some of these suggestions are summarized in Table 4-2. In the charity solicitation study, the authors attempted to minimize experimenter expectancy effects by using completely objective measures and by keeping the solicitors, as

well as the subjects, ignorant of the experimental hypothesis (termed a **double-blind procedure**). However, as Weyant (1984) has demonstrated, experimenter effects may still have been a problem.

Subject effects are distortions in research results caused by various response sets or temporary behavior patterns adopted by subjects contrary to the intentions of the researcher. Though some experiments have shown that subjects can be induced to be negativistic or cooperative (Christensen, 1977; Carr & Kroger, 1976), a thorough review of the relevant research literature has indicated that by far the most common subject effect is caused by **evaluation apprehension** (Weber & Cook, 1972). As the name implies, this produces attempts by subjects to act in socially desirable ways and "look good" out of concern about how other people (the experimenter or other research subjects) will evaluate them (Rosenberg, 1969). This can occur in any kind of research method, not just in experiments. It can be combatted by taking steps to reassure subjects and reduce their anxiety, and by disguising the experimental hypothesis and the expected behavior. Experiments in natural settings where subjects are unaware of being studied are a particularly good way of avoiding undue evaluation apprehension. In the charity solicitation experiment, whatever evaluation apprehension was present should have been equal in all conditions, and thus would not affect the study's hypotheses.

TABLE 4-2 Suggestions for Controlling Experimenter Expectancy Effects

1. Increase number of experimenters.
2. Observe behavior of experimenters.
3. Analyze experiment for order effects (changes in results between early and late data).
4. Analyze experiment for computational errors.
5. Develop experimenter-selection procedures.
6. Develop experimenter-training procedures.
7. Maintain blind conditions (in which experimenter does not know which group subjects are in).
8. Minimize experimenter-subject contact.
9. Use expectancy control groups (in which expectancies are created or not created to determine their effect separate from the effects of other variables).

Source: Oskamp, S. (1977). Methods of studying human behavior. In L. S. Wrighman, *Social Psychology* (2nd ed.) (Adapted from Rosenthal, 1966). Copyright © 1972, 1977 by Wadsworth Publishing Company, Inc. Reprinted by permission of the publisher, Brooks/Cole Publishing Company, Monterey, California.

Results Obtained

The results of the charity solicitation experiment were objective, simple, and straightforward. They leave little room for challenge or need for interpretation, but often this is not the case. In contrast to the large effect shown here, many studies display only small effects, which may not be practically important. The size of an empirical finding is usually evaluated in two ways: by a significance test to show whether the result could have occurred by chance, and by stating the effect size, which indicates the practical importance of the findings. Often in this book, we will mention both the statistical significance and the effect size when discussing research findings, and we will explain each procedure briefly here.

If the descriptive findings of a study show a difference between conditions, we want to know whether that is a "true" difference—i.e., one that would hold for the underlying population and not just for the sample of individuals that we studied. There is always some possibility that our findings could have occurred by chance, just because of the characteristics of the individuals that happened to be sampled, rather than because of our manipulation of conditions. A **significance test** indicates the likelihood that an obtained finding did *not* occur just by chance—i.e., that it is true of the population, and thus is dependable and real. Typically in psychology, we set a 95% confidence level for our findings; that is, we accept a 5% probability that our results are due to chance.

If our results are significant, a second issue is "how big is the effect?" An **effect size** measure shows the strength of the relationship between an independent and dependent variable, but is not influenced by the size of the sample. In contrast, significance tests are sensitive to the size of the sample, so that for large sample sizes (e.g., N = several hundred), small and even trivial effects can reach statistical significance. Of the several measures of effect size, the two most commonly used are r and d (Chow, 1988; Keppel, 1991). The first measure, r, is simply the correlation coefficient, which represents the strength of the relationship between two variables. Its value can range from $+1$ (a perfect positive relationship) to -1 (a perfect negative relationship), with 0 indicating no relationship at all. The second measure, d, is the standardized size of the difference between two conditions—the number of standard deviations between the means of the experimental and control conditions (for instance 1.5 would indicate 1 ½ standard deviations, and 0 would indicate no difference). Cohen (1992) has provided useful terms for evaluating both these measures—for example, a medium r is .30, and a medium d is .50 (half a standard deviation).

In considering research findings, it is often important to examine not only the main effect of one variable on another, but also **interaction effects**, in which two or more variables in combination have different effects than when alone. Interaction effects often occur with complex DVs (such as industrial production rates) which have multiple and complex determinants, so that changes in even a powerful single IV (such as wages) may not affect them sharply. As examples of interaction effects, wage increases might affect production levels for new workers but not for old ones, or they might increase productivity in the morning but not in the afternoon when workers are tired, or they might raise employee morale but not productivity. In charity solicitation research, Bull and Gibson-Robinson (1981) found an interaction effect showing that directness of the solicitor's gaze affected the amount of obtained donations more for casually dressed collectors than for smartly dressed ones.

Such interaction effects involve **moderator variables**, which are defined as variables that affect the strength or the direction of a relationship between an independent and a dependent variable (Baron & Kenny, 1986). In contrast to moderators, a **mediator variable** is an intervening variable that totally accounts for the relationship between an independent and a dependent variable, in the sense of showing the process by which one variable affects the other. For instance, hypothetically, if women solicitors received larger donations than men, but that effect was totally accounted for by their having greater eye contact with householders (that is, the gender difference disappeared when amount of eye contact was held constant), their eye contact would be a mediator variable, showing how and why the gender effect occurred.

Internal Validity and External Validity

If all confounding variables, experimental artifacts, lack of controls, or careless procedures are successfully avoided or minimized, an experiment may have internal validity, its most important requisite. **Internal validity** means that the study's conclusions can be accepted as correct—that is, the results were really caused by the operation of the independent variables. Cook, Campbell, and Perrachio (1990) have described internal validity as the most essential requirement of an experiment, without which no amount of social importance or real-world applicability has any value.

Cialdini and Schroeder's solicitation study seems to meet the test of internal validity very well. It has no apparent artifacts, careless procedures, or lack of controls that would cause us to challenge its results, except possibly the experimenter expectancy effect as an alternative explanation of the findings. However, in many studies that is not the case. A famous bad example was provided by some of the evaluation studies of the Head Start preschool program, which used control groups that were not really equivalent to the experimental group. As a result they were destined from the very beginning to find small or null effects of the Head Start program, but their findings were invalid because of the inadequate control procedures (Campbell & Erlebacher, 1970).

External validity refers to the **generalizability** of research results to other populations, settings, treatment variables, and measurement methods (Campbell & Stanley, 1966). Poor external validity can occur even when a study has excellent internal validity. In fact, this is a common occurrence in laboratory experiments because of their frequent artificiality, though artificiality alone is not a sure indication of poor generalizability (Aronson et al., 1985). If there is doubt about the generalizability of findings, the only safe approach is to try them out in other situations in which you are interested. That is the reason for the recommendation that laboratory findings be checked in field studies, and that the ideas developed in field studies be taken back into the laboratory for further analysis and more precise testing. However, even field research can be poor in generalizability, if it confines itself to atypical individuals, settings, or behaviors (e.g., only to male company presidents).

We have already discussed the external validity of the charity solicitation experiment at some length. Though its results clearly apply to real-life situations such as the one where it was carried out, there are undoubtedly some solicitation tasks and settings where its findings would not apply or would have to be appropriately modified. For example, Weyant and Smith (1987) showed that $5, rather than a penny, was an effective minimal contribution to mention in mail solicitations to residents of well-to-do neighborhoods.

Long-Term Effects

In many studies we want to know not just about immediate changes, but also and often more importantly, about long-term effects of the research variables. That question did not apply to the solicitation experiment, however, because the only change desired was the immediate one of contributing money at the moment when the request was made.

Unfortunately, though long-term change is often of great interest, it is rarely studied in research, largely because it is difficult and time-consuming to follow up research subjects and obtain additional data later on. As a consequence, much of our knowledge about attitude and behavior change is actually confined to *immediate* change. We should be aware that findings about how to create immediate changes *may not apply at all* to the issue of creating long-term changes. Or the findings may apply in part, but it would take additional research to show which parts apply and which do not (Cialdini, Petty, & Cacioppo, 1981).

Let us list a few examples of short-term versus long-term follow-up methods in the other interesting experiments mentioned at the beginning of this chapter. Studies of television violence, beer commercials, and blood donations have focused almost exclusively on immediate changes in attitudes and behaviors. A study that involved labeling of supermarket products according to their effect on the environment found that the labels led shoppers to change the products they purchased. However, an educational intervention aimed at increasing the effectiveness of the product labels did not produce any further changes in behavior (Linn et el., 1994).

Some studies have used longer follow-up periods. A Canadian study involving well-publicized police enforcement of laws requiring the use of auto seat belts found over half the increase in seat belt use still persisted six months after the enforcement program ended (Jonah et al., 1982). At the high end of the scale, Friedlander and Burtless (1995) examined the effects of job training and assistance in job searches on the work income and amount of welfare funds received by families on welfare over a 5-year period. The results showed significant increases in annual income, and significant reductions in the amount of welfare money received, compared to the control conditions. Similarly, Bushell (1978) traced the elementary school performance of children in an experimental Follow

Through program (subsequent to a summer school Head Start experience) for periods as long as six years, and he found continuing effects of the Follow Through training even after the children had left the special program.

Ethical Issues

The ethical guidelines discussed in Chapter 1 are particularly applicable to experimental research. In experiments, more than in any other research method, the investigator has real power over the subject, and this power must be used fairly, sympathetically, and unharmfully. Fortunately, it is now rare for psychological experiments to pose any real risk of **harmful consequences** to subjects, and most psychologists are sensitive to their responsibility to protect participants from any such risks. However, in the past, some experiments have used noxious situations that were physically or psychologically stressful to subjects (cf. Farr & Seaver, 1975; Greenberg & Ruback, 1992). An extreme example involved some military studies of stress, which exposed unsuspecting subjects to highly realistic simulations of radioactive contamination, aircraft engine failure in flight, or false information that their own errors with explosives had injured other soldiers (Berkun et al., 1962). Such stressful experiments would probably not be allowed under the federal regulations that have been in effect since the early 1970s. Since then, because of the ethical and legal issues involved in research with human participants, all proposed research procedures must be approved by an *institutional review board* (IRB) before being carried out.

Most experimenters in recent years have recognized their obligation to obtain **informed consent** from research participants, and the federal government has promulgated instructions about the way this should be done—for example, telling subjects the essential facts about the study, and informing them that they can refuse to take part or withdraw from participation at any time (U.S. Department of Health, Education, and Welfare, 1971). However, in field experiments, such as the solicitation experiments, obtaining informed consent is generally considered unnecessary if the experimental conditions are relatively natural situations to which the subjects might be exposed in everyday life. Though this procedure is somewhat controversial, it is similar to the situation in survey research, where informed consent is considered to have been given by the respondent's act of answering an interviewer's questions.

The two most common ethical problems in experiments are deception and debriefing. Because of the need to avoid experimental artifacts and to keep the subjects ignorant of the research hypotheses, **deception** has often been used in social psychological experiments. Recent surveys of the prevalence of deception in social psychological research showed that it is still widely used, though less than at its peak (Nicks, Korn, & Mainieri, in press; Sieber, Iannuzzo, & Rodriguez, 1995). For instance, in the *Journal of Personality and Social Psychology*, deception was used in 66% of the research reports published in 1969, 47% in 1978, 32% in 1986, and 47% in 1992. Undoubtedly deception has been overused and misused at times, and the practice has been severely criticized (Kelman, 1967). In recent decades, the scrutiny of proposed research procedures by IRBs has made investigators more careful to avoid unnecessary deception. Only where deception is necessary for the completion of the research and justified by the potential value of the research findings is it considered ethical, and there is still vigorous debate about this degree of permissiveness (Baumrind, 1985; Christensen, 1988; Soliday & Stanton, 1995).

Debriefing, on the other hand, is considered an ethical requirement for laboratory experiments. Even if a study involves no deception, it is still important to answer the participants' questions afterward and to be sure that they do not leave with any unallayed anxieties or misconceptions (Gurman, 1994). Helpful suggestions for a thorough debriefing routine have been offered by Mills (1976) and Rosnow and Rosenthal (1996). However, it is important to realize that the false impressions instilled in deception experiments can survive the traditional type of debriefing and therefore require much more thorough discussion with the research participants about the processes which cause false impressions to persist (Ross, Lepper, & Hubbard, 1975). In field experiments, debriefing is normally carried out only if the participants are aware that they have been in a study. In studies involving unobtrusive observation of public behavior, where the subjects are unaware of being studied and might become more upset to learn about it than to remain ignorant of it, both informed consent and debriefing are usually omitted. That was the case, for instance, in the charity solicitation experiment by Cialdini and Schroeder.

Finally, like atomic scientists after World War II, social researchers must face ethical issues about the **use of their findings**. Our research results are fortunately not so deadly, but they can certainly have major effects on some people's lives. Knowing that, what is our responsibility to the people who will use them, to the people on whom they will be used, and to the advancement of scientific knowledge? To take a mild example, if you were Cialdini and Schroeder, would you be just as content to have your research findings used by the Hare Krishnas (which has actually happened) as by the American Cancer Society? Or if, like Milton Rokeach (1979), you developed a strong method of changing people's values, would you be willing to have it used by the Ku Klux Klan or the American Nazi Party? If not, should you give up experimental research and turn to some less controversial occupation? Obviously there can be no final answer to these questions; all investigators must decide for themselves. However, the ethical code of the American Psychological Association (1992, p. 1600) reminds us:

> Psychologists are aware of their professional and scientific responsibilities to the community and the society in which they work and live. They apply and make public their knowledge of psychology in order to contribute to human welfare . . . [and] try to avoid misuse of their work.

THE NEED FOR AN EXPERIMENTING SOCIETY

The use, or misuse, of findings is a particularly crucial question for applied social psychologists. Because they are *applied* scientists, they are even more eager than other researchers to see their work used for the benefit of humanity, not just for the advancement of scientific knowledge.

One of the researcher's strongest tools is the experi-

ment, precisely because it so effectively demonstrates the nature and direction of causal relationships between variables. Despite the limitations of experiments, they can be effectively applied in answering vital social questions and evaluating important social programs. Donald Campbell (1969, 1988) advocated just such an approach in influential articles calling for social scientists to help build an "experimenting society." In such a society, experimental methods would be used rather than guesswork, superstition, popular stereotypes, or "common sense" in deciding important issues of public policy. For instance, research could be applied to questions such as:

- Do stiffer punishments reduce the amount of crime?
- Are single-parent families less successful than two-parent families in raising children to be responsible adults?
- Would a guaranteed annual income reduce people's incentive to work?

Often the results of such public policy research have provided surprising new insights about our society, and much more research evidence could be brought to bear on such questions if social investigators were encouraged to study them intensively. In future chapters, particularly Chapter 17, we will examine some findings on these kinds of questions.

SUMMARY

Experiments are studies in which there is a high degree of planned manipulation of conditions, control of other conditions, and precision of measurement. As a result they are the best research tool for isolating the effects of specific independent variables and determining the direction of causal relations between variables. The goal of all the many careful procedures involved in experiments is to achieve high internal validity of the results. However, experiments are often low in mundane realism, and because of this artificiality, there frequently are questions about how far their findings can be generalized to real-life situations.

The experimental realism (impact) of procedures in laboratory experiments is often limited by practical and ethical considerations, and consequently their results may be rather weak. Field experiments, on the other hand, though more natural in their settings and procedures, must also follow ethical procedures and may not allow as much control and precision as laboratory experiments. Social research advances best when a variety of research methods is employed, checking the results of any one method by the use of other methods and settings.

Cialdini and Schroeder's study on the wording of appeals for charitable donations illustrates many of the characteristics of experiments: theorizing, careful procedural planning, and controls to achieve the desired impact on subjects and avoid experimental artifacts, statistical tests of the results, and checks on other hypotheses. As a field experiment that involved no deception, its clear-cut results had an unusually high degree of mundane realism and external validity (generalizability).

Experiments that attempt to change socially important behaviors should be concerned with and measure long-range effects in addition to immediate changes. Fortunately, increasing numbers of social psycholo-gists are successfully applying careful, long-range procedures in the study of vital social issues. In doing so, they are helping to foster an "experimenting society."

SUGGESTED READINGS

Aronson, E., Brewer, M., & Carlsmith, J. M. (1985). Experimentation in social psychology. In G. Lindzey & E. Aronson (Eds.), *The handbook of social psychology* (3rd ed., Vol. 1, pp. 441–486). New York: Random House.—Presents a thorough rationale for experimental procedures combined with a helpful how-to guide that can aid experimenters in avoiding many costly mistakes.

Campbell, D. T. (1969). Reforms as experiments. *American Psychologist, 24,* 409–429.—An influential paper, which advocates applying experimental methods to solving social problems and deciding issues of public policy.

Rosnow, R., & Rosenthal, R. (1996). *Beginning behavioral research: A conceptual primer* (2nd ed.). New York: Macmillan.—A practical guide to experimental research, including sections on manipulation of independent variables, quantifying and measuring dependent variables, and ethical concerns.

CHAPTER 5

Correlational Research—Leadership

Men love to wonder, and that is the seed of science.

—Ralph Waldo Emerson

Scientists wonder about many things that they cannot study experimentally. In such situations they often turn to the **correlational method** of research. This is a *non-manipulative* approach, which focuses on *naturally occurring* events. In the area of social psychology, this means studying the naturally occurring characteristics of people, such as their abilities, personality traits, demographic characteristics, or interactions with other people. For a situation in which such research would be useful, consider the following example in the area of group leadership.

You are a new executive in a business organization, in charge of several departments of workers. The company has been having a hard time recently, suffering from vicious external competition, as well as internal feuding between and within departments. You want to lead the organization back to a constructive course, but how to do that is a puzzle. Should you:

(a) Crack down from the top, setting up rigid rules and enforcing them strictly?
(b) Choose a highly competent task specialist to head each department and hold each of them strictly responsible for achieving the department's goals?
(c) Choose department leaders who have good rapport with their workers and give them a free hand in determining operating procedures?
(d) Institute a company suggestion box and an incentive award scheme for good suggestions?
(e) Begin a group sensitivity training program for all managers and upper-level employees?

Which of these approaches would be helpful or harmful, and how can you know? To answer such questions, correlational research would usually be the method of choice. Because group leadership approaches are based largely on the personality traits and habits of the managers involved, it is difficult to modify them experimentally. Therefore, the typical method of research in such situations is correlational studies, which measure managers' naturally occurring behavior and relate it to its possible organizational consequences.

CHARACTERISTICS OF CORRELATIONAL RESEARCH

A detailed comparison of the correlational method and the experimental method referred to them as the "two disciplines of scientific psychology" (Cronbach, 1957). A prime example of the correlational approach in psychology is the longstanding and influential psychometric tradition, which has developed many widely used measures of intelligence, personality, interests, aptitudes, and attitudes. In this approach, individual differences are the focus of interest. In contrast, the experimental method considers individual differences as an annoying source of error variance and concentrates on manipulating situational or stimulus factors. As Cronbach (1957) put it: "The correlational psychologist is in love with just those variables the experimentalist left home to forget" (p. 674).

A typical approach when using the correlational method would be to measure two or more characteristics of each member of a group of people, and then to determine the relationship between the scores on one variable and those on each other variable. Despite the name of the method, it does not require the use of correlation coefficients, for there are many other statistical techniques for showing the degree of relationship between variables, including Chi square, *t* tests, factor analysis, and a variety of nonparametric tests. The method's focus on naturally occurring characteristics is valuable when:

- A variable cannot be experimentally manipulated (for example, age, gender, or personality).
- Ethical considerations prevent manipulation of a variable (such as physical danger, extreme stress, or love between two individuals).
- Manipulation of variables might be so obtrusive as to change the nature of the phenomenon being studied (for example, attempts to change the leadership styles of people experimentally).
- Even *measurement* of personal characteristics might be so obtrusive as to yield invalid results (for example, at-

tempts to measure dangerousness in incarcerated criminals)—then unobtrusive *observations* can be used as the data in a correlational study.

The major limitation of the correlational method is summarized in the old saying, "correlation does not mean causation." Thus, if we find a correlation between two variables—say, between people's liking for each other and their degree of interaction—what can we conclude about causal factors? There are several possibilities: (a) The relationship might be accidental and not indicate anything about a causal connection. (b) Liking may cause people to spend more time together. (c) Interaction may cause people to like each other better. (d) A third factor, such as personal similarity, might be the cause of both liking and interaction. (e) Liking and interaction may each be a cause of the other in a circular or reciprocal relationship. Without additional information, we cannot choose among these possibilities.

There are statistical techniques, such as structural equation modeling and cross-lagged panel correlation, that allow causation to be inferred from correlational data under some circumstances. In **structural equation modeling** (also referred to as covariance structure modeling, or causal modeling), a researcher first defines a **causal model**, which specifies theoretical causal relationships among several constructs of interest. Then the researcher tests the degree to which empirical data *fit* the model. Structural equations have advantages over traditional correlational methods (e.g., simple correlations, multiple regression) in that they deal with latent variables, which are theoretically free from the measurement error inherent in the assessment of any psychological construct, and they estimate the strength of the relationships among these error-free constructs. Though there are limitations and crucial assumptions involved in the use of this technique (cf. Bobko, 1990), some authorities have called it a notable advance in quantitative methodology because it helps correlational researchers to substantiate causal conclusions. Readable introductions to structural equation modeling can be found in Coovert, Penner, and Mac-Callum (1990), Hoyle (1995), and Olmstead and Bentler (1992).

In contrast to correlational studies, if we use the experimental method, we know that the independent variable we have manipulated is probably the cause of any changes in the dependent variable *if* we have controlled other crucial variables carefully and not overlooked any third factors that might be the true causes of the obtained results. In other words, in experiments we achieve a greater level of confidence about causal relationships by carefully controlling factors that may represent competing causal hypotheses. Correlational studies, by their very nature, cannot be controlled so thoroughly. However, some controls are possible, through careful selection of research participants and detailed specification of measurement methods and situations, which can help us avoid the introduction of rival causal factors into the data.

Though experiments have this advantage in providing stronger causal evidence, we should be careful to avoid two common misconceptions. First, experiments *do not prove* causal connections. In fact, causation is never proven in any final sense, for causation is an *inference* that we make based on all the relevant available information. Second, experiments are *not necessary* for the development of a science. The classic example of this is the field of astronomy. The first true science to develop during and after the Renaissance, it was based entirely on correlational data, for there was no way for astronomers to experiment by manipulating the courses of the celestial bodies. In Cronbach's delightful analogy:

> The experimentalist [is] an expert puppeteer, able to keep untangled the strands to half-a-dozen independent variables. The correlational psychologist is a mere observer of a play where Nature pulls a thousand strings; but his multivariate methods make him equally an expert, an expert in figuring out where to look for the hidden strings. (1957, p. 675)

With this brief background, let us examine some specific correlational studies in more depth, concentrating on the topic of group leadership.

EMPIRICAL RESEARCH ON LEADERSHIP

The area of leadership has had a great deal of scientific as well as practical interest over the years. One early approach was to search for traits that distinguished leaders from nonleaders, such as intelligence, initiative, and self-confidence. Though there are weak tendencies for these three traits and a few others to be higher in leaders than in nonleaders, in general this research found no consistent pattern of traits typical of leaders (Hollander, 1985; Yukl & Van Fleet, 1992).

A major reason for this finding seems to be that different types of situations, different kinds of groups, and different group tasks require different skills from a leader. A number of investigators have specified and studied different styles of leadership. In a famous series of studies, Lewin, Lippitt, and White (1939) experimentally created democratic, autocratic, and laissez-faire leadership styles among the adult leaders of boys clubs. These and many later studies led to the conclusion that democratic (egalitarian, friendly, permissive) leadership generally produces higher morale and quality of products, whereas autocratic (authoritarian, distant, controlling) leadership frequently results in higher quantitative productivity, at least as long as there is surveillance of the group by the leader (Hare et al., 1994).

Another famous series of studies, conducted by faculty members at Ohio State University, developed ways to measure the major functional activities of leadership and found two dimensions to be most important: **consideration**, which refers to leader behavior showing friendship, trust, respect, and warmth; and **initiating structure**, which refers to leader behavior that defines intragroup relationships, procedures, and patterns of organization and communication (Halpin, 1966). In theory, any leader could be high on both of these dimensions, but in reality the correlation between the two sets of characteristics is quite low, and few leaders are high on both (Greenwood & McNamara, 1969; Hare et al., 1994). These two functional aspects of leadership have also been referred to as *socio-emotional leadership* and *task leadership* (Bales, 1958; Hare et al., 1994).

Clearly, there is considerable similarity between Lewin's democratic versus autocratic styles of leadership and the Ohio State group's leader-activity dimensions of consideration versus initiating structure. However, as with the studies of leadership traits, later research did not find a single pattern of leadership styles or functional dimensions that was uniformly superior across different leadership situations and tasks. This fact has stimulated and shaped the direction of leadership research for the past 30 years, and has led to the development of contingency theories of leadership (Hare et al., 1994; Yukl & Van Fleet, 1992).

Contingency theories of leadership attempt to specify the match between leaders, their followers, the group task, and the situation. Thus, contingency theories focus on the *interaction* between leaders and the environment in which the group is functioning (Hollander, 1985, 1993). Since 1960, at least eight contingency theories have been developed—each focusing on different aspects of leader-environment interaction (Yukl & Van Fleet, 1992). In this chapter we will examine several of the correlational studies conducted by Fred Fiedler and his colleagues, which contributed to the first influential contingency theory—the LPC theory—and to the newer cognitive resources theory.

FIEDLER'S LPC THEORY OF LEADERSHIP

Triandis (1993) has divided research on leadership into two time periods—before Fiedler and after Fiedler:

> Before Fiedler, for almost 40 years, psychologists struggled to find personality attributes that would predict effective leadership. Stogdill's (1948) review told them to stop looking, but they kept looking for another 20 years! Finally, Fiedler pointed out that it is the fit of the person to the situation that results in effective performance. (p. 167)

Fiedler's LPC theory, like other contingency theories, specifies that effective leadership requires a match between the characteristics of the leader and the nature of the situation. A person-oriented, considerate, democratic leader will tend to be successful in certain types of situations, while a task-oriented, structure-initiating, autocratic leader will tend to be more successful in other types of situations.

Measurement

To assess the key characteristics of leaders, Fiedler developed two different but related measures, which are often used interchangeably. They both involve

Photograph courtesy of Fred Fiedler. Reprinted by permission.

Box 5-1

FRED FIEDLER, LEADERSHIP THEORIST

Internationally known as a researcher on leadership and managerial performance, Fred Fiedler has written over 200 articles and eight books on those subjects. Born in 1922, he served in the U.S. Army in World War II, and subsequently received his M.A. and Ph.D. from the University of Chicago. After brief teaching and research positions at the University of Chicago, he moved to the University of Illinois in 1951 and served for many years as director of its Group Effectiveness Laboratory. In 1969 he became the director of the Organizational Research Group at the University of Washington, where he is now Professor Emeritus.

Fiedler has directed a large number of research grants and

contracts from a wide variety of government agencies and private foundations, and he has also served as a consultant on management and leadership for many government agencies, nongovernmental organizations, and industrial corporations. He has received awards for outstanding research from the American Personnel and Guidance Association and from APA's Divisions of Consulting Psychology, Military Psychology, and Industrial and Organizational Psychology. He has also served as a consultant and task force member for Seattle and the state of Washington, as well as holding visiting professorships and lectureships in several foreign countries.

leaders' perceptions of their co-workers. The leaders being assessed are asked to think of all the individuals with whom they have ever worked. Then each leader describes: (a) his or her most preferred co-worker (MPC), and (b) his or her least preferred co-worker (LPC). These descriptions have generally been obtained on semantic differential scales (Fiedler & Gar-

cia, 1987)—8-point, bipolar adjective rating scales such as:

Pleasant   :-8-:-7-:-6-:-5-:-4-:-3-:-2-:-1-: Unpleasant
Rejecting   :-1-:-2-:-3-:-4-:-5-:-6-:-7-:-8-: Accepting

The simpler of Fiedler's two measures is just the sum of the LPC ratings. A person who has a low LPC score tends to be punitive and rejecting toward some co-workers, emphasizing task accomplishment rather than personal relationships. By contrast, a person with a higher LPC score shows relatively favorable feelings even toward inept co-workers, emphasizing personal relationships over task accomplishment (Fiedler & Garcia, 1987).

The second measure, called assumed similarity of opposites (ASo), is a more complex index involving the overall discrepancies between the person's MPC and LPC ratings. Because everyone rates their most preferred co-worker quite favorably, people with low LPC scores also perceive low similarity between their preferred and unpreferred colleagues, thus producing a low ASo score. On the other extreme, the leader who has a high LPC score sees more similarity between preferred and unpreferred co-workers and therefore has a higher ASo score. LPC and ASo scores have been found to correlate highly (from .70 to .93), which is why Fiedler came to use them interchangeably (Fiedler, 1964).

In examining a relatively simple questionnaire measure like the LPC score, you might wonder what it could have to do with leadership characteristics. Some scientific critics have raised the same issue, but nevertheless it has been found to be an important factor in leadership effectiveness in a long series of studies stretching over more than 30 years.

Illustrative Correlational Studies

One of the first of Fiedler's leadership studies was done with high school basketball teams. At this stage, the contingency theory of leadership had not yet been formulated, and the expectation in the study was that teams which had good interpersonal relations would be more successful. Because it takes good teamwork to win, it seemed logical that teams should win more games if the players got along well together.

The study was quite simple. Fiedler (1954) chose 14 teams in leagues of comparable high schools, and he defined group effectiveness as the percentage of games won by the middle of the basketball season. All team members were given sociometric questionnaires, asking them which three of their teammates they could co-

operate with best during games and which three they could cooperate with least well, as well as the MPC and LPC description tasks. The leader of the team was identified as the player who was the sociometric "star"—that is, the player who received the most sociometric nominations as a good cooperator. This player's ASo score was computed and compared with the criterion of the team's effectiveness, its proportion of winning games. Though the ASo scores were not highly reliable ($r = .61$), they had enough reliability to yield significant findings.

The surprising result of Fiedler's team study was that the leader's ASo score correlated *negatively* and significantly ($r = -.69$) with the team's success record. That is, teams whose informal leader was relatively punitive, psychologically distant, and task-oriented won a higher percentage of games than teams whose leader was friendly, warm, and supportive. Because a large number of scores had been computed and tested in this first exploratory study, Fiedler conducted a validational study using 12 other basketball teams near the end of the season. These data yielded a similar significant negative correlation ($r = -.58$). In addition, a parallel study of the performance of 22 university-student surveying teams also showed that the effective teams, as judged by instructors' ratings of their surveying accuracy in fieldwork, had low ASo leaders.

These findings were quite clear but, like any correlational study, they left the direction of causation unclear. Did the leader's task orientation help produce successful teams, or did winning teams choose as leaders someone who was task-oriented rather than relationship-oriented, or both? One way of beginning to tease out an answer was to study groups having appointed rather than emergent leaders, since this eliminated the possibility of the group choosing any given type of leader. So Fiedler (1955) moved on to study Air Force B-29 crews and Army tank crews.

In this military study there were two unrelated criteria of the effectiveness of the bomber crews (radar bombing accuracy and visual bombing accuracy) and two unrelated criteria of the tank crews' effectiveness (time to hit a target and time to travel to a new target). Here Fiedler found significant relations between the crew's performance and the leader's ASo score only for crews where the appointed leader was the most chosen member of the team sociometrically. He also discovered another crucial factor—whether the leader sociometrically chose or rejected the key team member for the given criterion task (such as the tank gunner for the gunnery task). When the leader endorsed the key team member, the relation between team performance and leader's ASo score was negative, as with the basketball teams (correlations of $-.81$, $-.32$, $.60$, and -33). However, when the leader rejected the key team member, the relation was reversed (correlations of $+.43$, $+.30$, $+.60$, and $+.43$).

The conclusion seemed to be that, when the leader liked the key team member, demanding, task-oriented leaders produced the best crew performance. However, when the leader didn't like the key team member, friendly, relationship-oriented leaders produced the best crew performance. To state the findings another way, task-oriented leaders stimulated the best team performance when they liked their key team members; whereas relationship-oriented leaders achieved the best team performance when they didn't especially like their key team members. This complex pattern of findings marked the birth of Fiedler's contingency theory of leadership.

Analysis and Critique of the Early Research

Like many correlational studies, these research projects used rather complex measurements (sociometric choices and ASo scores) but very simple procedures to relate these scores to the criteria of team performance. In the first study the *reliability* of the ASo scores was lower than desirable, but the degree of error variance was not great enough to prevent significant findings from emerging. In the study of surveying groups, the ASo scores had excellent reliability ($r = .93$), while in the bomber and tank crew studies their reliability was very nearly as high ($r = .86$ and $.91$ respectively). The sociometric choice scores could also vary over time, but their reliability was not reported. However, in the two military studies the reliability of the sociometric

scores was enhanced by pooling responses to several highly correlated questions and also by combining questionnaires given at three different points in time.

The reliability of the *criterion scores* also needs to be considered. In the basketball study, the criterion measure of proportion of games won was a perfectly objective score, but of course it could have been affected by teams having bad nights, or missing players, or opponents of varying difficulty. In the second basketball study this was checked by comparing team records for the first half of the season with those for the second half, and the criterion reliability was found to be very high ($r = .88$)—that is, winning teams continued to win and losing teams continued to lose. Criterion reliability was not reported in the surveying study. The measure was a subjective rating by instructors, but this was offset by the fact that the students were under "practically continuous supervision of their instructors" during a five-week summer field camp (Fiedler, 1954, p. 384). In the bombing study, much previous research had been done to establish the reliability of the criterion measures, and it was generally adequate though not high. Criterion reliability was not reported in the tank crew study, but it should have been quite high since the criterion scores were averages based on attacks on 25 targets over a three-month period.

A problem in interpreting these studies is that they were *exploratory* research projects. As Fiedler pointed out, many hypotheses and relationships were tested, and so reported significance levels need to be discounted to compensate for the likelihood of some chance findings in a large number of statistical tests.

Another disadvantage of these studies, but one having an opposite effect, was the *small number of cases* involved. Though many individuals took part, the team was the unit of analysis in each study; and it was undoubtedly difficult to gain the cooperation of a large number of teams, as well as to collect all the measures on them. Thus, in several of these studies the number of teams in a particular cell (such as winning teams) was as low as 5, 6, or 7. An inevitable consequence of these small samples was the difficulty of obtaining statistical significance, even when strong relationships were found; therefore the number of significant findings obtained in these studies is really quite impressive. In order for a correlation coefficient to be statistically significant ($p < .05$, two-tailed) with a sample size of 7, it must be .79 or larger!

In considering the *significance* of the findings, we need to note which relationships were actually significant and which were not. In general, correlations that do not reach significance, even if large, are not dependable because they are likely not to be replicated in further studies. In some of these studies, though not all of them, the negative correlations between leader's ASo score and team performance (where the leader liked the key team member) *were* significant. However, the positive correlations (where the leader didn't prefer the key team member over other co-workers) were generally *not* significant, even though quite large. Due to this lack of significance, we must be particularly cautious in accepting the latter part of the contingency hypothesis. The support for it is weaker because it comes only from the repeated pattern of fairly large correlations, and from the fact that the small Ns militated against obtaining significance. In addition, however, Fiedler reported that the *interaction* between leader ASo scores and team performance under the two conditions of leader-to-key-team-member relations was significant, so we certainly can't disregard the positive relationship as entirely unsupported. Instead we must seek further support for it in additional studies.

Replication of findings is one of the main strengths of these studies by Fiedler (1954, 1955). In each paper he repeated an initial exploratory study with one or two follow-up studies and several additional measures. The fact that he used somewhat different measuring instruments and quite different types of teams and criterion measures of team performance is an added strength, for repeated findings in somewhat different situations give greater confidence in the generality of the research conclusions. This approach has been called a **conceptual replication**, as contrasted with a literal replication of a study.

A final limitation of these studies is that the conclusions about the relation of the leader's ASo score to team performance only held for leaders who were the most-chosen member of their team. This was true for

less than half the crews in the bomber study, and for only two-thirds of the tank crews, so there were many leadership situations where the contingency theory conclusions did not apply, at least as Fiedler had stated them up to that point.

In summary, then, we can see both pluses and minuses of these research studies. They were quite carefully conducted, and the use of conceptual replications gave added weight to the repeated findings. However, the lack of significance for some of the findings caused doubts about them, and the scope of the theory still did not cover many leadership situations.

Developing the LPC Theory

At first Fiedler interpreted the results described above as indicating that a moderate psychological distance between leader and followers was necessary for good team performances—a generally warm, accepting leader should not be too close to key assistants, whereas a more distant, reserved leader should be friendly toward key assistants. After more research, however, the interpretation of ASo scores changed toward an emphasis on task-orientation versus person-orientation. As Fiedler continued to collect data on interacting work groups, he inductively developed a scheme to classify the degree of favorability of the group situation for the leader's (and the group's) success. He identified three aspects of the group situation that seemed to be crucial in determining how much the leader can influence the group. In descending order of importance, these three situational factors are:

1. Leader-Member Relations. This factor of affective relations was measured by the sociometric choices in Fiedler's early studies; but later it was measured by obtaining the leader's rating of the group atmosphere on a number of scales similar to those used for measuring LPC, such as:

```
Close   :-8-:-7-:-6-:-5-:-4-:-3-:-2-:-1-:   Distant
Bad     :-1-:-2-:-3-:-4-:-5-:-6-:-7-:-8-:   Good
```

Fiedler (1964) did not report the reliability of this measurement, but the format suggests that it should be quite high, like the LPC and ASo scores' reliability. This is the most important of the three factors, because leaders who are liked and respected do not need formal power; they can often influence the group and gain compliance even under very difficult external circumstances.

2. Task Structure. The second important factor is clarity versus ambiguity of the task. It has been measured by ratings of the task made by external judges on four 8-point scales; the four scales assess decision verifiability, goal clarity, lack of multiple goal paths, and solution specificity. Despite their forbidding sound, these scales are quite reliable; interrater agreement in using them to rate 35 tasks was .80 to .88 (Fiedler, 1964). The rationale of this factor is that the leader's job is much easier if the group task is highly structured (for example, assembling a piece of equipment) than if it is vague and ambiguous (for example, developing a policy to increase a company's profits).

3. Leader Position Power. This factor has been measured by a checklist of 18 items, of which the most heavily weighted were whether the leader is set apart from the members by official rank or status (such as military rank or elected office in an organization) and, in contrast, whether the group members can replace or depose the leader. Even a disliked leader who has a powerful office or position may be able to obtain compliance from the group. This factor was measured for 35 different group situations with an extremely high interrater agreement of .95 (Fiedler, 1964).

After defining these factors, Fiedler divided all group situations into eight "octants" according to whether they were high or moderately low on each of the three factors. In addition, research with real-life groups (as contrasted with experimental groups in the laboratory) led him to add a ninth cell to handle situations where the leader was strongly rejected by group members. Then he specified what kind of leader would be needed in order to obtain good group performance in each of these nine types of situations.

The general principle involved in this interaction of leader and situational characteristics is that a demanding, low-LPC leader will do best in either very favorable or very difficult situations; whereas a considerate, person-oriented, high-LPC leader will perform best in situations of moderate difficulty. This relationship and the empirical findings that established it are shown in Table 5-1 and Figure 5-1. These data summarize 60 different findings from about 20 different study settings, ranging from infantry squads to corporation boards of directors to church leadership workshops.

All the data points summarized in Table 5-1 are correlations between the leader's LPC or ASo score and the group's performance, arranged by octants according to the favorability of the group situation for the

TABLE 5-1   Median Correlations Between Leader LPC and Group Performance in Various Octants

	Leader-member relations	Task structure	Position power	Median correlation	Number of relations included in median
Octant I	Good	Structured	Strong	−.52	8
Octant II	Good	Structured	Weak	−.58	3
Octant III	Good	Unstructured	Strong	−.41	10
Octant IV	Good	Unstructured	Weak	.47	10
Octant V	Moder. poor	Structured	Strong	.42	6
Octant VI	Moder. poor	Structured	Weak	—	0
Octant VII	Moder. poor	Unstructured	Strong	.05	10
Octant VIII	Moder. poor	Unstructered	Weak	−.43	12
Octant V-A	Very poor	Structured	Strong	−.67	1

Source: Fiedler, F. E. A contingency model of leadership effectiveness. In L. Berkowitz (Ed.), *Advances in Experimental Social Psychology* (Vol. 1). New York: Academic Press, 1964. Reprinted by permission.

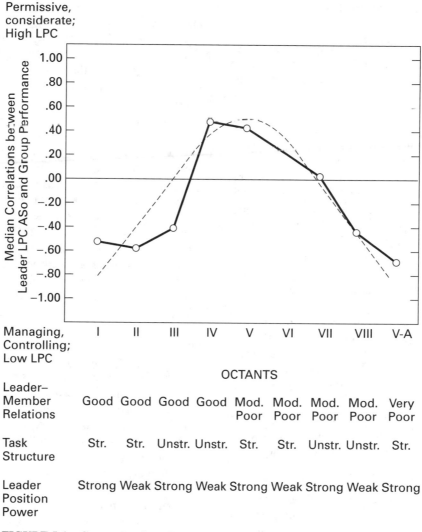

Permissive, considerate; High LPC

Managing, Controlling; Low LPC

OCTANTS

Leader–Member Relations	Good	Good	Good	Good	Mod. Poor	Mod. Poor	Mod. Poor	Mod. Poor	Very Poor
Task Structure	Str.	Str.	Unstr.	Unstr.	Str.	Str.	Unstr.	Unstr.	Str.
Leader Position Power	Strong	Weak	Strong	Weak	Strong	Weak	Strong	Weak	Strong

FIGURE 5-1   Curve showing relation of leader LPC to group performance for various group situations. (Source: Fiedler, F. E. A contingency model of leadership effectiveness. In L. Berkowitz (Ed.), *Advances in Experimental Social Psychology* (Vol. 1). New York: Academic Press, 1964. Reprinted by permission.)

leader. Thus, all the evidence so far cited for Fiedler's contingency theory comes from correlational research. Figure 5-1 displays the pattern of findings more clearly, showing that the hypothesized inverted U-curve was quite closely approximated by the obtained pattern of correlations across many different studies.

All the data contained in Table 5-1 and Figure 5-1

were available and considered by Fiedler in developing the principles of his LPC contingency theory of leadership. Therefore, they cannot be considered as strong evidence for the theory without further validating evidence. Fiedler realized this need and set out to collect just such data, as did a number of other leadership researchers.

Validational Research on the LPC Contingency Theory

Since Fiedler originally proposed his LPC theory, several hundred additional studies have been conducted on it. If we compare the data used by Fiedler to develop his LPC theory with subsequent validational studies, we find qualified support for the theory (Fiedler & Garcia, 1987; Peters, Hartke, & Pohlmann, 1985; Strube & Garcia, 1981). Figure 5-2 displays the validational findings summarized in a meta-analytic review of over 100 studies (Peters, Hartke, & Pohlmann, 1985), plotted against the original research data from Figure 5-1. This 1985 review calculated separate correlation coefficients for studies conducted in laboratory and field settings.

It is clear from the figure that the pattern of correlations from these later studies was quite similar to those of the earlier studies for studies conducted in field settings, but less so for laboratory experiments. The largest exception was Octant II, which did not fit the predicted overall pattern when assessed in the laboratory. Fiedler and Garcia (1987) suggested that this discrepancy might be caused by the difficulty of creating laboratory conditions with high task structure but low position power, and they pointed out that *field* studies in this octant had displayed the predicted negative correlations. Though we will not take the space to describe them here, some of the most carefully conducted *experimental* studies have been most supportive of the theory—for example, Chemers and Skrzypek's (1972) study with West Point cadets, which allowed strong manipulations of the three aspects of situational favorability.

Criticisms of LPC Theory

Despite the research support for Fiedler's LPC theory, several important questions remain. One problem is the choice of criterion measures of group performance. Because the theory doesn't indicate what specific measures of effectiveness should be used, the choice is usually made intuitively by the investigator. As a result, a wide variety of measures has been used, including proportion of winning games, accuracy of surveying, amount of production per unit of time, observers' rat-

ings of quality of performance, companies' net income, and judges' ratings of creativity of ideas. In any given study there might be several plausible alternate measures of group performance, and the theory doesn't tell the investigator whether any or all of them are appropriate to use—that is, whether the theory can hope to predict them or not.

Another concern is the situational favorableness measure. Fiedler (1978) changed its name to "situational control"—an indication of how much control or influence the leader has in the given situation. Though it is usually still measured in similar ways, there are discrepancies in the way it has been measured and weighted in several past studies. For instance, in a major validational study done with personnel of the Belgian Navy (Fiedler, 1966), several ad hoc combinations of variables were tried. The final scoring system added two new variables (the leader's main language—Dutch or French—and the sequence of tasks for the group), and it dropped the customary variable of task structure. There were also several explorations of how heavily to weight these added variables. These exploratory and nonstandard procedures led Graen et al. (1970) to dismiss the results of the study as incapable of providing *validational* evidence.

Critics have referred scathingly to Fiedler's approach as one of searching for new classificatory variables and trying them out until the obtained results fit the theoretical model (Graen et al., 1970). Because adding more variables increases the number of cells, it reduces still further the number of groups per cell, decreasing the reliability of findings, and making significance even more difficult to obtain. As a result, say these critics, it is impossible to disconfirm the oft-revised theory; and a theory that can't be disconfirmed is scientifically useless. Though this critique seems overstated, there is some truth to the criticism that revisions of the theory and its associated measuring instruments have been so frequent that validational studies have not been able to keep up with them.

Finally, the meaning of the LPC score has been a persistent question about the theory (Fiedler & Garcia, 1987; Schriesheim & Klich, 1991; Triandis, 1993). Over the years its interpretation has changed, from a measure of social distance, to an indication of task ori-

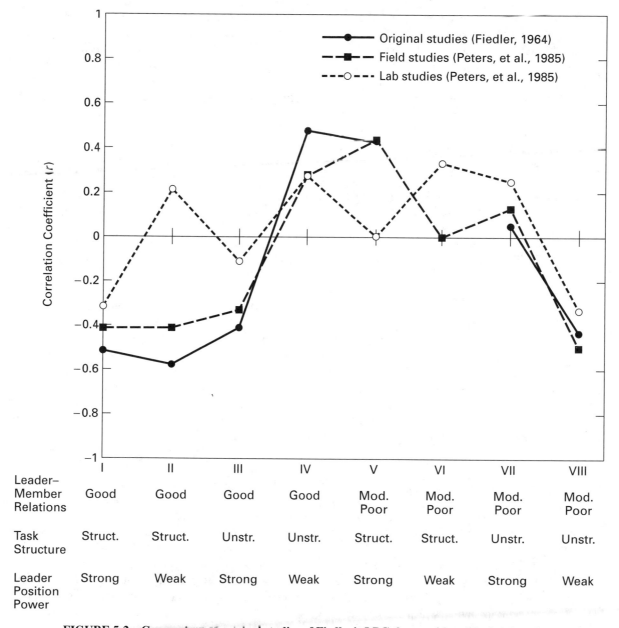

FIGURE 5-2 Comparison of original studies of Fiedler's LPC theory with validational studies conducted in field settings and in laboratories. (Source of data: Fiedler, 1978; Peters, Hartke, & Pohlmann, 1985.)

entation versus person orientation, to an index of the leader's hierarchy of motives. Fiedler (1993) believes that the LPC score is *not* a consistent predictor of the leader's behavior. That is, a high-LPC leader will not necessarily be considerate in all situations, for the leader's behavior is influenced by the favorableness of the situation. Rather, a high LPC score indicates the leader's **motive hierarchy**—the leader will be concerned first with friendly personal relations, and only secondarily with task accomplishment or other motives. In like manner, a low LPC score indicates a leader who will attend first to task considerations, and only secondarily to personal relationships.

COGNITIVE RESOURCES CONTINGENCY THEORY

A more recent contingency approach to leadership is Fiedler's cognitive resources theory (CRT—Fiedler, 1995). As mentioned earlier, psychological studies of leadership have long searched for qualities that would predict success among leaders—variables like intelligence, experience, and/or knowledge. However, research has failed to find strong correlations between these variables and success among leaders—most often correlations ranging from .00 to +.20 (Murphy, Blyth, & Fiedler, 1992). Despite these findings, Fiedler (1995) stated:

> It is very difficult to believe that intellectual abilities fail to contribute to such critical leadership functions as decision-making and coordinating and organizing work processes, or that leaders cannot learn from past events. There must be at least some conditions in which it is better for a leader to be relatively bright than stupid, and relatively experienced than inexperienced. (p. 6)

Following this line of reasoning, the cognitive resources theory is a contingency theory—an attempt to identify the conditions under which intelligence and experience correlate with the performance of leaders and their groups. Most of the research on these conditions has examined stressors like time pressure, task complexity, role ambiguity, or noxious working conditions (Fiedler, 1995). In brief, the theory holds that, under stressful conditions, leaders will have difficulty focusing on the job at hand and will rely instead on their experience. In contrast, under less stressful working

conditions, leaders will rely less on experience and more on their intellectual ability. Thus, CRT predicts an interaction between stress, experience, and intelligence. In stressful conditions, *experience* should be a strong positive correlate of performance; in nonstressful conditions, *intelligence* should be a strong positive correlate of performance.

The research has tended to support the predicted interaction (Fiedler, 1995; Fiedler & Link, 1994; Schonpflug, 1995). A clear example was the dissertation study of Borden (1980, described in Fiedler, 1995). This correlational study examined the effects of stress on the use of intelligence and experience by leaders in an Army combat infantry division. Participants in the study were 160 officers at various command levels and 167 noncommissioned officers such as platoon sergeants.

To test cognitive resources theory, Borden divided the leaders into those experiencing high, medium, and low stress with their immediate supervisor. For each group, correlation coefficients were calculated between the leaders' intelligence and experience, and their performance as rated by at least two supervisors. Results from the study are summarized in Table 5-2. As indicated in the table, under low stress the correlation between intelligence and performance was significantly positive while the correlation between experience and performance was nonsignificant. However, when stress was high, the correlation between intelligence and performance was nonsignificant, while the correlation between experience and performance was significantly positive.

These results, and similar findings from other studies (e.g., Potter & Fiedler, 1981), suggest that the relationships between intelligence, experience, and performance are contingent upon the situation—especially upon stress with the boss. However, as in any correlational study, a significant relationship may not be causal, because other variables may be influencing the results. Thus, additional research is needed to examine both the validity and generalizability of the findings.

One study that supported the earlier correlational findings through the results of an experimental manipulation was the dissertation research of Macaulay (1992, described by Fiedler, 1995). Macaulay examined the effects of experimentally induced stress on leaders

TABLE 5-2 **Correlations of Leader Intelligence and Experience with Rated Performance for Group Leaders Having High, Moderate, or Low Stress with Their Supervisor**

Variable	Stress with supervisor		
	Low	*Moderate*	*High*
Intelligence	.44	.31	−.02[a]
	(N=129)	(N=116)	(N=110)
Experience	−.02	−.06	.54[b]
	(N=131)	(N=123)	(N=114)

Note: Correlations above .26 are significant ($p < .01$).

[a] Correlations for low and high stress differ significantly ($p < .01$).

[b] Correlations for low and moderate stress differ significantly from high stress ($p < .01$).

Source: Borden (1980).

with high and low experience. Participants in the study were 180 college students, randomly assigned to 60 3-person teams. The leader's experience was measured as the amount of time he or she reported having spent in leadership positions (e.g., in high school, college, or work). A moderate level of stress was experimentally induced by informing half of the leaders that their performance would be evaluated by an expert, and by placing a video camera in the room. The teams worked on group decision-making tasks developed by NASA, which required the group to rank, in order of importance, 15 items used for survival in an imaginary plane crash in the desert. Performance was assessed by comparing the group's rankings against those made by a panel of desert survival experts.

The results from the study supported the prediction from CRT that less experienced leaders would be affected by the stress manipulation, while more experienced leaders would not be. Under low-stress conditions, less experienced leaders actually performed better than leaders high in experience. However, under moderate stress the effect was reversed, with high-experience leaders performing better than low-experience leaders.

Although the results from the studies on CRT provide solid evidence for interaction between stress and the leader's characteristics, many questions remain. These questions will undoubtedly be the topic of sub-

sequent research on CRT, both correlational and experimental, as Fiedler and his colleagues continue to develop and refine the theory.

APPLICATIONS OF CONTINGENCY THEORY TO LEADERSHIP TRAINING

An exciting offshoot of Fiedler's LPC contingency theory is a leader training program that attempts to improve organizational effectiveness by manipulating levels of situational control and leadership styles. Such an ability would provide an acid test for the theory, and Fiedler has gone out on a limb in using it in such applications. He believes that it is generally much easier to change leaders' levels of situational control than their leadership styles, and so he and his colleagues have developed a training program to teach leaders to modify their organizational situations to match their personalities.

This daring application of the contingency theory, called Leader Match, seems to have been very successful. Fiedler and Mahar (1979) reviewed 12 validation studies of the training program, 7 in military units, and 5 in civilian settings, ranging from volunteers in a public health agency to middle managers in a county government. In each study a training group and a control group were selected at random, and the performance criterion was evaluations by two or more superiors, made from two to six months after the training period. In all 12 studies, the group of leaders or managers trained with the Leader Match program performed significantly better than the untrained group.

Along lines similar to the Leader Match program, interventions have been developed within the context of cognitive resources theory. These training programs aim to reduce job stress, with the goal of increasing "the intellectual and creative productivity of individuals in leadership positions" (Fiedler, 1995, p. 24). Specifically, these programs attempt to improve the fit between leaders and their environment by teaching leaders to:

- reduce their level of stress through relaxation techniques.
- recognize and create conditions that facilitate performance among subordinate leaders.
- create a conducive work environment.

Although this work is not as fully established as the Leader Match program, some research has begun to examine each aspect of the program, and the preliminary evidence is encouraging (Jacobs, 1992; Link, 1992).

In short, the results from many studies indicate that the LPC and cognitive resources contingency theories can be put to work in practical, real-life settings to influence leaders' performance. Whether the training is about modifying work situations or controlling stress, the ultimate goal is to increase group performance, Findings from a wide range of studies provide strong evidence for the value of contingency theories. In addition, some of the studies have also demonstrated how experimental evidence can be used to buttress the findings from correlational research studies.

SUMMARY

Correlational research is a nonmanipulative approach for studying naturally occurring events and behavior, using a variety of statistical techniques. It is very useful when practical or ethical considerations prevent manipulation of variables. Though it is not as powerful as the experimental method in determining causal relationships, it is a perfectly adequate scientific method, as the science of astronomy amply demonstrates.

Correlational studies may often be vulnerable to methodological criticisms. For instance, Fiedler's early exploratory studies suffered from the likelihood of inflated significance levels due to their many statistical tests, but on the other hand their relatively small numbers of groups made it difficult to obtain significance. However, a great strength of his research came from the frequent replication of findings in new situations and with differing measures.

Fiedler's research on effective leadership provides many examples of correlational research. His contingency theory of leadership specifies that different types of situations require different leader characteristics in order to achieve effective group performance. The LPC contingency theory developed new conceptions and measures of situational favorability, and differentiated

hypotheses about which kind of leader would be effective in each of the eight types of situations called octants. Results from the many validational studies fit the theoretical model fairly well, and some exemplary experimental studies have provided especially strong support. Nevertheless, a number of critics have pointed out continuing methodological ambiguities and nonsupportive evidence.

A newer, but related, contingency theory is Fiedler's cognitive resources theory. A growing body of research, mostly correlational though some experimental, is showing that stressful work environments can have both positive and negative effects on performance, depending on the leader's characteristics. Under high stress, job performance is generally significantly and positively related to job-relevant experience, but not to intelligence; while under low stress, job performance is generally significantly and positively related to intelligence, but not to experience.

The principles of the LPC and cognitive resources contingency theories have been used in designing innovative training programs to help leaders learn how to change their group situations so as to achieve better group performance. These findings both demonstrate the theories' value and show how experimental evidence can add support to the findings of correlational research.

SUGGESTED READINGS

Cronbach, L. J. (1957). The two disciplines of scientific psychology. *American Psychologist, 12,* 671–684.—An insightful and interesting comparison of correlational methods with experimental methods, and an influential call for their collaboration and amalgamation.

Fiedler, F. E., & Garcia, J. (1987). *New approaches to effective leadership: Cognitive resources and organizational performance.* New York: Wiley.—Clearly summarizes both the LPC and cognitive resources theories, and provides a review of the supporting research.

Goodwin, J. (1995). *Research in psychology: Methods and design.* New York: Wiley.—A broad overview of research methods used in psychology, including a good discussion of correlational as well as experimental and quasi-experimental designs.

CHAPTER 6

Quasi-Experimental Studies—Effects of Television

✧✧✧

> *Science is simply common sense at its best—that is, rigidly accurate in observation, and merciless to fallacy in logic.*
>
> —Thomas H. Huxley

Suppose you are a researcher trying to study the results of a new educational or medical program—perhaps an educational TV program for children, or a new treatment procedure intended to prevent the recurrence of cancer after surgery. You might like to study the program's effects experimentally by randomly assigning individuals to various treatment and control conditions. However, the school authorities or the hospital administrators might not allow that, for students' class assignments or patients' treatment plans may already have been determined, based on nonexperimental considerations.

You could, of course, switch your research plans to a passive correlational design, and merely take data from the institution's records to relate the treatment program to students' or patients' later progress. But your choices are not limited to an active experimental design or a passive correlational design. Another research option is to use an active approach and plan a quasi-experimental study. Quasi-experimental methods fall between experiments and correlational research in their degree of rigor and control. They attempt to live up to Huxley's standards in the above quotation, for they particularly stress careful observation or measurement, and thorough logical analysis of all plausible causal relationships in the situation under investigation.

The prefix *quasi* means "almost." By definition **quasi-experiments** do not meet one of the defining characteristics of experiments: The investigator does not have full control over manipulation of the independent variable, and therefore cannot assign the subjects randomly to conditions. However, in other respects they can be just as rigorous, for the investigator does have control over how and when the dependent variable is measured, and usually also over what groups of subjects are measured. Campbell and Stanley (1966) pioneered the concept of quasi-experiments, and they have stressed that by carefully choosing measurement procedures and subject groups, we can con-

struct research designs that are close to true experimental designs in their power to produce valid causal inferences. Consequently, quasi-experimental designs are "deemed worthy of use *where better designs are not feasible*" (Campbell & Stanley, 1966, p. 34).

There are a large number of possible quasi-experimental designs, ranging from simple ones with many problematic aspects to complete ones, which guard against many of the likely threats to valid inference. Campbell and Stanley (1966), Cook and Campbell (1979), and Cook, Campbell, and Perrachio (1990) have full discussions of the possible designs and their strengths and weaknesses in refuting alternate causal hypotheses. In this chapter we will summarize the concept of threats to valid inference, as discussed by Cook et al. (1990), and describe two studies that illustrate two major types of quasi-experimental designs: *nonequivalent control group designs* and *time-series designs*.

A NONEQUIVALENT CONTROL GROUP STUDY: "SESAME STREET"

The award-winning TV program, "Sesame Street," attracted a great deal of attention and considerable scientific research in its early years. One of the studies was a dissertation project by Judith Minton (1975), in which she compared the school readiness of kindergarten children who had watched "Sesame Street" with that of quite comparable (but not randomly assigned) children who hadn't watched it—a **nonequivalent control group design**.

To see why Minton had to use a quasi-experimental research method, imagine how a randomized true experiment would be done with viewing of "Sesame Street" as the independent variable. Children would be randomly assigned to at least two conditions, and those in the viewing condition would be required to watch the program (perhaps during their kindergarten class), while those in the control condition would be prevented from watching it. The children would have to be in the same kindergarten class unless assignments to two or more classes had been made by strictly random methods (a rare procedure in school systems). If they were in the same class, the nonviewing group would probably resent missing out on the new program, and in any case they might be able to see the program after school or on weekends, or even hear about it from their classmates, thus damaging the experimental contrast. Though in some situations the experimenter might have enough control to accomplish a true, randomized experiment on TV viewing, such situations are certainly rare (and they would raise ethical issues about denying a possible benefit to the control group).

Minton did not have that amount of control, so she had to look for a situation where some children watched "Sesame Street" as part of their normal daily activities and others did not. A few such situations come readily to mind—a whole kindergarten class that watched the program during the school period versus one that didn't; children who had TV sets in their homes versus ones who didn't; and so on. However, the next step must be to ensure that the two groups of children, though not randomly assigned, are *as similar as possible* in all respects except for viewing "Sesame Street"; otherwise the nonviewing children would not be an adequate control group. This is a very tricky step because usually many other differences accompany any such contrast. For instance, families owning TV sets are apt to be more affluent, or (in the early days of TV) more technologically minded, than families without them. Similarly, two kindergarten classes, whose students have been assigned according to parental preferences, school-district judgments of compatibility or school readiness, or some other systematic approach, are likely to differ in many ways. If the classes are not from the same school, they are likely to differ still more because of demographic disparities in the areas served by the schools.

Methodology

As a result of such considerations, Minton chose to compare children who were in kindergarten during 1969–1970, the first year that "Sesame Street" was broadcast, with those who were kindergartners in the preceding few years. Thus she was able to ensure that the control group had *never* watched the program, and she was able to establish a control group from the same community, with similar backgrounds and other experiences to the experimental group. This is called a **cohort study**; it compares two **cohorts**, which are defined as *groups who have the same experience at about the same point in time*. For example, a birth cohort is composed of people born in the same year, and a marriage cohort includes couples who married in the same year. Though this was still a nonequivalent control group design, the two groups should be quite closely comparable, and Minton used some clever additional techniques to make them even more comparable.

The students chosen for study comprised all the kindergartners in a single school district with a heterogeneous population (about 500 each year for several years). The dependent variables were their scores on the Metropolitan Readiness Test (MRT), a standardized test routinely given to all kindergartners in the district each May. This, then, was an **archival study**, since the testing was a routine school district activity and the experimenter did not have to collect the school readiness scores herself; and consequently the research procedure was admirably free from any reactivity—as well as cheaper and more feasible to carry out.

The author compared the 1970 MRT scores with the previous years' scores for several different groups. Comparison 1 was for all the kindergartners in the district during those years. Comparison 2, one of the clever features, used a subset of the children who should be even more comparable than the total group: children who had siblings in the earlier kindergarten classes, with the older siblings' previous MRT scores serving as the control data. The author even included a control for any possible differences due to sibling order (older versus younger) by adding an analysis of data for 1969 kindergartners (before "Sesame Street" began) compared with *their* older siblings in previous years. Comparison 3, another look at a demographically more comparable subset of children, examined only the children who went on to parochial school. (Since the parochial school had no kindergarten, all children in the district went to the public kindergarten.) Finally, Comparison 4 examined the factor of socioeconomic status by comparing the scores of a group of "advantaged" youngsters from a notably affluent community in the district with the scores of a "disadvantaged" group of summer Head Start children whose parents were near the poverty level.

The MRT yields scores on six subtests and a total score. Though all of these scores might have been influenced by the information obtained from watching "Sesame Street," the subtest that was clearly most relevant to the program's content was Alphabet, a 10-item test of recognition of lower-case alphabetical letters. That point was established by an intensive content analysis of the program's first year, which showed that more time was devoted to teaching letters than to any other topic (Ball & Bogatz, 1970).

Results

Though tests were made on all the MRT scores, it turned out that significant differences were obtained only on the Alphabet subtest. This finding indicated some divergent validity in the data, since differences were found on the score where they would be most expected and not on any of the other scores.

Preliminary data analyses confirmed that the children were watching "Sesame Street" quite faithfully. In the total 1970 kindergarten group, 54% said they watched it every day, and 43% more said they watched it sometimes, while only 3% said "never."

The major results of the study are summarized in Table 6-1, which displays mean scores and significance levels for all four comparisons mentioned above on both the Alphabet subtest and the total MRT score. The table shows that the total kindergarten group performed significantly higher on the Alphabet subtest in 1970 than in previous years, and that the small increase in the MRT total score was not enough to be significant. Supporting this analysis were the results for the sibling groups and the parochial school students, both of which also showed highly significant increases in the Alphabet score in 1970. Similar significant findings were obtained for the small group of advantaged children, who had the highest mean scores of any group and also displayed a nonsignificant tendency toward a

TABLE 6-1   Major Effects of Watching "Sesame Street" on Kindergartners' Learning in Minton's Study

Comparison	Group	Year	N	Alphabet subtest Mean	F	Total MRT score Mean	F
1	Total	1968	482	9.00		61.36	
		1969	495	8.49	26.52***	60.44	1.15
		1970	524	10.45		62.08	
2	Siblings (older)	1966–1968	132	8.27		58.08	
	" (younger)	1969	132	8.63		62.38	
	" (older)	1967–1969	122	8.00	7.19**	58.77	0.01
	" (younger)	1970	122	10.42		62.81	
3	Parochial school	1968	68	9.30		63.82	
		1969	84	8.88	9.28***	64.17	0.86
		1970	87	11.32		66.50	
4	Advantaged	1968	37	11.13		69.94	
		1969	36	10.38	6.90**	70.41	2.49
		1970	34	13.58		76.05	
"	Disadvantaged	1968	70	6.40		46.04	
		1969	85	6.43	0.55	51.41	2.27
		1970	99	6.95		48.06	

$*p < .05$ $**p < .01$ $***p < .001$

Source: Adapted from Minton (1975, Tables 4, 5, 6, 8, and 9).

higher total score in 1970. The only group that did not show a marked increase in 1970 was the disadvantaged group, who also had the lowest mean scores.

These results provide considerable confirmation of the study's hypothesis that exposure to "Sesame Street" would increase children's school readiness. Though many comparisons were made in the study, it was not just a "fishing expedition," because the pattern of findings was highly consistent—improvement on the Alphabet subtest in almost every group of children, and no significant improvement on any of the other scores. Moreover, the additional tests made on the subgroups of children, particularly the groups of paired siblings, provide corroborative evidence based on treatment and control groups which are probably as comparable as could be attained without random assignment of matched pairs of children.

However, these laudatory comments do not mean that Minton's study was free from all dangers of reaching false conclusions, for it was not. To see why this is so, we will now discuss the many factors that can lead to incorrect causal inferences being made from research results.

THREATS TO VALID INFERENCE

Recall that a major goal in doing research is to reach conclusions about cause and effect relations between variables, and such conclusions *are always inferences*—never proven in any ultimate sense. We reach such conclusions by using all the available relevant information to help us interpret the results of research studies. In the process, many **threats to valid inference** may arise—factors that would lead us to incorrect causal conclusions. The better the research design, the fewer such threats will be present, but even the best research designs are apt to have some aspects that are not fully controlled or are open to differing interpretations. In general, experiments have relatively few threats to valid inference, while correlational studies have more. Quasi-experiments are in between and, depending on the particular design involved, they may range from very poor to very good in their safeguards against invalid conclusions.

What are some of these threats to valid inference? Cook et al. (1990) have described a large number and classified them under four main headings (see Table 6-2 for a convenient list). These are not the only threats to validity, for any particular research design may suffer from other idiosyncratic threats and may avoid many of these threats. Therefore this list should not be used in "cookbook" fashion. Rather, the important point is that any research design should be systematically analyzed for threats from rival hypotheses that could explain the findings.

Threats to Statistical Conclusion Validity

The first question in analyzing research findings is usually: Was there any effect? That is, were the presumed independent and dependent variables actually related? This is the question of **statistical conclusion validity.** Some of the major problems that can lead to incorrect answers to this question are:

1. Low Statistical Power. This can result from use of small samples or of statistical tests that have low power to detect effects. Also, each statistical test makes a set of underlying assumptions about the data, and these assumptions need to be checked, since violating some of them can lead to markedly distorted conclusions.

2. Fishing. A "fishing expedition," in which many different scores are compared statistically, will typically find some falsely "significant" comparisons simply because of chance factors. For example, of 100 tests, about 5% should be significant at the .05 level due to chance alone. In studies where many tests must be made, there are procedures for adjusting the error rate (alpha) to compensate for this problem.

3. Low Reliability of Measures. Instruments that are unreliable, or insensitive (for instance, ones having so few scale points that they give only a coarse score), can lead to false conclusions of "no effect." Where this problem is anticipated beforehand, there are several ways of increasing measurement reliability (cf. Sechrest, Perrin, & Bunker, 1990).

4. Low Reliability of Treatment Implementation (of the IV). This kind of nonstandardization often occurs when a given experimental treatment must be carried out many times by one person or by several different people. If the treatment is implemented in varying ways, its effectiveness may differ accordingly, and so the average results may be misleading.

5. Random Irrelevancies in the Experimental Setting. This threat often occurs in field situations where many aspects of the situation cannot be held constant (such as layoffs in work settings or weather in environmental studies). When such extraneous variables seem likely to have an effect on the dependent variable, they should be measured as carefully as possible and included as factors in the statistical analysis.

6. Random Heterogeneity of Respondents. The more heterogeneous a group of individuals, the more they will differ in their responses to a treatment. If some of their personal characteristics are related to their response to the treatment, that will increase the variance of the outcome measures, and thus make it harder to detect a treatment effect through statistical tests. This threat can be avoided by choosing a quite homogeneous group of respondents, such as male introductory psychology students (as was often done in past decades). However, that procedure tells us nothing about the characteristics of females or the generalizability of results to other age or educational groups (an issue of external validity). The best way to handle such problems is to measure the individual-difference variables and include them as factors in the data analysis.

Several ways of combatting these potential errors in statistical conclusions have been suggested. One is to estimate the sample size that would be necessary in order to detect an experimental effect of a reasonable or likely size (Lipsey, 1990). For instance, if a 20% decrease in the recidivism rate of juvenile delinquents seems a reasonable goal, how big a sample would be necessary to detect an actual change of that extent? Another way is to reduce the error term in the statistical analysis as much as possible. This can be done by using an *own-control design*, by matching subjects before their random assignment to treatments (a *randomized block design*), or by using analysis of covariance to remove the effect of extraneous respondent or situational variables on the dependent variable measure. A third approach is to improve the reliability or sensitivity of measures—for instance, by combining several items into a more reliable composite (Cook & Campbell, 1979; Cook et al., 1990).

TABLE 6-2   List of Possible Threats to Valid Causal Inference

Threats to Statistical Conclusion Validity
  1. Low statistical power
  2. Fishing (statistical tests of many different scores)
  3. Low reliability of measures
  4. Low reliability of treatment implementation
  5. Random irrelevancies in the experimental setting
  6. Random heterogeneity of respondents

Threats to Internal Validity
  1. History (extraneous contemporary events)
  2. Maturation (systematic changes in participants)
  3. Testing (effects of prior testing)
  4. Instrumentation (changes in a measuring instrument)
  5. Statistical regression (of extreme groups)
  6. Selection (nonequivalent comparison groups)
  7. Mortality (drop-outs)
  8. Interactions with selection
  9. Ambiguity about the direction of causal influence

Threats to Construct Validity of Causes and Effects
  1. Inadequate preoperational explication of constructs
  2. Mono-operation bias (only one operation for a construct)
  3. Mono-method bias (varied operations but only one measurement method)
  4. Interaction of procedure and treatment
  5. Diffusion or imitation of treatments
  6. Compensatory equalization of treatments
  7. Compensatory rivalry from other participants
  8. Resentful demoralization of other participants
  9. Hypothesis-guessing within experimental conditions
  10. Evaluation apprehension
  11. Experimenter expectancies
  12. Confounding of constructs with levels of constructs

Threats to External Validity
  1. Interaction of different treatments
  2. Interaction of testing and treatment
  3. Interaction of selection and treatment
  4. Interaction of setting and treatment
  5. Interaction of history and treatment

Source: Adapted from Cook, Campbell, & Peracchio (1990, pp. 498–510).

Threats to Internal Validity

If statistical tests show a significant effect (or if they do not), the next major question in research is: Is the demonstrated relationship a causal one rather than the result of some extraneous factor (or alternatively, are there confounding factors that prevented a causal relationship that actually exists from being demonstrated)?

These issues pertain to the **internal validity** of the study—that is, whether the independent variables really had a causal effect in this particular study. Among the many possible threats to internal validity are the following factors:

1. History. This term refers to the effect of some extraneous event during the course of a study. For instance, a war that broke out in the Middle East during a study of attitudes toward national defense would probably influence the study's dependent variable, and its effects might be mistaken for those of whatever independent variable was being studied (such as a presidential campaign featuring debates on military preparedness).

2. Maturation. This term refers to any systematic changes in the respondents during the course of a study, such as their becoming older, better informed, or more capable of performing certain tasks. It is a threat when any effects of these changes can be confounded with those of the independent variable. For instance, was an increase in a child's reading ability due to an instructional program or to normal developmental progress?

3. Testing. When pretests are used in a study, the experience of having been measured before can change responses on a later readministration of the same or a similar measuring device. For instance, an increase in measured IQ due to taking the same test a second time may be confused with the effects of the educational program being studied.

4. Instrumentation. Changes in a measuring instrument during the course of a study can distort the meaning of the results. Examples are changes in observers' rating standards as they become more experienced, or decreases in the difficulty of test items due to wide publicity about them, or revisions to the wording of items on a scale.

5. Statistical Regression. This is a threat whenever subjects are chosen for study partly or largely because they are unusually high or low on some characteristic, such as intelligence, activism, poverty, or achievement. Scores on any such personal characteristics always contain some error of measurement, as well as a true component. Consequently, because the extremity of the scores is partially due to measurement error, there is always a tendency for the extreme scor-

ers' later scores on the same or related instruments to regress toward the population mean (that is, to become less extreme). The problem here is that this statistical effect is likely to be confused with the effect of the independent variable under study. Such confusion has often occurred in studies of compensatory education programs, where intended "control" groups of low-performance students are apt to be more different from the mean of their population than the disadvantaged treatment recipients are from their population mean. As a result, the "control" group will usually regress more than the disadvantaged treatment group, and this effect opposes the effect of the educational treatment, tending to make it look ineffective even though it may be helpful.

6. Selection. This term refers to systematically different sorts of people being selected for various treatment groups. Naturally, their differences are apt to be confounded with the treatment effects. Since quasi-experimental research, by definition, involves situations where treatment groups cannot be chosen in ways that ensure their equivalence, selection effects are an ever-present danger.

7. Mortality, or Dropouts. Differential dropout can make even randomized, equivalent groups nonequivalent at a later time. Therefore, the amount of respondent attrition and the extremity of the individuals who drop out need to be checked within every group, and compared across groups.

8. Interactions with Selection. Several of the above threats to internal validity can combine with selection differences to produce effects that can easily be mistaken for treatment effects. For instance, a *selection-maturation interaction* occurs when two or more groups are maturing at different rates. Other common threats are a *selection-history interaction* or *selection-instrumentation interaction*.

9. Ambiguity About the Direction of Causal Influence. Even when the threats to internal validity have been reduced, the direction of causation between the variables may be unclear. This is not usually a problem in experiments, where the causal variable is normally the one that was manipulated. However, it is apt to be a problem in correlational or quasi-experimental research if all the measures are collected at the same time. For instance, does poor school achievement cause truancy, or does truancy cause poor school achievement, or does each have a causal influence on the other?

In deciding about internal validity, the investigator has to consider whether, and how, each of these possible threats could have affected the research data and then perform whatever tests are feasible to rule out as many potential threats as possible. In general, a randomized experiment will usually rule out all nine of these threats to internal validity, which is why experiments are so helpful in inferring causation. However, differential dropouts can be a problem in experiments, and in rare instances the other threats may occur (e.g., occasionally random assignment to conditions does not produce equivalent groups, so group pre-experimental measures need to be checked to rule out a selection threat).

Another important point about validity in quasi-experimental research is the value of *patched-up designs*. Even though a given design has inherent weaknesses (for instance, selection or history threats to internal validity), they can often be overcome by "patching it up" through additional internal data analyses, or by adding other control groups to check on the effect of particular threats to the validity of the basic design.

Threats to Construct Validity of Causes and Effects

After we have determined what causal conclusions we can reach in any specific study, the next question is: What do these particular research results mean in conceptual terms? As Cook and Campbell (1979, p. 38) expressed it, **construct validity** refers to "the fit between operations and conceptual definitions." In order to have construct validity, the research operations must correspond closely to the underlying concept that the investigator wants to study. The operations should embody all the important dimensions of the construct but no dimensions that are similar but irrelevant—that is, they should neither underrepresent nor overrepresent the construct.

Threats to construct validity come from **confounding**—"the possibility that the operational definition of a cause or effect can be construed in terms of more than one construct" (Cook et al., 1990, p. 503). For instance,

is it the medicine or the *placebo effect* (belief in the medicine and the doctor) that causes the sufferer to improve? Another way of putting it is that construct validity refers to the proper labeling of the "active ingredient" in the causal treatment and the true nature of the change in the observed effect.

Following the proposals of Campbell and Fiske (1959), Cook and Campbell (1979, p. 61) suggested two ways of assessing construct validity:

> first, testing for a convergence across *different* measures or manipulations of the same "thing" and, second, testing for a *divergence* between measures and manipulations of related but conceptually distinct "things."

For example, if we were interested in measuring alphabet ability among children, we could measure the number of seconds it takes each child to recite the alphabet, their ability to recognize English letters, or their scores on a word-recognition test made up of 3-letter words. If these three measures were highly related, they would have **convergent construct validity**. Our measures should also show **discriminant validity**—they should not correlate highly with theoretically different constructs. For instance, measures of alphabet ability should not correlate with measures of personality variables like self-esteem or extroversion, which are conceptually different.

Cook et al. (1990) also noted that applied research tends to be much more concerned about the construct validity of *effects* than of causes, because it often seems more important to have an impact on a particular social problem than to know exactly what dimensions of an ameliorative program *caused* the impact. For example, applied social scientists working on the topic of poverty would be very concerned that their measures adequately represented such concepts as "unemployment" or "family income" (the effect), but they would probably be less involved in measuring the impact of every separate component of an antipoverty program (the cause).

The topic of construct validity is often hard to grasp in the abstract, but it should be clarified through the following examples of different threats to construct validity:

1. Inadequate Preoperational Explication of Constructs. Before measures and manipulations can be designed, the various dimensions of all constructs involved in the study should be stated explicitly. For instance, if the construct of "aggression" is defined as doing *physical* harm to another person *intentionally*, the instruments developed to measure it should not consider *verbal* expressions of threat or abuse, nor *accidental* physical injury.

2. Mono-Operation Bias. If possible, it is always preferable to use two or more ways of operationalizing the causal construct, and two or more ways of measuring the effect construct. Thus, if helping behavior were the conceptual variable, the investigator might devise several different situations in which helping could be demonstrated and use each one with a different group of subjects. This procedure should both represent the definition of helping more adequately, and also diminish the effect of irrelevant aspects of the various situations, since each situation would probably contain different irrelevancies.

3. Mono-Method Bias. Even where multiple operations of a construct are used, they may still be measured in the same basic way, leading to a mono-method threat to validity. A common example is using several different scales to measure attitudes, but allowing them all to be paper-and-pencil, self-report measures. A better approach would include some behavioral measures and some observational measures of attitudes, as well as paper-and-pencil self-reports.

4. Interaction of Procedure and Treatment. Sometimes the context in which the independent variable occurs may influence the way in which participants react to the treatment—an example of confounding of two possible causal factors. For instance, the Income Maintenance Experiments conducted in New Jersey guaranteed participants a minimum income for three years. Thus, the effect of this treatment may have been produced by the payment, or alternatively by the knowledge that it would last for three years (Cook et al., 1990).

5. Diffusion or Imitation of Treatments. This may be a threat when people in various treatment and control groups are in close proximity and can communicate with each other. In consequence, the intended independent variable condition (such as special information) may be spread to the other groups and diminish or eliminate planned group differences. For example,

the pupils who saw "Sesame Street" might tell the non-viewing control group information they had learned from the program.

6. Compensatory Equalization of Treatments. This can occur when a planned treatment is valued by community members, as in the case of a Head Start program or an improved medical treatment. There are numerous instances in the literature where comparisons of such a treatment with an intended control group were subverted by authorities or administrators, who gave the "control" group a similar or offsetting benefit in order to avoid the appearance of unfair treatment of different individuals or groups. Unfortunately, such attempts at "fairness" can ruin crucial research procedures.

7. Compensatory Rivalry from Other Participants. This is similar to the equalization-of-treatment threat except that it is a response of participants in less-desirable treatment groups, rather than of administrators. When the assignment of people to treatment conditions is known publicly, those in the control group or the less-desirable treatments may work extra hard in order to show up well, and as a result the treatment comparisons may be invalidated. Saretsky (1972) pointed out examples of this in experimental educational programs where the control-group teachers saw their job security as being threatened. He called it the "John Henry effect," after the legendary railroad steel-drivin' man who won his contest with the newly invented steam drill, though he killed himself in the process.

8. Resentful Demoralization of Other Participants. This is the opposite of compensatory rivalry. If study participants in less-desirable conditions become resentful over their deprivation, they may intentionally or unintentionally reduce the quality or quantity of their work. This reduced output would not reflect their usual performance, of course, and so would not be a valid comparison for the other treatment conditions.

9. Hypothesis-Guessing Within Experimental Conditions. This is an aspect of **reactivity** in research, in which the act of studying something may change the phenomenon being studied. Wherever possible, it is best to disguise procedures so that research participants cannot guess the research hypothesis and change their behavior accordingly. However, as pointed out in

Chapter 4, there is relatively little empirical evidence of research subjects being consistently negativistic or consistently overcooperative, even when the research hypotheses are easily guessed.

10. Evaluation Apprehension. As described in Chapter 4, this is a subject effect that does seem to occur fairly frequently in laboratory studies. Though it is probably less common in field studies, it can still be a threat to validity because its effects can be confounded with the results of any other causal variables. Hence, efforts should be made to minimize it.

11. Experimenter Expectancies. This aspect of experimenter effects was also discussed in Chapter 4. Because experimenter expectancy effects can be confounded with effects of the intended causal variable, they should be avoided wherever possible, using the techniques described earlier.

12. Confounding Constructs with Levels of Constructs. Often research uses only one or two levels of a variable, and because of practical as well as ethical limitations, the levels used are apt to be weak ones. If the research results are nonsignificant, a conclusion of "no effect" of variable A on variable B may be drawn. In contrast, if a higher level of variable A had been used, a true effect might have been found. To avoid this threat, it is desirable to do **parametric research**, in which many levels of the independent variable are used. Otherwise, it is important to qualify research conclusions by specifically stating the levels of the variables involved.

One important way of assessing construct validity is to use **manipulation checks**, as discussed in Chapter 4. This procedure verifies whether the treatment actually created differences in the intended constructs and left unchanged other features that it was not intended to affect. After research data have been collected, another important approach to construct validity is to generate a **multitrait-multimethod (MTMM) matrix**. As discussed above, a study should use more than one measure of each main construct, and preferably these measures should employ different methods (e.g., self-report, observation, physiological measures, etc.). The MTMM matrix is simply a table of the correlation coefficients among the measures. *Convergent validity* is reflected in high correlations between various measures of the same construct, while *discriminant validity* is reflected in low correlations between measures of different constructs. More quantitative approaches to assessing construct validity are available through the use of a technique called confirmatory factor analysis (Gorsuch, 1983), which is a special type of the structural equation modeling procedure we mentioned in Chapter 5.

Threats to External Validity

The final question in assessing research findings is: To what extent can the findings be generalized to other persons, settings, and times? This question defines the **external validity**, or **generalizability**, of the research. When samples of participants are chosen because they are conveniently available (such as introductory psychology students), it is difficult to know what underlying population they represent, and even more difficult to know whether the findings apply to particular other groups. If a treatment has a given effect on one group of individuals but not on another group, this is a **statistical interaction**. Hence, the following threats to external validity are stated as interaction effects between the experimental treatment and some other condition.

1. Interaction of Different Treatments. Whenever subjects are exposed to more than one treatment, the combined or interaction effect of the treatments may be different from their separate effects. In such cases it is important to analyze the effect of each treatment separately as well as in combination. For instance, does an instructional program produce better learning *only* for students that have been given a motivational incentive, and not for others?

2. Interaction of Testing and Treatment. The measurement conditions of a study, such as repeated testing, may interact with the intended treatment to produce a combined effect. For example, a pretest measure may *sensitize* subjects to a later treatment (signaling them that there is something they should learn about a given topic), or it may *inoculate* subjects against the effect of a later treatment. Though careful research (e.g., Lana, 1969) has indicated

Rd p. 134 of P. lab Text to both grs ? about racism
Claire to one gr.
essay to one gr.

Quasi-Experimental Studies—Effects of Television **101**

that neither of these possible interactions is common in experimental studies, it is wise to take precautions against them. This would involve using posttest-only control groups, which, because they had no pretest, could not display a sensitization or an inoculation effect.

3. Interaction of Selection and Treatment. A treatment may work with one type of person (such as introverts) but not with another type (such as extroverts), or it may work differently with the two types. This threat can be combatted by making the group of participants as heterogeneous as possible, and one way to accomplish this is to make the research task so convenient that relatively few people will refuse or fail to participate.

4. Interaction of Setting and Treatment. Research findings in one setting (such as a school system) may not be applicable in another setting (such as a military combat team). "The solution here is to vary settings and to analyze for a causal relationship within each" (Cook & Campbell, 1979, p. 74). Fiedler's research on leadership (discussed in Chapter 5) provides many examples of this issue, and the above solution is exactly the one he adopted.

5. Interaction of History and Treatment. A given treatment may have different effects at one time (for instance, during a war scare, a gasoline shortage, or a recession) than at other times. To give greater confidence in the continuing applicability of findings, studies can be replicated at different times, or literature reviews can be conducted to search for previous supportive or contradictory evidence.

In addition to replicating studies, we can increase external validity by choosing research samples that are either *representative* of an important population or else as *heterogeneous* as possible. Since representative random sampling is often impossible in applied settings, a very useful model is to select settings for study that differ widely along important dimensions. For instance, in research on an innovative educational method, the treatment should be tried out in one or more of the "best" schools available, and in some of the "worst" problem schools, and in some "typical" schools. Racial composition and other important di-

mensions might be varied by similar means. Though this procedure does not guarantee generalizability to other schools in other geographic areas, it certainly increases its likelihood.

Relationships Among the Four Types of Validity

To summarize our discussion of the threats to various kinds of validity, we may note that statistical conclusion validity is a special case of internal validity. That is, they both deal with whether conclusions can properly be drawn from *the particular research data at hand*. Internal validity is concerned with sources of *systematic* bias, which can influence mean scores, whereas statistical conclusion validity is concerned with sources of *random* error, which can increase variability, and with the proper use of statistical tests (Cook et al. 1990; Cook & Shadish, 1994).

Similarly, construct validity and external validity are very closely related because they both deal with *making generalizations to other conditions*. In other words, they both bear on the conditions under which a causal relationship holds. The major difference between them is that external validity is concerned with generalization to *concrete, specific* examples of other persons, settings, and times, whereas construct validity is concerned with generalization to other examples of *concepts* like aggression, cooperation, or authoritarianism.

Some methods of increasing one type of validity are apt to decrease other types. For example, performing a randomized experiment will maximize internal validity, but the organizations (such as school systems or businesses) that will allow such procedures are likely to be atypical, which reduces external validity. Similarly, using heterogeneous subjects and settings will increase external validity but reduce statistical conclusion validity.

Cook et al. (1990) stressed that good internal validity is the single most important requirement for research studies, but that sometimes trade-offs to achieve it are simply too costly in the loss of other values. Since no single piece of research will ever avoid all validity problems, the best procedure is a program of replica-

Photograph courtesy of Donald Campbell and Lehigh University Office of Public Information. Reprinted by permission.

Box 6-1

DONALD CAMPBELL, GURU OF RESEARCH METHODOLOGY

In addition to his influential writings on psychological research methodology, which are highlighted in this chapter, Donald Campbell was honored for his work as a philosopher of science, as a field researcher as well as a laboratory experimenter, and for his contributions to sociology, anthropology, and political science. Among his outstanding honors in psychology were election as president of the American Psychological Association, receipt of the Distinguished Scientific Award of the APA, and election to the National Academy of Sciences and the American Academy of Arts and Sciences.

Born in Michigan in 1916, Campbell described in an autobiographical chapter how he worked on a turkey ranch after high school, attended a junior college, and did not have an article published until he was 33. After earning his B.A. at

the University of California, Berkeley, he served in the Navy and the OSS during World War II. Completing his Ph.D. at Berkeley in 1947, he taught for several years at Ohio State University and the University of Chicago. He settled at Northwestern University in 1953 and remained there until 1979, moving then to Syracuse and later to Lehigh University, where he died in 1996.

Despite his late start at publishing, Campbell coauthored over 10 books and 200 articles and book chapters. He was best known within psychology for his seminal works on quasi-experimental research methods, on unobtrusive research, on attitude measurement, and for his advocacy of planned experimentation on social and governmental programs.

tions using differing research methods and settings. Cook et al. (1990, p. 516) suggested that, for many applied social research topics, the importance of various types of validity runs from internal validity (highest) through external validity, construct validity of the effect, and statistical conclusion validity, down to construct validity of the cause.

ANALYSIS OF THE "SESAME STREET" STUDY

Now let us return to Minton's (1975) study on the effects of "Sesame Street" and analyze it in terms of the preceding list of threats to valid inference. To begin, we might diagram the study schematically, following

Cook et al.'s (1990) notation. In the following diagram, the experimental and control groups are shown on separate lines, with the broken line between them indicating that they are nonequivalent (since the children were not randomly assigned). The time sequence of events is shown by their position on the line, with earlier events farther left. The letter O stands for an observation (in this case the MRT administration) and the letter X for an experimental treatment (exposure to "Sesame Street"), while the numerical subscripts merely indicate the sequence of these events. Thus, the study can be diagrammed:

Control group:　　　　O_1
- - - - - - - - - - -
Experimental group:　　　X　O_2

This is an example of an **institutional-cycle** or **cohort design**, the basic feature of which, as mentioned earlier, is that the various cohorts (in this case annual entering classes) go through essentially the same institutional cycle (here, the kindergarten) at different times. Cohort designs are frequently useful, because it is often reasonable to assume that successive cohorts are highly similar to each other on most characteristics. Also, many institutions such as school districts or businesses keep careful archival records, which can sometimes be used for measures of the variables of interest and can also provide checks on the assumed comparability of the successive cohorts.

Statistical Conclusion Validity

Let's examine each of the major types of validity in turn. First, statistical conclusion validity seems good in Minton's study. In general, positive findings raise fewer questions about statistical conclusion validity than do negative results, and Minton's findings were strongly positive (on the Alphabet subtest). Therefore we can dismiss questions about low statistical power and poor reliability of measures (for that subtest at least), even though no reliability figures were given. In one instance Minton did report a check on assumptions of the analysis of variance, and it seems that violated statistical assumptions were not a problem there. Despite the number of significance tests made, the regu-

larity of the findings indicates that the study was not just a "fishing expedition."

The only threat to statistical conclusion validity that seems to be present is varying degrees of treatment implementation—that is, half the children watched "Sesame Street" every day, most others watched it sometimes, and a very few never saw it. In a quasi-experimental study like this where the treatment condition could not be assigned, such differences in implementation are inevitable, and fortunately Minton did present clear data on the extent of exposure to the program for all the subgroups of children. However, it would have been desirable for her to go one step further and present an analysis of the MRT scores for heavy viewers, lighter viewers, and nonviewers, since that would have been the clearest possible operationalization of watching "Sesame Street."

Internal Validity

*- as kindergarten progresses,
don't you become
more capable of
learning ABCs*

The crucial category of internal validity also seems quite good in Minton's study, though there are some lingering questions. Taking the good points first, there are no problems with maturation (all groups were the same age when tested), testing (no pretest was given), statistical regression (the whole kindergarten cohort was used for each year), or mortality (all children present in May were tested). Also, there is no ambiguity about the causal direction (from watching "Sesame Street" to MRT scores, rather than vice versa). Since all children in several similar cohorts were studied, there was little danger of interactions with selection (though this could have been a problem, for instance, if only the advantaged children's scores were compared with those of the disadvantaged group). Because the MRT is a standardized group test, threats due to instrumentation changes were unlikely (though they could conceivably occur if the testers in the earlier years were markedly inexperienced and so used different testing procedures from those used in 1970).

Only two factors pose plausible threats to internal validity: selection and history. Selection differences between the cohorts are still possible despite their general similarity. One obvious example is that the earlier years' cohorts would have a larger proportion of first-born children than would the 1970 cohort, and if first-born children performed less well on the MRT, that could be mistaken for a beneficial effect of watching "Sesame Street." It is probably more likely that first-borns would perform better, but in either case there is a possible confounding. However, Minton handled that problem very nicely by comparing the 1970 kindergartners and their older siblings *with the 1969 class and their older siblings*. Since the latter comparison showed no significant superiority in MRT scores for the younger siblings, the hypothesis that older siblings generally performed worse on the MRT could be convincingly dismissed.

History is the most common threat to internal validity in a design (like this one) that doesn't have a simultaneous control group. That is, *anything else* that happened to these children between May 1969 and May 1970 could be mistaken for the effect of watching "Sesame Street." Suppose, for instance, that the school district had instituted a new reading-readiness program in the kindergartens in the fall of 1969. Its effects might look just like those found in Minton's study.

One way of checking on the effects of gradual historical change is to have more than one earlier cohort, as Minton did. However, this procedure will not detect any historical occurrence that has a sudden onset at about the same time as the experimental treatment. A good control for the effects of history, which Minton could have used but didn't, would be to *partition* the experimental treatment into two or more levels (such as heavy and light viewers) and then check their comparative amount of learning. If higher levels of the purported experimental treatment produced significantly more learning than lower levels, that finding could not plausibly be explained as the effect of some other historical effect, such as a new school program. However, Minton used another procedure, which gave a somewhat similar safeguard against a threat from history. Instead of partitioning the independent variable, she divided the dependent variable into seven different MRT scores. Since only the score most closely related to the content of "Sesame Street" (the Alphabet subtest) showed significant findings, there is strong reason to believe that the causal factor was watching "Sesame Street." By contrast, if there had been a new school program aimed at improving school readiness, it would probably have influenced some of the other subtest

scores as well. Hence, a threat to the validity of Minton's study from unknown historical events, though not impossible, seems very unlikely.

The three preceding paragraphs give excellent examples of how a design can be "patched up" in order to overcome any inherent weaknesses it may have.

Construct Validity

The area of construct validity presents the most questions in Minton's study. In part, this is an inevitable result of the specificity of the research question about the effects of one particular TV program, "Sesame Street," on one particular test battery. Thus, the problems of mono-operation bias and mono-method bias were built into the study. As a result, we know the effects of that TV program on one test but not on other tests or measures of kindergarten performance, and we also don't know how other educational TV programs for children would affect the MRT or other measures. At a minimum, it would have been preferable to investigate *convergent validity* by including other tests of alphabet skills in the study. The ideals of construct validity would have been better met if both the independent variable and the dependent variable were considered as representatives of a class of educational programs and tests respectively, and if other representatives of each of these classes were also included in the study. Of course, this is a tall order, but only such large-scale multivariate studies can produce fuller knowledge of the general constructs. To put it another way, from this study we know that watching "Sesame Street" had an effect on children's MRT Alphabet scores, but we don't know why, nor what other effects it may have had.

One other construct validity problem is that the initial explication of constructs would have been better if the author had specified that Alphabet should be the only MRT score affected *before* doing the study rather than after the data were analyzed. Other threats in this category seem well controlled—for instance, there is no likelihood of hypothesis-guessing, evaluation apprehension, or experimenter expectancies affecting the results. There could be no diffusion of the treatment (the program wasn't on the air in previous years); and similarly, there was no chance for compensatory equalization of treatments, compensatory rivalry, or resentful demoralization on the part of the earlier control groups. Likewise, the other possible threats to construct validity seem minimal. Minton could have investigated the issue of confounding constructs with levels of constructs by analyzing the *regular* viewers of "Sesame Street" separately from those children who watched it less regularly, but this threat does not appear to seriously affect the construct validity of the study.

External Validity

The external validity of Minton's study seems good because it was done in a natural field setting with nonreactive procedures and measures. Because there was no pretest before the kindergarten year, there could be no interaction of testing and the treatment. Questions could be raised about each of the other threats in this category, but none of them seems very serious. For instance, there was only one treatment in the study (watching "Sesame Street") so there was no opportunity for it to interact with another treatment (e.g., a new kindergarten teaching method). There could be an interaction of selection and the treatment, but Minton checked on this with a variety of subgroups, and only the "disadvantaged" group was found not to have benefited significantly from watching "Sesame Street." An interaction of setting and the treatment would be present if Minton's results didn't hold for other school districts, or for children at other grade levels. However, there seems no reason to believe that children in other towns would respond differently to the TV program, and the kindergarten level is certainly an appropriate one on which to measure the show's effect. Finally, an interaction of history and the treatment would be illustrated if "Sesame Street" in its second year on the air or at some other time no longer had the same effects that Minton found. At the moment we can only speculate about such long-range questions, but they do not seem obvious threats to the validity of Minton's findings.

A TIME-SERIES STUDY: TV AND READING

We turn now, briefly, to the other major type of quasi-experimental research. The two essential characteristics of **interrupted time-series designs** are that sev-eral similar observations are made on a group of people or objects over a period of time (often a large number of weekly, monthly, or annual observations), and that sometime during that period an event occurs that is expected to change the level of the dependent variable observations. The event—the independent variable in the design—might be a new government program, a natural disaster such as a flood, an international event such as a war, or the introduction of new technology such as household videocassette recorders. If the specified experimental event in such a study is accompanied by a change in the dependent variable, thus distinguishing that time point from the pattern of the several preceding observations, the long series of observations can provide good protection against some of the major threats to valid inference (such as maturation, testing, instrumentation, and regression).

Interrupted time-series studies have been conducted on a variety of applied topics (Mark, Sanna, & Shotland, 1992). A famous example of an interrupted time-series study demonstrated the significant effect of the British "breathalyser" crackdown, a nationwide program in which British police began giving on-the-spot breath tests to drivers who were suspected of being drunk or committing traffic offenses (Ross, Campbell, & Glass, 1970). Other examples include studies on the effects of:

- Mandatory seat belt laws (Wegenaar, Maybee, & Sullivan, 1988)
- Publishing shoplifting and drunk driving offenders' names in a newspaper (Ross & White, 1987)
- Gun control ordinances (O'Carroll et al., 1991)
- Media publicity about an execution (Stack, 1993)
- The advent of television on crime rates (Hennigan et al., 1982)

The study we will discuss here was done by Edwin Parker and several colleagues and reported by Cook et al. (1990, pp. 566–568). It concerned the effects on public library book circulation of the advent of television in various Illinois communities in the 1940s and 1950s, and it followed the methodology pioneered in an earlier study by Parker (1963). The independent variable was the introduction of television reception in the various communities, and it was expected to cause a decrease in the dependent variable, a careful computation of per capita book circulation from each town's public library over a long period of years. Actually television broadcasting arrived at quite different times in different communities because the Federal Communications Commission put a freeze on the issuance of licenses for new TV stations in 1951 and did not lift it until 1953. Thus, some Illinois towns had television reception for several years before other towns obtained it.

This differential time of TV introduction allowed a replicated or **multiple time-series design**, in which the early-TV communities could be compared with the late-TV communities over a period of many years. If the pattern of changes in book circulation coinciding with the advent of TV reception was similar in the two groups of towns, that would give added support to the inference that the introduction of television caused the changes in circulation. Parker chose 55 pairs of early-TV and late-TV communities, which were matched on relevant variables such as population and library circulation. Thus, this design can be diagrammed as fol-

lows, indicating each group of communities by a line of observations, separated by a broken line to show that they were not completely equivalent (again O indicates an observation of the dependent variable, book circulation, and X indicates the experimental event, the introduction of TV reception).

Early-TV: O_1 O_2 O_3 X O_4 O_5 O_6 O_7 O_8 O_9
- -
Late-TV: O_1 O_2 O_3 O_4 O_5 O_6 X O_7 O_8 O_9

Results of the study are shown in Figure 6-1, which displays per capita annual library circulation for the years from 1945 to 1960. Looking at the upper curve, for the late-TV communities, you can see a drop in circulation for the years 1953 and 1954, which was exactly when TV was becoming available to them. Though a statistical test demonstrated the significance of that decrease, it would not be as conclusive in itself as it is in conjunction with the curve for the early-TV

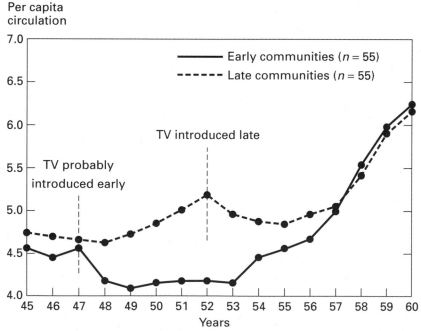

FIGURE 6-1   Results of the TV and reading study: per capita library circulation in two sets of Illinois communities as a function of the introduction of television.
(Source: Thomas D. Cook and Donald T. Campbell, *Quasi-Experimentation.* Copyright © 1979 by Houghton Mifflin Company. Used with permission.)

communities. There it can be seen that a very similar and even steeper drop in library circulation occurred in 1948 and 1949, the period when television was first becoming available in those communities; again, a statistical test showed that the drop was significant. The parallelism of these two curves, with the drops occurring as hypothesized at the times when TV was being introduced, is very strong evidence that the advent of TV really was the causal variable. Another notable feature is the virtual superimposition of the curves in the final years of the study (1957–1960), and their similar pattern before 1948, both of which support the conclusion that the two sets of matched towns really were comparable.

Analysis of the TV and Reading Study

> The power of the design derives from its control for most threats to internal validity and from its potential in extending external and construct validity. External validity is enhanced because an effect can be demonstrated with two populations in at least two settings at different moments in history. Moreover, there are likely to be different irrelevancies associated with application of each treatment and, if measures are unobtrusive, there need be no fear of the treatment's interacting with testing. (Cook et al., 1990, p. 566)

Despite these strengths, the study had some potential validity problems. In the area of internal validity, history could conceivably be a threat. A specific example of an historical event whose effects could mimic the predicted effects of TV in this study is the increased availability of paperback books. In fact, publication of paperbacks did increase markedly during this time period, and their availability at a low price might possibly account for the observed drop in library circulation. However, in order for this explanation to fit Parker's *replicated* time-series study, there would have to be a reason to expect paperbacks to affect the two groups of communities at different points in time—an interaction of selection and history. Though not too likely, that is at least possible, for the communities did differ in some relevant ways despite their matching. The early-TV communities in general were urban and relatively affluent, while the late-TV towns were mostly rural and poorer. Thus, it is conceivable that the impact of pa-

perback books could have hit the poorer communities five years later than the richer ones, and been the real cause (or a partial cause) of the decline in library circulation. One way of checking on this possibility further, as Parker (1963) did in his earlier study, would be to divide the variable of circulation into fiction and nonfiction books. In 14 pairs of Illinois communities, he found that the advent of television decreased the library circulation of fiction books significantly more than that of nonfiction ones. He had predicted this effect on the basis that TV, as a primarily fictional or fantasy medium, would be more likely to displace fictional reading; and this finding makes the explanation of lower circulation as being due to the increased availability of paperbacks even less plausible than before.

In general, the least impressive aspect of this study was its construct validity. As with Minton's study of "Sesame Street," this was largely the result of its mono-operation and mono-method approach. Library circulation is only one index of the amount of reading in a community (though perhaps the most readily available one), and a fuller understanding of the construct would have been gained by using a variety of measures of the dependent variable.

One other question about this study concerns the reliability of treatment implementation. The introduction of television into a community may occur at one precise moment when the local station begins broadcasting, but that doesn't mean that the whole community (or even an appreciable fraction of the population) will be affected by it at that time. In fact, it took from four to six years for the new technology to diffuse to the point that three-quarters of the homes in the Illinois communities had television sets (Cook et al., 1990, p. 567). Yet the dates of the library circulation decreases in Parker's study (1948 and 1953) were years when only 10% to 15% of the homes in the respective groups of communities had TV sets! Thus, it is unclear what process led to the decrease in library circulation. Was it accounted for by just 10% to 15% of the population? Or could it have been an anticipatory effect on the part of the remainder: getting ready for TV by reading less? These questions go beyond the observed *outcome* to ask about the *process* by which television's arrival affected reading and other community activities.

USING RANDOMIZATION IN FIELD RESEARCH

The last topic in our discussion of quasi-experiments is: When should one use randomized assignment of subjects to treatment conditions (that is, true experiments)? A crucial basic principle here is that randomization should be used whenever possible because it increases the strength of causal inferences (Cook & Shadish, 1994). As we discussed in Chapter 4, the great advantage of true experiments is that randomization equates the initial characteristics of the treatment subgroups, within specifiable limits of sampling error, and thus allows proper use of the most powerful statistical tests. However, remember that *initial* equivalence of experimental subgroups does not guarantee their *final* equivalence at the end of the experiment, because such factors as differential attrition, compensatory equalization of treatments, compensatory rivalry, or demoralization may produce marked discrepancies in final subgroup scores, entirely apart from any effect of the treatment variable. For that reason, checks on the presence of these factors should always be included in experimental research designs.

Randomized experiments have sometimes been criticized as too costly, in both money and time, to be widely used in social research. It is true that correlational research or quasi-experimental studies are apt to be quicker and cheaper than true experiments. However, many authors have insisted that the costs of research are far outweighed by the social costs of being wrong about research conclusions that affect national programs or even local affairs (Cook et al., 1990; Coyle, Boruch, & Turner, 1991; Manski & Garfinkel, 1992). Consider, for instance, the costs to the public of wrong decisions about the approval for sale of a hazardous drug like thalidomide, or about a prison early-release program involving still-dangerous convicts.

Despite the difficulties of conducting randomized experiments in field settings, there is a surprisingly long list of published experiments on social programs in areas such as education, law, mental health, and employment (Boruch, 1996; Cook & Shadish, 1994). Cook and Campbell (1979) presented a helpful list of types of situations where randomization may be possible and acceptable in social research. Among their examples, two fairly common ones are:

- Lotteries for the equitable distribution of scarce resources (such as new condominiums) or undesirable burdens (such as military service).
- Assignment of applicants for a social benefit to a treatment group or a waiting-list control group in circumstances where the demand exceeds either the supply (such as new medical techniques like kidney dialysis) or the distribution capacity (such as job-training programs).

Randomization in Quasi-Experimental Studies

There is one other way in which randomization can be useful, even in quasi-experimental studies where the researcher does not have full control over assignment of the treatment conditions. Recall that the definition of quasi-experimental research indicated that the investigator *does* have control over the timing and methods of *measurement*. Thus the investigator can randomly assign measurement to part of the total sample at one time and part at another time. One example is the *separate-sample pretest-posttest design*, which can be diagrammed as follows (R standing for random assignment):

$$\begin{array}{lllll} \text{Pretest-posttest group:} & R & O_1 & X & O_2 \\ \text{Posttest-only group:} & R & & X & O_3 \end{array}$$

Why would anyone want to use such a design? A major circumstance where it would be useful is when the whole population must undergo the treatment (for instance, a year of high school study), but the pretest measurement is reactive so that it affects the later learning of those exposed to it (for instance, a test of American history knowledge). In such a situation, giving the pretest to a random half of the students and only the posttest to the other random half will ensure that a nonreactive pre-post comparison can be made (by comparing the first group's O_1, with the second group's O_3), which would not be possible in any other common design. Though this design suffers from other threats to validity, they can be largely overcome by the principle of "patching-up" with additional control groups and measurements (Campbell & Stanley, 1966).

SUMMARY

In quasi-experimental research, the investigator does not have full control over manipulation of the independent variable, but does have control over how, when, and for whom the dependent variable is measured. The many quasi-experimental designs are useful when better designs are not possible, and they can often be "patched-up" to avoid most of the threats to valid inference. No single study is ever free from all inferential problems, but in general, quasi-experimental designs are weaker than experiments and stronger than correlational research.

The four major types of validity are: (1) statistical conclusion validity (was there a significant effect?), (2) internal validity (was it a causal effect?), (3) construct validity (what does the finding mean in conceptual terms, or in understanding of the "key ingredient" of a complex measure?), and (4) external validity (can the finding be generalized to other persons, settings, and times?). The first two deal with whether conclusions can properly be drawn from the particular data at hand, while the last two concern generalization to other conditions. Internal validity is usually the most essential characteristic, for without it other types of validity are meaningless. There are many specific problems in research design that constitute threats to each of these types of validity, and there are many corresponding ways of combatting the problems in order to reach valid conclusions.

Minton's study about the effects of the first year of the "Sesame Street" program on kindergarten children's school-readiness test scores illustrates possible threats to validity in one major class of quasi-experimental studies: nonequivalent control group designs. Similarly, Parker's study of how the introduction of television affected public library circulation exemplifies the other main class of quasi-experimental studies: interrupted time-series designs.

Randomized assignment of subjects to treatment conditions is the great strength of true experimental designs and should be used wherever possible in order to strengthen causal inferences. There are many social situations in which randomized experiments are possible, given careful forethought and planning. Even in quasi-experimental designs, randomization can be used very profitably to divide subject groups for different measurement procedures.

SUGGESTED READINGS

Campbell, D. T., & Fiske, D. W. (1959). Convergent and discriminant validation by the multitrait multimethod matrix. *Psychological Bulletin, 56,* 81–105.—This early paper is still a useful description of how to determine construct validity through a pattern of similar and dissimilar relationships.

Cook, T. D., Campbell, D. T., & Perrachio, L. (1990). Quasi experimentation. In M. Dunnette & L. Hough (Eds.), *Handbook of industrial and organizational psychology* (2nd ed., Vol. 1, pp. 491–576). Palo Alto, CA: Consulting Psychologists Press.—The most recent comprehensive overview of the four kinds of validity, the many types of quasi-experimental designs, and the typical threats to validity of each design.

Mark, M. M., Sanna, L. J., & Shotland, R. L. (1992). Time series methods in applied social research. In F. B. Bryant, J. Edwards, S. Tindale, E. Posavac, L. Heath, E. Henderson, & Y. Suarez-Balcazar (Eds.), *Methodological issues in applied social psychology: Social psychological applications to social issues* (pp. 111–133). New York: Plenum.

Ross, A., & Grant, M. (1994). *Experimental and nonexperimental designs in social psychology.* Madison, WI: Brown & Benchmark.—This short book gives an introduction to experimental design and an overview of the strengths and threats to validity of many research designs.

CHAPTER 7

Evaluation Research— Drug Prevention Programs

Program evaluations should contribute to enlightened discussion of alternative plans for social action.

—Lee J. Cronbach et al. (1980, p. 2)

Program evaluation, or evaluation research, attempts to evaluate the operation, impact, and effectiveness of public or private programs. The wide variety of such evaluative studies is illustrated by the following examples:

- A program to combat the disease beriberi was developed in the Philippines following World War II. Villages in one part of the Bataan Peninsula were supplied with fortified rice, while villages in another part of the peninsula got the usual white rice. After one year the incidence of beriberi in the experimental area had dropped from 14.3% to 1.5%, whereas in the control area it had risen from 6.7% to 8.7% (Salcedo, 1954).
- When the Salk polio vaccine was ready for mass trials in 1954, it was given to second grade students whose parents volunteered to participate, and first and third graders were used as untreated controls. Results for over a million children ("the biggest public health experiment ever") showed a reduction from 46 cases of polio per hundred thousand children in the control group, to 17 cases per hundred thousand among the vaccinated group (Meier, 1972).
- One outstanding social experiment was the Income Maintenance study, which investigated the effects of a possible future social policy—providing poor families with a guaranteed income instead of the normal welfare payments (Gueron, 1988; Kershaw & Fair, 1976; Moffitt, 1992; Rossi & Lyall, 1976). Following the original study in New Jersey, several large follow-up experiments were conducted with federal funding. These studies are discussed at greater length in Chapter 17.
- The Head Start program, initially established by the Economic Opportunity Act of 1964, was developed to provide children from poor families with the educational background needed to succeed in school—to make them "school ready." Results from a series of evaluations indicate that the benefits for students who participate in Head Start include improved academic performance, higher high school graduation rates, greater employment rates after graduation, less juvenile delinquency and criminality, and lower teen pregnancy rates (Kennedy, 1993; Zigler, Styfco, & Gilman, 1993). The results are discussed in more detail in Chapter 8.
- Full-scale evaluations of the first years of "Sesame Street," conducted by staff of the Educational Testing Service, showed remarkable levels of viewing and learning among preschool children (Ball & Bogatz, 1970; Bogatz & Ball, 1971). "Sesame Street" continues to undergo evaluation and improvement (Lovelace,

1990), and various other examples of research on media content and effects are discussed in Chapter 13.
- Recent evaluations of Students Against Driving Drunk (SADD) programs showed that there was no difference between schools with and without the SADD program in levels of driving while intoxicated, nor in riding with an intoxicated driver (Klitzner et al., 1994).
- Substance abuse prevention programs designed for school aged children have been developed over the past 30 years. Recent evaluations of these programs have provided mixed results. In later sections of this chapter we will present the results from evaluations of the D.A.R.E. program, together with lessons learned from other substance abuse interventions.

These examples include some of the best-known program evaluation studies in the research literature. Yet even with these famous and large-scale social innovations, it is clear that not all of them succeeded in accomplishing their goals. Indeed, reviews of a large number of social programs have found that many have no discernible effects, and some even have harmful effects (Lipsey et al., 1985; Shadish, Cook, & Leviton, 1991). This conclusion underlines the need for evaluation research. Whenever we try out a new social program, we want to know (1) whether the program is working or not, and (2) the underlying reasons for success or failure. To answer these questions, we turn to evaluation research.

CHARACTERISTICS OF EVALUATION RESEARCH

Evaluation research is not a particular type of research design or methodology. It may use any or all of the research methods we have discussed in previous chapters—survey research, correlational methods, experiments, or quasi-experimentation. Its uniqueness lies not in its research methods, but in its goal, which is to determine how well a particular social program is operating. An accepted definition is that **evaluation research** or **program evaluation** is:

directed at collecting, analyzing, and interpreting information on the need for, implementation of, and effectiveness and efficiency of intervention efforts to better the lot of humankind. . . .Evaluations are undertaken for a variety of reasons: to judge the worth of ongoing programs and to estimate the usefulness of attempts to improve them; to assess the utility of new programs and initiatives; to increase the effectiveness of program management and administration; and to satisfy the accountability requirements of program sponsors. (Rossi & Freeman, 1993, p. 3)

In line with our discussion in Chapter 1, note how this definition emphasizes the goal of improving the quality of life.

Development of Evaluation Research

Ever since governments were first formed, there has been a need to evaluate their activities, and both leaders and common citizens have formed judgments about the success of specific programs (Gredler, 1996). Usually these evaluations were literary and impressionistic, though sometimes they included quantitative aspects. The Pharaohs' accounting system, Julius Caesar's written report of the Gallic Wars, and Martin Luther's 95 Theses criticizing the Catholic church are just a few of the countless examples of evaluations of important public programs of their times.

As sciences developed, they were enlisted by governments to help in national programs, particularly during wars. Occasionally their help included efforts to evaluate and improve public programs, such as campaigns for literacy training and disease control around 1900. During World War I, intelligence tests were used to screen soldiers and assign them to appropriate duties, and by the time of World War II the military used scientific methods to assess the effectiveness of many training, personnel, and propaganda programs. Meanwhile, the Western Electric Hawthorne Plant studies (Roethlisberger & Dickson, 1939) and Kurt Lewin's research on overcoming resistance to job changes (Coch & French, 1948) were early forerunners of scientific evaluations of programs in business and industry. By the 1950s, large-scale evaluation research was becoming quite common, covering such topics as family planning programs, nutrition and health campaigns, and agricultural and community development in many foreign countries. In the United States, evaluation research was conducted on medical and psychotherapy

treatment procedures, public housing programs, crime prevention efforts, and many other local and national programs (Manski & Garfinkel, 1992; Rossi & Freeman, 1993).

Despite these early efforts, it is only since around 1970 that evaluation research has become a discipline, with widely known procedures and standards. Even the term *evaluation research* is a relatively new one, referring to portions of what would formerly have been labeled simply "applied social research." Since 1970 the demand for evaluation studies and the number of professionals working as evaluators has zoomed upward. Similarly, the literature has expanded rapidly, with influential text books (Gredler, 1996; Guttentag & Struening, 1975; Posavac & Carey, 1989; Rossi & Freeman, 1993; Shadish, Cook, & Leviton, 1991; Wholey, Hatry, & Newcomer, 1994), review chapters (Cook, Leviton, & Shadish, 1985; Sechrest & Figueredo, 1993), and hosts of collected readings (e.g., Szafran, 1994). The magazine *Evaluation* began publication in 1973 and the journal *Evaluation Quarterly* (now *Evaluation Review*) started in 1977, while the Evaluation Research Society was founded in 1976. With all this burgeoning activity, however, there are still many disputes and conflicts over procedures and standards in the field.

Our purpose in this chapter is to sketch a broad framework for understanding evaluation research, and then to examine one prominent area of evaluation research—substance abuse prevention programs—from a theory-driven perspective.

Perspectives on Evaluation Research

Not everyone agrees on the purposes and procedures for evaluation. Unqualified researchers or hidden motivations for evaluating programs can often lead to "pseudoevaluations" (Suchman, 1972). Examples include: "whitewash" (attempts to cover up program limitations or failures that have been discovered) and "postponement" (using the need for evaluation as an excuse for postponing or avoiding action). Though program managers and funding organizations are often accused of harboring these covert motives for evaluation, researchers too may sometimes be guilty of such hidden agendas.

Photograph courtesy of Peter Rossi. Reprinted by permission.

Box 7-1

PETER ROSSI, EVALUATION RESEARCH EXPERT

A sociologist known for his survey research on social issues, Peter Rossi is also coauthor of one of the most widely used texts on evaluation research. Born in New York City in 1921, he attended City College there and took his Ph.D. at Columbia in 1951. After four years of teaching at Harvard, he joined the faculty at the University of Chicago, where he also served as Director of the National Opinion Research Center for seven years. In 1967 he moved to Johns Hopkins, and in 1974 he became Professor of Sociology and Director of the Social and Demographic Research Institute at the University of Massachusetts, where he is now retired.

The honors showered on Rossi include editorships or associate editorships of many journals in sociology and evaluation research, and membership in the American Academy of

Arts and Sciences. He has been elected president of the American Sociological Association (ASA) and the Evaluation Research Society, and has received both organizations' awards for outstanding research contributions. He has strongly influenced the course of social research through his memberships on innumerable research committees of NIMH, NSF, and the National Academy of Sciences, including committees that reviewed national energy consumption, housing allowance programs, federal evaluation research, and program evaluations in education. His own research has resulted in 40 coauthored or edited books and over 225 journal articles and book chapters. Among his recent books are volumes on *Sentencing Guidelines and Public Opinion Compared* and evaluations of *Five Federal Nutrition Programs*.

On a more philosophical level, there are many different concepts of evaluation in the scientific literature (e.g., Gredler, 1996; Isaac & Michael, 1995). As Glass and Ellett (1980) put it, "Evaluation—more than any science—is what people say it is; and people currently are saying it is many different things" (p. 211).

An Applied Science. The approach stressed in this text may be termed the *applied science viewpoint*, because it uses the scientific principles of careful measurement, experimentation, and control to investigate causal relationships. It is the approach emphasized in the *Handbook in Research and Evaluation* (Isaac &

Michael, 1995) and by many other social scientists. However, it is important to recognize that there are risks and limitations in this approach (Cook & Shadish, 1994). A particular danger is that striving for scientific purity and high internal validity may hamper the achievement of relevance and high external validity. As Guttentag (1971, p. 77) noted: "The neatest job of fitting evaluation research into an experimental frame of reference often results in the least relevant evaluation." Cronbach (1982) went even further, declaring that for evaluation research, external validity is more important than internal validity because conclusions about the value of social programs need to be applicable to diverse local conditions and to varying program procedures as they evolve over a period of time.

Other competing concepts of evaluation research are relevant and helpful for certain purposes and types of situations, but each has its own limitations as well. Below are listed five alternative models of program evaluation, each of which places its emphasis on a different aspect of evaluation (Glass & Ellett, 1980; Isaac & Michael, 1995):

- **Decision-Oriented Evaluation.** This view equates evaluation with making choices between alternatives. However, decision makers may often ignore careful and useful evaluations, and evaluations have other uses in addition to determining policy decisions.
- **Goal-Oriented Evaluation.** The key idea here is that evaluation should assess the progress of program participants toward a predetermined goal state. This viewpoint is incomplete because evaluation research should consider not only a program's stated goals, but also its unstated goals and unintended consequences.
- **Adversarial Evaluation.** This concept of evaluation follows the legal adversarial model, with advocates for and against a program making the strongest case that they can. Its disadvantages are that its outcome depends on the debating strengths and weaknesses of the advocates, and that many value issues should not be resolved in an either-or manner.
- **Descriptive Evaluation.** This approach views evaluation merely as a full description of a program, obtained through a case study rather than through measurement and experimentation. In addition to the likely subjectivity of such an approach, it gives no clear-cut basis for evaluative decisions.
- **Goal-Free Evaluation.** This concept of evaluation is based on a utilitarian philosophy that applies observation and reasoning to determination of a program's op-

erations, effects, and costs, as well as its morality and the need for it (Scriven, 1973). It holds that a program should be evaluated on an a priori set of criteria, apart from the program's conceptual framework and goals. In practice, this approach may often resemble the applied science viewpoint, but its underlying rationale is philosophical rather than scientific.

These differing approaches all have in common an interest in both the outcome of the program, and the processes that lead to the outcome. Analysis of the process of a program is termed **formative evaluation**. Formative evaluation analyzes programs during their early stages, providing feedback to help guide their development and improve their operation. Formative research is often less elaborate than later evaluation research and less concerned with rigorous scientific designs and statistical significance. Instead, it focuses on discovering the processes, effects, and problems typical of its target program. It tries to assist programs to be successful, rather than judging them (Rossi & Freeman, 1993).

In contrast, **summative evaluation** is applied at a later stage than formative evaluation and is primarily focused on a program's outcomes rather than its processes. Its aim is verification rather than discovery—to sum up how well a program has met its goals and to evaluate any other effects it has had. As Scriven (1991) stated, summative evaluation is "done for or by any observers or decision makers who need evaluative conclusions for any reason other than development" (p. 20). The summative evaluator is apt to be an outsider, rather than a member of the program staff, and is likely to use careful measurement methods and rigorous research designs rather than informal or impressionistic methods.

Program Evaluability

Before an evaluation is carried out, an important preliminary procedure is evaluability assessment, to determine whether a program can be effectively evaluated (Shadish, Cook, & Leviton, 1991; Wholey, 1994). The process involves establishing the definition of the program from the viewpoints of both the evaluator and the users of the evaluation—clearly identifying the purpose of the program, the reality of the program, and its actual activities. As described by Wholey (1994, p. 16), there are several key requirements of evaluability assessment:

- Program goals, objectives, and important side effects are well defined, with at least implicit agreement on the performance indicators that will be used to manage and evaluate the program. In particular, there is agreement on the questions that should be answered by the program evaluation efforts.
- Program goals and objectives are plausible. There is some likelihood that the program goals and objectives will be achieved.
- Relevant performance data can be obtained. There are feasible measures of program performance, which can be gathered at reasonable cost.
- The intended users of the evaluation results have agreed on how they will use the information—for example, to improve program performance or to communicate the value of program activities to higher policy levels.

Some of the above information is gathered from documents (legislation, plans, operating instructions, and so on), but much of it comes from interviews with program managers, policy makers, and lower level managers. After analyzing the rhetoric about the program, it is often found that many of the objectives are not stated in measurable terms (e.g., improving clients' moral standards), and many of the assumed causal relationships linking program features to goals are untestable (e.g., requiring skills training for welfare recipients will lead to lower welfare expenditures). In such cases, Wholey recommends that the evaluator should toss the problems back to the management or policy makers and wait for them to agree on criterion measures of success and indicators of causal relationships.

From that point onward, the course of either formative or summative evaluation research is much like any other empirical research project. It involves specifying antecedent, intervening, and dependent variables; developing measuring instruments and checking their reliability and validity; planning a research design; and collecting and analyzing the data.

Stages of Program Planning and Evaluation

In the preceding sections we have described various contending conceptual approaches to program evalua-

tion. However, despite the disagreement among practitioners regarding these philosophical issues, program planning and evaluation typically progresses through four basic stages (Isaac & Michael, 1995). These stages are shown graphically in Figure 7-1.

Stage 1: Needs Assessment. In this first stage of an evaluation the researcher assesses the discrepancy between what is and what ought to be. These needs can then be used as program goals and as criteria for success—a program that reduces the discrepancy between the current state and the desired state is a successful one. Data collected on these needs and goals can be either qualitative or quantitative. Qualitative data typically come from interviews or open-ended questions. Quantitative data can be observations of behavior or self-report measures such as questionnaires.

Stage 2: Program Design. During this stage a program is designed to meet the needs identified in the first stage. Programs should be developed to reflect the accumulated research knowledge and theories about the effects of particular interventions—that is, program development should be theory-driven.

Stage 3: Implementation and Progress Evaluation. In this phase, researchers assess whether the program is operating as it was designed to, and whether it is reaching its designated target population. Because the program was developed to reflect a particular theory about specific interventions and their effects, monitoring the program should indicate if the targeted variables are being affected. If not, it is pointless to conduct the final stage of evaluation. Stage 3 includes the use of formative evaluation, which should result in any needed mid-course corrections in the program.

Stage 4: Outcome Evaluation. This phase of the evaluation is conducted when the program is mature enough to have stable outcomes for a sufficient number of participants. It should include an assessment of both program impact and efficiency (Kee, 1994). **Impact assessment** analyzes the extent to which the program is causing the desired changes in the target population. It should also assess unintended side effects and consider whether factors other than the intervention program may be causing the intended or unintended ef-

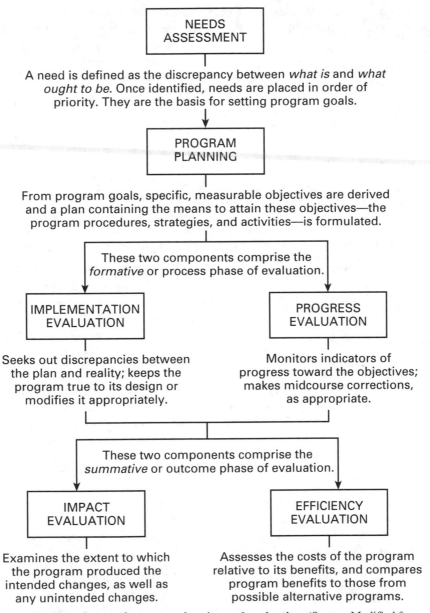

FIGURE 7-1 Stages of program planning and evaluation. (Source: Modified from Isaac & Michael, 1995, p. 11.)

fects. **Efficiency analysis** includes both *cost-benefit research* (relating program costs to program benefits) and *cost-effectiveness analysis* (comparing program benefits to those from possible alternative programs). This is the summative stage of the evaluation.

Many authorities advocate *comprehensive* evaluations—that is, evaluations that include program monitoring (implementation and progress evaluation) along with outcome evaluation (impact and efficiency assessment). This comprehensive approach gives the fullest possible picture of the program: how it is being implemented, its effects, and whether the effects are worth the effort and costs involved.

A detailed breakdown of the steps in planning an evaluation research study includes many steps typical of any empirical research project, but the early stage of evaluability assessment is unique to evaluation studies (Isaac & Michael, 1995). Evaluation research also differs from other research in that it is specifically designed to produce useful information for responsible decision makers. However, it can also illuminate relevant theoretical issues, assumptions underlying the particular program, and long-term policy questions that go beyond the current needs of program administrators and policy makers. That is a major reason why it should not restrict itself to the stated goals of the program, but should also consider unstated goals and unintended consequences.

ILLUSTRATIVE EVALUATION RESEARCH: PROJECT D.A.R.E.

The D.A.R.E. Program

Since the early 1970s, the United States and Canada have been conducting a large-scale anti-drug campaign. A major part of this campaign has been school-based drug-use prevention programs. As part of this initiative, D.A.R.E. (Drug Abuse Resistance Education) was developed. The program began in Southern California in 1983 with collaboration between the Los Angeles Police Department (LAPD) and the Los Angeles Unified School District. The D.A.R.E. program was founded on the ideas generated from several earlier school-based interventions, and from theoretical

research on persuasive communications (Hansen et al., 1988); however, no formative evaluations of its development have been published. The intention of the program developers was to design a school-based intervention that would provide children with the self-management skills necessary to resist peer pressures to start smoking, drinking, or using drugs (DeJong, 1986).

The D.A.R.E. program consists of 17 one-hour lessons delivered to students once a week by a uniformed police officer. The program targets children in the fifth and sixth grades, because they typically have not yet become drug users, and because they view police officers as highly credible sources of information. Table 7-1 summarizes the 17 weekly lessons of the program. As it makes clear, the program provides education in a variety of areas, including assertiveness training, resisting peer pressure, building self-esteem, and information on the effects of drugs. As Rogers (1993) stated, "It doesn't tell them to say 'no', it teaches them how to say 'no'" (p. 146).

During the summer of 1983, 10 police officers from the LAPD attended an intensive 2-week course in which they were trained to be D.A.R.E. officers. In September, each of the officers began the curriculum in five schools—one school each weekday. Since 1983 the original Los Angeles program has been adopted by over 2200 communities in Australia, Canada, New Zealand, and the United States. The program has reached over 4.5 million children, and receives both public and private funding (Rogers, 1993). In the sections below we will summarize a short-term evaluation study, a long-term evaluation study, and a meta-analysis of D.A.R.E. evaluations.

An Illustrative Short-Term Evaluation

Numerous evaluations of the D.A.R.E. program have been conducted since its implementation in 1983. One study, typical in design and findings, was an evaluation of D.A.R.E. in Charleston County, South Carolina (Harmon, 1993). In Charleston, as in most other U.S. states and Canadian provinces, surveys of high school students found high levels of self-reported alcohol consumption (77%), cigarette smoking (47%), and marijuana use (31%). These findings constituted the needs

TABLE 7-1   The 17 Lessons in the D.A.R.E. Program for 5th- and 6th-Graders

1. Personal Safety Practice—Acquaints students with the role of police and with practices for student safety.
2. Drug Use and Misuse—Helps students understand the harmful effects of drugs.
3. Consequences—Helps students understand the negative consequences of drug use and the positive consequences of saying "no" to drugs.
4. Resisting Pressures to Use Drugs—Makes students aware of kinds of peer pressure they may face and helps them learn to say "no" to offers to use drugs.
5. Resistance Techniques—Teaches students ways to say "no" in resisting various types of pressure.
6. Building Self-Esteem—Helps students understand that self-image results from positive and negative feelings and experiences.
7. Assertiveness. A Response Style—Teaches that assertiveness is a response style that enables a person to state his or her own rights without loss of self-esteem.
8. Managing Stress Without Taking Drugs—Helps students recognize stress and suggests ways to deal with it other than by taking drugs.
9. Media Influences on Drug Use—Helps students develop the understanding and skills needed to analyze and resist media presentations about alcohol and drugs.
10. Decision-Making and Risk-Taking—Helps students apply the decision-making process in evaluating the results of various kinds of risk-taking behavior, including that of drugs.
11. Alternatives to Drug Use—Helps students find out about activities that are interesting and rewarding and are better than taking drugs.
12. Role Modeling—Older student leaders and other positive role models that do not use drugs talk to younger students to clarify the misconception that drug users are in the majority.
13. Forming a Support System—Students develop positive relationships with many different people in order to form a support system.
14. Resisting Gang Pressure—Helps students to identify situations in which they may be pressured by gangs and to evaluate the consequences of the choices available to them.
15. D.A.R.E. Summary—Helps students summarize and assess what they learned from the program.
16. Taking a Stand—Students present their own commitment to the class, which helps them respond effectively when pressured to use drugs.
17. Culmination—Student graduation from the D.A.R.E. program.

Source: Rogers, E. M. (1993). Diffusion and re-invention of Project D.A.R.E. In T. Backer and E. Rogers (Eds.), *Organizational Aspects of Health Communication Campaigns: What Works?* (pp. 139–162), Copyright © 1993 by Sage Publications, Inc. Reprinted by permission of Sage Publications, Inc.

assessment—Stage 1 of the program design. The need determined by the program planners was to reduce the number of students using alcohol and other harmful substances.

In an attempt to reduce the prevalence of drug use in Charleston, the D.A.R.E. program described above was implemented. Using an established program eliminated the need for extensive program design and development—Stage 2 of program planning. In establishing the program, local Charleston police officers underwent an 80-hour training session in which they learned how to implement the D.A.R.E. program.

Formative evaluation of this program was not reported. Implementation is an important aspect of any program, and it is an unfortunate fact that research reports on D.A.R.E. programs have generally neglected to report on how the program operated, but instead have focused on the outcome. Often there is an implicit assumption (which may be incorrect) that if the summative evaluation shows significant results, then the program must have operated as expected. If its results are doubtful, however, data from the formative evaluation are crucial in trying to understand why.

Methodology. Harmon's (1993) summative evaluation of the D.A.R.E. program studied 708 fifth-grade students from 10 elementary schools. Of these children, 341 received the D.A.R.E. program, and 367 served as a control condition. The schools selected for the study represented a cross-section of the county's population. Each D.A.R.E. school was **matched** with a control school that did not receive the program—that is, the two schools were equivalent on specified dimensions. The schools in this study were matched on the number of students, the percentage of students receiving free lunches, the percentage of White students, the percentage of male students, and on standardized reading and math test scores.

The design for the study was a quasi-experiment, because neither the students nor the schools were randomly assigned to receive the D.A.R.E. program. Instead, the researchers took the schools that were designated by the school board to receive the program, and then selected matched comparison schools that did not receive the program. Because of the lack of random assignment, it is possible that the schools receiving the D.A.R.E. program were different from the comparison schools. The matching procedure was an attempt to rule out specific threats to the internal validity of the study, but *matching always underequates* because it is impossible to match on every relevant variable.

The D.A.R.E. schools received the 17-week program, delivered by well-trained, uniformed police officers. Each student completed a self-report questionnaire prior to beginning the program, and again 20 weeks later, shortly after the program ended. Equal percentages of the students in the treatment and comparison groups completed the surveys. The questionnaire contained 14 scales, including such variables as drug use, attitudes toward police, assertiveness, and self-esteem.

Results. The summative evaluation (Stage 4) tested for changes from the pretest to the posttest period on each of the variables targeted by the D.A.R.E. curriculum. For the control schools, none of the variables changed significantly. Results from the D.A.R.E. schools showed changes on some of the variables, but not on others. The D.A.R.E. children:

1. Initiated alcohol use less in the last year.
2. Had higher levels of belief in prosocial norms.
3. Reported less association with drug-using peers
4. Reported that more of their peer associations were positive.
5. Had more negative attitudes about substance use.
6. Were more assertive.

However, D.A.R.E. children did not change in the percentage reporting cigarette, tobacco, or marijuana use in the past year, or in the past month. Additionally, their reported attitudes toward the police, attachment to the

school, self-esteem, and rebellious behavior did not change (Harmon, 1993).

These results provide only partial support for the claim that D.A.R.E. reduced substance use by children. The largest changes for the children who received the D.A.R.E. program were in attitudes and peer relations. The program was effective at reducing alcohol initiation, but not at reducing the percentage of students using tobacco or marijuana. Although the results appear somewhat hopeful, some general questions need to be answered. First, how big are the changes produced by the D.A.R.E. program? Second, how long do these changes last? To get a stable answer to the first question, we can utilize the technique called *meta-analysis*.

A Meta-Analysis of D.A.R.E. Evaluations

From the above evaluation research study in one location, it appears that D.A.R.E. may be effective at reducing alcohol consumption among children, changing attitudes toward drug use, and increasing assertiveness. However, the program's inability to reduce other substance use was disappointing. If you were a stakeholder in this program (i.e., one of the developers or policy makers supporting D.A.R.E.), would you consider abandoning the program? Probably not. After all, this was just one study. The results were based on a sample of children in one county in South Carolina, and the study contained some of the threats to internal validity discussed in Chapter 6 (particularly selection, and possibly threats from mortality and instrumentation change). On the other hand, the positive results might be challenged as possibly due to a social desirability response set among the D.A.R.E. students, who had just completed a lengthy and highly publicized program. Other D.A.R.E. evaluations, conducted in other settings and with different children, have found somewhat different results (e.g., Aniskiewicz & Wysong, 1990; Clayton et al., 1991; DeJong, 1987; Dukes, Ullman, & Stein, 1995).

To reach an overall judgment on the value of D.A.R.E., these conflicting findings need to be resolved. The traditional way of doing this has been to conduct a literature review of many similar studies, analyze their quality, and base conclusions on the balance of results of the highest quality studies. However, even studies using the same careful methodology (e.g., quasi-experiments) often find different results, so some might show significant benefits and others might not.

Meta-analysis is a quantitative approach that is gaining popularity for resolving conflicting research findings such as these. It is a statistical procedure for combining the results from several independent studies to arrive at a conclusion with a stated degree of confidence (for a thorough discussion, see Cooper & Hedges, 1994, or Rosenthal, 1991). Meta-analysis has been used to study a variety of topics, and it often produces results different from those generated in traditional subjective literature reviews (Mann, 1994).

To understand how that can happen, consider a topic on which three studies have found significant positive results, and three others have found nonsignificant results, though in the same general direction. A traditional subjective literature review would probably conclude that the overall picture was not definitive. However, a statistical meta-analysis would combine the (low) probabilities of getting each of the significant results with the (somewhat higher) probabilities of getting nonsignificant findings in the same direction. If there were no studies with results in the opposite direction, the cumulative picture would be an extremely low statistical probability that such a pattern of six studies would occur by chance—in other words, a significant overall finding. In fact, that is the typical sort of result found in many meta-analyses—they have generally shown that psychological and social intervention programs in education, mental health, and many other areas *do* have fairly substantial positive effects (Lipsey & Wilson, 1993).

Fortunately, enough D.A.R.E. evaluations have been conducted to make a meta-analysis possible. As of 1994, 18 evaluations of the D.A.R.E. program were available from the U.S. and Canada. In determining studies to include in their meta-analysis, Ennett et al. (1994) selected only those studies that (a) used a control group, and (b) had both pretest and posttest measures. These criteria were selected to remove studies of low quality (i.e., studies with a greater number of threats to internal validity). These selection criteria reduced the number of studies to be analyzed from 18 to 8. (Because omitting so many studies due to their weak methodology sharply reduced the remaining sample of studies, a preferable alternative approach would have been to code the quality of each study, and then to compare the typical findings for studies with high versus low quality.)

For each of the 8 high-quality studies, the strength of D.A.R.E. effects was quantified using the statistics reported in the study. As we explained in Chapter 4, the strength of an effect, or **effect size**, can be measured in several ways. The two most common effect size measures are correlation coefficients (r), and standardized differences between group means (d). This meta-analysis used d, calculating the effect sizes by subtracting the control group's mean score from the D.A.R.E. group's mean score, and dividing the difference by the average standard deviation of the two groups. The resulting effect size was the number of standard deviations by which the means of the two groups differed. An effect size of .00 would indicate no difference. A useful rule of thumb is that an effect size (d) of .20 or less is small, .50 is a medium effect (i.e., half of a standard deviation), and .80 or higher is a large effect (Cohen, 1992).

The effect sizes from the D.A.R.E. program were calculated for six variables that were measured in all 8 studies: knowledge about drugs, attitudes about drugs, social skills, self-esteem, attitudes toward police, and drug use (including alcohol, tobacco, and marijuana). Because of the lack of long-term evaluation studies, this meta-analysis examined only short-term effects. Results for a total of 9317 students from 214 schools in the U.S. and Canada were combined. The results from this analysis are summarized in Figure 7-2. For each dependent variable, the figure shows the mean effect size and the 95% confidence interval around it. If the lower bound of the confidence interval is above zero, the effect for that variable is significant at the .05 level.

Results. The figure shows that D.A.R.E. is most effective at increasing knowledge about drugs. The effect sizes for attitudes toward drugs, social skills, self-esteem, and attitudes toward the police were small though significant. The effect size for drug use, the most important outcome variable, was extremely

Mean Effect Size

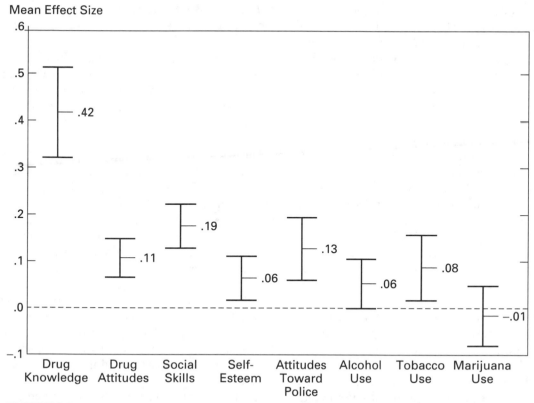

FIGURE 7-2 Magnitude of D.A.R.E.'s weighted mean effect size (and 95% CI), by outcome measure. (Source: Adapted from Ennett, S., Tobler, N., Ringwalt, C., & Flewelling, R. (1994). How effective is Drug Abuse Resistance Education? A meta-analysis of project DARE outcome evaluations. *American Journal of Public Health, 84,* 1394–1401. Copyright 1994 by American Public Health Association.)

small. Breaking down that score to show the effects of D.A.R.E. on different substances revealed that only on tobacco use was it statistically significant (effect size = .08); on alcohol (.06) and marijuana use (–.01) it was not significant (Ennett et al., 1994). Thus, the results from both this meta-analysis and the study by Harmon (1993) agree that, in the short-term, D.A.R.E. produces moderate increases in knowledge about drugs, some effects on attitudes, and small (though favorable) effects on substance use.

A Long-Term Study of D.A.R.E.

A remaining important question about D.A.R.E. is the *long-term* effects of the program. In 1994, Ennett et al. reported that there were not enough long-term

evaluation studies to conduct a meta-analysis, but a few more have been conducted recently. A good example is a study by Dukes, Ullman, and Stein (1996), which examined the effects of D.A.R.E. on participants over a 3-year period. Sixth-grade students in 21 schools in Colorado Springs received the D.A.R.E. program in the first semester that it was offered district-wide, while students in 17 equivalent schools served as a control group. The D.A.R.E. program was introduced to the control schools the following year, but the sixth-grade students who served as the control group went on to junior high school without ever receiving the program, and were contacted three years later.

A random sample of 940 ninth-graders completed a questionnaire about their participation in D.A.R.E., self-esteem, drug use, onset of experimentation with drugs, attitudes toward drug use, resistance to peer pressure, attitudes toward police, and relationships with parents. Due to elimination of students who incorrectly recalled receiving or not receiving drug education programs, the final sample comprised 849 students: 497 who had received the D.A.R.E. program and 352 who had not. This group was split into two randomly chosen subsamples—one used for an initial study and the second for a validation study to determine the replicability of the initial results.

The results from the research are summarized in Figure 7-3. The figure presents effect sizes for each of the seven above-mentioned dependent variables. The small size of these effects indicates that the D.A.R.E. program did not have a significant long-term effect on any of the outcome measures in the initial study, and had only one small effect in the validation study. This was true in spite of the fact that previous research in the same schools had shown immediate results of the D.A.R.E. program *stronger* than those of the meta-analysis reported by Ennett et al. (1994). Therefore, the authors concluded that the effects of the D.A.R.E. program are short-lived. On a more hopeful note, they speculated that several years of presenting D.A.R.E. to every sixth-grade student may have "created a climate in the junior high schools that was quite unfavorable to the use of alcohol, tobacco, or other drugs." They also stated that, although they "could not demonstrate a significant long-term impact of D.A.R.E. participation, in general, students in both the D.A.R.E. group and the control group were doing well—an encouraging outcome" (Dukes et al., 1996, p. 63).

An important part of any outcome evaluation is consideration of the program costs relative to the program effects (Kee, 1994). D.A.R.E. is a relatively expensive program, with costs in 1996 running approximately $100 per student (Dukes et al., 1996). Considering that the program appears more effective at modifying attitudes than behaviors, the benefits may not be worth the costs. Because the long-term evaluation by Dukes et al. indicated that the program has no discernible long-term effects on behavior, it would be wise to reexamine the program in an attempt to identify cheaper and more effective intervention strategies.

A Theory-Driven Alternative: Normative Education

Why is it that the D.A.R.E. program apparently has only a small effect on short-term substance use, and no long-term effects? To answer this question we turn to a newly emerging area of evaluation research—theory-driven program evaluation (cf. Chen, 1990).

To answer the question "why," we must understand the factors that lead to substance use, and then develop effective intervention strategies that target those factors. Several researchers have argued that successful prevention programs tend to enhance an adolescent's ability to resist passive social pressure (e.g., social modeling, and overestimation of drug use by peers), and that it is less important whether they are able to resist direct offers of drugs (i.e., are taught "refusal skills"—the ability to "just say no"). Donaldson et al. (1994, 1995) suggested that the small effect sizes observed for D.A.R.E. and other similar programs were not due to program failure but to theory failure. That is, the D.A.R.E. program may have been implemented correctly, but the theory behind the program may be flawed.

Donaldson et al. (1994, 1995) examined the effects of resistance training (like that provided in the D.A.R.E. program) as compared with normative education. **Normative education** targets students' beliefs about the prevalence and acceptability of substance use by their peers. In five lessons, this program "corrected erroneous perceptions of prevalence and acceptability of alcohol and drug use among peers and established a conservative normative school climate regarding substance use" (1994, p. 201). This intervention was based on prior research which had demonstrated that adolescents who believe that alcohol and drug use are accepted and commonly practiced by their peers are at a substantially higher risk for the early onset of drug and alcohol use. The intervention study, called the Adolescent Alcohol Prevention Trial, involved nearly 12,000 students in 130 school units (both public schools and private Catholic schools) in Los Angeles and San Diego Counties.

Results from the Donaldson et al. (1994) research indicated that resistance skills training, as expected,

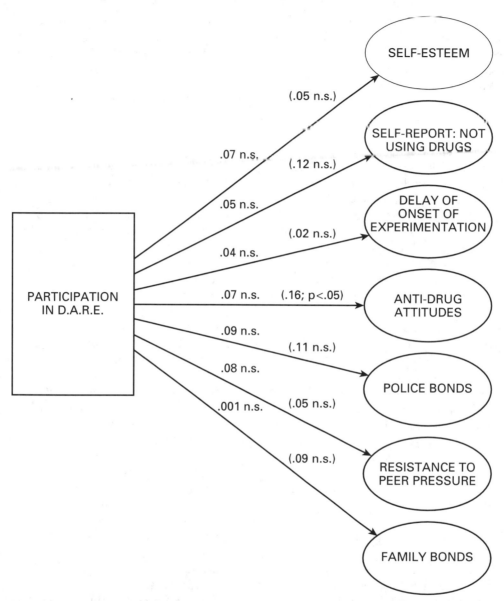

FIGURE 7-3   Structural model of participation in D.A.R.E. as a predictor of seven latent constructs. NOTE: Unstandardized regression coefficients are reported; validation sample coefficients are in parentheses. (Source: Dukes, R. Ullman, J. & Stein, J. (1996). Three-year follow-up of drug abuse resistance education (DARE). *Evaluation Review, 20,* pp. 49–66, copyright © 1996 by Sage Publications, Inc. Reprinted by permission of Sage Publications, Inc.)

did improve adolescents' refusal skills, but that refusal skills did *not* predict subsequent alcohol, tobacco, and marijuana use. Thus, part of the D.A.R.E. program's theory seems to be faulty. In contrast, normative edu-

cation, as predicted, reduced students' estimates of the prevalence of substance use and their beliefs that such use was acceptable; and those two belief changes in turn were associated with lower alcohol, tobacco, and marijuana use in eighth and ninth grades, one and two years after the intervention. Moreover, this same pattern of results was found for both boys and girls, various ethnic groups, students in public and private schools, and prior users and nonusers.

To probe why resistance training was not effective in reducing substance use, further studies were conducted comparing it with normative education and with an intervention combining the two approaches (Donaldson et al., 1995). Two important findings resulted. First, refusal skills predicted subsequent reduced alcohol use for those students who believed it was not acceptable for adolescents to drink alcohol, but *not* for those who believed it was acceptable to drink. Second, a harmful effect of resistance skills training was found among the students attending public schools—it increased their beliefs that there was a high level of prevalence of substance use in their schools. In contrast, normative education did not lead to an increase in those beliefs, and combining the two approaches led to the lowest level of prevalence estimates. These findings suggest that resistance training programs like D.A.R.E. may become more effective if they add lessons emphasizing beliefs in the low prevalence and unacceptability of adolescent substance use.

The virtue of this type of theory-driven program evaluation is that it helps policy makers, program designers, and researchers to understand the efficacy of a program, the mechanisms by which the program works or fails, and how to improve program effectiveness (Donaldson, 1995).

NEW TRENDS IN EVALUATION RESEARCH

As demonstrated by the substance abuse prevention studies described above, program evaluation is an important part of applied social psychology. In general, the recent proliferation of evaluation research provides evidence that this is one of the most fruitful applications of social science—one that society is eager to use and to adapt to new tasks and settings. Yet at the same time it should be recognized that program evaluation is not just a scientific activity but also a political activity, and it has to be carried out within the constraints of the social system. Doing evaluation research and focusing

it on public policy issues requires the researcher and the users of the research to adopt value positions about the desirable goals of social programs. (These ethical and value issues are discussed in more detail in Chapters 1 and 17.) The many diverse concepts of evaluation tend to encourage its use in widely varying ways and situations, though by the same token they impede agreement about its most appropriate methods and uses.

Some authors have advocated **naturalistic approaches** to evaluation, as a contrast to overly intrusive randomized field experiments (Guba & Lincoln, 1981; Rog, 1994). These approaches include case studies, informal interviews with key informants, archival research, and observational methods that do not disturb the natural functioning of the groups being evaluated. A parallel and overlapping development is the recognition that *qualitative methods* have much to offer as supplements to the usual scientific quantitative methods, and sometimes even as alternatives to them (Caudle, 1994; Patton, 1990; Sechrest & Sidani, 1995). Even such a hardheaded methodologist as Donald Campbell (1979) has acknowledged that important understanding of social systems can often be obtained through *conscientious, self-critical* case studies.

On the other end of the continuum, proponents of **full-scale social experiments** such as the income maintenance or "negative income tax" experiments still affirm that they are worth their heavy costs (Heckman, 1992). One advocate was Alice Rivlin (1973), the first head of the Congressional Budget Office, who had the unique role of being Congress's watchdog over program evaluations and budgetary cost-benefit analyses. However, she suggested that, to have the optimum policy influence, such experiments need to compare alternative detailed models of proposed legislative programs, so that the most successful models can be used as the basis for new laws.

Another approach that is proving useful in evaluation research is **cost-benefit analysis**. This technique attempts to estimate a dollar value for the costs of a program and for its benefits (including, as much as possible, its intangible social and psychological costs and benefits—for details, see Kee, 1994; Nas, 1996). Comparing these two figures in a benefit-to-cost ratio gives a measure of the program's efficiency. However, in this process it is important to discount the value of future benefits (or costs) in order to obtain their value in present dollars. Returning to the D.A.R.E. program described earlier, an examination of the costs suggests that the program is not justified. Although it is difficult to estimate in dollars the benefits of the program, the small short-term effects and nonexistent long-term effects suggest that the dollar figure would be small. In comparison, the salary for uniformed police officers (about $50,000) and the cost of course materials add up to about $100 per student.

Another recent development in evaluation research is the more widespread and directive use of **substantive theories**. In the past, many evaluations followed a set of fairly standard procedures or guidelines that could be uniformly applied to any program, without considering the unique context and features of the program. This "black box" approach to evaluation focused mainly on the relationship between the program inputs and outputs, and failed to take into consideration key aspects of the program setting, content, purpose, or participants. In short, the underlying theoretical factors which could cause program success or failure often were not examined (Lipsey, 1988). As Chen (1990) stated:

> Such simple input/output or black box evaluations may provide gross assessments of whether or not a program works, but fail to identify the underlying causal mechanisms that generate the treatment effects. (p. 18)

For a thorough introduction to the values and strategies of theory-driven program evaluation, see Chen (1990). The theory-driven approach to evaluation research is nicely demonstrated by the Donaldson et al. (1995) study on normative education in substance abuse prevention programs, discussed above.

A final recent trend in program evaluation is **critical multiplism**. This term describes research which systematically incorporates a variety of methods and procedures. A study may combine various quantitative methodologies (e.g., experimentation, survey research, quasi-experimentation, and correlational designs, as discussed in the preceding chapters) and also qualitative methodologies (e.g., interviews, case studies, or ethnographic methods). In addition, evaluations following this critical multiplism perspective typically examine many aspects of a program and not just those related to its stated goals (Shadish, 1993).

USE OF EVALUATION RESEARCH

There is no doubt that more and more evaluation research is being done. But is it being used? And if so, how, and how well? These questions have been raised by many writers, and there are wide differences of opinion about the answers. Glass and Ellett's (1980) early review asserted, "Considering that the interest and commitment to evaluation is widespread, it is surprising how little solid evidence of its value can be found" (p. 225).

This pessimistic conclusion has been echoed by many researchers in the area—evaluation research often is *not* used by program managers or policy makers (Sonnichsen, 1994). Some authors who hold this viewpoint attribute the limited use to managerial incompetence, or to conflict between evaluators and managers, or to nonrational "political" factors. Others claim that it is a reasonable course of action because most evaluation research doesn't monitor variables that can be controlled by, or are of specific interest to, program managers. For instance, summative evaluations tend to be concerned with long-range outcomes rather than with short-term components or processes of the program that a manager can influence.

A related point of view is that evaluations should be aimed specifically at the questions and topics that interest the program manager, so that they will be sure to be used. This viewpoint has been espoused by Patton (1986), who recommended that the users of the evaluation be identified at its very beginning, and that the research be designed to meet their needs for information about the issues they consider important. However, many authors see this approach as making the evaluator too subservient to the short-range needs of the program administrator and not responsive enough to society's longer-range needs to know the effects of particular programs and social policies. Undoubtedly, research can be useful without becoming a slave to the administrator's every whim.

Despite the pessimistic views about limited usage, there are techniques that evaluators can use to increase the likelihood that their evaluations will be useful (Sonnichsen, 1994). Carter (1994) suggested five ways to increase the use that is made of evaluation results. For instance, recommendations for change should focus on improvement, and should be specific and feasible. Also, the evaluator should present multiple uses of the study data—that is, make an effort to generalize the results beyond the setting of the program.

Another concern for evaluators is that evaluation research is often used only for its political effect—for instance, to defend decisions that have already been made on other grounds, to confirm strongly held prejudices, or to attack someone else's program plans (McLaughlin, 1975). A much more desirable political use of evaluation research can be seen in legislative requirements that new social programs must be thoroughly evaluated after a specified period of years, thus aiding the passage of the new programs by reassuring their critics and doubters that evidence of their success or failure will eventually be made available (Chelimsky, 1994).

A factor that often influences whether evaluation research is used or not is the source of its funding. Studies have shown that it is most likely to be used by the sponsoring agency or organization, and not used by other organizations even if they know about the findings (Bell, 1994; Caplan, Morrison, & Stambaugh, 1975). Similarly, evaluators who are "inside" employees generally have less power in planning the form and scope of the evaluation, but their findings are more likely to be used than those of outside evaluators (Bell, 1994).

Some authors have warned that it may be too much to expect that research findings will be used directly in making most decisions about program and policy options. Many factors must enter into most program decisions, and the evaluation findings will normally be just one component (Cronbach et al., 1980; Rossi & Freeman, 1993). Evaluation studies rarely cause dramatic shifts in major program decisions, but they frequently feed additional pieces of information into a gradual, evolutionary process of program development (Carter, 1994; Hatry, Newcomer, & Wholey, 1994; Patton et al., 1977). Also, research may have cumulative or delayed effects, taking months to be assimilated and to permeate the thinking of staff members before it has any obvious influence on program decisions.

Clearly, there is no simple answer to the question of whether and how evaluation information is used. In different situations it may be used in many different ways and to markedly different extents, whereas in some situations it may not be used at all. We will return to the issue of the use of research by public policy makers in Chapter 17.

Finally, we must mention ethical issues involved in the use of evaluation research findings in the policy arena. One key issue is: To whom is the evaluator responsible?—the program funding agency, the program managers, the program's clients, or the general public? It is often assumed that research findings will promote the general welfare, but that does not always happen, particularly when the evaluator has vested interests in serving one of these constituencies more fully than others. A related issue is the tendency of many person-oriented research reports to "blame the victims" of social problems such as poverty, crime, or poor health care, and to focus on modifying individuals' behavior rather than on changing pathological societal conditions (Caplan & Nelson, 1973). On the other side of the coin, some authors have emphasized that evaluation research can be used to empower local community groups in their efforts to improve local conditions (Fetterman, Kaftarian, & Wandersman, 1996).

The American Evaluation Association has developed an official statement of *Guiding Principles for Evaluators* and published it together with critical commentaries and discussions of its scope and application (Shadish et al., 1995). The five main topics that it states as professional requirements are systematic inquiry, competence, integrity/honesty, respect for people, and responsibilities for general and public welfare. Another useful volume on ethical issues in evaluation research is Newman and Brown (1996). The related ethical issues involved in promoting social change and influencing public policies are discussed in more detail in Chapters 16 and 17.

SUMMARY

Evaluation research has become a booming activity, with applications in many diverse government and business programs. Its goal is to evaluate the need for, implementation, and impact of programs designed to affect the quality of people's lives. Not a specific research technique itself, it uses any or all of the research methods discussed in previous chapters. Evaluations of public and private programs have been made for centuries, but only in recent years has evaluation research become a separate discipline.

This chapter has emphasized the applied science conception of evaluation research and given relatively little attention to the other contending concepts often found in the literature and the activities of some evaluators, such as the descriptive, decision-oriented, or adversarial viewpoints. Yet, at the same time, we have stressed the possible dangers to the relevance of results if an evaluator adopts an overly rigid, ultrascientific approach.

Formative evaluation provides feedback to administrators to help improve the operation of programs in their early stages. Summative evaluation focuses on a program's outcomes rather than its processes, and assesses its effects, including the degree of progress toward its goals. Formative evaluation includes needs assessment, program design, and monitoring of program implementation and progress. Summative evaluation includes assessment of impact, and efficiency analysis. Before evaluations are begun, an important preliminary is evaluability assessment, to determine whether the program is defined clearly enough to be evaluated.

The research on D.A.R.E. by Harmon (1993) provides a good example of a carefully planned evaluation project, including pretests and posttests of treated and matched control groups. Its results suggested that the D.A.R.E. program may be somewhat effective in reducing drug use among children. Results from a statistical meta-analysis of all high-quality published studies showed that the D.A.R.E. program produces short-term effects on drug knowledge and attitudes, as well as a tiny reduction in tobacco use. However, a recent long-term study showed that, after three years, no specific effects of the D.A.R.E. program were discernible among ninth-grade students. As an alternative to the D.A.R.E. approach, encouraging results have been found with a theory-driven intervention strategy which mainly targets normative beliefs about the prevalence and acceptability of drug use, not just resistance-skills training.

The debate over D.A.R.E.'s value illustrates that evaluation research is still a young discipline with many conflicting viewpoints and a wide variety of new techniques. The questions of how much and how well evaluation research is actually used and what ethical problems it raises are also the subject of debate. Between the optimistic claims and the pessimistic viewpoints, it is important to realize that evaluation research findings are only one of many factors that should influence policy decisions, and they often have gradual and cumulative effects on the course of social programs.

SUGGESTED READINGS

Backer, T., & Rogers, E. (Eds.). (1993). *Organizational aspects of health communication campaigns: What works*? Newbury Park, CA: Sage.—Provides excellent examples of evaluation research on drug prevention programs, community health programs, and family planning programs.

Ennett, S., Tobler, N., Ringwalt, C., & Flewelling, R. (1994). How effective is drug abuse resistance education? A meta-analysis of Project D.A.R.E. outcome evaluations. *American Journal of Public Health*, *84*, 1394–1401.—Presents a quantitative examination of the D.A.R.E. program, which nicely illustrates the technique of meta-analysis.

Isaac, S., & Michael, W. (1995). *Handbook in research and evaluation*. San Diego, CA: Edits.—A readable overview of the different philosophies and methodologies used in evaluation research.

Rosenthal, R. (1991). *Meta-analytic procedures for social research* (2nd ed.). Newbury Park, CA: Sage.—A clear and understandable overview of meta-analytic techniques.

Rossi, P. H., & Freeman, H. E. (1993). *Evaluation: A systematic approach* (5th ed.). Thousand Oaks, CA: Sage.—A comprehensive textbook on evaluation research written by two of the most respected workers in the field.

Wholey, J. (1994). Assessing the feasibility and likely usefulness of evaluation. In J. Wholey, H. Hatry, & K. Newcomer (Eds.), *Handbook of practical program evaluation* (pp. 15–39). San Francisco: Jossey-Bass.—A detailed examination of how to determine if a program is evaluable.

CHAPTER 8

Educational Settings—Intergroup Relations and Learning

Social science and school desegregation: Did we mislead the Supreme Court?

—Stuart W. Cook (1979, p. 420)

Of all the contemporary issues worked on by social psychologists, possibly their greatest public influence has been on the topic of school desegregation. Their research evidence was used in the famous 1954 Supreme Court school desegregation case, *Brown v. Board of Education of Topeka, Kansas*, and in the years since then many researchers have done studies on the process and effects of desegregation. In this chapter we will discuss some of the highlights of social science research on segregation and desegregation, as well as the educational topics of teacher expectations, preventing violence by students, and teaching students with differing abilities. This chapter is closely related to the following chapter on diversity issues, but it focuses primarily on intergroup relations in educational settings.

A BRIEF HISTORY OF SCHOOL DESEGREGATION

The movement for public schools in the United States started in the early 1800s, but it spread rather slowly from its origin in New England. At the time of the Civil War there was no public education for anyone in most parts of the South. In the North it was more common for Whites but was available to less than 7% of free Blacks (Stephan, 1980). After the Civil War, the Fourteenth Amendment guaranteed "equal protection of the laws" to all citizens of the United States, but it did not promise the right to an education to anyone, Black or White. The earliest Supreme Court ruling on the Fourteenth Amendment in 1880 interpreted it as prohibiting all state-imposed discriminations against Blacks (*Brown v. Board of Education*, 1954). However, after the end of Reconstruction, most southern states passed laws that prevented most Blacks from voting and imposed segregation in public transportation. Court cases challenging this discrimination on railroads eventually reached the Supreme Court and resulted in the *Plessy v. Ferguson* ruling of 1896, in which the court for the first time interpreted the Fourteenth Amendment as allowing "separate but equal" facilities.

Following the *Plessy* decision, legalized segregation became more and more pervasive in the South, spreading to public education, hotels and restaurants, hospitals, and government employment. One reaction on the part of Blacks was the founding of the National Association for the Advancement of Colored People (NAACP) in 1910. The NAACP fought against the widespread lynchings of that time, against unequal justice, and eventually against many other forms of discrimination. In 1930 the average per-pupil expenditure in U.S. public schools was $99; in the South it was $44 for White pupils but only $13 for Black students (Stephan, 1980). The NAACP attacked this overwhelming disparity, and in 1936 it began to win suits in the area of graduate education, aimed at getting Black students admitted to White law schools in states that had no Black law schools.

During and after World War II, race relations in all parts of the United States began to change more rapidly. President Roosevelt prohibited discrimination in war-related industries in 1941, and some military units were integrated during the war; but not until 1948 did President Truman order *all* the armed forces integrated. By 1950 the NAACP was ready to challenge segregation in elementary and secondary schools, on the grounds that it violated the "equal protection" clause of the Fourteenth Amendment—in other words, separate schools were inherently unequal. Eventually five separate cases from various states, all arguing this basic principle, were combined in the *Brown v. Board of Education* ruling.

In each of these five cases the NAACP made major use of social scientists to testify about the effects of segregated education on Black pupils. Many eminent social psychologists gave expert testimony before the lower courts about the effects of segregation (Stephan, 1980). One source frequently cited was Kenneth and Mamie Clark's famous studies involving projective questions about children's reactions to Black and White dolls (Clark & Clark, 1947), but there were many others as well. A particularly influential study was a survey of 517 social scientists who were professionally concerned with racial issues (Deutscher & Chein, 1948). When asked the effects of segregated education, even if equal facilities were provided to the two races, 90% of these authorities said it was detrimental to the minority group, and 83% said it was also detrimental to the majority group that enforced the segregation. Thus the informed professional opinion of the time was overwhelmingly against segregation.

When the *Brown* case reached the Supreme Court, there was no further oral testimony by social scientists, but a Social Science Statement was submitted as an appendix to the plaintiffs' legal briefs. In it, 32 eminent anthropologists, psychiatrists, psychologists, and sociologists summarized the scientific knowledge of that time regarding the effects of segregation and desegregation on students' self-esteem, school achievement, and race relations (Allport et al., 1953; for a description, see Cook, 1979). It is unknown which specific facts and arguments influenced the Supreme Court's *Brown* decision in 1954, but in a footnote the court did cite seven scientific sources, including Gunnar Myrdal's (1944) famous book on U.S. race relations, *An American Dilemma*. And the court agreed entirely with the NAACP's arguments that *a segregated education was inherently unequal.* Though the court cited social science findings, its decision was aimed squarely at the legal issue of constitutional rights under the Fourteenth Amendment. (For some of the highlights of the *Brown* decision, see Box 8-1.)

Box 8-1

EXTRACTS FROM THE SUPREME COURT'S DECISION IN THE CASE OF *BROWN V. BOARD OF EDUCATION*

In approaching this problem, we cannot turn the clock back to 1868 when the [fourteenth] amendment was adopted, or even to 1896 when *Plessy v. Ferguson* was written. We must consider public education in the light of its full development and its present place in American life throughout the Nation. Only in this way can it be determined if segregation in public schools deprives these plaintiffs of the equal protection of the laws.

Today, education is perhaps the most important function of State and local governments. . . . In these days, it is doubtful that any child may reasonably be expected to succeed in life if he is denied the opportunity of an education. Such an opportunity, where the State has undertaken to provide it, is a right which must be made available to all on equal terms.

We come then to the question presented: Does segregation of children in public schools solely on the basis of race, even though the physical facilities and other "tangible" factors may be equal, deprive the children of the minority group of equal educational opportunities? We believe that it does. . . .

To separate them from others of similar age and qualifications solely because of their race generates a feeling of inferiority as to their status in the community that may affect their hearts and minds in a way unlikely ever to be undone.

The effect of this separation on their educational opportunities was well stated by a finding in the Kansas case . . . :

> Segregation of white and colored children in public schools has a detrimental effect upon the colored children. The impact is greater when it has the sanction of the law; for the policy of separating the races is usually interpreted as denoting the inferiority of the Negro group. A sense of inferiority affects the motivation of a child to learn. Segregation with the sanction of law, therefore, has a tendency to [retard] the educational and mental development of Negro children and to deprive them of some of the benefits they would receive in a racial[ly] integrated school system.

Whatever may have been the extent of psychological knowledge at the time of *Plessy v. Ferguson*, this finding is amply supported by modern authority. Any language in *Plessy v. Ferguson* contrary to this finding is rejected.

We conclude that in the field of public education the doctrine of "separate but equal" has no place. Separate educational facilities are inherently unequal. Therefore, we hold that the plaintiffs . . . are . . . deprived of the equal protection of the laws guaranteed by the fourteenth amendment.

Source: *Brown v. Board of Education*, 347 U.S. 483 (1954).

What Has Happened Since *Brown*?

After another year of hearing further arguments, the Supreme Court ordered in 1955 that the *Brown* decision should be implemented by lower courts "with all deliberate speed." However, for about 10 years very little movement toward desegregation took place, due mainly to the effort and expense of court suits and to the widespread opposition of Whites. In 1964, 99% of Black school children were still attending segregated schools (Edelman, 1973), and the Supreme Court in another desegregation case declared that "there has been entirely too much deliberation and not enough speed" (*Griffin*, 1964).

In 1964, as a result of the swelling civil rights movement, Congress passed the first civil rights act since Reconstruction. Among other things, it authorized the cutoff of federal funds and the filing of court suits against school districts that did not comply with the 1954 *Brown* decision. Most of the enforcement efforts were directed at the South because its dual school systems were required by law (*de jure*), in contrast to the North's pattern of *de facto* segregation (segregation based on the fact of where people lived). By 1972, 44% of Black children in the South were attending predominantly White schools, while the figure was still only 29% in the North (Pettigrew, 1975).

The 1970s saw a continuing series of court rulings ordering desegregation of schools, not only for Black students, but also for Hispanics. Often the method by which this was accomplished was busing of students (usually the minority students) to different schools away from their homes. As a result, opponents of desegregation focused their attacks on busing, which appeared to be the most vulnerable part of school integration plans (Olzak, Shanahan, & West, 1994). Some communities, such as New Haven, Connecticut; Waterloo, Iowa; and San Diego, California, made voluntary efforts to desegregate their schools without the pressure of federal or court orders. Other cities, such as Boston and Los Angeles, dragged their heels and fought against court-ordered desegregation plans for many years (Mills, 1979).

In the 1970s, because of the rapidly increasing minority population in many large northern cities and the long-standing pattern of White migration to the sub-

urbs, it often developed that there were too few White school children left in a city to allow full-scale desegregation. For example, in Detroit, so many White families had moved to the suburbs that the remaining student population was 80% Black (Fiss, 1979; Rist, 1980). One proposed solution for this situation was combining the city and suburban school districts into a metropolitan desegregation plan. However, in the *Milliken v. Bradley* case (1974), the Supreme Court overturned a lower court's order for a Detroit metropolitan desegregation plan on the grounds that the only violation of students' constitutional rights had been within the Detroit school district and not within the suburbs, so that the only required desegregation was *within* the city of Detroit. Since that case and a similar one in Dayton, Ohio, in 1977, legal support for large-scale busing plans to remedy desegregation has declined steadily. However, as Russell and Hawley (1983) noted, the few studies that have examined the effect of riding a bus to school have consistently found no effects on academic achievement nor attitudes toward school that were attributable to the busing.

More recent statistics indicate that many schools remain segregated. The U.S. Commission on Civil Rights in 1987 reported that 70% of Black students were attending schools with some White students (5% or more). However, that means that 30% of Black students were attending all-minority schools! Among White students, only 31% attended a school that had 5% or more Blacks in the student body. Recent demographic trends suggest that the percentages of students attending truly desegregated schools will continue to decline (Stephan, 1991).

Should the U.S. continue to strive for a racially integrated school environment? To address this question, we need to understand the types of desegregation plans available, and the effects that desegregation has on children, as determined by empirical research.

RESEARCH ON SCHOOL DESEGREGATION

Types of Desegregation Plans

Several types of desegregation programs have been developed. That Blacks, Whites, Latinos, and Asians frequently live in largely segregated residential areas is not in dispute. Analyses of 1990 census data have demonstrated this using an index of ethnic dissimilarity, which would be 100 in the case of complete apartheid, and 0 if people were randomly distributed. In U.S. metropolitan areas, these analyses found scores of 69 for Blacks and Whites, 44 for Asians and Whites, and 48 for Latinos in relation to non-Hispanic Whites (Farley & Frey 1994). What has been hotly disputed is: how to produce desegregated schools in a segregated society.

Desegregation techniques can be classified as either mandated or voluntary. Mandatory programs may be ordered by the local school board or court-ordered, and they offer parents no choice as to whether they will participate in desegregation, as long as their child remains in public school. In contrast, voluntary programs allow parents to choose whether their child will be assigned to a desegregated school or remain in the neighborhood school (Rossell, 1983). Results from 20 years of research have consistently shown that mandatory programs are more successful at reducing segregation than are voluntary programs (Rossell, 1990; Welch & Light, 1987). Also, desegregation plans, either voluntary or mandatory, produce greater reductions in racial isolation if they are court-ordered (external) rather than school-board-ordered (internal). However, as in any complex area of social research, the most successful program for any given situation is determined by many variables. Furthermore, government-mandated programs, although producing less school segregation, can often elicit negative responses from those involved. (See Rossell, 1983, 1990, for an excellent comparison of mandatory versus voluntary desegregation programs.)

From the discussion above, it is clear that constitutional rights require the U.S. to have a desegregated education system, and that many local school systems have implemented programs to reach desegregation. Implicit in the drive for desegregation is the expectation that it should have positive effects on both minority and majority students, as the Social Science Statement submitted to the Supreme Court affirmed. But were its authors right? Or, as Stuart Cook (1979) put it, "did we mislead the Supreme Court?" From informa-

tion in the section that follows, you will see that desegregation can have both positive and negative effects, and that these effects are not limited to the minority group.

Reviews of the Research Literature

In the late 1960s and early 1970s, many research studies of desegregation programs in individual school districts were carried out, and since then many reviews of the research literature have been conducted. In an early review, St. John (1975) summarized more than 120 research reports and pointed out their complex pattern of findings on the many different dependent variables that had been studied. Another early review concluded:

> (a) desegregation generally does not reduce the prejudices of Whites toward Blacks, (b) the self-esteem of Blacks rarely increases in desegregated schools, (c) the achievement level of Blacks sometimes increases and rarely decreases in desegregated schools, and (d) desegregation leads to increases in Black prejudice toward Whites about as frequently as it leads to decreases. (Stephan, 1978, p. 217)

However, these conclusions must be qualified because of several major limitations in the research. In particular, most studies have investigated only short-term effects of desegregation, and the extent and methods of desegregation have varied tremendously from study to study and in different geographic regions. Also, crucial background factors such as social class and IQ were typically not used as control variables in assessing the effects of desegregation.

Other research reviews, despite considering somewhat different studies and methodological issues, have reached rather similar conclusions (e.g., Schofield & Sagar, 1983; Stephan, 1991). Some reviewers are more optimistic about Black school achievement, stressing that modest gains for desegregated students have been demonstrated in a majority of studies, particularly ones that allowed comparisons with control groups remaining in segregated schools (Crain & Mahard, 1978; Feagin, 1980). Other reviewers, concentrating on studies of interracial attitudes and behavior, have pointed out that very few of them were carefully controlled and even fewer were done under conditions where interracial contact could be expected to have favorable consequences (Schofield, 1986; Taylor & Moghaddam, 1994). For instance, Pettigrew et al. (1973) stressed that the *quality* of interracial interaction is crucial and that all aspects of a school situation must be equal in status before it can truly be considered "integrated" (that is, a balanced racial mix among teachers, principals, student council members, cheerleaders, and so on). However, a large-scale study in Indianapolis high schools by Patchen (1982) suggested that conditions which promote friendly interracial attitudes and behavior may produce poor academic achievement—a difficult dilemma to resolve.

In the sections that follow we will summarize research findings concerning the effects of school desegregation on key dependent variables, based on literature reviews and the findings of more recent studies.

Self-Esteem and Educational Aspirations

The Social Science Statement in *Brown* asserted that the self-esteem and educational aspirations of Black children had been diminished by government-enforced segregation, but it did not take a direct position on whether, or how soon, desegregation would reverse this effect. According to the available research, self-esteem and the educational and occupational *aspirations* of segregated Black students are at least as high as those of segregated Whites (Cook, 1979; Rosenberg, 1986). This apparent contrast with the Social Science Statement is hard to evaluate because of the possibility that the "Black pride" movement of the 1960s may have raised the overall level of Blacks' self-esteem (Hraba & Grant, 1970), and also because quite different measurement techniques were used in the pre-1954 studies and in the more recent research.

Some reviewers, though not all, have concluded that Black students' self-esteem may actually decrease in the first year or two of desegregation (e.g., Stephan, 1991). However, because many aspects of social status and of discrimination in our society (in addition to school segregation) would also influence Blacks' self-

esteem, Cook (1979) suggested that no sudden changes in self-esteem or other basic personality characteristics should be expected. Though reviews differ in their conclusions regarding short-term changes in self-esteem, the available data clearly indicate no long-term differences in self-esteem between Blacks who attended segregated schools and Blacks who attended desegregated schools. For instance, using a national probability sample of Blacks (the National Survey of Black Americans), Dawkins (1994) found no long-term difference in the self-esteem of Black adults who had attended desegregated versus segregated elementary and high schools. Thus, his results were contrary to the implicit expectations of the Social Science Statement. However, this type of study does not take into account the social atmosphere of the school, which, as pointed out above, is an important consideration in research on school desegregation.

Educational Achievement

Consistent with the Social Science Statement in *Brown*, much subsequent evidence shows Black (and Hispanic) students to be substantially behind White students educationally (Blackwell, 1990; Coleman et al., 1966). Desegregation does not necessarily change that picture; some studies have shown desegregation to improve Black students educationally, but only to a modest extent (Stephan, 1991). However, Cook (1979) stressed that better results have been obtained under conditions consistent with the Statement—specifically, when official policy has required desegregation, when students have spent their whole educational history in mixed schools, and when cumulative rather than short-term gains in achievement have been measured.

A famous study using a sample of over 645,000 Black and White students from all regions of the country was the Coleman Report on *Equality of Educational Opportunity* (Coleman et al., 1966). Using regression analysis and controlling for SES, it found that the greater the proportion of White students in a school, the better the achievement of Black students in the school, and that this relationship grew stronger in the higher school grades. A reanalysis of a portion of

Photograph courtesy of Kenneth B. Clark. Reprinted by permission.

Box 8-2

KENNETH B. CLARK, DESEGREGATION RESEARCHER AND ADVOCATE

The work of Kenneth B. Clark probably had more influence on the process of school desegregation in the United States than that of any other scientist, and it was specifically cited by the U.S. Supreme Court in its 1954 decision on *Brown v. Board of Education*. Born in Panama, Clark grew up in Harlem, earned his bachelor's degree at Howard University, and took his Ph.D. in psychology at Columbia in 1940. He spent brief periods in teaching and wartime research before joining the faculty at City College of New York, where he spent the rest of his career and is now Distinguished Professor of Psychology Emeritus. He has also served as president of the Metropolitan Applied Research Center, and after retiring, he and his wife, Mamie, founded a firm which consults on issues involving human relations, discrimination, and affirmative action.

Clark's early research with his wife, which was cited by the Supreme Court, concerned the self-images of black school children. In addition to serving as a consultant to many organizations and government agencies, he published books on *Prejudice and Your Child*, *The Negro American*, *Dark Ghetto*, *A Relevant War Against Poverty*, and *Pathos of Power*. He has been honored by election as president of the American Psychological Association and appointment to the New York State Board of Regents, which oversees higher education in the state.

the Coleman data for ninth-grade students from northern cities found that even more important than *school* desegregation was desegregation of the students' own *classroom*. That is, the average achievement of Black students increased in proportion to the percentage of Whites in their classroom (McPartland, 1969). These large-scale findings, coming at about the time of the major federal push to enforce desegregation rulings, provided important ammunition for the civil rights movement of the 1960s.

More recent reviews of the effects of school desegregation on achievement have found results similar to those of Coleman. Using survey data from the National Survey of Black Americans, Dawkins (1994) found that, in northern and western states, there was better educational attainment for African Americans who attended desegregated schools than for those who attended segregated schools, but in the southern states the effect was unclear. Researchers using meta-analytic procedures have also demonstrated greater achievement among minority students attending desegregated schools. For example, Schneider (1990) summarized the results from a series of meta-analyses showing that, in comparison to students educated in segregated schools, Black students educated in desegregated schools were superior in reading, but not in math.

Based on their review of research on desegregation and academic achievement, Mahard and Crain (1983) offered the conclusion:

> Desegregation is indeed beneficial [for the minority student], although it must begin in the earliest grades. We have also seen what research has led us to suspect for some time—that desegregation in a predominately White society requires predominately White schools, and desegregation in a society where Whites have run to the suburbs to establish a "White noose" around the decaying, predominately minority central cities requires metropolitan desegregation. We have also learned some things that were not expected. The discovery that a school can have too many White students and thus harm Black achievement confirms what up to now had been a largely speculative argument for a "critical mass" of Black students in desegregated schools. (p. 124)

Despite a general consensus that desegregation does have some favorable effects on academic achievement by minorities, nearly all of the reviews point out that many of the available studies have serious limitations. For example, the meta-analysis by Schneider (1990) started with 157 empirical studies of Black student achievement, but relied on only 19 after excluding those that did not meet the methodological standards established for inclusion in the review. As we discussed in Chapter 7, a broader picture would have been obtained by rating the methodological quality of studies and comparing the results for studies that met the preestablished criteria versus those that did not.

Setting aside the issue of desegregation for the moment, it is crystal clear that many minority groups in the U.S. fail to attain the same educational accomplishments as White students. On average, Blacks, Hispanics, and native Americans are less likely to graduate from high school, less likely to attend college if they do graduate, less likely to graduate from college if they do attend, less likely to pursue graduate education if they graduate from college, typically score lower on standardized tests, and ultimately earn less money than their White counterparts (Blackwell, 1990). Research on school desegregation indicates that it can help to reduce these differences between the White majority and ethnic minorities. Studies have found that Blacks who attended desegregated high schools are more likely to graduate from high school, attend and graduate from college, and attain higher GPAs than Blacks who attended segregated schools (Crain & McPartland, 1984; Stephan, 1991). Over the longer run, crucial longitudinal research has shown that Blacks who attended desegregated schools or colleges are more likely to work in desegregated employment settings and to achieve higher incomes than Blacks with segregated educational backgrounds (Braddock, 1985).

Effects on White Students

Though the Social Science Statement suggested that desegregation would have beneficial effects on Whites by reducing their unrealistic self-appraisals and their moral conflicts over discrimination, very few studies have attempted to measure such effects. Most reviewers agree that White students' school achievement has been unaffected by desegregation, though St. John (1975) pointed to a few instances of negative changes for Whites in predominantly Black schools.

Willie (1989) argued that school desegregation has had a greater positive effect on White students than on Black students. Desegregation, he feels, has helped White Americans to overcome a false sense of superiority, and to absorb the attitudes necessary to succeed in a diverse society. Without school desegregation, many White Americans would continue to believe in their inherent superiority and to oppress other racial and cultural groups. Several studies of White students attending Black colleges have found positive effects on their self-concept as well as more favorable race relations (Comer, 1980; Pascarella et al., 1987).

Interracial Tension, Conflict, and Prejudice

The Social Science Statement in *Brown* predicted that government-mandated desegregation would proceed with few difficulties, particularly if temporary incidents were met with forceful leadership. In general there have been few major difficulties, despite the highly publicized examples of troops being used to enforce court orders in Little Rock, Arkansas, in 1959, or crowds attacking school buses carrying Black students in Boston in 1974. By 1974 desegregation had been accomplished in over 5000 communities in the South without major crises (Cohen, 1974). A national sample of school superintendents reported that, in 82% of their districts, desegregation had occurred without serious disruption for more than two weeks (U.S. Commission on Civil Rights, 1977). Despite the negative experiences of the other 18% of districts, Cook concluded that "the peaceful process that characterized 82% of communities testifies to the near-miraculous orderliness with which a revolutionary change in strongly entrenched societal customs and practices was brought about" (1979, p. 430).

The Social Science Statement also predicted the possibility of friendlier race relations and more favorable racial attitudes, *if* the following qualifications were met:

> (1) simultaneous desegregation in all the schools of a school system, (2) consistent and firm endorsement by those in authority, (3) absence of competition among the students from the different racial groups, (4) equivalence of positions and functions among all student participants in desegregated schools, (5) interracial contacts of the type that permit learning about one another as individuals. (Cook, 1979, p. 430)

Other writers have indicated that the Social Science Statement gave relatively little attention to these qualifying conditions (Hennigan, Flay, & Cook, 1980). In any case, many reviewers who have examined interracial attitudes and behavior agree that the results in different districts are very inconsistent, ranging from positive to negative. However, most studies in this area are uninterpretable because they do not measure or report the crucial conditions and events within the schools. In many cases the school board or local community leaders opposed desegregation, and the conditions in most schools were probably far from equal in status or noncompetitive in nature. Thus, the above prediction could be tested only in a small number of relatively ideal school situations. However, those situations are the kind that authorities should be aiming at creating when they establish a school integration program.

White Flight

Much of the opposition to integration in northern and western cities seized on the use of busing as the focus for community protests. Some researchers, such as Coleman (1975), concluded that compulsory court-ordered busing led to "White flight" out of the city public schools—that is, an increase over the usual amount of White migration to the suburbs. However, White flight can take several forms. The most extreme form is the relocation of White families to the ethnically homogeneous suburbs, while a less extreme form is enrollment of White students in private schools. As Rossell (1983) has noted, most of the research has not made this distinction.

The research on White flight is controversial, and the data are often complex and contradictory (Rossell, 1990; Rossell & Hawley, 1983; Weigel & Pappas, 1981). However, the cumulative findings suggest that desegregation, especially mandated desegregation, does cause reductions in the percentage of White students enrolled in public schools. One excellent example reported data on White flight from 20 schools around the U.S., each of which had either a mandatory or voluntary desegregation program (Rossell, 1990). Approximately half of the schools had a minority student population of 30% or more, while the remaining half had a lower proportion of minorities. The variable of interest was the percentage of change in White student enrollment before, during, and after the time when desegregation procedures were implemented. Some of the results for the more-than-30% minority schools are summarized in Figure 8-1.

As the figure shows, there was already a steady decrease in the percentage of White students prior to desegregation (approximately a 5% annual reduction in

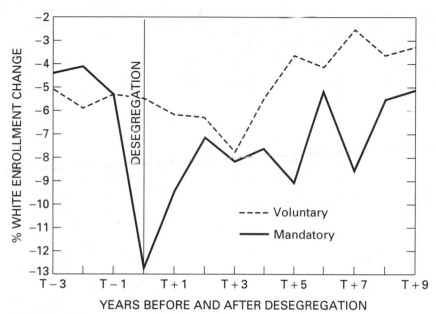

FIGURE 8-1 **Percentage of White enrollment change in districts with more than 30% minority enrollment, plotted separately for voluntary and mandatory desegregation programs.** (Source: Rossell, C. (1990). *The Carrot or the Stick for School Desegregation Policy: Magnet Schools or Forced Busing.* Philadelphia: Temple University Press.)

White students during each of the three years prior to desegregation). Then the first year of *mandatory* desegregation displayed a substantial drop in the number of White students, and later the decrease gradually returned to its original levels. However, for schools instituting voluntary programs, there was essentially no change in the rate of decrease during the first year of desegregation, and the decrease actually slowed in later years. A finding not shown in the figure is the somewhat different pattern found for schools in which minorities made up less than 30% of the student population. There the percentage of White students was initially more stable prior to desegregation, and it dropped by 7% for mandatory programs, but by less than 2% for voluntary programs in the year when the desegregation program began, later leveling off at about a 4% annual decrease.

These results clearly show that desegregation *can* lead to "White flight." However, it is important to note that, for schools in which 30% or more of the students were minority, there was already steady out-migration

of White students prior to desegregation, and that desegregation, especially mandatory desegregation, simply strengthened a change that was already occurring. In many cities, the result was a percentage of Whites nearly identical to what would have been predicted without any school desegregation whatsoever.

Ultimately, White flight has negative consequences for the (mostly minority) students that remain behind. A lower percentage of White students in a school district is associated with lower family incomes, lower property values, and increased crime rates. Note that these changes are not directly the result of a high concentration of minority residents, but occur simply because many of the more affluent families have left. These changes gradually lead to lower school budgets, less parental involvement, and less-qualified teachers—all in all, a lower quality education (Slaughter & Kuehne, 1989).

Conclusion. After surveying past desegregation research, Cook (1979) recommended that, instead of reactively studying whatever desegregation program local authorities devise, social scientists should devote their efforts to proposing and studying better ways of integrating students—ways in which the conditions for favorable intergroup relations could be met and the possibilities for educational benefits maximized. In contrast, Taylor and Moghaddam (1994) have suggested a different approach. They argue that research on conditions that facilitate positive interactions between groups is based on the assumption that relations between minority and majority groups are bad to begin with, and that interaction under the "right" conditions will help change the attitudes of those involved. Although this may have been true when desegregation first began, it definitely seems less true today. They suggest alternatively that the relations between groups are generally good, and that researchers should begin to examine the dynamics that lead to deviations from these good relations.

Second, Taylor and Moghaddam (1994) point out that researchers have assumed that desegregation would produce contact between the groups, which, if positive, would lead to reduction in intergroup hostilities. However, research shows that simply merging groups of students together in the same context may not produce real contact, even if the social conditions are favorable. Even within desegregated schools, students show a strong tendency to interact with students of their own ethnic group (Schofield & Sagar, 1977). Regarding contact between races in desegregated schools, Taylor & Moghaddam state:

> The results from quite different contexts converge to suggest that intergroup contact may not be as prevalent as believed. Even in situations that are apparently conducive to contact because of physical proximity and positive attitudes, there is less interaction than would be expected. (p. 183)

These facts suggest that simply forming desegregated schools may not be enough to promote positive intergroup relations. The typical school classroom is a highly competitive environment, and in order to promote positive contact between groups, it may be necessary to restructure the learning atmosphere—to create a more cooperative learning environment. That is the topic of our next section.

A MORE EFFECTIVE DESEGREGATION PROCESS

The current situation regarding desegregation is extremely mixed. On one hand, national surveys over the last 50 years have shown a steady decrease in racial prejudice and a strong increase in the favorability of Whites toward school integration (Dovidio & Gaertner, 1991; Farley et al., 1994); and the average level of school segregation in the United States is still declining. On the other hand, subtle forms of racial prejudice and discrimination remain common (Pettigrew, 1991), and schools in most major cities have become *more segregated* due to the increasing concentration of minorities in the cities and of Whites in the suburbs, so that some major city school districts now have *80%* or more minority students. Up until the 1980s, busing had been the remedy ordered by the courts for this racial concentration, but busing for purposes of desegregation is a very unpopular measure among all segments of White society (Ladd & Lipset, 1975). By 1976 busing was opposed by a majority of Blacks as well, in part because minority children were almost always the ones transported when one-way busing plans were adopted (Rist, 1980).

What can social scientists suggest in this situation to help promote meaningful integration in the schools? A number of social psychologists have suggested approaches that maximize the conditions necessary for positive intergroup contacts. In essence, these are **equal-status** and **cooperative learning** situations (Slavin & Madden, 1994). We will describe one example in detail to show how it works and how it differs from more customary classroom procedures.

Cooperative Learning in the Jigsaw Classroom

Elliot Aronson and his colleagues pioneered a new approach to education, designed to integrate formerly isolated and competitive students into a cohesive, cooperative classroom group (Aronson et al., 1978; Aronson & Osherow, 1980; see also Clarke, 1994). They began by noting Gordon Allport's theoretical analysis of prejudice and his prescription for the conditions necessary to reduce intergroup prejudice. In the same year as the Supreme Court's *Brown* decision, Allport (1954) specified that the reduction of prejudice between the members of two societal groups requires (a) equal-status contact, which is (b) aimed at common goals, and is (c) supported by authority or other institutional patterns. There is good research support for each of these principles, but it is striking to note how far the usual desegregated classroom deviates from these specifications. There is often official resistance to desegregation, and most American classrooms—desegregated or not—fail to meet the other two conditions as well. Their goal structure is usually one of fierce individual competition rather than cooperation, and there are usually marked status differences between the "good" students and the "poor" students, as well as between the majority group and any ethnic or national minority students in the class.

The Jigsaw Technique. Stimulated by the conflict attending the desegregation of schools in Austin, Texas, Aronson and his colleagues developed a scheme to implant Allport's three conditions in elementary

school classrooms. In the "jigsaw technique" (Figure 8-2), small groups of about five or six students meet together for about an hour several days a week to study one curriculum area. The structure for that period is one of *cooperative learning and peer teaching*. A typical way of accomplishing this is to split the day's material into five or six sections (for instance, different aspects of life in a particular historical period), and to give one to each group member. After reading it carefully, the student's responsibility is to teach it to the other members of his or her group and to listen and absorb their teaching of their sections of material—each member contributing a piece of the total picture, like a jigsaw puzzle. After a day or a few days of this procedure, students are tested on the material and graded individually. Thus, the group members are interdependent in studying the material, they gradually learn to help each other and to reward each other instead of competing, but their grade reflects their own individual learning so that they aren't penalized if other group members have learned less than they have.

That is the essential core of the jigsaw technique, but there are other clever supporting features. Often

FIGURE 8-2   A jigsaw classroom group in action.

one member from each group will meet briefly with counterparts from the other groups to discuss and learn their corresponding sections. That enables slower students or poor readers to get help in comprehending their section before teaching it to their own group members. Often pupils who have English language deficits are awkward in communicating their information to the group, but since the other students have to know that material to do well on the test, they become motivated to draw out the information and help the speaker communicate more clearly. Of course, distractions, conflicts, and name-calling may occur; but when they do, the circulating teacher is available to remind students of the task, point out the need for all members to contribute their own material, or suggest ways to improve the group process. Normally each group has a student leader appointed for a week or so to help with its organization, keep it on its task, and assist its functioning by focusing on group-process difficulties. At the end of each session, the group takes a few minutes to review its interaction and suggest improvements for the next time.

Preparation for Using the Technique. Effective group functioning with the jigsaw technique can develop quite rapidly, but it does require careful planning and preparation. Before their first full-scale, 6-week-long experiment with the technique in Austin, Texas, the researchers held a week-long summer workshop for fifth- and sixth-grade teachers (Blaney et al., 1977). Later, because cooperative learning is so unfamiliar in U.S. classrooms, the teachers organized preliminary team-building exercises and group discussions about the technique for their pupils. One simple beginning is the Broken Squares Game, where each group member starts with pieces of several different jigsaw puzzles and, in order to complete their own puzzle, all members must receive pieces from other members. However, the rules call for no communication, so each member has to notice and voluntarily give the other members the pieces they need. Other exercises may concentrate on listening skills, or use brainstorming to evoke ideas about how to improve cooperative interactions. Some exercises involving competition between groups may also be used to solidify each group into a more cooperative team.

After about two weeks of such preparation, the groups should have developed their cooperative skills and can then begin to focus on academic content. The original selection of members should make each group as heterogeneous as possible in sex, race, and academic ability, but close friends or bitter enemies should not be in the same group. Finally, if the jigsaw technique is used for more than six weeks or so, the authors recommend rotating members so that students can work closely with more classmates and learn to appreciate and respond to their individuality (Aronson et al., 1978).

Research on the Jigsaw Technique

Initial reports from teachers and classroom observers were highly enthusiastic about the jigsaw technique. Even visiting music and physical education teachers who didn't know about the experimental program remarked about the students' increased cooperation. However, though such testimonials are gratifying, they can give a selective and misleading picture about the success of any program. Therefore, careful experimental research was necessary to demonstrate that the program really worked and to show precisely what its effects were.

The first major study was a quasi-experiment (Blaney et al., 1977) comparing the fifth- and sixth-grade students in ten jigsaw classrooms with three control classrooms. The teachers who had volunteered to use the jigsaw method in their classes had attended the summer workshop and also received more training and exchanged useful experiences in several additional short workshops. The control teachers had been nominated as highly competent and committed to their own mode of teaching, and they agreed not to use any small-group or cooperative teaching techniques during the period of the research. There were two main measuring instruments for the dependent variables. One was a 22-item questionnaire concerning attitudes toward school and toward oneself, which was administered orally in the classroom with the students marking one of seven boxes in answer to each question. The second was a sociometric measure of liking for their classmates, which was presented as an imaginary visit to an exciting island in a small boat; they could take only a few classmates in each boatload, so they had to assign numbers to each classmate indicating in which boatload they wanted their classmates to come and join them on the island. These measures were administered to the experimental and control classrooms both before and after the 6-week jigsaw period, with the following results:

Liking for Classmates. At the beginning of the study the pupils liked their jigsaw group members slightly less than their other classmates, but by the end they liked them substantially more. However, this change did not diminish their liking for other classmates, which also increased, though only slightly.

Liking for School. This dimension was measured by a 3-item scale, which showed significant differences across time and between groups. The control-group students decreased their liking for school (a common classroom occurrence), while the jigsaw classroom students remained unchanged. Breaking the results down by ethnic group, the authors found that Anglos in the jigsaw groups gained in liking for school while Anglos in the control classes decreased. Black students in the jigsaw classes decreased slightly in their liking for school, but their peers in traditional classes decreased sharply. In contrast, Mexican Americans in the experimental classes increased only slightly, while those in the control classes showed a marked increase in their liking for school. Later research in Watsonville, California, suggested that this unexpected effect was due to Mexican American students with language difficulties being forced out of their accustomed silence and required to communicate regularly with their jigsaw group classmates. The Watsonville Mexican American children had been in a desegregated school situation for several years, and when they participated in jigsaw groups, their liking for school increased.

Self-Esteem. Self-esteem was a key variable because of the findings in many other studies that the self-esteem of minority students may decrease in desegregated classrooms. It was measured by a 4-item scale focusing mostly on feelings of success in the classroom. Happily, results showed that students in the jigsaw groups increased significantly in self-esteem, while the control students decreased.

Competitiveness. Responses to the item, "I would rather beat a classmate than help him," showed that the jigsaw students became less competitive during the study while the control students became more competitive.

Learning from Others. Responses to another item demonstrated that students in the jigsaw classrooms increasingly believed that they could learn from other students, whereas students in the traditional classrooms decreased in that belief. Altogether, the results were a resounding verification of the hypotheses behind the jigsaw technique of cooperative learning and peer teaching. Not only that, but the innovation became so popular that large numbers of elementary teachers in the school system began using small-group, cooperative learning methods (Aronson & Osherow, 1980).

School Performance. In the Blaney et al. (1977) study, the jigsaw students' classroom grades also improved, while the control students' grades decreased. However, this could have been due to a teacher expectancy effect, so a controlled experiment was designed to study school performance objectively (Lucker et al., 1977). For two weeks, 11 fifth- and sixth-grade classes in five Austin schools studied the same curriculum on colonial America. Six classes used jigsaw groups for about 45 minutes each day, while the other five were taught by highly competent teachers using the traditional method. All 11 classes were given a standardized test over the material both before and after they studied it. Results of the experiment are shown in Table 8-1.

The findings of this study are highly encouraging. Differences between the conditions were minute on the pretest, but the jigsaw group showed significantly more improvement on the posttest. This effect was primarily due to the minority students, who improved significantly more in the jigsaw classrooms than in the traditional classes. The Anglo students, on the other hand, were nonsignificantly different in the two conditions, so the jigsaw technique did not in any way interfere with their learning. Though this study was only two weeks long, its results are impressive: minority students profited markedly in achievement from use of the jigsaw technique, while Anglo students' performance was not hurt.

TABLE 8-1   Performance of Anglo and Minority Students in Jigsaw and Traditional Classrooms

Group	N	Performance	
		Pretest score	Adjusted posttest score*
Jigsaw			
Anglo	122	29.00	64.47
Minority	36	25.40	64.66
Traditional			
Anglo	120	29.40	62.65
Minority	25	26.20	57.02

*Raw posttest scores (which followed the same pattern) adjusted for reading level and pretest score by covariance analysis.
Source: Reprinted from Elliot Aronson and Neal Osherow, "Cooperation, Prosocial Behavior, and Academic Performance, Experiments in the Desegregated Classrooms," pp. 163–196 in Leonard Bickman, ed., *Applied Social Psychology Annual 1,* © 1980 by Society for the Psychological Study of Social Issues, Inc., with permission of Sage Publications, Inc.

Combining these findings on students' performance with the earlier data on improved peer liking, liking for school, self-esteem, and attitudes toward competitiveness and learning from others, there seems to be a strong case for using the jigsaw technique of cooperative learning in other desegregated classrooms. Considering various aspects of the classroom situation, Aronson stated, "School desegregation can open the door to increased understanding among students, but, by itself, is not the ultimate solution" (1992, p. 192). In order to achieve the full benefits of desegregated schools, it is necessary to restructure the classroom learning environment.

Cumulative Research on Cooperative Learning

The term **cooperative learning** is used to refer to any instructional program where small groups of students work together to maximize each other's learning (Johnson & Johnson, 1994). Aronson and his colleagues are only a few of the many social scientists working on cooperative learning approaches that might be useful in desegregated school situations. Sev-

eral other research groups have proposed and studied other innovative procedures based on various aspects of current social science theory. For a good overview of many other cooperative learning techniques, see volumes by Sharan (1994) or Thousand, Villa, and Nevin (1994).

The cumulative results from several hundred studies on the effects of cooperative, competitive, and individualistic learning environments have led to conclusions similar to those from the jigsaw classroom research. In recent reviews of 375 studies on cooperative learning environments, Johnson and Johnson (1989, 1994) found that working together to achieve a common goal produced higher achievement and greater productivity among students than did working alone or working competitively. They found support for a greater transfer of knowledge from one situation to another in cooperative environments, and demonstrated that cooperative learning promotes more positive relationships among the participants, even when they initially dislike each other. These results support Aronson's findings that intergroup relations improved in the jigsaw classroom, and they indicate that any heterogeneous group will be likely to show improved relationships in a cooperative learning atmosphere. See Slavin (1992) for an excellent summary of the research on cooperative learning.

Overall, the research results demonstrate that cooperative learning can have positive effects on student achievement, self-esteem, and intergroup relations. However, the long-term effects of cooperative learning environments have not yet been adequately studied. Most studies on cooperative learning have focused on a time-limited experimental intervention, and few schools have adopted it exclusively. Instead, most classroom environments continue with business as usual—mostly competitive, with an occasional cooperative activity thrown in for variety. This limitation has led some critics to question whether the effects of cooperative classrooms are due to the less-competitive learning environment, or simply to a Hawthorne effect.

One notable exception to the pattern of short-term research was a 2-year-long quasi-experiment with grade school children (Stevens & Slavin, 1995). The study included 1012 children from 45 classes in a large urban school district, with 21 of the classes adopting a cooperative learning model, and 24 classes serving as a matched control group. Data were collected at the beginning and end of each year for two years. The dependent variables were scores on standardized achievement tests, attitudes toward school work, and social relations among the children. After two years, students in the cooperative classrooms had significantly higher achievement than students in the more traditional control classrooms in reading vocabulary, reading comprehension, language expression, and math computations. These results were consistent across "normal" children, gifted children, and children with disabilities. There were also better social relations among these three groups of children in the cooperative classrooms. The results from this study clearly indicate that the benefits of a cooperative classroom are not short-term.

VIOLENCE AND YOUTH

We turn now from the topic of cooperation to a discussion of violence within school settings, and its prevention and treatment. For further study, a thorough overview of youth violence is contained in a volume stemming from the Commission on Violence and Youth of the American Psychological Association (Eron, Gentry, & Schlegel, 1994).

The United States is a violent society—in fact, one of the most violent in the world (Fingerhut & Kleinman, 1990). Homicide rates have risen sharply over recent decades, and by 1990 homicide was the second leading cause of death among young people aged 15 to 24. Death by violence claims even more young minority males and is the leading cause of death for young African American males (Bureau of Justice Statistics, 1990; Rodriguez, 1990). In addition to homicide, violent behaviors like assault, bullying, sexual abuse, rape, and physical abuse are also prevalent among youth in our society.

Schools have not been spared from these increases in violence, and surveys of urban high schools have found high rates of fighting, bullying, harassment, and the presence of weapons. Many students are bringing weapons to school in hopes of protecting themselves from this violence (Centers for Disease Control, 1991; Sheley, McGee, & Wright, 1992). For instance, a sur-

vey of students in a large urban high school in Southern California found 6% of the students reported bringing a gun to school at least once in the past year, and one-third of the students reported seeing a gun at school (Schultz & Schultz, 1996).

Given these alarming statistics, what can social psychologists do to reduce violence—both in school and out? Over the past 20 years, various interventions have been developed to treat and prevent aggressive behavior and violence among adolescents, primarily in school settings. These programs differ widely in their scope, targeted population, and theoretical framework (Guerra, Tolan, & Hammond, 1994). Early interventions were based on psychodynamic, humanistic, or behavioral theories, but in the late 1970s a new approach began to emerge—psychological skills training. Unlike its predecessors, this social psychological approach views violent behavior not as a behavior requiring psychotherapy, but as due to a deficiency in the skills necessary for effective interpersonal interactions (Goldstein, 1986).

Preventing Violence Through Social Competence

Social competence training is a broad term used to describe interventions that are based on the assumption that violence is frequently a response of persons who lack the skills necessary to manage conflict with others. Therefore, if a child learns how to assert needs, to express anger without hurting others, and to respond constructively to the anger of others, then he or she will be less likely to respond with violence. For many children, this approach is a novel way to solve problems, for they have been raised with the belief that some situations require a violent response (e.g., if your mother is insulted, or you are insulted in front of others, or you are directly challenged). Indeed, Prothrow-Stith and Weissman (1991) reported that 72% of the students they sampled agreed with the statement "a person ought to fight if challenged to fight."

Since the introduction of social competence training, many varied programs have been developed (Gable, 1986; Guerra et al., 1994). There are many ways in which these skills can be taught, and programs differ in their emphasis on behavioral techniques (like modeling and reinforcement), cognitive techniques (such as means-end thinking), or social techniques (such as social perspective-taking or normative interventions). Programs like H.A.W.K. (High Achievement, Wisdom, and Knowledge), B.U.I.L.D. (Broader Urban Involvement and Leadership Development), and S.A.V.E. (Students Against Violence Everywhere) all aim to reduce the frequency of violent behavior (Prothrow-Stith & Weissman, 1991). Most of these programs use a combination of the following techniques:

- **Monitoring**. Students are taught to observe their own thoughts, feelings, and behaviors. This is often accomplished through behavior-recording exercises, for example tallying the number of times they act in a particular way or experience a particular feeling.
- **Modeling**. Students observe nonviolent responses to a variety of provoking situations, such as failure, expressing a complaint, responding to anger, or being excluded.
- **Conflict Resolution**. Students are taught to recognize the early signs of a conflict, and they learn specific strategies to avoid escalation.
- **Role Playing**. Students engage in role playing, where they act out responses to a hypothetical conflict situation. Other students watch and evaluate these responses.
- **Peer Mediation**. Students are chosen (or sometimes elected by classmates) and trained to negotiate and resolve disputes between classmates. These mediators intervene quickly in peer conflicts in order to find nonviolent solutions that are agreeable to both sides. For a good example of such programs, see a research report by Johnson et al. (1996).

Does social skills training work? Major integrative reviews of conflict resolution programs in elementary and secondary schools are just beginning to appear (e.g., Johnson & Johnson, 1996). Given the findings described in Chapter 7 regarding the D.A.R.E. program (a substance abuse prevention program based on a rather similar knowledge-deficit assumption), you might expect that social skills training would not work. Indeed, interpersonal violence is a complex pattern of behaviors, and preventing it may hinge on many different factors (Staub, 1996).

One problem with work in this area is that many of the programs have not been empirically evaluated, making it difficult to know with any confidence whether they are producing any effects. However, a recent meta-analysis identified 49 published studies, ei-

ther experimental or quasi-experimental, conducted between 1981 and 1990 on the effects of social competence training (Beelmann, Pfingsten, & Losel, 1994). Most relevant for our discussion are the findings regarding social adjustment (i.e., less aggressiveness), and social interaction skills (positive social interactions). For the immediate effects (i.e., changes in behavior that occurred within two months of the program), the combined analysis showed an effect size (d) of .10 for social adjustment, and .34 for social interaction. That is, these programs were producing better adjustment (i.e., less aggressive behavior) and more positive social behavior than the control conditions. Moderator analyses revealed that the effects were strongest for younger children (ages 3 to 5) and at-risk children. However, in contrast to these immediate effects of the program, longer-term follow-up comparisons (defined as more than two months after the end of the program) showed disappointing results—the effect sizes for social adjustment ($d = -.07$) and social interaction skills ($d = .05$) were not significant.

The results from this meta-analysis suggest that, over the short term, social competency training programs can reduce aggressive behavior and improve social interaction skills. However, the long-term effects of these programs are in doubt, though some more-focused social competency interventions have been able to demonstrate long-term effects (e.g., Deffenbacher et al., 1996). One notable instance is the ACHIEVE program for at-risk youth (Knoff & Batsche, 1995). Unlike typical social competency training programs, ACHIEVE focuses on the classroom management and conflict resolution skills of *teachers*, rather than students. This program produced reductions in student disobedience, fighting, disruptiveness, abusive behavior, and disrespectfulness over a 3-year period. As an example, the number of referrals to the principal's office for fighting dropped from 215 in 1990–91 to 82 in 1992–93 (Knoff & Batsche, 1995).

Clearly there are many aspects of the school behavior setting that can influence the effectiveness of interventions against violence—the type of student, the school atmosphere, and the skills of teachers and students all need to be considered. This promises to be an area of active research and advancement in the next ten years.

TEACHER EXPECTANCIES— PYGMALION IN THE CLASSROOM

Another line of research that is particularly important in school settings is studying how the expectations held by a teacher can influence the social, emotional, and cognitive development of a student. This process has been termed the **Pygmalion effect**, named for the mythical sculptor who created the statue of a woman and brought it to life.

In a book entitled *Pygmalion in the Classroom*, Rosenthal and Jacobson (1968) evoked considerable controversy in both psychology and education. The book claimed that the expectations held by a teacher had a direct influence on the subsequent development of students, and it supported this claim with results from a study in which students in several classes had been randomly selected and identified to their teachers as likely to "bloom" that year. At the end of the school year, research data showed that these students had in fact "bloomed," showing a significant increase in intelligence scores in comparison to control students. The importance of this finding is not just in the positive effects of labeling, but also in the potential harm that teachers might do their students through low expectations (termed the **Golem effect**—Babad, Inbar, & Rosenthal, 1982).

The potential for negative consequences of teacher expectations is especially problematic in desegregated classrooms, where minority students may be more likely to receive expectations of lower ability. These expectations are then likely to be confirmed through student-teacher interactions. In the following sections we will address four key issues. First, do teacher expectations influence student performance? Second, how do the expectations become reality? Third, what are the expectations for minority students in comparison to White students? And finally, how can the research knowledge be used to increase student performance on a large scale?

Do Teachers' Expectations Influence Students' Performance?

This is the most fundamental question regarding the Pygmalion effect. Although the question may appear simple, it is difficult to determine if changes or differences in student performance are directly attributable to teachers' expectations, to the exclusion of any other variable. Many other potential variables (e.g., intelligence, motivation, level of aspiration, and/or parental support) could be responsible for what appears to be a teacher expectancy effect. The original Pygmalion study produced a flurry of research, and after nearly 30 years, it is possible to review and synthesize these studies into some solid conclusions.

A meta-analysis by Rosenthal and Rubin (1978) combined the results of 345 studies on interpersonal expectancies, and concluded that teacher expectations *do* influence student performance. This conclusion has been echoed in many subsequent studies and reviews (e.g., Harris & Rosenthal, 1985). These types of findings have led Cooper (1993) to call the effects of interpersonal expectations a "social fact"—a strong conclusion from a scientific approach that bases findings on probabilities and statistical analyses.

How large are the effects produced by teachers? Can a teacher's expectations turn a failing student into an honor student, or vice versa? Even if the research findings support the existence of a teacher expectancy effect, how much difference can a teacher's expectations really make in a student's performance? The research to date suggests that teacher expectancies can account for between 5% and 10% of the variance in student performance (Babad, 1993; Brophy, 1983). Brophy (1983) argued that this is a negligible effect. However, this is not the opinion of most researchers in the area, who maintain that 5%–10% is a substantial amount of variance to explain, especially regarding something as important as students' academic performance.

The Process of Expectancy Confirmation

Given that researchers have established that the expectations held by teachers can affect their students, the second question is how this process occurs. Methodologically, this question becomes a search for variables that mediate the expectation-confirmation relationship. As Cooper (1993) noted, a great many studies have investigated the process of expectancy mediation since publication of the original *Pygmalion* research. The cumulative results from these studies show that teachers behave in ways that lead students to act consistently with their expectations. For example, students who are perceived as low in ability tend to be called on less often in class, receive less eye contact from their teachers, and in general do not get the same amount of attention as students perceived to have high ability.

Research on the Pygmalion effect has attempted to pinpoint the types of teacher behaviors that lead students to act in ways consistent with their expectations. Rosenthal (1973) suggested a 4-factor theory for the mediation process (see also Harris, 1993; Harris & Rosenthal, 1985, 1986). The four factors are:

1. **Climate**—teachers' affective behaviors (e.g., warmth, support, smiling, eye contact) and the socio-emotional climate they create for high- and low-expectancy students.
2. **Feedback**—teachers' praise and criticism of students; their acceptance or acknowledgment of a student's statement or request.
3. **Input**—amount or difficulty of material presented to the student.
4. **Output**—opportunities for the student to respond (e.g., frequency of contact between the student and teacher, such as questions asked by the teacher).

Through these types of behaviors, teachers influence the actions of their students. More recent research suggests that the climate and feedback behaviors are the most crucial actions in the expectancy confirmation process (Harris, 1993).

Expectations Concerning Minority Students

One central assumption of the Pygmalion effect is that many expectations held by teachers are not accurate. Because students in an experiment must be randomly assigned to conditions, any experiment on teacher expectations must necessarily introduce biased information about the students in the study. However, some researchers have argued that, in real life, teachers generally form accurate expectations for their students, and that the Pygmalion effect research is misleading because the studies instill false expectations in teachers (Brophy, 1983, 1985; Jussim, 1989, 1993).

The belief that teachers form accurate expectations about their students rests on the assumption that humans are rational processors of information. It views teachers as unbiased perceivers who evaluate students solely on information that is relevant to their performance. However, cognitive and social psychological research on interpersonal perception demonstrates this is far from true. Expectations about behavior come from many sources irrelevant to the actual ability of the student, and they are subject to a multitude of cognitive biases. Particularly relevant to the issue of diversity in educational settings is the fact that expectations about a student are often based on *stereotypes* concerning categories of people that the student belongs to. These categories include gender, ethnicity, social class, and age, to name a few. Knowledge of these stereotypes can threaten the self-concepts and discourage the ambitions of students in the stereotyped group, as demonstrated in research by Claude Steele that is described in Chapter 9. In the following brief paragraphs we will focus on ethnicity as a category. For a discussion of expectations based on gender, see Good and Findley (1985), as well as Chapter 9.

Intuitively, it makes sense that students from minority groups, or other groups about which there are negative stereotypes, would be harmed by the Golem effect. That is, teachers would tend to form lower expectations for these students based not on their ability, but on stereotypes about the group (Alexander & Entwisle, 1988). Baron, Tom, and Cooper (1985) provided support for this intuition. In reviewing the research on teacher expectancies, they found that Black students tended to receive lower teacher expectations of mental ability and academic performance than did White students. Results from research on Mexican Americans paralleled those for African Americans. Another finding from the review was that students from a lower-class background consistently had lower teacher expectations for performance and ability than did middle-class students. Given the frequent relationship between ethnic minority status and lower social class, this finding adds strength to the notion that teachers will hold lower expectations for minority students.

Though these results indicate that teachers will tend to have lower expectations for minority children than for White children, this may not be the case for all teachers. Some types of teachers may be more resistant to forming lower expectations than others. For example, minority teachers may be less likely than White teachers to have low expectations of minority students. In contrast, teachers who score high on authoritarianism (see Chapter 2) may be more likely to form low expectations of minorities.

Applied Interventions to Increase Teacher Expectancies

The research on teacher expectations has prompted a national call to raise the expectations for all students, particularly those that are at risk for failure. If a teacher's expectations influence student performance, then raising expectations should produce a concomitant increase in student performance. To this end, many different interventions have been developed. These interventions are typically implemented in "in-service" training programs for teachers, and they attempt to heighten teachers' awareness of differential expectations, and to change behaviors that lead to confirmation of negative expectations (Babad, 1993; Weinstein, Madison, & Kuklinski, 1995; Weinstein et al., 1991).

One example of this type of intervention was reported by Weinstein et al. (1991). The purpose of the study was to increase teachers' awareness of the potential harm resulting from lower expectations for at-risk students, 90% of whom were minority. The participants in the study were all incoming ninth-grade students that were assigned to the lowest track of English classes at a single high school. Over a 2-year period, 158 students participated in the experimental intervention, and were contrasted with 154 comparable students from cohorts two years prior to the intervention. Thus, the study had a quasi-experimental design. The year-long intervention focused on changing the classroom environment for the ninth-grade students by raising the performance expectations of teachers. After one year of the intervention, students participating in the project had higher English and history grades than comparable students who did not participate in the project, as well as higher overall GPAs. A year after participating in the intervention, project students were less likely to drop out of high school, and less likely to attend a continuation school than were control students. However, the improvements in school grades were short-lived, and a year after participating in the program, there was no difference in grades between project students and control students. The results from this study are encouraging, and they suggest that interventions targeting teachers' expectations for student performance can be an effective technique to improve the educational experiences of at-risk students.

EDUCATING STUDENTS WITH DIFFERING ABILITIES

In any classroom, students will have a variety of abilities. The greater the diversity of students, the more difficult it is to educate them all simultaneously in a classroom setting. American schools, and most schools around the world, attempt to reduce the heterogeneity of student ability by grouping them according to chronological age, and classifying them at specific grade levels. However, no group of students will ever have completely equal abilities. Their differing abilities may be cognitive, social, or physical, and can facilitate or impede their education. In the section that follows we will discuss, from a social psychological perspective, some of the issues that arise in educating students with differing abilities.

Head Start

During the 1960s, government officials became aware that half of the 30 million Americans living in poverty were children, and a large percentage of poor households were headed by a person with only a grade-school education (Zigler & Muenchow, 1992; Zigler, Styfco, & Gilman, 1993). To help break the cycle of poverty, the federal government attempted to increase the education level of children living in poverty. It was recognized that, at home, many poor children did not receive the kind of educational background necessary to succeed in public school, and thus were behind from the beginning of the school process. In the Economic Opportunity Act of 1964, the Head Start program was established. The program was developed as a way to reach poor children and provide them with the background education necessary to succeed in school. (For a review of other educational interventions with at-risk children, see Slavin, Karweit, & Wasik, 1994.)

The ultimate goal of the Head Start program was for all children to be "school ready" by the time they entered the public education system. In this sense it was a preventive program, rather than a remedial one. It targeted children up to age 3, and it was anticipated to expand its coverage to grade-school-aged children (Kennedy, 1993). As with many government programs, when Head Start was first established, it was not based on a solid foundation of scientific evidence. As Zigler et al. (1993) noted: "Head Start began as a hastily assembled but immense program built more on professional intuition than on scientific fact" (p. 6).

Despite this lack of an initial research base, Head Start became a national laboratory, and has continued to be thoroughly studied and evaluated. Early evaluations of the Head Start program focused especially on increases in intelligence. Research showing higher IQ scores for children who graduated from Head Start than for comparable samples of non-Head Start children gained nationwide attention, despite a highly publicized Westinghouse research report claiming that the short-term gains in IQ and later school achievement "faded-out" over time (Cicirelli et al., 1969). More recent research has confirmed the short-term gains in intelligence, and has demonstrated a wide range of other advantages of the program, including better health, better social adjustment, improved academic performance, higher secondary school graduation rates, greater employment rates after graduation, less juvenile delinquency and criminality, and lower teen pregnancy rates (Berrueta-Clement et al., 1984; Copple, Cline, & Smith, 1987; Hebbeler, 1985; McKey et al., 1985).

A cost-benefit analysis of the savings to society produced by the Head Start program—from reductions in spending on special education, repetition of school grades, welfare, and criminal justice, as well as positive contributions to taxes due to higher employment rates—showed that for every dollar spent on Head Start programs, the government achieved a savings of between $3 and $6 (Barnett, 1985). This type of research helped increase the public and governmental support for the program, which allowed the program to expand and cover a wider range of ages. (The program currently extends services through age 5, and is projected to expand to cover all grade-school-aged children.) In fiscal year 1994, the program received approximately $7.7 billion dollars in federal funding, and served more than 541,000 children (Zigler et al., 1993).

Bilingual Classrooms

Another issue that arises in diverse classroom settings is **bilingual education**. National surveys of academic achievement have consistently found that minority students, especially those with low English proficiency, are at-risk for academic failure (Steinberg, Blinde, & Chan, 1984). Particularly in cities with a high immigrant population, an important question is whether the students with limited English proficiency should be taught in a bilingual classroom, where teachers speak both English and the student's native language, or whether these students should be immersed in an English-only instructional program. At issue are both the benefits to the child, and the costs to society. Many scholars have asserted that the public school system is intended to provide a similar education to our culturally and racially diverse populace, and therefore classroom environments in which immigrant students do not receive an equal quality of education because of a language barrier are detrimental to this goal (DeVillar, 1994). This viewpoint argues for teaching students in their own language, at least until they have developed adequate English proficiency. For this reason as well as others, the multicultural movement in the American education system advocates the need for bilingual education.

From a social psychological perspective, the central question is whether or not students with low English proficiency are better served by special classrooms, or by **mainstreaming** them with the other children. That is, which produces the most beneficial results for the student? In this line of research, "beneficial" results are usually measured in terms of subsequent academic achievement and levels of English proficiency. Costs and ideology aside, the available data indicate that low

English-proficiency students taught in a bilingual classroom require less time to master the English language and score higher on standardized math and vocabulary tests (Gonzalez, 1994; Ramirez, 1986; Willig, 1985). However, nearly all of the studies conducted in this area have been quasi-experiments, in which students enrolled in different types of programs are compared, and these comparison groups are never fully equivalent. Furthermore, many of the studies also have high attrition rates, they frequently lack complete data on many students, and no distinction is usually made between immigrant children and children who are not immigrants but whose parents do not speak English. Nevertheless, the available data do suggest that bilingual classrooms facilitate mastery of the English language, after which point their graduates can be mainstreamed with the other students.

SUMMARY

Social psychologists have worked on many educational issues, but none where they have had greater involvement or influence than the topic of school desegregation. Though the Supreme Court's 1954 *Brown v. Board of Education* desegregation decision was based on constitutional rights, it specifically cited social science evidence about the effects of segregation. More than 40 years later, thousands of U.S. communities have desegregated their schools with relatively little disruption, but some others have suffered through riots or protracted legal suits or massive local resistance and "White flight."

Many reviews of subsequent desegregation studies have found generally similar conclusions. Retrospective or cross-sectional surveys of Blacks who have gone to integrated schools generally show that their achievement is higher than segregated comparison groups', but these findings could be due to cultural change, self-selection, or other correlated personal characteristics. The few good longitudinal studies also show higher educational attainment over the long term, and higher employment income, for minorities who attended desegregated schools and/or colleges. In contrast, short-term studies of desegregation have sometimes shown decreases in the self-esteem of minority

students, and fairly frequent increases in racial tensions and prejudice on the part of both Whites and minorities. However, very few of these studies were done in situations where the conditions that should create favorable effects were present. In short, merely combining racial groups in a school is far from enough to create truly integrated conditions.

Consequently many social scientists have turned their efforts toward developing a more effective process of desegregation, typically stressing equal-status, cooperative learning situations. Aronson's version of this concept, called the jigsaw classroom, features cooperative learning and peer teaching in small groups for a few hours a week. Research with the jigsaw technique has found that it maintains students' liking for school and increases liking for group members, self-esteem, cooperativeness, and openness to learning from other students. Best of all, it improves the school performance of minority students while maintaining that of Whites.

A major problem of intergroup relations in schools is youth violence. Social competency training programs are interventions intended to reduce the level of violent behavior. These interventions use a combination of social psychological principles to teach students how to have positive interactions with others, and how to deal effectively with conflict. Evaluations of these programs have shown favorable short-term effects, but their long-term effects remain questionable.

Another important issue in the area of intergroup relations and learning is the effects of teacher expectations. The "Pygmalion effect" occurs when teachers act in ways that cause students to fulfill the teacher's expectations. This is especially problematic for students who come from a minority group about which teachers may have stereotypes and lower expectations, but cooperative learning environments may help to combat this problem.

A pioneering social program for teaching students with differing abilities is the Head Start program, which helps preschool students from a poor socioeconomic background acquire the skills necessary to succeed in school. Evaluations of the program have demonstrated short-term increases in IQ scores, as well as more long-term improvements in social adjustment, high school graduation rates, less teen pregnancy, and less juvenile delinquency. Other differentiated educational programs like bilingual education for low English-proficiency students often evoke much controversy. However, empirical data indicate that bilingual education produces faster English language and mathematics learning.

SUGGESTED READINGS

Allport, F. H., et al. (1953). The effects of segregation and the consequences of desegregation: A social science statement. *Minnesota Law Review*, *37*, 429–440.—This is the actual text of the statement, signed by 32 eminent social scientists, which was submitted to the Supreme Court as an appendix to the brief in the case of *Brown v. Board of Education*.

Aronson, E., Blaney, N., Stephan, C., Sikes, J., & Snapp, M. (1978). *The jigsaw classroom*. Beverly Hills, CA: Sage.—This short book gives a very readable description of the jigsaw technique and presents sample curriculum materials, team-building exercises, and procedures for teacher-training workshops.

Blanck, P. (Ed.). (1993). *Interpersonal expectations: Theory, research, and application*. New York: Cambridge University Press.—An excellent edited book on the effects of interpersonal expectations, with chapters by the leading researchers in the field, and stressing applications to education, organizations, and legal issues.

Eron, L. D., Gentry, J. H., & Schlegel, P. (Eds.). (1994). *Reason to hope: A psychosocial perspective on violence and youth*. Washington, DC: American Psychological Association.—Chapters written by outstanding authorities summarize many aspects of youth violence in our society and incorporate the recommendations of the Commission on Violence and Youth of the American Psychological Association.

Fife, B. L. (1992). *Desegregation in American schools: Comparative intervention strategies*. New York: Praeger.—A useful collection of chapters summarizing the historical and legal background of desegregation, including some case studies of events in specific cities, and several controversial proposals for future policy.

Stephan, W. G. (1991). School desegregation: Short-term and long-term effects. In H. Knopke, R. Norrell, & R. Rogers (Eds.), *Opening doors: Perspectives on race relations in contemporary America* (pp. 100–118). Tuscaloosa: University of Alabama Press.—Reviews the research literature on the short- and long-term consequences of school desegregation.

CHAPTER 9

Diversity Issues— Gender and Ethnicity

✧✧

We must recognize the whole gamut of human potentialities, and so weave a less arbitrary social fabric, one in which each diverse human gift will find a fitting place.

—Margaret Mead

Human beings differ on countless attributes—height, hair color, handedness, shoe size, age, national origin, rural-urban residence, amount of education, religious beliefs, physical abilities and disabilities, and so on. In a word, we are *diverse*. Yet we often react to other individuals by classifying them into categories on the basis of one or a few of these characteristics. In this chapter we will focus on two of the dimensions which are used most often in our society to classify individuals into social groups—gender and ethnicity.

The same principles that apply to these central dimensions are apt to be applicable to other less salient dimensions (Thomas, 1995). In a sense all of these differences are cultural ones, even the apparently physical and temporal ones like gender, height, and age. That is so because cultural beliefs and norms determine how people with these characteristics are treated. Some societies revere and defer to their elderly, while others treat them cruelly or patronizingly. Some societies limit women to child care and housework duties, while others expect them to do heavy labor outside of the home.

Diversity as a topic is a quite recent way of conceptualizing individual differences. A dictionary definition of the term is "the state of being varied, dissimilar, or unlike." There are still relatively few books on the topic, and almost all of them were written in the 1990s. In earlier years, it was more common to focus on single dimensions of individual differences, such as intelligence, age, sex, or race, rather than on the collection or mixture of characteristics. Use of the single term to include differences along all of these dimensions implies, as stated above, that people's responses to these differences follow many similar principles.

FRAMEWORK FOR STUDYING DIVERSITY

Figure 9-1 presents a schematic framework proposed by Triandis (1995) that can be used to analyze relationships between any differing groups—Bosnians and Serbs, African Americans and Euro-Americans, Hispanics and Anglos, or men and women.[1] In the figure the size of boxes does not have any intrinsic meaning, but the number of arrows coming to and/or leaving a box shows the centrality or importance of the concept in the box. One thing that the figure shows immediately is the very large number of variables that must be considered in order to understand intergroup relations (and this framework is admittedly a great simplification of real-life situations). In time span, these key variables range from the past history of the groups, and the degree of cultural distance between them (at the top of the diagram), through individuals' present knowledge about the other group, to their goals for the future. A second point is the centrality in this scheme of *perceived similarity* and *opportunity for positive contact* with members of the other group. Another of the key variables determining the progression of intergroup relationships is the *rewards* that participants feel as a result of the interaction. Finally, the outcome variables in this scheme (at the bottom of the figure) represent the degree of success in adapting to group differences, as shown by experiencing relatively little "culture shock" and by making appropriate accommodations.

A few of the terms in the framework may need brief explanation. One of the most important is **cultural dis-**

---

[1]For variety in expression, in this chapter we will switch between using the terms African American or Black and Euro-American or White, with a full realization that these shorthand terms are oversimplifications, and that each group has great within-group variability of characteristics. A recent national survey of Black adults about their preferred term showed that 17% preferred Black, 17% preferred African American, and 58% said it didn't matter—though a somewhat greater proportion of respondents under age 30 preferred African American (*Gallup Poll Monthly*, 1995, August).

In similar national polls, Americans of Spanish descent indicated by large margins that they preferred terms referring to their national origin, such as Mexican American (de La Garza et al., 1992). However, among pan-national terms, 62% preferred Hispanic, 10% preferred Latino, and 24% said it didn't matter (McAneny, 1994).

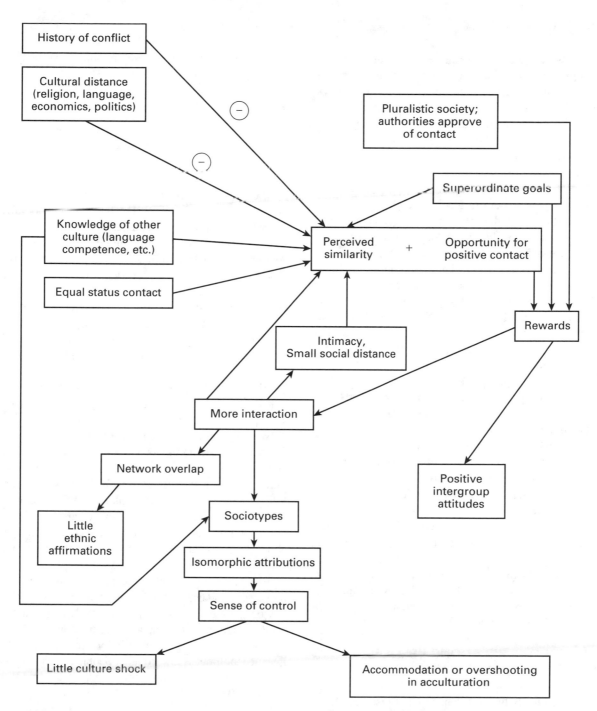

FIGURE 9-1 A theoretical model for the study of diversity. (Source: Modified and reproduced by special permission of the Publisher, Consulting Psychologists Press, Inc., Palo Alto, CA 94303 from **Handbook of Industrial and Organizational Psychology, Second Edition, Volume 4** by Marvin D. Dunnette and Leatta M. Hough, editors. Copyright 1994 by Consulting Psychologists Press, Inc. All rights reserved. Further reproduction is prohibited without the Publisher's written consent.)

tance, which refers to the degree of difference between groups in the important dimensions of language, religion, family structure, political, and economic systems. It may also include subjective, perceived differences in value systems, attitudes, customs, or practices between the groups. The central variable of **perceived similarity** is often dichotomized into perceived ingroup or outgroup membership, and the context of judgment may shift that perception dramatically. For instance, people who might be seen as different because of their gender, ethnicity, age, or language, in other contexts may be seen as ingroup members—part of "my team," "my company," or "my nation."

In this model, the variable of **contact** between groups has several important dimensions: its frequency, quality, and the degree to which it is individual and personal (Islam & Hewstone, 1993). With more interaction and higher quality interaction between groups, individuals' stereotyped beliefs about the other group are likely to become **sociotypes**, Triandis's term for valid stereotypes. Similarly, accurate perceptions of the other group are conducive to **isomorphic attributions**—that is, attributions or causal beliefs on which members of different groups agree. For instance, they attribute the same meaning to a given behavior, such as the idea that shaking one's head horizontally means "no" or that smiling indicates friendliness. Making isomorphic attributions increases another important variable, the *sense of predictability and control* that a person feels he/she has in an interaction. A sense of control indicates the possibility of favorable outcomes, and without it, a person is unlikely to want to continue the interaction. With a sense of control, individuals are more likely to avoid feelings of culture shock and successfully accommodate their behavior to new groups and situations (Triandis, 1995).

INTERGROUP RELATIONS—BELIEFS, ATTITUDES, AND BEHAVIOR

Relationships between groups are not just a matter of how their members behave toward each other. Fundamental to those intergroup behaviors are the beliefs and attitudes that their members hold, as well as the norms and institutionalized practices of the societies within

which they exist. All of these variables have had extensive study by social scientists.

Some Definitions

Stereotypes are sets of beliefs that a person holds about the characteristics of most members of a particular social group. By their very nature, stereotypes are highly simplified sets of beliefs; typically they contain clear evaluative elements and are rather rigidly resistant to change (Oskamp, 1991). Thus, they cannot fully describe the group's characteristics, and research shows that they are often inaccurate, though they may contain a "kernel of truth" about some aspect of the group (Brigham, 1971). However, inaccurate or not, stereotypes about other groups are *useful* to their holders in the sense that they reduce the complexity of the world into a few simple guidelines that suggest how members of those groups should be treated. When similar stereotypes are *shared* by many people, they have a powerful influence on patterns of intergroup behavior. For instance, the Nazis promulgated the stereotype that Jews were unclean and subhuman, and Germans were pressured to treat them accordingly.

We may define intergroup **attitudes** as feelings or emotions toward members of another group, involving evaluation or favorability (Oskamp, 1991). That is, attitudes are not just beliefs, but feelings of liking or disliking for the group—for example, preference for one's own group, or fear or antagonism toward a different group. **Values** are very important and central attitudes about the life goals that are important to one—strong favorable attitudes toward abstract concepts like freedom or justice, or toward more concrete goals such as money or good health. **Social norms** are patterns of behavior that are *expected* to be displayed in a particular social situation, though people's actual behavior is often found to diverge from verbally stated norms. For instance, politeness toward other people is normatively expected in our society, but many people are impolite in actual everyday situations.

Intergroup Biases

Next we will examine a number of more specific variables that influence intergroup relationships. **Inter-**

group biases are cognitive and emotional tendencies to evaluate and treat one's own group more favorably than outgroups. Classic research by Tajfel (1970) on the "minimal intergroup situation" has shown that these tendencies are not based on objective characteristics of the group, for they can be produced quickly and easily about any artificially created group, no matter how flimsy its basis for existence. For instance, in laboratory experiments a dot-estimation task has often been used, in which subjects are asked to estimate the number of dots that are quickly flashed on a screen. Then each person is (randomly) told that he or she under- or overestimated the number, and accordingly is assigned to a group of "underestimators" or "overestimators." No information is given about who else is in either group, the groups have no interaction, and no other rational basis for evaluating the groups is provided. Nevertheless, subjects will immediately show preferences for their group and discriminate against the outgroup, as shown by assigning higher monetary payoffs to anonymous "members" of their own "group," rating them more favorably, and so on. The same effect occurs even when the basis of categorization is explicitly made random, as in drawing letters A or B from a container (e.g., Crocker & Schwartz, 1985).

In real-life groups, similar but stronger tendencies occur. Cross-cultural research has found an apparently universal tendency to view one's own group as morally superior and more trustworthy than outgroups (Brewer, 1986). The tendency to rate one's own group as better than others is one major aspect of **ethnocentrism**, a personality trait which also includes rejection of outgroups and a view of one's own group as the standard against which all others should be judged.

Another useful concept is **social dominance orientation**, a general attitudinal preference for intergroup relations to be hierarchical, combined with the attitude that one's own group is superior to other groups and should dominate them (Pratto et al., 1994). People high in social dominance orientation tend to believe in ideologies such as racism, classism, and religious superiority and to enforce them actively. Research has shown that social dominance orientation is positively correlated with political-economic conservatism, nationalism, ethnic prejudice, and support for military pro-

grams and punitive criminal policies. As you might expect, it is negatively correlated with support for women's rights, government social programs in general, and programs aimed at helping racial minorities (Pratto et al., 1994).

Prejudice and Racism

Prejudice can be defined as an intolerant, unfair, or irrational unfavorable *attitude* toward another group of people (Oskamp, 1991, p. 373). Literally, it means "prejudgment" of others, which could be positive or negative, but in current use it generally means negative attitudes that aren't justified by the facts. **Discrimination** is unequal treatment or unfair *behavior* toward some people but not toward others. When strong prejudice is directed at an ethnic group, it becomes an aspect of **racism**, which is "hostility, discrimination, segregation, and other negative *action* expressed toward an ethnic group" (Marx, 1970, p. 101). Such racist behavior also inevitably has an ideological element—belief in the superiority of a particular race and its right to domination over others (Zuckerman, 1990).

Racism can be *individual*, as in cases where a person organizes much of his or her life around opposition to another racial group. An even more powerful form is **institutional racism**, which includes both formal laws and regulations as well as informal, but powerful, social norms that limit the opportunities and choices available to certain ethnic groups. Examples are segregated school systems, laws prohibiting interracial marriages, racial or religious restrictions on hiring or promotion, "White only" country clubs, and tests or other qualification requirements that unfairly discriminate against particular groups. Individual and institutional racism can act separately, but generally they are mutually reinforcing. Institutional racism cannot develop or survive without support from many individual racists, and individual racism is much less likely to be expressed and to spread without strong societal support.

Intergroup Anxiety

A concept which specifically spotlights the negative affect that is common in intergroup relations is the notion of **intergroup anxiety** (Stephan & Stephan,

1985). It can be defined as the cognitive worry and the physiological arousal that people may feel when interacting with members of an outgroup. Three main types of consequences have been predicted as reactions to the experience of intergroup anxiety. Behaviorally, avoidance of the anxiety-arousing situation would be a common response. However, if interaction does occur, a person's dominant responses to a situation would be amplified; thus, if the situation normally evoked politeness, anxious people would respond extremely— even excessively—politely. Similarly, emotional responses would be augmented and polarized, depending on the outcome of the interaction, toward strongly favorable or strongly unfavorable feelings about outgroup members. Cognitively, the worry and arousal that was experienced would be apt to strengthen information processing biases, such as relying on previous expectancies and stereotypes (Stephan, 1994).

Empirical research has supported several of this model's main points. For instance, even anticipating interacting with ethnic outgroup members typically elicits physiological signs of arousal (Vander Kolk, 1978), and intergroup anxiety is often accompanied by avoidance of interaction (e.g., Glick, Abbott, & Hotze, 1988).

Reactions of Stigmatized Groups

There is abundant evidence of prejudice and discrimination being directed at ethnic minorities and other stigmatized groups, such as people with physical disabilities. Turning to the reactions of members of these stigmatized and ill-treated groups, many psychological theories predict that they would suffer from low self-confidence and self-esteem because of their awareness of others devaluing and rejecting them (e.g., Cooley, 1956). However, despite the negative social and economic consequences of prejudice and discrimination, empirical studies show that members of stigmatized groups often do not display lowered self-esteem (Crocker & Major, 1989). In fact, they sometimes make a virtue of their stigmatizing condition, as in the "Black pride" movement.

Careful research on the general self-esteem of stigmatized or oppressed individuals has suggested several mechanisms by which they can protect themselves

from the negative appraisals of others (Crocker & Major, 1989). First, they may attribute any negative feedback or poor outcomes to prejudice on the part of others rather than to their own inadequacies. Second, they may compare their own outcomes to those of ingroup members rather than to those of advantaged outgroups. Third, when they recognize their less favorable position on some characteristic (e.g., athletic ability, or income), they are likely to minimize the size of the difference, selectively devalue the importance of that characteristic, or focus attention on other aspects where they feel superior.

Intergroup Behaviors—Discrimination and Hate Crimes

As mentioned above, discrimination is unequal or unfair treatment of people, based on their group membership. Though one would expect prejudiced attitudes and discriminatory behavior toward a social group to go hand-in-hand, there are many situations where that is not the case. Most of these are situations where social norms are opposed to private attitudes. For instance, a prejudiced person may fail to discriminate against members of a minority ethnic group because laws require equal treatment or because other majority group members in the setting are displaying patterns of equal treatment. On the other hand, a nonprejudiced person may go along with discriminatory treatment of a stigmatized person without thinking about the inconsistency, or due to ingroup pressure or fear of being ostracized.

The most extreme form of discrimination is **hate crimes**, such as spray-painting swastikas or racial epithets, burning down or vandalizing property, personal beatings, or murder. Violence against individuals from stigmatized groups increased substantially in the U.S. in the 1980s and 1990s. A recent volume analyzed a sample of hate crimes and classified them into three major types (Levin & McDevitt, 1993). The most common type is *thrill* hate crimes, which are usually committed quite randomly by small groups of young males, who are looking for "excitement" and find it by bashing a stranger who appears different from them. *Defensive* hate crimes are responses by highly prejudiced individuals to perceived "intrusions" by some stigmatized person into their neighborhood or workplace or campus. They are often committed by a single individual and frequently involve an escalating series of assaults. *Mission* hate crimes are the rarest but most serious category; they are committed by members of hate groups such as the Ku Klux Klan or Skinheads, who view them as attempts to rid the world of all members of some "inferior" or "treasonous" group. Examples include lynchings and the 1995 bombing of the federal building in Oklahoma City.

Institutionalized Norms and Practices

Institutionalized norms and practices frequently form patterns of institutional racism. In many cases though, practices that distinguish a certain group may have completely legitimate reasons, such as requiring identifying uniforms for police and fire personnel or protective hardhats for construction workers. However, such clothing distinctions can easily shade over into invidious discrimination, as in voluntary wearing of gang colors or the Nazi requirement for Jews to wear yellow stars. Similarly, voluntarily chosen costumes, such as punk attire or Hasidic beards, may provide stimuli for the expression of prejudice by others.

Some discriminatory practices may be required by law, for example, apartheid in South Africa or similar legal "Jim Crow" segregation in the American South up until the 1950s, which required separate schools, bus and railroad waiting rooms, and even separate drinking fountains for Blacks and Whites. Similar outcomes may be accomplished by informal means, such as "redlining" by realtors, which kept ethnic minorities out of desirable residential neighborhoods, or the "glass ceiling" which prevents most women employees from reaching higher management levels.

Sometimes these institutionalized practices are established for the supposed good of the stigmatized group, such as special education classes for slow learners or other special classes for students with physical disabilities. However, opponents of these practices point out that they perpetuate and expand the areas of unequal treatment, often far more than is necessary—for instance, a student in a wheelchair may be able to take an equal role in all school activities except physical education, and thus is being unfairly treated if seg-

regated from able-bodied students for the whole school day.

GENDER

The principles and concepts discussed above apply to many different categories of minority groups, though not equally to all. We turn now to discussion of research findings about males and females. Though not a numerical minority, women experience many of the same discriminatory treatments as small ethnic groups, so they have sometimes been called "the 52% minority."

Gender Comparisons

Though the term **gender** has been used in various ways, recently it has been most often used to designate the *socially determined* psychological and behavioral characteristics of males and females—that is, learned and culturally influenced ways of thinking, feeling, and acting. In contrast, **sex** now usually refers only to biologically determined differences between males and females, such as physiological characteristics and behaviors related to procreation and childbearing. We have adopted that usage for this volume. Thus, we consider **gender roles** as social expectations—learned cultural prescriptions for sex-appropriate personality and behavior (Oskamp, 1991).

Gender differences have been a topic of fascination for as long as human history has been recorded. Though they have been celebrated in myth, literature, and psychological theories, when careful empirical studies have been done, the extent of measured gender differences has been rather small. For example, a classic volume by Maccoby and Jacklin (1974) summarized decades of research and concluded that there were very few characteristics that displayed consistent gender differences between the average scores for males and females. Furthermore, even when consistent gender differences were found, the amount of variance they accounted for was small in comparison with the amount of variation within each gender. Some of the most clear-cut differences are that men average somewhat higher scores on tests of mathematical and spatial abilities, and in the domain of social behavior men are more often physically aggressive than women. Similarly, preschool-aged boys are much more inclined to rough-and-tumble play than are girls, both in the U.S. and in other cultures that have been studied (White, 1983). Women typically score much higher on tests of verbal associational fluency such as stating synonyms (Hines, 1990).

In recent years, meta-analyses combining the results of dozens of empirical studies on a particular type of behavior have more clearly pinpointed the nature and size of gender differences in several realms (Eagly, 1995). For example, using this methodology, Eagly (1987) reported that men are more likely than women to help a stranger who appears to need it, and that women are generally somewhat more influenceable than men. The male-female differences found in meta-analyses, though significant because of the large total number of people in the combined studies, were often small to moderate in size (Eagly, 1995). For instance, gender only accounted for 1% of the variance in influenceability. However, even this small a difference may have quite large practical effects in real-life situations (cf. Martell, Lane, & Emrich, 1996). An additional fact that made the picture more complex was that studies by male researchers typically found a gender difference in influenceability whereas studies by female researchers did not—suggesting that the finding stemmed partly from the nature of interactions between experimenters and research subjects (Eagly & Carli, 1981). These results illustrate the topic of experimenter expectancies, which we discussed in Chapter 4.

A new perspective which challenges past findings of minimal gender differences has been presented by Maccoby (1990), who studied the effect of the *interaction context* and reported that it led to large behavioral differences between boys and girls. Specifically, the sex of the child's interactive partner makes a great difference in the type of behavior displayed. Both boys and girls of preschool age have much higher levels of social interactive behavior when playing with a same-sex partner than with an opposite-sex partner. For example, the opposite of interactive behavior, passive behavior (merely watching the partner play with a toy) is a rather frequent response of girls in girl-boy pairs, though it is not more common overall among girls than among boys. It occurs very seldom in girl-girl pairs,

and somewhat more often in boy-boy pairs (Jacklin & Maccoby, 1978). Thus, the sex of the interaction partner greatly influences social behavior. Moreover, children are increasingly likely to choose same-sex playmates after their early-preschool years. As early as age 4, children spend about three times as much time with same-sex playmates as with opposite-sex ones, and that imbalance increases markedly by age 6 (to a ratio of 11 to 1—Maccoby & Jacklin, 1987).

We will return to findings about gender differences as we discuss some later topics, such as leadership.

Gender Stereotypes

Stereotypes about gender differences generally view them as being large on many key traits, and on some dimensions they diverge from the research findings about actual behavior that we have just summarized. Moreover, despite some variations across cultures and historical eras, they show a surprising degree of similarity in their major themes. This was demonstrated in all 25 of the nations, ranging from Peru to Malaysia, where gender stereotypes were studied by Williams and Best (1990). For instance, across these nations, women were seen as more sentimental, submissive, and superstitious, whereas men were seen as more adventurous, forceful, and independent. Studies in the U.S. indicate that our gender stereotypes have changed very little in the last 50 years (Deaux & Kite, 1993; Werner & La Russa, 1985).

Gender stereotypes typically include at least four main subtopics: personality traits, role behaviors, physical characteristics, and occupations that are expected of women or of men (Deaux & Lewis, 1984). In the personality area, women are typically viewed as more **expressive** (e.g., more emotional, sentimental, affectionate, and sensitive), while men are expected to be more **instrumental** (acting to reach a goal, forceful, aggressive). In terms of role behaviors, women are viewed as more **communal** (concerned about others, selfless, affectionate, appreciative), whereas men are seen as **agentic** (concerned for their own interests, forceful, self-assertive, active, ambitious)—(Block, 1973; Parsons, 1955). It is important to realize that some of these stereotype differences are probably not valid; for example, greater male assertiveness (as distinguished from aggressiveness) has not been supported by research findings (Matlin, 1987). Also, differences in personality or gender role behavior are often outweighed by *situational* demands; for instance, men and women supervisors typically display equal degrees of dominance when interacting with subordinates in work settings (Moskowitz, Suh, & Desaulniers, 1994). Similarly, on average, men and women leaders are equally effective (Eagly, Karau, & Makhijani, 1995). However, recent reviews have concluded that in many respects gender stereotypes are generally consistent with empirically measured sex differences (Eagly, 1995; Swim, 1994).

In the realm of expected occupations, gender stereotypes often reflect reality because many occupations in our society have been sex-segregated, and many still remain so despite great increases in women's employment rates (Reskin, 1993). For instance, nurses, secretaries, and bank tellers are more than 90% women, whereas carpenters, mechanics, engineers, and airline pilots are more than 90% men. Many other occupations are still quite sex-segregated, though gradually changing (U.S. Bureau of the Census, 1995).

On dimensions of physical characteristics, within any given ethnic group, the average man is taller, heavier, and stronger than the average woman. However, there are many tall, heavy, and/or strong women who are quite capable of doing what was formerly considered "men's work." Gender stereotypes often exaggerate the "kernel of truth" in the average physical and physiological differences. Moreover, it is a cultural fact that in most societies most women are lower in social status, prestige, and power over other people than are men; they typically control far fewer physical and financial resources, and thus weakness and powerlessness become salient parts of their stereotype (Fiske & Stevens, 1993).

Gender stereotypes seem to be more *prescriptive* than other stereotypes; they specify that women *should be* nurturing, selfless, submissive, sentimental, and so on. That fact poses a difficult dilemma for a woman who wants to pursue a formerly "male" career, such as law, and act in ways appropriate to it. She will be criticized as "unfeminine" if she acts in the occupationally

appropriate assertive way, and she will be criticized as "incompetent" if she acts in the stereotypical feminine way—a double bind that is very difficult to resolve (Fiske & Stevens, 1993).

Sources of Gender Stereotypes. Examples of gender stereotypes are everywhere around us, from birth to death. Prominent among the sources from which we learn them are parents, teachers, and peer-group members, children's literature, textbooks, psychotherapists, everyday language, and the mass media (Oskamp, 1991). Typical aspects of gender role portrayals in the mass media are discussed at some length in Chapter 13.

Sexism

Sexism is a term parallel to racism; it means prejudiced attitudes or discriminatory behavior based on the presumed inferiority or difference of women from men. Usually it refers to viewpoints derogatory to women, but it is equally applicable to anti-male attitudes or behavior. Since behavior unfavorable to women has been by far the most common form, we will focus on it in this section.

Though some individual women in our society have achieved success and power, women as a group have experienced institutionalized sexism for centuries. This has been universally true in other countries as well (Jacobson, 1992; Rhoodie, 1989). For example, most of the world's religions have presented rationales for women's subordination, and women's inferior status has been enforced in education, politics, sexual restrictions, and occupational exclusion. In English common law, wives were "wards"—meaning that their husbands held custody of their person, property, and earnings. In the U.S., women did not get the right to vote until 1920, more than half a century after all men (including former slaves) received it. From 1920 through the early 1980s, the average employed woman earned only about 63% as much as the average employed man (Marini, 1989). Even in positions where women's and men's work was identical, women's pay averaged substantially less than men's (Nieva & Gutek, 1981). Until 1964, it was legal in the U.S. for employers to refuse to hire women for certain positions or job levels, or to require higher qualifications of women. Though laws requiring equal pay and equal opportunity in employment were passed by Congress in 1963 and 1964, these patterns have changed very slowly. By 1994, data for *full-time* working women indicated that they still earned only 76% as much as full-time working men (U.S. Bureau of the Census, 1995).

Recently, research on sexism has demonstrated two aspects of sexist attitudes and behavior. Glick and Fiske (1994) have labeled these aspects hostile sexism and benevolent sexism and have constructed an Ambivalent Sexism Inventory to measure them. **Hostile sexism** is antipathy toward women, including beliefs that women exaggerate their problems, seek power over men, and try to control men sexually. In contrast, **benevolent sexism** emphasizes positive reactions to women, though still stereotyping their behavior and restricting their roles. It has three components: protective paternalism, complementary gender differentiation, and heterosexual intimacy. Sample items will convey its flavor: "Women should be cherished and protected by men," "Women, as compared to men, tend to have a more refined sense of culture and good taste," and "Every man ought to have a woman whom he adores."

It may surprise you that in many samples hostile sexism and benevolent sexism are positively correlated in the .4 to .5 range—thus showing that many people, both men and women, are ambivalent about women's characteristics and proper roles in society. However, less surprisingly, some men have been found to separate these two aspects of sexism and believe in one or the other, but not both. As expected, men score higher than women on both sexism scales, but the difference is much smaller on benevolent sexism—that is, more women support those beliefs than the hostile sexist beliefs (Glick & Fiske, 1994).

Women's Attitudes and Performance

An important issue is, What are the effects on women of the stereotypes and sexism that we have been discussing? A few examples will illustrate the wide range of topics and findings where this issue has been studied.

Mathematics. Interest and performance in mathematics is one of the areas where gender stereotypes predict a lower standing for women than for men. However, in elementary school, girls like math just as much as boys do, perform slightly better on standardized mathematics tests, and consistently get better school grades in math than boys (Chipman & Wilson, 1985; Hyde, Fennema, & Lamon, 1990; Kimball, 1989). Nevertheless, many parents and teachers believe the negative stereotypes and accordingly discourage girls from taking mathematics or related science courses. In turn, this affects the girls' self-concepts and their choices of activities and courses (Eccles et al., 1993). One result is that, by high school, girls take fewer math courses than boys, and that course experience is one major factor contributing to boys' math performance (Wilder & Powell, 1989). By the end of high school, many more boys than girls score high on the math section of the Scholastic Aptitude Test (SAT) and accordingly are counseled to pursue math-related careers (Dorans & Livingston, 1987). Though it is possible that biological factors may be partly responsible for this apparent superiority of males in advanced mathematics, it is incontestable that the image of math as a male field and the early discouragement that girls receive about pursuing it lead many girls to see math as incompatible with their self-concept and future goals (Eccles, 1989; Murray, 1995).

Aspirations. Related to girls' discouragement about taking math is the general topic of their aspirations and motives to achieve. We have seen that many occupations in industrialized nations are substantially sex-segregated, and it is also true that employed women have a more limited choice of jobs than do men. Over half of employed women are in clerical, sales, and service occupations, and relatively few in skilled and semi-skilled production jobs of all kinds (U.S. Bureau of the Census, 1995). Most of the top ten occupations for women are "pink-collar" jobs that have low status and provide poor pay and benefits and few opportunities for advancement (Reskin, 1993). Though the more prestigious "women's fields" of teaching, nursing, and social work offer more intellectual challenges, they typically have rather low pay and restricted working conditions, which have led them to be dubbed "semi-professions" (Etzioni, 1969). Girls and women learn these facts, and most of their role models are in traditional women's positions, so it is not surprising that most young women grow up with limited expectations for careers (England & McCreary, 1987).

Most of the research done on the topic of achievement motivation has focused on males rather than females. Early research by Horner (1972) suggested that women have a greater **fear of success** than men, which might lead them to give up their goals easily or choose less challenging fields of work. However, later research showed that result only held true in achievement areas that were generally considered "sex-inappropriate" (as it did for men also), and that men and women were similar in their degree of fear of success (Paludi, 1984). On objective tests of achievement motivation, men generally score higher on dimensions of competitiveness and mastery (liking for challenges), while women score higher on liking to work hard (Spence & Helmreich, 1983). When employed women are asked what they value about their jobs, they are likely to say pleasant working conditions and congenial co-workers, whereas more men mention their pay or opportunities for promotion—a difference that is probably both a cause and an effect of women's limited prospects for advancement.

Another aspect of aspirations and expectations is people's feelings of entitlement in social and job situations. It is a surprising fact that, despite lower pay and poorer job prospects than men, employed women report the same levels of job satisfaction as men (Crosby, 1982). Careful research by Major (1987) on reasons for their satisfaction has shown that women generally have lower feelings of **entitlement**—that is, in situations where pay or other benefits are to be allocated, women expect less and feel they deserve less for themselves than do men (also see Chapter 10). The apparent reason for this is that both women and men tend to rely on same-sex comparisons when judging the appropriateness of their rewards, and thus women generally have a lower level of expectation against which to evaluate their pay. A policy suggestion that derives from these findings is that women's standards of comparison should be changed (e.g., by publishing pay norms for both sexes in the same or comparable jobs), and that they should be made aware of any unfairness in the procedures by which rewards are allocated (Major,

1987). These suggestions bear on the topic of affirmative action programs, which we will discuss later.

Leadership. Another area where common North American stereotypes portray women as less competent than men is in group leadership (e.g., Craig & Sherif, 1986; Lott, 1985). Women's typical behavior contributes to this result. Both men and women view a directive, autocratic style of interaction as associated with effective leadership, but that style is inconsistent with the stereotype of desirable feminine behavior, and women in mixed-sex groups are less likely than men to display it (Eagly & Johnson, 1990). When people are asked hypothetically whether they would prefer a man or a woman as a boss, both male and female respondents are more likely to say a man, and women say that more often than men do (Moore & Gallup, 1993). Similarly, women who are *appointed* leaders in laboratory groups are evaluated somewhat less favorably than appointed male leaders (e.g., Butler & Geis, 1990).

In studies of **leadership emergence**, women are also less likely to *seek* leadership in most types of situations. In fact, dominant women in mixed-sex dyads often lead in a subtle, self-effacing way by suggesting that the man be the official leader or spokesperson (Megargee, 1969; Nyquist & Spence, 1986)—this is apt to be a diplomatic action, for men feel more stress from threats to their status than women do (Brinkerhoff & Booth, 1984). In small-group studies, women are chosen as leaders of mixed-sex groups far less often than men (Dion, 1985). Meta-analytic studies of leadership emergence show that women have a harder time than men in becoming viewed as leaders in formerly leaderless, mixed-sex groups. However, that disadvantage is reduced when the focus is on stereotypically "feminine" tasks or behaviors, such as ones involving social relationships, and also in research situations lasting longer than 20 minutes, in which participants might gain some actual knowledge about each other (Eagly & Karau, 1991).

Beyond the topic of leadership emergence, an important question is the actual comparative *behavior* of men and women who have become leaders in real-life organizational settings. There, meta-analyses have shown that women and men are very similar in their leadership behavior. Across many studies, women leaders in organizations were found to be just as task-oriented as men, though they did display a somewhat more democratic, participatory style of decision making (Eagly & Johnson, 1990). Importantly, across all organizational settings, men and women leaders were also found to be equally *effective* (Eagly, Karau, & Makhijani, 1995). In settings and roles that were defined in relatively masculine terms (e.g., military organizations), men were more effective leaders, but in settings and roles that were relatively feminine (e.g., education and social service), women were more effective leaders.

Discrimination Against Women

Historically, and still in most industrialized societies, women are expected to do most of the housework and child care without pay and with little social prestige. Their relative lack of income is a major factor in re-

Photograph courtesy of Alice Eagly. Reprinted by permission.

Box 9-1

ALICE EAGLY, EXPERT ON GENDER ROLES AND LEADERSHIP

Known particularly for her research on differences between men and women in leadership styles and effectiveness, Alice Eagly is an authority on the study of attitudes and persuasion. She graduated from Radcliffe College and earned her Ph.D. from the University of Michigan in 1965. After two years of teaching at Michigan State University, she moved to the University of Massachusetts, where she rose to Full Professor. In 1980 she joined the faculty at Purdue, and in 1995 she moved her research program to Northwestern.

Many of Eagly's nearly 100 scientific articles are meta-analyses of gender differences, and she has authored influential volumes on *Sex Differences in Social Behavior* and *The Psychology of Attitudes*. In addition, she has chaired the APA Board of Scientific Affairs and been elected president of the APA Division of Personality and Social Psychology. She has also served on the editorial boards of 14 different journals, on the executive committees of the Interamerican Society of Psychology and the Society of Experimental Social Psychology, and as a Visiting Professor in Tubingen, Germany.

ducing women's power in society (Burn, 1996). U.S. women spend about 20 hours a week doing housework, compared to about 10 hours a week for men, and in addition women do the great bulk of the child care (Robinson, 1988). Even when women are employed, as well over half of U.S. women are, this unequal picture changes very little (Antill & Cotton, 1988). These discrepancies exist in contradiction to the expressed views of a majority of married couples that household tasks should be shared responsibilities (Hiller & Philliber, 1986).

One way that discrimination against women is displayed is in **distancing behavior** by males. Lott (1995) has studied behavioral indicators of interpersonal distancing, such as ignoring, excluding, and devaluing women, and she sees them as a part of a continuum of behaviors that range from negative humor and put-downs to physical abuse and even murder. Developmentally, these actions begin before age 6 in boys' avoidance of and negative reactions to girls (Maccoby, 1988). Among adults, examples include sales clerks giving poorer and slower service to women than to men (e.g., Rafaeli, 1989).

A form of discrimination against women that has very serious consequences is unequal employment treatment. We have already mentioned the differential pay received by women, even when performing the same job as men (Marini, 1989). There are many examples of unequal treatment of women at all stages of getting and holding jobs. For instance, it has been common for career counselors to advise women against considering nontraditional job areas (Harway, 1980). When men and women applicants are equally qualified, the women are less likely to be hired, and they are frequently offered lower-level jobs or lower initial pay levels for the same job (Betz & Fitzgerald, 1987; Gerhart, 1990). This negative discrimination occurs most often when the job requirements are ambiguous or the candidate's qualifications are unclear. After being hired, it is common though not universal for women to be given fewer promotions and raises than men, even when their performance evaluations are equally high—as demonstrated in studies of various major corporations (Cannings & Montmarquette, 1991; Gupta, Jenkins, & Beehr, 1983).

Another frequent practice is omitting women employees from social interactions, such as informal lunches and after-hours sessions where valuable information may be exchanged (Sonnert & Holton, 1995). Women may also receive unfair job evaluations, particularly in traditionally male job areas, because many male supervisors hold stereotypic views of women workers as being less capable and less rational than men (Rosen & Jerdee, 1978). Another serious problem for women in many work settings is greater difficulty in obtaining support and mentoring from a senior administrator who can help to advance the protege's career (Ragins & Cotton, 1991). One area where women are still very rare is the highest paid levels of officers and directors; a study in 799 of the largest U.S. companies found that women held less than half of 1% of the positions at that level in 1989 (19 out of 4012—Fierman, 1990). This "glass ceiling" barrier has been targeted for reduction by the Civil Rights Act of 1991 (Federal Glass Ceiling Commission, 1995).

A particularly serious form of discriminatory treatment, which is often directed at women, is sexual harassment, which we will discuss a bit later.

Correctives to Discrimination. One major method of correcting for the unequal employment treatment of women and ethnic minorities is *affirmative action*, which we will discuss at some length at the end of this chapter. Another corrective that has been proposed is ensuring pay equity between men and women—often called **comparable worth**. There are differing explanations for the overall gender-related wage gap, with some authors attributing it to lower qualifications and commitment of women workers (e.g., O'Neill, 1985). Though *equal pay* for jobs involving equal work and qualifications has been the law in the U.S. since the Equal Pay Act of 1963, only a minority of workers are in situations where both men and women do the same jobs. A majority are in largely sex-segregated jobs or positions (e.g., telephone operators and telephone linemen), and therefore "equal work" cannot be clearly established.

Consequently, comparable worth proposals go further than "equal work" solutions, and attempt to equalize pay for sex-segregated jobs of different content but equal value, within a firm or agency (Patten, 1988). The problem in doing this, of course, is establishing "equal value" for jobs as different as secretaries and mechanics, bookkeepers and salespersons. Many factors need to be considered, including educational requirements, special skills, physical effort, responsibility, dangerous working conditions, and so on. This requires *job evaluation* on all these key dimensions and combining the dimensions to get an overall job-worth score for any position (cf. Gerhart & Milkovich, 1992). Though this is a complex process, its principles have been used in U.S. industry for over 50 years to determine employee compensation. In the last decade these procedures have been widely applied to comparison of male-dominated and female-dominated jobs, and many examples of successful application of pay equity schemes are now available (Orazem & Matilla, 1989; Wittig & Lowe, 1989). In fact, England, Canada, and Australia have all passed comparable worth laws, whereas only a small minority of U.S. states have begun broad implementation of pay equity. A comprehensive overview of comparable worth concepts, procedures, and implementation issues is presented in a volume by Lowe and Wittig (1989).

In recent years, the many approaches to reducing gender-based inequities and discrimination have made substantial progress. People working today can remember the time, a few decades back, when there were no women in graduate business school classes, and very few in law and medical schools, whereas now women make up large proportions. Breaking into formerly male *blue-collar* occupations has been harder. Table 9–1 shows what percentage of workers in various selected fields were women as of 1994, and the amount of increase in the proportion of women since 1983. In that decade, the proportion of women increased markedly in almost all of these occupations, even though the percentage still remained low in some fields.

Violence Against Women

Unfortunately, the progress in women's employment and income has been accompanied by a continuing and increasing amount of violence directed against women.

Table 9-1   Percentage of Women in Selected Occupations in 1994, and Percentage of Increase Since 1983

Occupation	% of women in 1994	% of increase since 1983
Psychologists	59	3
Economists	47	25
Math & computer scientists	34	14
Natural scientists	31	51
Lawyers & judges	25	57
Physicians	22	41
Telephone installers & repairers	17	70
Police & detectives	16	66
Dentists	13	99
Clergy	11	98
Engineers	8	43
Mechanics & repairers	5	50
Truck drivers	5	45
Airplane pilots & navigators	3	24
Firefighters	2	110
Construction trades	2	22

Source: U.S. Bureau of the Census (1995, pp. 411–413).

It takes several different forms, of which we will briefly discuss sexual harassment, abuse and rape, and pornography.

Sexual harassment has been defined as "unwelcome sexual advances, requests for sexual favors, and other verbal or physical conduct of a sexual nature" (Equal Employment Opportunity Commission [EEOC], 1980, p. 74677). It is an age-old pattern of behavior, but the term was codified and studies on it begun in the 1970s, and in 1980 the EEOC regulations established it as a form of sexual discrimination—a federal offense—under the 1964 Civil Rights Act. It includes behavior ranging from ogling, "wolf whistles," and vulgar comments, to sexual touching, propositions, threats of job loss for noncompliance, and even rape. The concept received dramatic publicity in 1991 in the charges made by Anita Hill against Clarence Thomas's nomination to the U.S. Supreme Court. Recently it has gained a great deal of research attention (e.g., Stockdale, 1996; Pryor & McKinney, 1995).

Because harassment is subjectively defined by the

recipient, it may mean different things to different people. Though there is general agreement about behaviors that are harassing, men are somewhat less likely than women to classify various behaviors as harassment, especially verbal comments or nonverbal behavior such as leering or touching (Frazier et al., 1995; Gutek, 1995). Thus, a man may consider such actions as "flirting," while a woman may deeply resent them. A review of many research findings indicates that about half of all U.S. women are sexually harassed sometime in their lives in academic or work settings (Fitzgerald, 1993). One study of a representative sample of over 1200 workers indicated that 53% of women and 37% of men reported having experienced sexual harassment during their employment; a more conservative estimate by trained raters concluded that the events described by 21% of the women and 9% of the men qualified as sexual harassment (Gutek, 1985).

Research on the effects of sexual harassment shows that women are very likely to find it stressful—more so than men (Frazier, Cochran, & Olson, 1995). In a sample of women workers, about half of their harassers were supervisors and two-thirds were married, whereas the typical harasser described by male workers was a young, attractive, unmarried, nonsupervisory woman (Gutek, 1985). Over 20% of women report having quit a job or a job application, or having been transferred or fired as a result of sexual harassment (Gutek, 1985). In a study of women who had registered a complaint about being harassed, two-thirds had quit their job or been fired (Crull, 1980). Sexual harassment is often reported by women in blue-collar jobs (e.g., Baker, 1989; Gruber & Bjorn, 1982), and it seems to be most common in work settings where few women have traditionally been employed—e.g., in the armed forces and in "masculine cultures" where incoming women have a "token" or solo status (Fiske & Glick, 1995; Newell, Rosenfeld, & Culbertson, 1995). In addition to the likelihood of job loss, women who are harassed typically experience lowered self-esteem, self-blame, deteriorating social relationships, and lowered life satisfaction (Gutek, 1993).

Though sexual harassment is now a criminal offense, there are still many work settings where it is at least overlooked or tacitly condoned; and women who complain are often considered "troublemakers," ostracized, or treated as irrational and neurotic (for a dramatic example, see Gutek, 1993). There are many different reactions to the experience of harassment (Fitzgerald, Swan, & Fischer, 1995). Among the most frequent are trying to ignore it or to avoid the harasser; also common are attempts to appease the harasser without either compliance or direct confrontation, and seeking social support by discussing the problem with co-workers, friends, or family. Studies indicate that less than half of harassed women directly asked the harasser to stop, and less than 20%, even of those who have experienced serious harassment, ever reported it to any authority. That figure may be increasing as the concept of sexual harassment and the laws against it become better known.

Both employers and universities are now required to have policies in place and specific officials named as responsible for handling sexual harassment complaints. Individuals who are experiencing harassment should first clearly tell the offender that the actions are unwelcome, and then if they do not cease, keep records of them and report the problem to the designated organizational official (Wagner, 1992).

Abuse. More extreme forms of violence against women include physical and sexual abuse and rape. Reports from a national sample of over 4000 college students indicated that *in the previous year* over 80% of both men and women had engaged in some verbal aggression in a heterosexual relationship, and about 35% of each sex had resorted to physical aggression, ranging from throwing objects at someone to pushing, shoving, and hitting (White & Koss, 1991). Though these data show that physical aggression is reciprocal, men report that they aggress to intimidate or get their way, whereas women more often use force in self-defense, and they are much more likely than men to be seriously injured in the process (Makepeace, 1986). Factors that increase the likelihood of being involved in such "courtship violence" include having learned patterns of violence in one's family, and associating with peers who are accepting of violence (Gwartney-Gibbs, Stockard, & Brohmer, 1983). Unfortunately, such abusive patterns in courtship often carry over to even more serious battering in later marriages (Roscoe & Benaske, 1985).

Sexual assault includes various forms of unwanted sexual contact such as fondling and kissing, of which the most serious is **rape**—forced sexual intercourse, without consent. The fear of being raped affects a large proportion of women in our society, casting a lifelong pall over their freedom of action (Koss, 1993). Current U.S. data indicate that one woman in five will be raped sometime in her life, though 80% or more of these events are not reported to authorities (Frazier et al., 1994). Many rape victims are so traumatized that they are afraid to tell anyone about the attack. Major reasons for the low reporting of rapes are realistic fears of being stigmatized, and mistrust of the police and courts. In the U.S. legal system, about 80% of rape cases do not even have charges filed, and the victim often is treated as if her actions were responsible for the crime (Frazier et al., 1994).

About 85% of all sexual assaults are committed by someone known to the victim, over half by romantic partners (Koss, 1990). In one major study of college students, about three-quarters of victimized women did not label their own experiences of forced intercourse as rape (Koss, Gidycz, & Wisniewski, 1987). The same survey found that 8% of college males admitted to having attempted or committed rape, and 17% more admitted to some lesser form of sexual coercion. After a few dates, some males may expect to have sex in return for their paying for dinner or entertainment, they may think of their own behavior as "seduction" rather than coercion, or they may employ other justifications (Shotland, 1989).

Unfortunately, in our society there are many *rape myths* that support the view that rape is not a serious offense, that men sometimes can't control their sexual urges, that women really want to be raped and could avoid it if they tried, or that only "bad women" are raped (Burt, 1980). Recent research has shown that hostility toward women is a central element in acceptance of these rape myths (Lonsway & Fitzgerald, 1995). There is no evidence to support these myths, and changing legal codes are underlining the principle that a woman always has the right to say "no" to sexual overtures.

The emotional effects of rape on its victims are far-reaching: fear, anxiety, depression, and lowered self-esteem that may continue for many months or years following an assault (Ellis, 1983). Research has shown victims of a single date rape to be just as distressed as victims of repeated childhood sexual abuse, and generally more distressed than victims of rape by a stranger (Roth, Wayland, & Woolsey, 1990). The trauma resulting from rape has recently been considered an example of *post traumatic stress disorder (PTSD)*, like the delayed reactions of war veterans to their horrific battlefield experiences (Roth, Dye, & Lebowitz, 1988). A related example of PTSD is the *battered woman's syndrome*, proposed by Lenore Walker (1984) to describe the psychological reactions of women who remain with abusive men because they feel helpless to protect themselves or to escape. More extensive discussions of psychological factors in sexual assault and rape can be found in Matlin (1987) and Unger and Crawford (1992).

Pornography. One of the main forces in our society that perpetuates the rape myths and traditional patterns of male control over women's lives is media portrayals of sexual violence. **Pornography** has been defined as "sexually explicit material that [approvingly] represents or describes degrading or abusive sexual behavior" (Longino, 1980, p. 44). In the 1980s and 1990s there has been a marked increase in the depiction of sexual violence in mainstream movies and prime-time television. However, this is pale in comparison to "slasher films," which show women being tied up, beaten, tortured, mutilated, and/or murdered, usually interspersed with sexually suggestive scenes (Donnerstein & Linz, 1994). Courts in the U.S. have generally treated such depictions as constitutionally protected speech, sharply in contrast to the 1992 Canadian Supreme Court decision to prohibit such speech because it was harmful to society in general and to women's equality and self-esteem in particular (*Harvard Law Review*, 1993).

A fitting summary is: "Pornography is just one link in the chain of a patriarchal culture that subordinates women" (Jensen, 1991, p. 13). In Chapter 13 we present more details about sexual content in the media and its effects on audience members' attitudes and behavior.

ETHNICITY

Many of the principles discussed above in relation to gender issues also apply to ethnic groups, often with even greater force. Thus, this section will primarily highlight principles and findings that are different from those regarding gender.

"Race" as a Term

Ethnic groups are often referred to as "racial" groups. Historically, physical anthropologists have divided humankind into at least three large biological categories (e.g., Negroid, Caucasoid, and Mongoloid), which were differentiated by their inherited patterns of physical features, such as the color of their skin, hair, and eyes, shape of their head, nose, and mouth, stature, and so on. However, it has long been realized that in our era there are no pure races, if there ever were any. The natives of different geographic areas have various combinations of the characteristics of the supposedly "pure" original races; moreover, in many areas of the world, people from different races have interbred extensively. Consequently, there are tremendous variations in genetic and physical characteristics among persons who are nominally classified as of the same "race," and stating a person's race is not a biological fact, but a social and linguistic convention (a "folk taxonomy"—Fish, 1995).

In the common lay use of the term, a person's race is an all-or-nothing affair—either Black or White or Oriental, etc. However, genetic studies of blood groups and other evidence indicate that, in the U.S., about 70% of "Blacks" have some White ancestry and about 20% of "Whites" have some Black ancestry (Reed, 1969; Stuckert, 1964). Nevertheless, in the U.S. South, it has been traditional to classify as Negro or Black a person who had as little as 1/16 Black ancestry. Yet such a person might have white skin and blue eyes, as did Walter White, a famous early leader of the National Association for the Advancement of Colored People (NAACP).

Because the term "race" carries the false implication of an objective genetic classification, many social scientists have abandoned use of that term. This change carried particular social significance because the idea of "racial superiority" had often been invoked as a reason for national aggression and genocide, as in the Nazi extermination of Europe's Jews. As early as 1950, the United Nations Educational, Scientific, and Cultural Organization (UNESCO) promulgated a statement that race was a misleading and dangerous concept, and recommended use of the term *ethnic group* instead (Montagu, 1951). Members of an **ethnic group** share a language, culture, and traditions, as well as some physical similarities. Though the terms "race" and "ethnic group" have generally been used interchangeably, recent writings have emphasized the pernicious implications inherent in the concept of race (Yee et al., 1993). Consequently, we will avoid that term and refer to ethnic groups instead. In doing so, it is important to understand that many people have mixed ethnic heritages and, for some individuals, their ethnic group may be a matter of personal self-identification—for example, as in choice of a religious affiliation, adoption of an ancestral name, or emphasis on particular cultural values.

Research on Ethnic Groups

Similarly, when ethnic group comparisons are reported in research, it must be understood that they do not involve "pure" groups with homogeneous biological and genetic backgrounds, but rather groups having varying degrees of biological, linguistic, and cultural similarity. In studies of psychological variables, such as temperament or personality characteristics, it is almost inevitable to find "much more variation within groups designated as races than between such groups" (Zuckerman, 1990, p. 1297).

Psychological research on ethnic group differences in the U.S. has focused mostly on African Americans, the earliest and largest minority nationwide (Ackerman & Humphreys, 1990). A crucial aspect of their social and cultural history leading to their disadvantaged status is that most of their ancestors came to the U.S. as slaves (the first Black slave was brought to this country in 1619, the year before the Pilgrims landed). Their unique position as a minority group resulted from that background of slavery—an issue that ignited the U.S. Civil War—and from the legalized segregation imposed on them after their emancipation. Though Hispanics have lived in the Southwestern states even longer, and are now a rapidly growing minority group, they have received much less research attention. A key factor affecting their status in the U.S. is their linguistic uniqueness as Spanish-speaking; in addition, many of them are recent immigrants, so length of time in this country is a crucial variable in understanding their adjustment and other characteristics. A third important minority group is Asian Americans, who have only recently begun to receive any research attention. Like Hispanics, all Asians have critical linguistic differences from the English-speaking majority, but they come from many diverse countries with quite different languages and cultural patterns and cannot meaningfully be lumped together on many variables. In addition, all the major Asian national groups in this country except Japanese have a majority of foreign-born members, so they particularly experience the challenge of trying to understand a new culture and unfamiliar customs.

Stereotypes and Intergroup Differences

As with most past psychological research, we will focus here mainly on the situation of African Americans. Stereotypes of Blacks in America have been studied empirically since the early years of social psychology. An influential early study, done with Princeton undergraduates, found that more than 75% of them agreed that, as a group, "Negroes" were superstitious and lazy, and 25% or more agreed that they were ignorant, ostentatious, but also happy-go-lucky, and musical (Katz & Braly, 1933). Studies since then have shown a general fading of sharp ethnic stereotypes and a growing reluctance to attribute traits to whole ethnic groups. However, raters typically show much higher levels of agreement when they are asked what traits *others* attribute to Blacks than when asked about their own perceptions. Because the topic is a pejorative one, national surveys rarely ask directly about ethnic stereotypes, and most studies in recent years have been done with samples of college students. One careful study showed that over 50% of a small student sample considered

each of the following characteristics as part of the stereotype of Blacks: poor, aggressive/tough, criminal, low intelligence, uneducated, lazy, sexually perverse, and athletic (Devine, 1989). Whether or not individuals share these stereotypic views, it is clear that most Americans are well aware of the negative stereotypes about Blacks.

One of the most prominent stereotypes about U.S. Blacks is that they are intellectually inferior to Whites (and to Asians, who have recently gained a stereotypic reputation as a "model minority"). Though this stereotype long predates organized mental testing, it has gained some empirical support from many studies of measured intergroup differences between African Americans and other groups. On cognitive measures, such as standardized individual intelligence tests and group school achievement tests, it is common to find that the average score for Euro-Americans is as much as one standard deviation higher than the average for African Americans (Ackerman & Humphreys, 1990; Neisser et al., 1996). We will briefly cite some of this research as background for the study described in the next section.

In school performance, by sixth grade, African American students in most U.S. school districts are about two grade levels behind their Euro-American classmates on standardized achievement tests (Gerard, 1983). In high school the Black dropout rate is higher than for Whites, and in college, 70% of Blacks who enter do not complete a bachelor's degree within six years, compared to 42% of Whites (American Council on Education, 1990). Those Blacks who do graduate have an average GPA two-thirds of a letter grade lower than White graduates (Nettles, 1988, cited in Steele & Aronson, 1995).

The causes behind these educational differentials are the subject of great dispute. A recent controversial volume, *The Bell Curve* (Herrnstein & Murray, 1994), attributed them largely to genetic ability, as did an earlier widely debated overview by Jensen (1969). However, this viewpoint resurrects the old nature-versus-nurture argument, and it is undeniable that the differentials reflect huge discrepancies in the typical environments of Blacks and Whites (Neisser et al., 1996). In part, these are a function of lower social class or socioeconomic status (SES), which often prevents families from providing their children with many of the physical necessities of life, let alone the early experiences and advantages that stimulate motivation and achievement in academic areas. The same economic forces frequently lead students to drop out of school to make money, or to carry jobs that interfere with their continuing education.

These economic factors are just a part of overwhelming differences in the environmental influences which shape the behavior and outcomes of Blacks, Whites, and other ethnic groups. A central background factor is African Americans' long history of slavery, oppression, segregation, and discrimination, making many of them an underclass or caste-like minority (Ogbu, 1978). Other authors have pointed to deep-rooted elements of African American culture, such as communalism, that are incompatible with Euro-Americans' typical individualistic cultural expectations (Boykin, 1994). An important *psychological* influence has been demonstrated in recent influential research by Claude Steele on the topic of stereotype threat, which we discuss next.

Stereotype Threat—Illustrative Studies

This research examines the largely unstudied question of what effect stereotypes have on *those who are stereotyped.* For example, since Blacks as well as non-Blacks in America know about the widespread negative stereotype concerning Blacks' intellectual ability, what effect does that have on Blacks' performance? Steele and Aronson (1995) proposed that it created a **stereotype threat** to Blacks' self-evaluation, and they did several experiments to demonstrate the effects of this threat. They predicted that stereotype threat would be particularly high in intellectual achievement situations which are difficult or frustrating, but not in those that are less demanding, and that it would depress performance in the demanding situations, regardless of whether participants themselves believed the stereotype.

The experiments they conducted to test their hypotheses are models of creativity, rigorous design, and applied social importance. They recruited Black and White college students of exceptional capability (e.g., Scholastic Aptitude Test [SAT] scores around 600 or higher) and gave them a 25-minute test of very difficult items taken from the Graduate Record Exam (GRE) study guides. In one representative experiment, equal proportions of 20 Black and 20 White students were randomly assigned to two conditions in which the instructions differed only in their stress on diagnosing the participants' abilities. In the diagnostic condition they were told that the test involved "reading and verbal reasoning abilities" and that after the test they would be given feedback about their "strengths and weaknesses." In the nondiagnostic condition they were told that the test concerned "psychological factors involved in solving verbal problems" and that the feedback would inform them about "the kinds of problems that appear on tests [they] may encounter in the future" (Steele & Aronson, 1995, p. 799). Both groups were told that the test was so difficult they should not expect to get many items correct, and both were instructed to make a strong effort on the test despite its difficulty.

A key dependent variable in this study was the number of problems answered correctly, adjusted by using their SAT scores as a covariate or baseline measure of problem-solving ability. The results are displayed in Figure 9-2, which shows a strong interaction effect ($p < .01$), with the Black group in the diagnostic condition performing significantly worse than any of the

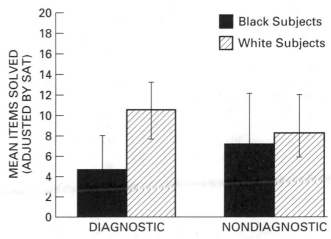

FIGURE 9-2 Mean test performance for Black and White subjects. (Source: Steele, C. M., & Aronson, J. (1995). Stereotype threat and the intellectual test performance of African Americans. *Journal of Personality and Social Psychology, 69,* 797–811. Copyright © 1995 by the American Psychological Association. Reprinted with permission.

Photograph courtesy of Claude Steele. Reprinted by permission.

Box 9-2

CLAUDE STEELE, INVESTIGATOR OF STEREOTYPE THREAT

Claude Steele earned his B.A. at Hiram College in Ohio and his Ph.D. at Ohio State University in 1971. He taught briefly at the University of Utah, spent 14 years at the University of Washington, moved to the University of Michigan for four years, and then settled at Stanford in 1991. His major areas of research have been processes in alcohol and drug abuse, and academic achievement of ethnic minorities. This chapter discusses his recent research on performance decrements due to individuals' knowledge of negative social stereotypes about their group. He has also conducted action research that established college dormitory programs which aimed to overcome the effects of stereotype threat on minority students by providing them extra academic challenges rather than remedial instruction.

In professional activities, Steele has been chosen as a member of the American Academy of Arts and Sciences, and elected head of the prestigious Society of Experimental Social Psychology, president of the Western Psychological Association, and member of the Board of Directors of the American Psychological Society. His research has been funded by major grants from the National Institute of Alcohol Abuse and Alcoholism, the National Institute of Mental Health, and the Russell Sage Foundation. He has served on the editorial board of six psychological journals and also been chosen as a Master Lecturer at the APA annual convention.

other three groups. In fact, their adjusted score was only about half the number of items that the Black non-diagnostic group answered correctly. Similarly, the Black diagnostic group was lowest in their accuracy score (the number of items correct over the number attempted—interaction $p < .05$), and also lowest in the number of items they attempted. Thus, being warned that the test measured their abilities slowed down the Blacks, but not the Whites, as well as diminishing their proportion of correct answers.

Further studies replicated this basic finding and demonstrated several of the processes involved in the stereotype threat effect (Steele & Aronson, 1995). Measures of thought associations showed that several processes were activated in African American participants by the diagnostic instructions. First, associations regarding their ethnic group membership were activated significantly more for Blacks in the diagnostic condition than for any of the other groups. Second, self-doubt associations were activated significantly more for that group—over twice as many as for any of the other groups. Third, on a self-report measure of activity preferences and personality characteristics, Blacks in the diagnostic condition *avoided* agreeing with ethnically stereotypic descriptions, significantly more so than any of the other groups. Fourth, only 25% of that key group indicated their race on the postexperimental questionnaire, whereas all members of the other groups did so (a significant interaction, $p < .01$). Finally, three items assessing *self-handicapping* responses were also significantly highest for the Black diagnostic group (claiming fewer hours of sleep the night before, stating a lower ability to focus, and reporting that they typically found standardized tests more tricky/unfair than the other groups did). These findings all indicate a strong feeling of **evaluation apprehension** arising from the stereotype threat situation.

A final experiment demonstrated how easily this stereotype threat could be invoked. Here the same very difficult test was given to participants, but no mention was made of it testing their ability; instead the nondiagnostic instructions from the previous studies were used. The key manipulation of stereotype threat was in a brief questionnaire given just before the test. It merely asked the participant's age, year in school, major, number of siblings, parents' education—and, for the threat group, their race. Despite its simplicity and apparent triviality, this *priming* event strongly activated the stereotype threat, as shown by a significant interaction effect in which the Black primed group had significantly lower SAT-adjusted scores on the test than the other three groups, and also significantly lower adjusted accuracy scores and lower numbers of completed items. Yet participants were not aware of this effect on their performance, and claimed not to have been distracted by recording their race. In postexperimental interviews many stated that they had paid

no attention to recording their race because it was a common event in their lives. The researchers concluded:

> stereotype threat—established by quite subtle instructional differences—can impair the intellectual test performance of Black students, and . . . lifting it can dramatically improve that performance. (Steele & Aronson, 1995, p. 808)

One of the important implications from this research is the ease with which stereotype threat can be invoked, by apparently innocuous or well-meaning actions or references. Steele's (1996) theory goes further and proposes that many threatened individuals respond by **protective disidentification**—that is, ceasing to identify with the threatening domain of activity or to use it as a basis of self-evaluation. This action protects their self-esteem, which is thus unlinked from achievement in that area. In addition, peer groups may apply pressure and threats of rejection to enforce this disidentification as a group norm (the norm of the "gentleman's C" on ivy league campuses is an example). On the other hand, the nondiagnostic condition instructions in Steele and Aronson's research offer a model for ways to avoid stereotype threat—*describe a task as difficult and challenging, but not as an indicator of the participant's abilities*. This is a hopeful suggestion that ways can be found to remedy Black underachievement by making changes in the testing situation. Further, these results propose at least a partial explanation of mechanisms leading to the pervasive finding of deficits for Blacks on standardized achievement and ability tests (e.g., IQ, SAT) such as we described above.

Application to Women and Mathematics. Another crucial implication is that this stereotype threat effect is applicable to individuals from any group on tasks where a well known stereotype indicates that their group is inferior. An obvious example is women's performance in mathematics, and some past research findings are consistent with the theory's principles. For instance, an intriguing finding by Dreyden and Gallagher (1989) showed that adding a time limit on a difficult math test—an apparently trivial change like asking one's race—sharply depressed the performance of talented girls in comparison to boys, whereas without the time limit girls took no more time but performed just as well as boys.

Steele has done experimental research on this topic as well, and his results support the theory of stereotype threat. In one study, mathematically talented men and women college students were given either a very difficult math test or one that was more within their skills. Women underperformed men on the difficult test but not on the easier one (Spencer, Steele, & Quinn, 1996). However, this result might be interpreted as consistent with the suggestions of some authors, mentioned in an earlier section, that there is a genetic limit on women's ability in very high levels of mathematics. To disprove that interpretation, Spencer et al. conducted a similar experiment, using the same difficult math test as before for all participants. However, half of each gender group were told that the test generally displayed gender differences, while the other half were told that it did not do so. As predicted, women dramatically underperformed men in the first condition, but they performed as well as men when the stereotype threat was removed by the instructions that the test did not show gender differences.

Implications for Education. Steele (1996) has built on these experimental findings to propose a system of "wise" education, which will help stereotype-threatened individuals make the most of their academic potential. To remove the sense of stereotype threat and prevent threatened students from disidentifying with academic work, he suggests several approaches. First, teachers and other adults should affirm that the students have good learning potential—that is, they should openly attribute this ability to the students. Second, they should present highly challenging assignments rather than remedial work to make up for past deficits. Also, they should stress the expandability of human abilities, and encourage students to work together in groups, which can overcome the threatened student's *pluralistic ignorance* in thinking that he or she is unique in experiencing frustration and difficulty in learning.

As evidence that such approaches can elicit much improved academic performance from minority group students, Steele cites the success of Jaime Escalante in challenging urban ghetto high schoolers to outstanding performance in math and calculus. Similarly, Treisman (1985) developed a very effective challenge-oriented program to teach calculus to Black university students. In an even more ambitious program at the University of Michigan, Steele and his colleagues recruited representative freshmen, but with an oversampling of ethnic minorities, to live together in one wing of a large dorm during their freshman year. The program was presented as honorific and challenging, not remedial, and members were offered special challenge workshops and discussion groups, held in the dorm, which were related to freshman courses and adjustment issues. Early results from this program are very encouraging. Black students in Steele's program performed much better in their first semester courses than Black students in parallel remedial programs at the university or those in no special program. They also showed almost no underachievement in relation to White freshmen, and follow-ups showed that they continued to do well through their sophomore year. Only 4% of them dropped out in their first two years compared with 25% of Black students in the remedial program (Steele, 1996). These results provide impressive support for the use of psychological theory to modify some very difficult and important social problems.

Prejudice, Discrimination, and Racism

Let us now return to the attitudes and actions of majority group members that create this climate of inequality. The widespread ethnic stereotypes discussed above are one important constituent of the phenomenon of ethnic prejudice. However, as defined earlier in this chapter, **prejudice** also includes *attitudes* that are intolerant, unfair, or irrationally unfavorable toward another group. In that section, we also defined the related concepts of ethnic **discrimination**, **racism**, and **institutional racism.** How common are such patterns within American society?

A recent volume by Clayton (1996) has summarized the current status of race relations in America, about 50 years after the publication of Myrdal's (1944) classic analysis of racism, *An American Dilemma.* Gaines and Reed (1995) have emphasized that the era of slavery still has a legacy in current patterns of racism, and that African Americans live in a divided world, torn between their identification as Americans and their socially inferior status as Blacks. Every African American grows up in an environment where many daily events emphasize their subordinate status, and to a lesser extent the same is true for other ethnic minorities. For example, children may be markedly affected by the fact that teachers' expectations regarding academic performance are generally lower for Blacks than for Whites, and are especially low for Black males (Ross & Jackson, 1991).

Here are a few specific indicators of *institutional racism*, quoted from Campbell (1995, p. 23):

- Income for White families averages $36,915; for Black families, $21,423.
- Although 8.8% of White Americans live in poverty, 31.9% of Black Americans do.
- The infant mortality rate for White Americans is 7 per 1000 live births; for Black Americans, 17 per 1000 (National Center for Health Statistics, 1995).
- 24.4% of White Americans have attended 4 or more years of college; 12.7% of Black Americans have.
- Black Americans make up less than 13% of the general population, but more than 45% of the prison population.

Moreover, these disadvantages cumulate for individuals who are low on two or more status dimensions, such as ethnicity, gender, and social class. For example, a study of the salaries of government employees in the Miami metropolitan area found, after controlling for level of education and job category or classification, that White women's salaries were 75% of White men's, Hispanic women's salaries were 72% of White women's, and Black women were lowest on the totem pole with salaries only 62% of White women's—i.e., less than half of White men's (Idson & Price, 1992). This kind of systemic inequality has serious consequences that affect almost all ethnic minority individuals.

In addition to this pattern of institutional discrimination, there are countless examples of *interpersonal racism and discrimination* which have recently been reviewed by Maluso (1995). Illustrative findings include a study of White attendants' behavior in physically restraining adolescent patients in a psychiatric hospital; the average number of violent acts committed by White and Black patients did not differ, but Blacks were four times as likely to be physically restrained as Whites (Bond, DiCandia, & MacKinnon, 1988). Similarly, in a south Florida school district, Black students received proportionately more of the corporal punishments and school suspensions than did White students (McFadden et al., 1992).

The prevalence and societal importance of ethnic prejudice is suggested by the fact that it is one of the most studied topics in social science. Many differing analyses of prejudice and racism have been made by psychologists in recent years. We will quickly sketch some of the most important approaches. **Traditional racist** attitudes in the U.S. involved support for segregation laws and beliefs in the moral and intellectual inferiority of Blacks. Since the civil rights movement of the 1960s, this blatant form of prejudice has been abandoned by most citizens except for a small percentage who are sympathetic to extremist groups such as the Ku Klux Klan or the White Aryan Resistance. For instance, 40 years after the (originally controversial) U.S. Supreme Court's decision that racially segregated public schools were illegal, 87% of a national sample of Americans said they approved of that decision (McAneny & Saad, 1994).

In contrast, **modern racist** attitudes are more subtle, less extreme indications of negative feelings toward Blacks (McConahay, 1986). They are measured, for instance, by endorsement of statements indicating that American racial problems have been largely solved, that civil rights groups' goals are too extreme, or that Blacks have gotten more respect and benefits than they deserve. As examples, in a nationally representative survey in 1993, 47% of Whites said that Black civil rights groups are asking for too much, whereas only 7% of Blacks agreed with that view. Similarly, 70% of Whites but only 30% of Blacks said that Blacks had as good a chance as Whites in their community to get a job for which they were qualified (Wheeler, 1993). The same distinction between blatant and subtle prejudice has been supported in research from other nations, for instance in various countries of western Europe (Pettigrew & Meertens, 1995).

Quite similar to modern racism is the concept of **symbolic racism**, which is defined as a blend of anti-

Black attitudes with belief in traditional American values such as individualism, self-reliance, and the work ethic (Kinder & Sears, 1981). This concept highlights the symbolic importance of these values, and it explains people's opposition to welfare, busing, and government programs designed to help poor people and/or minority groups as being largely based on the belief that the programs violate these traditional values.

Another aspect of racism has been called **aversive racism** (Gaertner & Dovidio, 1986). This term describes people who have grown up with the almost unavoidable racial biases produced by socialization and cultural patterns in the U.S., but who also have internalized American values of fairness and equality so that they sympathize with victims of injustice. The result is a kind of ambivalence—their conscious feelings and beliefs are nondiscriminatory, but they also have some negative feelings of discomfort or fear toward minorities, and these negative feelings are often unconscious. Typically, the two aspects will be expressed in different situations. Where norms for equal treatment are clear, such people will follow them and not discriminate against minorities. However, where the social norms are ambiguous, they will tend to be avoidant or unhelpful (an aversive reaction), but will justify or rationalize such actions as being based on factors other than race (e.g., the person's need for assistance wasn't clear). This pattern is consistent with Stephan's (1994) concept of *intergroup anxiety*, and research by Kleinpenning and Hagendoorn (1993) has classified it as a milder form of prejudice than symbolic racism. Though this pattern is passive and generally nonhostile, it nevertheless helps to perpetuate the prevalent institutional patterns that keep ethnic minorities as second-class citizens. A pertinent quotation is Edmund Burke's statement that "The only thing necessary for the triumph of evil is for good men to do nothing."

A more hopeful view—that **prejudice is a habit** and can be broken—has been advanced by Devine (1989; Devine et al., 1991). Her research has shown that both low-prejudice and high-prejudice Americans are aware of the negative stereotypes about ethnic minorities, but they differ in that, when responding intentionally, low-prejudice individuals try to act in ways consistent with their beliefs and to avoid acting in ways consistent with the stereotypes. However, because the stereotypes are well-learned, this is difficult and requires inhibiting automatic, unthinking responses. Consequently, well-meaning people sometimes slip up and fail to act upon their beliefs, and when that happens they feel guilt or *prejudice with compunction*. The Devine et al. (1991; Zuwerink et al., 1996) research suggests that the guilt felt by low-prejudice people when they fail to act in accordance with their beliefs is a motivating force that helps them to go farther toward breaking the habit of prejudice. Certainly there is good evidence for this learning process in the changes experienced by many Americans in the last 50 years. During the era of segregation, even sitting next to or shaking hands with a Black person was unthinkable for many White Americans, whereas now such contact is accepted by most without a thought.

Reducing Prejudice, Discrimination, and Racism

This point leads us to the question of what techniques can be used to reduce prejudice and its expression. In this area, the **contact hypothesis** has had a long history of theory and research. Allport (1954) predicted that intergroup contact would lead to decreased prejudice and increased liking, but only under the following four conditions: (a) equal status between the groups in the situation, (b) common goals, (c) lack of competition between the groups, and (d) support by authorities for the contact. Other researchers have suggested additional conditions, such as an intimate situation which allows personalized understanding of members of the other group (Amir, 1976; Brewer & Miller, 1984), and participants low in authoritarianism (Weigel & Howes, 1985).

The contact hypothesis, in its several variations, has received support in many studies, conducted in various situations and with different social groups, ranging from foreign students to the elderly (e.g., Ellison & Powers, 1994; Gaertner et al., 1994; Sigelman & Welch, 1993; for a review, see Stephan, 1987). We have summarized some of these findings in Chapter 8. Among the most successful applications of this principle have been cooperative learning programs for elementary and secondary school students, such as the jigsaw classroom studies (Aronson et al., 1978). Recently Pettigrew (1994) summarized research findings concerning foreign immigrants in several European countries, which suggest that three key processes are involved in effective intergroup contact. They are: learning about the outgroup, developing positive affect toward the outgroup, and reappraising the nature of one's ingroup, which Pettigrew calls *deprovincialization.* Deprovincialization is a process of becoming less ethnocentric, and a hopeful conclusion from this research is that successful contact with members of one outgroup can generalize to greater tolerance of and willingness to interact with other outgroups.

In addition to intergroup contact, other methods have been used successfully to reduce intergroup prejudice. One approach is to provide majority-group members with a *planned, personal experience of discrimination,* such as minority-group individuals undergo every day. This experience should make them more empathetic and understanding of the problems of minorities, and this method has been used both in elementary classrooms and in sensitivity training for public officials such as police officers (e.g., Pfister, 1975; Sata, 1975; Weiner & Wright, 1973). Another approach to reducing prejudice is *spotlighting people's value conflicts,* which can motivate them to change their beliefs and behavior in the direction of consistency with their underlying values, such as fairness and equality. Rokeach and his colleagues demonstrated that long-lasting attitude and behavioral changes could be produced with this relatively simple technique (e.g., Ball-Rokeach, Rokeach, & Grube, 1984; Rokeach, 1971).

This necessarily brief overview of methods for reducing individual prejudice and discrimination can be supplemented with more comprehensive reviews (e.g., Eberhardt & Fiske, 1996; Hewstone, 1996; Hewstone & Brown, 1986). However, such individual-level interventions have little cumulative effect on the patterns of institutionalized racism in our society that we have discussed earlier in this chapter. Therefore, we turn finally to a discussion of one of the major *structural* attempts to reduce institutionalized patterns of unequal treatment—affirmative action programs.

AFFIRMATIVE ACTION

What Is It?

Affirmative action is a policy that was designed to help women, ethnic minorities, and other groups that had formerly been discriminated against in employment and educational settings. In the previous sections of this chapter we have given examples of how extensively women and ethnic minorities have been and still are disadvantaged and treated as second-class citizens, both in employment and in many other areas of society. For centuries, White males have benefited from favoritism; and even within that group, males with the "right" education, religion, social class, and connections received extra favoritism.

The first approach to ending that favoritism was **equal opportunity** laws and regulations, which aimed to give everyone an equal chance to be chosen for positions, based on their personal qualifications and not on their sex or race. This was an appealing goal, but as a policy it had two major drawbacks. First, it didn't work as intended, for a long series of U.S. presidential executive orders concerning equal opportunity, starting in 1941, did not produce equal outcomes for people with equal qualifications (Lindgren & Taub, 1988). Second, even if it had worked as intended, it did nothing to remedy the effects of past discrimination against "underrepresented groups." Thus, the background of poverty that led to poor education, and the past job discrimination that led to low pay and undeveloped skills, were not corrected or even considered in equal opportunity procedures, which were supposed to be "color-blind" and "gender-blind."

Consequently, **affirmative action** policies were developed to begin to compensate for the history of discrimination against affected groups.

> Affirmative action mandates a consideration of race, ethnicity, and gender. Remedial measures may be court ordered, in response to a finding of previous discrimination; they may be required by law, as they are for federal contractors and subcontractors; or they may be voluntarily adopted. (Clayton & Crosby, 1992, p. 3)

The first affirmative action programs were begun after passage of the Civil Rights Act of 1964. They require a two-step process: First the employer's work force is analyzed to see whether the percentages of race, sex, and ethnic groups in each job category are comparable to the percentages in the labor pool of people qualified for that job. Second, if the percentages do not match, the source of the exclusion is determined, and various positive measures are put into effect to counteract it.

> Examples of such action include targeted recruitment, career advancement training, validation of selection instruments, and in general efforts to search out those who might otherwise not be identified for hiring and promotion, to ensure that they are not missed through the application of inappropriate criteria, and to provide them with special training where necessary and appropriate. (Clayton & Crosby, 1992, p. 19)

Thus, affirmative action often involves special efforts at recruiting underrepresented groups into applicant pools, frequently involves goals for eventual future representation of target groups, but as a result of the Supreme Court's ruling in the 1978 *Bakke* case, it *cannot* involve fixed numerical quotas for hiring or selection (Taylor, 1991). There is no question that it has been very effective in increasing access to employment and education for both women and ethnic minorities in the U.S. (Clayton & Crosby, 1992).

Attitudes Toward Affirmative Action

Starting about 1989, the Supreme Court has increasingly limited the conditions under which it would approve of affirmative action (AA) plans and the types of remedies it would endorse (Taylor, 1991). Following the election of 1994, the Republican majority in Congress began to mount legislative attacks to cut back on affirmative action and on welfare programs in general. Concomitantly, the mood of public opinion seems to have become more critical of the general concept of affirmative action. For instance, in 1995, over 55% of a national sample said that AA programs were no longer needed for either women or ethnic minorities. In contrast, 86% of the same sample strongly agreed that when AA programs were begun 30 years before, they *were* needed, and over 70% agreed that they had helped women and minorities (Moore, 1995).

However, responses about AA in general obscure a great deal of complexity due to differences in people's minds about what constitutes affirmative action (Steeh & Krysan, 1996). Thus, "someone who claims to oppose 'affirmative action programs' may actually support many . . . types of programs" (Norman, 1995, p. 49). In 1995, a national sample showed a surprising amount of support for some specific types of plans:

- 82% approved of job training programs to help make minorities and women better qualified.
- 75% approved of special college-preparatory classes for minorities and women.
- 73% approved of companies making special efforts to find and recruit qualified minorities and women (Norman, 1995, p. 49).

In contrast, large majorities of all groups, including women and Blacks, disapproved of hiring a minority applicant instead of a better qualified White applicant, and a two-thirds majority disapproved of setting aside scholarships for minorities or women.

Overall, more respondents approved of AA programs for women than for minorities. Minority respondents were much more strongly favorable than Whites to AA programs for either women or minorities, and women approved of both kinds more than did men (Moore, 1995). About half of Blacks and one-quarter of women respondents said they felt that discrimination had cost them a job or promotion or admission to college. About one-quarter of White men said they felt they had lost a job or promotion due to AA, and about the same number believed they had seen a woman or minority get an undeserved job due to AA (Norman, 1995).

Criticisms of AA for previously underrepresented groups typically overlook the fact that there have always been various forms of favoritism for privileged groups in society, such as special college admissions for children of large donors or past alumni ("affirmative action for the rich"). They also overlook the cultural bias that is inevitably built into employment and academic tests that are used to screen job and educational applicants. Most basically, they overlook the societal inequities in economic conditions and educational access that make many minority group members less well prepared for jobs or advanced education (Wittig, 1996). Strong steps are needed to repair those inequities, and

AA is one of the few current mechanisms that addresses those problems (cf. Skedsvold & Mann, 1996).

A close parallel to the possible preference that women or minorities may get from AA programs is the preference for military veterans that is a long-established part of hiring for many jobs in civil service and some in industry. However, the veterans' preference has not been attacked during the 1990s debates over AA.

Among the most important recent developments, the University of California Board of Regents voted in 1995 to end all AA in student admissions at all branches of the university, and a federal appeals court in 1996 ordered the University of Texas not to use different admission standards for minorities than for White applicants (Gwynne, 1996). Statewide initiative campaigns and court appeals are following up on these events.

Psychological Research

Until recently, there has been very little empirical research on the implementation and consequences of AA. Psychological research on AA confirms that it is very poorly understood and that it has been implemented in an immense variety of ways (Turner & Pratkanis, 1994a). A number of studies have found that the way in which it is implemented can produce either favorable or detrimental effects on organizations and on its intended beneficiaries. Research shows that some of the resistance to AA is due to aversive racism; however, other resistance stems from it being presented without sufficient explanation and justification (Murrell et al., 1994). The issue of **procedural justice**—developing procedures that are perceived as fair and equitable—importantly affects reactions to AA programs (Nacoste, 1994).

One of the main questions investigated has been AA's effects on recipients. Affirmative action hirees often face a situation of triple jeopardy: solo status as a member of a formerly unrepresented group in the workplace, racial or gender prejudice, and stigma because AA hirees may be perceived as less qualified (de Vries & Pettigrew, 1994). Both theory and empirical research indicate that recipients can disparage their own competence and performance in situations where AA programs rely mainly on target group membership as the criterion for selection (Turner & Pratkanis, 1994b). However, it is important to realize that most of these research findings come from laboratory studies with relatively artificial and short-term tasks. The one survey based on a representative national sample found no negative effects on any social psychological variables for women or African Americans who were employed at firms that practiced AA versus firms that did not. In addition, Black workers at AA firms showed greater occupational ambition and more belief in people's helpfulness (Taylor, 1994).

From a theoretical standpoint, the occasional finding of low self-evaluation by AA recipients can be interpreted as due to attributions of low personal deservingness (Major, Feinstein, & Crocker, 1994) or due to the effects of stereotype threat (Steele, 1996). In either case, it indicates that AA procedures ought to be explained as stressing the primacy of the recipients' qualifications, not just their group membership. This policy recommendation also advances the perception of procedural justice, which increases public acceptance of AA programs. More detailed and specific policies for the effective management of AA programs have been presented by Taylor (1996) and by Turner and Pratkanis (1994b).

A WORD ABOUT CULTURE

Our focus in this chapter has been on gender and ethnicity. In our definition of ethnicity, we indicated that it included similarities in culture, language, traditions, and so on. However, it is important to realize that within any ethnic group there may be great variations in cultural backgrounds—for example, Hispanics born in Central America, Mexico, or the U.S.; Euro-Americans who are Protestant, Catholic, or Jewish; Blacks who are middle-class or lower-class, etc. In particular, social class dimensions involving different degrees of poverty and of education often overlap with other ethnic differences, and form the basis for **classism**—discrimination based on social class differences. When the many dimensions of **culture**, including language, religion, social class, national background, values, traditional practices, and so on, are added to the picture, intergroup relations become incredibly more complex than when only gender and "race" differences are considered. Much more research on varied cultural groups is needed (cf. Loo, Fong, & Iwamasa, 1988). This complexity will make understanding and adapting to other diverse groups even more difficult. However, this is a task that cannot be avoided because, in our fast-shrinking and multiply interconnected world, exposure to members of such diverse groups is becoming more and more inevitable.

Cultural psychology can help in this process, and we will list here a few key references for those who want to read further in this area. The just-published 3-volume *Handbook of Cross-Cultural Psychology* is a massive resource (e.g., Segall, Berry, & Kagitcibasi, 1997), and two recent review chapters give highly compressed summaries of recent empirical and theoretical approaches (Bond & Smith, 1996; Shweder & Sullivan, 1993). For readers seeking an initial general orientation to the field, four articles present helpful conceptual views of issues in studying cultural aspects of behavior (Betancourt & Lopez, 1993; Fiske, 1995; Fowers & Richardson, 1996; Triandis, 1996).

SUMMARY

Human diversity has myriad dimensions, but in our society gender and ethnicity are two of the most important ones. Relationships between different societal groups are influenced by the cultural distance between them, their members' perceived similarity and opportunities for positive contact, and many other variables. Stereotyped beliefs about members of another group and intergroup biases are important elements of prejudiced attitudes or feelings. Behavioral variables related to prejudice are discrimination (unequal or unfair treatment) and racism (a general pattern of negative actions toward an ethnic group), which may be either individual or institutionalized. Other useful concepts in studying intergroup relations include social dominance orientation, intergroup anxiety, and the self-protective reactions of stigmatized groups.

Gender comparisons have been widely studied by psychologists, and in recent years meta-analyses have

provided more complete and objective conclusions about the size of gender differences in various realms. On single dimensions, these differences are typically small even if significant, but the gender of an interaction partner can cause large differences in individuals' behavior. Gender stereotypes in many societies portray women as more expressive and communal, men as more instrumental and agentic in their behavior. Many occupations are strongly gender stereotyped, despite the growth of alternatives in recent decades. The mass media are a major influence in developing and perpetuating gender stereotypes, and also ethnic ones.

Sexism is systematic prejudice and/or discrimination against women, and it is often displayed in institutionalized practices. Individually, it can be either hostile or benevolent in its tone. Stereotypes and sexism have affected women in many ways—in decreased mathematical interests, reduced aspirations, lower feelings of entitlement, challenges to their leadership abilities, and discrimination in employment. A more extreme outgrowth of sexism is violence against women, in the form of sexual harassment, abuse, sexual assault, rape, and the prevalence of pornography.

It is incorrect to call ethnic groups "races," and research on ethnic groups in the U.S. rarely ever contrasts two "pure," homogeneous categories. African Americans' legacy of slavery and legal segregation makes their history unique, but Hispanic and Asian groups also have special distinctive cultural and situational characteristics. Stereotypes about Blacks are largely negative, and are well-known to most Americans. On average, Blacks do tend to score lower than Whites on many cognitive measures, but there is no agreement about how much of the difference is biological and how much is due to centuries of environmental impoverishment.

Claude Steele's creative research has shown that knowledge of a negative stereotype about one's social group can be a potent threat in performance situations relevant to the stereotype. Studies show that this stereotype threat can depress Blacks' test scores and women's mathematics performance. It is very easy to arouse, and it encourages individuals to protectively disidentify from the threatening domain of activity. Steele's research has also shown that techniques of strong teacher support, challenging assignments rather than remediation, and group cooperative learning can help to avoid or lessen the impact of stereotype threat.

Institutionalized racism still keeps minority groups at a strong disadvantage in America, and patterns of prejudice and discrimination are still widespread, though now they are subtler and more indirect than in the era of segregation. Psychologists have done extensive research on modern racism, symbolic racism, aversive racism, and ways to break habits of prejudice. Intergroup contact, under favorable conditions, has been shown to increase understanding and reduce prejudice, especially in cooperative learning situations.

However, broader structural solutions, such as affirmative action programs, are necessary to compensate for the long history of institutionalized racism in our society. Though affirmative action is widely misunderstood, and some of its aspects are currently controversial in the U.S., other aspects are supported by large majorities of the public. There is no doubt that it has been very effective in increasing access to employment and education for both women and ethnic minorities. Recently, psychological research has demonstrated that the way in which affirmative action is implemented can produce either favorable or detrimental effects on organizations and on its intended beneficiaries. Displaying procedural justice and emphasizing the qualifications of those hired are important in gaining public approval of affirmative action programs.

SUGGESTED READINGS

Clayton, O., Jr. (Ed.). (1996). *An American dilemma revisited: Race relations in a changing world.* New York: Russell Sage Foundation.—A collection of chapters analyzing how the status of African Americans has changed in the last 50 years, and prospects for the future of race relations.

Douglas, S. J. (1995). *Where the girls are: Growing up female with the mass media.* New York: Times Books.—A bitingly witty, authoritative, and thought-provoking description and critique of mass media portrayals of desirable gender roles.

Katz, P. A., & Taylor, D. A. (Eds.). (1988). *Eliminating racism: Profiles in controversy.* New York: Plenum.—This volume presents social scientific analyses, often from opposing viewpoints, of many aspects of racism, desegregation, busing, intergroup conflict, and affirmative action.

Macrae, C. N., Stangor, C., & Hewstone, M. (Eds.). (1996). *Stereotypes and stereotyping.* New York: Guilford.—An up-to-date and far-reaching set of chapters covering all aspects of stereotypes, written by many of the most active researchers in the field.

Turner, M. E., & Pratkanis, A. R. (Eds.). (1994c). Social psychological perspectives on affirmative action [Special issue]. *Basic and Applied Social Psychology, 15,* 1–220.—This journal issue contains some of the best recent empirical research on the implementation and consequences of affirmative action programs.

CHAPTER 10

Organizational Settings— Job Satisfaction

It's a pretty good day layin' stone or brick. Not tiring. Anything you like to do isn't tiresome.

Thirty-five, thirty-six seconds to do your job—that includes the walking, the picking up of the parts, the assembly. Go to the next job, with never a letup, never a second to stand and think.

(Reprinted from Terkel, 1974, pp. xlvi & 191)

These are quotes from two men who work with their hands in two different occupations. What characteristics of their jobs could lead workers to such diametrically opposed viewpoints? And what steps could employers take to make workers more satisfied with their jobs?

About 100 years ago in New York City, employees in a carriage shop worked a 13-hour day, six days a week, and on Sundays the employer required that they all be "in the Lord's House" (Bass, Shackleton, & Rosenstein, 1979). Working conditions have changed greatly since then, but a multitude of organizations still control much of our lives: the way we work, much of our recreation, and the running of our communities.

Today, at General Motor's Saturn division, cars are built in an environment markedly different from the typical, monotonous, high-pressure, deafening assembly line. The factory operates with many small work teams where everyone has the authority to solve problems or suggest improvements. Line workers who find a defective part can call the team that supplied it directly, without going through a management bureaucracy. This unusual arrangement is reported to foster efficient production and to reduce absenteeism and job turnover markedly (Woodruff, 1992). What can it tell us about desirable ways to organize industrial jobs?

Applied social psychologists have contributed to the understanding and improved functioning of organizations in many ways—from job design and personnel selection to leadership and labor-management relations. This chapter begins with a brief introduction to several organizational topics on which applied social psychologists have worked constructively. Then, among these important areas, we will concentrate on the topics of job satisfaction and the quality of working life. Clearly, people's satisfaction with their work is one of the most important variables in the area of organizational behavior, and it continues the theme from Chapter 3 of the *quality of life* as a major goal in the work of applied social psychologists. Furthermore, job satisfaction is an area where a social psychological point of view adds important dimensions to the approaches of other social scientists such as economists and political scientists.

For fuller presentations of applied social psychology in organizational settings, see books edited by Carroll (1990) and Murnighan (1993). Many of the following topics are given extended treatment in the massive four-volume *Handbook of Industrial and Organizational Psychology* edited by Marvin Dunnette and colleagues (Dunnette & Hough, 1990–1994).

SOME AREAS OF ORGANIZATIONAL PSYCHOLOGY

Personnel Selection

Personnel selection is the process of selecting from the available candidates for a job the one who can most effectively meet the demands of the position. Though this is often done informally, it can be conceived of as a three-step process. The first step is **job analysis**—determining the requirements for the position. This can be accomplished through observations, interviews, or surveys of people who have worked or are still working in that position, and many standardized instruments have been developed for this purpose.

After the demands of the position have been determined, the second step is selecting the right candidate from the available applicants. This process attempts to use information gained about applicants to predict their performance in that position. The information may come from interviews, an application form, or letters of reference, and this information is then "matched" to

Photograph courtesy of Marvin Dunnette. Reprinted by permission.

Box 10-1

MARVIN DUNNETTE, ORGANIZATIONAL RESEARCHER

Among his 200+ publications, Marvin Dunnette is probably best known for supervising two editions of the *Handbook of Industrial and Organizational Psychology*, which is frequently referred to in this chapter. Born in 1926, he attended the University of California at Berkeley and the University of Minnesota, earning a bachelor's degree in chemical engineering in 1948. After a brief period in engineering research, he shifted to psychology and completed his Ph.D. at the University of Minnesota in 1954. He then worked as Manager of Employee Relations Research for the 3M Company, developing methods for selecting and evaluating employees. In 1960 he returned to teaching at the University of Minnesota, where he is still a professor of psychology.

Dunnette also founded two companies specializing in management consulting and research on better utilization of human resources. Over the years, he has helped to improve selection procedures for many occupations, ranging from police officers, salesmen, firefighters, and power plant operators to lawyers, managers, and Navy recruiters. He has also done research on motivation, morale, job satisfaction, appraisal of job performance, and adolescent drug use. He has consulted for scores of organizations as diverse as AT&T, Frito-Lay, insurance companies, school boards, the U.S. Air Force, and the Civil Service Commission. He has been elected president of the APA Division of Industrial and Organizational Psychology and has written *Personnel Selection and Placement*, *Managerial Behavior, Performance, and Effectiveness*, *Work and Non-Work in the Year 2001*, and *Psychology Applied to Industry*.

the demands of the job (Landy, Shankster, & Kohler, 1994). The third stage of personnel selection is a later evaluation of the success of the selected candidates in order to help refine the selection procedure.

Research on the best predictors of job performance has consistently found that standardized tests of cognitive ability yield the most accurate prediction of performance. Biographical inventories, structured interviews, and personality measures are typically significant contributors to the prediction equation, but not as strong as cognitive ability (Ree, Earles, & Teachout, 1994). Other less-structured sources of information, such as the typical informal job interview, have not been found to be good predictors of performance (Campbell, 1990; McDaniel et al., 1994). This finding is most likely due to the fact that interviewers typically focus on confirming their initial impressions of the candidate, and fail to assess the applicant characteristics that are most crucial to a high level of performance in the position (Dougherty, Turban, & Callender, 1994). Several comprehensive volumes on the selection of personnel are available (e.g., Schmitt & Borman, 1993).

Training and Development

Another area of applied social psychology in organizations is improving the work of employees. Training may be aimed at increasing knowledge, improving skills, or developing new abilities. Training programs typically follow a four-stage sequence (Goldstein, 1991). First, an assessment is made of where the changes are needed, who needs to change, and what behaviors need to be targeted. Next, the objectives of training are established: What are the participants expected to learn, and how will their behavior change? Third, the program is implemented, very often through "in-house" seminars that use lectures, role-playing, films, and/or games. The final step of a training program is an evaluation, which attempts to assess the effectiveness of the program in changing the targeted behaviors. For a detailed overview of training programs, see Craig (1987).

Evaluating Job Performance

Evaluating job performance is an important aspect of work settings. All workers need feedback about their accomplishments and shortcomings. Employers benefit too because evaluations allow them to identify the strengths and weaknesses of their workers, to compare employees' abilities, to document personnel selection, and to assess training needs (Cleveland, Murphy, & Williams, 1989).

One interesting line of research has examined the process of performance evaluations by supervisors and the common errors that they make. A particularly pervasive error is due to the **halo effect**. This term refers to an evaluator not making differential ratings of a per-

son's characteristics, but instead relying on an overall impression (Lance, LaPointe, & Stewart, 1994). For example, a person who is rated low for punctuality and social skills may erroneously also be rated low on intelligence, productivity, and ability. Note that the halo effect denotes similar ratings on several specific traits, but not necessarily favorable ones. This is just one of the many possible errors that are made in the process of evaluating employee performance.

Leadership

Research on leadership has direct implications for the work environment. The simple question is: Who makes the best leader? However, the answer to this question is not yet clear. As we discussed in Chapter 5, research on leadership suggests that although some traits of leaders are correlated with having more productive groups, any particular person's effectiveness as a leader also depends on the task that the group is working on. Furthermore, different styles of leadership lead to different behaviors on the part of group members, so there are also interactions between the characteristics of the leader and the group members.

Group Processes

A group consists of two or more individuals interacting with each other (Forsyth, 1990). Groups are a pervasive part of our everyday lives. They help to give us self-identity, and they have a powerful influence on the ways in which we act. Social psychologists have studied many aspects of group processes, including how groups form, the roles that group members take in their interactions, group cohesiveness, and the emergence of group norms.

One line of research on group processes that is particularly relevant to the work environment is the difference between work done in a group versus an individual working alone. Which performs better, the group or the individual? Research indicates that groups can have both positive and negative effects on productivity. On the positive side, small groups of people interacting with each other will usually produce more creative ideas and/or complete a complex task faster than will individuals working alone (Forsyth, 1990).

On the negative side, when people work in a group they may have a tendency to coast—to diminish their efforts and rely on others to take up the slack—a phenomenon termed **social loafing**. Whether the group is discussing everyday tasks, considering major organizational changes, or simply deciding where to eat lunch, some people will work harder than others (Kerr, 1989). Research shows that social loafing is more likely to occur in large groups, on tasks that are trivial or only moderately important, and under conditions where each person's contribution cannot be assessed (Karau & Williams, 1993). As an applied example, workers in an automobile factory will tend to be more careful about their work and less likely to deliver defective components if they are required to sign for each piece of work they complete (Shepperd, 1993).

JOB SATISFACTION

Now let's turn to the important topic of job satisfaction, and examine what causes it, and the consequences it has on the behavior of employees. Job satisfaction can have a tremendous effect on many aspects of an organization. Early studies of attitudes toward work started before World War I and were actively pursued in Great Britain and Europe as well as in the United States. Among the central topics was the question of how to combat monotony and boredom on the job, and as early as the 1920s the suggested antidotes included piece-work pay, rest periods, increased variety of work, social interaction, and even background music.

In the United States, probably the most influential research on the effects of working conditions on job satisfaction and productivity was the famous Hawthorne studies, named for the Hawthorne plant of the Western Electric Company, where they were conducted (Mayo, 1933; Roethlisberger & Dickson, 1939). The conclusion traditionally drawn from those studies was that the physical working conditions (such as lighting and rest periods) were far less important in affecting satisfaction and productivity than were the friendly informality of the work group and the fact that management was paying attention to them and giving them a special status as an experimental group. This conclusion led to the term **Hawthorne effect**, referring

to any artifactual improvement in performance due to people being given special or experimental treatment. It also gave great impetus to the **human relations movement** in industrial management, which stressed interpersonal relations and supervisory practices designed to maintain employee motivation.

Ironically, however, critical reanalyses of the Hawthorne studies' data have developed evidence that working conditions *were* major causes of the workers' productivity gains, after all (Parsons, 1974, 1992). Specifically, the pay system was changed to provide incentives based on the production of the small experimental group, and the workers received regular feedback of information about their production levels, based on the detailed performance records kept by the experimenters. In addition, the workers' hourly productivity fell when rest periods were eliminated and rose when they were reintroduced. These factors, rather than the friendly, informal supervision may have been responsible for most of the effects obtained in the research. Consequently, the causes and effects of job satisfaction must be studied anew, with better research designs and better data than in the early studies.

Measuring Job Satisfaction

The usual measuring instruments for job satisfaction are self-report rating scales, and the typical research design in the area is a correlational one, relating satisfaction to one or more hypothesized antecedents or consequents. Perhaps the most widely used and carefully constructed measuring instrument is the Job Descriptive Index (JDI), developed at Cornell (Smith, 1974). On it respondents write *yes* or *no* beside several adjectives or brief phrases that describe each of five aspects of their work situation: the work itself, supervision, co-workers, pay, and opportunities for promotion. Another well-designed instrument is the Minnesota Satisfaction Questionnaire (MSQ), which obtains Likert-type ratings of the respondent's degree of satisfaction on five items for each of 20 scales, including ability utilization, creativity of the job, variety of work, job security, and physical working conditions (Weiss et al., 1967).

Each of these approaches to measuring job satisfaction assumes that it is a function of a finite and stable set of situational and personal variables that can be measured validly at a single point in time. Some critics have proposed that job satisfaction is mostly dispositional (i.e., a personality trait), rather than being closely tied to characteristics of the job (e.g., Staw & Ross, 1985). However, more careful analyses of the current and retrospective reports of people who have changed jobs have supported the validity of job satisfaction ratings by showing that they are more sensitive to aspects of the specific job than to general aspects of the employing organization or to stable personality characteristics (Gutek & Winter, 1992). Another criticism with some research support is that job satisfaction may also be partly determined by respondents' short-term emotional state when they complete the survey (Quartstein et al., 1992). As a trivial example, one study found that giving workers a cookie before they completed a measure of job satisfaction increased their overall ratings in comparison to a control group (Brief, Butcher, & Roberson, 1995).

Theories of Job Satisfaction

The major theoretical conceptions of job satisfaction are the following:

- **Expectancy theories** consider satisfaction to be determined by how fully one's expectations are matched by one's achievements, and dissatisfaction to be caused by failing to meet one's expectations.
- **Need theories** view satisfaction as a function of the degree of fulfillment of a person's needs, including both physical and psychological needs. Needs are conceptualized as objective human requirements, similar for all people, whereas values are viewed as subjective desires, which vary from person to person.
- **Value theories** see job satisfaction as determined by whether the job allows attainment of the individual's own personal values.

Organizational psychologists have often cited Maslow's (1970) **need-hierarchy theory** as applicable to job satisfaction. The theory posits five kinds of human needs. Arranged from most to least fundamental, they are: physiological needs (such as food, water, and air), safety needs (such as freedom from danger and economic security), social needs (for love, acceptance,

and group belongingness), esteem or ego needs (achievement, recognition, approval, and feelings of self-worth), and self-actualization needs (seeking to fulfill one's potential to the utmost). According to Maslow, only when the more fundamental needs are relatively well met will the higher needs become operative. Hence, job satisfaction should be determined by how well the job meets the needs that are dominant for a given individual (the most fundamental needs which are not already well-fulfilled). For one individual, that might be a need for economic security, while for another it might be a need for self-actualization, so naturally the same job could give them drastically different levels of satisfaction.

Another theory of job satisfaction is Herzberg's (1966) two-factor theory. He posited two kinds of needs (roughly parallel to Maslow's categories): physical needs and psychological needs. According to Herzberg, these two kinds of needs operate on two different principles. Physical needs operate to avoid pain or discomfort; factors that counteract these needs (Herzberg called them hygiene factors) can reduce or avoid discomfort, but cannot produce pleasure. On the other hand, psychological needs, such as striving for growth, knowledge, achievement, creativity, and individuality, operate on a pleasure principle; their satisfiers (called motivators) can produce pleasure, but their lack or absence does not produce displeasure or discomfort. Thus, the two dimensions of satisfaction and dissatisfaction are viewed by Herzberg as independent of each other. Either may be present or absent in any degree, regardless of the other, and it is possible to be simultaneously satisfied and dissatisfied with different aspects of the same job.

Though all the theories of job satisfaction sound plausible and seem to fit many work situations, they are mutually incompatible at various points. For instance, Maslow's theory indicates that a satisfied need does not continue to motivate future behavior, whereas Herzberg disagrees. Maslow's theory ignores the importance of values, as contrasted with needs, in determining satisfaction. Herzberg's theory makes an extreme and unwarranted mind-body distinction between the physical and psychological needs. At this stage of the field, there is relatively little empirical evidence supporting any of these theories, though there is considerable nonsupportive evidence about Herzberg's concept that the factors governing satisfaction and dissatisfaction are independent of each other (Waters & Waters, 1972).

Combining the most reasonable and compatible aspects of all of these theories, Locke (1976) presented the following tentative definition of **job satisfaction**:

> Job satisfaction results from the appraisal of one's job as attaining or allowing the attainment of one's important job values, providing these values are congruent with or help to fulfill one's basic needs. These needs are of two separable but interdependent types: bodily or physical needs and psychological needs, especially the need for growth. Growth is made possible mainly by the nature of the work itself. (p. 1319)

Note how this definition includes both needs and values, while maintaining the distinction between them. It also emphasizes the different types of needs that a job can fulfill, and it stresses the nature of the work itself more strongly than the many context factors (such as pay, working conditions, relations with co-workers, and supervision), though it recognizes that the context factors can also contribute to job satisfaction.

There is one marked limitation of all the available theories: they fail to consider family-related factors. As Bruce and Blackburn (1992) pointed out:

> Any considerations of job satisfaction and performance must view the worker as an integral part of a family, both away from work and at the worksite. (p. 120)

This limitation is especially important given the recent changes toward a more gender-balanced workforce (Romzek, 1991). Traditionally, in both organizational research and organizational policies, the family has been disregarded, but there is a growing recognition that an important factor to include in job satisfaction models is how the work meshes with the worker's family situation.

A Model of Job Satisfaction

A useful model of the process of achieving job satisfaction and the factors that affect it has been presented by Ferratt and Starke (1977). A schematic diagram of the model is shown in Figure 10–1, but it needs some explanation to make its implications clear.

A convenient starting place in the model is the left-hand box labeled "employee need structure." It is one determinant of job motivation, which influences productivity, which in turn affects rewards. However, at each of these steps there are "other determinants," shown in the boxes above, which combine with the immediately preceding causal factor to help determine the next succeeding factor. For instance, job motivation is one factor in productivity but not the only one. Productivity is also influenced by task design (easy or difficult); individual personal factors like skills and abilities; group factors such as norms that encourage or discourage production; organizational factors, such as communication with other work groups that are also involved in the overall task; and so on. Next, the rewards that workers receive are posited to determine their need satisfaction in the work situation, but needs can also be satisfied off the job (as indicated in the lower left-hand box), so these two types of need satisfaction combine and cycle back to determine the individual's overall need structure. Similarly, need satisfaction on the job is not the only determinant of overall job satisfaction, for workers' perception of the equity of their rewards and their expectations of future need satisfaction (shown in the large lower box) are also important factors in determining job satisfaction. Finally, overall job satisfaction does directly determine continuing on the job versus quitting, and naturally only employees who stay on the job can continue to receive rewards and potential need satisfaction there.

Note that in this model job satisfaction does *not* lead to productivity, as has often been expected by organizational managers. Instead, the model shows the reverse direction of relationship, with productivity being one of the factors that combine to determine job satisfaction (cf. Locke & Latham, 1990). Though the model summarizes many research findings, it is mainly a heuristic guide to the variables involved rather than a final and definitive conclusion about the whole area. For instance, it seems that a number of context factors not shown in the model (such as working conditions, relations with co-workers, and supervision) are determinants of job satisfaction, in addition to the direct rewards of the job itself. Perhaps the greatest value of the model is to underline the complexity of the area and the many factors and relationships involved.

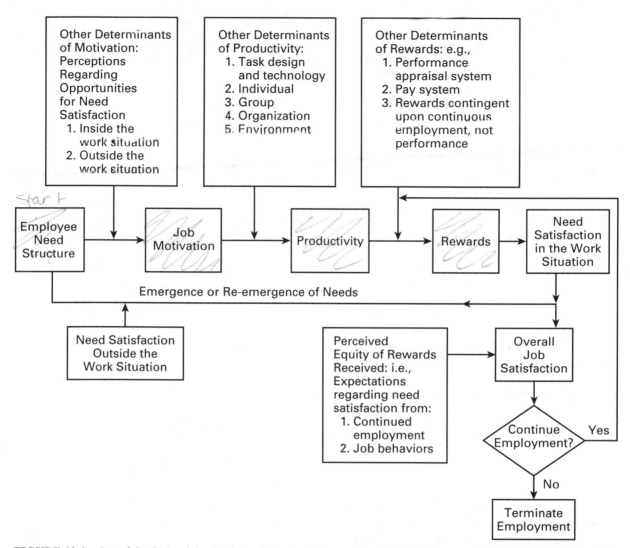

FIGURE 10-1 A model relating job satisfaction to motivation and productivity. (Source: Ferratt, T. W., & Starke, F. A. Satisfaction, motivation, and productivity: The complex connection. In J. L. Gray & F. A. Starke (Eds.), *Readings in Organizational Behavior: Concepts and Applications* (p. 84). Columbus, OH: Merrill, 1977. Reprinted with permission.)

CAUSAL FACTORS INFLUENCING JOB SATISFACTION

When measured by self-report surveys, job satisfaction levels of American workers have generally been found to be high. For example, in national survey studies, from 85% to 90% of American workers have reported that they are either "somewhat satisfied" or "very satisfied" with their jobs, with about half saying that they are "very satisfied" (Quinn & Stalnes, 1979). Even in assembly-line work, which psychologists have described as monotonous, meaningless, and dehumanizing, a very high percentage of workers report general job satisfaction. Figures for factory workers have ranged from a high of 95% satisfaction for a group of 576 union members working in an auto plant to a low of 76% satisfaction for 440 employees in a paper mill—still a surprisingly high level (Taylor, 1977).

These reported levels of job satisfaction are higher than the levels expected by researchers, by members of the lay public, or even by workers themselves when they are asked to estimate the satisfaction of their co-workers (Gutek, 1978). Consequently, *absolute* levels of job satisfaction should be interpreted with caution. In some cases they probably represent an offhand or guarded response to an interviewer's question; in other cases they may indicate resigned adjustment to an undesirable work situation (Taylor, 1977).

Though absolute levels of job satisfaction must be interpreted cautiously, *relative* levels can still be very informative concerning the conditions that increase or decrease satisfaction. Relative levels are involved when research reports compare the job satisfaction of two or more groups or of various treatment conditions. Let us examine the kinds of factors that are causal influences on workers' job satisfaction. In the section that follows, the many factors affecting job satisfaction will be divided into **intrinsic, content factors**—those inherent in the work itself—and **extrinsic, context factors**, which in turn can be divided into **working conditions**—impersonal circumstances of the job—and **interpersonal relations** on the job.

The Work Itself

Research has shown many work attributes to be related to job satisfaction. Most of these job attributes seem to share the element of personal challenge (Locke, 1976).

Probably the most basic attribute here is that the work must be **personally interesting and meaningful** to the individual in question (Herzberg, Mausner, & Snyderman, 1959; Nord, 1977). Obviously, this specification makes work satisfaction subject to a wide range of individual differences, for individuals with one set of values, abilities, and backgrounds may find a particular kind of work personally interesting, while people with different values, abilities, and backgrounds may find the same work completely unmeaningful. A more objective aspect of meaningfulness is **task significance**—the impact of the work on the lives of other people, or in the overall organizational work process (Mottaz, 1988). For example, a worker riveting aircraft wings has a more significant job than one riveting trash containers, and is likely to feel more satisfaction with it. A somewhat similar work attribute is **task identity**—doing a "whole" job, or at least a portion where one's personal contribution is clear and visible.

Various other characteristics of the job have been found to be positively related to job satisfaction (Griffin et al., 1980; Gruneberg, 1979; Hackman & Lawler, 1971). **Application of skill** is a job feature that workers often boast about. Another important job aspect is **job autonomy**—the worker having a say in when and how to perform the job.

The negative effect of monotonous, repetitive work on job satisfaction has been well documented (Cox, 1985). On assembly lines and other jobs that involve much repetitive work, the amount of **variety** in the job has frequently been found to be positively related to job satisfaction (e.g., Ross & Reskin, 1992). As an example, "utility workers" and others who rotate from job to job usually show higher satisfaction than workers who perform only one operation all day long, and this finding has been the basis of many "job enrichment" schemes. However, research indicates that people's *perception* of their job as being boring or monotonous is a more important determinant of dissatisfaction than any objective measure of the demands of the work (Melamed et al., 1995). Furthermore, jobs with so much challenge that the worker cannot cope with it may lead to failure, job stress, and job dissatisfaction.

Working Conditions (Impersonal)

Pay. Pay is one of the most important working conditions for almost all occupational groups (Lawler, 1981, 1990). Yet even here there is conflicting evidence, for some studies have found pay to be relatively unimportant in determining job satisfaction for certain groups of workers (Berkowitz et al., 1987). In his book on *Understanding Job Satisfaction*, Gruneberg (1979) concluded:

> It appears that money means different things to different groups, and is likely to have greater importance for individuals who cannot gain other satisfactions from their job. (p. 62)

Perhaps for that reason, pay is the job aspect about which the largest proportion of employees are dissatisfied (Lawler, 1981). This is consistent with Herzberg's theoretical contention that pay is a "hygiene factor"—that is, a factor that can be a source of dissatisfaction if it is low, but cannot produce satisfaction if it is high.

However, this viewpoint overlooks the many symbolic meanings of workers' pay levels—such as being signs of achievement, recognition, esteem, and value to the employer—which can contribute to job satisfaction.

Yet pay is not just a simple and objective factor. Contrary to theories of economic determinism, psychologists have emphasized that there are many individual differences in the meaning of money, varying with the worker's stage in life, personal experiences, gender, economic status, and personality characteristics (Berkowitz et al., 1987). For example, research on gender differences indicates that women tend to be just as satisfied as men even when their pay is less than men's (Jackson, 1989). Thus, no single formula can determine people's satisfaction with their pay.

Theories of social comparison, relative deprivation,

Photograph courtesy of Edward Lawler. Reprinted by permission.

Box 10-2

EDWARD LAWLER, ORGANIZATIONAL THEORIST

A leader in the field of organizational research, Edward E. Lawler was born in 1938. He competed in varsity football and track at Brown University and later earned his Ph.D. in psychology from the University of California at Berkeley in 1964. After teaching at Yale for eight years, he was appointed a professor of psychology at the University of Michigan, where he also served as a program director in the Survey Research Center. In 1978 he moved to the University of Southern California as a professor of organizational behavior in the School of Business Administration and as founding director of the Center for Effective Organizations.

Lawler has authored or coauthored over 200 articles, and his work has been translated into seven languages. His 25 books include *Strategic Pay, Employee Involvement, Motivation in Work Organizations, Managing Organizational Behavior,* and *Creating High Performance Organizations.* His research has won awards from the American Compensation Association and the American College of Hospital Administrators. As a consultant or board member, he has provided advice to over 100 organizations, including the U.S. Department of Commerce, the Work in America Institute, and the American Center for the Quality of Work Life—activities that are closely connected with the topic of this chapter.

and equity are particularly relevant to the topic of pay levels. Whatever one's background or actual level of pay, it appears that satisfaction with one's paycheck is usually a function of the *relative* level of pay, in comparison with other similar workers, rather than of the *absolute* level of pay (Berkowitz et al., 1987; Orpen & Nonnici, 1990). For example, women who are satisfied with less pay than men may be using other women as their reference group (Bylsma & Major, 1994; Major, 1987). Some research suggests that the recent changes toward a more gender-balanced work context are changing women's judgments about what is a fair salary (Loscocco & Spitze, 1991). This shift toward more similar male-female expectations about pay is also related to a general reduction in job satisfaction among women. Although this line of research indicates that perceptions of pay equity are an important part of one's job satisfaction, the processes by which one chooses a reference group with which to compare oneself are still only poorly understood.

Another aspect of pay is the system by which wages are determined. Most studies have found that hourly pay is preferred to piecework systems by most workers, and straight salaries are preferred to incentive schemes (Brown & Huber, 1992; Thierry, 1987). One reason for this is that incentive schemes tend to disrupt social relationships on the job, which are another major source of worker satisfactions. However, there is an interesting paradox here, for wage incentive schemes generally result in greater *productivity* than does hourly pay (Heneman, 1992; Warr & Wall, 1975), and productivity often is associated with job satisfaction.

Job Security. Job security is also a crucial aspect of working conditions, and a strong determinant of job satisfaction, as well as life satisfaction and physical health. A longitudinal study of automobile workers found that those who did not have secure positions were less satisfied with their job and experienced more physical ailments than secure workers (Heaney, Israel, & House, 1994). The authors suggested that job insecurity leads to job stress, and that the resulting stress causes the health and attitudinal differences. In the following section of this chapter the effects of job stress are discussed in more detail.

Role Ambiguity. Role ambiguity is another aspect of working conditions that contributes to dissatisfaction (House & Rizzo, 1972; Itzhaky, 1993). Examples of role ambiguity are unclear job duties and expectations, or vague criteria for obtaining promotions and raises. Such ambiguity has been found to be particularly hard on workers with a high need for achievement, but less of a problem for workers with high ability (Johnson & Stinson, 1975; Schuler, 1977).

Organizational Structure. Organizational structure includes a number of aspects. Organizational size often interacts with personal values in influencing satisfaction. For instance, workers in very large organizations are often attracted by their high pay levels, while workers in very small firms tend to be motivated more by job variety and social relationships (Bruce & Blackburn, 1992; Ingham, 1970). Hierarchical bureaucratic structures with a large number of job levels can lead to poor communication and worker alienation. In particular, managers, teachers, and salesmen have all been found to be more satisfied in "flat," nonbureaucratic organizational structures than in "tall," bureaucratic ones (Palardy, 1992; Porter & Lawler, 1968).

Physical Working Conditions. Physical working conditions, as you would expect, generally produce more satisfaction if they are comfortable and not dangerous. Moderate levels of temperature, humidity, ventilation, lighting, and noise are preferred over either extreme of the continuum (Locke, 1976). A recent quasi-experimental study of over 2000 office employees investigated the effect of renovations to the office areas on job satisfaction and performance. Prior to renovations, noise was found to correlate negatively with job satisfaction, but not with productivity. Following renovations, workers whose office environments had become quieter reported more job satisfaction, whereas employees who were experiencing more noise were less satisfied. However, no changes were observed for productivity following the renovations (Sundstrom et al., 1994).

Environmental Factors. Environmental factors outside the workplace can also influence job satisfaction (Bruce & Blackburn, 1992). Generally, being located in small cities leads to more job satisfaction than living in very large cities. Weather conditions, housing, shopping facilities, recreational facilities, and cost of living in the area have also been found to be important. Workers often trade off unpleasant environmental conditions, such as service in a "hardship post," for advantages in pay, job security, or advancement. On the other hand, living in prosperous, high status communities does not necessarily produce high job satisfaction because satisfaction is *relative* to the conditions of other people in the community—workers tend to be more satisfied when their own circumstances are better than those of other people in the same area.

Interpersonal Relations

Co-Worker Relations. Co-worker relations are frequently the most important factor of all in determining job satisfaction or dissatisfaction (Herzberg et al., 1957). In an early study by Van Zelst (1952), when employees were allowed to choose their own workmates, their job satisfaction increased, and turnover and work costs decreased. Other studies have found that job satisfaction is positively influenced by popularity with other workers and by degree of group cohesiveness (Adams & Slocum, 1971; Van Zelst, 1951). Even off-the-job social relations can contribute to job satisfaction or dissatisfaction (Gruneberg, Startup, & Tapsfield, 1974). Argyle (1988, 1989) has demonstrated that much of the sociable interaction in work settings occurs nonverbally. Friendship is established and maintained through expressing attitudes of approval in facial expressions, mutual gaze, and body language.

Supervision. Supervision has historically been regarded as a very important job dimension, though reports by employees indicate that it is considerably less important to them than co-worker relationships (Herzberg et al., 1957). Typically, 60% or more of the employees in any organization report that the worst or most stressful part of their job is their supervisor, and some researchers have suggested that 60% or more of American managers are incompetent in supervision (Hogan, Raskin, & Fazzini, 1990). The research data here are related to our discussion of leadership in Chapter 5. Many U.S. studies have found that consid-

erate supervision produces greater job satisfaction than does task-oriented supervision, and that supervisors high on both dimensions are liked best of all (Newsome & Pillari, 1991; Zaccaro, Craig, & Quinn, 1991).

However, there are exceptions to this pattern. Some research suggests that compatibility in beliefs among supervisors and subordinates is an important determinant of job satisfaction (Rowley, Rosse, & Harvey, 1992). For example, workers with authoritarian personality structures may prefer autocratic, directive leadership rather than a more democratic leader. This pattern of findings regarding satisfaction fits well with contingency theories of leadership, which specify that differing work circumstances call for different types of leadership.

Participation in Decision Making. Participation in decision making is partly a work-conditions factor, and partly an interpersonal factor. In most surveys of worker opinions, employees report that they want to participate in decision making about their own job situation, and those who have experienced participation generally retain favorable attitudes toward the experience afterwards. Correlational research and meta-analyses of the literature have consistently found significant positive relationships between participation in decision making and job satisfaction (Cotton, 1993; Packard, 1989). However, studies are also consistent in showing little or no positive effect of employee participation on *job performance*. For an excellent overview of the research on employee involvement in decision making, see Cotton (1993).

Job Stress. The term *job stress* is used to designate the many sources of stress that result from working in an organizational environment. Stress can be produced by both social and physical aspects of the working environment, and psychologists have made extensive studies of a long list of contributory factors (Sauter, Murphy, & Hurrell, 1990). There are many different theories of job stress, each with its own definition of stress (Kahn & Byosiere, 1992). Despite the variety of theories, they all focus on a similar sequence of events: Some characteristic of the work environment leads to stress; stress produces a physiological response in the worker; the worker attempts to cope with the stress;

and ultimately some effect occurs. This sequence suggests that stress is a mediating variable between the many different impinging factors and the ultimate job dissatisfaction. That is, it is an essential intervening condition.

The major causes of job stress seem to be work demands, role ambiguity, and role conflict. One source of job stress is a mismatch between the abilities of the individual and the demands of the job (Jamal, 1990). For example, a person with weak creative or artistic skills is not a good fit in a work environment like advertising that requires these skills. However, many characteristics of the individual can mediate the effects of stress resulting from different work environments. The social structure, one's personality, and one's coping mechanisms can help lessen (or increase) the impact of job stress (Berry & Houston, 1993).

So what is the relationship between job stress and job satisfaction? By and large, research on this issue has found a consistently strong negative relationship between job stress and job satisfaction. However, because the data regarding job stress are correlational, it is difficult to identify whether job dissatisfaction causes stress, or stress causes job dissatisfaction, or both. A true experiment to resolve this causal problem would be both unethical and very difficult to conduct, because people do not want to be randomly assigned to job-match versus job-mismatch conditions. Instead, as we discussed in Chapter 5, researchers have used causal modeling techniques in attempts to demonstrate likely causal links between job stress and job satisfaction. A recent study employing causal modeling found that job satisfaction and job stress both have a causal effect on each other, in a reciprocal manner (Judge, Boudreau, & Bretz, 1994).

PUTTING IT ALL TOGETHER—
AN ILLUSTRATIVE STUDY

In the preceding section, we have presented many variables that have been found to affect job satisfaction—at least 16 major sources plus various other minor sources. A resulting question is how well these variables can predict who is satisfied with their job, and who is not. That is, if we measure all of these variables,

and use them to predict job satisfaction, how accurate will the prediction be?

Methodology

A recent study by Agho, Mueller, and Price (1993) attempted to answer this question. The organization studied was a Veterans Administration Medical Center. Its 823 employees were a diverse group, including both white-collar workers (e.g., clerks, nurses, social workers, psychologists, dentists, and physicians), and blue-collar ones (e.g., housekeeping, maintenance, and grounds workers).

Data were collected through questionnaires completed at two points in time, with three months between the first and second collection times. The longitudinal design was used to examine causal links between the predictor and criterion variables. In the first wave of data collection, the questionnaire contained measures of the independent variables used to predict job satisfaction, as well as an initial measure of job satisfaction. The predictor variables included many of the work-related features discussed above, as well as personality variables and demographic variables (see Table 10–1 for a brief definition of each of these variables). The second wave of data collection only obtained measures of job satisfaction, plus information on changes in work experiences, including promotions, pay raises, supervisor changes, and transfers.

Of the 823 employees surveyed, 550 returned their questionnaires on the first wave, and 419 of these returned the second-wave questionnaire. The researchers dropped 14 respondents because they had experienced one of the changes in work experiences listed above. The remaining 405 consisted of 40% men and 60% women; 58% white-collar and 42% blue-collar, 84% full-time and 16% part-time workers.

Several preliminary tests were conducted. Because the sample comprised only 50% of the employees, it was important to know whether the respondents in the sample were different from those who did not respond. Analyses showed that the sample was similar to the total group of employees in terms of gender, white-collar/blue-collar, and full-time/part-time workers. Second, differences between part-time and full-time workers were examined, and the results indicated that

**TABLE 10-1   Definitions of Predictor Variables
of Job Satisfaction**

Opportunity: availability of alternative jobs in the
organization's environment.

Autonomy: degree to which employees have freedom to act
independently on the job.

Role ambiguity: degree to which role expectations are
unclear.

Role conflict: degree to which role expectations are
incompatible.

Role overload: degree to which various role expectations
exceed the amount of time and resources available for
their accomplishment.

Distributive justice: degree to which rewards and
punishments are related to performance inputs.

Supervisory support: degree to which supervisors are
helpful in job-related matters.

Internal labor market: degree to which the organization job
structure is characterized by job ladders, entry limited to
the bottom, and upward mobility which is accompanied
by a progressive development of skill and knowledge.

Task significance: degree to which an individual's job
contributes to the overall organizational work process.

Integration: extent to which employees have close friends
in their immediate work unit.

Pay: money and its equivalent received by employees for
their services.

Routinization: degree to which a job is repetitive.

Work motivation: belief in the centrality of the work role in
one's life.

Positive affectivity: degree to which an individual is
predisposed to be happy.

Negative affectivity: degree to which an individual is
predisposed to experience discomfort.

Job satisfaction: degree to which individuals like their jobs.

Kinship responsibility: Involvement in kinship groups in
the community.

Source: Adapted from Agho, A., Mueller, C., & Price, J. (1993). Determinants of employee satisfaction: An empirical test of a causal
model. *Human Relations, 46,* 1012. Reprinted with permission.

they only differed on demographic variables, and not
on any of the work related variables.

To provide an accurate and reliable measure of each
construct, all of the work-related variables in this study
were measured with multiple questions (with the exception of pay, which was obtained from personnel
records). For example, job satisfaction was measured
with a 6-item global satisfaction index which had been
used in previous studies. The reliability coefficients for
the measures were good, ranging from .72 to .95, with
an average of .85.

Results

Recall that the purpose of this study was to test how
well the variables described above could predict job
satisfaction. Table 10–2 summarizes the results from
two analyses conducted in the study. The first and simplest way to find the contribution of each variable to
satisfaction is to examine its correlation coefficient
with satisfaction. The first column of Table 10–2 presents these correlations for the second-wave satisfaction measure. These correlation coefficients indicate
that, with the exception of role overload, all of the
work-related predictor variables were significantly related to job satisfaction. Also, the personality variables
of work motivation and positive and negative affectivity were significant predictors of job satisfaction—e.g.,
employees who were predisposed to be happy across
time and situations were more likely to be satisfied
with their jobs. Further, job satisfaction was found to
have a significant degree of stability—i.e., employees
who were satisfied at the first wave of measurement
tended to be satisfied at the second wave as well,
though the relationship was not high.

A problem with any such set of zero-order correlation coefficients is that they do not consider the relationships *among* the predictor variables, but only those
between each predictor variable and the criterion, job
satisfaction. It is typical for many of the predictors to
be related to each other (e.g., routinization was negatively related to autonomy, $r = -.49$). For this reason,
a second analysis was conducted, using a statistical
procedure that accounted for the overlap among predictor variables as well as the relationship between
each predictor and satisfaction. The authors used structural equation modeling procedures, and the results
from this analysis are summarized in the final column
of Table 10–2. The coefficients listed there represent
the true, unique strength of the relationship between
each predictor variable and job satisfaction, independent of the other overlapping predictors. The results
show that opportunity, distributive justice, routinization, work motivation, and positive affectivity were

TABLE 10-2   Findings in Predicting Job Satisfaction at Wave 2

Predictor variables	Zero-order correlations	Combined model
Opportunity	−.11*	−.09*
Autonomy	.48**	.10
Role ambiguity	−.34**	−.07
Role conflict	−.28**	−.01
Role overload	−.04	−.04
Distributive justice	.52**	.22**
Supervisory support	.40**	.05
Internal labor market	.19*	−.07
Task significance	.37**	.01
Integration	.27**	−.03
Pay	.24**	−.02
Routinization	−.54**	−.35**
Work motivation	.35*	.16**
Positive affectivity	.44**	.24**
Negative affectivity	−.27**	−.09
Age	.23**	
Sex	.06	
Education	.11*	
Occupation	.05	
Tenure	.02	
Marital status	.02	
Job satisfaction (wave 1)	.19**	
Combined R^2 (% of variance explained)		.57

*$p < .05$.   **$p < .01$.

Source: Adapted from Agho, A., Mueller, C., & Price, J. (1993). Determinants of employee satisfaction: An empirical test of a causal model. *Human Relations, 46,* 1020. Reprinted with permission.

the only variables that made unique contributions to the prediction of satisfaction. Combined, the predictor variables accounted for 57% of the variance in job satisfaction—a gratifyingly large amount.

Conclusions. The results from this study demonstrate that many of the variables discussed in the previous section of this chapter make significant and independent contributions to job satisfaction. In this study of medical center employees, low routinization, high distributive justice, and low availability of alternative jobs within the organization were the three work-related characteristics that independently predicted job satisfaction. In addition, people who were typically happy and who saw the work role as central in their life tended to be more satisfied. Finally, the re-

sults indicated that job satisfaction was a somewhat stable attitude across time, though they raised an interesting question as to why its stability was not higher. However, the results also showed that we cannot fully explain why people are satisfied or dissatisfied with their jobs (since over 40% of the variance was still not explained), suggesting that additional predictor variables need to be considered.

CONSEQUENCES OF JOB SATISFACTION

Productivity

What are the consequences of workers being satisfied or dissatisfied with their jobs? In the minds of many managers, a likely and important outcome is *productivity*, on the theory that "a happy worker is a productive worker." Unfortunately however, this theory has often been refuted in empirical research. Thorough reviews of the literature have usually found little or no relationship between satisfaction and work productivity (Iaffaldano & Muchinsky, 1985; Organ, 1988). Instead, job satisfaction appears to be correlated with "citizenship behaviors." People who are more satisfied with their work tend to interact with people in a more friendly and congenial manner. Organ (1988) defined **citizenship behaviors** as "helpful, constructive gestures exhibited by organization members and valued or appreciated by officials, but not related directly to individual productivity nor inhering in the enforcement requirements of the individual's role" (p. 548).

An alternative way of viewing the satisfaction-productivity relationship was suggested by Porter and Lawler (1968). They argued that productivity should be considered as one of the causes of job satisfaction, rather than the other way around. (Note that this causal order was indicated by the diagram in Figure 10–1.) The reasoning behind this directional relationship is that high productivity often leads to rewards, such as high earnings, recognition, and promotion, and to attainment of the worker's important job values, such as success and achievement. In turn these factors will lead to satisfaction with the job, provided that the productivity was not achieved at too high a cost in effort or damaged family relationships.

The traditionally expected directional relationship (satisfaction leading to productivity), though intuitively plausible to the lay person, assumes the operation of much more complex and questionable mediating processes. For instance, if the worker's satisfaction with the job were based on working conditions, such as the level of pay, or on social interactions on the job, and neither of these were contingent on productivity, there is little reason to think that satisfaction would lead to high production. Locke (1976) pointed out many other mediating variables that must not be overlooked: for instance, whether a worker has enough ability and knowledge to achieve a high level of production, what goals workers set for themselves, and the action alternatives that a worker chooses in response to feelings of

satisfaction (such as slacking off, switching jobs, or continuing to work hard).

Absenteeism

In contrast with the findings on productivity, there is more research agreement on the causal relation of job satisfaction to absenteeism. Most reviews have concluded that there is a direct negative correlation between job satisfaction and absenteeism (Brooke & Price, 1989). Three separate meta-analyses have included an assessment of the relationship between absenteeism and job satisfaction. The findings across 23, 26, and 31 studies (Hackett & Guion, 1985; McShane, 1984; Scott & Taylor, 1985) were average correlation coefficients of $-.19$, $-.25$, and $-.13$ between absenteeism and job satisfaction. Hackett (1989) reexamined these meta-analyses and conservatively estimated the correlation between overall job satisfaction and frequency of absence at $-.09$ ($N = 3767$), and the correlation between overall job satisfaction and duration of absence at $-.15$ ($N = 974$).

The significant correlations reported above indicate that job satisfaction is related to absenteeism, but the relationship may not necessarily be a causal one. Tharenou (1993) suggested that absenteeism may be a cause of job dissatisfaction as well as the other way around. In addition, many different job circumstances can dilute the typical negative relationship between satisfaction and absenteeism. A generous sick-leave policy may encourage absences even among satisfied workers. On the other hand, dissatisfied workers may come to work regularly due to a feeling of obligation or fear of being fired for absences. Other factors that can influence attendance are social rewards on the job, financial need, and the availability of other jobs.

Employee Turnover

Quitting one's job has often been considered an extension and final stage of absenteeism, and many studies have found that absenteeism is a good predictor of later job termination. A meta-analysis of the relationship between absenteeism and job turnover found an average correlation of .33 (Mitra, Jenkins, & Gupta, 1992).

Similarly, there is strong evidence that low job satisfaction fosters employee turnover (e.g., Cramer,

1993). Cotton and Tuttle (1986) conducted a meta-analysis of over 120 studies on correlates of employee turnover. They found six work-related variables that were strongly associated with employee turnover. Job satisfaction had a strong negative relationship, as did the variables of pay, organizational commitment, and satisfaction with supervision. Cotton and Tuttle (1986) also identified nine personal factors associated with turnover, including lower age, higher education, single marital status, and a low number of dependent children. These findings portray people who are likely to leave an organization as mobile because they are young, well-educated, and do not have a large family to support.

Despite the temptation to conclude that job dissatisfaction *causes* employee turnover, some recent research indicates that the relationship is more complex than expected. Results show that job dissatisfaction and low commitment to the organization reciprocally influence each other, and together lead to turnover (Farkas & Tetrick, 1989). Some researchers have suggested that job satisfaction, as it is generally measured, may not be conceptually distinct from organizational commitment—that is, both measures may be tapping the same underlying construct.

The findings regarding dissatisfaction and turnover hold not only for individuals, but also at the aggregate, organizational level. That is, a company that takes action to increase employees' job satisfaction (or commitment) is likely to achieve a concomitant decrease in turnover (Mobley et al., 1979).

Other Worker Actions

Employee complaints and filing of grievances are frequent results of job dissatisfaction (Locke, 1976). More extreme but much rarer is "whistle-blowing"—reporting of superiors or colleagues for improper or illegal policies or actions on the job. Accidents on the job may also be related to dissatisfaction at times, though the empirical evidence on this topic is limited. Counterproductive behavior such as sabotage, theft, intentional poor work, or starting trouble on the job is also somewhat related to dissatisfaction, according to a study by Mangione and Quinn (1975). Relying on workers' self-reports of these behaviors, this study found that

they were most common among male employees under age 30, but only among male employees over 30 were they consistently linked to job dissatisfaction.

Physical Health

There are many reports in the literature of links between job dissatisfaction and physical symptoms of illnesses, ranging from fatigue and headaches to ulcers and heart disease (e.g., Cooper & Marshall, 1976; Wright, Bengtsson, & Frankenberg, 1994). The connection is a logical one since job dissatisfaction can be a source of stress, and stress is a contributory cause of many physical illnesses (see Chapter 12). Sales and House (1971) found high negative correlations between average job satisfaction and coronary mortality rates for various occupational groups. In a longitudinal study of individual workers, Palmore (1969) found work satisfaction to be the best predictor of long life, though the correlation was only .26.

It is important to realize that all these studies of physical health, even the careful longitudinal ones, are correlational in nature. As a result, many concomitant variables cannot be controlled, and the evidence for causal mechanisms in illness is necessarily speculative (Argyle, 1987). However, within those limitations, it seems that job satisfaction does play a role in influencing health or illness.

Mental Health

In the area of mental health, also, the necessity of correlational research requires cautious interpretations. Several studies have reported relationships between poor mental health (e.g., anxiety, depression) and job dissatisfaction, for instance among industrial workers, financial dealers, teachers, and nurses (Kahn & Cooper, 1990; Khaleque, Hossain, & Hoque, 1992; Melamed et al., 1995; Travers & Cooper, 1993). However, the relationships are generally small, and their interpretation is unclear because low-level, unsatisfying work is usually associated with other environmental problems that can cause stress (Kasl, 1973). Also, severely dissatisfied workers tend to leave a job before it drives them to the extremes of emotional maladjustment, and emotionally unstable individuals can be found in almost all occupations and in both satisfying and unsatisfying jobs.

General Life Satisfaction

The question of how job satisfaction is related to general life satisfaction has generated two opposing theories. **Compensation theory** posits that a person whose job is unsatisfying will find compensating satisfactions in other areas of life. **Spillover theory** holds that "unhappiness at work is likely to affect one's whole life" (Gruneberg, 1979, p. 125). The available research data clearly support spillover theory and indicate that job and life satisfaction are positively related (e.g., Judge & Watanabe, 1993). In a test of a causal model of job satisfaction among executives, Judge, Boudreau, and Bretz (1994) found that both life and job satisfaction had a causal effect on each other, but it appeared that job satisfaction had the stronger effect.

In summary, we can conclude that job *dis*satisfaction:

- Is usually not a causal factor in productivity (though occasionally success in productivity may increase job satisfaction).
- Is a factor contributing to absenteeism, but not at a strong level.
- Is a strong predictor, and frequently a cause, of employee turnover.
- Is weakly related to counterproductive job behavior, at least among older male workers.
- Can play a role in producing some kinds of physical illnesses.
- Can contribute to mental illnesses.
- Is clearly correlated with, and may help produce, general life dissatisfaction.

A NATIONWIDE STUDY OF THE QUALITY OF WORKING LIFE

Most of the studies of job satisfaction cited so far—including the illustrative study we described—have been carried out within a single company or a single occupational group, or at most with a small number of companies or occupational groups. Therefore, their results may be idiosyncratic to the setting in which they were done. Because a large proportion of such studies have been done with male professional or managerial em-

ployees in profit-making businesses, they do not fill the need for objective, nationwide data that can be used as social indicators of the general *quality of working life*. Fortunately, in the 1970s that need was recognized and met by a series of national survey studies done by the Survey Research Center at the University of Michigan in 1969, 1973, and 1977 (Quinn & Staines, 1979). Because of the importance of these Quality of Employment Surveys, we will describe their methods and results in some detail, after which we will present a few results from more recent but less thorough studies.

Methodology

Each of the Quality of Employment Surveys contacted a representative, nationwide, multi-stage, probability sample of housing units; within each selected housing unit, a single interview was conducted with an employed adult, if any lived there. The household interviews lasted an average of 80 minutes and included extensive coverage of many aspects of working life. Each survey interviewed about 1500 respondents, with a completion rate of approximately 75%. In addition, the 1977 survey reinterviewed almost 1100 members of the 1973 panel of respondents to obtain a longitudinal view of American working life.

Work-Related Problems

The surveys covered a list of problems on the job which had earlier been determined to be both important in terms of public policy questions and relatively frequent in their occurrence. The respondents reported whether they experienced each problem in their employment and, if so, how severe it was. A summary of their reports on the frequency of these problems is displayed in Table 10–3.

In general the table shows marked differences in the prevalence of various problems, but relative stability in their frequency from one period to the next. The most common problems, experienced by close to 40% of all U.S. workers, were desire for additional fringe benefits, exposure to one or more health and safety problems, inconvenient or excessive hours, transportation problems, and unpleasant physical conditions. Concerning exposure to health and safety problems, the

TABLE 10-3   Frequency of Selected Work-Related Problems during 1969, 1973, and 1977

Problem area	Percentage of workers reporting one problem or more in each area*		
	1969	*1973*	*1977*
Inadequacy of family income for meeting monthly expenses	26% >	21%	21%
Desire for additional fringe benefits, all workers	39	40	46***
Wage and salaried workers only**	45	45	55***
Exposure to one or more health and safety problems	38	42	78***
Work related illness or injury during last three years	13	14	16
Occupational handicap(s)	9	9	10
Inconvenient or excessive hours	30 <	39 >	34
Age discrimination	5	4	6
Sex discrimination, all workers	3	5	5
Women only**	8 <	14	12
Race or national origin discrimination, all workers	3	3	6
Blacks only**	17	15	16
Unsteady employment	11	9	9
Transportation problems	35	40	38
Unpleasant physical conditions****	33 <	40	37

*Statistically significant changes are indicated by the symbol < or >.

**An indented row description indicates that the percentage is based on the subsample thus described.

***The 1969 and 1973 data are not comparable to those from 1977 due to changes in measurement methods.

****Includes only those who work at one place or building.

Source: Adapted from page 289 in Quinn, R. P., & Staines, G. L. *The 1977 Quality of Employment Survey: Descriptive Statistics, with Comparison Data from the 1969–70 and the 1972–73 Surveys.* Ann Arbor: Institute for Social Research, University of Michigan, 1979. Copyright © 1979 by the Institute for Social Research, University of Michigan. Reprinted by permission.

four hazards most often reported were air pollution (40%), fire or shock (30%), noise (30%), and dangerous chemicals (29%). The safety area was singled out by respondents as the one area in which employees should have the greatest say in work-related decisions.

Moderately common work problems (experienced by about 15% to 25% of workers) were inadequate family income, and a work-related illness or injury in the last three years. Problems experienced by 10% or less of workers included occupational handicaps, unsteady employment, age discrimination, sex discrimination, and racial or nationality discrimination (though women and Blacks reported higher levels of problems in the latter two categories). Of course, these lower-frequency problems can be very severe for the individuals concerned, and in fact, all of these problems were rated as relatively severe by the workers who had experienced them.

Job Satisfaction

The Quinn and Staines studies gave psychologists their first opportunity to examine job satisfaction over an extended period of time, and they provided a base line for comparing future changes in job satisfaction as well. The short-term changes during the 1970s turned out to be striking and fascinating. As shown in Table 10–4, a variety of measures of job satisfaction remained stable from 1969 to 1973 and then turned sharply downward from 1973 to 1977. This was true for the overall job satisfaction measure as well as the facet-free measure (five questions about the job in general) and the facet-specific measure (33 questions about specific aspects of the job, covering six different dimensions). All six of these dimensions, except satisfaction with co-worker relationships, showed the same pattern. Results also showed that every group except

TABLE 10-4   Trends in Indicators of Job Satisfaction

Job satisfaction indicator	Mean values**				
	1969		*1973*		*1977*
Overall Job Satisfaction*	0		−2	>	−24
Facet-free job satisfaction	3.75		3.79	>	3.66
Facet-specific job satisfaction	3.24		3.20	>	3.05
Comfort	3.14	>	3.03	>	2.87
Challenge	3.26		3.21	>	3.06
Financial rewards	3.06		3.10	>	2.89
Relations with co-workers	3.41		3.34		3.40
Resource adequacy	3.45		3.44	>	3.28
Promotions	—		2.63	>	2.46

*Overall Job Satisfaction is an equally weighted combination of the Facet-free and Facet-specific job satisfaction indexes, transformed to a mean of zero in 1969.

**Statistically significant changes are indicated by the symbol >.

Source: Adapted from page 304 in Quinn, R. P., & Staines, G. L. *The 1977 Quality of Employment Survey: Descriptive Statistics, with Comparison Data from the 1969–70 and the 1972–73 Surveys.* Ann Arbor: Institute for Social Research, University of Michigan, 1979. Copyright © 1979 by the Institute for Social Research, University of Michigan. Reprinted by permission.

workers under age 21 displayed marked drops in satisfaction. In 1977 only a few demographic groups remained above the 1969 overall population mean—notably workers age 65 or older, the self-employed, farmers and farm managers, and (barely) workers with a graduate education.

In attempts to explain the sharp drop in job satisfaction, Quinn and Staines (1979) tested three plausible explanatory hypotheses: (1) the composition of the labor force changed, (2) objective qualities of the working environment deteriorated, or (3) workers' expectations about work rose but were unfulfilled. However, they found no evidence for any of these hypotheses, though they had less data with which to test the third one than the other two. They therefore concluded that the changes in U.S. workers' job satisfaction were probably due to a complex set of factors, which might well be different for the different segments of the labor force.

Although the surveys by Quinn and Staines did not continue beyond 1977, the Gallup Poll has measured general job satisfaction from time to time, using single-item measures. The results from these polls, though not directly comparable with the results from Quinn and Staines, provide a useful update of these earlier stud-

ies. A 1994 telephone survey of randomly selected U.S. residents asked, "How satisfied are you with your current job?" Of the respondents who were employed, 39% were completely satisfied, 47% were somewhat satisfied, 11% were somewhat dissatisfied, and 3% were completely dissatisfied (Gallup, 1995). In the preceding year, the same question had yielded slightly higher average satisfaction (Gallup, 1994). With respect to *specific* job characteristics, the 1993 Gallup Poll reported that 46% of employed respondents were completely satisfied with job security, and 50% were completely satisfied with their amount of vacation time, whereas only 24% were completely satisfied with the amount of on-the-job stress. The results from these more recent surveys suggest that, although there are yearly fluctuations in global job satisfaction, overall it remains at a fairly stable and high level in the U.S.

Unfortunately, since the 1970s, no comparable nationwide study has been done to update the Quality of Employment Surveys. In 1993 a report appeared describing the first wave of a new large-scale, longitudinal study of work life (Galinsky, Bond, & Friedman, 1993). This study was based on hour-long telephone interviews with nearly 3000 wage or salary workers across the U.S. in 1992. However, comparisons with earlier findings were limited because, instead of repeating the earlier items, its authors focused much more on topics of interest to employers, and the initial report presented relatively sparse quantitative data. Among the most interesting findings were documentation of contemporary job insecurity among American workers; 42% of respondents had experienced "downsizing" or permanent cutbacks in the work force at their place of business, and 15% of workers felt they had been discriminated against at their current jobs (22% of minority employees and 13% of nonminority employees). On the positive side, flextime had become quite common and popular; 24% of respondents were able to work regularly at home, and up to 47% had some degree of flexibility in their work hours. Of those who didn't have such job features, roughly one-quarter said they would be willing to switch jobs to obtain them (Galinsky et al., 1993). Future reports on later waves of this study should yield valuable new knowledge about working conditions in America.

Life Satisfaction

As a final topic, the Quality of Employment Surveys of the 1970s also measured overall life satisfaction. The methodology was similar to the job satisfaction measures: one subscale with general questions on satisfaction with life, and another composed of more specific adjective-rating scales. Just as with job satisfaction, both components were found to take a sharp nose-dive between 1973 and 1977. Thus, it appears that there were some pervasive forces operating in the mid-1970s, which reduced the average U.S. citizen's satisfaction with life in general as well as with the quality of life on the job.

IMPROVING THE QUALITY OF WORKING LIFE

The research described above demonstrated several organizational-level variables that can lead to job stress and job dissatisfaction. Armed with this knowledge, applied social psychologists have attempted to improve the quality of working life by reducing job stress and increasing job satisfaction. In the sections that fol-

low, some definitional issues are discussed, and then two general methods for improving the quality of working life are described: participative management, and job design.

Defining the Quality of Working Life

What is the **quality of working life (QWL)**? It is more than simple job satisfaction (since some workers can be satisfied with miserable working conditions) but it is less than life satisfaction. In fact, the quality of working life means different things to different people. In a review of the literature, Nadler and Lawler (1983) described six different definitions for QWL, including conceptions of it as a variable, an approach, a set of methods, or a movement. However, most of the research on QWL has considered it as an approach—for example, any program "designed to increase employee involvement and to help both the worker and the organization" (Nadler & Lawler, 1983, p. 157).

Clearly, job satisfaction is one important aspect, but QWL also includes more objective aspects of working conditions, such as safety, cleanliness, pay, security, hours, and adequacy of equipment (Seashore, 1975). In addition, it may also include objective indices of behavioral outcomes, such as absenteeism, turnover, and even productivity (Graber, 1980); and worker's individual differences in abilities, values, and expectations should also be considered (Seashore, 1975). For instance, some workers want job variety while others prefer routine. In sum, the quality of working life is generally viewed as a combination of several different factors, but there is no general agreement yet on exactly which aspects to include and how to weight them.

Participative Management

One of the early approaches to improving working life was the **participative management** movement, which emphasized employee participation in decision making about aspects of their jobs. Stemming directly from Kurt Lewin's (1947) theorizing about group decision processes, empirical studies of group decision making in industry (such as Coch & French, 1948) eventually led to major theories about human relations approaches to organizational management (e.g., Likert, 1961;

McGregor, 1960). This movement has stressed the participation of employees in small decision-making groups at all levels of an organization to consider problems and procedures for their own job area. See Bruce and Blackburn (1992) for a good review of approaches to participative management.

Reports on the results of participative management have often been strongly favorable, with long-lasting increases in both worker satisfaction and productivity following changes toward group-centered supervisory practices (e.g., Packard, 1989; Schwarz, 1989). However, reviews of the area have also found cases where the method did not have these favorable consequences (Bramel & Friend, 1987). It appears that participative methods interact with characteristics of the workers and the work situation. For example, participative workgroups may not be successful if they are perceived as a way to control the workers. The success of participative management programs may depend largely on the reasons that they are implemented, and the support they receive from management (Long, 1988).

One time-tested version of participative management is the **Scanlon Plan**, which was developed to increase cooperation between labor and management in improving organizational effectiveness and productivity (Kovac, 1986; Miller & Schuster, 1987). In this scheme every department forms a production committee, consisting of both supervisors and workers, to discuss ideas about production offered by the employees in that department. Similar committees are also formed at higher management levels. The other major feature of the plan is that labor costs are measured objectively, and a large percentage of any savings in labor costs is put into a bonus pool to be shared by all employees. Results of this plan have often included increased productivity—not surprisingly, considering its heavy emphasis on production—as well as increased satisfaction with the work, better co-worker relationships, and more favorable attitudes toward the organization. However, some attempts to use the Scanlon Plan have failed, particularly if labor-management relations were poor or if there was a union that was split into factions regarding the plan (Alderfer, 1976).

The most popular form of work-improvement group since the 1980s has been **quality circles** (Griffin, 1988;

Lawler, 1992). In this technique, small groups of employees meet weekly to brainstorm about ways to improve productivity or cut company costs. Successful ideas often save the company tens or hundreds of thousands of dollars, and a portion of the savings is shared by the members of the circle that suggested the idea (Lawler & Mohrman, 1985). However, results from empirical studies on quality circles have often failed to find the expected benefits. For example, in a quasi-experiment, Bush and Raban (1990) compared the effects of quality circles on the quality of work, absenteeism, and productivity. Results showed significant differences in workers' attitudes, with quality circle participants scoring more positively than the control group, but no differences in absenteeism or productivity. Reviewing the literature on quality circles, Lawler (1992) concluded that their long-term effectiveness is "questionable."

Many European companies have gone beyond U.S. systems of participative management, in a movement termed **industrial democracy**. Many countries have passed legislation requiring large companies to have worker representatives on their boards of directors as well as on lower-level management committees (Bass et al., 1979; Industrial Democracy in Europe, 1993). In the U.S., the first notable example of worker representation at the board of directors level was the addition of the United Automobile Workers president to the board of the financially troubled Chrysler Corporation in 1979, in return for the union's agreement to renegotiate contract provisions downward. However, few other companies have followed that example as a precedent.

Potentially the most extensive form of participative management is **employee ownership** of their company. In the 1970s, U.S. tax legislation favorable to Employee Stock Ownership Plans (ESOP) served as the impetus for the establishment of many such programs, and by 1986 about 7% of all U.S. workers owned company stock (Wichman, 1994). Research on employee ownership programs indicates that they can be an effective way to improve both commitment to the organization and productivity (National Center for Employee Ownership, 1993). However, these gains are often found only when employee ownership is coupled with a participative management scheme. Further, employee ownership appears to be most effective with workers who stand to gain more from it—those with more skills, and who are employed at higher levels of the organization (Buchko, 1992; Wichman, 1994). See Rosen and Young (1991) for a good overview of employee ownership programs in both America and Europe.

Job Design

Short of full-scale industrial democracy or participative management, many steps can be taken to improve the quality of working life by **job design**. This approach arose as a reaction against earlier industrial trends toward automation and extreme job specialization, which were designed to "de-skill" jobs to the point where anyone could do them with a minimum of training, knowledge, and ability. In the last 30 years a contrary movement has gained strength, aimed at attacking the monotony and meaninglessness of such de-skilled jobs by redesigning them.

There are several methods of redesigning jobs to combat specialization (Neuman, Edwards, & Raju, 1989). The simplest method is **job rotation**, in which assembly-line workers take turns doing each of several different jobs on the line. Even such simple changes as this have often been opposed by management and frequently by unions as well. As a result, they have sometimes been instituted unofficially without management approval, as by assembly-line workers in an automobile plant "doubling up" and relieving each other on adjacent work stations (Kremen, 1973).

Job enlargement is a planned program of increasing the number of job operations performed by each worker. It is sometimes referred to as "horizontal" job extension because each of the worker's new functions is at the same level of skill and responsibility. As far back as 1952, Walker and Guest found that this procedure increased the job satisfaction of assembly-line workers. Current research indicates that while job enlargement programs typically increase job satisfaction, they also tend to require more training of employees, which can be costly for organizations (Campion & McClelland, 1991).

A further step in job extension is the creation of **autonomous work groups**, which are relatively small teams that take responsibility for a whole sequence of steps in a production process (Jessup, 1990). As a result, the group's output will have a clear "task identity," in which they can take pride (Hackman & Lawler, 1971). Probably the most surprising example of this approach is its use on some automobile assembly lines, in Sweden's Volvo plants and General Motors' Saturn plants, where work teams take responsibility for a complete car assembly job (Gyllenhammar, 1977; Woodruff, 1992). In some companies, autonomous work groups may control many aspects of the working environment, such as deciding about work practices, scheduling tasks, determining rest breaks, and allocating jobs (Pearson, 1992). Because they are responsible for a variety of tasks, they must have members with a wide range of relevant skills. Rather like students in the jigsaw classroom (discussed in Chapter 8), each worker may have a unique set of skills that are required for the group to complete its tasks. The few empirical studies that have been conducted on autonomous work groups suggest that they are a promising new method for organizing working environments (Pearson, 1992).

Another innovation in job redesign features is the option of flexible work hours, sometimes called **flextime** (Golembiewski & Proehl, 1978; Pierce et al., 1989). Flextime programs in industry first began in the mid-1960s, and as of 1988 nearly five million American workers were on a flextime program (Ralston, 1989). Features of these programs range from merely allowing employees a choice of starting and stopping hours, to allowing variable numbers of hours of work per day or per week, as in the Swedish Volvo plant (Loeb, 1979). In a study on the benefits of flextime programs among government workers, Ralston (1989) found that they decreased commuting time, improved coordination of work and family responsibilities, reduced tardiness, and increased job satisfaction. However, they did not improve employee-employer relations, or increase productivity. For an excellent review of the research on flextime and other alternate work schedules, see Pierce et al. (1989).

A final type of job redesign is **job enrichment**,

which entails both horizontal and vertical extension of the job. That is, it includes not only more varied activities but also more responsibility and autonomy in planning and doing the work. For instance, a machine operator might be given responsibility for deciding on the sequence of jobs, ordering parts, inspecting finished products, repairing and maintaining equipment, and so on. Hackman et al. (1975) mentioned two additional ways in which jobs can be enriched: providing more feedback about the quality of performance, and having the worker maintain contact with the organization's clients or customers.

Because job enrichment schemes generally institute many of these job changes at the same time, it is usually impossible to tell which of the specific changes were responsible for any subsequent effects. However, it seems likely that the combined impact of several simultaneous changes in the job is necessary to achieve any very noticeable changes in job satisfaction, productivity, or other dependent variables. Field studies of job enrichment have frequently shown a variety of favorable effects. Most common are increases in job satisfaction and in the *quality* of job performance. Other frequent effects are drops in absenteeism and worker turnover and increases in the quantity of production (Lawler, 1992). However, individual differences in workers and differences in job settings can markedly influence the success of job enrichment schemes (Katzell et al., 1975).

SUMMARY

Of all the topics studied by applied social psychologists in organizational settings, job satisfaction has been one of the most important continuing areas of research. Different theories of job satisfaction have stressed (a) expectations in relation to actual circumstances, (b) the degree of fulfillment of physical and psychological needs, or (c) the level of attainment of the individual's important personal values. Probably all three factors contribute to job satisfaction.

The major causal factors influencing job satisfaction are intrinsic aspects of the work itself (such as meaningfulness, skill, autonomy, and variety), imper-

sonal working conditions (including pay, job security, role clarity, and other features), and interpersonal relations on the job.

Though many managers expect job satisfaction to lead to increased productivity, the opposite order of events seems to occur more often. Absenteeism, and especially employee turnover, are the best established consequences of job dissatisfaction. Other possible consequences are employee grievances, reduced physical and mental health, and a spillover effect shown in lower satisfaction with life in general.

Quinn and Staine's nationwide survey studies provided important information on the quality of working life for typical U.S. workers. The most common work-related problems were found to be insufficient fringe benefits, health and safety risks, inconvenient or excessive hours, and unpleasant physical conditions.

Any definition of the quality of working life needs to include both subjective ratings of job satisfaction and also objective measures such as working conditions. One of the major approaches to improving the quality of working life has been the movement toward participative management, in which groups of workers and supervisors meet to discuss and make decisions about job problems and procedures. Job design is another way to improve the quality of working life, by combatting extreme job specialization and "de-skilled" jobs. Both of these approaches have produced greater worker satisfaction and increased quantity or quality of productivity in some settings, but in other settings research findings have shown no positive effect. Research is beginning to show that these types of program are most effective when management is committed to making them work, and when workers see the likelihood of benefiting from them personally.

SUGGESTED READINGS

Argyle, M. (1989). *The social psychology of work*. New York: Penguin.—A readable overview of many areas of organizational behavior to which social psychology has contributed, including job design, motivation, job satisfaction, unemployment, and retirement.

Arvey, R. D., Carter, G. W., & Buerkley, D. K. (1991). Job satisfaction: Dispositional and situational influences. In

C. L. Cooper & I. J. Robertson (Eds.), *International review of industrial and organizational psychology* (pp. 359–383). Chichester, England: Wiley.—A good summary of the research on factors related to job satisfaction.

Bruce, W., & Blackburn, J. W. (1992). *Balancing job satisfaction and performance*. Westport, CT: Quorum.—Based on social psychological research, this readable book describes the necessity of and techniques for balancing organizational needs with the needs of employees.

Cotton, J. L. (1993). *Employee involvement: Methods for improving performance and work attitudes*. Newbury Park, CA: Sage.—This volume summarizes many different participative management and job design programs intended to improve job satisfaction and worker productivity.

CHAPTER 11

Environmental Issues— Energy and Resource Conservation

*There are real and growing dangers to our simple and most precious pos-
sessions: the air we breathe, the water we drink, and the land which sus-
tains us.*

—President Jimmy Carter, 1981

*Humanity stands at a defining moment in history. We are confronted with
. . . the continuing deterioration of the ecosystems on which we depend for
our well-being.*

—UN Conference on Environment and Development (1992, p. 6)

In recent years social scientists have become increasingly sensitized to the many environmental conditions
that affect people's behavior or are caused by people's
behavior. Consequently the field of environmental psychology has developed, largely as an offshoot of social
psychology, but with its own agenda regarding central
topics and preferred research methods (Proshansky,
1987, 1990; Saegert & Winkel, 1990; Stokols, 1995;
Sundstrom et al., 1996). **Environmental psychology**
studies the interactions and relations between people
and their environments (McAndrew, 1993; Proshansky, 1990).

Traditionally, the field of environmental psychology
has emphasized how the physical environment affects
human thoughts, feelings, and behaviors. However,
much recent environmental research has stressed the
other side of the coin—how human actions affect the
environment. Thus, the topics studied range from the
design of offices and homes to the effects of environmental pollution. Environmental psychologists study
all aspects of person-environment relations, frequently
adopting an interdisciplinary stance and working cooperatively with architects, city planners, geographers,
sociologists, anthropologists, political scientists, or engineers.

We will begin this chapter with a brief survey of
some of the environmental topics that have been of
great interest to applied social psychologists. The topics in this brief overview focus primarily on research
investigating the ways in which the environment influences people's thoughts, feelings, and behaviors. The
later, more in-depth part of the chapter will concentrate
on understanding the impact of human actions on the

natural environment, and on promoting environmentally responsible behavior.

SOME APPLIED AREAS
OF ENVIRONMENTAL PSYCHOLOGY

Crowding. One of the most heavily studied topics
in environmental psychology has been the effects of
crowding. Research has found, contrary to common
opinion, that the presence of many people in one place
does not always produce the feeling of being crowded.
The term **density** refers to the number of people in a
given space, while **crowding** refers to the negative
subjective feeling that there are too many people in a
given space (McAndrew, 1993). High density conditions may decrease human performance, but they do
not always do so because people are often able to adapt
to them and continue to function effectively (Freedman, 1975). In general, the feeling of being crowded is
a stressor that can have physiological, psychological,
and social consequences for both humans and animals
(Baum & Paulus, 1987). However, some of the negative
impacts of crowding can be reduced if people feel that
they have some control over their crowded conditions.

Most of the research on crowding has been done in
short-term laboratory studies, and it is not clear to what
extent the findings apply to long-continued extreme
crowding in real-life situations like slum housing, prisons, subways, or department store sales. Long-term experiments on density and crowding are difficult to conduct. For practical reasons, most are performed in
college dormitories, or in prisons (Baum & Paulus,

1987). In prisons, correlational studies have shown that higher density is associated with higher blood pressure (D'Atri & Ostfeld, 1975), more complaints of illness (Wener & Keys, 1988), and even higher death rates (Paulus, McCain, & Cox, 1978). However, just as with the findings from short-term studies, allowing prisoners to feel a sense of control over their environment appears to lessen the impact of high density living (Ruback, Carr, & Hopper, 1986).

Psychological theories and research have also been devoted to other aspects of human spatial behavior, including personal space, the desire for privacy, and territorial behavior. *Too Close for Comfort* (Insel & Lindgren, 1978) is an enjoyable paperback volume covering all these topics.

Environmental Stress. This term refers to environmental conditions that interfere with optimal human functioning (Evans & Cohen, 1987). Possible sources of stress include cataclysmic events, stressful life events, daily hassles, and ambient stressors like noise or crowding (e.g., Staples, 1996). Just as with stress from crowding, exposure to excessive noise can produce negative effects on current performance and on later performance after the noise is terminated, but it does not always do so. Also, as with crowding, the perception that one can control the noise often alleviates its negative effects, even if the control is never used (Cohen & Weinstein, 1982; Glass & Singer, 1972). Thus, there is a complex relationship between the physical stressor and people's mental and emotional adjustment to it.

Studies of long-continued noise in natural settings, such as noisy factories, or schools and homes near jet airports, have shown a variety of negative effects. For example, a study on children who lived close to the flight path of airplanes landing at Los Angeles International Airport found that, in comparison to other children of similar ethnicity and economic status, they were more likely to have high blood pressure, had lower average math achievement scores, and were less capable and persistent at solving problems (Cohen et al., 1980, 1986).

Environmental Risks. Another area of research is on people's perceptions of the risk posed by environ-

mental problems, and their reactions to this perceived risk (Dake, 1992; Hallman & Wandersman, 1992). Each day of our lives we choose to take some risks and to avoid others. The foods we eat, the transportation we use, the area where we live—all aspects of our lives pose some risk to our health. Empirical studies of risk perception have included the topics of natural disasters, various diseases, pollution, food contamination, transportation accidents, and nuclear power (Covello & Mumpower, 1995; Rosa & Dunlap, 1994; Wilson & Crouch, 1995).

Behavior Settings. The physical and social settings where people live, work, and play have a tremendous influence on their behavior. However, few social psychologists have worked in this research area, with the exception of a dedicated group at the University of Kansas under Roger Barker (for summaries of this work, see Barker, 1987; Wicker, 1979, 1987). Following Barker's pioneering research and theorizing, many environmental psychologists have begun to study the behavioral effects of the physical and temporal settings that individuals move through in their daily lives. For instance, when people are in church, they usually act sedate, but when they leave church and go to a ball game, they are generally boisterous. An enjoyable autobiographical account of Barker's life's work has been published (Barker, 1979).

Architectural Psychology. When dedicating the rebuilt House of Commons after its destruction in World War II, Winston Churchill made the insightful observation: "We shape our buildings, and afterwards our buildings shape us." The subfield of architectural psychology focuses on this area of interaction between environment and behavior, asking how to design the built environment in accordance with human needs for safety, comfort, and happiness. Thus, it takes into account findings from the studies of crowding, privacy, territoriality, and other areas of the field. Architectural psychologists have studied a wide variety of settings, including homes and offices, playgrounds and parks, university dormitories, hospital wards, high-rise apartment buildings, schools, prisons, and mass transit vehicles. See Lang (1987) for a good review of this work.

Photograph by Hixson Studio, Lawrence, Kansas, courtesy of Roger Barker. Reprinted by permission.

Box 11-1

ROGER BARKER, PRE-EMINENT ENVIRONMENTAL RESEARCHER

Demonstrating his life-long belief in the importance of environmental influences on people's behavior, Roger Barker (1979) wrote a colorful article describing the settings and individuals that shaped his professional career. Born in Iowa in 1903, he contracted osteomyelitis in his hip and knee at age 13—a painful and periodically incapacitating bone disease, which recurred in acute episodes for many years. As a result, his education was prolonged, and he received his B.A. in 1928 and his Ph.D. in 1934, both from Stanford. In that Depression period, faculty positions were unavailable, so Barker was fortunate to continue as a research associate at Stanford and then to receive a postdoctoral fellowship at the University of Iowa with Kurt Lewin, who had an indelible influence on his later career. After brief teaching positions at Harvard, the University of Illinois, Stanford, and Clark University, Barker finally settled down at the University of Kansas in 1947.

At Kansas, Barker founded the Midwest Psychological Field Station in a nearby village and carried on pioneering research in environmental psychology for 25 years. He continued active research and writing until his death in 1990. His research aimed to discover and classify the environments a town provides, to observe and record the behavior of children in various environments, and to study how the settings influenced their behavior. He and his colleagues also studied the behavioral differences in small and large schools and in an American and an English town. Among Barker's many influential books are *Adjustment to Handicap and Illness*, *One Boy's Day*, *Midwest and Its Children*, and *Ecological Psychology*. Barker's years of pace-setting research were recognized by his receipt of APA's Distinguished Scientific Contribution Award.

Assessing Environments. Environmental assessment is the attempt to describe and predict how the physical attributes of places affect human thoughts, feelings, and behaviors (Craik & Feimer, 1987). A major goal in assessing environments is to provide reliable and valid information that will be useful in environmental planning and design, in environmental impact analyses, and in management decision making (Zube, 1991). Among the numerous ways of evaluating the perceived quality of the physical and social environment, the most widely used methods have been scales for assessing the perceived "social climates" of organizational or institutional settings—e.g., college dormitories, hospitals, correctional facilities, high school classes, military groups, work settings, and families. See Craik and Feimer (1987) for a description of many of these scales.

The Natural Environment. When people think of physical recreation, or plan family vacations, research shows that they typically prefer a natural environment over a built environment (Ulrich, 1986). Some of the favorite activities of people around the world include outdoor recreation such as fishing, camping, and hiking (Knopf, 1987).

Following the first Earth Day in 1970, people around the world became increasingly aware that their actions were harming the environment. Pollution of the air, water, and land was becoming more visible, and there was a growing recognition that the planet's resources were not endless. Behavioral scientists also began to consider these issues, as illustrated by the following quotation, which appeared in a review of social psychological research on cooperation and competition:

> The great needs of our times are the three E's—energy, economy, and environment—in a world of suddenly limited resources relative to increased population. (Davis, Laughlin, & Komorita, 1976, p. 525)

Because of the great importance of this issue, we will devote the remainder of this chapter to an exploration of how human actions affect the natural environment. We will explore the topics of people's environmental concern, the nature of environmental problems, studies of environmentally responsible behavior, public policy on various environmental issues, and essential steps toward achieving a sustainable future for the world.

CONCERN FOR THE ENVIRONMENT

Recognition of the negative impact of human behavior on the environment has grown into a global environmental movement, whose main goal is to alter the ethical and worldview bases of environmental concern

in the U.S. and other countries (Gardner & Stern, 1996). In examining these developments, we will first discuss changes in people's level of concern for the environment, and second, various aspects of people's worldviews.

Trends in Environmental Concern

Opinion polls from the United States and many other nations show that public concern for environmental issues is currently very high. In the U.S., concern over environmental problems began to emerge as one of the most pressing social issues in the late 1960s and early 1970s, sparked by the first Earth Day in 1970 (Dunlap, 1991). Public concern continued to rise fairly steadily throughout the 1970s and 1980s and reached an all-time peak in the mid-1990s (Bosso, 1994; Kempton, Boster, & Hartley, 1995).

An example of the high level of environmental concern in the U.S. is a 1990 nationwide survey which found that 71% of respondents believed the U.S. is spending "too little" on "improving and protecting the environment," while only 4% stated "too much" (Dunlap, 1991). Similar results were found in a series of CBS/*New York Times* polls which repeated the same question about the environment from 1981 to 1990: "Do you agree or disagree with the following statement? Protecting the environment is *so* important that requirements and standards cannot be too high, and continuing environmental improvements must be made *regardless* of cost." The data from seven surveys over ten years showed a steady increase in the number of people who agreed, with an extra jump in 1989 following the grounding of the oil tanker *Exxon Valdez*, which spread oil sludge over hundreds of miles of ocean and beaches in Alaska (Dunlap, 1991—see Figure 11–1). The figure also shows that there was a steady decrease in the number of people who disagreed with this statement, and similar results have been found in several other independent public opinion polls (Bosso, 1994; Dunlap & Scarce, 1991).

Concern for environmental issues is not solely an American or Western phenomenon. Recent research has found high levels of support for environmental protection from countries around the world (Dunlap,

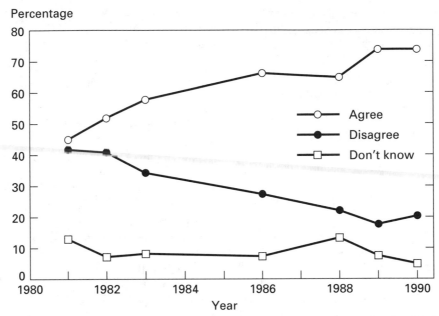

FIGURE 11-1   Support for environmental protection, "regardless of cost," 1981–1990. (Source: Data from Dunlap, 1991, p. 300.)

Gallup, & Gallup, 1993). The Gallup Organization surveyed approximately 1000 people in each of 22 countries, which ranged widely in economic development, political structure, and geographic region. In all but 2 of the countries, respondents listed environmental protection as the top social concern. Furthermore, in 16 of the countries, people stated a willingness to pay more for products that were less harmful to the environment.

Types of Environmental Paradigms

Environmental concern can be broadly defined as a set of proenvironmental beliefs, attitudes, and values about the relationship between humans and the natural environment—a viewpoint that considers the environment as valuable in its own right and as worthy of protection, care, and preservation by humans. Gardner and Stern (1996) discussed several movements that are attempting to raise the level of environmental consciousness in industrial societies—that is, to change people's *worldviews.* We will briefly describe three here: ecotheology, deep ecology, and ecofeminism. See Tucker and Grim (1993) for a discussion of other worldviews.

Ecotheology. To what extent do Christianity and other Western religious beliefs contribute to environmental problems? Some religious philosophers (e.g., Ophuls, 1977; White, 1967) have argued that the materialism of Western societies is largely the result of Christian beliefs.

> The sickness of the earth reflects the sickness in the soul of modern industrial man, whose whole life is given over to gain, to the disease of endless getting and spending that can never satisfy deeper aspirations and must eventually end in cultural, spiritual, and physical death. (Ophuls, 1977, p. 232)

A related problem stems from the fact that many passages from the Bible indicate that humans were created to rule over nature. One of the clearest examples can be found in Genesis 1:28, which instructs humans to:

> Be fruitful and multiply, and replenish the earth, and subdue it, and have dominion over the fish of the sea, and over the fowl of the air, and over every living thing that moves upon the earth.

(Despite this clear directive for humans to "subdue" the earth, it is encouraging that research, both in the

U.S. and internationally, has not found a clear negative relationship between Judeo-Christian beliefs and environmental concern—Eckberg & Blocker, 1989; Greeley, 1993; Kanagy & Willits, 1993).

Ecotheology is a new religious movement, based on reinterpretation of various Biblical passages, which aims to reconcile environmentalism with Judeo-Christian beliefs. Ecotheologists argue that Judeo-Christian scripture supports a *stewardship* of the earth, rather than domination and exploitation (Gelderloos, 1992; Whitney, 1993). A related but more far-reaching approach, proposed by Thomas Berry (1988), is a new religion that is earth-centered, rather than human-centered. Berry suggested returning to the view of many native peoples that the environment is sacred—but incorporating a scientific understanding of the interconnectedness of all aspects of the earth and its environment. He argued that modern sciences (e.g., physics, astronomy, biology) are just beginning to understand the "oneness" of all things.

Deep Ecology. Deep ecology is in many respects the antithesis of the dominant Western paradigm (Naess, 1989). The traditional Western belief system about the environment is human-centered—stressing materialism, economic growth, dominance over nature, and reliance on technology to solve environmental problems. From this stance, the quote from President Jimmy Carter presented at the beginning of this chapter can be seen as a shallow perspective on the environment because it states that the resources of the earth are "our possessions." In contrast, the deep-ecology paradigm is nature-centered—it holds that nature does not exist for human use, but has inherent value in itself. Among its goals, this movement advocates a major reduction in human population, living a lifestyle that is "voluntarily simple," and reconnecting with nature through outdoor experiences like hiking. Further, it argues that in order to save humankind and the environment from destruction, we must radically change our thinking. See Box 11–2 for more details of its beliefs.

Box 11-2

HOW DEEP ARE YOU?—LEVELS OF ENVIRONMENTAL CONSCIOUSNESS

Level One—Shallow Ecology: Concern About Pollution and Resource Depletion. Acute and visible cases of environmental degradation are a cause of serious concern and action. Different environmental problems are seen as largely unrelated, and are to be corrected on a case-by-case basis. Natural resources should not be squandered, but should be consumed efficiently. Nature exists for humans and human use, but it is in our own self-interest that nature be managed wisely.

Level Two—Intermediate-Depth Ecology: The Spaceship Earth Analogy. Nature exists for human use, but humans are polluting and despoiling it badly. We must more fully understand the high degree of human dependence on nature, the finite ability of nature to absorb pollution and yield resources, the interrelatedness of all life forms, and the complexity of global ecosystems. With advanced scientific knowledge and management, and with proper laws, regulations, and other existing societal institutions, we should be able to manage the planet wisely, so that humans will continue to prosper materially into the foreseeable future.

Level Three—Deep Ecology: Bioequality. Morally speaking, humans are not more important than nonhuman life forms and are not fundamentally different than, or separate from, them. All forms of life have a basic right to exist. Humans and human science and technology will never be able to fully understand and manage global ecosystems; to assume so is merely human ignorance. Nature can't be bent to the ways of humans. Pursuit of material comforts is intrinsically unrewarding; a lifestyle of voluntary simplicity is rewarding. We must replace our Western worldview with that of Eastern and native religions, and develop a spiritual/religious bond with the earth and all its creatures, including fellow humans of all cultures and countries.

Source: Gardner & Stern (1996, p. 54). Adapted from Miller (1990) and Devall & Sessions (1985).

Ecofeminism. The ecofeminist movement is directed toward solving both gender inequality and environmental problems. Ecofeminists argue that both sexism and environmental problems are created by Western male thinking, and can only be solved by developing a new paradigm. The Western view of nature, developed by men, treats nonhuman life forms as inferior and exploits them for human gain. Similarly, in Western tradition, women have been treated as inferior and historically were subjugated and exploited (and many authors argue that they are still—Salleh, 1992; Shiva, 1989). In contrast to the male paradigm (discrimination, domination, exploitation), the female paradigm is described as nurturing, accepting, and equalitarian. Thus, the ecofeminism movement holds that solving the problems of sexism and environmental destruction requires acceptance of the feminine paradigm and rejection of the male paradigm.

All three of these environmental movements share a rejection of the traditional Western worldview (Gardner & Stern, 1996), which includes beliefs that earth's resources and the growth of human activities can be limitless, that humans are exempt from nature's constraints, and that nature is impervious to human impacts. In contrast, the **new environmental paradigm** that is advanced by these movements holds that there are limits to growth, that people cannot dominate and control nature's processes, and that the balance of nature is easily upset by human actions (Dunlap & Van Liere, 1978).

A related way of classifying environmental attitudes posits three basic orientations concerning the issue of human domination and control over nature (Merchant, 1992; Stern & Dietz, 1994). An **egocentric** orientation pursues individual self-interest (e.g., pollution of air, water, or land is acceptable if it leads to corporate profits or economic growth). It is the dominant Western paradigm. In contrast, an **anthropocentric** orientation focuses on the needs of all people, rather than on individual gain or environmental good (e.g., such pollution would be judged unacceptable if it led to widespread human health problems). Finally, an **ecocentric** orientation judges acts according to their effect on the *biosphere*, rather than on individuals or on humanity (e.g., pollution would be condemned if it damaged the replenishment capability of forests, lakes and streams, or the atmosphere).

ENVIRONMENTAL PROBLEMS

Human actions are destroying the natural environment. However, this destruction is not new; human actions have always had impacts on the environment. Thousands of years ago, irrigation of the Tigris and Euphrates valleys eventually poisoned the land with salt. In Biblical times, overgrazing turned the once-fertile lands of the Middle East into deserts (DiSilvestro, 1995). More recently, deforestation of Africa, Asia, and Latin America has eroded the topsoil and created new deserts. Similarly, many signs of environmental destruction can be seen in the U.S. For instance, acid rain has killed all fish and vegetation in many lakes and rivers, and runoff of toxic fertilizers from agricultural lands has killed innumerable animals and birds.

As we have seen in the previous section, most people in the U.S. today agree that it is important to protect the environment. However, the severity of environmental problems, as well as the steps needed to protect the environment, are heatedly disputed (for contrasting viewpoints see Easterbrook, 1991; Ray & Guzzo, 1990). The next sections briefly discuss four areas in which human behavior is negatively affecting the environment: population, pollution, energy use, and natural resources.

Population

A basic underlying cause of the threats to the environment is the number of humans living on the planet. More humans mean more pollution, less space, and a greater demand for natural resources.

> The time needed to add a billion people to the world's population has become ever shorter. It took nearly one century (1830–1930) to advance from 1 billion to 2 billion people, 30 years (1930–1960) to advance to 3 billion people, 15 years (1960–1975) to attain a fourth billion, and 12 years (1975–1987) to grow from four billion to 5 billion people. (David, 1994, p. 334)

Countries with the fastest population growth tend to be mostly in less developed and poor regions of Southeast Asia, Latin America, Africa, and the Indian subcontinent (Simmons, 1991). Thus, the greatest growth is occurring in countries that economically cannot support their populations.

No one knows how many humans the earth can support. Determining the **carrying capacity** of the planet for human life depends largely on the amount of food that can be produced, and on the quality of life that is desired (Brown, 1994). As the number of people living on the planet increases, the resources available to each individual decrease. Some responsible environmental scientists have estimated that we have already overshot the *long-term* carrying capacity of the earth, which may be *less than half* of the number of humans who are alive today (Meadows, Meadows, & Randers, 1992; Pimentel et al., 1994).

Pollution

In 1969, the Cuyahoga River in Cleveland, Ohio, caught fire because its water was so heavily polluted with petroleum chemicals. At that time, industrial smokestacks around the country billowed toxic smoke into the air freely, and there were few regulations to prevent toxic pollution of water and land, such as the poisonous products dumped at Love Canal in Buffalo, New York. In the U.S. today, many of these blatantly harmful actions have been curtailed through environmental legislation. However, other developing countries around the world, in their quest for an industrial society, have been increasing their polluting actions (Gore, 1992).

Air Pollution. Air pollution is caused by the release of chemical by-products into the air. These chemicals come primarily from the generation of energy which powers our automobiles, heats our houses, and produces electricity. Other extremely serious air pollutants are compounds of chlorine, such as the chlorofluorocarbons (CFCs), which are used in air-conditioning systems. These pollutants have been linked to many environmental problems, including acid rain, holes in the ozone layer, and the greenhouse effect.

Acid rain is produced when sulfur from burning coal, and nitrogen from burning gasoline, combine with oxygen in the atmosphere to form acids. These acids are then returned to the earth in the form of rain and snow, damaging many plants and trees, and killing all the life in many rivers and lakes.

Air pollution is also seriously damaging the **ozone**
layer. Ozone is a relatively rare and active gas. At the earth's surface it is an eye-irritating part of the smog formed by automobile exhausts. However, in the earth's upper atmosphere it forms a protective layer which is crucial to human, plant, and animal health because it blocks much of the deadly ultraviolet radiation coming from the sun. Reductions in the amount of atmospheric ozone mean that more ultraviolet radiation will hit the earth, producing increases in human skin cancer and cataracts, and reductions in agricultural yields due to injury to many animals and plants, including plankton in the oceans (Brown, 1994).

In the 1980s, scientists first discovered reductions in the amount of ozone in a large region over the Antarctic. Today, it is clear that there is a similar ozone hole over the north polar region as well, and an 8% reduction in the amount of ozone in the Northern Hemisphere was documented between 1979 and 1990 (Gribbon & Gribbon, 1993). This ozone depletion is caused by chlorine atoms chemically reacting with ozone to produce a new compound. The primary source of chlorine in the upper atmosphere is CFCs such as freon, a chemical manufactured for use as a coolant in air conditioners and refrigerators, and formerly as a propellant in spray cans. Almost all of the world's nations have signed a treaty, called the Montreal Convention, agreeing to phase out the production of CFCs, but unfortunately that treaty has been attacked as unnecessary by ill-advised politicians in the U.S. and other countries (Wager, 1995–1996).

The **greenhouse effect** is another result of gases in the upper atmosphere. The term refers to an increase in the earth's average temperature, which occurs through a process rather similar to the way that glass panes in a greenhouse let in warming sunlight but prevent warm air from escaping. Energy from the sun constantly heats the earth's surface, but much of this energy is reflected back into space either as visible light or as infrared radiation. In the upper atmosphere, several types of gases allow visible light to penetrate, but reflect the earth's infrared radiation back to earth, thus heating it further. The primary one of these "greenhouse gases" is carbon dioxide, which is produced by the burning of fossil fuels such as natural gas or petroleum, in industries, homes, and automobile engines (Walsh, 1993).

The result of the greenhouse effect is that the earth's temperature will gradually increase. Global warming is already occurring and is predicted to drastically change life as we know it (Flavin & Tunali, 1996; Wyman, 1991). It will change rainfall patterns, flooding some areas while creating deserts elsewhere in place of current agricultural lands, disrupting food production, and causing the extinction of many species. Eventually, melting of the earth's icecaps will slightly raise the level of the oceans and flood many low-lying seacoast areas. Research data on the average temperature of the earth's surface show a steady rise over the last 100 years, as illustrated in Figure 11–2. The most frightening aspect of these data is that such changes, once underway, may be irreversible. As Stern (1992) stated:

> Global changes may be impossible to control once they get started; by the time a catastrophe is foreseen, it may already be too late to prevent it. Humanity is conducting a grand experiment on its natural environment, and cannot afford to fail. We have only one earth on which to experiment. (p. 271)

The Energy Crisis

1973 was a watershed year for the world's energy situation, separating us from a past that we can never recapture. That fall an Arab-Israeli war broke out, and subsequently the Arab nations of the Organization of Petroleum Exporting Countries (OPEC) refused to sell oil to the United States and other Western nations. Since the U.S. imported a large part of the oil it used, shortages of gasoline and heating oil quickly became widespread. Drivers often had to sit in gas lines for an hour or more, and frequently there was no gasoline available at all. National frustration was intense!

Fortunately, the embargo ended after six months, and the shortages and gas lines disappeared. But since then there have been many wrenching changes in the energy picture. Initially, OPEC more than quadrupled the list price of oil from about $2.50 per barrel to about $11, and after the Iranian revolution the price tripled again to over $30 in 1981, later leveling off around $20 in the 1990s. These price increases drove some poorer nations close to bankruptcy, and oil imports cost the

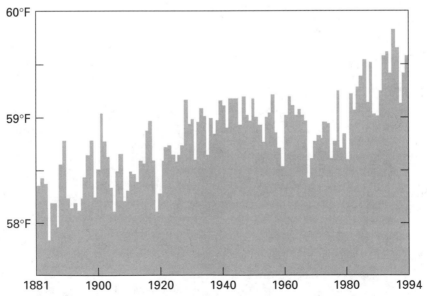

FIGURE 11-2 Global average temperature, annually, 1881–1994. (Source: Environmental Defense Fund, 1995, p. 1. Data from Vinnikov et al., 1994, *Trends '93*, Oak Ridge National Laboratory.)

United States $80 billion in 1980, more than 25 times their cost only ten years earlier (Weaver, 1981). Individual consumers suffered the drastic effects of inflation as gasoline prices quadrupled.

Yet despite this national and individual suffering, the United States did almost nothing to diminish its dangerous dependence on imported oil. In spite of national programs for "energy independence" dramatically announced by Presidents Nixon, Ford, and Carter, our reliance on oil as an energy source has increased rather than diminished, and we now import over half of our oil from politically unstable areas of the world such as the Near East. In 1991, the U.S. imported over 2 billion barrels of crude oil, dramatically up from 483 million barrels in 1970 (U.S. Bureau of the Census, 1994). However, this situation—and the whole international energy picture—is unstable and cannot last for long without further marked changes. The Persian Gulf War of 1991 and continuing international conflict and terrorism in the Middle East demonstrate how vulnerable to disruption is the world's supply of petroleum, which keeps production and transportation running in every nation.

Natural Resources

The earth's resources are finite. Many of the materials that are used in manufacturing processes are not from renewable sources (e.g., oil, minerals, underground water supplies). However, industries and consumers act as if there is an unlimited supply. Estimates of natural resource supplies remaining are typically calculated as the number of years the resources will last at the present annual consumption rate. In the late 1980s, there was an estimated 14-year supply of lead, 65 years of nickel, 179 years of iron ore, and 25 years of zinc (Simmons, 1991). However, these estimates are based on average annual consumption figures, and these rates have been steadily increasing over the last 100 years (Brown, 1995).

The United States is by far the largest consumer of the world's production of raw materials (Brown, 1994). Nevertheless, we continue to discard about 83% of all materials after using them only once, rather than reusing or recycling them into new products (Khator, 1993). Though we can postpone the final depletion of resource supplies by digging deeper, using less-concentrated mineral bodies, and finding substitutes for depleted raw materials, our practice of using up the earth's resources must eventually stop. Instead, we must adopt a new lifestyle of reducing our consumption, reusing products that still have useful life, and recycling the materials in products that are no longer serviceable (U.S. Environmental Protection Agency, 1992).

Social Science Can Help. Psychologists can make important contributions to preserving the earth's resources and the natural environment. The necessary changes are largely *behavioral* in nature, and even where they involve technological change, psychological approaches will be needed to inform and motivate people to adopt the new technology. One major example of contributions by behavioral scientists is research on people's proenvironmental behaviors, such as recycling and energy conservation, which is reviewed in the following section.

ENCOURAGING PROENVIRONMENTAL BEHAVIORS

Earlier in this chapter we discussed environmental attitudes such as general environmental concern. However, the real benefit to the environment comes from ecologically responsible *behavior*—not just awareness of environmental problems or favorable attitudes. Many psychologists have begun to concentrate on studying such behavior (for reviews, see Oskamp, 1995a; Schultz, Oskamp, & Mainieri, 1995). Of the two main research approaches in this area, one is applied behavior analysis, which stems from the Skinnerian tradition of behavior modification and is based on learning theory. Researchers using that theoretical approach have conducted many successful experiments on decreasing littering and encouraging recycling—areas that have clear-cut criteria, which make behavioral studies convenient. The other main approach is studies involving a more dynamic-motivational tradition, emphasizing processes of social interaction and persuasion.

We will mention examples of both kinds of research, focusing largely on the area of recycling and to a lesser extent on energy conservation. We will begin by examining predictors of proenvironmental behavior and then focus on interventions designed to increase these behaviors.

Predicting Who Recycles

Research on recycling behaviors conducted over the last 25 years has investigated characteristics of people that are associated with recycling. These studies have explored demographic variables, knowledge about recycling, environmental attitudes, and personality variables (see Schultz et al., 1995, for a review).

Demographics. The four most commonly studied demographic predictors of recycling are age, gender, income, and education. Early research indicated that recyclers on average tended to be young, White, better educated, and more affluent than people who did not recycle. However, more recent research suggests that the relationship between demographic variables and recycling is decreasing (Derksen & Gartrell, 1993). As recycling becomes more convenient and commonplace, many types of people will be recycling, and for a variety of different reasons.

Knowledge. Knowledge about recycling has been found to predict recycling behavior. In general, the more knowledge a person has about which materials are recyclable, or where recyclables are collected, the more likely that person is to recycle. However, research findings in this area are correlational, and the direction of causation between knowledge and behavior is unclear. Two further qualifications about knowledge are important. First, research suggests that knowledge about the *specifics* of the recycling program is a better predictor of actual behavior than is knowledge about recycling in general (Oskamp et al., 1991). Second, while knowledge is a necessary antecedent to recycling, it is not a sufficient condition. In order for knowledge to be translated into behavior, there must be something to motivate the person to recycle—either an external incentive, or an internal motive.

Environmental Concern. One potential internal motive for recycling is concern for the environment, which we have touched on above. However, research

indicates that general environmental concern is not always a good predictor of recycling (Oskamp, 1995b; Schultz et al., 1995). The theory of planned behavior (Ajzen, 1991), discussed in Chapters 2 and 14, holds that behavior is determined by individuals' attitudes, their perceptions of social norms regarding the behavior, and their perceived ability to perform the behavior. Clearly, attitudes are just one of the factors producing behavior. That theory also holds that attitudes about a specific behavior are better predictors of the behavior than are more general attitudes. This point is clearly supported in recycling research (Boldero, 1995; Gamba & Oskamp, 1994). Attitudes specific to recycling (e.g., about the benefits of recycling, or the difficulties of recycling) are frequently better predictors of whether a person will or won't recycle than are broad attitudes of general environmental concern.

Personality. Another potential motivating force for recycling is personality characteristics, but research attempting to identify a "recycling personality" has been largely unsuccessful. The one suggestive finding from this line of research is that recyclers are more likely than nonrecyclers to feel a sense of responsibility for protecting the environment. However, as Simmons and Widmar (1990) pointed out, feeling that your behaviors can make a difference is not enough; it must be coupled with knowledge about the recycling process, and a supportive social context.

Behavioral Interventions

We turn now to an examination of interventions to increase proenvironmental behaviors. Typically, these interventions are based on social psychological theories and, as mentioned above, they can be divided into behavioral interventions and social interaction interventions. We will discuss five kinds of behavioral interventions: information about recycling, prompts, modeling procedures, monetary incentives, and feedback.

Information campaigns are a favorite influence technique of government agencies and private organizations (e.g., public utilities, waste disposal companies, and energy producers). Information strategies are intended to make people more knowledgeable—about recycling, for instance—which in turn is often expected to lead to an increase in recycling behavior. However, findings on the effectiveness of information interventions in increasing proenvironmental behaviors are mixed and typically show only weak effects (Gardner & Stern, 1996; Leeming et al., 1993). Nevertheless, information campaigns are often used in attempts to change behavior—in part because they are relatively inexpensive and easy to implement.

It is probable that long-continued information campaigns do have cumulative effects, but research suggests that they are not likely to be successful (e.g., in reducing energy use) unless conducted as part of a larger conservation program, including widespread distribution or marketing of energy-saving devices and materials. For instance, it does little good to inform people about the value of low-flow showerheads if they have no idea where to obtain one (Gardner & Stern, 1996).

Prompts are brief signals about what actions to take. They can vary from general ("Please recycle") to specific ("Place all aluminum cans in this bin"). There is good research evidence that more specific prompts are more successful, so they should be phrased to indicate the who, what, and when of the desired actions. Geller (1981) reported that prompts are more successful if they are polite rather than demanding, request a response that is easy to perform (such as turning off a light switch, as contrasted with taking materials to a drop-off recycling center), and are administered close to the point of response (for example, a sign near the light switch and room exit, or above a recycling bin).

Prompts and information are **antecedent strategies**—that is, they are stimuli occurring before the desired response. As such, they are rarely as effective as **consequent strategies**—ones that occur after and are contingent on performance of the desired response—e.g., reinforcement or feedback. Though prompts have had some success in influencing easy-to-perform actions, they are generally more effective when combined with reinforcing consequences (Austin et al., 1993).

Modeling is also an antecedent procedure which presents information, but in ways that make it concrete and easy to learn. By definition, modeling involves demonstration of desired behaviors or practices (Bandura, 1977). This can be done very efficiently through TV or films, or more expensively through in-person demonstrations, where participants can try out the desired behaviors and receive feedback and further individualized instruction. Such methods have been used effectively to strengthen desired behaviors such as dieting, and variables that help to determine their effectiveness have been summarized by Bandura (1977).

An example of the use of modeling to influence environmental behavior was a field experiment in which antilittering behavior was modeled to unsuspecting subjects (Reno, Cialdini, & Kallgren, 1993). As people left a local library and approached their cars, a confederate walked by and picked up a fast-food bag that had been placed on the ground near the car, and threw it in a trash can. When the subjects reached their cars, they found a handbill on the windshield. Results showed that only 7% of the subjects in the modeling condition tossed the handbill on the ground, while 37% did so in the control condition.

Monetary incentives, as reinforcement theory predicts, have been found effective in increasing a wide range of proenvironmental behaviors, including energy conservation, recycling, using public transportation, and ride sharing (Everett & Watson, 1987; Gardner & Stern, 1996; Geller, 1989). An excellent example of research on monetary incentives was Deslauriers and Everett's (1977) study, which attempted to increase patronage of a university campus bus system. The authors rewarded the behavior with either a continuous, or a variable-ratio, reinforcement schedule, giving riders tokens that could be exchanged for discounts at many local stores. In the continuous condition, riders received one token for each trip, whereas in the variable-ratio condition every third rider received a token. Results for a control condition showed no change in ridership from the baseline level. In contrast, there was a 27% ridership increase in the continuous reinforcement condition, and a 30% increase in the variable-ratio condition. The findings from this study have been applied by transportation systems in Spokane and Seattle, WA, Portland, OR, and Bridgeport, CT. However, the results across these cities were mixed (Everett & Watson, 1987).

Although the research on monetary incentives indicates that they can be an effective tool for increasing proenvironmental behaviors, there are three important practical considerations: the amount of behavior change, the cost of the incentive, and the long-term effects of the intervention. In contrast to the impressive findings of Deslauriers and Everett's (1977) transportation study, most incentive studies have not achieved very large changes in behavior—typically not much more than 10% from the original level. Thus, it was frequently true that the amount of monetary incentives paid was greater than the value of the behavior change (e.g., energy savings). Such experimental procedures can demonstrate that reinforcement principles work, but because they are not cost-effective, they are not useful as a basis for public policy to encourage conservation (Winett & Neale, 1979). More economically feasible approaches have been demonstrated by studies using partial reinforcement procedures, or reinforcement of a random subgroup of participants, or contests or lotteries to determine the winners from among a group of successful energy conservers (Needleman & Geller, 1992).

Another problem is that the change in behavior produced by reward programs tends to be short-lived, and once the intervention is terminated, behaviors typically return to their original levels (or in some cases, to lower levels). One factor here is that rewarding people for actions that they already enjoy may lead them to make an external attribution for the behavior. For instance, they may come to believe that they are recycling because of the reward rather than for more intrinsic motives (Boggiano et al., 1987; Lepper & Greene, 1979). In such cases, when the reward stops, the justification for the behavior no longer exists, and the frequency of the behavior decreases.

In contrast to positive reinforcement, **punishments** such as fines or penalties are usually less successful in shaping long-term behavior. Yet government attempts to achieve desirable social ends usually rely mostly on laws and regulations with built-in penalties. One valuable exception to this rule is the "bottle bills" which have been passed by ten states. In the field of energy conservation and recycling, these laws, which specify a monetary payment for returning beverage containers for recycling, are the only large-scale, positive reinforcement procedures adopted by governments in the United States. They have been outstandingly successful in increasing the percentage of returned containers, to levels as high as 90%, and thus have dramatically reduced the amount of roadside litter (Shireman, 1993). Yet unfortunately, they have generally been opposed by industry.

Monetary *dis*incentives, such as increasing costs of gasoline and electricity or higher energy taxes, do have effects on behavior (O'Brien & Zoumbaris, 1993). For example, countries with high energy taxes provide a strong disincentive to use or waste energy. As an illustration, in most Western European countries gasoline costs about $4 per gallon, and consequently consumers there use it much more sparingly than in the U.S. and Canada. Cheap energy in the U.S. is undoubtedly one of the major reasons for our overconsumption of oil—more than twice the per capita rate of Western European countries and Japan ("Wasting Opportunities," 1990).

An example of monetary disincentives from the recycling area is a per-bag waste disposal fee. In these types of programs, householders are required to purchase stickers that must be placed on all garbage at the curbside for pickup, whereas recyclables are collected free of charge. The Environmental Protection Agency (EPA) conservatively estimates that this simple approach can reduce the amount of trash by at least 10% (Cohn, 1992), but a report from Seattle indicated that the number of bins of trash set out per week declined by 60% after this system was inaugurated (Shireman, 1993).

Feedback means providing people with specific information about their own behaviors. Feedback has been used in a variety of environmental arenas: to influence home energy use, water consumption, gas mileage in cars, and recycling programs (Schultz, in press). In the area of home energy use, feedback interventions have often been found to produce energy savings of 10% to 15% (Seligman, Becker, & Darley, 1981). Also, some experiments have shown them to have continuing effects for several months after the experimental treatment was discontinued (Pallak, Cook, & Sullivan, 1980; Winett, Neale, & Grier, 1979). For best results, feedback needs to occur at least daily, rather than weekly or monthly as happens with the feedback provided on utility bills. A theoretical analysis of why feedback appears more effective than other behavioral techniques suggests that it has both informational properties (as do prompts), and also, since it shows progress toward a goal, motivational properties (as do incentives)—(Ellis & Gaskell, 1978).

Feedback also has the potential for being more cost-effective than incentive approaches *if* it can be made relatively automatic, thus dispensing with the need to pay a person to provide the feedback. Two

ways of accomplishing this are self-monitoring and mechanization. Using an example from the area of energy consumption, **self-monitoring** could involve train-ing householders to read and record the utility meter every day, and this approach has typically produced energy savings of a bit below 10%. In a study of winter heating of all-electric townhouses, self-monitoring produced an average saving of $11 per month

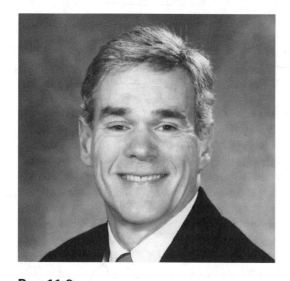

Photograph courtesy of Scott Geller. Reprinted by permission.

Box 11-3

E. SCOTT GELLER, PIONEER IN ENVIRONMENTAL BEHAVIOR RESEARCH

Scott Geller is a noted authority on the application of behavioral analysis methods to the solution of community and corporate problems, particularly in the areas of health, safety, and environmental protection. Born in Pennsylvania in 1942, he attended Wooster College in Ohio and earned his M.A. and Ph.D. in experimental psychology from Southern Illinois University. Since receiving his Ph.D. in 1969, he has taught at Virginia Polytechnic Institute and State University, where he has shaped the Applied Behavioral Science program.

Geller has published over 250 papers, many of which have been on environmental topics such as litter control, energy conservation, resource recovery, shoplifting prevention,

seatbelt use, and transportation efficiency. He has also written extensively on cognitive processes, decision making, and behavior modification, and he has been the principal investigator on over 50 research grants. His seven books include *Preserving the Environment: New Strategies for Behavior Change*, *Motivating Health Behavior*, and *The Psychology of Safety*. Recently, directing his work at safety in industrial workplaces, he has developed a training series entitled *Actively Caring for Safety*. He has also served on the editorial boards of several journals and has won an award for outstanding teaching from APA's Division of Teaching of Psychology.

(Winett, Neale, & Grier, 1979). This simple procedure seems so effective that Geller (1981) suggested that power companies should give residents the option of reading their own meters and phoning in the reading each month, with only an annual checkup by the utility meter reader.

Mechanization of feedback, which can be accomplished with a wide range of inexpensive signaling devices, is also a very promising approach to encouraging proenvironmental behaviors. In a study on the use of mechanized feedback, Becker and Seligman (1978) installed a flashing blue light in a randomly chosen set of 10 identical townhouses of families who agreed to participate in an energy conservation study. The device was installed by the wall phone in a central location, and blinked continuously when the outside temperature was 68 degrees or lower, *and* the air conditioner inside the townhouse was on. Significant results showed that, when compared to a 10-week baseline period, families with the mechanized feedback used 16% less electricity. At that rate of savings, the device would pay for itself in about two years.

An Illustrative Feedback Experiment

Feedback has also been used to improve curbside recycling. In order to examine the effectiveness of feedback on recycling, Schultz (in press) conducted an experiment comparing two types of feedback and two types of information as ways to increase recycling. The study was done with households served by a residential curbside recycling program which required separation of four types of recyclable materials (newspapers, cans, bottles, and plastics #1 and #2).

Participants in the study were 605 single-family homes in a middle-class residential suburb of Los Angeles. Approximately 120 houses were systematically assigned to each of five experimental conditions: individual written feedback, group written feedback, information, plea-only, and control. For convenience in data gathering, households were grouped by small contiguous geographic areas, ranging in size from 5 to 16 houses, and these small areas were randomly assigned to experimental conditions. To reduce possible diffusion of the treatment, households were grouped so that

discussion between residents in different conditions would be minimized. This was done by using natural barriers (e.g., trees, walls, cross streets, empty lots, etc.) as boundaries of the contiguous areas. In assigning the housing groups to conditions, the conditions were equated on their members' past recycling participation, as measured during a previous unobtrusive study. The assignment to conditions produced 5 groups of approximately 120 households, with each possessing an average baseline rate of recycling participation within 1% of each other.

Households had been observed for eight weeks in order to establish this recycling baseline. Later, when the interventions began, all households except for those assigned to the control condition received a plea to recycle. The plea stated: "In order for [the city] to achieve the benefits of recycling, please try to recycle as much as possible." This information was printed on one side of a green door hanger and placed on the doorknob of each household in the four experimental conditions. The plea served two purposes. First, it signaled to these four groups that a study was being conducted. Second, its effects as a manipulation were tested by having it as the only intervention for the plea-only group.

Beginning on the second week of the experimental period, houses in the other three experimental conditions (individual feedback, group feedback, and information) received four weeks of information or feedback, presented on green door hangers on their front doorknob. The door hangers were delivered on the morning of the trash pickup day, after the observers had completed observations of recycling for all households in the area.

Households in the individual written feedback condition received four weeks of feedback about their specific recycling behaviors. The feedback informed each household about the amount of each type of recyclable material collected the previous week, the amount of each type of material collected the current week, and the total amount of each material collected for the duration of the study. This information was handwritten on preprinted door hangers.

Households in the group written feedback condition received a preprinted door hanger similar to the individual feedback condition, for the same 4-week period, but with feedback information about the recycling amounts for their residential area (that is, approximately 200 contiguous houses of their SES level—high, medium, or low).

Households assigned to the information condition received four green door hangers during the 4-week intervention, each with a different type of information. The first door hanger reminded householders which materials were recyclable in the recycling program, and the second gave a list of nonrecyclable materials and frequent contaminants. The third door hanger described important features of the recycling process, from collection to reuse of recycled materials. The final door hanger gave information about the conservation of energy, landfill space, and natural resources that results from recycling.

After the 4-week interventions, the recycling of all households was observed for an additional four weeks in follow-up observations.

Results. The data analysis was based on the three time periods: baseline, intervention, and follow-up. Repeated-measures analysis of variance, using the three time periods as the repeated measure, and the five experimental conditions as a second independent variable, showed a significant increase in (a) the frequency of participation and (b) the amount of material recycled for the individual feedback and group feedback conditions, but not for the information, plea-only, nor control conditions. On the average, households in the individual feedback condition recycled 15% more often and 23% more material per week during the 4-week follow-up period than they did during the baseline period. For the group feedback condition, results showed an 18% increase in the frequency of participation, and a 20% increase in the amount of material recycled.

Thus, the theoretically predicted effect of feedback was found to occur at a substantial level in this experiment, demonstrating a relatively easy way to encourage people to recycle more often and greater amounts of material. The approximately 20% increase in the amount of recycled materials observed in this study is consistent with results from feedback studies in the area of home energy use (e.g., Becker & Seligman, 1978; Van Houwelingen & Van Raaij, 1989).

Social Interaction Interventions

In contrast with the behavioral research described above, social psychologists from a more dynamic-motivational tradition have taken other approaches in studying proenvironmental behavior. Building on social psychological theories and principles (such as those summarized in Chapter 2), they have used persuasion methods and social incentives; investigated social influence situations like foot-in-the-door, group decision, and public commitment; removed obstacles to attitude-consistent behavior; and analyzed the effects of group processes such as "social traps" (Gardner & Stern, 1996).

Persuasion has been a favorite topic of social psychologists for decades. In the energy area, researchers have used persuasive messages featuring appeals to fear, highly credible sources of information, and recommendations to take specific actions, as well as other techniques. Generally these persuasion approaches have been aimed at changing attitudes or intentions, while changes in actual behavior have seldom been measured. Though it is often assumed that changed attitudes will lead to changed behavior, there is much evidence in the literature that this sequence often does not occur (Lipsey, 1977). Therefore, it is highly desirable to study actual behavior as well as attitude change, and to measure the behavior by means other than self-report.

In a study on the effects of persuasive communications, Gonzales, Aronson, and Costanzo (1988) examined compliance by householders with recommendations from an energy specialist (see also Aronson & Gonzales, 1990). Trained energy auditors made a free home inspection for householders who requested it, and stated recommendations on how to reduce the amount of energy used in the home. Initial baseline measurements found that only 20% of households actually implemented the changes suggested by the auditor. Subsequently, the auditors were trained to describe the problems in each home in more vivid and persuasive terms. For example:

> Look at all the cracks under that door! It may not seem like much to you, but if you were to add up all the cracks around and under each of these doors, you'd have the equivalent of a hole the size and circumference of a basketball. (p. 1054)

Similarly, attics without insulation were described as a "naked attic." When the auditors used these vivid terms for making recommendations, 61% of the homeowners made the suggested changes—a dramatic increase, and a very cost-effective intervention since the vivid recommendations took no more time nor effort than the previous more technical ones.

Social incentives, such as approval or public recognition, according to reinforcement theory, should have behavioral effects similar to those of monetary incentives. An early review found only two energy-related studies of this sort, but both showed significant effects on actual energy consumption (Cook & Berrenberg, 1981).

Social influence techniques, such as the foot-in-the-door approach or use of cognitive dissonance, have also been applied to environmental problems. For instance, Dickerson et al. (1992) used an intervention that aroused cognitive dissonance to reduce the amount of water used in a gym shower. Female subjects were approached by a researcher as they left the swimming pool on their way to the showers. Some were interviewed about their shower habits, and some were interviewed about another topic. The subjects were then asked to sign a petition urging people to reduce their water consumption. A female confederate then showered nearby each subject and measured the amount of time the water was running during the subject's shower. Results showed that subjects who were interviewed about their habits, and who signed a petition to reduce water, used significantly less water during their shower. Stated technically, their attitudes about water conservation were *primed*, and then they made a **public commitment** to water conservation. However, as illustrated by this study, social influence techniques are apt to be difficult to apply on a large scale, because they require personal contacts with individual participants.

Removing obstacles to proenvironmental actions is an approach that can be used in large-scale government or industry programs. In recycling research, for example, reducing the distance that a person has to travel to reach a recycling bin has been found to increase the amount of material that is recycled. In a study by Luy-ben and Bailey (1979), placing an additional six bins around a mobile home park produced an increase of 47% in the amount of recycled newspapers.

Similar results have been obtained for other proenvironmental behaviors. For instance, providing vans or offering priority parking spaces to encourage vanpools and carpools has been found to increase the likelihood that people will rideshare (see reviews by Reichel & Geller, 1981; Zerega, 1981). Other examples of this approach involve removing financial obstacles to energy-saving actions such as home insulation or weatherizing. A variety of government and utility-company programs of this sort have been developed, such as income-tax rebates, low-interest loans, and loans that can be repaid through monthly charges on the utility bill.

Social Traps. Social traps are social situations that motivate people to pursue their individual self-interest rather than acting in the long-term common interest (Platt, 1973). They have also been described as creating "the tragedy of the commons" (Edney, 1980; Hardin, 1968). Essentially, they are situations where a scarce resource, such as grazing land or world petroleum supplies, is overused and depleted because each user is intent on improving his or her own short-term outcomes. Psychologists have analyzed social traps in game-theory terms and have done considerable laboratory research on simple analogs of the commons dilemma (Feeny et al., 1990).

Many studies have been conducted in attempts to find possible ways out of these social traps. Results from this research indicate that there are many potential solutions, ranging from pleas to morality or personal trust, to changes in the ways in which participants interact (e.g., Martichuski & Bell, 1991). One clear improvement is to foster communication. In an illustrative study, college students who participated in a simulated social trap made more cooperative choices (i.e., choices that benefited everyone) rather than competitive choices (i.e., choices that only benefited themselves) when they were allowed to talk together for 10 minutes. The communication gave participants a chance to learn whether the other group members were going to act competitively or cooperatively, and to gain assurances from other group members about their future decisions (Orbell, van de Kragt, & Dawes, 1988).

PUBLIC POLICY ON ENVIRONMENTAL ISSUES

Public policy about environmental problems largely begins in the government—federal, state, or local (see Chapter 17). In every U.S. presidential campaign since the 1970s, environmental quality has been an important issue (Dwyer & Leeming, 1995). In principle, one of the primary functions of the government should be to protect the environment from destructive human behaviors. However, attempts to protect the environment through legislation and political action invariably involve balancing the short-term gains from economic development and production against the long-term, less visible considerations of adverse environmental impacts (Dwyer & Leeming, 1995).

Energy

It seems reasonable, in view of the energy crisis that has resulted from our reliance on nonrenewable energy sources, that the government would promote policies to help reduce energy consumption and to boost the use of renewable forms of energy (e.g., solar and wind energy). However, this has not been the case. Throughout the 1980s, the U.S. government resisted legislation that would promote energy conservation, relying instead on the forces of a free market, and claiming that mandated conservation programs were an infringement on personal freedoms (Kempton, Darley, & Stern, 1992).

Although this reasoning prevented major changes from the energy policies implemented by the previous administrations of Ford and Carter, a few useful laws were passed. The Energy Labeling Program, which was part of the Energy and Conservation Policy Act of 1975, mandated that certain types of information be made available to consumers concerning energy efficiency (e.g., energy use by appliances, fuel economy in cars), so that they could compare the relative energy consumption of products. However, a manufacturers' lobby then succeeded in getting the requirement for some products changed to an index

number rather than the more meaningful dollar figure. At that time, some research was done, primarily on the legibility of the labels, but in the 20 years following passage of the law, very little research has been conducted to determine if, and how, these informational labels are used by consumers in their purchase decisions. Though the basic idea of energy effectiveness labeling is an excellent one, this is a sad story of the non-use of social science expertise! (U.S. EPA, 1994; Watson, 1989).

Solid Waste

The amount of trash generated by Americans, and by other nations, continues to rise dramatically. In the U.S., nearly 200 million tons of trash are buried in landfills each year (about 1600 pounds for every man, woman, and child in the country). The solid waste stream is composed of many potentially reusable materials (e.g., paper, metal, plastic, and glass), as well as organic materials (e.g., grass, food), and trace amounts of toxic chemicals (e.g., lead, mercury, cadmium). However, only recently has public policy about solid waste turned toward recycling.

In 1989, the EPA warned that U.S. landfill capacity was becoming exhausted and announced a national goal of reducing landfill use. In the years since this announcement, all 50 states have passed legislation requiring cities and counties to reduce the amount of trash sent to landfills. Most of these laws leave the methods of reduction to local officials, and simply require a percentage reduction in the amount of trash that is buried. In California, for example, a 1989 law required cities to reduce the amount of trash sent to landfills 25% by 1995, and 50% by the year 2000. Cities that did not comply could be fined $10,000 per day! (Shireman, 1993).

In the 1990s, curbside recycling programs are the most common strategy in the effort to reduce landfill use. Nationally, by 1993, over 5000 curbside recycling programs served more than 15 million households, and the number was growing rapidly (Boerner & Chilton, 1994). Results from these programs in California indicate that by 1995 the statewide amount of trash sent to landfills was reduced by 25% (California Integrated Waste Management Board, 1995). However, most of this reduction occurred from the startup of new city recycling programs, and it is unclear whether the goal of 50% reduction by the year 2000 will be attainable.

Pollution

In the early 1970s, the federal government passed the first set of comprehensive standards to control the quality of the environment. The Clean Water Act of 1970 and the Clean Air Act of 1972 (as well as later amendments) established limits on the types and quantities of pollutants that could be released into the air and surface water of the U.S. Clearly this type of legislation is critical in changing the way humans interact with the environment. Such laws require individuals and corporations to act in ways that are good for the population at large, rather than making the competitive, individualistic decisions often displayed in "social trap" situations.

However, one crucial missing component of most such laws is a mandated evaluation. Are these programs effective at controlling the quality of the air and water? Though these environmental programs aim in the right direction, most have not been adequately evaluated, and there is some doubt about their effectiveness (Bartlett, 1994). The Clean Air Act is estimated to cost $50 billion per year (Portney, 1990), and the Clean Water Act is estimated to cost $30 billion per year (Freeman, 1994). With such large expenditures, there should be large positive effects on the environment, but recent examinations of these two programs suggest mixed results.

Research on the quality of the environment shows both improvements and continuing problems. On the improvement side, the air in the U.S. is getting cleaner. Between 1983 and 1992 airborne lead fell 89% as leaded gasoline was phased out. Carbon monoxide fell 34%, largely because of catalytic converters on cars and scrubbers on factory smokestacks. Furthermore, recent requirements that gasoline be oxygenated—a procedure which raises the consumer cost by 5 cents per gallon but causes cleaner burning—has produced a 13% reduction in CO_2 in 28 metropolitan areas. All three of these improvements are directly attributable to the 1972 Clean Air Act and the 1990 Amendment to the Clean Air Act (Nixon, 1995). On the down side, however, a 5-year EPA study on the presence of 60 toxic chemicals in 119 species of fish across 314 bodies of water in the U.S. showed many of the harmful chemicals in more than 90% of the sites, and dangerous amounts of every pollutant in the study were found in at least one location (Adler, 1994). Since these toxic chemicals accumulate in the tissues of living organisms, they can be dangerous or even fatal to people who eat the fish, and there is no labeling system available to warn people of the danger.

Environmental Justice

Environmental justice is a broad term which raises the issue of whether environmental policies about the production and disposal of toxic products unfairly put poor people and people of color at a substantially greater risk of exposure than wealthier, White people (Been, 1995). The threats involved stem from pollution of air, water, and land, and from all kinds of wastes disposed of within the U.S., as well as the 20 million tons of hazardous waste shipped each year from the U.S. to developing countries (Foster, 1995).

As one example, Mohai and Bryant (1992) investigated the distance of poor and minority households from commercial hazardous waste facilities. They collected data in face-to-face interviews with 793 residents whose households were selected using a stratified random sample of all households in the three counties surrounding Detroit. The distance from each house to the closest one of 16 commercial hazardous waste treatment or storage facilities was measured to the nearest tenth of a mile. Minorities were defined as individuals who identified themselves as Black, other non-White, or Hispanic. Results showed a clear racist and classist pattern of proximity to hazardous waste facilities. Of households which were more than 1.5 miles away from the nearest facility, 18% were minority and 10% were poor. Among households located from 1 to 1.5 miles away, 39% were minority and 18% were poor. Finally, of households less than 1 mile away, 48% were minority, and 29% were poor. The authors also tested the relative strength of race and income as influences on distance from hazardous waste sites. Results from a regression analysis showed that both poverty and minority ethnicity were significant independent predictors of distance from a site, and that minority ethnicity was the strongest predictor.

Much past research on environmental problems shows that people only get mobilized to combat threats when the threats are dramatically present, such as an oil spill like the *Exxon Valdez*, or when there is heavy media attention to them (Lipsey, 1977). In such situations, rich and poor alike may perceive the threat and unite to take action against it. By contrast, people who live in daily contact with a noxious condition like a polluting factory or a toxic waste disposal site are less likely to mobilize against it, particularly if they or their neighbors' income or employment is linked to the polluting source (Creer, Gray, & Treshow, 1970).

These considerations suggest that, if affluent members of our society were clearly threatened by environmental risks, as poor people often are, there would be more political action to reduce those risks. However, in the 1990s, a contrary political trend occurred, in which Congress attacked and eliminated many environmental regulations, using the justification of saving money or increasing government efficiency. The result will be greater environmental dangers to all citizens—e.g., uninspected food, more carcinogens in the air and water supplies—but this threat will fall most heavily on the poor and on ethnic minorities (Wright, Bryant, & Bullard, 1995).

TOWARD A SUSTAINABLE FUTURE

In view of the environmental problems that we have discussed, the findings of psychological research on promoting proenvironmental behaviors, and public policy developments concerning environmental issues, what can we expect for the future? The social sciences have theories about how our expectations for future events can become self-fulfilling prophecies. History, anthropology, sociology, economics, and psychology all make reference to ways in which people's expectations about the future can influence their actions and make what they expect become a reality (Boulding, 1966; Olson, 1995). For this reason, building a vision

of a sustainable future for the world is an important step toward protecting the environment.

The term **sustainable development** has been succinctly defined by the report of the World Commission on Environment and Development (1987), as a process that "meets the needs of the present without compromising the ability of future generations to meet their own needs" (p. 363). Is it possible for our society and the world as a whole to become a sustainable one? We must work unceasingly toward that goal, for the alternative to sustainable living is eventual destruction of human life and activities, due to destruction of much of the earth's ecosystem.

One way to explore what it will take to become a sustainable society is the IPAT formula (Ehrlich & Ehrlich, 1991). This formula can be used to estimate the environmental impacts from population growth, changed levels of consumption, and advances in technology:

$$I = P \times A \times T$$

where (I), the impact on the environment of any society, is equal to (P) the population, times (A) the amount of consumption per person (affluence), times the environmental damage or protection stemming from particular (T) technologies that support that level of affluence. For instance, if the population doubles, and the affluence and the environmental impact of the technology remain constant, there will be twice as much impact on the environment (twice as much resource use, pollution, and other degradation). However, if in addition the technology became four times as efficient in making use of natural resources, then the combined impact would be only half the original level.

Setting the IPAT formula equal to one for a given year, say 1995, will provide a baseline against which to compare the environmental impact of future growth and economic development. In order for a society to be sustainable indefinitely, it is believed that the environmental impact (I) must be below this 1995 state of the world. Olson (1995) analyzed four models that have been proposed for future societal development, and used the IPAT formula to assess whether each one could produce a sustainable society.

The Brundtland Model

Named for Gro Brundtland, the chairperson of the World Commission on Environment and Development, the Commission's report (WCED, 1987) was widely heralded as offering an optimistic view of a potentially sustainable world. However, this model forecast a world population of 8.2 billion by the year 2025, and 10 billion by 2050, nearly twice its present size. It estimated that the world economy would expand to 5 to 10 times its present size by 2050. It expected technological advancements to reduce the impact of pollution and to be more energy-efficient, thus reducing T by one half. Using the IPAT formula, Olson estimated that these components would produce an environmental impact of 2.5 to 5 times the 1995 level—a clearly *non*sustainable society.

Slow Growth

Slow growth models emphasize the need to control the human population (Meadows et al., 1992). The key to slow growth and a sustainable future is for the world's population to level off at around 8 billion people (about 1.5 times the current level). Economic growth must be slowed substantially (for example, affluence per person should only double by 2100). This model also projects much more efficient technology and energy consumption (reducing T by a factor of 10 to .1 by 2100). Using the IPAT formula, Olson estimated this model could produce an environmental impact of .3, roughly one-third of today's level, which probably would be a sustainable society.

Technology Transformation

A third model for a sustainable future is based on a radical transformation in technology. In this scenario, all the technologies of energy production, transportation, construction, agriculture, etc., must become drastically more efficient—Olson projected them to become over 1500 times as efficient. In this model, pollution would be reduced by utilizing renewable energy sources and materials that are recycled and reused. Olson estimated that this sort of development, with a doubling in population and a 10-fold increase in affluence per person,

would lead to an environmental impact of .012, about 1/80 of the present level—which is clearly sustainable. However, the thought that technology efficiency could increase by such a huge amount seems closer to science fiction than to a realistic possibility.

Sustainable Community

This model proposes a path to sustainability through social transformations, rather than technological ones. In describing this vision, Olson (1991) argued that instead of growing bigger, we need to grow better. Our current preoccupation with consumption and a growing economy must be changed. In this model, instead of looking for new technologies to solve environmental problems, society would move back to smaller communities where people live, work, shop, and socialize. Walking and bicycling would become the dominant modes of travel. This model predicts that, with such sweeping social changes, the world population in 2050 would level off at 1.5 times the 1995 level, and the level of affluence per person would rise to 4 times its 1995 level. Olson estimated that the technological impact could be reduced to .02 of its current level by changes in behavioral patterns, rather than through substantial new technological developments. Using the IPAT formula, Olson calculated the environmental impact of this scenario to be .12 by 2050—again, a sustainable society, but again one where the predicted increases in technological efficiency boggle the imagination.

These four models of societal growth and development provide an important vision by suggesting that a sustainable society is possible—three of the four models discussed apparently reach sustainability. However, some of the assumptions behind these models seem unrealistic. First, all of the models assume that the earth's population will level off at between 1.5 and 2 times the current level. Given the current rate of growth, this may be a faulty assumption behind all of these models (although it would appear necessary in order to reach a sustainable society). Second, both the technology transformation and sustainable community models propose what seem to be unrealistic changes in technological efficiency. It seems exceedingly unlikely that in the next 50 years, technology will lessen the impact of human activity by a factor of 1500, or even 50—nor that Olson's radical social changes toward a less mechanized society will occur. Of the four models presented, the most likely sustainable society seems the slow growth model, but even that scenario requires stringent population control and dramatic advances in technology.

Thus, it is crucial for everyone to become aware of these issues and to do all they can toward achieving a sustainable society. Social science has a major role to play in this effort, and many of its research findings are directly applicable to creating essential changes in people's behavior and lifestyles (Vlek, 1995). One good example is provided by a book that highlights community-based techniques of social marketing that can be used to promote a sustainable future (McKenzie-Mohr, 1996). Another important contribution is efforts to increase the ecologically sustainable practices of managers and organizations ("Special Topic Forum," 1995). Only through the heroic efforts of all kinds of scientists, policy makers, and common citizens will we have a chance to change the behavior of nations, corporations, and individuals enough to avoid the progressive destruction of earth's life-giving environment.

SUMMARY

Ecological issues of people's relationship to their environment, both natural and human-made, have assumed crucial importance to our quality of life, and even to the survival capacity of humanity. This chapter has provided a brief overview of psychological research on how the built environment affects human behavior, and discussed several aspects of research on how human actions affect the natural environment. Environmental problems of drastic population growth, serious pollution of air, water, and land, and crises in the use of energy and other natural resources provide critical challenges for social scientists who hope to change people's behavioral patterns and thus lessen these grave problems.

Attitude studies indicate that environmental concern has grown to very high levels among the American public and in many other nations. Some individuals have gone further and adopted new worldviews,

such as deep ecology, which reject traditional Western materialistic values. However, behavioral research has shown that actions often do not follow attitudes. It frequently requires an awareness of serious personal consequences or a strong proconservation personal norm to get people to make environmentally responsible choices.

Researchers have investigated demographic and personality characteristics, as well as knowledge and attitudinal variables, that are associated with proenvironmental behaviors such as recycling or energy conservation. Behavioral research aiming to encourage such behaviors has shown that the antecedent strategies of presenting information and prompts are generally not very effective unless combined with behavioral consequences, such as reinforcement or feedback. Social interaction studies have investigated persuasion, social influence, removing obstacles, and avoiding social traps as ways to increase desired environmental behaviors.

U.S. energy policies have frequently been harmfully resistant to energy conservation and use of renewable sources. However, in the areas of solid waste and pollution, federal programs to save landfill capacity through recycling, and laws to improve air and water quality, have reached desirable goals, though their degree of efficiency has rarely been systematically evaluated. Poor people and ethnic minorities suffer more than other Americans from exposure to environmental hazards.

If humanity is to have a future on the earth, it is crucial that we move speedily to a world with a sustainable level of population, economic activity, and technology. Conceivable scenarios of the future indicate that a sustainable society is a possible goal, but that it will take heroic efforts to limit population and to counteract the frequently negative effects of economic activity and technology.

SUGGESTED READINGS

Bell, P., Greene, T., Baum, A., & Fisher, J. (1997). *Environmental psychology* (4th ed.). Fort Worth, TX: Harcourt Brace Jovanovich.—This textbook provides a clear and readable overview of the field of environmental psychology, with chapters on many aspects of the built and natural environments.

Gardner, G. T., & Stern, P. C. (1996). *Environmental problems and human behavior*. Boston: Allyn & Bacon.—An excellent overview of how human behavior is affecting the environment, and the psychological research done to understand and change these behaviors.

Goldfarb, T. D. (1995). *Taking sides: Clashing views on controversial environmental issues*. New York: Dushkin.—This book presents chapters with opposing viewpoints on many different environmental issues, particularly on environmental public policy.

Petrikin, J. (Ed.). (1995). *Environmental justice*. San Diego, CA: Greenhaven.—This volume describes both sides of the controversy over environmental racism, the disproportionate exposure of poor and minority individuals to dangerous environments.

Tucker, M. E., & Grim, J. (Eds.). (1993). *Worldviews and ecology*. London, England: Bucknell University Press.—Discusses many different paradigms of the relationship between humans and the natural environment, including many varied cultural and religious perspectives.

Winter, D. D. (1996). *Ecological psychology: Healing the split between planet and self*. New York: Harper-Collins.—A fascinating book, showing the relevance of central psychological topics to the goal of building an ecologically sustainable world.

CHAPTER 12

Health and Health Care—Smoking

Control of the present major health problems in the United States depends directly on modification of the individual's behavior and habits of living.

—John H. Knowles, M.D. (1977, p. 61)

The processes that determine tobacco addiction are similar to those that determine addiction to drugs such as heroin and cocaine.

—C. Everett Koop, M.D. (1988, p. iii)

Perhaps you have had a relative or an acquaintance who had cancer, or a heart attack or stroke, or some other life-threatening illness. If so, a psychologist might have helped them cope with their situation by counseling them about new lifestyle patterns, providing relaxation training, offering rehabilitation assistance, or conducting follow-up interviews or visits.

More than 10,000 American psychologists work full-time in medical settings. Though a majority are clinical psychologists, mostly employed in psychiatric units, medical psychologists also teach in medical schools and work in physical medicine, pediatrics, physical therapy, social work, occupational therapy, dietetics, family medicine, cardiology, neurology, physiology, pain and sleep clinics, aftercare services, chronic illness programs, mental health and the law, and of course in research (Carmody & Matarazzo, 1991; McNett, 1981).

APPLIED SOCIAL PSYCHOLOGY AND HEALTH

Where do applied social psychologists fit into the health care picture? On the surface, physical health might appear beyond the boundaries of psychology. However, during the 1900s a change has occurred in the causes of illness and death in United States. In prior centuries, the leading causes of death in the U.S. were infectious diseases like pneumonia, influenza, and tuberculosis. Today, the two leading causes of death are heart disease and cancer (National Center for Health Statistics, 1993). These chronic illnesses, unlike infectious diseases which are transmitted from person to person, are primarily caused by *patterns of behavior.* For example, the chances of developing heart disease can be greatly reduced by proper diet and exercise, and by lowering

stress levels. Similarly, cancer is caused by exposure to a carcinogen (cancer-causing substance) on a repeated basis, and the chances of developing cancer can be lowered by reducing the behaviors that lead to exposure.

This is where social psychology comes into the picture. Because the diseases that account for most of the deaths in our society are largely caused by human behaviors, the field of applied social psychology can help to change the way people act, to help them live longer and healthier lives. In the last 20 years there has been a rapid growth and crystallization of the field that has come to be called behavioral medicine, and of the subfield termed health psychology. The field of health psychology is "devoted to understanding psychological influences on how people stay healthy, how they become ill, and how they respond when they get well" (Taylor, 1995, p. 3).

Major handbooks or comprehensive summaries of the many applications of psychology to health issues have been published by Maes et al. (1988) and Taylor (1995). In the following sections we will examine a few of the health areas to which applied social psychologists have been contributing their skills, knowledge, and methods. We will then turn our attention to one particularly harmful behavior—smoking.

Health Topics Studied by Psychologists

Health Care Policy. Reforming the health care system has been called one of the most urgent issues facing American society (Daschle, Cohen, & Rice, 1993). The cost of health care in the U.S. has become prohibitively expensive, both to individuals and to the nation. The U.S. spends more money on health care per person than any other nation—a total of $820 billion in 1992, well over $3000 per man, woman, and child—and total health care expenditures have grown from 6% of the gross national product in 1966 to an estimated 16% in 1998 (O'Donnell & Harris, 1994). And yet, at any given time in the 1990s, one-quarter of all U.S. residents had no health insurance and so had no regular access to routine medical care (Frank & VandenBos, 1994). All too often people who are ill fail to seek early treatment for their symptoms because of the costs involved.

An urgently needed solution to this problem is to adopt a nationwide healthcare program, and in planning for such a system the contrast between Canada and the U.S. is illuminating. In Canada, all residents are covered by the government-sponsored health care system, in which every Canadian has coverage, and per capita health care costs are much lower than in the U.S. (nearly 30% less per person in 1989). In Canada, though there may be longer waits for some high-technology medical procedures, 91% of citizens and most health care providers view their system as better than the U.S. system. In contrast, in the U.S. a large proportion of citizens and health care providers are dissatisfied with the fractionated and inefficient system, and only 26% of citizens view it as better than the Canadian system (Hugick, 1991). However, the U.S. system is avidly supported by the large insurance companies and health care organizations and physicians who profit from it most strongly.

Historically, health care in the U.S. has been an individual fee-for-service system, with many people covering much of their medical bills through purchasing health insurance. In recent years a rapidly growing alternative has been **managed care**, in which health maintenance organizations (HMOs) collect prepaid monthly dues from their members and contract with health care providers to treat the members at set fees. As of 1993 more than 33 million Americans received medical services through an HMO. HMOs generally concentrate on keeping their members healthy, not just treating them when they are ill, and research indicates that, by moving away from a fee-for-service orientation, they may actually promote early detection of life-threatening illnesses (Riley et al., 1994). However, research on HMOs also suggests that, although they are good at meeting the physical needs of the patients, the emotional and psychological needs typically met by a familiar physician often are not met by an HMO (Barr,

1983; Freudenheim, 1993). The trend toward managed care has been increasing the role of HMOs in American health care, but the direction that reform of the U.S. nonsystem will take in the future is still unclear.

Smoking. One of the greatest burdens on the health care system is the health consequences of smoking cigarettes. Smoking is a major risk factor for cancer and heart attacks, as well as strokes, bronchitis, emphysema, and other serious conditions. Indeed, "Smoking is the largest preventable cause of death in America" (U.S. DHEW, 1979, p. ii). Since 1964, a series of massive government research reports has documented these links, and the more recent social psychological research has concentrated heavily on breaking the smoking habit, on public policy regarding smoking, and on studying the effects of warning labels. Another promising line of research has focused on prevention of smoking in young children before they ever get started (Bruvold, 1993; U.S. DHHS, 1994). Regarding the health costs of smoking, former Secretary of Health and Human Services Joseph Califano stated in an editorial in the *Journal of the American Medical Association:*

> At least $3 billion that Medicaid spent [and] . . . $16 billion that Medicare spent on health inpatient hospital care in fiscal 1994 was attributable to the long-term effects of smoking cigarettes. . . . Smoking is the largest single drain on the Medicare trust fund, and is poised to take $800 billion over the next 20 years. (1994, p. 1217)

Because of the tremendous costs of smoking to both human health and national expenditures, the later sections of this chapter focus on the causes, effects, and prevention of smoking cigarettes.

Pain Control. Some of the greatest advances in medical and psychological science in the last 50 years have been in the control of pain. Currently there are dozens of pain management centers around the country. Pain management aims to enable patients to reduce their experiences of pain in order to live more enjoyable, rewarding lives (Rains, Penzien, & Jamison, 1992). Research has found that such programs are often successful in reducing patient's experiences of pain (Flor, Fydrich, & Turk, 1992). Often treatments are aimed at reducing the dosages of pain medications. Such treatments may involve behavioral therapy, changing cognitions, learning new psychological coping mechanisms, or even altering family dynamics.

Effects of Stress. Stress can be defined as the perception of having too many demands on our personal resources (Lazarus & Folkman, 1984). Stress occurs when we believe that we do not have the capability to handle the demands of a situation. Effects of the stress involved in major life events, such as marriage, divorce, job changes, and moving, have been extensively studied by psychologists (e.g., Crandall, Priesler, & Aussprung, 1992). In addition, research has begun to study the health effects of long-continued environmental conditions, such as noise, crowding, pollution, and even anxiety about nuclear radiation (Baum, Fleming, & Singer, 1982; Cohen, Glass, & Phillips, 1979; Topf, 1989; Zuravin, 1986; also see Chapter 11). Even the cumulative frustration of minor everyday hassles can be a source of stress, with which individuals may or may not learn to cope effectively (Bolger et al., 1989; Stone, Neal, & Schiffman, 1993).

Research has identified a strong link between stress and personal health. Some scientists estimate that stress may play a role in 50% to 70% of all physical illnesses (Frese, 1985; Lin & Ensel, 1989). Stress has been linked to such serious illnesses as heart disease, high blood pressure, ulcers, diabetes, and suppression of the immune system, to list just a few. In an interesting demonstration of the effects of stress, Cohen, Tyrrell, and Smith (1993) randomly exposed volunteers to the cold virus. They found that, while those exposed to the virus were more likely to develop cold symptoms, people who scored higher on measures of stress, regardless of whether or not they were exposed to the virus, were also more likely to develop cold symptoms.

Obesity. Research has shown that overeating in humans is influenced by a variety of factors, including biology, social class, social and cultural pressures, and stress (Lingsweiler, Crowter, & Stephens, 1987; Sobel & Stunkard, 1989). Because obesity is associated with overeating, psychological research can be useful in producing behavior changes and the possibility of weight loss. However, research has found that obesity is difficult to modify (Rodin & Ickovics, 1990). Treatments often involve a variety of strategies including dieting, exercise, appetite-suppressing drugs, behavior

modification, and even surgery. Unfortunately, most weight-loss programs, even if successful in the short-term, rarely produce long-lasting changes in weight. This finding has prompted researchers to speculate about the possibility of homeostatic mechanisms that prevent large changes in body weight (Sperry, 1994). One promising explanation for the difficulty in maintaining weight loss is the notion of a **set-point**—i.e., that individuals have a biologically determined weight which cannot be easily altered (Brownell & Wadden, 1992). However, research continues to examine possible techniques to help people lose weight effectively and permanently (Brownell & Rodin, 1994; Friedman & Brownell, 1995).

High Blood Pressure and Heart Disease. In the United States, hypertension (chronically high levels of systolic and diastolic blood pressure) is estimated to be a problem for about 60 million people. Hypertension has been directly linked to such medical problems as heart attacks and strokes (Knowles, 1977). Because its symptoms are often unnoticeable, many sufferers do not even know they have high blood pressure, and patients' adherence to antihypertensive programs is frequently very poor (Dunbar-Jacob, Dwyer, & Dunning, 1991; Shapiro & Goldstein, 1982). Mass screening to identify all cases in the population would not justify its costs, but research directed at increasing patients' adherence to their prescribed treatment regimen is badly needed.

Though heart disease is by far the largest cause of death in the United States, its death toll was reduced 20% between 1965 and 1980, apparently due largely to reductions in smoking and in the amount of animal fat in Americans' diets (Stachnik, 1980). Perhaps more than any other leading cause of death, the risk factors in heart disease are lifestyle and behavioral patterns, such as exercise, diet, smoking, and drinking. Consequently, social psychologists have been heavily involved in research on the relationships between personality, social, and environmental characteristics and the risk of coronary disease (Adler & Mathews, 1994; Fortmann et al., 1995; Rodin & Salovey, 1989). A major behavioral pattern found in many coronary heart disease sufferers is a syndrome of competitive, urgent, aggressive characteristics termed **Type A behavior** (Booth-Kewley & Friedman, 1987). However, re-

Photograph courtesy of Shelley Taylor. Reprinted by permission.

Box 12-1

SHELLEY TAYLOR, AUTHORITY ON HEALTH PSYCHOLOGY

Born near New York City, Shelley Taylor went to Connecticut College and earned her Ph.D. at Yale in the areas of attribution theory and social cognition. She taught for seven years at Harvard before moving in 1979 to UCLA, where she remains. At Harvard she directed her research more toward real-world contexts and began her health psychology work with a study of breast cancer patients. At UCLA she developed a training program in health psychology and wrote her widely cited text on *Health Psychology*.

Taylor's health research areas have included heart disease, cancer, and HIV/AIDS. Some of her applied work in social cognition has focused on social comparison processes and the value of positive illusions in maintaining people's mental health. She has published over 150 papers and coauthored a pioneering text on *Social Cognition* as well as a popular text on *Social Psychology*. Among the many honors she has received are the APA Award for Distinguished Scientific Contribution, the presidency of the Western Psychological Association, and awards for distinguished research from societies in social psychology and health psychology.

search is beginning to suggest that the Type A behavior pattern is multidimensional, and that it may be the aggressive aspect of it that is related to heart disease (Adler & Mathews, 1994).

Cancer. Cancer is the second leading cause of death in the United States; one out of every four people will develop cancer in their lifetime. The causes of cancer are still not well understood, but the link to behavior patterns is apparently more indirect than in the case of heart disease. One stream of social psychological re-

search has concentrated on cancer patients' reactions to their illness, their fears and anxieties, defense mechanisms, and methods of adjusting to and coping with the disease (Manne et al., 1994; Taylor & Levin, 1976). Findings indicate that combative cancer patients—those who become angry at their illness, doctors, and family members—often live longer than polite, nonaggressive people who quietly undergo treatment (Levy et al., 1985; Levy, 1990). Recently, treatment research has focused on rehabilitative interventions for cancer patients that attempt to help them cope with pain, changes in lifestyle, and the side-effects of various treatments (Vasterling et al., 1993).

AIDS. Acquired Immune Deficiency Syndrome is a disease that reduces the body's natural ability to fight off infections, ultimately leading to death. AIDS is the result of an infection with the HIV retrovirus. The first case of AIDS in the U.S. was detected in 1981, and since then its prevalence has grown dramatically. As of 1993, the number of cases of AIDS in the U.S. was estimated at 83,000, with over 1 million Americans being infected with the HIV virus. Worldwide, it was estimated that there were 13 million people infected with the HIV virus in 1993 (Merson, 1993). The HIV virus can only be transmitted through the exchange of body fluids with an infected person (e.g., blood transfusions, sharing needles, sexual intercourse). Because AIDS is primarily caused by a person's behavior, applied social psychology can help people to avoid it by identifying and promoting safer behaviors.

Early psychological interventions were aimed at teaching people about AIDS and its modes of transmission. However, research has found that knowledge about AIDS is not a very good predictor of avoiding risky behaviors, and that motivational factors are crucial to consider (Fisher & Fisher, 1992; Winslow, Franzini, & Hwang, 1992). Other interventions, based on the theory of planned behavior (which is described in Chapter 14), have targeted self-efficacy—an individual's perception of being able to control risk-related behaviors (Abraham et al., 1992). These interventions have been successful in changing the behaviors of people from different ages, cultural backgrounds, and sexual orientations (Jemmott & Jones, 1993; McKusick et al., 1990; Oskamp & Thompson, 1996).

Alcoholism. Alcoholism was officially recognized as a disease by the American Medical Association in 1957. Alcohol consumption is a cause of a variety of health problems, including cirrhosis of the liver in adults and fetal alcohol syndrome in infants. It is also partially responsible for nearly 50% of all highway driving fatalities (Finney & Moos, 1991). Because alcoholism is a behavioral disorder, social psychologists can study its causes and help to design effective interventions that reduce or eliminate alcohol consumption. A variety of interventions have been developed to help

people stop drinking, including social skills training, self-control training, motivational counseling, behavioral therapy, community interventions, and stress management (Holder et al., 1991; Lewis, 1994). Combining the results of all these available treatments, it is estimated that approximately one-third of alcoholics are able to stop drinking with minimal help (Moos & Finney, 1983).

In recent years, there has been a changing emphasis from short-term treatment of alcoholism to long-term maintenance of adaptive behaviors and avoidance of recidivism (Mejta, Naylor, & Maslar, 1994). An interesting question emerging from research on the treatment of alcohol abuse is whether it is possible for a recovered alcoholic ever to drink in moderation. Many treatment groups such as Alcoholics Anonymous claim that alcoholics are alcoholics for life, and that a single drink can push them to binge drinking again. By and large, this claim is supported by the research (Rychtarik et al., 1987).

Aging. People today live considerably longer than they did in the past, and typically have a substantial period of retirement after their employment ends. In addition to the medical problems of old age, psychologists have recently begun to study the processes and problems of normal aging, including physiological, cognitive, behavioral, and social changes. The roles of family members, activities, and social contacts have been shown to be very important in maintaining adequate functioning in old age, and there is much that the elderly themselves can do to sustain their productivity and emotional adjustment (Rodin, Bohm, & Wack, 1982; Skinner, 1982). There is a wealth of reviews of social science research on aging (Fry, 1992; Green et al., 1980; Myers, Poidevant, & Dean, 1991).

Death and Dying. The end of life has been studied increasingly by psychologists since about 1960. Topics investigated include conceptions of and attitudes toward death, fear and other reactions to imminent death, family and medical-staff interactions with terminally ill patients, and methods of counseling dying patients and their families (Corr, Nabe, & Corr, 1994; Sankar, 1994). One interesting line of research has attempted to describe the ways in which people cope with death. In a ground-breaking book, Kubler-Ross (1969) argued that all people go through the same sequence of stages when faced with death: denial, anger, bargaining, depression, and acceptance.

Because social psychologists have contributed to so many of these health topics, it would be impossible to include detailed discussion of them in this chapter. Instead, we will concentrate here on full presentation of just one topic—smoking, which is the greatest preventable health risk of our era. It is also a phenomenon with many behavioral aspects, and accordingly one to which psychologists have made numerous important research contributions (Azar, 1994).

A BRIEF SOCIAL HISTORY OF SMOKING

Unlike many products and diseases that originated in Europe, tobacco was brought to Europe from the New World. In 1492, Christopher Columbus found the natives of the West Indies smoking crude cigars. Tobacco was introduced into Europe in 1558, and in the late 1500s Sir Walter Raleigh popularized pipe smoking in England. In the early 1600s King James I tried to eliminate the use of tobacco in England. He wrote a *Counterblast to Tobacco,* in which he called tobacco a "sotweed" and declared that smoking is "a custom loathsome to the eye, harmful to the braine, dangerous to the lungs" (Borgatta, 1968).

Despite King James and others who denounced tobacco, such as the Puritans, use of snuff and cigar and pipe smoking remained familiar though not widespread customs into the 1800s. Since then, smoking has increased tremendously, many of the boosts to its popularity occurring during the social upheaval of warfare. Cigarette smoking became popular in Europe following the Crimean War of 1854–1856, when French and British soldiers copied Turkish soldiers' habit of smoking hand-rolled "paper cigars."

In the United States, the Civil War marked the beginning of the rise of cigarette smoking. In 1880 chewing tobacco was the principal form in use in the United States, and cigarettes were still manufactured by hand processes. But in 1883, technology entered the picture when an automatic cigarette-making machine was developed, and by 1890 cigarette sales had increased fivefold. During World War I, cigarette sales zoomed upward, and in World War II there was another huge increase. In addition to the stresses of wartime, this increase was partly due to the fact that cigarettes were distributed free or very cheaply to U.S. servicemen overseas. From 1880 to 1960, the annual consumption of cigarettes in the United States soared from about 15 to over 4000 per person age 18 or over (including nonsmokers as well as smokers). In 1993, U.S. smokers consumed nearly one trillion cigarettes (DuMelle, 1993).

Smoking was almost entirely a male activity until approximately 1900. By the early 1920s about 50% of U.S. adult males (age 18 and older) smoked cigarettes, compared to only about 5% of adult women. In some urban areas, nearly 90% of adult men used tobacco in some form, and the percentage of male smokers in the United States as a whole continued to rise until the late 1940s. Due to strong social taboos, increases in the proportion of female smokers lagged 25 to 30 years behind increases in male smokers. The proportion of adult women who smoked did not reach 25% until World War II, and it peaked at 33% in 1965—ironically confirming the cigarette ad slogan, "You've come a long way, baby."

Recent History

Survey research has revealed much information about smoking in recent decades. Worldwide, smoking has been increasing sharply, particularly in developing countries like China (Chandler, 1988), but the picture is dramatically different in the United States. Since the 1950s the percentage of adult men in the U.S. who smoke cigarettes has declined markedly from 53% to 26% in 1992. The percentage of adult women who smoke remained very close to 33% through 1976, but decreased to 25% by 1992 (Fiore et al., 1993; U.S. DHHS, 1994). The annual per capita consumption of cigarettes has also decreased from about 4350 per year in 1963 to about 2500 in 1994 (U.S. Department of Agriculture, 1995–96)—see Figure 12-1.

A major reason for the recent declines in the number of U.S. smokers has been a long series of research reports of health risks associated with smoking. In 1954 the first major empirical paper on the results of smoking was delivered at the American Medical Association convention, based on mortality figures for a sample of over 187,000 men (Hammond & Horn, 1958). At that point total U.S. cigarette sales dipped sharply, but then increased again until 1964. In that year the first Surgeon General's report on Smoking and Health was released (U.S. DHEW, 1964), containing much additional information on health risks, and cigarette sales again tumbled. Subsequently, the cigarette companies spent the next 30 years trying to stifle or deny all information about health risks from smoking, to control the content of research reports, and to advertise their deadly products as contributing to enjoyment of life (Glantz et al., 1996).

Since 1964, an ever-increasing series of research reports on the health risks of smoking has begun to reinterpret tobacco use as a community public health concern rather than an individual behavior problem. As a result, many cities and states have established laws that regulate smoking in public places, further restrict access to tobacco by children and youths, and limit ad-

vertising of tobacco products (Novotny et al., 1992). By 1990, 45 states had passed laws regulating smoking in public areas, such as government offices, private workplaces, and, most recently, restaurants. Many states have increased their taxes on cigarettes, leading to a drop in sales, and a few states and cities have started to restrict the billboard advertising and free distribution of tobacco products (Novotny et al., 1992).

A new phase in U.S. discouragement of smoking began in 1994, when the Food and Drug Administration (FDA) first asserted its jurisdiction over tobacco products and proposed to regulate cigarettes as drug-delivery devices. In 1996, after a period of public comment, the FDA issued detailed regulations based on the strategy of breaking the cycle of addiction by restricting the advertising and sale of tobacco products to children

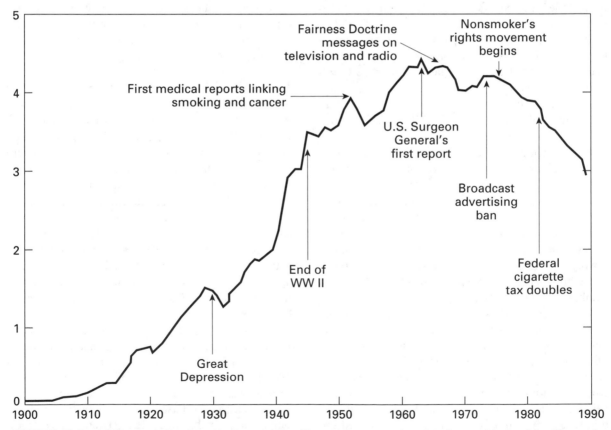

FIGURE 12-1 **Adult per capita cigarette consumption (thousands per year) and major smoking and health events, United States, 1900–1990.** (Source: Novotny et al., 1992, p. 297.) With permission, from the Annual Review of Public Health, Volume 13, © 1992, by Annual Reviews, Inc.

and adolescents (Kessler et al., 1996). In 1997, a federal judge in North Carolina ruled that the FDA had the right to regulate tobacco products because nicotine is a drug (Cimons, 1997).

Further dramatic events followed quickly in 1997 as a result of a court suit by 40 states against the tobacco companies, seeking to recoup the huge health care costs of treating their citizens for smoking-related diseases. In an historic agreement with the states' Attorneys General, the major U.S. tobacco companies agreed to pay over $368 billion in compensatory and punitive damages to reimburse state health care expenses and to fund related health programs and anti-smoking campaigns. The industry also agreed to regulatory control by the FDA, expanded health warnings on cigarette packs, and an extensive ban on outdoor advertising and vending machine sales (Weinstein & Levin, 1997). In return, the agreement gave the industry immunity from future class-action lawsuits on behalf of ill smokers and an annual cap on punitive payments for past wrongdoing— both points of contention in the public health community. Before it could become law, the agreement had to overcome such criticisms and receive approval by Congress and the President (Smolowe, 1997).

Despite the U.S. national trends toward decreased smoking, smokers have incurred increased risks from two sources. Before the reports on the hazardous contents of cigarette brands became publicly available, some manufacturers actually increased their "tar" and nicotine content to counterbalance the effect of adding filters. In addition, smokers of "low-tar" cigarettes have been found to inhale more deeply, smoke down to a shorter butt, and in many cases smoke more cigarettes— thus increasing their intake of dangerous products.

On the other side of the ledger, the number of ex-smokers in the United States has grown steadily in recent years to more than 40 million in 1990. Each year about one-fourth of adult smokers report trying to quit smoking, but only about one-fifth of those who try to quit report success. Of the smokers that do successfully quit, about 60% go back to smoking within the first year, a relapse rate very similar to that for alcohol and heroin (Taylor, 1995). In addition to ex-smokers, the decline in the total number of U.S. smokers is also due to a decrease in the number of young men who begin smoking. Among the male cohort born between 1951

and 1960, only 40% have become smokers, compared with figures of 60% to 70% in the five previous cohorts. Among young women, however, only a very small decrease has occurred; and for the first time in history, the proportion of young women in the United States who become smokers is now as high or even higher than the proportion among young men (U.S. DHHS, 1990).

SCIENTIFIC KNOWLEDGE AND PUBLIC POLICY ABOUT SMOKING

Research Links Between Smoking and Disease

The 1964 Surgeon General's report on *Smoking and Health* was an historic document, gathering a mass of evidence on causal links between cigarette smoking and cancer of the lungs and larynx, and chronic bronchitis (U.S. DHEW, 1964). It also described statistical associations between smoking and overall mortality rates, heart disease, and various other serious ailments. Representatives of the tobacco industry have tried to rebut this evidence in various ways. Primarily they have pointed out that a statistical association or correlation does not prove a causal relationship, and that many puzzling aspects of the medical data cast doubt on whether there is a direct causal relationship. For instance, 10% to 20% of lung cancers occur in non-smokers, so it is clear that smoking is not their only cause (that is, not an essential cause). A conservative way of stating this conclusion is: "Cigarette smoking is neither a necessary nor a sufficient condition for the development of any disease" (Guilford, 1968).

Most experts now agree that overwhelming evidence shows smoking to be a major contributory cause of several serious or fatal diseases, including cancer of the lungs, mouth, larynx, and esophagus; heart disease; bronchitis; and emphysema. Supporting these conclusions, the Surgeon General published another report on *Smoking and Health* in 1979, totaling nearly 1200 pages of recent scientific findings (U.S. DHEW, 1979). In it the Secretary of Health, Education, and Welfare declared that "smoking is Public Health Enemy Number One in America" (p. ii) because it is directly related to over 300,000 deaths each year from the above-mentioned diseases. More recent reports by the Surgeon

General have taken the link between smoking and cancer as a given (U.S. DHHS, 1990, 1991, 1994).

Studies of brain chemistry and behavior have shown that nicotine has an addictive effect very similar to that of cocaine or morphine (e.g., Nash, 1997; Pontieri et al., 1996). In 1997, the Liggett Group became the first of the major cigarette manufacturers to admit publicly that its officials had known for years that tobacco is addictive and causes cancer (Solomon & Rogers, 1997).

Second-Hand Smoke

Even for nonsmokers, recent research shows that there can be health dangers from "second-hand smoking"—the involuntary exposure to carbon monoxide and other cigarette combustion products as a result of sharing enclosed spaces with smokers. This is more tech-

nically termed **environmental tobacco smoke (ETS)**. ETS is the smoke given off by the burning ends of cigarettes, pipes, and cigars, or exhaled from the lungs of smokers, and it is estimated to cause lung cancer in 3000 Americans each year (Browner, 1993). Besides death, ETS has been linked to other respiratory problems of adult nonsmokers including coughing, phlegm production, chest discomfort, and reduced lung capacity (Repace, 1993).

The health consequences of ETS were first raised in a 1972 Surgeon General's report. Public concern about ETS heightened in the 1980s when several large-scale studies of the wives and children of smoking men were published (Greenberg et al., 1984; Hirayama, 1980). By 1987, an entire volume of the Surgeon General's report on smoking was devoted to ETS. Many cartoons, like the one in Figure 12-2, articulate the point. How-

Steve Kelley cartoon. Reprinted with permission of Copley News Service.

FIGURE 12-2 A possible reaction to second-hand smoke. (Steve Kelley cartoon. Reprinted with permission of Copley News Service.)

ever, this concern was slow in being translated into law. As of 1993, four states (KY, MS, AL, and GA) had no statewide limitations on smoking in public, 19 had minimal limitations, 23 moderate, and 4 extensive (MN, NH, NY, VT), while no state had comprehensive restrictions about smoking in public (DuMelle, 1993). (*Extensive* restrictions ban smoking in most public areas, but permit some designated areas, whereas *comprehensive* restrictions ban smoking in *all* public places). In 1993, the Environmental Protection Agency (EPA) classified ETS as a Class A carcinogen. Class A substances (e.g., asbestos and radon) are defined as being extremely harmful to human health.

For years, tobacco companies have attempted to refute the research showing a link between lung cancer and cigarettes, and ETS is no exception. In June 1993, the tobacco industry filed a lawsuit against the EPA, claiming that the classification of ETS as a Group A carcinogen was "arbitrary." However, the EPA's claim that ETS causes lung cancer has been endorsed by many scientific associations including the American Medical Association, American Public Health Association, the American Lung Association, and the American Cancer Association.

How then, despite strong support from many legitimate research organizations, can the tobacco industry deny the research findings? The simple answer is research methodology. To date, there is no true experiment linking cigarette smoke with lung cancer in humans. You will recall that the best evidence for a causal association is revealed by a true experiment with random assignment. The problem is, humans won't volunteer for random assignment in smoking research. Much of the research on ETS has examined nonsmoking children or wives of smoking men. In fact, one study found that even the *dogs* of smokers had a 50% greater risk of lung cancer and early death than dogs of nonsmokers (Reif at al., 1992). However, all of this research is correlational in design (cf. Chapter 3). Experiments have been performed, but only on mice, monkeys, or other animals that cannot refuse to be randomly assigned to a smoke-filled or smoke-free experimental condition. And of course the tobacco industry claims that experimental findings on other species cannot be applied to humans.

Public Attitudes Toward Smoking

Survey studies of public opinion have found that, in general, Americans believe the health warnings that scientists have issued about smoking. For instance, back in 1950 approximately 45% of adults believed that cigarette smoking *causes* lung cancer. By 1986, 85% of smokers, and 92% of the general population believed cigarettes cause cancer (U.S. DHHS, 1989). Similar increases were found, for both smokers and nonsmokers, in the percentage that believed cigarette smoking caused heart disease, emphysema, and bronchitis. Interestingly, even 93% of prominent scientists employed on research grants provided by the Council for Tobacco Research "strongly believed" that most lung cancer deaths are *caused* by smoking.

Public opinion regarding smoking has shown a marked decline in the social acceptability of smoking in public. For example, in 1964, 46% of Americans found it annoying to be near someone who was smoking, whereas by 1986, this percentage had grown to 69%. Similarly, a majority of the public favors policies restricting smoking in public places and worksites, increasing taxes on cigarettes, and even banning cigarette advertising altogether (U.S. DHHS, 1989).

Cigarette Advertising and Government Policy

Cigarette companies spend huge sums of money on advertisements. In 1990, U.S. cigarette companies spent nearly $4 billion to promote their products. Cigarette companies are the second leading industry in the total amount of money spent to advertise in magazines and newspapers (automobile manufacturers spend slightly more), and they are first in billboard advertising. They were the leading advertisers on television and radio until 1971 when Congress banned such advertising.

Federal legislation regarding the advertising of cigarettes has a long and fascinating history. Cigarette companies, because of their wealth, have substantial power to influence public policy (cf. Gibson, 1997). The 1971 law banning cigarette advertising on TV and radio was seen by many anti-smoking advocates as a major victory, but the 1965 law requiring labels on cigarette packages had the effect of protecting the tobacco companies from lawsuits filed by relatives of lung cancer victims, charging that they were selling lethal products. Recently, however, a few such suits have been successful in winning large damages for the families of deceased smokers (Kelder & Daynard, 1997).

Cigarette Advertising and Public Policy in Other Countries

A major reason that governments don't crack down harder on cigarettes is that they depend on them for very large amounts of tax revenue. In 1990 the U.S. federal government collected over $4 billion in cigarette taxes from the 16 cent tax on each pack of 20 cigarettes (the per box tax has increased considerably since 1990) (Warner, 1993). The picture is similar in other countries. France, for example, collected $2.3 billion in cigarette taxes in 1992. Nevertheless, Great Britain, Canada, Ireland, Norway, Japan, Peru, and a number of other nations around the world have also banned advertising of cigarettes from TV and radio.

Several Asian countries have made sweeping attempts to curtail smoking. Singapore is striving to become the world's first smoke-free city. To this end, cigarettes are banned in public places, vending machines are outlawed, and tobacco companies are not allowed to sponsor public events. In an effort to reduce the 16% of residents who still smoke, Singapore is considering banning smoking in bars. Hong Kong has matched Singapore's low 16% smoking rate, doing so by means of a 300% tax increase on cigarettes in 1983 and another 100% increase in 1992. However, no such policies have been adopted in mainland China and many other developing countries, where smoking is increasing dramatically (Chandler, 1988).

RESEARCH ON SMOKING BEHAVIOR

Many of the research findings mentioned above have been established by social psychologists. Now however, we will turn to research that is directed specifically at psychological variables in smoking. As far back as the Surgeon General's report in 1964, it was generally agreed that psychological factors were crucial aspects in understanding smoking. That report declared that:

> The overwhelming evidence points to the conclusion that smoking—its beginning, habituation and occasional discontinuance—is to a large extent psychologically and socially determined. (U.S. DHEW, 1979, pp. 1–9)

Since that is the case, let us consider the major areas of social psychological research on smoking. These main research topics are developmental stages in smoking, measurement issues, motives for smoking, treatment approaches to help people quit, and smoking prevention.

Stages of Smoking

In an excellent review of research on smoking, Leventhal and Cleary (1980) discussed four stages in the development of smoking: preparation, initiation, becoming a smoker, and maintenance of smoking. Similar stages have been found in a variety of studies reviewed by Flay (1993).

Preparation. Preparation occurs before the individual ever tries a cigarette. It involves developing attitudes and intentions about smoking and images of what smoking is like—both from personal observations of parents or acquaintances and from the inescapable media inputs of our society. Leventhal and Cleary (1980) suggested that three different sets of attitudes incline young people toward smoking. One is the tough, "cool" image of smoking, which is attractive to youngsters who would like to be viewed as independent, grown-up, tough, and rebellious toward authority. A second attitudinal set is an inadequate, anxious, approval-seeking pattern; it disposes a youth to try smoking in order to gain peer approval and be part of the crowd. A third preparatory set is the notion that smoking can be helpful in keeping calm under stress and performing well in work or academic situations.

Initiation. Initiation of smoking is a critical step. It often occurs at the urging of peers, but smoking by family members reduces the barriers to taking this step and also makes cigarettes more readily available for experimentation (Conrad, Flay, & Hill, 1992; Gorsuch & Butler, 1976). Data show that young people who smoke just *ten* cigarettes have more than an 80% chance of becoming regular smokers (Salber, Freeman, & Abelin, 1968). Fortunately, however, many beginners never get as far as their tenth cigarette. In 1990, 62% of high school students had tried at least one cigarette, but only about 30% actually became regular smokers (U.S. DHHS, 1991). Negative reactions to the heat, smoke, and harsh taste of cigarettes are undoubtedly a factor here, but it appears that some people learn to interpret noxious bodily sensations as minor and unimportant, and that this encourages them to ignore the sensations and adapt to smoking (Leventhal & Everhart, 1979).

Becoming a Smoker. Becoming a smoker is the third stage. Various studies have indicated that it typically takes about two years for an individual to move from initial experimentation to regular, steady smoking (Leventhal, Fleming, & Glynn, 1988). However, it is less clear whether many individuals make this transition rapidly while others take many years, or whether the process is similar for most smokers. This stage involves a process akin to concept formation—learning when and how to smoke and incorporating the role of smoker into one's self-concept. It is clear that during this stage a tolerance develops for the physiological effects of smoking (Russell et al., 1979). Young people are generally unaware of how dependent adults become on cigarettes, and many people believe that smoking is bad for others, particularly for older or unhealthy individuals, but not for themselves (Leventhal & Everhart, 1979). This same phenomenon of overlooking risks to oneself is found in many areas of safety research, from avoiding use of seat belts to ignoring warning signs of heart disease or cancer.

Recent findings show that young people are becoming more aware of the health hazards of smoking. For example, the percentage of high school seniors who strongly agreed with the statement, "people risk harming themselves if they smoke one or more packs of cigarettes per day" was 69% in 1992, up from 56% in 1976 (U.S. DHHS, 1994). Similarly, the 1993 survey showed that only 14% of high school seniors surveyed agreed with the statement, "The harmful effects of cigarettes have been exaggerated."

Maintenance of Smoking. Maintenance of smoking is the final stage, when both psychological factors and biological mechanisms combine to perpetuate the learned behavior patterns. Research studies have found a variety of psychological reasons for smoking (Ikard, Green, & Horn, 1969; Leventhal & Avis, 1976). Among them are:

- Habit
- Addiction
- Reduction of anxiety and tension
- Pleasurable relaxation
- Sociability and obtaining social rewards
- Stimulation and arousal
- Handling the smoking materials

Among the biological mechanisms that maintain smoking behavior, two factors have received most attention: the reinforcing effects of nicotine, and the conditioned need to keep a certain level of nicotine in the bloodstream. These maintenance mechanisms will be discussed further in the section on motives for smoking.

Measurement Issues in Studying Smoking

Many studies have focused on discovering why people smoke. By far the most commonly used measures of smoking behavior are *self-report* methods, such as asking people to indicate their agreement or disagreement with statements about various reasons for smoking (e.g., "I smoke cigarettes to stimulate me, to perk myself up"). This method might seem to have many flaws, for smokers might not understand the reasons behind their behavior, or they might be motivated to cover up reasons about which they feel sensitive or ashamed. Nevertheless, there are few feasible alternative ways of developing a typology of reasons for smoking. Observational methods are very tedious, and use of other objective measures such as kinds or amounts of smoking would not get at the underlying reasons. Therefore, self-report methods are the most commonly used technique to measure smoking behaviors and the motives for smoking. Most studies agree in specifying from six to eight different factors or reasons for smoking, such as the list presented in the paragraph above (Leventhal & Cleary, 1980).

Validity. Smokers' responses not only show consistency in their self-ascribed reasons for smoking, but also appear to be quite valid. Studies by Leventhal and Avis (1976) used experimentally manipulated conditions and studied actual smoking behavior to check on the validity of smokers' self-reports. Smokers were divided into low- and high-scoring groups on each of the reasons for smoking, and then presented with relevant experimental situations. For instance, during a few hours of smoking abstinence, addictive smokers reported more craving and difficulty than other groups. When given cigarettes soaked in vinegar to smoke for a two-day period, smokers high on the pleasure-taste scale reduced their level of smoking quite markedly, whereas other groups did not. When required to monitor their behavior for several days by filling out a card on each cigarette smoked, habit smokers reduced their amount of smoking significantly more than pleasure-taste smokers. Thus, some behavioral evidence supports smokers' self-reports of their reasons for smoking, and this evidence may provide a basis for differential approaches to help different kinds of smokers quit smoking—a topic which we will consider later in this chapter.

Among some groups, such as schoolchildren or clients of anti-smoking clinics, smoking is a socially disapproved behavior, and consequently the validity of self-reports of smoking may be questionable. One central issue is the situation where the questionnaire is completed. Research shows that among 12- through 17-year-olds, self-reported smoking is 10% to 30% higher if surveys are completed at school, rather than at home (Turner, Lessler, & Gfroerer, 1992). A valuable adjunct in such situations is a *nicotine-in-saliva test;* its use has been found to increase the number of students who report that they smoke (Horning et al., 1973).

The use of an observational measure to improve self-reports has also been investigated in a **bogus pipeline** procedure (Jones & Sigall, 1971). In this procedure, students are falsely informed that the researcher has a biochemical test that will accurately assess their smoking patterns, and that it will be given after they complete the survey. Research on this procedure has found that students typically report more smoking after this announcement than without it (Murray & Perry, 1987).

Motives for Smoking

Why do people smoke? Research findings on the motives for smoking suggest that there are many factors involved. Smoking is determined by a variety of psychological, social, biological, and even genetic factors (Fisher, Lichtenstein, & Haire-Joshu, 1993; Lichtenstein & Glasgow, 1992).

Psychological Factors. The self-report questionnaires described above have identified many psychological factors that motivate smoking. In general they fall into several major categories. One category is smoking from *habit,* without other positive or negative motives. A second category is smoking to produce *positive emotional reactions*—including stimulation and arousal, pleasure, relaxation, enjoying the taste, and handling the smoking materials. The third category is smoking to *decrease negative emotional reactions*—to reduce tension, general anxiety, or social anxiety about interactions with other people. A partially overlapping fourth category is smoking for *social reasons,* such as group belongingness, identification with other smokers, and defining one's self-image (Mausner & Platt, 1971). Of course, many people smoke for a combination of reasons. A fifth category of motives for smoking derived from the self-report questionnaires—smoking due to *addiction or craving*—properly falls under the next heading, biological mechanisms.

One limitation with this research on psychological factors that motivate smoking behavior is a lack of consideration for cultural differences. Some researchers have argued that psychological and social factors that motivate Euro-Americans may not apply equally to cultural minorities within America. For example, research suggests that among African Americans, low levels of social support are a crucial factor in leading women to smoke (Romano, Bloom, & Syme, 1991). Similarly, among Hispanic Americans, familial support plays an important role in smoking behavior (Perez et al., 1993).

Biological Mechanisms. Most evidence points to the nicotine in cigarettes as the chemical agent that leads to physiological dependency on smoking, but much is still being learned about what specific mechanisms cause the addictive effect (cf. Ponticri et al., 1996). Taylor (1995) described four theoretical views. The simplest view is the **fixed effects model**—that nicotine has certain fixed reinforcing effects on the nervous system—for instance, it changes the levels of neuro-amines in the blood, speeds up the heart rate, and produces relaxation of the skeletal muscles. However, these are short-term effects, and their reinforcing nature does not explain why smoking is so persistent or so difficult to quit successfully.

A second view, the **nicotine regulation model**, holds that smoking is reinforcing only when the amount of nicotine in the body falls below a given level—thus, addicted individuals smoke to maintain their internal nicotine level at or above that point. There is considerable experimental evidence for this view, such as the fact that smokers who change to low-nicotine cigarettes commonly increase the number of cigarettes smoked, smoke each cigarette farther down, and inhale more deeply (Jarvik, 1973; Schachter, 1977).

However, many facts that are inconsistent with the nicotine regulation model can also be cited (Leventhal & Cleary, 1980; McMorrow & Foxx, 1983). For instance, there are high relapse rates for stop-smoking programs several months after cessation, even though blood nicotine levels return to zero within a few days after quitting. Also, in experiments, smokers will smoke cigarettes made of lettuce, which contain no nicotine at all, and the level of their smoking is quite responsive to transitory emotional states and to levels of environmental stress. In addition, it is relatively easy to quit smoking in protected situations such as sensory deprivation chambers. For reasons such as these, Leventhal and Cleary (1980) proposed a **multiple regulation model** of smoking, which posits that *emotional states* are the key factor connecting bodily nicotine lev-

els to smoking behavior. This model "assumes that the smoker is regulating emotional states and that nicotine levels are being regulated because certain emotional states have become conditioned to them in a variety of settings" (p. 391).

A fourth viewpoint, a **performance regulation model**, was developed by Pomerleau and Pomerleau (1984, 1989). It holds that smoking is used by individuals to help regulate their performance and emotion levels. Nicotine alters the availability of several neurotransmitters (acetylcholine, norepinephrine, and dopamine), and nicotine levels influence anxiety and tension reduction, as well as performance on a variety of memory and psychomotor tasks. Consequently, smokers learn to use nicotine to regulate their behavior in order to perform better on many different tasks.

In sum, the psychological reasons for smoking, mentioned above, provide cues for lighting up, and over long periods of time they generally combine to develop heavy levels of smoking. As a result, the physiologically addicted smoker smokes, not just to maintain bodily nicotine levels, but also because drops in bodily nicotine levels have become associated with emotionally stressful cues, and with poorer task performance.

Genetics. A new approach to understanding why people smoke is based on genetics. In a study of 4775 pairs of identical and fraternal twins, Carmelli et al. (1992) found that identical twins are somewhat more likely than fraternal twins to show similarities in smoking patterns—whether the pattern is smoking occasionally, quitting smoking, or chain-smoking. This finding lends support to the notion that genetics play a role in smoking behaviors.

TREATMENTS TO HELP PEOPLE QUIT SMOKING

The motives for smoking discussed above are important considerations in planning interventions to help smokers "kick the habit." We will discuss three main types of treatment intervention: behavioral approaches, verbal approaches, and community campaigns.

Photograph courtesy of Howard Leventhal. Reprinted by permission.

Box 12-2

HOWARD LEVENTHAL, HEALTH RESEARCHER

One of the outstanding authorities in the growing field of health psychology, Howard Leventhal is a professor at Rutgers University in New Jersey. He was born in Brooklyn in 1931 and studied at New York's City College and Queens College. After completing his Ph.D. at the University of North Carolina, he served as a social psychologist in the U.S. Public Health Service and taught at Yale for nine years before moving to the University of Wisconsin in 1967 and later to Rutgers in 1988.

In addition to Leventhal's research on smoking behavior, he is also known for his work on cancer, pain in physical illness, and compliance with prescribed medical treatments.

His reputation in health research is shown by his service on the editorial boards of several major journals in psychology or health sciences. He has consulted on a wide range of topics, including long-duration manned spaceflight, children's television programs, dental public health, heart disease, drug abuse, hypertension, aging, cigarette smoking, and smoking prevention. Among his 100+ published papers, he is particularly known for research on the effects of fear-arousing messages, the relationship of attitudes and behavior, human stress responses, psychosocial factors in patient care, and studies of anti-smoking programs. As a contrast, he has also published research on the appreciation of humor.

Behavioral Treatments

Behavioral approaches treat smoking as a highly over-learned behavior, and attempt to modify the behavior using operant and classical learning principles (Lando, 1993). Behavioral approaches to smoking cessation can be classified as either nonaversive or aversive techniques.

Nonaversive strategies are those that attempt to assist quitters by providing them with reinforcement and stimulus-control procedures needed to abstain from smoking. Four commonly used nonaversive strategies are relaxation training, contingency contracting, social support, and the nicotine patch.

Relaxation training involves practicing relaxation in the presence of stressful internal cues or situational stimuli that ordinarily lead to the desire to smoke. Though this technique has been quite successful in treating some types of psychological problems such as phobias, its use in anti-smoking programs has not led to appreciable increases in long-term abstinence rates (Lando, 1993). Instead, relaxation training is often incorporated into treatments with other strategies.

Contingency contracting is a behavioral technique that has produced more encouraging results. In it, the smoker deposits a sizable sum of money with the therapist, and portions of the deposit are returned if the smoker meets certain specified treatment goals, such as quitting for a given period of time. In one illustrative study, Winett (1973) found 50% of contingency contracting smokers were abstinent at a six-month follow-up, compared with 24% of anti-smoking program participants who received a noncontingent repayment. Recent developments in contingency contracting are worksite and community contests in which smokers compete to see who can abstain from smoking the longest. Despite the appeal of contingency management programs, a recent review concluded that while they appear to be effective for short-term abstinence, long-term results are disappointing (Lando, 1993).

Research has consistently shown that support from friends and family is strongly related to success in smoking cessation. This being the case, a logical extension is to systematically manipulate **social support** by asking friends, family members, or co-workers to help in the quitting effort. However, such attempts have proven largely unsuccessful (Lando, 1993; Lichtenstein & Glasgow, 1992). Current research is attempting to identify the reasons for the failure, and to incorporate social support manipulations into comprehensive treatment programs (Lando, 1993).

Many treatment programs begin with a **nicotine replacement** system. Nicotine chewing gum was one of the first replacement systems used to help smokers change their behavioral patterns without feeling the symptoms of nicotine withdrawal. The rationale was

that once the smoking habits had been changed, the smoker would have an easier time coping with the lack of nicotine in their system. However, results from studies of nicotine gum showed minimal success (Orleans et al., 1993). In part, the lack of success was caused by the time needed for the nicotine from the gum to be absorbed—unlike nicotine in cigarette smoke, which is absorbed extremely quickly.

More recently, a skin patch was developed that can deliver nicotine to the bloodstream steadily. Research suggests that the nicotine patch, coupled with other types of therapy, can be an effective tool to help smokers break the habit (Lichtenstein & Glasgow, 1992). In an experiment on the nicotine patch, Richmond, Harris, and de Almeida (1994) randomly assigned participants in a smoking cessation program to receive either a nicotine patch or an identical patch that did not contain nicotine (placebo). Each participant in the study also received two hours of group therapy each week for five weeks. The experiment was double-blind, so neither the researchers nor the participants knew which condition they were in. The results showed that the participants that received the nicotine patch were more successful at abstaining from cigarettes than participants who received the placebo, after three months (48% versus 21%) and after six months (33% versus 14%).

Aversion strategies are ones that attempt to reduce smoking by pairing aversive stimuli with the act of smoking or thoughts about smoking. The aversive stimuli most frequently used are cigarette smoke, electric shock, and vivid thoughts of nauseous or unpleasant scenes (a procedure called **cognitive sensitization**) (Carlson, 1994; Lando, 1993). Some early aversion studies used an apparatus which blew warm, stale cigarette smoke in the face of treatment participants while they sat in a small cubicle and smoked rapidly until they could tolerate the situation no longer. Such treatment sessions were repeated regularly until the participant was abstinent from smoking for at least 24 hours and felt confident of remaining abstinent. One study using this method reported 100% success at the end of treatment and 57% continued abstinence at the end of six months (Schmahl, Lichtenstein, & Harris, 1972). Most subsequent studies adopted a simpler procedure, involving **rapid smoking**—inhaling every six seconds until the participant felt ill and could tolerate no more—without the use of the smoke-blowing apparatus. This procedure has also produced good results in many studies. In a review of 49 rapid-smoking studies, Schwartz (1987) found the median cessation rate after 1 year to be 25%. Lando (1993) concluded that aversion techniques may be more effective for immediate cessation rates (i.e., less than six months), but that long-term changes are best produced when aversion techniques are combined with nonaversive techniques.

The research findings suggest that the most promising behavioral treatment approaches are **multimodal interventions**, in which aversion techniques and nonaversive techniques (sometimes referred to as *self-management* techniques) are combined in a coordinated package (Carlson, 1994). In one carefully conducted study of this sort, over 60% of the participants were initially successful, and over 30% remained abstinent in a verified one-year follow-up (Pomerleau, Adkins, & Pertschuk, 1978). Another multimodal study investigated the separate and combined effects of three different treatments (Tongas, 1979). It achieved spectacular levels of success for a combination of verbal group therapy, a rapid-smoking aversive treatment, and covert conditioning consisting of vivid visualizations of disgusting, nauseating scenes associated with smoking and pleasant, highly rewarding scenes associated with nonsmoking. Of the participants completing the five days of treatment, 77% reported abstinence at one year, and 62% at two years.

Verbal Treatments

Verbal treatments rely on discussion or advice rather than direct experience with a noxious or rewarding situation. The simplest form of verbal intervention is **advice from a physician** to give up (or cut down on) smoking. Of course, doctors are perceived as experts on health matters, so their advice may carry special weight. In addition, large numbers of physicians have stopped smoking themselves, so they may also serve as a reference group who demonstrate that quitting is possible and desirable. Controlled studies have found 17% to 38% self-reported cessation of smoking following a physician's advice to quit, compared with about 10% for control groups who received no such advice (Lichtenstein & Holis, 1992; Russell et al., 1979).

Beyond simple advice-giving, many forms of **psychological therapy and counseling** have been tried as anti-smoking treatments. However, approaches used by private therapists, if reported at all, are usually published as subjective clinical reports of experience with a few cases and are rarely analyzed in controlled empirical studies. One careful study compared seven different treatment approaches, involving 8-week programs of individual counseling, group counseling, and/or prescription of tranquilizers, as well as two control groups (Schwartz & Dubitzky, 1968). At the end of treatment, the individual counseling and group counseling conditions appeared to have had moderate success in diminishing smoking; but at the one-year follow-up, none of the seven treatment groups did significantly better than the control groups, which had an 18% cessation rate.

Clinic Procedures. Clinic procedures to help smokers quit smoking have been developed in many settings, both public and private. Two of the most widespread programs are the group counseling program of the American Cancer Society and the Five-Day Plan of the Seventh-Day Adventist Church. The Cancer Society program stresses group support, development of personal insight, and individual determination of when and how to quit smoking. The Adventists' Five-Day Plan emphasizes immediate quitting, using films about health threats, buddy support systems, and encouraging attitudinal, exercise, and dietary changes to reduce the effects of nicotine withdrawal. Unfortunately, because these programs have a strong service orientation—trying to help smokers kick their habit—rather than a research orientation, they have rarely been compared with no-treatment control conditions. Some reports have claimed initial success rates of about 75%, but relapse rates in the first few months after treatment are usually quite high. Interestingly, male participants in these programs usually achieve somewhat higher abstinence rates than women (Lando, 1993).

Typical studies of anti-smoking clinics have found that about half the participants stop smoking, but only about 20% of the participants are still abstinent a year or more later (Lewis, Sperry, & Carlson, 1993; Pomerleau, 1979). Since early relapse rates are so high, considerable attention has been given to procedures aimed at maintaining abstinence, such as occasional booster sessions or supportive phone calls to reinforce non-smoking. However, research on these procedures has rarely demonstrated improved abstinence rates, and paradoxically, some studies have found significantly poorer long-term results (Best, Bass, & Owen, 1977; Elliott & Denney, 1978). It appears that any maintenance programs that are used should be offered in such a way that they do not detract from clients' self-attributions of responsibility for their own success.

Though a majority of American smokers say that they would like to quit, only a small proportion of them are motivated to begin anti-smoking clinic programs, and some efforts to get smokers involved in smoking cessation groups have been "spectacularly unsuccessful" (Rosenblatt & Allen, 1968). Based on the research evidence, some reviewers have concluded that the achieved success of clinic programs is little if any better than the rate of self-initiated quitting in the public at large—that is, without benefit of any special programs (Leventhal & Cleary, 1980; Orleans et al., 1993). In fact, 90% of ex-smokers have quit without the help of a formal treatment program (Fiore et al., 1990).

Recently several programs have been designed to help smokers quit on their own. These self-help aids are often similar to correspondence classes, including pamphlets, information, and video. Evaluations of these programs have found that over a 6-month period, between 9% and 20% of the smokers successfully quit (Jeffery, Hellerstedt, & Schmid, 1990; Schwartz, 1987). These percentages are similar to those found for clinical and community interventions. Furthermore, self-help programs that specifically target the stage of the smoker have been found to be even more effective (Prochaska et al., 1993). These results emphasize that many people are able to quit smoking without professional help, and that cumulative "lifetime" success rates over many years of trying are much greater than the rates reported for single attempts to quit smoking—a hopeful note for the high proportion of smokers who want to stop!

It should also be recognized that gradual changes in social norms regarding smoking may be partially responsible for the improved success of both clinic anti-smoking programs and self-help programs. However, some of the treatment methods discussed above appear to have achieved levels of success over and above those attributable to general social change, and they provide guides for constructing even more effective future interventions. With verbal psychological treatments, as with behavioral treatments, it appears that multimodal interventions are the most promising approaches, particularly when they are carried out by treatment teams who are highly skillful and knowledgeable about the kinds of problems that can lead ex-smokers to relapse (Elliott & Denney, 1978).

Problems with Behavioral and Verbal Treatments

Neither behavioral nor verbal treatment methods are yet differentiated enough to respond directly to all the needs of the would-be ex-smoker. Interventions are usually presented as if they are equally applicable to all smokers—a stretch-sock approach ("one size fits everyone"). This approach largely ignores the implications of Leventhal and Cleary's multiple regulation model, which stresses that smoking is regulated not only by the physiological effects of nicotine addiction, but also by the psychological effects of numerous conditioned emotional states associated with smoking. This oversight may explain the relatively slow progress of anti-smoking treatment research in the last 30 years. Most treatment programs largely ignore the obstacles to successful treatment which stem from the many conditioned emotional factors in smoking together with their cognitive, sensory, and physiological concomitants. Incorporating such complex factors into differentiated treatment procedures for individual smokers seems necessary in order to achieve higher levels of long-term smoking abstinence.

Community Campaigns

In contrast to individual or small-group treatment programs, community campaigns against smoking follow a *public health approach*, stressing mass communication techniques for changing attitudes and behavior. (Many of the principles discussed in Chapter 13 on the mass media are relevant here.) Because exposure and attention to the campaign messages are always variable and frequently do not exceed a very low level, public information or action campaigns often have weak or negligible effects. Individual and group treatment approaches, on the other hand, can be tailored specifically to their audiences, and exposure and attention to their messages can be assured. As a result, they might be expected to have much stronger effects than community campaigns, but Leventhal and Cleary (1980) have pointed out some arguments to the contrary:

> It is usually assumed that intensive, individual therapy can generate the most significant impact on smoking, but the opposite may in fact be true. Intensive efforts to alter societal, community, and group values and norms might be more effective in producing change in smoking behavior. Restricting smoking in public buildings, requiring nonsmoking sections in airplanes and restaurants and changing attitudes about the rights of nonsmokers might do more to change smoking habits than intensive procedures directed at individuals. (p. 381)

There are many dramatic examples of this point, such as the huge reduction in smoking during college classes and public meetings during the last few decades. As part of this trend, several major community-wide smoking prevention campaigns have been undertaken in the last 20 years (e.g., Wallack & Russell, 1991).

AN ILLUSTRATIVE STUDY—
THE STANFORD FIVE-CITY PROJECT

Probably the most widely publicized of such community programs was the Stanford Five-City Project. Initiated in 1978 by a group of Stanford researchers, the project was designed to reduce the risk of cardiovascular disease among residents of two treatment communities (Farquhar et al., 1990; Fortmann et al., 1990, 1993, 1995). The study was unprecedented in its scope and audience. It presented a community-wide education program that targeted behaviors known to increase the risk of cardiovascular disease (e.g., smoking, lack of exercise, eating habits) and included 92,000 people aged 12–74 in the treatment groups and 141,000 in the

control groups. The health education intervention included television programs, radio segments, newspaper ads and articles, booklets and pamphlets, and face-to-face conversations. Outcome measures included systolic and diastolic blood pressure, weight, cholesterol levels, and behavior changes in diet, exercise, and smoking. For the purposes of this chapter, we will focus on the effectiveness of the education intervention in reducing smoking levels in the target communities, and in inducing smoking cessation.

In 1978, five California cities were chosen for the study based on their location, size, and media market: Monterey, Salinas, Modesto, San Luis Obispo, and Santa Maria. Monterey ($N = 40,600$) and Salinas ($N = 82,000$) were selected as treatment communities, while Modesto ($N = 161,600$) and San Luis Obispo ($N = 35,900$) were selected as control communities. The city of Santa Maria was monitored for morbidity and mortality only, and measures of cigarette smoking there are not available. Thus, we will examine behavior changes among the two treatment and two control communities. Because it was impossible to randomly assign community members to receive or not receive the mass-media-based educational campaign within each city, the study was quasi-experimental—examining changes within and between the four existing groups.

Baseline measures and subsequent changes were assessed in two ways. First, fresh random samples of residents within each community were obtained every two years. The selected households were recruited by mail, telephone, and in person, and invited to stop by a survey center. At the center, each respondent completed a detailed questionnaire and was interviewed by trained health professionals. Additionally, cholesterol, blood pressure, and expired-air carbon monoxide levels were taken. The second assessment method studied behavior changes of the initial cohort of baseline respondents through longitudinal follow-ups made every two years.

Intervention Program

A smoking cessation intervention was distributed throughout each of the two treatment communities. It was aimed at increasing knowledge about the dangers of smoking and the advantages of quitting, reducing positive attitudes toward smoking, increasing smokers' confidence in their ability to quit, and encouraging smoking prevention, cessation, and maintenance of non-smoking (Fortmann et al., 1993). The smoking program began in 1980 and lasted 6 years. It contained a total of 955 combined media messages, distributed across television (106), radio (22), newspapers (574), other print (59), and face-to-face presentations (96). In addition, a four-page "quit kit" was developed and distributed to 20,555 individuals through community physicians and nurses. A longer self-help guide titled *Cool Turkey* was distributed in both English and Spanish.

Evaluation

As is clear from the above description, the educational intervention was designed to reach every person in the treatment communities. Fortmann et al. (1993) reported on the effectiveness of these community interventions in reducing smoking behavior.

Baseline Data. Prior to beginning the educational intervention, baseline data were obtained from a random sample in each of the four cities. A summary of these data showed that the treatment and control cities could not be exactly matched, and there were significant differences in ethnicity, education, income, smoking prevalence, and intentions to quit.

Independent Samples. Independent random samples of community residents were obtained every two years. The smoking results from these surveys are shown in Table 12-1, which demonstrates that smoking rates declined for *all* of the communities between 1979 and 1986. For the treatment communities, smoking rates fell 10.5%, but for the control cities, they fell 10.7% for the same period. The expected time-by-treatment interaction was not significant.

Cohort Sample. The 1703 initial baseline respondents were contacted and remeasured every two years. One ever-present problem in such longitudinal research is dropout, and in this study, almost half of the baseline participants did not continue in the cohort follow-up. The majority of these dropouts were people who moved out of the community (67%). Most of the dropouts occurred between the baseline measures and the first round of follow-ups (70%). The participants who dropped out of the study were more likely to be smokers, less educated, younger, poorer, and Hispanic. Dropout rates were fairly equal across the four communities.

Results from the cohort samples are presented in Table 12-2. As in the cross-sectional samples, smoking rates across all four cities dropped sharply during the six-year period. However, in contrast to the cross-

TABLE 12-1 Smoking Rates per 100 and Sample Sizes for Each Independent, Cross-Sectional Survey Among Participants Aged 25–74, Stanford Five-City Project, 1979–1986

	Independent surveys			
	1979–1980	*1981–1982*	*1983–1984*	*1985–1986*
Condition				
Treatment	33.8 (905)	31.5 (920)	27.1 (897)	23.3 (930)
Control	32.8 (798)	29.1 (774)	27.8 (932)	22.1 (825)
City				
Monterey	28.5 (460)	35.2 (472)	27.1 (454)	22.7 (490)
Salinas	39.3 (445)	27.7 (448)	27.1 (443)	24.1 (440)
Modesto	38.5 (442)	34.3 (388)	30.2 (480)	27.7 (463)
San Luis Obispo	25.8 (356)	23.8 (386)	25.2 (452)	14.9 (362)

Note: Sample size in parentheses.

Source: Table 3 in Fortmann, S. P., Taylor, C. B., Flora, J. A., & Jatulis, D. E. (1993). Changes in adult cigarette smoking prevalence after 5 years of community health education: The Stanford Five-City Project. *American Journal of Epidemiology, 137,* 82–96. Reprinted with permission of the Johns Hopkins University School of Hygiene and Public Health.

TABLE 12-2   **Smoking Rates per 100 for Each Cohort Survey Among Participants Aged 25–74, Stanford Five-City Project, 1979–1985**

	Cohort surveys			
	1979–1980	*1980–1981*	*1982–1983*	*1984–1985*
Condition				
Treatment (*N*=413)	28.1	25.4	23.2	20.6
Control (*N*=392)	26.5	26.3	25.5	22.5
City				
Monterey (*N*=242)	22.7	20.3	19.0	16.5
Salinas (*N*=171)	35.7	32.8	29.2	26.3
Modesto (*N*=202)	33.2	32.7	31.7	29.2
San Luis Obispo (*N*=190)	19.5	19.5	19.0	15.3

Note: Sample size in parentheses.

Source: Table 2 in Fortmann, S. P., Taylor, C. B., Flora, J. A., & Jatulis, D. E. (1993). Changes in adult cigarette smoking prevalence after 5 years of community health education: The Stanford Five-City Project. *American Journal of Epidemiology, 137,* 82–96. Reprinted with permission of the Johns Hopkins University School of Hygiene and Public Health.

sectional samples, in the cohort samples the rate of smoking decline was larger for the treatment cities than for the control cities. Smoking rates in the treatment communities fell 7.5% between 1979 and 1985, while smoking rates in the control communities fell only 4% (a difference significant at $p<.10$).

The researchers pointed out that the small cohort effects and nonsignificant independent sample effects may be due to the nature of the educational intervention. The campaign primarily targeted smoking cessation, and not smoking prevention. Thus, the researchers examined the quit rates among the baseline smokers in both the treatment and control conditions. Over time, nearly 40% of the cohort smokers in the treatment communities quit smoking, while only 23% in the control communities quit ($p<.006$). Subsequent analyses suggested that a slightly uneven dropout rate between smokers and nonsmokers may have affected the overall smoking rates in such a way that the comparisons between treatment and controls described above for the independent samples were not significant.

In addition to the data on smoking, another important finding was that other risk factors for heart disease (particularly blood pressure readings) also declined more in the treatment cities than in the control cities (Fortmann et al., 1990).

Summary. Overall, the Stanford Five-City Project is an excellent example of a community-based smoking intervention. The program attempted to increase cessation rates and to reduce overall smoking rates through a large-scale mass media campaign. The results suggest that such a campaign can be an effective way to encourage quitting among smokers. However, the effects on overall smoking rates were small, reiterating a point made throughout this book—it is difficult to produce large changes in behavior through campaigns that are primarily educational.

PREVENTING CHILDREN FROM STARTING TO SMOKE

Perhaps even more important than helping current smokers quit is the goal of keeping children and youths from endangering their health by starting to smoke. Unfortunately, American young people are starting to smoke at younger and younger ages. In a 1991 national survey, 70% of high school students reported that they had tried cigarette smoking (Centers for Disease Control, 1992). The percentage of high school seniors who are daily smokers hit a high point of 29% in 1976. Since then it declined rather steadily to a low of 17% in 1992, but rose disturbingly to 22% by 1995. Reports of daily smoking by 8th and 10th graders, though lower overall, also showed the same type of rise from 1992 to 1995 (U.S. DHHS, 1996).

For many years anti-smoking campaigns of various sorts have been conducted in our schools. The American Cancer Society, American Heart Association, and American Lung Association have all developed curriculum materials and supported demonstration and research projects aimed at health education and smoking prevention. The age groups targeted by these programs have ranged from high school all the way down to kindergarten. In addition, various federal agencies, universities, and public school districts have developed teaching guides and launched numerous experimental projects to prevent children from smoking. For a review of these programs, see the 1994 U.S. Surgeon General's report, *Preventing Tobacco Use Among Young People* (U.S. DHHS, 1994).

Early Approaches. Early school-based interventions, conducted in the 1960s and 1970s, were often based on the assumption that children who smoked simply didn't understand the health consequences of smoking. The logic was that, because they were not informed, presenting them with information about smoking should lead to reductions in the number of students who smoked. This approach is commonly referred to as an **information deficit model** and is characteristic of many early interventions in a variety of areas, including AIDS prevention, drug prevention, and teen-pregnancy programs. These early smoking interventions bombarded students with information, through films, pamphlets, posters, speakers, etc.. However, reviews of these types of information campaigns found that information alone was not an effective strategy to prevent smoking (Thompson, 1978).

Social Influences. A new wave of school-based interventions began in the 1980s and has continued to the present. These interventions are based on social psychological theories of human behavior, such as Fishbein and Ajzen's (1975) theory of reasoned action (see Chapter 14 for fuller details). According to this approach, behavior is determined by one's beliefs about the consequences of the behavior *and* by one's perceptions of how other people view the behavior, termed *social norms*. This new wave of school-based smoking interventions not only targets beliefs and knowledge about smoking, but also social norms, and aims to provide students with the skills to resist pressures to smoke. The drug prevention programs discussed in Chapter 7 represent similar examples. Recent evaluations of these types of programs have found them to be more successful than information campaigns (Bruvold, 1993). However, recall that the changes resulting from the D.A.R.E. program were primarily attitudinal, and the changes it produced in substance use were short-lived. Examining a variety of effective school-based anti-smoking interventions, Glynn (1989) identified eight essential keys to success for such programs. These central factors are listed in Table 12-3.

As we have seen in this chapter, smoking cessation and smoking prevention are important health topics, to which social psychology has contributed a great deal. The field of health psychology, as one area of applied social psychology, promises to grow tremendously over the next decade as people around the world strive for healthier lifestyles.

TABLE 12-3   Essential Elements of School-Based Smoking-Prevention Programs

1. Classroom sessions should be delivered at least five times per year in each of two years in the sixth through ninth grades.
2. The program should emphasize the social influences that affect smoking onset, short-term physiological and social consequences of smoking, and refusal skills.
3. The program should be incorporated into the existing school curricula.
4. The program should be introduced during the transition from elementary school to junior high or middle school (sixth or seventh grades).
5. Selected student peers should be involved as assistants to teachers in the presentation and delivery of the program.
6. Parental support is important, and parental involvement should be encouraged.
7. Teachers should be adequately trained and committed to the program.
8. The program should conform to community norms and be acceptable to all the various constituencies involved in the school system.

Source: Adapted from Glynn (1989).

SUMMARY

Many applied social psychologists are now working in the field of health psychology, in areas ranging from community health care, stress, and obesity, to heart disease, cancer, and alcoholism. An area where they have made numerous contributions is research on and treatment of smoking, which is the greatest preventable health risk of our era.

Psychological variables are crucial factors in understanding many aspects of smoking. Stages in the development of smoking include (a) attitudinal preparation, (b) initiation of the first tries at smoking under a wide variety of social influences, (c) becoming a more regular smoker through a social learning process over a period of months or years, and (d) maintenance of smoking, with both psychological factors and biological mechanisms combining to perpetuate the learned smoking patterns.

The psychological motives for smoking established by research studies include habit, reduction of anxiety or tension, pleasurable relaxation, sociability and social rewards, stimulation and arousal, and handling the smoking materials. Physiological addiction, which helps maintain smoking, may be based on the reinforcing effects of nicotine, on the conditioned need to keep a certain level of nicotine in the bloodstream, on a learned association of smoking with improvements in task performance, or more likely, on a multiple-regulation process in which emotional states have become conditioned to nicotine levels and are an important source of pressure to keep smoking.

Useful programs to help people quit smoking include the behavioral techniques of contingency contracting, aversive treatment using warm, stale, smoky air or sustained rapid smoking, and coordinated combinations of nonaversion and aversion techniques. The simplest verbal treatment is merely a physician's advice to stop smoking, but it has a potential for widespread use and effectiveness. Neither behavioral treatments nor psychological counseling approaches are yet differentiated enough to respond to the widely varying needs and motives of different smokers.

Community anti-smoking campaigns follow a pub-lic health or communication model, and since public attention is often very low, they generally have weak or negligible effects. However, a few carefully planned and highly publicized campaigns, such as the Stanford Five-City Project, have shown socially important effects on reduction of smoking and of risk factors for heart disease. Also, the *cumulative* impact of all the negative publicity about smoking in the last 30 years seems to have curtailed U.S. nationwide cigarette consumption by a large amount.

SUGGESTED READINGS

Adler, N., & Mathews, K. (1994). Health psychology: Why do some people get sick and some stay well? *Annual Review of Psychology, 45,* 229–259.—A very readable overview of current research in health psychology.

Edwards, J., Tindale, R. S., Heath, L., & Posavac, E. (Eds.). (1990). *Social influence processes and prevention.* New York: Plenum.—This book covers a wide variety of health topics including AIDS, smoking, alcoholism, and heart disease. Its focus is on strategies of social influence to decrease social problems.

Fortmann, S., Taylor, C. B., Flora, J., & Jatulis, D. (1993). Changes in adult cigarette smoking prevalence after 5 years of community health education: The Stanford Five-City Project. *American Journal of Epidemiology, 137,* 82–96.—One of several reports from the Stanford Five-City Project that evaluated the effects of the program on smoking.

Sussman, S., Dent, C., Burton, D., Stacy, A., & Flay, B. (1995). *Developing school-based tobacco use prevention and cessation programs.* Thousand Oaks, CA: Sage.—This book discusses effective school-based tobacco interventions, synthesizes a wide variety of programs, and presents a clear framework for developing and understanding effective interventions.

Taylor, S. (1995). *Health psychology* (3rd ed.). New York: McGraw-Hill.—An excellent overview of the growing field of health psychology, covering a variety of health topics including smoking, drug abuse, stress, and AIDS prevention.

U.S. Department of Health and Human Services. (1994). *Preventing tobacco use among young people: A report of the Surgeon General.* Washington DC: U.S. Government Printing Office.—Provides up-to-date, clearly summarized information on current patterns of cigarette smoking and the resulting medical risks, with breakdowns by gender, age, and ethnicity.

CHAPTER 13

Mass Communication— Media Content and Effects

The most important educational institution in the country is not Harvard or Yale or Caltech—it's television.

—Newton Minow (1979)

We do not believe any reasonable person can view a typical eight to twelve noon Saturday morning period on any of the major television networks and fail to recognize the need for fundamental change in the way our society is using its most powerful and persuasive medium of communication to entertain and enlighten the very young.

—Kenneth Mason (in Sheikh, 1978)

There would probably be little disagreement about the great educational potential of television, but its performance has often failed to measure up to its potential. The mass media have been among the most praised and criticized, the "most cussed and discussed" aspects of modern society.

Social psychologists and other communication researchers have studied many different aspects of the mass media of communication, ranging from *content* of the media, to characteristics of their *audience,* to ways in which the media are *used,* to *effects* of the media on attitudes and behaviors. Several books provide excellent overviews of this literature (Bryant & Zillmann, 1994; Comstock, 1991; Liebert & Sprafkin, 1988). In this chapter we will briefly touch on some of the major areas of social psychological research and then focus more heavily on the most studied aspects of media content and media effects.

PRINT MEDIA, RADIO, AND TELEVISION

The term **media** refers to the channels by which communications are transmitted to a large group of people. Currently, television is by far the most heavily studied medium of communication, but books, newspapers, radio, the Internet, movies, and many other transmission methods are also important types of media. However, very little research attention has recently been paid to these other forms of media (Huston, Zillmann, & Bryant, 1994). Newspapers have had some study, and movies have been the focus of sporadic research. Because of this imbalance in research, television will be the focus of our attention in this chapter also.

Since the rise to dominance of television, the other media have all been dramatically affected. As the number of hours people spent watching television increased, the average amount of time devoted to movies, radio, books, magazines, and newspapers decreased, as did their share of the consumer's entertainment expenditures. More striking still were the resulting changes in their form and function. In attempts to compete with TV, movies have become more violent and more explicitly sexual (the latter is a change that TV could not completely imitate for fear of offending portions of its mass home audience).

Radio was initially a national mass medium of network news and entertainment. It transmitted such programs as Franklin D. Roosevelt's "fireside chats" to the whole nation, as well as news bulletins during World War II, Jack Benny's comedy, and the adventures of "Jack Armstrong, the All-American Boy." After the growth of television, radio became a local medium, fractionated into many separate stations with specialized programming aimed at homogeneous audiences (such as top 40 tunes, country and western, and talk programs). In a similar manner, many large-circulation, general-interest magazines died (e.g., *Saturday Evening Post* and *Life*), while specialty magazines like *Playboy, Rolling Stone, Ms.,* and *Motor Trend* prospered. Even the sales of comic books decreased by half, and the percentage of drama, poetry, and fiction books put out by publishers declined (Comstock, 1993; Comstock et al., 1978). Thus, there is abundant evidence of the impact of television in changing our society's sources of information and entertainment.

The average U.S. household is exposed to approximately 55 hours of television per week (*8 hours* per day), with the average viewer over the age of two watching more than 3 hours per day (Andreasen, 1994; Comstock, 1991; Gerbner, Gross, et al., 1994). For the average American, almost from birth up through old age, television constitutes a large part of the daily activities. In fact, next to sleeping and school (or work), television is the activity that occupies the largest amount of the U.S. public's time. With this in mind, let's examine the uses of television, the content of television, and the effects that television has on people's thoughts, feelings, and behaviors.

USES OF THE MEDIA

A booming research area in recent years has been the study of media "uses and gratifications." This approach delves behind the manifest content of the media to ask: What are people's motives for spending time with the media? It stresses a view of audience members as active and seeking to satisfy their individual needs, in contrast to earlier alarmist views of a passive audience mesmerized by the "boob tube."

Among the numerous needs that have been suggested, many studies have converged on four basic clusters of functions that the media can serve: (a) entertainment and diversion, (b) information and knowledge about the world, (c) social contact (providing both vicarious contact and topics to talk about with acquaintances), and (d) personal identity and self-definition (comparison of one's own experiences and views with those in the media) (Murray & Kippax, 1979; Rubin, 1994). Some research has indicated that television is the broadest, least-specialized medium, capable of satisfying all four clusters of needs, and that radio has much the same breadth. By contrast, books have been described as primarily serving personal identity needs, newspapers as fulfilling information needs, and movies as satisfying entertainment needs (Katz, Gurevitch, & Haas, 1973). Studies in several countries have generally supported these views, except that newspapers also appear to have broader functions. Within the medium of television, selection of specific programs to watch is also largely influenced by the viewer's needs (Murray & Kippax, 1979).

However, reasonable as this uses-and-gratifications research sounds, various questions have been raised about it. Though entertainment is by far the predomi-

nant use made of most media (Tannenbaum, 1980), the bulk of research has been done on the information function, for instance in the areas of news and political information. There is also an atheoretical circularity to some of the research, based on the reasoning that viewers who use a given medium must have the corresponding need. Moreover, because the research uses self-report data, it relies on respondents' conscious self-understanding; and it encourages them to describe all media exposure as purposefully chosen, rather than as the result of habit, accident, or social pressures (Roberts & Bachen, 1981). Despite these deserved criticisms of some research, studies have begun to establish valid independent measures of personal needs, to show that different media often do satisfy different needs, and also to caution that the gratifications sought through media use may sometimes be different from those actually obtained (e.g., Perse & Rubin, 1990; Rubin & Bantz, 1989).

MEDIA CONTENT

Social researchers have studied many different aspects of media content. Here we will summarize the findings concerning portrayals of ethnic minorities, women and gender roles, violence, sexuality, and advertising. In a later section of this chapter we will discuss the *effects* of these media portrayals. The research findings in these sections are drawn from a wide variety of sources, and they are illustrated by several tables from a content analysis by Rothman, Lichter, and Lichter (1992). These authors surveyed the content of three decades of television programming (1955–1984), focusing on television series and prime-time shows. Their samples of television programs were selected randomly from ones stored in the Library of Congress and the New York Museum of Broadcasting.

Ethnic Minorities

Research findings can rarely keep up with the fast-changing pace of new television programs, or even current trends in the other media. However, a large body of studies documents the dramatic changes in depiction of ethnic minorities in the media. A typical progression includes three stages, moving from nonrecognition of the existence of minorities, through ridicule (as in

Amos and Andy or Jack Benny's servant, Rochester), to inclusion (Clark, 1969). For an excellent review of the changes in ethnic representation in the media over the past 30 years, see Greenberg and Brand (1993).

In 1967–68, in response to social pressures including threatened boycotts, the television networks adopted a policy of increasing the presentation of Blacks, and marked changes took place in the next two years (Dominick & Greenberg, 1970). The number of commercials featuring Blacks more than doubled (to 11%), and the number of Blacks in major roles in soap operas and prime-time dramas rose sharply. In the early 1970s, Black characters were still presented on TV only about half as often as their proportion of the population, but they were frequently shown as "good" characters in high status occupations, whereas non-Americans and Hispanic characters were usually depicted in lower status activities (Seggar, Hafen, & Hannonen-Gladden, 1981; Seggar & Wheeler, 1973). Blacks were still somewhat less likely than Whites to have major roles, but Hispanics were much farther behind. Another study found, in comparison with real-life statistics, that non-Whites were markedly underrepresented both in criminal roles and as victims of crime on TV (Dominick, 1973).

By 1975, the proportion of non-White characters on prime-time TV had leveled off at about 13%—still below the population figures. The most recent figures show that the 13% figure held steady, and that minority characters comprised only 10% of the characters in prime-time TV commercials (Cantor & Cantor, 1992; Gerbner, 1993; Greenberg & Brand, 1993). The non-White characters shown on prime-time television were predominately Black (11% of all characters), whereas only 3% were Asian or Hispanic, and non-White characters were heavily concentrated in comedy programs—22% of characters there as compared with only 3% in drama programs (Weigel, Loomis, & Soja, 1980). Additionally, the minorities featured in sitcoms tended to be clustered in nearly all-Black or nearly all-Asian shows. For instance, 75% of the total number of Blacks depicted on television were in 18% of the shows (Weigel, Loomis, & Soja, 1980). Situation comedies like "In Living Color," "Martin," "The Cosby Show," and "American Girl" contained almost entirely one minority ethnic group.

The overall results from the Rothman et al. (1992) content analyses of prime-time depictions of ethnic minorities across three decades are presented in Table 13-1.

In contrast to the increase in the percentage of Blacks depicted on prime-time television, weekend morning network television, a time slot that is almost entirely directed at children, is nearly devoid of any minorities. Gerbner's (1993) content analysis found that minority characters comprised less than 5% of the codable characters on Saturday morning TV. Summarizing their survey, Greenberg and Brand (1993) stated:

> not a single program on the . . . morning lineup featured or displayed a minority in any regular role or even a major role on a single episode. . . . From *Muppet Babies* at 8 a.m. through *Waldo* at noon, we did not identify any such regular minority character. (p. 133)

In fact, Hispanic characters made an appearance on Saturday morning TV only once every two weeks, on average (Gerbner, 1993). However, unlike network television, children's shows on the Public Broadcasting System (PBS) all showed ethnically diverse groups of children interacting. "Barney and Friends," "Zoobilee Zoo," "Sesame Street," "Mister Rogers' Neighborhood," and "Reading Rainbow" all contained many ethnically diverse characters.

Women and Gender Roles

There are numerous ways, both subtle and blatant, in which gender-role norms are transmitted through many different media. Cameron (1977) summarized gender-role portrayals contained in the popular writings of psychotherapists and historians, in textbooks for marriage and family classes, and in children's literature. Books for children may be especially influential because they often aim to teach socially valued behavior. Yet most of them are amazingly lopsided in their presentation of gender roles. Boys and men have predominated in the central roles in children's books, and they are much more likely than girls or women to be portrayed as heroic, adventurous, and clever. In the past, women and girls were typically depicted in passive activities or doing domestic work, in difficulties and needing to be rescued, or acting as supportive helpers or admirers for their menfolk (Kolbe & LaVoie, 1981; Women on Words and Images, 1975). However, these

TABLE 13-1 Prime-Time Television Depictions of Race and Ethnicity Across Three Decades

		Years			
	Measure	*1955–64*	*1965–74*	*1975–84*	*Total*
Minorities as % of all characters	(%)	4.0	12.7	14.7	11.0
Blacks as % of all characters	(%)	0.6	6.7	9.1	5.9
Hispanics as % of all characters	(%)	1.7	3.0	2.1	2.2
Frequency of treatment of race and ethnicity theme	(N)	41	73	65	179
minorities will be successful only if they give up most or all of cultural heritage**	(%)	7.3	1.4	0.0	2.2
minorities are different but can work differences out to fit into society**	(%)	12.2	12.3	6.2	10.1
minorities are basically the same as other Americans**	(%)	26.8	24.7	40.0	30.7
minorities are treated fairly**	(%)	22.0	27.4	35.4	29.1
Frequency of interracial/ethnic personal relations theme	(N)	38	63	105	206
interracial/ethnic relations are acceptable**	(%)	100.0	98.4	97.1	98.4
Frequency of problems in interracial/ethnic relations theme	(N)	26	36	72	134
no problems**	(%)	65.4	66.7	83.3	75.0
problems imposed by outsider**	(%)	15.4	11.1	8.3	10.5
combination of inherent and imposed problem**	(%)	3.9	8.3	2.8	4.5
Frequency of Blacks	(N)	12	150	271	433
% of Blacks commit crime	(%)	0.0	6.0	8.5	7.4
Frequency of Hispanics	(N)	36	66	63	165
% of Hispanics commit crime	(%)	13.9	27.3	22.2	22.2

**Totals do not add to 100% due to categories not listed.

Source: Rothman et al. (1992, p. 244).

patterns are gradually changing in a more egalitarian direction (Williams et al., 1987; Oskamp, Kaufman, & Wolterbeek, 1996).

In the major women's magazines, fictional stories also present a highly unrealistic view of life. As late as the 1970s, the majority of female characters in such stories were described as never having held a job, and most of those who had been employed held only low-status jobs, which they gave up when they married (Franzwa, 1974). In prize-winning children's picture books too, women's occupations were almost completely limited to wife and mother (Williams et al., 1987). In advertising, there has been a slight trend in recent years toward less stereotypic gender-role portrayals for both men and women. However, for men depicted in magazine ads, the chief change has been from showing traditional "manly" activities to a greater frequency of purely "decorative," nonfunctional roles (Skelly & Lundstrom, 1981).

In other mass media, gender-role stereotypes are also very pervasive (Butler & Paisley, 1980; Chavez, 1985). Since the beginning of TV nearly 50 years ago, men have consistently outnumbered women in prime-time programming by at least 2 to 1 (Gerbner, 1993; Signorielli, 1989). Women are more often minor characters, usually unemployed or in low-status jobs, and twice as likely as men to be portrayed as incompetent (Steenland, 1990). In general, men are depicted as more powerful, smart, rational, and stable, but also more violent and "bad"; women characters are generally younger, more attractive, warmer, and happier

than men (Durkin, 1985; Tedesco, 1974). On children's television, a similar pattern is found: aggressive and constructive men, ineffective and deferential women (Signorielli, 1993). However, there is a fascinating exception to this pattern on the daytime "soap operas," where the viewers are mostly housewives. Contrary to many people's image of soap operas, they actually portray women as much more equal to men in power and in professional occupations, and they generally show housewives as intelligent, self-reliant, and articulate (Downing, 1974; Gerbner, 1993; Katzman, 1972).

Other details about the portrayal of women on primetime television over a period of three decades are summarized in Table 13-2.

In television commercials, women also play a sub-

TABLE 13-2   Prime-Time Television Depictions of Women and Men Across Three Decades

		Years			
	Measure	*1955–64*	*1965–74*	*1975–84*	*Total*
Frequency of female characters	(N)	479	594	984	2057
Frequency of male characters	(N)	1659	1638	2007	5304
*% Women succeed in aims	(%)	69.7	66.0	72.1	70.0
	N=	(317)	(412)	(674)	
*% Men succeed in aims	(%)	64.5	62.9	62.7	63.0
	N=	(1125)	(1203)	(1442)	
% Women who are mature adult	(%)	47.4	51.7	48.2	49.3
% Men who are mature adult	(%)	69.7	71.7	67.8	69.6
% Women in personal context	(%)	68.9	60.8	53.7	59.3
% Men in personal context	(%)	35.8	30.6	32.6	33.0
% Women in occupational context	(%)	17.5	23.4	23.5	22.1
% Men in occupational context	(%)	50.5	55.6	45.5	50.2
% Women who are professionals	(%)	4.1	3.4	5.8	4.9
% Men who are professionals	(%)	16.6	13.8	13.4	14.2
Frequency of equal treatment for women theme	(N)	11	11	15	37
Women are not treated equally but should be**	(%)	54.5	72.7	93.3	75.7

*Based on fewer cases. Some characters not applicable.

**Totals do not add to 100% due to categories not listed.

Source: Rothman et al. (1992, p. 232).

ordinate role. They appear about as frequently as men, but most often as housewives being advised or persuaded to use a kitchen or bathroom product, while the salesperson is usually a man, and the authoritative off-screen voice summarizing the product's benefits is almost always a man (Courtney & Whipple, 1983; Craig, 1992). In commercials on children's TV programs, the spokesperson for products is a male about 90% of the time (Bretl & Cantor, 1988). Moreover, commercials directed at boys contain more action and aggression, while those aimed at girls have more frequent fades, dissolves, and soft background music—subtle cues of the children's expected gender roles (Welch et al., 1979). Some magazine and newspaper ads seem to be moving away from these stereotypes, however—particularly cigarette and soft drink ads, which have been showing many more women in nontraditional activities and occupations (Sexton & Haberman, 1974).

In summary, though women are not invisible in the media, as women and minorities once were, they are still very often treated as second-class citizens. The effects of this kind of treatment are discussed later in this chapter.

Violence in the Media

The presentation of violence in TV programs has been a hotly debated public issue since the advent of television in the late 1940s, and consequently it has generated four times as many empirical studies as all other television research combined. About 80% of all TV dramatic programs contain one or more violent episodes, while in some seasons 100% of network children's programs and cartoons have contained violent episodes (Gerbner, Morgan, & Signorielli, 1994; Liebert & Sprafkin, 1988). Put another way, prime-time TV dramas have an average of about 5 acts of violence during each program hour, but children's cartoons average about 25 violent acts per hour (see Figure 13-1). Even more violent are children's TV commercials, if nonhuman aggression is counted as violence, for the ads have about three times as much aggression per minute as do the children's programs (Schuetz & Sprafkin, 1979). The overall pattern of violence on TV has been one of cyclic variations around

a continuing high level of violent programming (Gerbner et al., 1978, 1980, 1994). Figure 13-1 displays a 20-year plot of these trends in television violence and dramatically shows how much more violence is depicted in Saturday morning children's shows than even in adult prime-time dramas.

The likelihood of a television dramatic character becoming the victim of violence is 50 times greater than a U.S. citizen's average real life likelihood (Comstock et al., 1978). Extensive research by Craig Haney and John Manzolati has shown that:

> violent crime, particularly murder, occurs far more frequently on the tube than it does in real life. In contrast, white-collar or corporate crime—like consumer fraud and industrial pollution—and victimless crime—like drunkenness—appear far less often on the screen than in the real world. (Rice, 1980)

Government Investigation. The effect of all this video violence, especially on children, became such a public issue that the U.S. Surgeon General appointed a special scientific committee to investigate the problem and commissioned five volumes of research studies, which were published to accompany the committee's report (Comstock & Rubinstein, 1972; Surgeon General's Scientific Advisory Committee, 1972). Despite controversy about whether the television industry had too much influence over choosing the committee, the unanimous committee report concluded that TV violence could encourage viewer aggressiveness under some conditions (Cater & Strickland, 1975; Eysenck & Nias, 1978). Ten years later, a follow-up report from the National Institute of Mental Health (1982) summarized the extensive research findings of the intervening years. It concluded that they had significantly strengthened the earlier report's conclusions, and that there was now "overwhelm-ing" evidence that excessive violence on U.S. television caused aggressive behavior in children who watched it (Rubinstein, 1983). Governmental investigations into media violence have continued sporadically in response to pressing social concerns, as evidenced by the "National Consultation on Violence" and the "Violence Summit," both conducted in 1993 (Gerbner, Morgan, & Signorielli, 1994). In 1996, the first of a series of reports from a new in-depth National Television Violence Study was published (University of California, 1996).

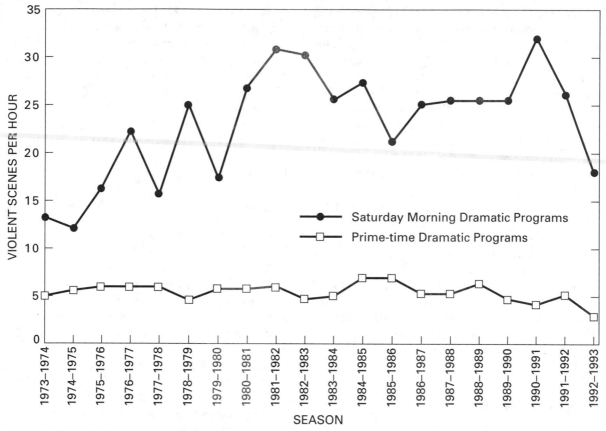

FIGURE 13-1 **Violent scenes per hour on television networks' prime-time and Saturday morning dramatic programs, 1973–1993.** (Data from Gerbner, Morgan, & Signorielli, 1994, Tables 1 & 5.)

The history of attempts to limit the amount of violence on television is a fascinating story of the struggle between private industry and public pressures leading to governmental restrictions. A recent development in this long struggle was the 1989 Television Violence Act. This was the first law that specifically targeted reductions in the amount of violence on TV. The act granted television executives the authority to discuss the issue of TV violence together without being in violation of anti-trust acts, but it did nothing directly to reduce the amount of violence on television—it only opened the door for possible cooperation across all TV stations (Congressional Digest, 1993).

More recently, the Federal Telecommunications Bill of 1996 required that all new TV sets have a built-in **V-chip**—an electronic device that will allow parents and other viewers to block out programs that have certain content codes (e.g., for violent or sexual content). The television networks have agreed to develop a content-rating system, perhaps similar to the one used with movies, and to broadcast these ratings with each program. The Federal Communications Commission is overseeing the process of development to ensure that the V-chip system will work effectively ("Getting Ready," 1996; Rich, 1996).

Measurement of TV Violence. Measuring the amount of violence on TV is a highly complicated undertaking, and the networks have often complained that violence scores such as those cited above do not fairly describe their programming. The major research attempt to monitor TV violence has been a continuing annual **violence profile** published every year since 1967 by George Gerbner and his colleagues at the University of Pennsylvania (e.g., Gerbner, Morgan, & Signorielli, 1994). The findings of this research program have been very influential, so its methodology is important in indicating its possible limitations. The data are based on samples of network prime-time and weekend morning programs during the fall season, so they exclude all independent stations' programming. Analysis is limited to fictional programs that tell a story, so news, sports, variety programs, documentaries, and specials are excluded. The definition of *violence* used is "the overt expression of physical force, with or without a weapon, against self or other, compelling action against one's will on pain of being hurt or killed, or actually hurting or killing" (Gerbner et al., 1978, p. 179). The data are carefully coded from videotapes and used to compute a **violence index**, which includes the prevalence of programs containing any violence, the frequency of violent episodes, and the proportion of characters who are either perpetrators or victims of violence.

Some of the criticisms of the Gerbner violence profile are justified while others are minor or unsupported. For instance, their samples based on a single week of programs in the fall have been criticized as unrepresentative, but some studies have shown good stability of the measures when other periods of programming were analyzed (Gerbner et al., 1977). Similarly, the exclusion of news programs is not a serious problem, for television drama, television news, and newspaper front pages have been found to be similar in the proportion of violent stories or programs (Comstock et al., 1978). The exclusion of variety shows and specials undoubtedly makes the index higher than it would be if they were included, but the rationale for the index is to analyze programs that tell a story, not all programs. The inclusion in the index of "accidental" violence and violence in the context of humor has been defended on the basis that such episodes are carefully planned by the writers and producers and carry an implicit mes-

sage of *potential victimization* to the audience, regardless of the intent of the characters in the episode. Research by CBS developed some measures that excluded comic violence and violence having nonhuman sources or targets. Naturally, the resulting data showed a lower level of violence, but the pattern of year-to-year changes still roughly paralleled the comparable measures of Gerbner and his colleagues (Comstock et al., 1978).

The greatest problem in interpreting the Gerbner data arises from the violence index, which arbitrarily combines scores based on programs, on episodes, and on characters into an overall index, the meaning of which is obscure because it can be pushed in different directions by its different components. However, data on the separate components are also readily available, such as those shown in Figure 13-1; and this objection does not hold for them, for they have relatively clearcut interpretations. Also, independent research has shown quite high agreement between the Gerbner measures for individual programs and rankings of violence made by the viewing public and by TV critics (Greenberg & Gordon, 1972).

Conclusions About Violent Content. Certainly it is safe to conclude from all the research that there is a very high level of violence on most types of TV programs, and that the level has fluctuated somewhat in various years, apparently largely in response to public pressures on the broadcasting industry. The most pronounced decrease in TV violence occurred in the frequency of killings, a change which Comstock et al. (1978) referred to as a relatively minor "sanitizing" one, because other aspects of violence have changed far less. The industry seems to have concluded that violence is a necessary ingredient to attract and hold audiences, and whenever the audience ratings of violent programs are high, the networks tend to present more such programs in the following year (Clark & Blankenburg, 1972). However, some research has suggested that there is no correlation between the amount of violence on a TV series and the popularity of the series as shown by Nielsen ratings (e.g., Diener & DeFour, 1978; Himmelweit, Swift, & Jaeger, 1980). It appears

Photograph courtesy of George Gerbner. Reprinted by permission.

Box 13-1

GEORGE GERBNER, WATCHDOG ON TV VIOLENCE

George Gerbner was born in Budapest, Hungary, in 1919 and won first prize in a national literary competition as a teenager. In 1939 he emigrated to the United States, where he quickly achieved an outstanding command of the language and earned a B.A. in journalism from the University of California at Berkeley in 1942. After a brief period as a reporter and columnist for the *San Francisco Chronicle*, he became a U.S. citizen in 1943 and enlisted in the army. He served overseas with the secret services and received a field commission and Bronze Star for operations behind enemy lines.

After the war Gerbner worked as an editor for the U.S. Information Service and taught at junior colleges before earning his Ph.D. in communication at the University of Southern California in 1955. He was a faculty member at the University of Illinois until 1964, when he moved to the University of Pennsylvania, where he later served for many years as Dean of the Annenberg School of Communication. Since

1989 he has been Dean Emeritus and has held visiting professorships at universities in five countries.

Gerbner directed many research projects on mass communications, with funding from the National Science Foundation, the U.S. Office of Education, UNESCO, the International Sociological Association, the President's Commission on the Causes and Prevention of Violence, and many other organizations. He studied topics as diverse as the portrayal of mental illness in the media, images of teachers and schools, film heroes, media treatments of aging, press coverage of foreign news, and violence on television. The longtime editor of the *Journal of Communication*, he is especially noted for his theories about the "cultivation effect" of television in influencing viewers' norms of expected social behavior, and for heading a project to develop "cultural indicators" through analysis of trends in television content and effects.

that *action,* rather than violence, may be the program element that most strongly attracts viewers. This conclusion has been supported by the popularity in recent years of series that featured relatively nonviolent ac-

tion in hospitals or rescue situations, such as "ER" or "Rescue 911."

In a later section of this chapter we will consider the effects that media violence has on the behavior of adults and children. In the meantime, we will focus on two other aspects of media content, sexuality and commercial advertising.

Sexuality in the Media

Next to violence, the presentation of sexuality has been the second most controversial public issue regarding the media. Public concern about the notably increasing amount of sex in movies was a major factor in the film industry's 1968 adoption of its system for rating offensiveness (using categories of G, PG, R, and X), and the recent additions of PG-13 and NC-17 ratings (meaning not suitable for children under 13 and 17 respectively). As mentioned above, substantial minorities of survey respondents have often expressed criticism of the amount of sex on TV—mostly in relation to its availability to children.

Content analysis studies show that sexuality on TV has increased since 1975, particularly after 9 p.m. Though explicit sexual intercourse seldom appears on TV, the frequency of sexual references and seductive behavior has increased over the past 25 years, and these portrayals have been becoming more and more explicit (Brown, Childers, & Waszak, 1990; Silverman, Sprafkin, & Rubinstein, 1979). Research also indicates that different types of TV shows portray sexuality differently (Greenberg, 1994). For example, nighttime soap operas typically depict the relationships surrounding sexual activity, detective shows frequently focus on the sexual underworld, and news shows often discuss deviant or extraordinary sexual behavior (Smith, 1991). Interestingly, the music television channel (MTV), which is particularly popular among adolescents, tends to depict men as dominant, and women as sexual and subservient recipients of both implied and explicit sexual advances (Sommers-Flanagan, Sommers-Flanagan, & Davis, 1993).

Patterns of changes in the portrayal of sexuality on television over three decades are summarized in Table 13-3.

Advertising

A final important category of media content is commercials and advertising. In our capitalistic system, almost all the media are in the business of delivering a

mass audience of consumers to advertisers. Even the "noncommercial" stations of the Public Broadcasting System have to keep holding fundraising campaigns to pay their operating budgets. Though the Public Broadcasting System receives some government funding, in the U.S. we have nothing close to the government-subsidized but independently run networks of the British Broadcasting Corporation, the Canadian Broadcasting Corporation, or similar systems in European countries (Day, 1995). Because advertisers support the U.S. media, advertising is a central part of broadcasting and almost as important in the print media.

On television, the average amount of audience attention to commercials is lower than for other types of programming; they provide occasions for the refrigerator raid and the bathroom break. Even allowing for that, commercials still occupy about 15% of the audience's actual viewing time (Bechtel, Achelpohl, & Akers, 1972). However, in recent years, so much effort and money have been lavished on TV commercials that they are often more riveting than the programs they interrupt. On children's morning programs, commercials make up 20% of the air time on weekends, and 17.5% on weekdays—ceiling limits which were mandated by the 1990 Children's Television Act. In the 1970s it was estimated that the average American child, watching TV about four hours a day, was exposed to over 20,000 commercials every year (Adler et al., 1977). That figure is even higher today due to increased advertising minutes and shorter commercials (Kunkel & Roberts, 1991).

One factor slightly offsetting this avalanche of advertising is that public television stations do not show product commercials, and they devote more than 50% of their air time to children's programs, compared with less than 10% for commercial stations (Hoynes, 1994; Twentieth Century Fund, 1993). As of 1991, 98% of all U.S. households had access to a public television station, and 54% of them watched at least one public television show each week—that's 45 million viewers! However, public television's average share of the nationwide TV audience at any given time is only about 2%. Although this share is very small compared to the networks, it represents more viewers than CNN, the Discovery Channel, and A&E combined (Twentieth Century Fund, 1993).

TABLE 13-3   Prime-Time Television's Portrayal of Sexuality Across Three Decades

		Years			
	Measure	*1955–64*	*1965–74*	*1975–84*	*Total*
Extra-marital sex theme frequency	(*N*)	4	18	41	63
Extra-marital sex, no judgment or OK as recreation	(%)	25.0	77.8	78.1	74.6
Extra-marital sex is acceptable if people are in love	(%)	25.0	16.7	14.6	15.9
Extra-marital sex is wrong in all cases	(%)	50.0	5.6	7.3	9.5
Prostitution theme frequency	(*N*)	0	8	9	17
Prostitution is fact of life/ sympathetic to prostitutes	(%)	0.0	25.0	22.2	23.5
No judgment about prostitutes/ view is unclear	(%)	0.0	75.0	66.7	70.6
Prostitution is acceptable	(%)	0.0	0.0	11.1	5.9
*Adultery theme frequency	(*N*)	10	8	18	36
No judgment about adultery**	(%)	70.0	62.5	77.8	72.2
Homosexuality theme frequency	(*N*)	0	1	5	6
Homosexuality is a viable alternative	(%)	0.0	0.0	40.0	33.3
Unclear if homosexuality is right or wrong	(%)	0.0	100.0	60.0	66.7

*Adultery is defined as sex where at least one person is currently married to someone other than the sexual partner.

**Totals do not add to 100% due to categories not listed.

Source: Rothman et al. (1992, p. 230).

Because of the pervasiveness of television commercials, much of the recent research on media advertising has focused on questions of how these TV commercials affect the child viewer—a topic discussed in the next section.

EFFECTS OF THE MEDIA

We turn now from discussing media content to considering the *effects* of the media on people's attitudes and behavior. Because social psychology is the study of how humans are influenced by others, the ways in which television portrayals of "others" affect our thoughts, feelings, and behaviors are central topics in applied social psychology. Due to the ubiquity of TV in our daily lives, it is common to find correlations of TV viewing with various behaviors or attitudes, such as aggression or gender-role beliefs. Yet, it must be admitted that the very pervasiveness of TV and other media exposure causes great difficulty for research in establishing conclusive evidence of a *causal connection* between viewing specific media content and a resulting specific behavior or attitude.

Before taking up media effects in more specific areas, we will mention two general effects of the mass media: the processes of enculturation and attitude change. A third general effect, agenda-setting, will be discussed later under political effects.

Enculturation

Enculturation is the process of instilling and reinforcing the values, beliefs, traditions, behavioral standards, and views of reality that are held by most members of a given culture. This has always been one of the main functions of the media—from the oral storytellers in the time of Homer, to the books handcopied by scribes and monks before the invention of printing, to television today. Because this effect is so pervasive throughout a society and its results are so consistent with existing cultural patterns, it is often overlooked. Recently, however, enculturation has begun to receive considerable research attention as one of the most important of all media effects. Katz (1980) described the media as having "ideological" effects, which almost invariably support and defend the interests of the established power structure in a society; and Gerbner et al. (1980, 1994) are known for their theory about how TV "cultivates" or inculcates in its audience a set of standard assumptions about the nature of social reality—particularly views of who has the power in society. These enculturation effects of the media will be especially relevant when we consider the areas of political beliefs, violence, and sex-role presentations.

A process related to enculturation is **political socialization**—the process by which children become informed about and involved in public affairs and political issues. Compared to other socialization agents, such as parents, schools, and peers, the communication media play important roles in this process. Children from age 7 upward preponderantly list the mass media, particularly TV, as the best source of political information. When measures of actual political information are used as the criterion, there is a negative relationship to the overall amount of children's TV viewing (that is, for entertainment) but a positive relationship to children's TV news viewing (Atkin & Gantz, 1978). As with adults, there is a strong positive relationship between children's newspaper use and their amount of political information (Chaffee et al., 1977; Newspaper Advertising Bureau, 1980). Taken together, all these data point to the mass media's important role as an agent of enculturation.

Attitude Change

The mass media not only have the power to enculturate people and form attitudes, they also have the power to change attitudes and behaviors. The billions of dollars spent on advertising in the U.S. each year attest to the belief in this ability (McGuire, 1986). The topic of attitudes and attitude change is a central one in the field of social psychology, and there have been many theories proposed to explain who will change their attitudes and when. For good reviews of these theories see Eagly and Chaiken (1993), Oskamp (1991), or Petty, Priester, and Wegener (1994).

The first attempts to understand the effects of mass media on human attitudes and behaviors, conducted in the 1920s and 1930s, followed a **direct effects model**. Research during this time assumed that the mass media at that time (radio, newspapers, and films) produced direct effects on their audience (Doob, 1935; Lippmann, 1922). Much of the support for this position came from anecdotal evidence like reactions to the 1929 stock market crash, the public hysteria following Orson Welles's radio broadcast of "War of the Worlds," and the propaganda techniques used in Adolf Hitler's rise to power (Petty & Priester, 1994; Sears & Kosterman, 1994).

A second wave of research, beginning in the 1940s, posited an **indirect effects model** for the influence of the mass media. This model viewed the recipient of a mass communication as an active, thinking, reasoning person, processing and interpreting the message. This was in stark contrast to the "captive, attentive, and gullible" audience that "sat glued to the radio, helpless victims," as viewed by the direct effects model (Sears & Kosterman, 1994). Much of the research supporting this perspective converged on the conclusion that mass media influence usually resulted in crystallizing or sharpening people's beliefs and reinforcing their previous attitudes, rather than dramatically changing their attitudes and determining their behavior.

Contemporary approaches to understanding how the media affect attitudes and behaviors have focused on the *process* of influence and the *conditions* under which the media will or won't have an effect (Petty & Priester, 1994). A major current theory of influence is the **elaboration likelihood model** (Petty & Cacioppo, 1986). According to this theory, mass media communications can influence attitudes through either of two routes—peripheral or central. The **central route** involves effortful processing of information, in which the recipient of the message listens, processes, and evaluates it with respect to existing beliefs and attitudes. Under this type of scrutiny, a message high in objective information will be more likely to lead to attitude change. In contrast, the **peripheral route** to persuasion is a noneffortful processing of the message, relying on cues and heuristics to evaluate the message. Information irrelevant to the message (e.g., the attractiveness of the source, surrounding scenes, or humor) can lead to persuasion. Recent research on this theory has made substantial progress toward understanding when central processing will occur and when peripheral processing will occur. For more details about the theory and its applications, see Chapter 14.

Advertising and Children

Children are influenced by the mass of advertising to which they are exposed (Atkin, 1980; Unnikrishnan & Bajpai, 1996). Children who are heavy TV viewers make about twice as many requests as light TV viewers for their parents to buy the advertised products. Many studies have shown moderately strong relationships between the amount of children's TV viewing and their consumption of candy, heavily sugared cereals, snack foods, soda pop, hot dogs, and empty-calorie foods (Dussere, 1976). Atkin (1980) found that heavy TV viewing increases children's general desire for many kinds of cereals and candies, not just for the advertised brands. Mothers report that by far the most common reason their children give for requesting a particular cereal is the premium offer featured in the cereal ad, and that nutritional reasons are rarely given. The power of advertising aimed at child consumers has been graphically described in this quote from an advertising executive:

> When you sell a kid on your product, if he can't get it, he will throw himself on the floor, stamp his feet and cry. You can't get a reaction like that out of an adult. (*Advertising Age*, 1965, p. 41)

Children also accept quite uncritically the health claims and implications contained in commercials. Young children in particular often accept cartoon characters such as Fred Flintstone as knowledgeable sources of information about what cereals are good for them. Almost two-thirds of a sample of 4- to 7-year-olds stated the belief that an advertised cereal would make them strong after seeing an ad of a circus strongman eating it. Many children do not realize that sugared cereals promote tooth decay, and heavy viewers of TV commercials are twice as likely as light viewers to express the belief that sugared cereals and candies are highly nutritious (Atkin, 1980). The pictures showing ingredients of a "balanced breakfast" in cereal ads do not register on most young children, and two-thirds of a group of preschoolers thought that a bowl of cereal alone would provide the desirable balance.

Of course, it is possible for some of the same advertising techniques to be used toward pronutritional goals. Studies have shown that noncommercial public service announcements can influence children's behavior and attitudes in healthy directions (Goldberg, Gorn, & Gibson, 1978). Also, it should be remembered that the mass media have sometimes been used successfully in campaigns to improve public health, as we discussed in Chapter 12 (McAlister et al., 1980). A wide variety of research on the impact of television on children is summarized in a volume by Berry and Asamen (1993).

Fortunately, children become less susceptible to commercials' claims and implications as they grow older (Dorr, 1986). Before the age of 7, less than half understand that the intent of commercials is to sell products (Ward, Wackman, & Wartella, 1977). Even after children become aware of commercials' selling intent, however, they may still be oblivious to the resulting biased presentation of information and emotional appeals (Roberts & Bachen, 1981). By age 8, a majority of children who are asked whether commercials always tell the truth will answer "no," and by age 10 a large majority say "no" (Ward et al., 1977). However, lower-class and Black children are generally more trusting of advertising claims than are other groups (Wartella, 1980). Even after children develop skepticism about commercials, their defenses can be worn down by a continuing advertising campaign, as in the barrage of pre-Christmas toy ads (Rossiter & Robertson, 1974).

Evidence that children (especially those younger than 8 years old) are especially susceptible to advertising has prompted public concern and governmental hearings. In 1978 the FTC held regulatory hearings concerning the issue of broadcast advertising to children. However, the nation's businesses, advertisers, and broadcasters combined their resources and put together a war chest of over $15 million to fight all attempts to cut down or eliminate ads to children. They generated so much pressure on Congress that it cut back on the FTC's powers and funding and threatened for a time to kill the agency completely (Choate, 1980). This led to a period of deregulation in the 1980s during which many of the hard-fought gains of the 1970s were repealed, and only recently with the passage of the Children's Television Act of 1990 has the pendulum begun to swing back in the other direction.

One particularly controversial type of advertising strategy is the "program-length commercial." These are television shows targeted at children that are based on a line of toys. The ban on these types of shows was removed during the deregulatory trend of the early 1980s, and toy manufacturers again joined forces with the television industry and advertisers to develop product-based shows (Greenfield et al., 1993). The shows that emerged included "Transformers," "Teenage Mutant Ninja Turtles," and "Power Rangers." However, despite the controversial nature of these types of television shows, there has been little research on the psychological effects they have on the children who watch them.

The Children's Television Act, which went into effect in 1992, was a rare piece of legislation because it required four key changes in television programming (Kunkel, 1993). First, television stations were required to broadcast educational programming for children, though the types and amount of educational programming were not specified. Secondly, on children's programs, advertising was limited to 12 minutes per hour on weekends, and 10.5 minutes per hour on weekdays.

Third, the act created a National Endowment for Children's Educational Television; and finally, it ordered the FCC to reexamine its 1984 decision to end the ban on program-length commercials. The act also specified that any station that does not follow these requirements may not have its license renewed in the every-5-year renewal process, though such sanctions have hardly ever been employed. In 1996, President Clinton added the element of persuasion, initiating a campaign for the TV networks to commit themselves to providing a few hours each week of truly educational programs for children.

Political Effects

A question of major social importance is: How do the media affect people's political knowledge, attitudes, and behavior? We will discuss four effects that the mass media have on politics: acquisition of information, cognitive effects, voting behavior, and effects on the political system (McLeod, Kosicki, & McLeod, 1994). For a thorough overview of the effects of the media on political attitudes and behaviors, see Lenart (1994).

Acquisition of Information. A large proportion of the studies on political information has dealt with three topics—the Watergate scandal, the Vietnam War, and the presidential candidate debates during several election campaigns. As one might expect, almost all adults say that they get most of their information about such world and national events from the mass media (Mayer, 1993)—after all, the main other possibilities are first-hand experience or conversations with other people.

In general, these reports are confirmed by the basic findings of many studies that people with high exposure to the media news are typically somewhat (though not greatly) better informed about current affairs than people who use the media less (Roberts & Bachen, 1981). This informational effect is usually stronger for the print media, and it often does not hold for exposure to television news. TV's inferiority in this regard appears largely due to its search for exciting visual events (e.g., demonstrations, or crowd reactions to a candi-

Photograph courtesy of George Comstock. Reprinted by permission.

Box 13-2

GEORGE COMSTOCK, AUTHORITY ON TELEVISION AND HUMAN BEHAVIOR

George Comstock holds the S. I. Newhouse chair in Public Communications at Syracuse University. He received his B.A. in journalism and economics at the University of Washington in 1954 and spent three years in the U.S. Air Force before returning to take an M.A. in communication at Stanford University. After two years as a reporter for the *San Francisco Examiner* and two more years in Bogota, Columbia, as director of a Peace Corps television research project, he earned his Ph.D. in communication from Stanford in 1967. He worked as a research coordinator at the National Institute of Mental Health and as a senior social psychologist at the Rand Corporation before moving to Syracuse University in 1977.

Comstock's job while at NIMH was Science Advisor and Senior Research Coordinator for the Surgeon General's Scientific Advisory Committee on Television and Social Behavior. As such, he was co-editor of the committee's 5-volume series of research reports. At the Rand Corporation, he was senior author of four more volumes summarizing research on *Television and Human Behavior*, and he has also written less technical books such as *Television in America*. Among his other activities, Comstock has served on the National Broadcasting Company (NBC) social science advisory panel, the National Council for Children and Television, editorial boards of journals in the communication field, and as a visiting professor at the Chinese University of Hong Kong.

date) and its corresponding neglect of important substantive political issues. Indeed, Patterson and Mc-Clure (1976) declared, "Network news may be fascinating. It may be highly entertaining. But it is simply not informative" (p. 54). However, this emphasis on the TV news programs overlooks other informative as-

pects of television. Special programs targeted specifically at disseminating political information, like candidate debates and conventions, do convey knowledge to the viewers (Conover & Feldman, 1989). For instance, studies of 1992 Clinton-Bush-Perot debates showed that viewers gained increased information about the candidates and their stands on campaign issues (Zhu, Milavsky, & Biswas, 1994).

Cognitive Effects. Another very important political effect of the media is **agenda-setting**—their influence in telling people, not what to think, but "what to think *about*" (Cohen, 1963, p. 13). The basic theoretical notion here is that the true characteristics of world events and issues (to the extent that they can be objectively described) are only partly reflected in media accounts, and that people's attention and concern are influenced more by the media portrayal than by the actual real-world situation. For example, if the media carry many crime stories, people may become convinced that there is a "crime wave" regardless of whether the actual number of crimes is increasing, decreasing, or remaining constant. In fact, this media focus on crime has occurred in the 1980s and 1990s, even though the total number of crimes in the U.S. has been decreasing ever since its peak year of 1981 (Beckett, 1994; Bureau of Justice Statistics, 1992). Thus, the media content can determine the "public agenda"—the topics that people attend to, are interested in, and try to respond to.

Research on agenda-setting faces a number of complications: for instance, in objectively measuring the real-world situation, defining the media coverage and the public agenda, and trying to determine the presence and direction of causal relationships among these variables (McCombs, 1994). In spite of these difficulties, there is increasing evidence that media emphasis often does differ from the nature of real-life events, and that public concern follows the media emphasis rather than the actual events (Iyengar & Kinder, 1987). For instance, media coverage of the Vietnam War reached a peak and started to decline before action in the war reached a peak; and meanwhile, people's poll responses about the most important national problem followed the media coverage rather than the actual events of the war (Funkhouser, 1973).

Voting Behavior. Studies on voting behavior have typically looked for direct effects, and for the most part, have been unsuccessful. What is presented on television and in other media does not appear to *directly* change the way a person will vote. More recent research has treated voting as a complex behavior that

can be indirectly influenced by a variety of sources, including the mass media such as television.

In general, the media are much more likely to *reinforce* voting intentions than to change them (Comstock et al., 1978; Katz, 1971). Media advertising typically has much less effect in political campaigns than in product sales campaigns because other determining factors, such as personal involvement and party identification, are more important in the political sphere. The media's main role in elections is to focus attention on the campaign and to provide information about the candidates and issues. Even the historic presidential-candidate debates have had mostly informational effects, though they have apparently also influenced the votes of a relatively small but possibly decisive group of voters (Kraus, 1979).

Although the media may not have a strong direct effect on changing votes, they can affect *how many* votes are cast in an election. Noelle-Neumann (1984, 1992) suggested that people implicitly make judgments about which side is winning in a close race, or on a hotly debated issue. These personal judgments, which are strongly influenced by the media, lead to a reduction in the number of votes cast for the losing side. Early coverage of elections, or reports from random surveys, can foster these judgments about who is winning, and can lead to a **spiral of silence** among the perceived losers.

Effects on the Political System. Television, since its first major role in U.S. politics in the 1952 election, has increasingly transformed the whole political system. It can not only influence politics by focusing, crystallizing, or swaying public opinion, but it can also greatly affect the politicians who make policy decisions. Because of its large audiences, television has increasingly determined the nature of campaign activities and expenditures. In most close races, the politician who spends the most money on advertising wins the election (Dawson & Zinser, 1971). The media—through publicity, paid advertisements, and news coverage—also have a strong ability to directly influence the amount of money raised for a campaign. Because of the importance of media coverage in an election, campaign staffs and the candidates themselves have had to become media experts.

Effects on Gender Roles

The data that we presented earlier in this chapter on the gender-role content of mass media presentations provide the starting point for a classic example of an enculturation effect. Because women are typically presented as domestic, passive, weak, or even absent, will girls and women learn and accept these gender-role behaviors as appropriate for them? And complementarily, will boys and men learn that they should be strong, unemotional, violent, and controlling?

Research on such effects is difficult to conduct. Unexposed control groups are unavailable because traditional gender-role presentations are so pervasive that everyone has been exposed to them frequently, and nontraditional gender-role presentations are still relatively rare (Pingree & Hawkins, 1980). However, children who watch much television have been found to give more traditional gender-role descriptions than do those who watch less (Freuh & McGhee, 1975). Children who viewed non-gender-stereotyped programs were more accepting of nontraditional occupational roles, and similar findings occurred with 5- and 6-year-old girls who saw cartoons with nonstereotypic gender roles (Davidson, Yasuna, & Tower, 1979; Miller & Reeves, 1976). Girls who watched a large number of TV beauty ads were more likely than others to believe that beauty was a necessary condition for popularity with men (Tan, 1979). And even among college women, heavy viewers of soap operas were found to give significantly higher estimates of the number of problems of illegitimacy, serious operations, nervous breakdowns, abortions, and divorces in the real world (Buerkel-Rothfuss & Mayes, 1981).

An encouraging report on how to change such stereotypic attitudes and perceptions came from an evaluation study of "Freestyle," a television series that was designed to reduce gender-role stereotypes and increase career orientations in grade-school girls. Viewers became more accepting of girls in nontraditional gender roles, and this effect was larger and persisted for as long as nine months among children who had seen the program in school, accompanied by a class discussion (Johnston & Davidson, 1980).

All the above data provide evidence for an enculturation theory of the media's impact on gender-role development, or what has also been called a "cultivation effect" (Gerbner et al., 1994)—i.e., an emphasis on stereotyped perceptions and attitudes.

Effects on Violence and Aggression

As with gender-role attitudes, research on media violence has also been interpreted as evidence of a **cultivation effect**, a term originating in Gerbner's extensive work on TV violence. That is, the violence that is so pervasive in many of the mass media is seen as having a conditioning or adaptation effect on viewers, implanting and cultivating the idea that violence in society is common, natural, and acceptable. Gerbner et al. (1978, 1980, 1994) have presented data showing that heavy viewers of TV are more likely than light viewers to perceive high chances of encountering violence, to be afraid to walk around their neighborhood at night, to feel mistrustful of other people, and to believe that they live in a "mean world" (see Cantor, 1994, for a review). However, this cultivation theory is still controversial, for the effect of TV viewing was markedly reduced or eliminated in some reanalyses of comparable survey data when controls were introduced for demographic variables that might produce similar paranoid perceptions, such as being a woman, being Black, or living in a large city or a high-crime area (Doob & Macdonald, 1979; Hughes, 1980).

Going beyond cultivation effects, much social psychological research has focused on the question of a direct causal effect of TV violence in making viewers *more violent or aggressive themselves*. This causal hypothesis was supported by the Surgeon General's Scientific Advisory Committee (1972), which concluded that television violence was probably a contributory cause of increased aggressive behavior among young viewers, and it was advanced even more strongly by the ten-year follow-up report from the National Institute of Mental Health (1982). What is the scientific evidence for this view?

Laboratory Experiments. Some of the evidence began back around 1960 with Bandura's famous laboratory studies, in which children who had seen filmed aggressive acts against large Bobo dolls later *imitated* the same actions themselves (Bandura, Ross, & Ross, 1963). Subsequent experiments showed that young boys and girls would also imitate filmed aggressive acts against live human beings (Bandura, 1985; Hanratty, 1969). The laboratory studies since the 1960s have consistently shown that viewing violence on television can cause an increase in aggression immediately following the exposure (Hearold, 1986). Furthermore, these effects are more pronounced among people who are already predisposed to act in an aggressive manner (Josephson, 1987). Even Freedman (1988), who critically reviewed the results of other types of research on TV violence, agreed that the findings in laboratory studies showed a causal relationship between viewing television violence and displaying aggression.

Another effect of viewing media violence that has been demonstrated in laboratory experiments is **desensitization**, or lowered emotional sensitivity to violence (Cline, Croft, & Courrier, 1973). Other studies indicate that this can increase children's and college students' tolerance for real-life aggression (Thomas et al., 1977).

A major question about all such laboratory experiments is their external validity. They take place in circumstances so different from normal TV viewing or other media use that their findings may not be applicable to real-world media issues. Therefore, many correlational studies and field experiments have been done in more realistic settings in order to investigate questions about the effects of media violence. Here the emphasis is usually not on imitation of a specific act seen in the media, but rather on the relationship between continued exposure to media violence and a pattern of heightened aggressive behavior of many sorts in everyday situations—that is, a pattern of general **disinhibition of aggression** (Liebert & Schwartzberg, 1977).

Correlational Research. Studies using correlational methods have typically found positive relationships between viewing televised violence and various measures of aggressiveness in daily life. Studies that measured violence in children's total TV viewing schedule have usually found stronger relationships than those using violence measures based on a few favorite programs (Comstock et al., 1978). In a number of studies

with children ranging from third grade through high school, the dependent measures which showed significant relationships to violent TV viewing included the following: deviant acts such as petty delinquency by both boys and girls (McIntyre & Teevan, 1972); having gotten into serious fights or hurt someone else badly (Belson, 1978; Robinson & Bachman, 1972); conflict with parents, fighting, and delinquent behavior (McCarthy et al., 1975); and perceived effectiveness of aggression and stated willingness to use it oneself, in both American and English samples of boys and girls (Greenberg, 1974; McLeod, Atkin, & Chaffee, 1972). Many of these relationships held up well even when statistical controls were introduced by holding constant the children's social class, school grades, or amount of exposure to nonviolent television.

The most impressive of the correlational studies were a series of longitudinal studies of children's aggression and television viewing habits conducted by Huesmann and his colleagues (Eron et al., 1972; Eron & Huesmann, 1984; Huesmann, 1986; Huesmann & Miller, 1994). In the first of several studies, the same sample of New York schoolchildren were measured at ages 8, 18, and 30 (Huesmann & Miller, 1994; Lefkowitz et al., 1977). Results showed that the boys in the sample were strikingly different from the girls in their aggression scores, and they showed much stronger patterns of relationships between variables. In spite of all the intervening years, and the resulting chances for countervailing effects of other variables, the boys' amount of exposure to TV violence at age 8 was a significant predictor of peer-rated aggression both 10 years later and 22 years later (the results from the 10-year follow-up are presented in Figure 13-2). Moreover, the amount of aggression at age 8 was not related to viewing violent TV 10 years later. The logic involved here is that a cause must come before its effect, so a relationship between two variables across time can indicate the direction of causation between the variables. This design is called a **cross-lagged correlational study**, meaning that the key relationships between measures are the diagonal ones, which *cross* between measures of two different concepts and over a *lag* in time (in this case, 10 years). If one variable (in this case, watching violent TV) is the cause of another,

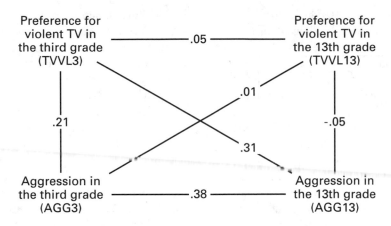

FIGURE 13-2   Correlations between a preference for violent television and peer-rated aggression for 211 boys over a 10-year lag. (*Source:* Eron et al., 1972, p. 257.)

the diagonal correlation of its time-1 measure with the time-2 measure of the other variable should be significant, and the other diagonal should be substantially smaller.

As Figure 13-2 shows, boys' early viewing of violent TV predicted aggression 10 years later ($r = .31$)—the hypothesized causal cross-correlation—whereas early aggression did not predict viewing of violent TV 10 years later ($r = .01$). This is suggestive evidence of the hypothesized relationship: that the early viewing may be a cause of the later aggressiveness. Though early aggression also was significantly correlated with later aggression, and thus is a likely additional causal factor, the authors were able to show statistically that early aggression could not be the *sole* cause of both early viewing of TV violence and aggression 10 years later. In further reanalyses they have continued to find evidence that this effect of boys' early violence viewing on their later aggression is a causal one, not just a spurious concomitant relationship (Huesmann et al., 1973). Similar results were found for the 22-year follow-up (Huesman et al., 1984), as well as for a second series of longitudinal studies with 1297 children in Australia, Finland, Israel, Poland, and the United States (Huesmann & Eron, 1986). For a thorough overview of the longitudinal studies of television violence and aggression, see Huesmann and Miller (1994).

Field Experiments. As we have discussed in Chapter 4, experiments, which entail random assignment of subjects to conditions, provide the most convincing evidence of causal relationships. In the television violence area, a number of such experiments have been done in real-life settings, and most of them support the link between TV violence and aggression (Comstock, 1978; Wood, Wong, & Chachere, 1991).

Adding together the findings from laboratory experiments, correlational studies, and field experiments, the principle that media violence can increase viewers' interpersonal aggression seems to be thoroughly established (Friedrich-Cofer & Huston, 1986; Murray & Kippax, 1979), though there are a few reviewers who still favor the null hypothesis—that is, that there is no demonstrated relationship (Fisher, 1983; Freedman, 1984, 1988). The conclusion that media violence leads to an increase in aggression was supported in two recent meta-analyses that summarized all types of studies on the effects of television on aggressive behavior in children and adolescents (Paik & Comstock, 1994; Wood et al., 1991). The results indicated that viewing media violence significantly increased aggressive interactions, by both boys and girls, with strangers, classmates, and friends, in both field and laboratory settings. The results were strongest for laboratory studies and for preschool-aged children, but they were significant for all age groups including adults, and for all types of studies.

Interacting Variables. As a result of this rather overwhelming evidence of the main effect of media violence, many recent studies have turned toward a search for conditions that amplify or minimize that basic effect. Several of the field experiments described above suggest that delinquents may be particularly susceptible to media violence effects. Similarly, other studies have shown larger effects for the initially more aggressive children within normal school-age groups than for their less aggressive peers (Huesman & Miller, 1994; Surgeon General's Scientific Advisory Committee, 1972).

Several kinds of studies show that the presence of negative implications about media violence can decrease its aggressive effects. For instance, when an adult criticizes filmed aggression, 10-year-old children are less likely to imitate it later (Grusec, 1973). Violence that is perpetrated for a mixture of good and bad motives stimulates more aggression in child audiences than violence performed for entirely bad motives (Collins & Zimmerman, 1975). Similarly, among college students, seeing "justified" violence or ambiguous or unexplained violence leads to more aggressive behavior than viewing unjustified violence (Meyer, 1972). Ironically, however, these findings indicate that seeing a TV "good guy" beating up the villain is more likely to produce later viewer aggression than is seeing the villain beating up his victims—an unanticipated effect of the traditional movie code that the villain has to get his comeuppance in the end. Finally, the absence or delay of negative consequences for filmed violence will encourage more aggression among children than if negative consequences are promptly and clearly portrayed (Collins, 1973). Comstock et al. (1978, p. 249) summed up the research evidence in this area as follows:

> When violence is portrayed as punished, aggressiveness is more likely to be inhibited. When portrayed as rewarded, when portrayed as leading to no consequences, when portrayed as justified, and when performed by an attractive character—all common characteristics of contemporary television programming—the probability of subsequent aggression increases.

Another kind of interacting variable is the similarity between the media situation and the viewer's later environment. A long series of studies by Berkowitz and his colleagues has shown that more aggressive responses will be displayed by viewers of media violence if the cues in their subsequent environment are highly similar to those in the media portrayal—for instance, if similar potential weapons are present, or potential victims with similar names (Geen & Berkowitz, 1967).

An important redeeming feature of the media is that they can reduce the expression of viewer aggression by distracting and entertaining viewers. Several laboratory studies in which subjects were angered and then shown nonaggressive films have demonstrated that the distraction from the film reduced the amount of aggression that was subsequently displayed (Donnerstein, Donnerstein, & Barrett, 1976).

Pornography and Effects on Sexuality

Many important social issues revolve around human sexuality—for instance, teen pregnancy, the AIDS epidemic, and sexual assault. A great deal of information about sex is conveyed through mass media, including music, magazines, videos, television, and movies (Harris, 1994). Thus, it is important to ask the question: What effect does viewing sexually explicit material have on people?

Social psychological research on *pornography* or *erotica* (a more neutral term) has taken several paths. There is general agreement among research studies that viewing of sexually explicit material may produce sexual arousal. For instance, among undergraduates, over 80% of both males and females reported genital sensations in response to viewing an erotic film, but such arousal effects decrease with repeated exposures (Eccles, Marshall, & Barbaree, 1988; Howard, Reifler, & Liptzin, 1970). An interesting research finding, consistent with many people's personal experience, is that less explicit sexual scenes may be more arousing than highly explicit portrayals (Byrne & Lamberth, 1970).

Values and Attitudes. A frequent concern among parents is that exposing their children to sexual material in the mass media may desensitize them to certain expressions of sexuality (Harris, 1994). Some research suggests that viewing idealized bodies in the media can lead to less satisfaction with the viewer's own body and with their partner's body (McKenzie-Mohr & Zanna, 1990; Weaver, Masland, & Zillmann, 1984). For example, shows like soap operas or "Baywatch" present an idealized image of attractiveness to which few of us can measure up in real life. Exposure to erotic material can also lead to an overestimation of the popularity of certain sexual practices, as well as the frequency with which people have sex (Zillmann & Bryant, 1984—in this regard, recall the findings in Chapter 3 about the average frequency of sexual intercourse). Exposure to sexual material also causes less satisfaction with affection, a greater acceptance of sex without emotional involvement, a greater acceptance of violence toward women, and a greater acceptance of premarital and extramarital sex (Zillmann & Bryant, 1982, 1988).

Behaviors. Though exposure to sexual material can change attitudes, it doesn't necessarily mean that viewing sexual material will lead to acting-out or criminal sexual behavior. In fact, the report of the U.S. Commission on Obscenity and Pornography (1970) concluded that there was no convincing evidence of damaging personal or social effects of pornography, specifically mentioning lack of evidence for increased delinquency or criminal sexual behavior. However, more recent assessments (Donnerstein & Linz, 1994; Donnerstein, Linz, & Penrod, 1987; Final Report of the Surgeon General's Commission on Pornography, 1986; Reed, 1994) have indicated that violence, or violence mixed with sexuality, though not sexuality alone, can have harmful effects on subsequent behavior (see below for more details).

There are competing theories for the effects of sexuality in the media. According to the Freudian concept of **catharsis**, viewing sex in the media should relieve sexual urges and lead to a gratification that does not require sexual intercourse or interaction with another person. A counter hypothesis is **disinhibition**—the theory that watching sex in the media will make a person less likely to inhibit sexual urges and more likely to act on them.

The research on this topic, although clearly not supporting the catharsis hypothesis, does not strongly support the disinhibition hypothesis either. Establishing a causal link between viewing sexually explicit material and sexual deviance is difficult, primarily because it is impossible to study the topic experimentally. The correlational data, though suggestive, do not provide firm evidence of a causal connection. For example, the number of cases of rape has increased in most Western countries over the past 20 years, and during this same time period, the availability of sexually explicit material has also risen. Evidence for a positive correlation between rape and pornography has been found in Japan, Australia, and the United States (Abramson & Hayashi, 1984; Harris, 1994). In a U.S. study, Baron and Straus (1989) found a correlation coefficient of +.64 between rape rates and circulation rates of eight sex magazines across the 50 states.

In contrast with research on media sexuality alone, research on the effects of *violent sexuality* is clear (Donnerstein & Linz, 1994; Lyons, Anderson, & Larson, 1994). Violent sexuality refers to media portrayals of sexual scenes combined with rape, torture, or mutilation of women—a topic included in one out of every eight Hollywood films (Wilson et al., 1992). These types of media portrayals can lead to the development of the false belief that women enjoy forcible sex and find it exciting—a **rape myth** (Lonsway & Fitzgerald, 1994). Research indicates that watching scenes of violent sexuality significantly increases male viewers' acceptance of aggression against women and tends to increase their acceptance of rape myths. Interestingly, these effects are reversed for women (Malamuth & Check, 1981). In summarizing this research, Donnerstein and Linz (1994) stated that it:

> consistently indicates that exposure to depictions of violence against women, either juxtaposed with mildly erotic scenes (slasher films) or in the form of sexually explicit or nonexplicit rape scenes, results in callousness toward female victims of violence, especially rape victims, and in other antisocial attitudinal, perceptual, and behavioral effects. (p. 15)

Prosocial Effects

As mentioned earlier, media portrayals can also have favorable effects. We will limit this discussion of their effects on **prosocial behavior** to its central aspects—

actions such as cooperation, sharing, and helping others—though other desirable behaviors studied under this general heading have included empathy, friendliness, self-control, creativity, diminishing fears, and avoidance of stereotyping (Hearold, 1986; Huston, Watkins, & Kunkel, 1989; Rushton, 1979). However, research in this area has been relatively rare, and has been conducted almost entirely with children. It is one of the areas where additional media research is most needed.

Almost all the studies of prosocial effects have been done in some sort of laboratory situation, even if they used actual TV or movie programs. Studies using very short audiovisual messages have shown that even brief public service messages illustrating cooperative behavior can encourage children's subsequent cooperation (Forge & Phemister, 1987; Liebert, Sprafkin, & Poulos, 1975). Just as in the area of media violence, the presence and nature of consequences are important. Seeing models who shared some of their money or candy stimulated viewers to share, and the effect was stronger if the model was rewarded and an explicit reason for the reward was stated (Elliott & Vasta, 1970). Viewers who saw models punished for not sharing also shared more later on (Morris, Marshall, & Miller, 1973). In situations where the model practiced either generosity or greediness and preached the other, child viewers' imitation generally followed the models' behavior rather than their exhortations (Bryan & Schwartz, 1971).

Several studies with actual TV or movie programs have shown prosocial effects. There is ample evidence that children do perceive and recall prosocial messages or themes from media programs (Columbia Broadcasting System, 1977). Some TV series such as "Sesame Street," "Mister Rogers' Neighborhood," and "Barney and Friends" have been designed with goals of prosocial learning in mind. Studies of preschool children's responses to these types of shows have typically found some increases in prosocial behavior in comparison with control groups that viewed other programs, but the effects were usually brief and confined to situations quite like those in the programs (Friedrich & Stein, 1973; Paulson, 1974). However, combining the program with similar emphases by the teacher (for

instance, using verbal labeling or role playing) led to considerably stronger subsequent prosocial behavior (Ahammer & Murray, 1979; Friedrich & Stein, 1975). In a major review, Hearold (1986) concluded that the effect of prosocial television on behavior was twice as large as the effect of TV violence on aggression. However, studies of these effects were short-term and limited to laboratory settings.

Thus, there is considerable evidence that seeing prosocial media presentations has the potential for positive effects on children's behavior—in the lab. However, long-term correlational studies have indicated that grade school children's normal everyday viewing of prosocial TV had a very low, almost nonexistent relationship to their prosocial behavior in school (Sprafkin & Rubinstein, 1979; Wiegman, Kuttschreuter, & Baarda, 1992). Wiegman et al. (1992) examined the long-term effects of viewing prosocial television on prosocial behavior among Dutch elementary school children and their parents over a 3-year period. The results from this careful study showed that watching prosocial television was *not* correlated with prosocial behaviors. The likely explanations for this finding center around the fact that prosocial TV constitutes a very small part of television programming. In fact, viewing prosocial TV was strongly correlated ($r = +.90$) with viewing violent television! Thus, children who were watching the prosocial TV also were watching a great deal of violent TV, and because of the disparity in the overall levels of prosocial and violent programming, they were exposed to substantially more violent scenes.

In summary, research on prosocial television indicates that it *can* have a positive effect on behavior. However, this effect appears to be limited to controlled laboratory settings and is short-lived. There is no current evidence that in real life, children who watch prosocial TV act any differently than children who do not.

Summary of Effects. Overall, the research on the effects of television and other mass media on attitudes, politics, aggression, sexuality, gender roles, and prosocial behaviors tends to show that the media do influence people. These effects are usually stronger in controlled laboratory studies than in field experiments. Today, most researchers on the effects of media communication agree that television can have both direct and indirect effects on human thought, feeling, and action. However, the causal link between viewing television and subsequent changes is complex and is moderated by many other variables (McGuire, 1986, 1992).

INTERVENTIONS TO REDUCE TELEVISION'S HARMFUL EFFECTS

TV's potential for harmful consequences is demonstrated by the research findings that watching violent television can cause an increase in aggressive behavior, that children watch more than 30 hours of TV per week, and that children's television is particularly violent. Faced with such findings, researchers in the 1980s began to develop interventions aimed at reducing or eliminating the link between watching violent television and aggressive behavior. Most of these interventions were directed at children in school classrooms (Neuman, 1991).

Critical Television Viewing Skills

In a series of large-scale studies sponsored by the Office of Education and the National PTA, educators and social psychologists developed curricula intended to make children more critical consumers of television. These programs were designed to (a) demystify the television process by showing children how TV shows were made, and (b) teach children to critically evaluate the messages they received from TV. Unfortunately, only a few of these **critical-viewing** projects were systematically evaluated (e.g., Dorr, Graves, & Phelps, 1980; Singer, Zuckerman, & Singer, 1980). Their results showed that the critical-viewing interventions did increase the *amount of information* a child could remember after watching a show, but they did not make the children more critical of the content. Similarly, more recent studies have demonstrated significant changes in knowledge or attitudes, but have typically not found (or not examined) changes in behavior (e.g., Vooijs & Van der Voort, 1993; Watkins et al., 1988).

One often-cited example of effective critical-viewing interventions was a longitudinal study by Huesmann et al. (1983), which began with 672 first- and third-grade children. Of these children, the 25% who watched the most television were selected for an experiment. These 169 high-violence viewers were randomly assigned to either the experimental condition or a placebo condition. Unlike other critical-viewing studies, the experimental condition used social psychological persuasion techniques to change the children's attitudes toward television. The goal was to persuade the children that "watching TV violence was not desirable and that they should not imitate violent television programs" (p. 904). To produce these attitudes, the researchers used counterattitudinal advocacy techniques, where the children wrote arguments that were counter to their original attitude. The results showed that the technique did in fact change attitudes. More importantly, four months after the intervention, children in the experimental condition were significantly less aggressive (as rated by their peers) than children in the control condition (effect size $d = -.39$).

Despite encouraging results such as these, the amount of research devoted to the issue of critical television viewing fell off sharply after 1983. In the 1990s the pendulum appears to have swung back toward regulation, such as the law requiring V-chips in TV sets, mentioned earlier. Instead of relying on parents to supervise their children's use of television, more emphasis has been placed on controlling the content of TV shows. Accordingly, we turn to the final issue in our discussion of the mass media—the role of social psychologists in the formation and evaluation of mass media policies.

MEDIA POLICY ISSUES AND SOCIAL RESEARCH

The television industry, like other media, is subject to legislative, judicial, and executive regulation; the regulations imposed can either determine its organizational structure or attempt to circumscribe its social effects. However, governmental purview over the content of the mass media is sharply limited by the

First Amendment guarantee of free speech. Less formally, the industry is also subject to pressures from the general public, from specialized advocacy organizations, and from various interested agencies and groups, all seeking to influence industry practices or regulatory rulings. The media respond to the governmental regulations, threats of regulation, informal public pressures, and organized group actions in ways that they feel will allow them to continue doing their job with the maximum freedom, effectiveness, and profitability. To forestall greater formal regulation, they sometimes adopt formal self-regulation standards and often adapt informally to current public opinion and governmental concerns as they understand them. However, though the major TV networks and movie studios may adapt to social change in ways that *reflect* societal trends, in the United States they almost never take a leading role in *initiating* social change. For instance, they began hiring ethnic minority actors and reporters as a result of pressure from government and private groups, not as an attempt to pioneer in equal-opportunity employment.

Some of the most prominent suggested areas for control of the media include the ban on TV or radio cigarette commercials, the attempt to remove drug commercials from children's normal viewing hours, and the concern about TV advertising in general, particularly the amount and types of ads on children's programs. In addition, violence, sexuality, obscenity, the depiction of women and ethnic minorities, and the question of public service programming have all excited attempts to regulate the media more closely.

Here is a list of various ways in which social psychological research can contribute to media policy issues:

1. Regulatory hearings. In the hearings concerning the issues of TV advertising and violence, social science data have had an impact, and this trend should increase in the future.

2. Public attitudes. Surveys of media consumer attitudes are of great interest to the media and the advertisers who support them.

3. Media content. Surveys of media content, such as the Gerbner et al. (1994) violence profile, have become vital tools in monitoring trends in programming.

4. Audience patterns. As one example, an important study determined that only 15% of the total amount of children's TV viewing occurs during the late afternoon and Saturday-morning periods that have special children's programming and industry self-regulations on advertising (Adler et al., 1977). This fact led advocacy organizations to press for further controls on both commercials and programming at times when large numbers of children are in the viewing audience.

5. Social effects. All the data on the effects of violence, of stereotyped gender and ethnic roles, of advertising, and so forth, have contributed to the overall climate of public opinion, which led to pressures for regulation.

6. Evaluation of regulations and practices. For instance, are the FTC-required disclaimers in children's commercials (e.g., "some assembly required" for toy kits) understandable to children?—finding: not nearly as understandable as simpler language (Liebert et al., 1977).

7. Evaluation of alternative practices. For instance, if violence in children's programs is presented as unjustified, will the young viewers' subsequent aggressiveness be less than if violence is presented as justified?—finding: yes, it will (Meyer, 1972).

8. Satisfaction of audience needs. For instance, although the national network news doesn't add to audience members' knowledge of issues or candidates during elections (Patterson & McClure, 1976), local TV news *does* add to viewers' local public affairs information (Lucas & Possner, 1975).

We may conclude, with Comstock et al. (1978, p. 485): "The potential role of behavioral and social science in television policy-making, which is many-leveled and complex, is large."

SUMMARY

The mass media have tremendous potential to influence social behavior, and there have been many controversies about their actual role in our society. Social psychologists and other communication researchers have studied many aspects of the media, but have paid by far the most attention to television. Research on people's *use* of the media depicts audience members not as passive recipients, but as active in attempts to satisfy their personal needs for entertainment, information, social contact, or individual self-definition.

The *content* of the mass media has shown rather stable patterns. Though ethnic minority individuals have become more common in TV programs and commercials since the late 1960s, they are still somewhat underrepresented and heavily concentrated in comedy programs. Women's roles have also been treated stereotypically in all the media, with a typical emphasis on passivity, domesticity, and lack of careerism. Violence on TV programs has remained at a relatively high level for the past 30 years, with Saturday morning children's television consistently showing far more violent scenes than prime-time shows. Sexuality and advertising in the media are two other controversial issues, which are particularly criticized for their potential impact on children. Recent trends indicate that sexuality on television is becoming ever more explicit, despite the voluntary self-regulation of sexuality attempted by both the movie and television industries.

The *effects* of the media on human behavior comprise the most studied area of communication research. There is general agreement that the media contribute greatly to enculturation (spreading a society's typical views about the nature of social reality), to attitude changes, and to agenda-setting (indicating what topics people should think about). Research on political effects of the media has studied the areas of acquisition of information, political socialization, voting, and effects on the overall political system. Television has transformed the political system, concentrating attention on the party conventions and largely determining the nature of campaign activities and expenditures. The quantity and quality of political advertisements frequently have a major impact on vote totals.

Research has shown that media sexuality can produce sexual arousal and make viewers' attitudes toward erotica more accepting. There are also clear research findings that viewing violent sexuality can increase males' callous and aggressive attitudes toward women and their acceptance of rape myths. In the 25 years since the 1972 report of the Surgeon General's Scientific Advisory Committee, strong convergent findings from laboratory experiments, correlational studies, and field experiments have indicated that viewing violence can lead to imitative acts, lowered emotional sensitivity, and generalized patterns of higher aggression in viewers' everyday behavior.

Recent studies have turned toward pinpointing interacting variables that amplify or minimize the effects of media violence (for instance, the presence of negative implications or consequences). There has also been some success in developing critical-viewing interventions that will help children to resist harmful influences of TV on their attitudes and/or behavior. Fortunately, the media can also promote prosocial effects, such as increases in cooperation, sharing, or helping behavior.

In developing these kinds of findings, applied social psychological research can contribute to resolving media policy issues by providing evidence for regulatory hearings, industry self-regulation, or citizen pressure groups.

SUGGESTED READINGS

Bryant, J., & Zillmann, D. (Eds.). (1994). *Media effects: Advances in theory and research.* Hillsdale, NJ: Erlbaum.—An excellent summary of many ways in which the mass media can affect human thought, feeling, and behavior, with chapters written by many of the leading researchers in the area.

Comstock, G. (1991). *Television in America* (2nd ed.). Newbury Park, CA: Sage.—A fine overview of research on the content, effects, and public policy implications of television.

Gerbner, G., Morgan, M., & Signorielli, N. (1994). *Television violence profile no. 16: The turning point from research to action.* Philadelphia: Annenberg School for Communication, University of Pennsylvania.—One of the latest in a long series of articles assessing the current level of TV violence and how it cultivates viewers' perceptions of a "mean world."

Iyengar, S., & Kinder, D. R. (1987). *News that matters: Agenda-setting and priming in a television age.* Chicago: University of Chicago Press.—An overview of the agenda-setting effects of television news.

Kunkel, D. (1993). Policy and the future of children's television. In G. Berry & J. Asamen (Eds.), *Children and television: Images in a changing sociocultural world* (pp. 273–290). Newbury Park, CA: Sage.—Discusses public policy regarding television, including desirable future directions of these policies.

Rothman, S., Lichter, S., & Lichter, L. (1992). Television's America. In S. Rothman (Ed.), *The mass media in liberal democratic societies* (pp. 221–266). New York: Paragon House.—Reports the results of content analyses of television programming over a 30-year period.

CHAPTER 14

Consumer Issues— Advertising

Advertisements are now so numerous that they are very negligently perused, and it is therefore become necessary to gain attention by magnificence of promises and by eloquence sometimes sublime and sometimes pathetick.

—Samuel Johnson (1758)

Think for a minute about what leads you to buy a product such as a box of cereal. What factors do you consider in deciding which one to buy? What have the manufacturer and the advertiser done to get you to buy their product? What protection do you have, or should you have, from receiving an inferior or dangerous product? If the product involved were a major purchase, such as an automobile, would your answer to any of these questions be different? These are some of the issues studied by consumer psychologists.

In this chapter we will consider three major approaches used to study consumer issues. The first approach is to investigate the attitudes and behavior of consumers as they absorb information and make decisions about products. The second is to examine the techniques used by marketers to persuade people to buy and consume their products. The third approach is to consider consumer protection issues and policies.

CONSUMER ATTITUDES AND BEHAVIOR

This first approach studies consumers themselves, and it draws on and contributes to the empirical findings and theories developed by social psychologists concerning people's attitudes and behavior. It was not until the 1960s that consumer-oriented research on these topics became widespread. In this section we will summarize three of the major social psychological theories of attitudes and behavior and illustrate how they apply to consumers.

The Yale Model of Persuasive Communication

Think again about the steps that you might go through between the time you first heard about a new product—for example, a cereal with the unlikely name of Blueberry Morning—and the time that you bought it in a store. One of the main theories of persuasive communication, developed by a well-known team of researchers at Yale University, lists the major steps as **exposure**, **attention**, **comprehension**, **acceptance**, **retention**, and **action** (cf. Hovland, Janis, & Kelley, 1953; McGuire, 1985). Normally, these steps occur in the sequence stated, and if any step is not completed, the chain of persuasion is broken.

To reach the first step in this process, the product manufacturer hires a team to design an advertising campaign, and buys advertising space or time in print and/or broadcast media. When the campaign begins, you, the potential consumer, may or may not see an ad in your local paper or on TV. If this exposure attempt fails, you won't carry out any of the other steps unless you see the product on your supermarket shelf or hear about it from someone who has been exposed. If you do see the ad, you may be aware of seeing it, or you may skip right over it without giving it any attention. If you do attend to it, distracting or confusing elements may prevent you from comprehending what it is about—for instance, that happened with initial TV ads for the Infiniti automobile, which showed beautiful scenery but didn't focus clearly on the car that they were advertising.

In turn, comprehension of the message is usually necessary but definitely not sufficient for its acceptance. You may understand the ad for Blueberry Morning, but be allergic to blueberries or unconvinced that they would taste good in cold cereal. Even if you accept the message and resolve to buy the product, you may forget about it before the next time you shop for groceries. Finally, even if you remember the message and your intention to buy the product, you may fail to buy it because you didn't find it on the shelf, or because lack of money or attention to other purchases prevented you from following through.

Research studies have established several facts about these steps in persuasion. First, as just illustrated, the steps are "loosely linked" so that successfully taking one step does not necessarily lead to accomplishing the next one. Second, particular aspects of the persuasive message may have different effects on the various steps. Here are two examples: (a) a message that is simple may be easily understood but be unconvincing and therefore not accepted; (b) a picture of a beautiful woman or a handsome man standing by an expensive sports car may be eagerly viewed and well remembered, but may not produce intentions to buy that kind of car. Third, different characteristics of the perceiver may help to determine success or failure at the various steps in persuasion. For example, competing activities such as a "bathroom break" may prevent exposure to a TV commercial; distraction by ongoing conversation may hinder attention to it; or low intelligence may decrease its comprehension. On the other hand, high intelligence or a high level of knowledge about the topic may reduce acceptance of a message, while lack of opportunity or lack of money may prevent acting as the message recommended.

Thus, the effects of persuasive communication are a complex result of many variables interacting with each other. Though the final stage in the process, actual purchase behavior, is the payoff for manufacturers, advertisers, and retailers, the great majority of consumer research studies have measured earlier stages of the persuasion process and hoped that there would be a linkage to the final stage of buying. For instance, the Nielsen ratings of TV viewership pertain to exposure, while studies of recall of ads measure attention, and experiments on persuasion typically measure acceptance of messages.

In the following paragraphs, we will briefly illustrate research on each of these stages of persuasion with a few representative and interesting findings about the effects of persuasive messages. Much fuller presentations can be found in recent reviews of research on consumer behavior (e.g., Foxall & Goldsmith, 1994; Mullen & Johnson, 1990; Tybout & Artz, 1994). A major limitation of much of the careful experimental research on consumer psychology is that investigators' emphasis on experimental control has often led them to conduct laboratory studies with college students as subjects, the results of which may not

generalize to real-world settings with diverse types of people and chaotic exposure conditions (Wells, 1993).

Studies of Exposure. As mentioned in the preceding chapter, television is by far the dominant medium of communication in the United States and in most other industrialized countries. The average U.S. adult or child watches TV for about three hours per day, though there are wide individual differences related to age, sex, education, social class, and employment (Gerbner et al., 1994). During three hours of network television, viewers may be exposed to over 70 TV commercials per day (*American Demographics*, 1989). However, advertisements are so ubiquitous in our society—not only on TV and radio, but also in newspapers and magazines, on billboards, placards in buses and trains, signs on buildings, and on posters everywhere—that it has been estimated that most adults are exposed to about 1500 every day. In other regards, though, people are rather selective in the information to which they voluntarily expose themselves (e.g., which books, magazines, or TV programs) and also in their patterns of travel and locations for shopping or recreation (Foxall & Goldsmith, 1994).

Repetition of exposure to information has been shown to increase attitudinal favorability, but seeing or hearing the same message several times within an hour or two produces a "saturation effect," after which exposure to the identical content causes a decrease in favorability (Gorn & Goldberg, 1980; Rethans, Swasy, & Marks, 1986). Thus, repetition of noticeably different commercials for the same product may yield the greatest favorability (Schumann, Petty, & Clemons, 1990).

Studies of Attention. Among the countless visual and auditory stimuli that bombard each of us, there is a severe limit on the number that we can pay attention to (Cohen & Chakravarti, 1990). In general, people pay more attention to topics that are important or motivating to them. Though most Americans give some regular attention to the mass media, the quality of their attention is generally low. For instance, in "reading" a newspaper, less than half of the readers even examine the front-page stories, while the comics, entertainment, and sports sections get the largest amount of attention (Cutlip, 1954; Frank & Greenberg, 1980). Similarly

- bombarded, ... must be sel've w/ attn
- pay attn to ads that are imp or motivating to us
- usu entertainmt > info
- kids - quantity; adults - quality

Consumer Issues—Advertising **283**

with television, entertainment generally takes precedence over information, and even viewers who watch the TV news can only recall about one-fourth of the stories a few hours later (Stauffer, Frost, & Rybolt, 1983).

In advertising, children who watch more TV commercials have been found to be more aware of the advertised products (Goldberg, 1990). However, with adults, the frequency of presentation of ads *per se* generally does not produce higher levels of attention, but the quality of the ads does. Ads are better attended to if they are entertaining, usefully informative, humorous, professional in appearance, or feature novel or contrasting elements (Atkin et al., 1973). Advertisers often use humor, fear stimuli, visual imagery, or sexual suggestions to attract attention to their messages. In a pioneering study, Bauer and Greyser (1968) reported that the average consumer only notices about 75 ads each day out of the 1500 or so that impinge on his/her eyes or ears, and that only about a dozen are important enough to be classified as enjoyable, informative, annoying, or offensive.

Studies of Comprehension. Comprehension is usually measured by giving objective tests of the amount of knowledge gained from a program, story, or ad. Though some studies have demonstrated successful communication of knowledge, for instance through TV documentaries, many other studies have shown very little comprehension of informative programs or stories. For instance, research using magazine stories and ads found that more than one-third of the respondents could not correctly state what they had read (Jacoby & Hoyer, 1989). In general, people who are more involved in a given topic will display both more attention and better comprehension of messages about that topic (Celsi & Olson, 1988). However, comprehension is often unrelated to acceptance of the message (Patterson & McClure, 1976).

Studies of Acceptance. Acceptance of the persuasive message (sometimes referred to as "yielding") is the dependent variable most often studied in the voluminous research literature on attitude change. Though yielding cannot occur without reception of the message (that is, attention and comprehension, the two stages just discussed), the amount of yielding is not necessarily related to the degree of reception. One reason for the lack of relationship is that many personal characteristics (e.g., intelligence, or self-esteem) that are positively related to reception are negatively related to acceptance, and vice versa. For instance, in the political arena, political involvement increases exposure and attention to political advertisements but decreases acceptance of them (McGuire, 1968a; Zaller, 1987).

Several types of yielding or attitude change have been distinguished by Kelman (1958). **Compliance** is public yielding without private acceptance, usually motivated by hope of gaining rewards or avoiding punishments—a common response to in-person influence attempts by powerful individuals such as parents or bosses. **Identification** is attitude change in an attempt to be like an admired individual or reference group. **Internalization** is attitude change in which the new attitude is intrinsically rewarding, useful, or consistent with one's value system. Advertisers usually try to achieve identification (e.g., by presenting a celebrity spokesperson for their product) or internalization (e.g., by having an expert source present factual information about the value of the product to potential consumers).

As discussed in Chapter 13, mass media messages rarely convert people to dramatically new and different points of view; instead they usually reinforce existing attitudes or produce minor changes in them. Though occasionally a particular message may have a powerful effect on an audience, usually attitude change attempts have *minimal effects* (McGuire, 1986). This is especially true in the advertising arena, where message exposure, attention, and comprehension are often chaotic, and people are typically exposed to offsetting messages for other competing products. However, mass communication can be most effective where people's attitudes are weak, and that is often true in product advertising—particularly so when new products are being introduced.

Studies of Retention. Memory and forgetting have been extensively studied in laboratory experiments by researchers interested in learning processes. In naturalistic research, however, retention is the least-studied step in the persuasion process, largely because of the

Photograph courtesy of Yale University Office of Public Information. Reprinted by permission.

Box 14-1

WILLIAM MCGUIRE, ATTITUDE THEORIST AND PERSUASION RESEARCHER

William McGuire made a multiple reputation in social psychology as an experimentalist, theorist, systematizer, editor, and administrator. Born in New York City in 1925, he attended Catholic schools, enlisted in the army in World War II, and then earned his B.A. and M.A. from Fordham. Moving to Yale for his Ph.D., he was one of the fruitful group of scholars who did experimental research on communication and attitude change and jointly developed the Yale model of persuasive communication. After teaching briefly at Yale and Illinois, he spent a longer period on the faculty of Columbia and three years at the University of California at San Diego. In 1970 he returned to Yale and served as chair of the psychology department, where he remains as an active scholar.

McGuire was influential as editor of the *Journal of Personality and Social Psychology*, and as author of two landmark handbook chapters on attitudes and attitude change, as well as an astounding number of systematic reviews of various topics in personality and social psychology. He is also known for his theoretical contributions regarding cognitive consistency and other aspects of thought processes, immunization against persuasion, and the self-concept. As a visionary and prophet for the field, he called for more multivariate research in real-world settings and for a complex systems view of attitude and behavioral change. His seminal research and writing were recognized by the Distinguished Scientific Contribution Award of the APA in 1988.

practical difficulties involved in conducting delayed tests of the effects of a message. Even more difficult, but a particularly needed area of work, is research on the continuing and cumulative impact of multiple media messages over a prolonged period of time (e.g., many messages suggesting the prevalence of crime,

or implying that heavy consumption of material goods is necessary for personal happiness—cf. Comstock, 1985).

Two types of retention are of interest: retention of message content and retention of attitude change, if any occurred. In general, these two variables usually

Retention - least studied area
- 2 types; content, att Δ (low-mod +ve correl.)
- sleeper effect

show a low-to-moderate positive correlation ($r = +.2$ to $+.5$), though some studies have demonstrated that recall of specific message content is not essential to continuing attitude change (e.g., Cacioppo & Petty, 1979). A rare but fascinating finding, termed the **sleeper effect**, is the occurrence of delayed attitude change in the direction of a persuasive message that was originally rejected because it was untrustworthy or came from a noncredible source. Apparently in these cases the source is forgotten faster than the message, leading to a delayed increase in agreement with the message (e.g., Pratkanis et al., 1988).

As is true of any learned information, retention of both content and attitude change normally drops off fairly sharply in the hours after exposure to the message, and then gradually stabilizes at a level that is typically less than half of the original post-message level. Some experimental studies have shown persisting significant attitude change for periods of six months or longer, and repetition of a persuasive message normally reinforces and prolongs any initial attitude change (Cook & Flay, 1978; McGuire, 1969).

Studies of Action. Research findings show that the relationship between attitudinal acceptance of a persuasive message and acting on it may range from zero to very strongly positive, and a wide range of interacting variables can moderate the strength of that relationship (Tybout & Artz, 1994). In the political arena, ads for candidates generally have quite small effects on voting, but in most races the candidates' expenditures for media ads are positively related to their aggregate vote totals, so it is clear that political advertising does have an effect (Grush, 1980).

Product advertising is most likely to have a strong influence with audiences who haven't been exposed to it much before, such as adults in developing countries without pervasive mass media, or children who haven't yet learned to discount it. For instance, a study in the U.S. showed that children's exposure to more TV commercials was related to having more kinds of cereals in the home (Goldberg, 1990). This relationship occurred because a large proportion of American parents yield to their children's preference for cereals; to a lesser extent the same is true for snack foods, toys, and games (Ward & Wackman, 1972).

In industrialized countries, much media advertising to adults is aimed at reinforcing existing preferences and maintaining the product's current market share, more than at converting new purchasers (Alsop, 1989). Multimillion dollar advertising campaigns often produce only small increases in sales, but it should be realized that even a mere 1% increase in sales or in market share may mean huge increases in revenues and profits (Assmus, Farley, & Lehmann, 1984; Gorn & Goldberg, 1982).

This completes our overview of the stages of persuasive communication specified in the Yale model. Next we will briefly describe a popular theory which focuses on how different cognitive and attitudinal components combine to produce behavioral actions.

The Theory of Reasoned Action

For over 20 years, probably the most widely cited and studied theory of attitudes and behavior has been the **theory of reasoned action**, formulated by Fishbein and Ajzen (1975). As its name implies, it proposes that people generally act in ways that are reasoned—in the sense of being based on their beliefs and attitudes and understanding of social norms—though it does not claim that their reasoning is strictly logical. The theory proposes several postulates about factors that can predict a person taking a specific action during a specified time period:

1. The best predictor of a person's specific **action or behavior** (B) is his or her behavioral intention (I) concerning taking that action—e.g., an intention to buy a particular kind of food: $I \rightarrow B$.
2. **Behavioral intention**, in turn, is a weighted additive function of your own attitude (A) toward the action and your subjective norm (SN) about what relevant other people think you should do: $I = Aw_1 + SNw_2$.
3. Your **attitude**, in turn, is the sum of all your relevant **behavioral beliefs** (b) about the consequences of taking the action, with each belief being multiplied by your **evaluation** (e) of the importance of that consequence: $A = \Sigma (b_i e_i)$. To take a simple example using

only two beliefs, you might believe strongly that eating a certain kind of food would be good for your cholesterol level, but also that the food tastes bad. Then, if you evaluated a better cholesterol level as more important than the bad taste, your attitude toward eating the food would be moderately positive; but if you evaluated the bad taste as more important, your attitude would be moderately negative.

4. Your **subjective norm**, similarly, is the sum of your **normative beliefs** (n)—beliefs about what each of the relevant other individuals or groups in your life thinks you should do regarding the action—with each normative belief being multiplied by your **motivation to comply** (m) with that individual's or group's wishes: $SN = \Sigma (n_i m_i)$. Again, to take a simple example with only two groups, your parents might want you to eat the food in question and you might be motivated to comply with their wishes, but your friends might not want you to eat it and you might also be motivated to comply with them. In that case, the two sets of beliefs and motives would offset each other, producing a neutral subjective norm component. This would then be combined with the attitude component to form your behavioral intention.

Of course, people often act in a flash. They don't usually stop to think about each element; they don't score their beliefs, attitudes, and subjective norms mathematically and compute their behavioral intention before taking action. However, the theory of reasoned action posits that their actions are normally based on just such an implicit process of reasoning. The proof of the theory's value is in its ability to predict behaviors correctly, and on this score it has generally been quite accurate. It has been used successfully to predict behaviors ranging from engaging in premarital intercourse, to using birth control pills, to attending church regularly, to buying many types of consumer products. In these studies the average multiple correlation for predicting intentions was as high as +.7 or +.8, and the correlation between intentions and overt behavior ranged from +.4 to as high as +.9 (Ajzen, 1988, pp. 114, 119; Fishbein & Ajzen, 1975, pp. 310–311, 373–374).

One exception to the theory's coverage is its specification that the behavior in question must be *under the person's volitional control*. Thus, the theory wouldn't apply, for instance, to an addiction which might override all of a person's logical reasons for avoiding an action such as taking a drug. Similarly, it wouldn't apply to a behavior that was beyond a person's capability, such as running a four-minute mile (for most of us). Ajzen (1988) has added this factor of **perceived control** over the behavior to a more recent variation of the theory, which he calls the **theory of planned behavior**. Research has found that including this variable leads to better prediction of some kinds of behavior, such as attempted weight loss (Schifter & Ajzen, 1985) and avoiding problem drinking (Schlegel et al., 1988).

Another type of behavior that the theory may not handle adequately is habitual behavior—actions that are so overlearned that people never think about them—such as which shoe you put on first, or saying "you know" frequently, or using automobile seat belts. Triandis (1977) has included **habit** in his variation of this theory, and it has been found to add to the predictability of behaviors such as wearing seat belts and attending college classes regularly (Fredricks & Dossett, 1983; Wittenbraker, Gibbs, & Kahle, 1983).

In the realm of consumer behavior, the theory of reasoned action has been used frequently, and it has usually shown good to excellent ability to predict buying intentions and behavior. As examples, it has predicted purchase of clothing (Miniard & Cohen, 1981), using cents-off coupons (Shimp & Kavas, 1984), eating at a fast food restaurant (Brinberg & Durand, 1983), buying generic prescription drugs (Brinberg & Cummings, 1983), and buying Miller beer (Ajzen & Fishbein, 1980).

A wide-ranging meta-analysis of 87 studies (including many studies of consumption behaviors as well as other behaviors, such as going to church) confirmed that the theory of reasoned action has strong utility for predicting both intentions (average correlation = .66) and behaviors (average correlation = .53). This study also demonstrated three moderator variables that affected the theory's level of prediction: the theory performed best when it predicted (1) intentions rather than estimates of expected behavior, (2) behaviors rather than goals (outcomes that result from behaviors, such as losing 10 pounds), and (3) a choice

Photograph courtesy of Martin Fishbein. Reprinted by permission. Photograph courtesy of Icek Ajzen. Reprinted by permission.

Box 14-2

MARTIN FISHBEIN AND ICEK AJZEN, AUTHORS OF THE THEORY OF REASONED ACTION

Linked together in theory authorship as well as 15 years of empirical research, Martin Fishbein and Icek Ajzen are central figures in the study of attitudes and behavior. Their collaboration began at the University of Illinois in the late 1960s and resulted in development of the theory of reasoned action and coauthorship of two influential books, *Belief, Attitude, Intention, and Behavior* (1975), and *Understanding Attitudes and Predicting Social Behavior* (1980).

Fishbein received his B.A. from Reed College in Oregon and his Ph.D. from UCLA in 1961. His first faculty position was at the University of Illinois, where he still remains as a professor in psychology and in communications research. He has received several awards for his research in the areas of consumer psychology and marketing, especially for the recorded music industry, and he has been elected president of the Society for Consumer Psychology and the Interamerican Society of Psychology. The relevance of his research to consumer behavior is stressed in this chapter, and Chapter 16 il-

lustrates how the same theories and research are being used in community programs to prevent the spread of AIDS. Fishbein has become deeply involved in AIDS prevention, as a member of the NIMH AIDS Research Review Committee and as Acting Branch Chief in the Centers for Disease Control and Prevention.

Ajzen earned his B.A. in sociology at the Hebrew University of Jerusalem but switched to social psychology at the University of Illinois, where he received his Ph.D. in 1969. He taught there briefly before moving to the University of Massachusetts, where he remains as a professor except for occasional visiting professorships in Israel. He has extended his fruitful collaboration with Fishbein by proposing the theory of planned behavior, which is mentioned in this chapter. In addition, he has written *Attitudes, Personality, and Behavior* and conducted research on attitude-behavior relationships in areas such as decision making, health behavior, and leisure activities.

among alternative behaviors rather than performance of a single behavior (Sheppard, Hartwick, & Warshaw, 1988).

We move now to describing a cognitive response theory, which is currently the most popular theoretical approach to studying consumer behavior.

The Elaboration Likelihood Model

This theory holds that people are *active* processors of information rather than mere passive recipients. When they receive a persuasive message, they try to relate its arguments to their own knowledge, attitudes, and beliefs on the topic, and in doing so they generate a number of thoughts that are not part of the message itself. These **cognitive responses** may be favorable to the message, or opposing counterarguments, or thoughts that are neutral or irrelevant to it. Usually some mix of these three types of thoughts occurs (Petty, Ostrom, & Brock, 1981).

Cognitive response theory views attitude change as largely a process of self-persuasion; that is, "a person's own thoughts are a more powerful determinant of persuasion than is information that originates externally" (Petty & Cacioppo, 1981, p. 251). Thus, the theory proposes that it is not the arguments in the message itself that produce attitude change in a recipient; rather, the balance of favorable or unfavorable *self-generated* thoughts will determine the success of the persuasive message. Stated differently, the cognitive responses *mediate* between characteristics of the message or the recipient and the effect of the message, and they are considered to be crucial in determining what effect the message will have. In the terminology of the Yale model of persuasion, they represent an intermediate step between comprehension of the message and yielding to or accepting it (cf. McGuire, 1985). Thus, the **elaboration likelihood model** of attitude change stresses that an individual's *cognitive elaboration* of favorable or unfavorable issue-relevant arguments is the key factor in determining attitude change and persistence (Petty & Cacioppo, 1981).

Why should people's self-generated thoughts be so crucial in attitude change? One answer is that people *value* the arguments that they generate themselves more than other people value them, and more than they value other people's arguments. Second, they are able to *recall* their own arguments on a topic better and longer than arguments presented by someone else (Greenwald & Albert, 1968). Concerning advertised products, the main types of cognitive responses are support arguments (ones that support the message claims), counterarguments, source approval, and source derogation (negative responses concerning the source of the message).

A key issue in this theoretical approach is how these self-generated thoughts can be measured and studied empirically, since they are subjective and fleeting. The most commonly used method is the **thought-listing technique**. In it, participants are given a specified short period of time, such as three minutes, and asked to write down or dictate brief statements of the thoughts they had as they listened to or read the persuasive message. Later, judges code these thoughts as being favorable, unfavorable, or neutral to the position advocated in the persuasive message (Cacioppo & Petty, 1981b).

An important principle is the role of **involvement** in this theory. People who are highly involved in an issue will be more motivated to generate thoughts on the topic, and so exposure to a message on that topic will normally cause their attitudes to become more extreme than those of less-involved individuals who generate fewer relevant thoughts. If the message is one they already agree with, exposure to it will tend to make the attitude of highly involved individuals more extreme in the advocated direction; however, if the message is contrary to their current views, exposure to it will push involved individuals farther in the direction opposite to the message (Petty & Cacioppo, 1979).

Central Versus Peripheral Routes to Persuasion. The elaboration likelihood model has identified some important principles regarding two possible routes to attitude change (Petty & Cacioppo, 1986). The **central route** is based on *information* concerning the topic—for example, a person's prior knowledge and interest in the topic, learning from the message, and self-generated thoughts regarding the topic. Though it is not necessarily logical or unbiased, its hallmark is *thoughtful* consideration of information. In the consumer research literature, this has sometimes been called *systematic processing* or *extended problem solving* (Engel, Blackwell, & Miniard, 1993).

Photograph courtesy of Richard Petty. Reprinted by permission.

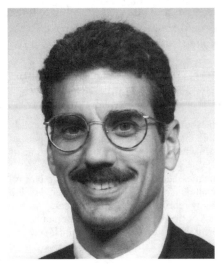

Photograph courtesy of John Cacioppo. Reprinted by permission.

Box 14-3

RICHARD PETTY AND JOHN CACIOPPO, DEVELOPERS OF THE ELABORATION LIKELIHOOD MODEL

Famed for their research on attitude change, Richard Petty and John Cacioppo have been prolific collaborators for 20 years, sharing authorship on more than 60 papers and 5 volumes. This chapter summarizes their research on cognitive response theory and the elaboration likelihood model, which are fully described in their volumes *Attitudes and Persuasion* (1981) and *Communication and Persuasion: Central and Peripheral Routes to Attitude Change* (1986). They began their collaboration as fellow graduate students at Ohio State University, continued it long-distance for a dozen years, and then were reunited as fellow faculty members at Ohio State.

Petty graduated from the University of Virginia and earned his Ph.D. in 1977. In eight years of teaching at the University of Missouri, he rose to hold a named chair as a full professor, before returning to Ohio State in 1987. In 20 years, he wrote seven books and over 130 articles and book chap-

ters. In addition, he was editor of the *Personality and Social Psychology Bulletin* and served on the editorial board of seven other journals. His most recent volume is *Attitude Strength: Antecedents and Consequences.*

Cacioppo was born in Texas, graduated from the University of Missouri, and also earned his Ph.D. in 1977. He taught for two years at Notre Dame and ten years at the University of Iowa before returning to Ohio State in 1989. His special focus in attitude research is physiological measurement, reflected in his volumes on *Perspectives in Cardiovascular Psychophysiology* and *Social Psychophysiology: A Sourcebook,* both prepared jointly with Petty. His other main research area is emotion and affect in information processing, as illustrated in his recent volume, *Emotional Contagion.* He has published over 200 scientific papers and served as the editor of *Psychophysiology.*

In contrast, the **peripheral route** is less thoughtful, and it is used when a person is low in information and interest concerning the topic or in motivation or ability to process the message content. It relies on cues peripheral to the content of the message, instead of on the arguments in the message and the relevant thoughts that it arouses. These peripheral cues provide a *short-cut procedure* by which a person can decide how to respond to a message without taking the trouble to think about all the pros and cons. This is also referred to as *heuristic processing* (Chaiken, 1987) or *limited problem solving*.

The cues that a person relies on when using the peripheral route may be any of the following:

- Aspects of the source—e.g., a source that is apparently expert, likeable, handsome, or famous may be persuasive to a person who is not thinking about the arguments in a message.
- Aspects of the message that are associated with past rewards or punishments—e.g., commercials that develop a mood of happy relaxation or sexual arousal.
- Characteristics of the recipient—e.g., the person's own current cheerful or depressed mood may influence acceptance or rejection of a message.

- The medium of transmission—e.g., a person may accept slick television commercials uncritically or reject written material as too complex to think about.

Though the peripheral route is cognitively "lazy," it is not necessarily unwise. You cannot possibly think in detail about every persuasive message, ad, or commercial that you are exposed to. So, for example, it may often make sense to rely on your opinion of the source—especially if the topic is not important to you.

The central route is likely to be used if the person is interested in the topic, motivated to think about it, and has the ability to process the information (due to clarity of the message, lack of distractions, etc.). If these conditions do not hold, the person is likely to use one or more peripheral cues to determine his or her response. The *consequences* of the two routes to persua-

TABLE 14-1   An Overview of the Differences Between Extended Problem Solving (EPS) and Limited Problem Solving (LPS)

Aspect	*Extended Problem Solving (EPS)*	*Limited Problem Solving (LPS)*
Motivation and need recognition	High involvement.	Low involvement.
Search for information	Strong motivation to search.	Low motivation to search.
	Information processed actively and rigorously.	Information processing not deep.
	Buying action influenced by brand recall.	Buying action influenced by brand recognition.
Alternative evaluation	Rigorous evaluation before purchase.	Nonrigorous evaluation mostly after purchase.
	Multiple evaluative criteria used.	Limited number of criteria used.
	Alternatives perceived as significantly different.	Alternatives perceived as essentially similar.
	Social compliance often an important motivator.	Social compliance not important.
Purchase	Will shop many outlets if needed.	Not motivated to shop extensively.
	Personal selling influences choice.	Choice often prompted by display and point-of-sale incentives.
Outcomes	Satisfaction improves brand loyalty.	Satisfaction motivates repurchase because of inertia, not loyalty.

Source: Engel, J. F., Warshaw, M. R., and Kinnear, T. C, (1994). Promotional strategy: Managing the marketing communications process. Copyright 1994 by Richard D. Irwin, Inc. Reprinted with permission.

sion are particularly important. Persuasion via the peripheral route is apt to be weak, temporary, and susceptible to counterpressures, whereas persuasion via the central route is usually stronger, relatively persistent, and resistant to counterattack (Petty & Cacioppo, 1986). See Table 14-1 for other aspects of the two routes as applied to purchase behavior.

Use in Consumer Research. The elaboration likelihood model has been widely used in research on consumer behavior. Many studies have corroborated that the elaboration process mediates judgments that people make, and that their amount of personal elaboration is influenced by the cognitive resources available for this task (intelligence, attention, interest in the task, etc.—Tybout & Artz, 1994). Also, involvement in the issue increases the amount of elaboration by message recipients (e.g., Celsi & Olson, 1988; Costley, 1988). However, other variables, such as the recipient's price consciousness and novelty-seeking motivation, may also affect the amount of elaboration.

People tend to use the effortful central route much more when considering large or important purchases, such as a car or a vacation, whereas peripheral cues are frequently relied on in small and repetitive buying decisions, such as for toiletries, beverages, or laundry products. However, as the elaboration likelihood model proposes, even with small decisions, a high level of involvement and strong arguments can produce central-level processing, more elaboration, and greater persuasion (e.g., Andrews & Shimp, 1990).

Of course, many ads do not make factual or rational claims, which would encourage central-route processing. They may rely instead on creating a mood or establishing peripheral cues, such as pairing the product with a beautiful model or with a celebrity spokesperson—think back to the many such ads you've seen. In these cases of peripheral-route persuasion, the effect is usually greater if the audience is *distracted* from noticing the lack of substantive arguments by an intriguing story, or by catchy music, or by the inclusion of humor. When factual arguments are presented, recipients who are motivated to process them are influenced by the *strength of the arguments*, and they often generate unfavorable thoughts if the arguments are weak.

These examples illustrate one of the great strengths of the central-peripheral distinction concerning persuasion process—namely, that it helps to clarify the complex *interaction effects* that often occur when several variables are combined in a persuasive message. For instance, *message repetition* allows an opportunity for more cognitive elaboration, which could lead to more persuasion. This holds true if the arguments in the message are strong ones, but if they are weak, message repetition can quickly lead to counterarguing and unfavorable attitude change (Petty & Cacioppo, 1981). Similarly, presenting a larger *number of arguments* in a message also allows for more cognitive elaboration. Again, if these arguments are strong ones, more persuasion will usually result, but if they are weak, more counterarguing and less favorable attitude change will occur (Harkins & Petty, 1981).

Somewhat related to the process of elaboration is the variable of **accessibility** of an attitude—that is, its ease of retrieval from memory. Based on a stimulus-response learning viewpoint, Fazio (1986) proposed that attitudes are most predictive of behavior when they are easily accessible. Two factors that increase an attitude's accessibility are its being based on the person's direct experience, and its having been repeatedly expressed by the person in the past. For example, consumers' buying behavior is more closely related to their product attitudes if they have had direct experience with the product in the past than if they have merely seen ads for it (Fazio, Powell, & Williams, 1989). Similarly, a person who has frequently rehearsed or stated a positive opinion about a product, such as a brand of beer, is likely to buy that product on the next relevant occasion.

ADVERTISING AND MARKETING RESEARCH

Next we turn to a more detailed discussion of how advertisers and marketers have used these and other theories of persuasion in their efforts to sell products and services to the public. In the research literature, this topic is often referred to as "responses to marketer-initiated stimuli." Good sources for research of this kind are the *Journal of Advertising Research* and the *Journal of Marketing Research*. In this section we will discuss advertising and people's attitudes toward it, product promotions and pricing, and market segmentation and psychographics.

Advertising

Print advertising has been in use at least since 1700, and the first U.S. advertising agency was founded in 1841 (Boone & Kurtz, 1992). However, the volume of advertising has grown explosively in the last 50 years. In 1994 the total annual expenditure for advertising in the United States was $55 billion—approximately $200 for every man, woman, and child (*World Almanac*, 1994). The U.S. company with the largest advertising budget, Procter & Gamble, spent nearly $1.5 billion for ads in that year alone. Among the industries with the highest advertising costs as a percent of sales are games/toys, industrial chemicals (about 15% each), beverages, and cosmetics (about 10% each)—Schonfeld & Associates (1989).

What do these companies get for all their expenditures, and how do consumers react to the deluge of advertising? We will summarize some of the main dimensions of advertising that can increase consumers' attention, acceptance, and purchase behavior.

Vividness. In general, ads with vivid language and/or pictures receive high attention, leading to more elaboration and retention in memory, and producing more accessible attitudes (e.g., Smith, 1991; Tybout & Artz, 1994). Ads that arouse emotions are better remembered than others, even months later (Friestad & Thorson, 1986). While it is important to realize that higher attention and retention do not necessarily cause buying, aspects of vividness that increase audience members' attention to ads include the following (Williams, 1982, p. 413):

- Large size
- Movement or the appearance of movement
- Intensity (bright color, large headlines, loud commercials)
- Novelty or unexpectedness
- Contrast with background or surroundings
- Color
- Position (upper left-hand portion of a page is best)
- Shape (taller than wide is best)
- Isolation (particularly from other similar stimuli)
- Multiple-sensory messages (e.g., sight, sound, movement, scent, feel)

Pictures in ads not only attract attention, but they also can make implicit claims (e.g., about a product aiding romantic success) that would be rejected if stated verbally (Messaris, 1996).

Incompleteness. A general principle underlying cognitive response theory is that *active participation* is more likely to lead to attitude change than is passive reception of a message (Oskamp, 1991). Advertisers sometimes make use of this principle by leaving a message incomplete and counting on the audience member to complete it (e.g., with the product name or slogan). This works well *if* the desired completion is obvious, and if the recipient is motivated to respond to it. Examples include omitting the conclusion at the end of a message, or asking a question rather than stating the conclusion (e.g., Howard & Burnkrant, 1990; Sawyer & Howard, 1991).

Brand Names. A basic principle of association learning is that, for optimum learning, the product brand name must be displayed clearly and prominently. A surprisingly large proportion of ads ignore or violate this principle, leaving audience members in the dark as to their goals. This principle also suggests that the brand name and other key facts should be repeated within the ad, but this must be done carefully and with restraint, so as not to exceed the audience's irritation threshold and cause unfavorable attitude change. A wise guideline here is the same as for repetition of whole commercials: using varied forms of the basic message is the optimum strategy to avoid *ad wearout* (Schumann et al., 1990).

Celebrities. Inclusion of sports heroes, movie stars, or famous entertainers in ads draws much audience attention. If the ad integrates them with the product, they should increase product recognition, which is an important goal in the competitive media environment of *ad clutter* from many contending advertisers (Boone & Kurtz, 1992). The celebrity should be a credible and admired person, and for best results, should have a logical connection with the product, such as an athlete recommending sporting equipment, but not life insurance.

As we have discussed in Chapter 13, an ironic effect of the use of beautiful or handsome models and spokespersons in so many ads is that viewers are apt to raise their standards of ideal attractiveness and become dissatisfied with their own appearance. Richins (1991) demonstrated that effect, but found that it did not prevent favorable attitudes toward the ad and the product.

Music. Music in commercials can contribute to persuasion through either the central or peripheral route (MacInnis & Park, 1991) As a peripheral cue, it can influence the listener's mood and also suggest characteristics of the product. Attention to the music also occupies some of the listener's processing resources, leaving less resources for processing information about the product. This can result in less recall of product information, but it may also postpone wearout of repeated ads. Through the central route, music may communicate ideas about the product in ways that are less likely to produce counterarguing than if the information was stated verbally—e.g., its luxury or excitement (Scott, 1990; Tybout & Artz, 1994).

Comparative Ads. In the last decade, ads making explicit comparisons to other products have become much more common. These ads work best when used by a new product or one with a low market share. Comparison of this brand with a prestigious brand provides a highly favorable anchor and thus lifts the evaluation of the advertised product (Snyder, 1992). Comparative ads also have more perceived message relevance, and thus they generate more involvement, attention to the ad, and cognitive elaboration of its contents (Muehling, Stoltman, & Grossbart, 1990). However, if they are used by a popular brand, they may just call attention to competitive brands and confuse viewers about which to prefer (Pechmann & Stewart, 1990). For instance, in 1995–1996, a major war of comparative ads was waged between Tylenol and Advil, each warning about the potential dangerous side effects of the other, and leading to much consumer confusion and anxiety (Greenwald, 1996).

Humor. You probably have noticed that many TV and radio commercials nowadays have humor in them, but you may not be aware that that is a greatly increased trend in the last 10 to 20 years. In the advertising community there are strong conflicting viewpoints for and against using humor in ads. However, there is general agreement that humor does not succeed for all products, populations, and forms of advertising, and that it is necessary to be extremely careful in incorporating humor into ads.

Early research, summarized by Sternthal and Craig (1973), established that humor in commercials attracts attention, so it is generally helpful at the first step of the persuasion process. However, humor may decrease comprehension of the ad, both because many people may not "get the joke" and because attention to the humor may distract from understanding of the sales message. At the third step, acceptance of the message, humor may be helpful for two reasons: it may establish a favorable feeling toward the ad, which may generalize to liking the product, and it may distract people from counterarguing and so increase persuasion. On the other hand, it is also possible that the response of laughing may generalize to laughing at the product—definitely undesirable to the advertiser—or that repeated exposure may "kill the humor." In addition, some people may find the humor tasteless or offensive and generalize those negative feelings to the product. Typically, humor is apt to enhance the credibility and likability of the *source*, because audience members perceive the source as not a "stuffed shirt," but that liking may or may not extend to the product. There are few clear data about the effect of humor on sales, except for case studies of particular highly praised campaigns, such as Stan Freberg's commercials for Sunsweet prunes, which joked about removing their pits and wrinkles (Engel, Warshaw, & Kinnear, 1994).

Recent research has shown that humor is effective only for some types of products—it would definitely not be recommended for mortuaries! Also, it works best when the humor is closely linked to the product—for instance, showing a small boy challenging a famous athlete not to steal his soft drink (Scott, Klein, & Bryant, 1990, Weinberger & Campbell, 1990/1991). Finally, the effect of humor depends on the recipient's prior attitude toward the product; humor increases persuasiveness for consumers with favorable preexisting attitudes, but may be counterproductive for those with unfavorable prior attitudes (Chattopadhyay & Basu, 1990). To quote Stan Freberg, "Humor in advertising is like a gun in the hands of a child. You have to know how to do it. Otherwise it can blow up on you" (*Advertising Age*, 1992, p. 52).

Attitudes Toward the Ad and Attitudes Toward the Product

A crucial question for advertisers is: Does a favorable attitude toward a likable or enjoyable ad "rub off" on the product? The general conclusion of much research is that it does. A recent meta-analysis demonstrated that people's attitudes toward the ad itself can influence their attitudes toward the product in two separate ways—a **dual-mediation model** (Brown & Stayman, 1992). First, attitudes toward the ad may carry over directly to the product, and this is usually the stronger of the two effects. It occurs most often when the person's involvement in the message is low, so that product claims made in the ad are ignored, and the general attitude toward the ad is the primary determinant of attitudes toward the product (an example of peripheral-route processing). Second, there may be an indirect effect, based on the person's attitude toward the claims for the product made by the ad. This is the kind of effect proposed in Fishbein and Ajzen's theory of reasoned action and, interestingly, it is usually the weaker of the two effects. It occurs most often when the person is involved and motivated to attend to the claims made in the ad (an example of central-route processing). For many people and many ads, both direct and indirect effects of the attitude toward the ad may occur (Droge, 1989; Homer, 1990; Miniard, Batla, & Rose, 1990).

These conclusions certainly suggest that advertisers would be wise to create ads that consumers will like. However, even with this apparent implication, there are questions. A recent study reported that, over time, the effects of a likable ad dissipate (Chattopadhyay & Nedungadi, 1992). Thus, if the advertiser hopes that the audience will use central-route processing to elaborate on the claims made in the ad, there may be dangers in having an ad that is so likable that it obscures attention to the product claims. However, another study found a carryover effect of feelings and attitudes toward the ad on attitudes toward the product after a four-week delay (Burke & Edell, 1989). With these questions still unresolved, the only safe conclusion is that there is great complexity in the relationship between people's responses to ads and their responses to the products that the ads promote.

An Illustrative Study

As an example of the kind of studies typically done in research on advertising effects, we will briefly describe an article closely related to this discussion of attitudes toward the ad and toward the product (Edell & Burke, 1987, Study 2). The ads used were six actual 30-second TV commercials for six different products, ranging from potato chips to a bank. Neither the commercials nor the products had been seen in the area where the study was conducted, so they were novel stimuli. They, and four other filler ads, were embedded within a 30-minute segment of a classic movie (e.g., *Casablanca*), which was shown in a movie theater, ostensibly as the first of several daily installments of the movie. The respondents were 32 people recruited through newspaper ads and fliers, who watched the movie segment and ads and then answered a questionnaire about the programming. Next they were shown each of the ads again, one at a time, and for each ad they filled out many measures—their overall evaluation of the ad, the extent to which it had elicited each of 56 feelings, their cognitive judgments of the ad on 25 adjectives, beliefs about four key attributes of the product, and evaluation of these attributes. Finally, after doing this for all the ads, they gave their overall attitude toward the product for each of the products. The measurement scales for each of the variables had been carefully developed in past research, and had high internal consistency.

The statistical procedure employed in analyzing the data was multiple regression, in which several scales were used in combination to predict one of the dependent variables. The findings showed that the overall attitude toward the ad was predicted very strongly by three dimensions of feelings and by three dimensions of judgments. The R^2 figures, which indicate the amount of variance in the dependent variable accounted for by the predictors, were .67 and .72 respectively, and when scales for all six dimensions were used as predictors, the R^2 increased significantly to .76—that is, feelings and judgments about the ad accounted for over 3/4 of the variance in attitudes toward the ad.

Next, the same general procedure was used to predict the overall attitude toward the product. Again, the feelings elicited by the ad were highly significant predictors ($R^2 = .50$), as were the judgments about the ad ($R^2 = .56$), and using all six scales increased the predictability significantly ($R^2 = .59$). Thus, both judgments about the ad and the feelings it generated carried over to affect attitudes toward the product (an example of peripheral route effects).

Finally, the indirect path was tested, to see whether the ad influenced beliefs about attributes of the product, and they in turn helped to determine attitudes toward the product (which would be an example of central-route processing). A belief score for each product was formed by multiplying each of the four attribute-likelihood scores by the respondent's rating of how good or bad it was for the product to have that attribute, and summing across the attributes. Findings showed that the ad-feelings and ad-judgments scores predicted these product-belief scores significantly but accounted for relatively little variance ($R^2 = .10$ and .11, respectively, and $R^2 = .16$ together). However, when product-beliefs were added to attitudes toward the ad, ad-feelings, and ad-judgments to predict overall attitudes toward the product, the variance accounted for increased significantly to .63. Moreover, the data showed that the ad-feelings were mediated by (i.e., had their effect through) the product-beliefs and attitudes toward the ad in influencing attitudes toward the product. The overall pattern of findings is illustrated in Figure 14-1.

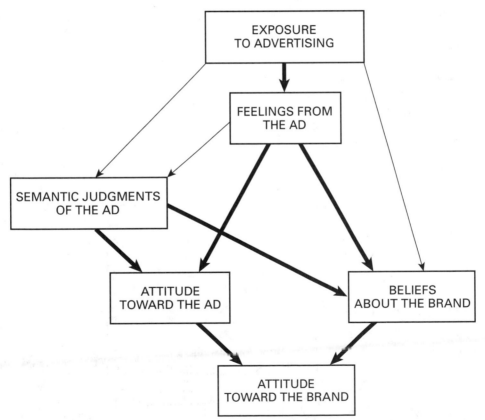

FIGURE 14-1   A conceptual model of the role of feelings in advertising. The heavy lines indicate relationships demonstrated in Edell and Burke's research. (Source: Edell, J. A. and Burke, M. C. (1987). The power of feelings in understanding advertising effects. *Journal of Consumer Research, 14,* 421–433. Copyright 1987 by The University of Chicago Press. Reprinted with permission.)

Though the results of this study were fairly clear-cut, it had a number of limitations, as does any single study. First, since the ads and products were unfamiliar, it was a study of *attitude formation*, and the results would probably be different for products or ads that were already quite familiar. Second, all of the measures were taken at the same sitting and on similar paper-and-pencil measures, so it is not surprising that there were high correlations among the variables. More important, the similarity and contemporaneity of the measures may have created artifacts affecting which variables were important predictors of other variables. Also, though the program and ads were viewed in a fairly realistic situation, the respondents were relatively few and undoubtedly were not representative of all potential ad viewers, so the results may not be generalizable to other populations and settings. Finally, note that no behavioral outcomes were studied, such as buying behavior.

Consequently, we can only conclude that, in this situation and for these respondents, feelings elicited by ads and cognitive judgments about the ads did carry over to attitudes toward products that the respondents had not experienced before (peripheral-route processing). Also, these feelings and judgments about the novel ads and products influenced respondents' beliefs about the products' attributes, and these beliefs helped to mediate the ads' effects on attitudes toward the product (central-route processing). Adding these results together with those of many other studies provides strong evidence that both of these persuasion routes can affect people's product attitudes (i.e., the findings support the dual-mediation model).

Product Promotions and Pricing

In addition to advertising, manufacturers spend a large proportion of their marketing budgets on special product promotions of various types—between $25 billion and $30 billion annually in the U.S. in recent years (Engel et al., 1994). The different types of promotions include providing samples of products, coupons, cents-off offers, rebates, contests and sweepstakes, and added premiums with the product. Whereas it usually takes months to develop and implement a nation-wide advertising campaign, such product promotions can be launched more quickly, and they usually cost less. In many instances, their goal is to produce a fast short-term increase in a product's market share, and in contrast to advertising, their results can often be determined more easily (e.g., by the number of coupons redeemed—Engel et al., 1994).

Providing samples of products is most often done to introduce new products nationwide, particularly with snack foods, cleaning products, or health-and-beauty items. It puts the sample into consumers' hands, thus getting far more widespread attention than any other method. Frequently this is done by mailing small packages to homes, but it may also be accomplished through special dispenser displays placed in stores (Boone & Kurtz, 1992). Giving samples to consumers can be particularly helpful to demonstrate some advantage of the product that would be hard to describe (e.g., taste, convenience, or fragrance). However, the cost of such a huge effort is very great, and it can only be justified if it stimulates a substantial level of later purchases. One successful example was the introduction of Agree shampoo, which distributed over 30 million samples and eventually achieved a 20% market share (Engel et al., 1994).

Coupons and cents-off offers are the most common ways of offering price reductions to consumers. Their use has skyrocketed in recent decades, from 5.3 billion coupons distributed in 1962 to *330 billion* in 1992. In 1992, U.S. consumers redeemed 8.3 billion coupons, or $2\frac{1}{2}\%$ of all those distributed, at an average face value of 59 cents (Hume, 1992). The main method of distribution is leaflets inserted in newspapers (80%), but in-store distribution has increased rapidly in the last decade to 5% in 1992. Coupons have the advantages that a specified time limit may stimulate relatively quick sales, and the price reduction is limited to customers who use them while all others pay the regular price. However, in addition to the lost sales income, manufacturers have to pay for redemption services, including a usual fee of 8 cents per coupon to retailers; and the cost of spurious redemptions to customers who did not actually buy the product and other fraudulent practices is estimated at $1 billion per year in the U.S. (Engel et al., 1994).

Premiums are offers of added items, either free or at a bargain price, to induce customers to buy a product. They may range from tiny items in a box of Cracker Jack, to toys that can be ordered in return for cereal box tops, to costly beauty-care kits offered with a basic cosmetic purchase. For best results, there should be a clear connection between the product and the premium, which will make the recipient more likely to reorder the product. Thoughtfully designed premiums have often been effective in getting people to try a new product or to change brands. A highly successful example was a three-inch-high figure of a dancing raisin that was offered for 99 cents with a proof of purchase seal from a package of California raisins (Engel et al., 1994).

Contests and sweepstakes are promotions that get consumers involved with a manufacturer's advertising and marketing programs, often though not necessarily in combination with a purchase. **Contests** are competitions that involve skill or knowledge, as in writing a product slogan or creating a cake recipe. **Sweepstakes** are games of chance in which valuable prizes are given away to people who send in entry blanks connected with a particular product—for example, magazine sales campaigns by Publishers' Clearinghouse. Since the prizes are often large, both contests and sweepstakes create attention, excitement, and involvement among customers; and they may gain additional support from retailers, who stand to profit from any increased sales. Usually thousands of consumers enter these promotions, but the total cost of prizes may be relatively small, so the advertising profession generally considers these as strong marketing techniques. However, even so, they sometimes fail to win consumer enthusiasm, or they may garner bad publicity because of foul-ups in picking winners or allegations of cheating or favoritism (Engel et al., 1994).

Price reductions are another way of trying to increase a product's market share. A conceptual approach to studying price effects is to compare an advertised price of a product with consumers' **internal reference price**—the approximate price they expect to pay, based on their past experience. Prices noticeably below the consumer's internal reference price generally lead to more favorable short-term attitudes and increased like-

lihood of purchase. In contrast, prices higher than expected lead to less favorable attitudes, which are often asymmetrically stronger (Kalwani et al., 1990). However, a price that is set extremely low may lead to suspicion about poor quality or deception, and so to unfavorable attitudes (Williams, 1982).

In the longer term, one's internal reference price will change toward the prices that one experiences—an example of **adaptation-level theory**. For instance, a low introductory price may come to be seen as the expected price, leading to consumer resistance when the price is later raised. However, when consumers are relatively ignorant of prices or uninvolved in the product, they may respond favorably to a promotion featuring prices, even if prices have been cut little or none (an example of peripheral processing)—Inman, McAlister, and Hoyer (1990). You may have seen this technique in use in your supermarket, where prices prominently marked on a large end-of-aisle display often gain attention and stimulate purchases even though prices haven't been reduced.

Success of Promotions. How successful are the above kinds of promotions in influencing consumers? There is less published research than desirable about their results, in large part because companies that use them typically keep the results secret as proprietary information. Psychological theories, such as self-perception theory or reference price theory, predict that promotions offering an incentive for short-term sales may have a negative long-term effect on brand loyalty, which would be shown in reduced repurchase behavior after the promotion is ended. Some research findings support this viewpoint, though others are conflicting (Tybout & Artz, 1994).

One example of the negative effect of price cuts on later purchases is consumers who wait to purchase a car until the next manufacturer rebate offer. Another example is that many consumers heuristically use a product's price as an indication of its quality, so a price cut may suggest dubious quality rather than attractive value (Lichtenstein & Burton, 1989; Tellis & Gaeth, 1990). In fact, much advertising for luxury products seeks to strengthen this perceived tie between price and product quality (e.g., "it's expensive, but you're worth it"). A related finding is that consumers' price consciousness is generally negatively related to their ratings of product importance, so that uninvolved consumers will be the ones who are most sensitive to price considerations (Lichtenstein, Bloch, & Black, 1988).

Promotions to Retailers. A final major aspect of promotions is the incentives offered to retailers to carry and display the product. Most consumers are oblivious to this aspect, but when you stop to consider it, it is obvious that if retailers did not stock the product, consumers could not buy it, and manufacturers could not sell it, except through direct mail channels. This fact gives retailers much leverage, and they do not hesitate to use it. One practice that has become widespread in the U.S. is retailers charging manufacturers **slotting fees** to provide shelf space for their products. With the flood of new products, these fees have increased to as much as $10,000 per store, just to get the manufacturer's products on the shelf (Engel et al., 1994).

In addition to paying slotting fees, manufacturers may use many other techniques to encourage stores to display and sell their products enthusiastically. A common technique is to build **in-store displays**, such as special plastic or cardboard containers to showcase a product dramatically, and offer them to stores. One report found that special displays in supermarkets more than tripled sales of featured frozen dinners and laundry detergents, and more than doubled sales of salty snacks, soft drinks, and soups (Deveny, 1992).

Market Segmentation and Psychographics

A final aspect of marketing that we will discuss is **market segmentation**, the process of addressing advertising and marketing appeals to special subgroups of consumers. People in each subgroup are ones who are similar in some important ways that affect their consumer attitudes and/or purchases. The similarities may be demographic ones, such as age, income, sex, family size, educational level, region of the country, etc. Or they may be psychological needs or personality characteristics or lifestyle factors that are linked to consumer behaviors such as perception of and use of products. **Psychographics** is the process of determining and measuring these psychological similarities of population subgroups. Once measured, these similarities can be used in creating and advertising products so that they will appeal to a particular subgroup of people.

An early example of psychographic research was directed at defining different motives for drinking beer (Ackoff & Emshoff, 1975). The authors did extensive preliminary research, which led them to a typology of four main motivational patterns—for example, *indulgent* drinkers are seeking to become more introverted and withdrawn, whereas *social* drinkers drink to stimulate friendliness and sociability. Then the researchers recruited regular beer drinkers, ostensibly to help a major beer manufacturer decide which of four new beers to bring to market. After taking a test that classified them into one of these four types, the participants were shown four commercials for the four new beers, each of which was designed to appeal particularly to one of the psychographic types. Then they tasted samples of the supposed four new beers, all of which were actually the same beer, but labeled with the names from the four commercials.

You might think that the participants couldn't or wouldn't distinguish between the four (identical) beers, but if so, you would be wrong. The authors reported that all the participants believed the brands were different, and that most stated strong likes and dislikes among them. The beer that they chose as most preferred was usually the brand that had been shown as satisfying their type of motivation in the commercials (Ackoff & Emshoff, 1975). These findings are a spectacular example of how advertising can *create* preferences, not just reinforce them or provide supporting beliefs—among products that, in this case, were objectively identical.

The above example also illustrates that psychographic systems can be customized to a particular type of product. However, they can also be general in nature, and the most widely used general system is VALS™ 2 (Values and Lifestyles), developed by SRI International (1989). It classifies people into eight consumer groups, based on answers to 4 demographic questions and 35 attitudinal statements such as "I often crave excitement" and "I would rather make something than buy it." The eight consumer groups are identified by their position on two key dimensions: self-orientation and resources. *Self-orientation* classifies people as:

Principle-oriented—guided largely by a set of strongly held beliefs, ideals, or morals.
Status-oriented—influenced by actions, opinions, and approval of others.
Action-oriented—seek social or physical activity, variety, and adventure.

A cross-cutting dimension, called *resources,* is categorized into two levels, based not only on income and education, but also on psychological resources such as health, self-confidence, and eagerness to buy. These six categories are illustrated in Figure 14-2, which also shows two additional groups, one higher than the others on resources, and the other much lower. In the spring of 1996, the groups ranged in size from 10% to 17% of the U.S. population. A brief description of the eight groups is as follows:

- Actualizers—successful, sophisticated, daring; difficult to categorize by self-orientation because of wide experience and high self-confidence.

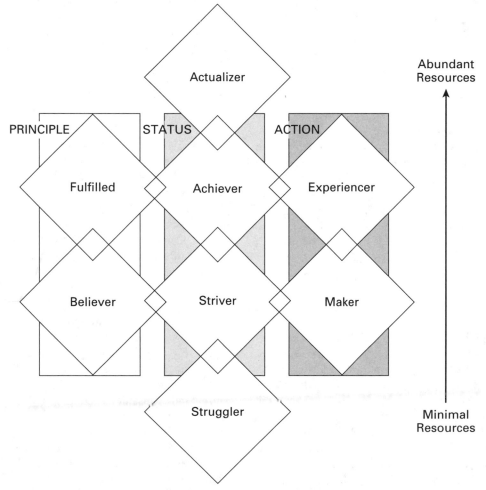

FIGURE 14-2   The 8 psychographic categories of the VALS 2 Lifestyle System. (Courtesy of SRI International.)

- Fulfilled—principle-oriented; mature, satisfied, knowledgeable, home-oriented, value order; relatively high income.
- Believers—principle-oriented; traditional values, family- and community-oriented, brand-loyal, tend to be older; modest resources. The largest group in 1996.
- Achievers—status-oriented; relatively affluent, aware of social position, career-oriented, conventional, buy prestige products.
- Strivers—status-oriented; financially insecure, impulsive, aware of social position and work to improve it, try to be stylish.
- Experiencers—action-oriented; enthusiastic, impulsive, dislike conformity, tend to be single and young, avid consumers.
- Makers—action-oriented; practical, independent, self-sufficient, traditional interests, unimpressed by prestige products.
- Strugglers—few resources, poor, concerned for security and safety, restricted consumption, tend to be old. Smallest group in 1996.

Using a scheme such as VALS 2, it is possible for manufacturers or advertisers to target their messages toward particular consumer psychographic groups. First, they can use words and images that appeal to a particular group. Next, they can place advertising in media that mainly serve particular psychographic segments (e.g., *Good Housekeeping*, sports and travel magazines, MTV, the Disney Channel). Also, they can send direct mail advertisements to specific zip codes, or to small portions of cities that have a particular psychographic profile—in fact, in major U.S. cities, psychographic profiles have been pinpointed to areas as small as a city block (Engel et al., 1994).

CONSUMER PROTECTION ISSUES

Finally, we turn to the important topic of how the interests of consumers can be protected from dangerous products and spurious advertising appeals. This topic has had much less concentrated research attention than the study of consumer behavior and of marketing and advertising techniques. For instance, textbooks in consumer behavior or marketing typically have many chapters on products and promotion, but at most a few pages on consumer rights or protection. Much of the work in this area has been done by consumer advocates

like Ralph Nader and activist organizations such as the Center for Law in the Public Interest. Empirical research reports can be found in journals such as the *Journal of Public Policy and Marketing*, in volumes such as Hill (1996), and in a special issue of the *Journal of Social Issues* (Friedman, 1991b).

A Brief History of Consumerism in the U.S.

Until the industrial revolution, most production and consumption of goods and foodstuffs was local in nature, so reputational knowledge about producers offered some measure of protection to consumers. However, the prevailing doctrine has always been *caveat emptor*—"let the buyer beware." In the United States, following the Civil War, Congress passed a number of laws to curb animal diseases, and national meat inspection began in the 1880s. In the field of public health, the first major law was the Pure Food and Drug Act of 1906, and its history illustrates the combination of forces that are usually necessary to pass major legislation to protect the public over the determined opposition of business leaders and conservative politicians (Nadel, 1971).

A key issue of the 1890s was health risks from opiates in patent medicines or from toxic substances such as formaldehyde or copper sulfate that canneries added to foodstuffs to preserve their appearance (Hermann, 1982). However, over ten years of efforts to pass regulatory laws in Congress had not succeeded. In 1905, President Theodore Roosevelt added his popular voice to the pressures for a law, and the American Medical Association began a supportive campaign. Even that influence was still not enough to get a bill out of committees in the House until the publication of Upton Sinclair's book, *The Jungle*. It was an expose of the nauseatingly unsanitary conditions in the Chicago meatpacking houses, and it was widely read by a revolted public. The publicity generated by this scandal finally carried the day, and a stiffer meat inspection bill and the Pure Food and Drug Act were both passed in 1906 (Hermann, 1982).

A similar combination of forces proved necessary to pass further consumer protection laws in later eras. In the 1930s, there was a campaign for more regulation of drugs and cosmetics to prevent horrible examples of disfigurement, blindness, poisoning, and death. Despite the pressure of women's groups, the American Medical Association, and President F. D. Roosevelt, commercial opposition stymied legislation until a scandal occurred, when 107 people died from taking a new sulfa drug combined with a toxic solvent that had never been tested for safety. With that impetus, the Federal Food, Drug, and Cosmetic Act was passed in 1938, requiring warnings and labels, and giving the Food and Drug Administration (FDA) power to approve drugs before they were marketed (Nadel, 1971).

In the 1960s, new consumer issues came to the fore and ended in passage of new legislation. A set of strengthening amendments to the Pure Food and Drug Act was passed in 1962, but only after Senator Kefauver broke the dramatic story of the sedative thalidomide causing physical deformities in fetuses, and how that drug had been kept off of the U.S. market by an FDA employee's insistence on further safety testing. Another central issue was automobile and tire safety, and House and Senate hearings were bolstered by publication of Ralph Nader's *Unsafe at Any Speed*, which demonstrated the major role of faulty design and construction in auto accidents and injuries. Public irritation with the automakers surged after revelations that General Motors was investigating and harassing Nader. Both Presidents Kennedy and Johnson called for legislation, and a number of bills were ultimately passed: the Vehicle Safety Act of 1966, a Truth-in-Packaging Act in 1966, a Truth-in-Lending Act in 1968, and several others (Hermann, 1982; Nadel, 1971).

Part of the push in consumer legislation in the 1960s was stimulated by President Kennedy, who in 1962 proposed to Congress a Consumer Bill of Rights. It stated the following key consumer rights:

- the right to safety from hazardous products
- the right to be informed about products (and not be deceived)
- the right to choose among competing products (instead of monopolies)
- the right to be heard (by sellers, manufacturers, and government)

These topics still form the core of consumer protection issues. However, a fifth right is now generally accepted as well (Aaker & Day, 1982):

- the right to recourse and redress (i.e., fair settlement of just claims)

This brief history of some of the major consumer protection campaigns in the U.S. illustrates that business leaders have typically opposed new laws or regulations as unnecessary or improper infringements on their activities. Pressure from an aroused and irate public has usually been a key ingredient. But that pressure has to be channeled by organized consumer groups, professional associations, and national leaders that can effectively lobby for change. Finally, the occurrence of and wide publicity about a major scandal have often been necessary to overcome opposition and legislative inertia.

In the current era, there has been a change toward deregulation of many businesses, such as airlines, railroads, banks, and oil, natural gas, and telecommunication companies. That trend offers important new topics for study to social researchers and new challenges to public policy aimed at protecting consumers (Brobeck, 1991).

Social Science Contributions to Consumer Protection

In the long cumulative process of legal and political maneuvering that leads to consumer reforms, there are many roles and possible contributions for social scientists. In this section we will present brief examples of some of the varied contributions of applied social psychological research to consumer protection issues.

Dangerous Products. A major role for social science research is establishing the degree of danger from unsafe products—problems such as the occurrence of injuries from flammable pajamas or automobile gas tanks that explode in accidents. For instance, toys alone injure about 700,000 U.S. children each year (Best, 1981). When dangers are demonstrated, government agencies may require the recall of unsafe products; for example, 5 million toy missiles for Mattel's

Battlestar Galactica were recalled as unsafe for children (Guzzardi, 1982).

Social science research is essential in establishing the way that people use potentially dangerous products as well as protective safety devices. For instance, many studies have investigated why people don't use automobile seat belts regularly, and ways in which their use could be made more widespread and effective (e.g., Geller, Paterson, & Talbott, 1982). Also, the results of protective regulations need to be studied, to ensure that they are working effectively. Such research demonstrated that poisonings of infants by baby aspirin decreased about 50% after passage of legislation that required childproof caps and bottles containing fewer pills (Walton, 1982). In another recent example, researchers showed that after Canada banned tobacco advertising in 1989, smoking among Canadians decreased about 8% per year (Koeppel, 1991).

Deceptive Advertising. The Federal Trade Commission (FTC) is charged with preventing unfair or deceptive advertising in the U.S., but definition of what is unfair or deceptive is a complex and contentious process. A certain amount of exaggeration, or "puffery," is expected in advertising, but false statements that a naive or trusting person might believe are forbidden, as are omissions of important facts affecting purchase (e.g., that a toy does not include batteries, or has to be assembled)—Aaker (1982).

In blatant cases of deception, the FTC can assess fines against offending manufacturers and advertising agencies, as it did for the TV ad showing a Volvo car as the only one with a roof that couldn't be crushed by a monster pickup truck driving over it. The picture was found to have been rigged by giving the Volvo extra internal supports and weakening the other cars' roof supports (Lipman, 1991). In less clearcut cases, consumer research is often helpful to determine what average citizens believe about the claims for a product. For instance, Firestone was allowed to continue applying the name Safety Champion to one of its tires after survey research showed that less than 2% of people surveyed understood that name as indicating that the tire had

special performance or safety characteristics (Cohen, 1980).

Another remedy sometimes ordered by the FTC is *corrective advertising*, to counteract past deceptive advertising. In one famous case, the makers of Listerine mouthwash had advertised for almost 50 years that Listerine could prevent or lessen the severity of common colds. In 1975 the FTC ruled that these claims could not be substantiated, and ordered that a corrective statement be put in the next $10 million of advertising for the product. An appeals court upheld this ruling, so for 18 months TV ads stated "Listerine will not help prevent colds or sore throats or lessen their severity." However, consumer research showed that people understood that message in different ways. There was a 40% decrease in people using Listerine for colds and sore throats, but about 40% still believed that effectiveness against colds and sore throats was a principal advertising theme of Listerine and used it for that purpose. Thus, research showed how difficult it was to extinguish people's past "learning" about a product's characteristics (FTC, 1981).

Advertising to Children. In Quebec, commercial advertising to persons under age 13 is forbidden by law! Imagine the difference between that situation and U.S. television's "kidvid," which allows up to 12 minutes of advertising in each weekend hour of children's programming. True, the FTC has more than once held public hearings on proposals to eliminate advertising to young children, and on milder recommendations to stop advertising of sugared food products directed at older children (because they produce dental health risks). However, because of pressure from product manufacturers and from Congress, each time the FTC has refused to set any restrictions of this sort (Armstrong & Brucks, 1988). Instead, it relies on voluntary groups—the major TV networks and the Children's Advertising Review Unit of the Council of Better Business Bureaus—to monitor ads directed at children and investigate ones that violate their guidelines.

As we discussed in Chapter 13, the average U.S. child is exposed to well over 20,000 TV commercials a year. This overwhelming exposure to ads has led to much psychological research about how children of various ages understand and react to TV advertising. Well-established findings indicate that young children do not distinguish clearly between programs and commercials, do not understand the persuasive intent of commercials, and tend to believe them uncritically and be influenced by them (Kunkel & Roberts, 1991). Findings like these led to the ban on children's ads in Quebec and to the unsuccessful efforts in the U.S. to establish controls on children's TV ads. However, contrary to these efforts, the deregulation movement of the 1990s even led to an *increase* in the amount of commercial time allowed on U.S. children's TV programs. A recent review article concluded:

> The history of regulatory attempts demonstrates that research findings are not a dominant influence on policy decisions. Rather, policy is a result of competing value orientations (e.g., protection of the marketplace or protection of the child) and the political maneuverings they engender. (Kunkel & Roberts, 1991, p. 57)

Provision of Information to Consumers. Consistent with American traditions of a free marketplace and free speech, U.S. laws and regulations have typically avoided limiting manufacturers' and advertisers' claims. Instead, much consumer protection research has been directed at providing consumers with offsetting objective information to help them make wise purchasing decisions. One example of this approach is the consumer product testing movement, pioneered by Consumers Union and Consumers' Research, Inc. in the 1920s, and the resulting large number of informative consumer magazines and books. However, only a relatively small proportion of better-educated citizens typically take advantage of these sources of information.

Another approach is legislation requiring fuller disclosure of information about products—a more limited goal than preventing or restricting their sale or requiring them to incorporate safety features. Many U.S. consumer protection laws have had this goal. Much research has been done about the degree of successful use of consumer information but much more is needed. Unfortunately, "information disclosure requirements

have the least effect on those buyers who have the greatest need for consumer protection" (Day, 1982, p. 162)—for example, low income, poorly educated, or non-English-reading consumers. Warning labels, in particular, are often disregarded by people from all socioeconomic groups. Research has shown that one way of increasing understanding and compliance is to use simple pictorial symbols in addition to words, as has been done systematically in Canada for hazard labeling that will be appropriate for both English- and French-speakers (Hadden, 1991).

Consumer Dissatisfaction and Complaints. Many surveys have been conducted to determine levels of consumer dissatisfaction with various types of services or products (e.g., Hunt, 1991). One large-scale study asked consumers about their most recent purchase in 34 different product categories, and found that 10% of all purchases were considered "somewhat unsatisfactory" or "unsatisfactory," plus another 10% for which problems were reported in response to an additional question about whether the purchase could have been better in some way. Combining these two responses, the categories that had the greatest percentages of problems (other than price) were car repairs (35%), car sales (32%), mail orders (31%), toys (31%), appliance repairs (30%), home repairs (28%), clothing (28%), vacuum cleaners (27%), and grocery items (26%)—Best and Andreasen (1976). Research also shows that actual customer complaints are a minority of the cases of dissatisfaction. In the above study, only 31% of those experiencing problems complained to the manufacturer or retailer, while another 1% complained to some other agency such as the Better Business Bureau or the courts.

What happens when consumers do complain? On average, about two-thirds of complaints are resolved to the consumer's satisfaction. However, in many cases, the retailer handles the problem, so that the manufacturer doesn't hear about it and can't take needed steps to correct it. Hence, many manufacturers have set up "consumer hot lines" with toll-free numbers to receive and respond to consumer complaints. General Electric's hot line receives 3 million calls each year and costs the company $10 million, but the payoff in retaining customers is considered to be far greater than the cost (Hawkins, Best, & Coney, 1992). Unfortunately, many companies try to avoid hearing about and redressing customer complaints, and whole books have been written reporting empirical research on problems in consumer complaint resolution (e.g., Best, 1981). Among the evasive techniques that companies use are the runaround, the silent treatment, legal gimmicks, blaming the victim, partial restitution, and rejection of requests for policy changes (Best, 1981).

The most extreme form of customer retaliation is organizing mass boycotts of an offending company or industry. Such boycotts aim to change the firm's offensive actions, either directly by reducing its sales, or indirectly through the media by damaging its public image until it reforms. An example was the consumer boycott against apple growers in 1989, which led them to stop using the pesticide Alar because of fears about its toxic residue in the fruit (Friedman, 1991a).

SUMMARY

A major approach in studying consumer issues is empirical and theoretical research on consumers' attitudes and behavior. Several well-known social psychological theories are highly relevant here. The Yale model of persuasive communication posits steps of exposure, attention, comprehension, acceptance, retention, and action in the consumer decision-making process; and much research has been done on each of these steps. The widely cited theory of reasoned action focuses on how different cognitive and attitudinal components combine to produce behavioral actions; it has generally been quite successful in predicting buying intentions and behavior. The currently popular elaboration likelihood model is a cognitive-response theory, which holds that attitude change is largely a process of self-persuasion; that is, one's own thoughts while processing a persuasive message—not the message itself—are the most crucial determinant of persuasive impact. The elaboration likelihood model also posits two routes to attitude and behavior change: the central route (systematic processing) involves a relatively thoughtful consideration of information and arguments about the topic, whereas the peripheral route (heuristic processing) is a less thoughtful, shortcut process, which relies on other cues and is used when a person is low in interest, motivation, or ability to process the message content.

A second major approach to consumer research focuses on the techniques used by marketers in their efforts to sell products and services to the public. Advertising is ubiquitous in our society, and is widely studied in consumer research. Some of the key dimensions of ads that can increase their effectiveness are vividness, incomplete elements (to stimulate audience members' active participation and elaboration), clear display of brand names, use of celebrities, and music. Comparative ads and use of humor are common today, but often are ineffective unless used extremely carefully. Attitudes toward a likable ad can and often do generalize to the product that it is promoting, either by the peripheral persuasion route or the central route or both.

Product promotions and pricing are other techniques used to encourage sales. Among them are giving samples to consumers, coupons and cents-off offers, premiums included with the product, contests and sweepstakes, and price reductions. The results of each of these short-term promotional techniques are often easier to assess than the more diffuse effects of advertising, but a danger with all of them is potential negative effects on consumers' brand loyalty. Most marketing today uses market segmentation—aiming advertising and marketing appeals at special subgroups of consumers—and the psychological similarities of these subgroups are measured with psychographic methods.

Consumer protection issues and policies deserve much more research than they have received. The consumer movement in the U.S. is over 100 years old, but it has usually succeeded in passing new protective legislation only when pressure from organized consumer groups and key national leaders has coincided with aroused public opinion due to some major scandal. Among the main social science contributions to consumer protection are research on dangerous products, deceptive advertising, advertising to children, effects of providing consumer information to the public, and consumer dissatisfaction and complaints.

SUGGESTED READINGS

Aaker, D. A., & Day, G. S. (Eds.). (1982). *Consumerism: Search for the consumer interest* (4th ed.). New York: Free Press.—A volume of collected readings, organized according to consumer issues that occur before purchase, at purchase, or after purchase, and containing both defenses and critiques of consumerism.

Friedman, M. (Ed.). (1991). Consumer protection issues. *Journal of Social Issues, 47*(1), 1–191.—This journal issue addresses many of the central topics of social science research on consumer protection.

Hawkins, D. I., Best, R. J., & Coney, K. A. (1992). *Consumer behavior: Implications for marketing strategy* (5th ed.). Homewood, IL: Irwin.—A comprehensive recent textbook which emphasizes the viewpoints and interests of marketers.

Hill, R. P. (Ed.). (1996). *Marketing and consumer research in the public interest.* Thousand Oaks, CA: Sage.—This recent collection of chapters mainly emphasizes critiques of current marketing practices.

Tybout, A. M., & Artz, N. (1994). Consumer psychology. *Annual Review of Psychology, 45,* 131–169.—The most recent of regular quadrennial reviews of current research findings and theoretical advances.

CHAPTER 15

Legal Issues—Research on the Legal System

How long we shall continue to blunder along without the aid of unpartisan and authoritative scientific assistance in the administration of justice, no one knows, but all fair persons not conventionalized by provincial legal habits of mind ought, I should think, unite to effect some such advance.

—Judge Learned Hand, 1911

Though Judge Hand issued this call for cooperation between social science and the legal system long ago in 1911, his call was rarely answered. In 1979 Anastasi echoed Judge Hand's statement:

> Current laws as well as judicial procedures are often based upon outdated theories of human behavior and are at variance with experimentally established facts. . . . The psychological principles actually followed in legal practice are sometimes so manifestly obsolete as to be almost unanimously rejected by psychologists. (p. 503)

However, in the past 20 years, the field of legal psychology has grown tremendously. Recent assessments of the field indicate that it is flourishing, both within the U.S. and internationally (Lösel, 1992). In this chapter we will consider the relationship of social psychology to the legal system and review many of the areas of legal psychology.

THE BACKGROUND OF LEGAL PSYCHOLOGY

Many aspects of the U.S. legal system are older than the country itself, having been imported bodily from the British system of common law. By its nature, the system stresses previous precedents and is highly resistant to change. It is interesting to note that in the early years of scientific psychology, at the beginning of this century, psychologists took an active research interest in some legal questions. The topic of witness testimony was one of the first areas of applied psychology, and was brought to widespread public attention by Hugo Munsterberg's (1908) book entitled *On the Witness Stand*.

However, in the 1920s, psychological research on legal issues diminished to a trickle, and it only began to revive again in the 1970s. Since then it has become a burgeoning and active field with a large number of investigators studying many different aspects of the legal system (Kagehiro & Laufer, 1992; Lösel, 1992). Among the signs of its vitality are the establishment of organizations dedicated to law and psychology in several countries, the founding of interdisciplinary journals such as *Law and Human Behavior* and *Behavioral Science and the Law*, and publication of many volumes containing research reports and summaries (e.g., Bartol & Bartol, 1994; Lösel, Bender, & Bliesener, 1992; Sporer, Malpass, & Koehnken, 1996).

One of the earliest examples of psychological applications to the law was in 1908 by Louis Brandeis, whose famous brief used research findings about widespread public opinion to convince the Supreme Court that the workday for women employed in laundries should be limited to 10 hours. A high point in the legal use of social science was the 1954 *Brown* decision on school desegregation (discussed in Chapter 8). Some of the other applications of social psychology to the legal system include questions of jury composition and jury size, regulations concerning bail and pretrial detention, findings of public opinion regarding trademarks, research on eyewitness testimony, arguments for and against the death penalty, and the effects of gun control laws.

When people speak of the U.S. legal system, they are often thinking primarily of courts and juries. It is easy to forget that the courts are only a small part of the legal system. In the civil justice system, only about 2% of the cases filed are ultimately settled by a court decision. In the criminal justice area, less than 10% of the cases where an arrest is made finally go to trial (Saks & Hastie, 1978; U.S. Department of Justice, 1990). Figure 15-1 presents a schematic picture of the number of cases at each of the many decision points in the U.S. criminal justice system during a typical year. As it shows, only about 20% of criminal sentences result from court trials; the rest stem from admissions of guilt and from **plea-bargains**, in which a person charged

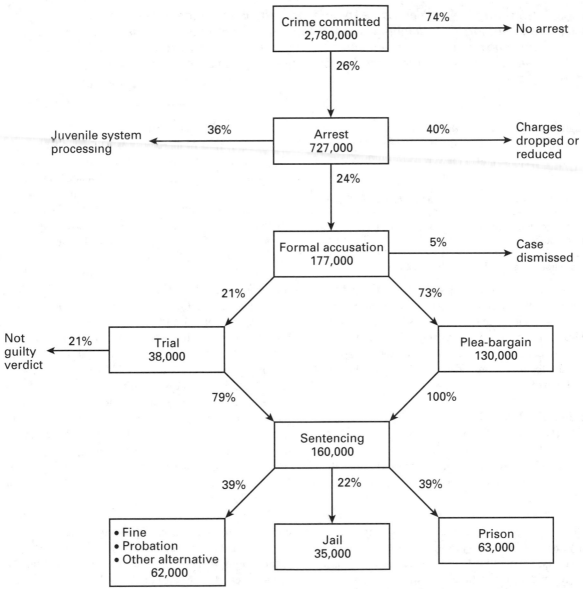

FIGURE 15-1 **The American criminal justice system: number and percentage of cases at major decision points in a typical year.** (Data for 1965 from President's Commission on Law Enforcement and Administration of Justice, 1967, pp. 262–263.)

with a crime agrees to plead guilty in return for a reduced sentence. Thus, the vast network of private lawyers, district attorneys, and public defenders has a numerically larger role than court trials. Other crucial parts of the system are the police, prisons, parole and probation agencies, and juvenile authorities. All these actors and settings have been studied by social psychologists.

SOCIAL PSYCHOLOGICAL CONTRIBUTIONS

Jury Selection Procedures

Juries are supposed to be composed of a representative cross-section of citizens in their community, but it is well-known that they often seriously fail to meet that test. Many studies have shown that juries typically have an overrepresentation of middle-class, White, and older individuals. When challenges to the composition of jury pools are raised, social psychological methods can be used to determine their representativeness. Surveys of the demographic characteristics of community members and statistical comparisons with jury pool lists can give quite precise measures of the degree of bias in the lists, and they have often been used as a basis for legal challenges of the composition of jury pools (Kairys, Schulman, & Harring, 1975).

At the beginning of court trials, the trial attorneys or the judge customarily question prospective jurors in the jury selection process called *voir dire*. The purpose is to eliminate any jurors who have biases regarding the case (for instance, ones who are acquainted with any of the parties), and to pick jurors who will be impartial (or possibly favorable to one's own side of the case). Since the time of Clarence Darrow and before, lawyers have propounded theories about which kinds of jurors will be most sympathetic and how it is possible to recognize them from their *voir dire* answers. However, empirical research indicates that lawyers differ widely on what juror characteristics they consider important and desirable, and that none of the characteristics they use are apt to be appreciably related to the jurors' ultimate decisions about guilt or innocence (Olczak, Kaplan, & Penrod, 1991).

Given this situation, considerable interest was aroused by social psychologists' attempts to use systematic scientific methods to aid attorneys in juror selection. The early uses of these methods in the 1970s were usually in major trials having a prominent political aspect, and usually by the defense team—for instance, in trials of the American Indian Movement leaders who occupied the village of Wounded Knee, defendants in the Watergate cover-up scandal, the Mc-

Martin child abuse trial, and the rape trial of William Kennedy Smith. More recently, a number of large corporations have used these techniques when they were being sued for millions of dollars in product liability or antitrust cases (Abramson, 1994).

What kinds of scientific techniques can identify sympathetic jurors? Scientific jury selection typically begins by collecting data from a representative sample of citizens in the local area where the trial will be held. The purpose is to determine which demographic characteristics, such as age, sex, race, education, and occupation, are related within that community to attitudes that are expected to be relevant to the trial, such as trust in government, authoritarianism, punitiveness, or racial prejudice. Once the key variables have been determined, the prospective jurors are evaluated on each of the variables, either through a checklist or even through interviews with community residents who are acquainted with individual members of the pool of prospective jurors. Third, additional information is obtained by monitoring nonverbal behaviors while prospective jurors answer *voir dire* questions (Christie 1976; Schulman et al., 1987).

There has been much controversy over the propriety of using these scientific jury selection methods (Penrod & Cutler, 1987). However, they are really only extensions of lawyers' traditional techniques of screening jurors. In addition, there is little evidence regarding the effectiveness of these scientific approaches (Abramson, 1994), though some research suggests that they may have a slight advantage over the traditional intuitive procedures used by lawyers (Moran, Cutler, & De-Lisa, 1994). In any event, the great effort and expense involved in these scientific methods will probably ensure that they will be used only in major cases where crucial social principles or millions of dollars are at stake.

Detecting Deception

The ability to determine when a person is lying versus telling the truth would be invaluable to the legal system. Many approaches to lie detection have been developed. Some common-sense approaches include attention to nonverbal cues like agitation, lack of eye contact, dryness of mouth, and voice tones. One ancient Chinese technique required people to put rice powder in their mouth and spit it out. If the powder was dry, the person was lying (B. Smith, 1967).

The most systematic and well-known approach to detecting deception is the **polygraph** or "lie detector." The polygraph measures several bodily responses that accompany stress. In its most commonly used form, physiological changes in heart rate, blood pressure, and galvanic skin response are studied, comparing an individual's reactions to relevant questions with reactions to control questions that are arousing but irrelevant (Saxe, 1994). For example, physiological responses to the question, "Have you ever stolen money from your employer" might be compared with physiological responses to the question, "Did you ever hurt anyone when you were a child." Lie detectors are used primarily in personnel selection and police investigations (Saxe, 1994). Traditionally, courts have not allowed the use of polygraph evidence, but recent rulings by the Supreme Court have ended this stringent rejection, and instead encouraged courts to consider its relevance to the case (Honts & Perry, 1992). As of 1994, there were still 28 states that did not allow evidence from polygraph tests, largely because of controversy over their accuracy (Bartol & Bartol, 1994).

Assessing the accuracy of a polygraph is a complex task. The type of questions, the person being questioned, the questioner, the context, and the questioner's training are a few of the variables that could affect the results (Abrams, 1989; DePaulo & Pfeiffer, 1986; Saxe, 1994). A review of empirical studies found that when tests were conducted by experienced administrators in a laboratory setting, 89% of guilty responses and 83% of innocent responses were correctly detected; in field settings, accuracy was slightly lower (Elaad, 1990). Overall, lie detectors are likely to be about 85% accurate on any given question (Ekman, 1992). Untrained observers without a polygraph are usually able to detect whether a person is lying at a somewhat better than chance level, but success when using lie detectors is substantially better than with an intuitive approach (DePaulo, 1992; DePaulo, Stone, & Lassiter, 1985). Nevertheless, the likely error rate of at least 15% raises serious questions about relying on such procedures in legal cases.

Bail Setting and Sentencing

The process by which judges set bail for defendants is an important one because it applies to a large proportion of criminal defendants, rather than only the 10% or so who end up in jury trials. Bail hearings are generally held in open court shortly after a person is indicted for a crime. Their purpose is to set the amount of **bail**—money that the accused will have to put up as security in order to be released from prison while awaiting trial. The judge can decide on any amount of bail, or can release accused persons on their own recognizance without bail, or can deny bail and hold them in jail.

In practice, the bail system discriminates against poor people who cannot afford to put up the bail themselves or to pay a bail bondsman's fee (usually 10% of the amount of bail) in order to be released. This often results in injustice, since about 70% of defendants who are held in jail because they cannot pay bail are later acquitted or else convicted but not given jail sentences. Furthermore, research has shown that one of the main influences on the judge's final sentence following a guilty verdict is the situation of the defendant before trial—in jail, released on bail, or on own recognizance—and the bail setting system is often a factor in keeping poorer defendants in jail until their trial (Ebbesen & Konecni, 1982).

Other research on plea bargaining in the sentencing process observed New York City's special "guilty plea courts" (McConville & Mirsky, 1995). There, judges often dispose of 50 or more cases in one day, and court-appointed attorneys typically have not interviewed their clients until minutes before they are arraigned and their bail is set. Not surprisingly, about 80% of these cases are resolved by guilty pleas. In this threatening situation, innocent defendants who were mistakenly rounded up in police raids were strongly encouraged to plead "guilty" in return for a promise of probation and to avoid the threat of possibly serving several years in prison. The researchers summarized this system as a "social disciplinary model," apparently designed to impose surveillance and control on the urban underclass, with little concern about defendants' actual guilt or innocence (McConville & Mirsky, 1995, p. 217).

Public Attitudes Toward Crime

In 1995, when asked about the most pressing problem facing their nation, more U.S. residents mentioned crime than any other factor. More than half perceived crime as increasing in their areas, while less than 10% felt it was decreasing. (In fact, crime has been decreasing, nationwide—see the next section.) Nearly half of the respondents said they felt afraid to walk alone at night in areas near their home, and international polls in Great Britain and Canada showed similar results (*Index to International Public Opinion,* 1995).

However, the fear of crime is often out of proportion to the actual incidence of crime. Research has shown that high levels of media coverage devoted to crime stories, particularly to the most violent crimes, can give viewers a distorted picture of local crime and may lead to increased fear of crime (Doob, 1982; McAneny, 1993). Surprisingly, groups of people who express a high fear of crime, such as women and the elderly, often have lower victimization rates than do men and younger people (Conklin, 1975). Some attempts to explain this situation have stressed personal feelings of control versus lack of control over the crime situation as an explanatory factor.

Kidder and Cohn (1979) suggested a useful distinction between **crime prevention** (actions aimed at cutting down the number of offenders) and **victimization prevention** (actions intended to reduce the likelihood that one will become a victim of crime). In terms of psychological theory, crime prevention is the equivalent of reactance—fighting against outside constraints—while victimization prevention is analogous to learned helplessness—giving up much of one's freedom because of a feeling of lack of control over outside situations. Crime prevention includes crime reporting, police-community relations programs, victim or witness assistance programs, and youth services. Victim-

Table 15–1 Steps Taken by Americans to Avoid Being a Victim of Crime: 1981 and 1993

Steps Taken	% in 1981	% in 1993
Not walk alone at night	20	40
Keep a dog for protection	20	38
Bought a gun for protection	16	30
Installed special locks	13	43
Installed a burglar alarm	5	18
Carry a whistle	5	10
Other measures	8	NA
No measures	8	NA

Source: McAneny (1993, p. 22).

ization prevention includes avoidance of risky areas, property protection such as locks and burglar alarms, escort services, citizen patrols, block organizing, and streetlight improvements.

What steps are most often taken to avoid crime? Table 15-1 lists the percentages of respondents in a representative national survey who said they had taken various actions, comparing responses in 1993 with an earlier 1981 survey (McAneny, 1993). The data indicate that almost everyone in the U.S. population (92% in 1981) had taken some actions to avoid crime, and almost all of the actions asked about were victimization-prevention measures. Additionally, the study showed that by 1993 a much larger number of people had taken prevention measures in *every* surveyed category than in 1981.

Another aspect of attitudes toward crime concerns the *punishments* that people think are appropriate for various crimes. From the 1970s through the 1990s, an increasing majority of Americans stated a belief that we should have stronger law enforcement, both by the police and the courts, and more severe punishments (Finckenauer, 1978; McAneny, 1993). A 1993 Gallup poll found 86% of respondents believed that the courts in their area were not harsh enough with criminals, a majority favored more restrictive bail and more difficult paroles, and 43% favored a complete ban on plea bargaining. Yet Americans are conflicted about punishment, for almost three-quarters of respondents indicated that the proper function of prisons should be rehabilitation, while at the same time a majority admitted that in actuality prisons mostly accomplished punishment and isolation of prisoners from society, rather than rehabilitation (McAneny, 1993).

Measuring Crime

The problem of determining the actual frequency of crimes is by no means a simple one. The best-known compilation of data on the national level is the *Uniform Crime Reports* (UCR), published annually by the FBI. It includes data from about 10,000 local jurisdictions, covering more than 90% of the country's population. However, its main focus is on the seven so-called Index crimes (murder, rape, aggravated assault, robbery, burglary, larceny, and auto theft), and it provides much less information on other crimes—particularly white-collar crimes like forgery, embezzlement, fraud, price fixing, and corporate law-breaking.

Even for the crimes that the UCR covers, there are problems. Though standard reporting forms are used, state and local definitions of crime, record-keeping practices, and reporting criteria may vary widely. There are also great fluctuations among jurisdictions in the extent of reporting crimes to the police. This can lead to an anomalous situation in which an effective police department may have a high rate of reported crime—because the local citizens trust the department and believe it will work hard to solve any crimes they report—whereas a slipshod department may have a low reported crime rate because no one bothers to report most crimes. Moreover, arrest rates and rates of "clearance" of crimes (by arrests or by failure of the victim to prosecute) have very serious problems of inaccuracy, inconsistency, and lack of comparability across jurisdictions. For instance, they can be easily inflated if the police make many low-quality arrests that fail to produce convictions or are thrown out by the district attorney before trial.

A final problem with the UCR, probably the most serious one of all, is that most crimes in the United States are never reported, so they do not enter into the official statistics. The way this is determined is through large-scale sample surveys which ask respondents about **crime victimization**. National sample studies have shown from three to five times as much crime in several major categories as was reported to police. A central example is the National Crime Victimization Survey of 75,000 households, conducted by the U.S. Department of Justice (1994). This study of the occurrence and reporting of major categories of crime during 1992 showed that over 60% of all crimes went unreported. Of course, since these data came from self-reports, they also have built-in sources of inaccuracy, but they are probably much closer than the UCR data to the true state of affairs (Schneider, 1981).

On the other hand, some crimes are reported to the police much more often than others; these include auto thefts (75% are reported), aggravated assaults (62% are reported), and other serious property or personal crimes that involve large losses or bodily injury. Hence, the crime reports are more accurate for them than for small-scale larceny, theft, or minor assault. Despite their flaws, the *Uniform Crime Reports* are valuable for showing trends in major categories of crime over time. Contrary to the impression that most people have gained from media sensationalization of crime stories, the occurrence of most major types of crime in the U.S. has been *declining* since a peak in 1981. Violent crimes have decreased on a per capita basis, and the absolute number of thefts and household crimes such as burglary decreased over 20% between 1981 and 1992 (Bureau of Justice Statistics, 1994).

Crime Reduction Laws

An important question for applied social psychologists is the effectiveness of laws designed to reduce crime. Studies of crime reduction and prevention have mostly taken the form of evaluation research. The examples of gun control laws and the death penalty will illustrate this research.

Gun control is a pressing social problem in many nations—particularly in the U.S., which has been dubbed "the homicide capital of the world" (Podell & Archer, 1994). Approximately 25,000 U.S. citizens are killed each year by firearms, a rate substantially higher than any other country in the world (Archer & Gartner, 1987). A variety of gun control laws have been proposed over the years, including:

- Mandatory sentencing for felonies committed with a firearm.
- Restricted ownership—usually, prohibiting convicted felons from owning guns.
- Prohibition of certain types of firearms like assault rifles.
- Purchase delays or waiting periods before a person can purchase a gun.
- Licensing laws that set requirements such as training for gun ownership

In an excellent review, Podell and Archer (1994) examined the effects of these gun control laws on a variety of criminal acts. Their results clearly showed that "major legal firearm reforms reduce violent death rates" (p. 50), even though they don't decrease the number of assaults. They concluded "it may be that firearm control laws do not affect the number of conflicts in a society, but only their lethality" (p. 58).

The death penalty provides another example of social psychological research on laws aimed at reducing crime. Most Americans report that they favor capital punishment—the figure has climbed from a low of 42% in 1966 to 77% in 1995 who stated that they supported the death penalty "for persons convicted of murder" (Moore, 1995). However, when people are asked more specific questions (e.g., about how they would vote in a particular capital trial), support for the death penalty drops sharply (Bohm, 1991). Reasons that those who favor capital punishment cite for their support include revenge (50%), deterrence (13%), elimination of possible future crime (19%), and the cost of a life-in-prison sentence (11%) (Gallup & Newport, 1991).

The issues of deterrence and cost have received considerable study, and the results indicate that popular conceptions of the death penalty are incorrect. First, there is no evidence that capital punishment is a deterrent to other potential criminals. In fact, there is evidence that capital punishment laws may actually increase the homicide rate (Bowers, 1988). Additionally, the legal costs of trying and convicting a defendant, and going through the "due-process" appeals required to impose a death sentence, are higher than the cost of life-in-prison (Costanzo & Costanzo, 1994; Dieter, 1993).

Related to the research on the death penalty is the issue of **death-qualified jurors** (ones in murder cases who state that they would be conscientiously able to vote for the death penalty). Research has consistently shown that death-qualified jurors are much more likely to vote "guilty" than are other, "excluded" jurors (e.g., Cowan, Thompson, & Ellsworth, 1984; Haney, Hurtado, & Vega, 1994). This finding raises an important issue regarding the fairness of trials for plaintiffs facing the death penalty. In 1986 the U.S. Supreme Court considered the issue of fairness regarding death-qualified jurors (*Lockhart v. McCree,* 1986). The American Psychological Association submitted a thorough review of over 20 years of psychological research, which demonstrated that death-qualified juries are more likely to convict defendants than are other juries (Bersoff & Ogden, 1987). However, on a 5–4 vote, the court rejected the empirical evidence as irrelevant to the constitutional issue, and ruled that death-qualified juries do not violate a defendant's right to a fair trial (Bersoff, 1987; Elliot, 1991).

Psychologists as Expert Witnesses

One way that psychological knowledge, such as the research about death-qualified juries or lie detection, could be used in court proceedings would be to have psychologists testify as expert witnesses about research findings that are relevant to a specific case. This procedure is becoming increasingly common. In recent years psychologists have testified in courts on a variety of topics, including dimensions of psychopathology, battered woman's syndrome, witness accuracy, the testimony of children, the adequacy of product warning labels, fraudulent advertising, and sexual abuse cases (DeAngelis, 1994; Loftus, 1991). Though many judges have refused to admit the testimony of psychologists as experts who have specialized knowledge, some of these exclusionary decisions have been reversed by appeals courts (Penrod, Fulero, & Cutler, 1995).

One topic that psychologists have frequently testified about in recent years is research on the accuracy of eyewitness testimony. The next section of this chapter will examine that topic in some detail. However, it should be noted that there is still controversy about whether expert psychological testimony will improve

Photograph courtesy of Elizabeth Loftus. Reprinted by permission.

Box 15-1

ELIZABETH LOFTUS, EXPERT ON EYEWITNESS TESTIMONY

Elizabeth Loftus is a cognitive psychologist who has done extensive work on the relationship of psychology to various legal issues. Born in Los Angeles in 1944, she graduated from UCLA and earned her Ph.D. at Stanford in 1970. After three years on the faculty of the New School for Social Research in New York, she moved to the University of Washington, where she quickly became a full professor in psychology and an adjunct professor in the law school. A prolific author, she has published 18 books and over 250 scientific articles. She has also been elected president of the Western Psychological Association and of two divisions of the APA (Experimental, and Psychology and Law).

Best known for her research on human memory and eyewitness testimony, Loftus has also written on communication in emergency situations, the wording of questions in legal interrogations, expert testimony, juror verdicts, improving jurors' understanding of legal instructions, advertising and jury awards, effects of drugs on memory, inducing resistance to misleading information, the topic of repressed memories, and issues of informed consent and affirmative action. She received a National Media Award from the APA for her book *Eyewitness Testimony*, and has held the unusual position of representative from her university faculty to the Washington legislature. She has served as an expert witness or consultant in hundreds of legal cases, including such famous ones as the McMartin Preschool molestation case, the Hillside Strangler, and the Menendez brothers.

jurors' evaluation of eyewitness testimony (Cutler & Penrod, 1995; Loftus & Ketcham, 1991).

Important issues about the form and content of expert testimony have also been reviewed (Hambacher, 1994). For instance, how should questions about the internal validity and external generalizability of research findings be handled? In cases where psychologists disagree about the interpretation of findings, does an expert witness have a duty to present both sides? How can the probabilistic, rather than certain, nature of research conclusions be explained understandably to jurors? Should scientific evidence be presented by expert witnesses hired by the parties in the case, or by a more impartial panel of experts (Chesler, Kalmuss, & Sanders, 1983; Slovenko, 1993)? Many more psychologists will have to face these issues as psychological expert testimony becomes more widely sought and accepted.

EYEWITNESS IDENTIFICATION AND TESTIMONY

This oldest area of applied legal psychology is still the focus of great research interest; in fact, "psychologists have conducted more research dealing with eyewitness testimony than with any other question of law" (Lipton, 1996, p. 7). Hence, we will examine the topic in some detail. Many findings of traditional experimental psychology are relevant here, particularly facts about sensory acuity, perceptual processes, and memory. For example, in a court case, individuals' accuracy in estimating short intervals of time or the speed of moving vehicles is often crucial in determining the value of their testimony.

The accuracy of witnesses' perception and recall has often been studied by unexpectedly staging an exciting incident before a group of unforewarned observers. For instance, during a college class, two students might get into an argument, escalating into name calling, book throwing, blows, and a hasty exit—after which the instructor might ask class members to write down all that they remember about the incident. In order to achieve greater control over the stimulus situation, incidents of this sort are now usually filmed or videotaped. Thus, they can be shown repeatedly to many different audiences, and the instructions to the observer and conditions of viewing can be varied experimentally (Wells & Lindsay, 1980; Yuille & Tollestrup, 1992).

The predominant conclusion of this kind of research—contrary to the beliefs of most average citizens, and of many judges and jurors—is the untrustworthiness of much eyewitness testimony (Tollestrup, Turtle, & Yuille, 1994). For instance, take the case of a police lineup where a witness is trying to identify which, if any, of several men committed a crime. Under most circumstances such testimony is apt to be unreliable (Wells & Luus, 1990). In fact, eyewitness

*mis*identification is the leading cause of wrongful conviction in U.S. trials. In a systematic review of 205 wrongful conviction cases, Rattner (1988) found mistaken identification to be a major contributing factor in 52%. In the following sections we will examine factors that contribute to misidentification, as well as the controversial issue of children's eyewitness testimony.

Factors Affecting Witness Accuracy

Generally speaking, in remembering a witnessed event, people tend to focus on information that fits with their expectations. Recollections about who did what can be influenced by many extraneous variables like style of dress, race, gender, time of day, or facial expression (Diges, Rubio, & Rodriguez, 1992; Jalbert & Getting, 1992; Lindsay, 1994a). For example, when asked to identify an assailant, witnesses often erroneously select innocent bystanders if they "look like" a criminal in their style of dress or appearance (Yarmey, 1993). Social psychological research has shown that witnesses generally fill in the gaps in their observations with plausible details that fit the general context (Narby, Cutler, & Penrod, 1996; Read, 1994). In this section we will examine seven factors which research has clearly shown can lead to errors in identification: question wording, police lineups, mug shot bias, post-event information, accuracy versus confidence, cross-race bias, and weapon focus (Kassin et al., 1989). Table 15-2 presents a brief overview of key findings on each of these topics. For a thorough review of other factors see Narby et al. (1996).

Question Wording. Experimental research has consistently found that human memory can be influenced by the words used to prompt recall of a person or an event. In the typical research paradigm, after witnessing an event, subjects are prompted to recall specific information about the details of their experience. This type of research has demonstrated that people who hear misleading suggestions about the details of an event typically recall the event less accurately than do control subjects (Lindsay, 1994b). Allowing people to report events in their own words tends to yield information on fewer details, but also produces a higher percentage of accurate recall than does direct ques-

TABLE 15–2   Eyewitness Factors About Which Enough Is Known to Present Research Evidence in Court   *[handwritten: source misattro.]*

1. Wording of questions	An eyewitness's testimony about an event can be affected by how the questions put to that witness are worded.
2. Lineup instructions	Police instructions can affect an eyewitness's willingness to make an identification and/or the likelihood that he or she will identify a particular person.
3. Mug shot bias	Eyewitnesses sometimes identify as a culprit someone that they have seen in another situation or context.
4. Post-event information	Eyewitness testimony about an event often reflects not only what the witness actually saw but also information obtained later on.
5. Accuracy vs. confidence	An eyewitness's confidence is not a good predictor of his or her identification accuracy.
6. Cross-race bias	Eyewitnesses are better at identifying others of the same race than they are at identifying members of another race.
7. Weapon focus	The presence of a weapon impairs an eyewitness's ability to accurately identify the perpetrator's face.

[handwritten left margin: memory construct faulty memory 7 confidant ID to identify]

Data were obtained from a sample of 63 experts who were asked to rank statements according to the amount of research supporting them. (Source: Extracts from Kassin, S. M., Ellsworth, P. C., and Smith, V. L. [1989]. The "general acceptance" of psychological research on eyewitness testimony: A survey of the experts. *American Psychologist, 44,* 1089–1098.)

tioning (Marquis, Marshall, & Oskamp, 1972; Saywitz et al., 1991).

Under hostile or leading questions, accuracy may drop still further (Brennan & Brennan, 1988; Lipton, 1977). Even the grammatical wording of a question may influence the response. "Wasn't the woman holding a purse?" is more suggestive than "Was the woman holding a purse?", which in turn is more suggestive and less likely to be answered accurately than "Did you see a purse?" (Loftus, 1975; Loftus & Zanni, 1975). These types of misleading questions produce what has been termed **source misattribution**: a mistake in the source to which the person attributes their memory (Johnson, Hashtroudi, & Lindsay, 1993). Research has shown that misleading questions can change individuals' memory for a witnessed event, and that these individuals then come to believe that the constructed memory is an accurate one because they incorrectly attribute the source of the memory to their experience and not to the misleading question (Weingardt, Toland, & Loftus, 1994). An interesting collection of cases where persons mistakenly came to believe in the accuracy of their memory was presented by Loftus and Ketcham (1991).

Police Lineups. An eyewitness identification of a suspect in a police lineup is often the most influential evidence in a criminal trial (Wells, 1993). When police make an arrest, they often asked witnesses to identify the perpetrator from among a group of other individuals. This procedure can take place anywhere from a few hours to many months after the original event. There are several features of the police lineup that can lead to misidentification. Two of the most pervasive involve the lineup construction and the instructions to the witness.

1. Lineup construction. To be fair, a lineup should include several innocent people who match the description of the perpetrator, or who resemble the suspect's general appearance (Luus & Wells, 1994). Indeed, distinctive features are usually a sure sign of identification—or misidentification, as the case may be. An example is the case of Steve Titus, who was mistakenly accused of rape. During a police lineup, Titus's picture was shown to the victim along with five "similar" others. However, his picture was distinct—it was the only one without a border, it was smaller than the others, and he was the only man smiling (Loftus & Ketcham, 1991).

2. Instructions. During the police lineup, the instructions given to the witness can dramatically alter the likelihood of misidentification. For example, instructions that lead the witness to believe the culprit is among those in the lineup lead people to feel compelled to identify someone (Malpass & Devine, 1981). Returning to the case of Steve Titus, the police asked the witness to pick the assailant from among the six pictures. After she scanned the pictures and shook her head, police urged her to concentrate and make a choice. Finally she identified the one that was "closest" in appearance to the culprit, and concluded that "it had to be the one" (Loftus & Ketcham, 1991, p. 38).

Mug Shot Bias. A strategy often used by police is to ask the witness to search through a series of mug shots. Research has clearly demonstrated that viewing pictures of potential suspects can reduce the accuracy of the identification (Narby et al., 1996). If one of the people from the mug shots appears in a subsequent lineup, the witness is just as likely to identify him/her as to identify the actual culprit. The findings regarding mug shots are part of the broader phenomenon in which witness identifications are influenced by experiences since the key event, and *source misattribution* produces a tendency to identify as the culprit a person who is familiar. For example, witnesses may identify as the culprit a person they have seen in a newspaper or on the news if they can't remember the source of their memory.

Post-Event Information. The memory for a witnessed event may be influenced by information obtained subsequent to the event. We have already seen examples of post-event information in the mug shot bias and the wording of questions. The general phenomenon of **memory construction**—the tendency to remember an event as consistent with current beliefs—can often lead to errors in witness identification.

Accuracy Versus Confidence. It is not just misidentifications of culprits by eyewitnesses that lead to false convictions in the criminal trial, but "the certainty with which such false identifications are sometimes made" (Wells, 1993, p. 564). After making an identification, witnesses are typically asked how confident they are about their identification. Research on witnesses' confidence has been divided into confidence in their *ability* to make a correct identification and confidence in *having correctly identified* the culprit. Regarding confidence to make an identification (an estimate made before the witness is asked to identify the culprit), the research evidence clearly indicates that there is little or no relationship between perceived ability and actual performance (Cutler & Penrod, 1989; Narby et al., 1996).

Once a witness has made an identification, what is the relationship between his/her confidence in the identification and its accuracy? Results from meta-analyses indicate that postidentification confidence judgments do have a low positive relationship to accuracy—an average correlation of + .25 (Bothwell, Deffenbacher, & Brigham, 1987; Luus & Wells, 1994). This modest correlation indicates that witnesses' confidence gives at best only a hint about their likely accuracy. Other research has demonstrated that the confidence-accuracy relationship is stronger under conditions where identification is easy—for example, when the culprit is clearly visible, and the witness is exposed for a long period of time. However, under less optimal conditions (e.g., when the culprit wears a mask, or is only seen for a short period) the confidence-accuracy correlation is weaker (Bothwell et al., 1987; Brigham, 1990)

A little-known principle, which has been demonstrated by Wells and Lindsay (1980), is that witnesses' *failures to identify* a lineup member as the suspect are more likely to be accurate than are positive identifications, even ones made confidently. However, despite the research findings regarding witness identification, jurors (and judges) are generally overly accepting of the accuracy of eyewitness testimony (Leippe, Manion, & Romanczyk, 1992; Lindsay, 1994b). This problem has been acknowledged in Britain, where a government committee reported to the House of Commons:

> We do however wish to insure that in ordinary cases prosecutions are not brought on eyewitness evidence only and that, if brought, they will fail. We think that they ought to fail, since in our opinion it is only in exceptional cases that identification evidence is by itself sufficiently reliable to exclude a reasonable doubt about guilt. (Devlin, 1976)

Cross-Race Bias. Research has demonstrated that people are better at identifying a person of their own race than members of another race (Chance & Goldstein, 1996). Most of this research has examined differences between Blacks and Whites, so much less is known about other ethnic groups (Shapiro & Penrod, 1986). In a meta-analysis of this research, Bothwell et al. (1989) found a large overall difference (effect size d around .70 of a standard deviation) for accuracy with own versus other race, for both Blacks and Whites.

An extension of this research is an examination of a similar gender bias. Are men better able to identify male culprits than women, and vice versa? A meta-analysis by Shapiro and Penrod (1986) suggested that there is little difference. On average, witnesses in laboratory studies were able to identify own-gender offenders correctly an average of 41% of the time, while cross-gender recognitions were correct 37% of the time.

Weapon Focus. If a weapon is used during a crime, it tends to capture the attention of observers. If witnesses are focused on the weapon, they do not pay as much attention to other aspects of the scene, leaving them less accurate in their identification. Loftus, Loftus, and Messo (1987) monitored the eye movements of individuals as they watched slides depicting crimes. Results indicated that they spent more time looking at the weapon than any other aspect of the image. Cutler, Penrod, and Martens (1987) showed people videotaped robbery scenes where the criminal either displayed a gun or kept the gun hidden in his jacket. Subjects who observed the videotape where the gun was visible correctly identified the robber in a lineup 26% of the time, compared with 46% for subjects who observed the same scene but with the gun concealed. A meta-analysis of similar studies found a small but significant difference between laboratory studies where a weapon was or was not displayed (Stelbay, 1992—effect size d = .13 of a standard deviation).

Many other conditions can affect accuracy of reporting: the type of incident—salient or trivial; the characteristics of the observer—age, intelligence, interests, expectations; the conditions of observation—distance, visibility, distractions; the time intervening between the incident and the report; and the conditions under which the report is given. However, the research on these topics is less consistent and not as widely agreed upon by researchers (Lindsay, 1994b; Narby et al., 1996).

An Illustrative Real-World Study

Most of the research that we have discussed so far, concerning factors that can lead eyewitnesses to make inaccurate identifications, has been laboratory-based. Typically, witnesses watch a staged or video event and then are asked to recall specific features of the event. These scenes are occasionally violent, but ethical constraints mute the degree of violence, and witnesses are not in any danger—they are unaffected observers. In the real world, many eyewitnesses are victims, and other observers of crimes may feel threatened and/or emotionally aroused. These differences raise questions about the generalizability of the laboratory findings reviewed above.

Three Canadian researchers responded to this issue by conducting a field study to test the generality of laboratory findings (Tollestrup, Turtle, & Yuille, 1994). They obtained data from the Royal Canadian Mounted Police regarding all of the robbery and fraud cases reported in a suburb of Vancouver between 1987 and 1989. Fraud cases were selected because they resemble the typical laboratory setting in that witnesses are unaffected observers. Fraud cases included passing bad checks, use of counterfeit money, credit card fraud, and insurance fraud. In contrast, robbery cases (ranging from purse snatching to armed robbery) were selected because they are markedly different from the typical laboratory setting in the level of observers' emotional involvement. The authors predicted that the results from witnesses to fraud would be similar to the results found in laboratory studies, while results from robbery cases would be different.

In all, 77 robbery cases and 21 cases of fraud were analyzed. Each of the cases was coded for descriptive information about the crime: location, date, time, number of eyewitnesses, number of perpetrators, and use of a weapon. The researchers collected demographic information on both the witnesses and perpetrators, and recorded the police preidentification procedures such as use of mug shots and lineups.

Results. Three sets of analyses were conducted. First, the authors examined the amount of detail provided by victims of robbery and fraud, as well as by nonvictim witnesses of robbery cases. As examples, nonvictim witnesses of a robbery were able to recall 6.4 descriptive details concerning clothing, robbery victims 4.9, and fraud victims only 1.5. Regarding physical appearance details, robbery witnesses recalled 8.4 details, robbery victims 9.8, and fraud victims 7.6.

The authors then compared the descriptions of physical appearance given by robbery victims and witnesses with the actual data collected by the police. Differences were calculated separately for age, height, and weight. For age, both victims and witnesses overestimated the perpetrator's age, victims by 2.9 years, and witnesses by 3.4 years. For height, both victims and witnesses underestimated the perpetrator's height, victims by 1.9 inches, witnesses by .5 inches. Finally, for weight, victims underestimated by 7.6 pounds, and witnesses underestimated by 4.8 pounds. Summarizing the results from the descriptions, robbery victims provided less detailed descriptions of clothing than did witnesses, and more inaccurate estimates of height and weight. However, they were able to give more details about physical appearance and more accurate estimates of age.

The second set of analyses examined the identification procedures and outcomes for the same group of 98 cases. In total, 170 identification attempts were made, 91% of which were photo spreads—only 10 police lineups were conducted. The first set of comparisons examined the percentage of cases in which the eyewitness identified the police suspect from the photo spread (termed "accuracy" by the authors). Results indicated that robbery victims were most accurate (46%), robbery witnesses second (33%), and fraud victims least accurate (25%). Additionally, witnesses were more accurate in cases where implicating evidence was available, and also in cases where the suspect confessed. The effect of delays between the witnessed event and the identification attempt is displayed in Table 15-3. As shown in the table, for both fraud and robbery, the amount of time between the event and the identification was negatively related to the proportion of positive identifications. The longer the time, the less accurate the identification.

TABLE 15–3 Range of Average Delay in Days Between Exposure to Perpetrator and Identification Attempt in Cases of Robbery and Fraud

Delay	Average	Sample Size	% Positive IDs
Robbery			
0–1	0.50	14	71.43
3–5	3.60	15	46.67
7–34	18.90	21	33.33
38–191	120.21	14	14.29
Fraud			
7–62	32.94	18	77.78
70–90	74.40	18	5.55
107–154	131.67	15	20.00
170–382	200.42	17	17.65

Source: Tollestrup, P. A., Turtle, J., and Yuille, J. (1994). Range and average delay in days between exposure to perpetrature and identification attempt in cases of robbery and fraud. In David Frank Ross, J. Don Read, and Michael P. Toglia (Eds.), *Adult eyewitness testimony: Current trends and developments* (p. 155). New York: Cambridge University Press.

The third set of analyses examined the issue of "weapon focus." In this real-life Canadian study, 43 of the 77 robberies were committed with a weapon. Table 15-4 displays the average number of details provided by eyewitnesses when weapons were used and when they were not used. Results showed that, unlike in laboratory studies, the presence of a weapon actually *increased* the number of details provided. A possible hypothesis might be that the presence of a weapon led to more detailed, but less accurate, descriptions. However, comparing the accuracy of age, height, and weight estimates, the authors found no significant differences. That is, the presence of a weapon did not affect the accuracy of these descriptions.

Summary. This archival study by Tollestrup et al. (1994) found several clear results. First, robbery victims tended to provide about as detailed and as accurate descriptions as did nonvictim witnesses; however, fraud victims recalled fewer and less accurate details than robbery victims. Second, the amount of time that elapsed between the event and the identification was negatively related to accuracy of the identification. Finally, a negative effect of weapon presence on accuracy

TABLE 15-4   **Average Number of Details Reported, by Eyewitness Type and Presence Versus Absence of Weapon**

Type of detail	Weapon in Case		No Weapon Used	
	Victim	*Witness*	*Victim*	*Witness*
Clothing	5.07	4.89	2.96	2.20
Physical appearance	7.92	5.16	5.91	4.45
Total	12.98	10.05	8.88	6.65
N	59	80	57	20

Source: Tollestrup, P. A., Turtle, J., and Yuille, J. (1994). Average number of details by eyewitness type and presence versus absence of weapon. In David Frank Ross, J. Don Read, and Michael P. Toglia (Eds.), *Adult eyewitness testimony: Current trends and developments* (p. 156). New York: Cambridge University Press.

of reporting, which is consistently found in laboratory research, was *not* present in these actual crime cases.

Children as Witnesses

A little earlier, we summarized research evidence concerning a variety of factors that lead to eyewitness misidentification in both laboratory and field settings. An interesting related question is the accuracy of children as eyewitnesses. In recent years, the number of cases in which children have testified has increased dramatically (Davies, 1996; McGough, 1994). The majority of these cases involved allegations of sexual abuse. Some well-known examples were charges by children in the McMartin Preschool trial, and in allegations against Michael Jackson and Woody Allen. Prior to 1991, children had to demonstrate "competency" before their testimony could be used in a court trial. However, the 1991 Criminal Justice Act removed the requirement for a "competency test." Now any child can provide evidence in a court, provided that the judge views the testimony as relevant and of interest to the court (Davies, 1996). In this section we will briefly examine the ability and fallibility of children as witnesses.

Ability. In many ways, the ability of a child (beyond the age of about three) to perceive and remember an event is very similar to that of an adult (Davies, 1996). However, children lack many of the cognitive abilities that adults possess. A recent summary of the research literature stated:

age differences in performance [as a witness] are most marked on those tasks that make the greatest demand on detailed knowledge of facial or bodily appearance, such as descriptions and composite production. Least differences due to age appear in tasks like identification, which rely more on recognition than spontaneous recall. (Davies, 1996, pp. 252–253)

As with adults, children's accuracy in reporting a witnessed event is better if they are allowed free recall (Leippe, Romanczyk, & Manion, 1992). Although children tend to recall fewer details, the accuracy of their accounts is only slightly lower than that of adults. In other aspects of memory, children are markedly inferior—most notably in long-term memory (Brainerd & Ornstein, 1991). However, a different research picture emerges when children and adults are asked leading or suggestive questions.

Memory Suggestibility in Children. The term **suggestibility** refers to "the extent to which individuals come to accept and subsequently incorporate postevent information into their memory recollections" (Gudjonsson, 1986, p. 195). A study illustrating how suggestibility can be demonstrated was described by Ceci (1994). In it, preschoolers played a game similar to "Simon says," in which they touched different body parts (e.g., stomach, nose, or toes). One month later, a social worker interviewed each child about what had happened in the game, guided by a one-page report that contained either accurate or inaccurate information about the events. Results showed that when interviewers were given accurate information, the children correctly recalled 95% of all events. However, when the interviewers were given inaccurate information, 34% of 3- and 4-year-olds and 18% of 5- and 6-year-olds falsely reported at least one of the nonevents. Similar results have been found in a variety of studies (Ceci & Bruck, 1995).

Findings like these have profound implications for many court cases where the evidence may be unclear, including ones involving sexual abuse. How should such cases be handled in court? This question is a controversial one, and psychologists line up on both sides. Some authors have suggested that "many of the mass-allegation daycare cases, as well as some other cases involving sexual abuse, stem from the phenomenon of interviewer's bias" (Ceci & Bruck, 1995, p. 93). A related issue, which was central in the 1990 Supreme Court case of *Maryland v. Craig,* is the suggestion that sexually abused children may not be reliable witnesses, especially when confronted face-to-face by an accused defendant (Goodman et al., 1991). Clearly, strong conclusions on such issues are controversial, and each individual case must be treated on its own merits. The research evidence has shown that children's memories are susceptible to bias that can be introduced during the context of an interview. But this is true of adults' memories also, so it is an open question as to whether there should be different rules for children and adults being allowed to testify in court.

Some interview techniques are more likely to lead to false information than others. For example, Lepore and Sesco (1994) showed how a judgmental interview with children between the ages of 4 and 6 could distort their reports. Each child interacted with a man who performed some preplanned actions, including taking off his sweater, and later an interviewer asked the children to recall the events that occurred. For half of the children, the interviewer remained neutral when the child recalled an event. For the other children, the interviewer added value judgments after each of the child's statements like, "He wasn't supposed to do that," or "That was bad; what else did he do?" All the children were then asked highly suggestive yes/no questions like "Didn't he take off some of your clothes too?" and were provided the opportunity to elaborate on their answers. Results showed that children in the judgmental-interviewer condition reported more inaccurate infor-

mation to questions like "Did he ever touch other kids at the school?"

Although incriminating interview techniques, like those just described, can lead to errors in children's recollections, other interview techniques can help promote more accurate recall. For example, questioning children about an event in the presence of trusted adults tends to produce more accurate recall, as does adopting a warm, rather than cold, questioning style (Moston & Engelberg, 1992). A more systematic interview strategy is the **cognitive interview**—an attempt, based on scientific evidence, to improve the accuracy of recalled information (Fisher, McCauley, & Geiselman, 1994). One aspect of this strategy is to allow witnesses to recall, in their own words, everything about their experience even if it seems unimportant. Another aspect involves encouraging the witness to think about particular features of the event. For example, if the witness is having difficulty remembering a name, the interviewer might ask the person to start with the length of the name, long or short, and to build from there. The cognitive interview has been used widely for both children and adults, often with notable success.

RESEARCH ON JURY SIZE AND VOTING RULE

In this section we will move from issues involving witnesses and their testimony, to focus on the process by which jurors come to a decision about the guilt or innocence of a suspect. This topic is an essential one for us to consider, for it is here that social science research has probably had its greatest effect on court decisions. However, as we shall see, that does *not* mean that social science findings have been correctly used and interpreted by the courts.

In 1966, Kalven and Zeisel published *The American Jury*, a monumental and pioneering empirical effort to describe the American jury system as it actually functions, and one that has been cited as an authority in subsequent Supreme Court rulings. It primarily adopted a broad sociological approach, presenting data about the percentages of convictions, acquittals, and hung juries in various types of cases, and so on. *The American Jury* was a product of the University of Chicago jury research project, which also attempted to collect data through tape recordings of actual juries, made with the judge's permission but without the jurors' knowledge. This procedure was the first and last serious scientific study of how actual juries deliberate and decide cases, for it led to considerable criticism of the undisclosed recording procedure, and a subsequent federal law prohibited any recording or observation of jury deliberations (Wrightsman, 1978).

The jury is a remarkable social invention for incorporating local community standards into official decisions. A jury is made up of untrained citizens, chosen haphazardly from eligible community members, and brought together briefly for a particular trial. The members are assigned important official responsibilities, required to deliberate in secret, and allowed to declare their verdict without any explanation or accountability to anyone, after which they return to their private lives.

The tradition of a unanimous, 12-person jury was established in England by the end of the fourteenth century (Abramson, 1994). The reason for having 12 members is unknown, but it is probably related to the British penchant for 12-unit measurement systems (such as 12 inches in a foot, 12 pence in a shilling). The tradition was brought to the American colonies and incorporated into the U.S. legal system. Though suggestions of smaller juries or nonunanimous decisions were occasionally made, such issues remained theoretical until the 1960s. In 1966 the British legal system adopted a new standard of 10 out of 12 members as sufficient for a decision. In 1970 the U.S. Supreme Court ruled that juries as small as 6 members were constitutionally permissible; and in 1972 it ruled that unanimity was not required for a decision, and that majorities as low as 9 out of 12 were sufficient.

In five related decisions between 1970 to 1978, the U.S. Supreme Court increasingly relied on social science evidence in reaching its decisions about the effects of jury size and decision rules (Monahan & Walker, 1994). But how well did it understand and interpret that evidence?

Jury Size

In the first of these cases (*Williams v. Florida*, 1970), the Supreme Court ruled that 6-member juries were

permissible after comparing them with 12-member juries and reaching this conclusion:

> What few experiments have occurred—usually in the civil area—indicate that there is no discernible difference between the results reached by the two different sized juries. (p. 102)

In a footnote the court cited six "experiments" to support this conclusion. However, these so-called experiments were based on casual observations or intuitive arguments devoid of any systematic empirical evidence (Saks, 1977). Zeisel (1971) condemned these studies as "scant evidence by any standards" (p. 715), and went further to demonstrate by statistical procedures that a 6-member jury was less likely than a 12-member one to be representative of the community from which it was drawn.

The Supreme Court ruling did cite Asch's (1958) famous study of group pressure, which demonstrated the likelihood of conformity or yielding among individuals faced by a strong majority who opposed their perception of a situation. However, the court cited this study to support its conclusion that the minority juror in a 5 to 1 split faces the same kind of pressure as in a 10 to 2 split, whereas Asch's findings emphasized the importance of having even a single ally as a factor encouraging resistance to conformity pressures. As Wrightsman (1978, p. 140) commented:

> Surely a label of law and psychology in conflict seems appropriate when a legal decision is based on a misreading of research results.

In 1973 the Supreme Court again took up the question of jury size in the case of *Colgrove v. Battin*. The court again held that a 6-member jury was adequate, and it again cited social science studies in a footnote as "convincing empirical evidence" to support its conclusion that different sizes of juries did not produce different verdicts (p. 159). However, all four of the studies had serious methodological problems that rendered their conclusions suspect, and only one of the four studies was a true experiment that used random assignment (Zeisel & Diamond, 1974).

In reviewing the court's decisions, Zeisel and Diamond (1974) concluded that the Supreme Court justices should have had enough skepticism and caution to evaluate these studies' methodological flaws and not accept their conclusions at face value. Saks (1974, p. 18) agreed, stating:

> The quality of social science scholarship displayed in [the court's] decisions would not win a passing grade in a high school psychology class.

In the 1978 case of *Ballew v. Georgia* the court considered the adequacy of a 5 member jury, and it ruled unanimously that 6 members was the minimum allowable size for a state criminal jury (Monahan & Walker, 1994). The *Ballew* ruling was unique in that it was "the first case in which the Court openly embraced empirical behavioral science data and where the wisdom of doing so was actively asserted" (Saks, 1978, p. 4). In fact, social science data occupied 14 paragraphs of the 32-paragraph opinion delivered by Justice Blackmun, and 25 different studies were cited concerning the effects of group size on jury decision making (Loftus & Monahan, 1980). The court concluded that:

> The purpose and functioning of the jury in a criminal trial is seriously impaired, and to a constitutional degree, by a reduction in size to below six members. (p. 4222)

However, in their concurring opinion, Justices Powell, Burger, and Rehnquist took issue with the use of empirical and statistical data, calling it "heavy reliance on numerology derived from statistical studies" (p. 4246). Thus, social science evidence was by no means fully accepted yet by the Supreme Court.

In addition, the court's use of social science in the *Ballew* decision presents a more basic problem. As Grofman (1980) has pointed out, all the research studies on jury size cited by Justice Blackmun referred only to differences between 6-person and 12-person juries. Therefore, if these studies are to be used as the basis for concluding that small juries are inadequate and unconstitutional, then *6-person* juries should be outlawed, not just *5-person* juries.

Major Jury-Size Effects. Justice Blackmun's opinion in the *Ballew* case very nicely summarized the main findings of research studies on the differences between 6- and 12-member juries, including an important study by Saks (1977), which presented a realistic videotaped trial to 58 experimental juries made up of actual recent jurors. The major differences he listed were that smaller juries generally produce

- Less-effective group deliberation
- Lower verdict accuracy
- Lower verdict reliability
- Inadequate community representation (Grofman, 1980, p. 761).

Grofman concluded that these findings by Justice Blackmun were heavily supported by the social science evidence, and that the previous Supreme Court decisions on jury size were essentially wrong.

The Court's Use of Social Science. Based on the record of the cases described above, we must agree with Grofman's (1980) conclusion that the Supreme Court has so far proved itself inept in integrating social science findings into legal rulings. As he stated (p. 764):

> Justices have confused speculation with evidence, willfully distorted social science data, ignored findings which they were unable to rebut, and shown great difficulty in telling good social science from bad.

Much the same criticisms can be made against the Supreme Court's ruling in the case of *Lockhart v. McCree* (1986) regarding death-qualified juries, where it considered the empirical research evidence irrelevant to the constitutional issue of the right to a fair trial.

Jury Decision Rule

The other, closely related issue taken up by the court is the question of whether jury decisions must be unanimous. In U.S. Supreme Court rulings, this traditional decision rule was first overturned in 1972 in the case of *Johnson v. Louisiana*. In this case, the court ruled, by a 5–4 margin, that at least 9 out of 12 jurors in agreement was enough to reach a verdict. Johnson's appeal argued that using a 9 of 12 decision rule was unfair to him, because it was easier to convict under that rule than under the unanimous standard. The court majority rejected his arguments, stating that neither the verdicts of juries nor their deliberative processes would be substantially affected by dropping the requirement of unanimous jury decisions. However, four justices in the minority vigorously challenged this ruling on several grounds, including the argument that under it, instead of engaging in full deliberation and confrontation of opposing viewpoints, "nine jurors can simply ignore the views of their fellow panel members" (*Johnson v. Louisiana*, 1972, p. 397).

In 1972 little empirical evidence was available on the issue of nonunanimous rulings. The Supreme Court majority relied primarily on unsupported assertions about the probable effects on deliberation processes of not requiring juries to reach unanimity. However, there were some facts about nonunanimous juries that could have been cited. Kalven and Zeisel's (1966) data showed that small minorities on a jury at the outset of deliberations rarely ever produce deadlocked final votes; it usually takes an initial minority of 4 or more out of 12 jurors to cause a hung jury. Thus, where unanimity was required to reach a verdict in the United States, the average rate of nonunanimous outcomes was less than 6%, whereas when Oregon stopped requiring unanimity, its rate of nonunanimous verdicts rose to 25% (Kalven & Zeisel, 1966). These data suggest that when a jury reaches the required majority, it simply stops deliberating, thereby preventing the minority from having any further influence which could conceivably change some votes to their position. Similarly, evidence from small-group research shows that groups required to reach unanimous decisions exert more pressure for unanimity than do groups required only to reach substantial majority decisions (Zajonc, Wolosin, & Wolosin, 1972). The excellent study by Saks (1977), which used actual past jurors as subjects, showed that there was a greater proportion of hung juries under a unanimous decision rule than under a 2/3 majority rule, and concluded that "only in unanimous juries could the minority effectively alter the course set by the majority" (p. 106).

Recent Developments. Following all this legal dispute and scientific research about the issues of jury size and decision rules, the Supreme Court has become more cautious. In 1979 it ruled, in the case of *Burch v. Louisiana,* that decisions by 6-member criminal juries must be unanimous. However, instead of citing empirical research findings, the decision by Justice Rehnquist stated as its authority "the near-uniform judgment

of the Nation" (Tanke & Tanke, 1979). And it declined to rule on the constitutionality of nonunanimous verdicts by juries larger than 6 members.

As of 1994, the current state of affairs on jury size was that more than 30 U.S. states allowed juries with fewer than 12 people, mostly for civil cases, but a few states allowed smaller juries for criminal cases as well (Abramson, 1994).

RESEARCH ON JURY DECISIONS

It is a striking fact that U.S. juries make up about 80% of all the jury trials in the world (Kalven & Zeisel, 1966). Thus, it is not surprising that jury decision making is the aspect of the legal system that has been most often studied by social psychologists. Therefore, we need to examine carefully the problems stemming from the typical methodological procedures that have been used.

Methodological Procedures in Jury Research

A crucial initial consideration is the fact that it is currently unlawful to observe or record actual jury deliberations in the United States. Therefore, there are basically five other methods of studying jury processes (Konecni & Ebbesen, 1992). We will mention them starting with the procedure closest to the actual jury situation and moving to increasingly distant analogs.

1. Interviewing Past Jurors. Thorough and probing interviews can recreate much of the jury deliberation process, including the reactions and motivations of individual jurors. The method has rarely been used by psychological researchers, probably because it is so time-consuming and the findings are limited to the particular case being studied. However, some systematic research of this sort has been conducted (Costanzo & Costanzo, 1994; Meza, 1982), and it can bring us closer to the actual processes of jury deliberation and decision making than any other method.

2. Archival Research. Archival studies of juror characteristics and jury decisions in various jurisdictions can tell us much about trial outcomes and some of the factors that affect them. This was the approach used in much of the sociological research of Kalven and Zeisel (1966). However, except by distant inference, such data reveal little or nothing about the *processes* of jury deliberation.

3. Mock Trials. This is an experimental procedure. A situation is created that simulates some aspects of a trial, and some measures are taken of the mock jurors' behavior or decisions. Mock trials can range very widely in realism, from a careful simulation of almost all aspects of a real trial to a highly simplistic written summary of some trial elements and a written "vote" by individuals without any group deliberation. They can also study a host of different variables, from the characteristics of the mock jurors, to the events and personages of the trial, to the procedures for reaching a verdict. By far the majority of social psychological jury research has used this method (Konecni & Ebbesen, 1992). Its disadvantage, of course, is its lack of the realism and complexity that are present in an actual court trial. Its chief advantage is the virtue of the experimental method—the ability to hold many aspects constant, carefully vary only a few, and reach strong conclusions about cause-and-effect relations.

4. Surveys of Legal Attitudes and Beliefs. Even without any simulation of a trial, one can survey citizens and learn about beliefs and attitudes that may be relevant to procedures or decisions in a trial. For instance, we have earlier described public attitudes toward crime and the punishments that should be invoked. One can also study people's understanding of legal concepts, such as the principle of proof beyond a reasonable doubt, or their levels of personal prejudice or authoritarianism, as was done in the jury selection research described earlier in this chapter.

5. Statistical and Probability Computations. Researchers starting with the findings of archival studies, and making certain assumptions about jury decision processes, can construct models of decision outcomes, including not only verdicts but also factors such as length of deliberation and likelihood of reversing an initial vote. Often predictions from these models have been found to correspond closely to data collected from the legal system or from mock juries (Hastie, 1993; Kerr, 1993). However, they primarily simulate the *outcomes* and tell us relatively little about the *individual processes* or *group dynamics* responsible for creating the outcomes.

The Issue of Realism

There are two aspects of realism in experiments, as we discussed in Chapter 4, experimental realism and mundane realism (Aronson et al., 1985). The requirement of **experimental realism** refers to the believability and impact of the experimental manipulations and instructions. Even though some aspects of the situation are quite artificial (that is, different from the everyday world), mock jury studies may still have good experimental realism. For instance, in one laboratory experiment with college student "jurors" and a videotaped trial, presenting slightly different wording in the judge's instructions about the criterion of "reasonable doubt" (using phrases specified in current courtroom guidelines) led to quite large differences in the percentage of guilty verdicts. A stringent standard for reasonable doubt produced guilty verdicts in 24% of juries; a more lax standard yielded 50% guilty verdicts; and instructions that left the standard undefined produced an intermediate level of 36% guilty verdicts (Kerr et al., 1976).

The most pervasive problem of mock jury research is its lack of **mundane realism**. This means similarity to situations and processes in the everyday world—in this case, to settings and events occurring in the actual legal system. Let us consider the many ways in which mock jury research often fails to resemble the real courtroom situation.

1. Subjects. The mock jurors in most experimental studies have been college students, due to their ready availability, and college students have been found to be significantly more lenient than heterogeneous adults in the length of the sentences they recommended (Feild & Barnett, 1978).

2. Setting. In decreasing order of mundane realism, very few experiments have used courtroom settings, whereas most have been conducted in classrooms or laboratories, or even by sending materials for people to read and decide about in their own homes.

3. Medium of Presentation. About half of all jury studies have used the least realistic medium, a written presentation—frequently a brief summary of evidence, or sometimes a fuller transcript. For greater realism, some have used audiotape, and a few have used film, videotape, or a live presentation. One study, comparing a black-and-white videotape presentation with audiotape, a written transcript of the tape, and a written summary, found that the videotape presentation produced significantly more guilty verdicts than the other conditions (Juhnke et al., 1979).

4. Nature of Trial Participants. In audio, video, or live presentations, the people who take roles in the trial may vary, from average citizens (whoever is available) to actors to professional legal personnel, such as judges, lawyers, policemen, and bailiffs taking their real-life roles.

5. Length of Trial. At the low end, some experiments have used a written summary that could be read in 10 minutes. Video or audiotapes are usually limited to an hour or so, but if carefully developed, they may still carry all the usual contents of a short trial. At the high end, Dillehay and Nietzel's (1980) student jurors spent a whole day in court, and studies using members of a jury pool may take even more than one day. However, even these examples are far from the months-long periods and the accompanying stress of murder trials, for instance.

6. Use of *Voir Dire*. Hardly any mock jury experiments have bothered to include a *voir dire* phase, in which potential jury members are questioned to eliminate any who might be biased against one side or the other. However, legal lore and court procedures strongly suggest that this process makes an important difference. Findings of a mock jury experiment by Horowitz (1980) suggest that the use of *voir dire* in selecting jurors might yield fewer convictions than an unselected jury.

7. Jury Size. In addition to juries of 6 or 12 members, some studies have used assorted other sizes—primarily for convenience rather than theoretical reasons—and the size factor may make a difference in the results.

8. Group Versus Individual Presentation. This variable refers both to the situation in which mock jurors are exposed to the trial information—usually in groups, but sometimes as separate individuals—and to the form of decision required of them. Though decisions in jury trials are always group judgments rather than individual ones, a surprisingly high proportion of studies has used only the unrealistic procedure of individual decisions as the dependent variable.

9. Presence of Deliberation. This factor tends to accompany group decisions, though group votes have occasionally been taken without prior deliberation. In legal writings, the confrontation of juror viewpoints, which takes place during deliberation, is often considered the central and essential hallmark of the jury system; and some experimental studies have shown significant effects of group discussion (Kerr & MacCoun, 1987). Certainly mock jury studies that omit deliberation are ignoring one of the major aspects of jury decisions.

10. Length of Deliberation. Even the relatively few studies that include deliberation may set unrealistic limits on its length due to constraints on the schedules of experimenters and subjects. Most such studies have set limits ranging from 10 minutes to 30 minutes, which is almost certainly too short a time for an adequate exchange of juror views in most trials.

11. Number of Votes. Like length of deliberation, this factor has generally been arbitrarily limited by the experimenter.

12. Nature of Jurors' Decision. In real criminal trials, jurors make a dichotomous choice between guilty and innocent, whereas many studies have required decisions on a continuous scale measuring degree of guilt. Many have also required mock jurors to recommend sentences, such as number of years in prison, which is never done in real criminal cases.

13. Consequences of the Decision. In real court cases, of course, the jury's decision has important—even crucial—consequences for the defendant and the other parties. Unfortunately, this aspect of reality is almost impossible to incorporate into experimental studies, and it is probably the most important of all the missing factors (Monahan & Loftus, 1982). A few attempts have been made, as where college students thought they were making disciplinary decisions that would affect the fate of other students (Kerr, Nerenz, & Herrick, 1979), but obviously such cases are relatively minor compared to most in the criminal justice system. When mock jury members are led to believe that their decisions will have real consequences, it appears that they are less likely to vote "guilty" than when the consequences are hypothetical (Wilson & Donnerstein, 1977).

The above list covers most of the ways in which mock jury experiments have been unrealistic or unfaithful to the real jury situation. The large number of such factors makes it impossible to avoid all of them, so no single experimental study can be realistic on all of these dimensions at once. However, within the limits of feasibility, researchers who hope to influence the legal system should try for as much mundane realism as possible. Without it, their studies will not be taken seriously as having any practical, applied value. On this score, the vast majority of mock jury research has been sadly lacking.

Independent Variables Frequently Studied

The kinds of independent variables most often selected or manipulated in mock jury research fall into three major categories: characteristics of the mock jurors, characteristics of other persons in the trial, and various aspects of the trial procedure.

Characteristics of Mock Jurors. Several studies have found that male mock jurors tend to participate more than women in the jury discussion, but sex differences in verdicts have been inconsistent in different studies—women are less severe in some situations but more likely to convict in rape cases, for instance. Education and other demographic characteristics of mock jurors have also affected their decisions in some studies (Davis et al., 1977). Considering personality, people who are authoritarian, high in internal control, or believe in a just world have generally been found more likely to hold a defendant responsible, and therefore they frequently favor more severe sentences than other jurors.

Characteristics of Other Persons in the Trial. Characteristics of the defendant, such as race, social status, or physical attractiveness, have often been found to influence mock jurors' evaluations of the case.

By a similar principle, when the victim is presented in a sympathetic light, the defendant is often treated more severely (Gerbasi et al., 1977).

Aspects of Trial Procedure. Naturally the type of offense—its seriousness, violence, presence of extenuating circumstances, and so on—is often an important influence on jurors' decisions. Similarly, the strength of the evidence or convincingness of the testimony has sometimes been varied experimentally and found to affect verdicts and sentences. Among legal issues, the judge's instructions to the jury have had some study, and the typical conclusion has been that they are rather poorly understood (Tanford, 1990). In particular, the instruction to disregard inadmissible evidence seems to be frequently ignored by jurors (Tanford & Cox, 1987). When only an extreme decision, such as first-degree murder, is available to the jury, there will be fewer guilty verdicts than with less extreme options such as manslaughter, or with more alternative verdicts (Gerbasi et al., 1977).

The issue of using videotaped testimony in courtrooms may become increasingly important as the legal system considers various proposals to expedite trials and standardize the presentation of evidence (one suggestion is to edit inadmissible evidence out of the tape). Preliminary research evidence is reassuring in indicating no difference in jurors' decisions between videotaped presentations and "live" trials (Miller et al., 1974).

The general conclusion from the large body of mock jury research is that many extraneous, nonevidential factors can influence jury verdicts. However, we must be cautious in accepting the results of these studies, because we must keep in mind questions about the validity of the research.

Validity of Mock Jury Research

A central question about mock jury research is its validity. To answer this question, we must consider several different kinds of validity, as described in Chapters 4 and 6 on experiments and quasi-experimental research. First, the *internal validity* of mock jury studies is generally good because they are typically experimental in nature; if they are well-done, experiments

FIGURE 15-2 Can mock jury research capture the important elements that are present in a complex court trial? (Photograph courtesy of UPI/Corbis–Bettmann.)

usually allow us to make confident statements about causes and effects in the experimental situation. However, there are some mock jury experiments with low internal validity—for instance, ones where the manipulation of the independent variable was not noticed or believed by the subjects.

The *external validity* of mock jury research, on the other hand, is usually very questionable, due to the many unrealistic aspects discussed above (Konecni & Ebbesen, 1992). This means that findings, even if clearly established in the experimental situation, may not generalize to the quite different courtroom situation, and no one knows which findings are generalizable and which are not. However, the findings of experiments that differ from legal situations on several dimensions seem more questionable than those of studies with fewer unrealistic aspects (Meza, 1982). Mock jury experiments are essentially role-playing situations, in which subjects are asked to act "as if" they were real jurors; and the findings of many role-playing studies have shown that role-playing subjects frequently behave differently from people in a similar real-life situation (Freedman, 1969).

Even experimental findings that turn out to be externally valid in some real-life settings may suffer from another liability which was pointed out by Dillehay

and Nietzel (1980). That is, their real-life importance, or **applied explanatory power**, may be very low. Thus, a mock-jury finding may hold true in a real courtroom, but it may be such a minor factor in the context of a complete trial that it could just as well be ignored. For instance, this might be true of the experimental findings regarding the effects of the defendant's physical attractiveness, for in a real trial the jurors have many more indications of a person's true character than just their physical appearance.

Another kind of validity is **construct validity**, which refers to how well specific research operations match their intended general theoretical constructs (Cook & Campbell, 1979). In order to satisfy this criterion, the research operations should neither underrepresent the key aspects of the concept nor overrepresent them by including other extraneous aspects. For example, many experiments that ask mock jurors to make individual decisions both overinclude the elements involved in real juries (by requiring decisions about prison sentences) and underinclude them (by omitting deliberation). Another threat to construct validity that is typical in most mock jury research is confounding levels of constructs with the constructs themselves (e.g., by using only a single case with a particular level of incriminating evidence).

SUMMARY

The fields of social psychology and the law have much to offer each other despite a history of only sporadic collaboration in the past. In an upsurge of research interest since about 1970, social psychologists have applied their knowledge and skills, not only to criminal court procedures, but also to the civil law system; legal bargaining and negotiation; and studies of the police, prisons, juvenile agencies, and other legal settings.

Among the major topics studied by psychologists have been jury selection procedures, means of detecting deception such as the polygraph, and the fairness of procedures in bail-setting and sentencing. Psychologists have also traced trends in public attitudes toward crime and punishment and shown an increase in the number of people adopting protective measures to avoid becoming crime victims. Measurement of crime frequency has many complications, but surveys of crime victimization indicate a much higher crime rate than official police reports. Another contribution of psychologists has been evaluating the effectiveness of laws designed to reduce crime.

The oldest research area of applied legal psychology, witness testimony, has shown how untrustworthy eyewitness reports often are, and also identified many conditions that can increase or decrease their accuracy. Laboratory studies have demonstrated that question wording, police lineups, post-event information, mugshot bias, cross-race bias, and weapon focus can all affect the accuracy of witnesses' memory. An important finding is that witnesses' confidence in their identification of a culprit is at best a weak predictor of their accuracy. Field research by Tollestrup et al., using an archival analysis of fraud and robbery cases, supported some of the results from lab studies, but also suggested clear limitations to several of these findings.

The topics of jury size and voting decision rule are ones where psychological research has most clearly affected court decisions. Unfortunately, however, in this area the Supreme Court was unable to tell good social research from bad, and it even misinterpreted the findings of several key studies. As a result it mistakenly held that 6-member juries were equivalent to 12-member juries in their community representativeness and verdicts, and that nonunanimous decision rules were constitutionally acceptable because, under them, both jury deliberation processes and verdicts would be similar to those under unanimous decision rules.

The aspect of the legal system that has had the most social science research is jury decision making. However, the great bulk of social research on this topic has been with mock trials, which usually have poor mundane realism on a large number of dimensions such as setting, medium of presentation, length, lack of deliberation, and lack of consequences. Many experimental studies have investigated the effects of juror characteristics, other trial participants' characteristics, or procedural aspects of the trial. Unfortunately, even if these studies have good internal validity, they almost all suffer from poor external validity and construct validity. Consequently, we are only beginning the task of developing a science of jury behavior.

SUGGESTED READINGS

Lösel, F., Bender, D., & Bliesener, T. (Eds.). (1992). *Psychology and law: International perspectives.* Berlin: de Gruyter.—Provides a thorough overview of many areas of legal research.

Narby, D. J., Cutler, B. L., & Penrod, S. D. (1996). The effects of witness, target, and situational factors on eyewitness identification. In S. Sporer, R. Malpass, & G. Koehnken (Eds.), *Psychological issues in eyewitness identification* (pp. 21–52). Mahwah, NJ: Erlbaum.—The most current overview of the research on factors that impair eyewitness identification.

Ross, D., Read, J. D., & Toglia, M. (Eds.). (1994). *Adult eyewitness testimony: Current trends and developments.* New York: Cambridge University Press.—This comprehensive book has chapters covering many aspects of eyewitness testimony.

Tollestrup, P. A., Turtle, J., & Yuille, J. (1994). Actual victims and witnesses to robbery and fraud. An archival analysis. In D. Ross, J. Read, & M. Toglia (Eds.), *Adult eyewitness testimony: Current trends and developments* (pp. 144–162). New York: Cambridge University Press.—An excellent real-world study.

Wrightsman, L., Kassin, S., & Willis, C. (Eds.). (1987). *In the jury box: Controversies in the courtroom.* Newbury Park, CA: Sage.—An interesting edited book containing classic articles summarizing the social psychological evidence on the jury system.

CHAPTER 16

Activism for Social Change

Democracy comes hard and goes easy. To make democracy work, it takes work—citizen work.

—Ralph Nader (1973, p. xii)

Never doubt that a small group of thoughtful, committed citizens can change the world. Indeed it is the only thing that ever does.

—Margaret Mead

Social activism is an unfamiliar role for most psychologists. Yet it is a vital role in accomplishing important social goals, and it is one that applied psychologists need to know about, whether or not they choose to adopt it themselves. We will define activism in a general way as *any activities directed at accomplishing social change or attacking social problems.*

Most psychologists and other social scientists have not concentrated their efforts in the fields of social change or social problems, but there are some outstanding exceptions. Daniel Katz (1974) provided a conceptual framework describing types of social change processes and factors that encourage or hinder them. A historical summary of the views of social scientists who have become involved in social action shows several phases in the last 50 years—ranging from idealistic optimism through rising doubts to instances of bitter disillusionment about the effectiveness of scientific approaches in achieving social change (McGrath, 1980; Pilisuk, McAllister, & Rothman, 1996).

In the past, when psychologists have done applied work, it has most often been in the service of the status quo and the establishment, rather than aimed at social change (Prilleltensky, 1990). As a result, many individually oriented psychologists have unfortunately tended to "blame the victims" of social ills by studying their "deficits," rather than attacking the underlying social problems such as poverty, poor health care, inadequate educational systems, and so on (Caplan & Nelson, 1973). Consultation to the poor and weak is an unusual role for most psychologists, as Morton Deutsch (1969) pointed out:

> If we have given any advice at all, it has been to those in high power. The unwitting consequence of this one-sided consultant role has been that we have too often assumed

that the social pathology has been in the ghetto rather than in those who have built the walls to surround it, that the "disadvantaged" are the ones who need to be changed rather than the people and the institutions who have kept the disadvantaged in a submerged position. (p. 33)

The customary activities of psychologists have been confined to four main types of roles: research, evaluation, dissemination of knowledge, and utilization of knowledge. Previous chapters of this book have presented many examples of the *research* projects and the *evaluation* activities of social psychologists. **Dissemination of knowledge** includes teaching, scholarly writing, and the less common activity of popularizing psychological knowledge to the general public. Dissemination is not usually activism, but occasionally it may be, as in manuals developed to summarize knowledge about persuasion techniques that could be used by activists working for peace organizations (Abelson & Zimbardo, 1970; Wollman, 1985). The **utilization of knowledge** role includes the typical nonactivist work of clinical and counseling psychologists, as well as a growing activist literature on using social science findings to produce social change by attacking many kinds of social problems (e.g., Heller, 1990; Levine, Toro, & Perkins, 1993; Seidman, 1983).

ACTIVIST ROLES FOR SOCIAL SCIENTISTS

In this chapter we will describe many of the forms of activism engaged in by social scientists. In doing so, we should recognize our debt to Kurt Lewin, who pioneered the concept of **action research**, in which research to advance knowledge was integrated into social action projects in a mutually beneficial merger. He was also instrumental in founding the *group dynamics* approach, which has subsequently expanded into a broad movement stressing personal growth and organizational development (including such techniques as T-groups, sensitivity training, encounter groups, etc.). Many of the people working within that movement are still faithfully pursuing Lewin's concept of applying social science knowledge to create beneficial changes in interacting individuals, groups, and organizations (e.g., Johnson & Johnson, 1995; Vanderslice, 1995; Wheelan, Pepitone, & Abt, 1990). Finally, in his *field theory*, Lewin presented theoretical ideas about how planned social change could be accomplished—for instance, through "unfreezing," moving, and "refreezing" group norms and standards (Lewin, 1951).

Followers of Lewin have systematically expanded on his theories and procedures for encouraging social change (e.g., Alderfer, 1993). One of the foremost of those disciples was Ronald Lippitt, who coined the term **change agent** to describe an activist who tries to apply social science principles and knowledge to produce planned changes in society. The work of a change agent can include any or all of the forms of activism discussed below (cf. Ottaway, 1983).

A useful classification of the intervention activities of change agents lists four kinds of relationships they can have to the system they are trying to change: expert, collaborative, advocacy, or coercive (Hornstein, 1975). The latter two approaches have also been described as social reformer and agitator roles. In the next several sections we will give some examples of how social psychologists can take each of these activist roles, beginning with an example of the expert role.

USING RESEARCH FOR SOCIAL CHANGE

An Illustrative Study

In the **expert role**, the change agent uses his or her expert methodology and knowledge to foster social change. An outstanding early example was displayed in a paper by Claire Selltiz (1955). She led a research project that was developed as part of a campaign against racial discrimination in restaurants around the United Nations building in New York City—a multi-

ethnic area that hosts visiting diplomats from all over the world.

The research method was one that has been used frequently in testing compliance with antidiscrimination ordinances in many localities. A stratified sample of 62 restaurants in the target area was chosen, and each selected restaurant was visited by two teams of diners—one consisting of two Blacks, the other of two Whites who were matched to the Black team on sex, age, and middle-class dress and behavior. During the weekday dinner hour, at a time when very few of the restaurants were full, a White team entered each restaurant, followed within a minute by its matched Black team. After being seated, each team ordered and ate typical middle-priced meals, while carefully observing how they were treated. Then they returned immediately to the sponsoring group's headquarters, where each team filled out a detailed factual report on their experience without consulting with the other team. The two teams who had tested a given restaurant then came together and compared their reports under the guidance of a research supervisor. A committee of eight coders made the final judgment about whether the two teams had received approximately equal treatment by examining the written reports.

The possible types of discriminatory treatment that were considered in the study included refusal of service, telling the Black team that reservations were required, and making them wait indefinitely before being seated. In Manhattan in the 1950s, none of these blatant forms of discrimination were found; and the Black teams were not overcharged or given spoiled or over-spiced foods, as has sometimes been observed in other cities. However, the study found more subtle forms of discrimination in 42% of the restaurants tested. This unequal treatment took two main forms: giving the Black teams undesirable locations (near the kitchen or lavatory, or away from other diners), giving them poor service (rudeness, long waits for service, or hurrying them through their meal to get them to leave quickly), or both. This discriminatory treatment was found in the following percentage of restaurants:

Undesirable location only	8%
Poor service or rudeness only	15%
Both undesirable location and poor service	19%

There was much less discrimination in the lower-middle-price restaurants, whereas more than half of those in the upper-middle-price range discriminated against the team of Black diners.

The researchers reported these results to their parent organization, the Committee on Civil Rights in East Manhattan, and the committee used this expert information in several ways:

1. The committee approached associations of restaurant owners and unions of restaurant employees in the area, discussed the study and the problem of discrimination with their officers, and asked for and obtained signed pledges of equal treatment for all restaurant patrons.
2. The study findings and the organizational pledges of nondiscrimination were described in a press release, and the story was carried in major New York newspapers and over several radio stations.
3. The committee sent letters to the owner or manager of each of the restaurants in the district, describing the research findings and the organizational pledges, and requesting each owner or manager to sign a similar pledge of equal treatment. After several contacts, 35% of the restaurants returned signed pledges.
4. Though the restaurants that had discriminated were not named in any public discussions, the committee sent representatives who attempted to talk with each of their managers about the study findings and the problem of discrimination. This approach received a mixed reaction, ranging from cooperation to denial and hostility.
5. The committee met with numerous community groups to inform them of the results of the study and of the follow-up program. It also printed the information in a popular pamphlet and distributed 10,000 copies.

Two years later, another study was conducted in the same area to see if patterns of discrimination had changed. This time 93 restaurants were tested, including all of those that had discriminated in the earlier study, half of those that had not, and 50 restaurants that had not been tested before. The testing, recording, and coding procedures were essentially the same as before. In this study, only 16% of the restaurants gave inferior treatment to the team of Black diners—a significantly lower figure than in the first study. As before, the main kinds of discrimination shown were offering poor service or an undesirable location; about 8% of the restaurants did both. However, there was no difference in the frequency of discrimination between the previously tested establishments and the new ones, or between restaurants having different price ranges.

This study by Selltiz illustrates many of the things that can be done with research findings to attempt to create social change. However, it is not implied that the observed decrease in restaurant discrimination was solely due to the committee's efforts or the use of the research data. Other social and legal developments occurring at the same time in New York probably tended in the same direction. Nevertheless, the net result was a noticeable and meaningful change in the public social climate for minority groups in East Manhattan (Selltiz, 1955).

Interestingly, the Selltiz study was replicated again about 30 years later in the same area of New York City to investigate the possibility of changes in racial discrimination during that period (Schuman et al., 1983). The procedures were as similar as possible to the earlier study, and the conclusion was that a substantial amount of discrimination was still present (about 20%), though apparently less than in the first of Selltiz's earlier surveys. This is consistent with other studies showing prejudice and racism still prevalent in the United States, but in subtler and more symbolic forms than in earlier decades (see Chapter 9). The replication study researchers, too, took steps to protest and attempt to change the policies of the discriminatory restaurants.

Other Research for Social Change

Researchers working in the Lewinian action-research tradition have developed procedures for giving feedback to organizations about the attitudes, perceptions, relationships, and problems of their staff members. These data, from various forms of research, can be used as an important input to groups at all hierarchical levels in the organization. The goal in such procedures is usually to improve the attitudes, relationships, and work satisfaction of the organization's staff members, particularly concentrating on interactions between supervisory personnel and their subordinates.

Another illustration of the potential power of research is seen in **international problem-solving workshops** that have brought together unofficial representatives of contending factions in international and interethnic disputes for several intensive days to examine each other's perspectives through informal but analytical discussion. These discussions are facilitated by social scientists knowledgeable about group dynamics and about the history of the conflict (Lumsden & Wolfe, 1996), and their procedures are informed by a large body of social psychological research on negotiation and third-party mediation (e.g., Bercovitch & Rubin, 1992). Such workshops have been employed effectively for over 20 years in the Israeli-Palestinian dispute by Kelman and his colleagues (Kelman, 1995), and recently also in the Northern Ireland conflict and the Greek-Turkish dispute on Cyprus (Fisher, 1993). These workshops have been credited with contributing importantly to ongoing, official-level peace discussions (Kelman, 1995), particularly since a number of their past participants have later held important policy-making positions (Lumsden & Wolfe, 1996). For other examples of influencing public policy, see the following chapter.

Conditions for Using Expert Knowledge

Hornstein (1975) has suggested several conditions under which expert information is most likely to be successful in accomplishing social change. In contrast to the collaborative, advocacy, or coercive approaches, change agents using an expert approach present their findings and then turn over responsibility for acting on them to the parties concerned. Thus, in order for subsequent action and change to occur, at least three conditions are necessary: (1) the responsible authorities must feel a need for change, (2) proposed changes must be within the perceived capabilities and desires of organization members, and (3) the affected individuals must be motivated to engage in the required behaviors. Even if these conditions are present, resistance to the proposed changes may arise from several causes: divergent goals and conflict within the organization, key members of the organization who feel threatened by the proposed changes, ingrained custom and inertia, or the research findings being seen as irrelevant to the organization's problems (Hornstein, 1975).

DOING ACTION RESEARCH

The social scientist can also take a **collaborative role**, maintaining a continuing relationship with the organization and sharing the responsibility for designing the research and implementing the changes that evolve from the research findings. In other words, the research is an integral part of a program of social action, and the results of the action program contribute to new theoretical and empirical knowledge. Recent examples have been provided by Alderfer (1993), Elden and Chisholm (1993), and Whyte (1991). Because Kurt Lewin originated this concept, many of his students and followers have done outstanding action research studies. One classic example was the study conducted by Coch and French (1948) in a garment factory. There they used group-discussion and group-decision methods to decrease workers' resistance to the frequent necessary changes in work activities as different types of garments were produced. Some of the results of this approach included better worker morale, less disruption of production, increased productivity, and reduced employee turnover.

A more recent industrial example was a project at a Xerox plant in New York (Whyte, Greenwood, & Lazes, 1991). There, management had proposed the necessity of closing a major department and laying off its 180 workers in order to save over $3 million per year. Instead, for an interim period, a cooperative labor-management "cost study team" was formed. This newly formed team of two management and six union members worked full-time for six months, and was given full access to management financial information and an adequate budget, as well as the right to propose changes in work rules and labor contracts. Creatively addressing formerly out-of-bounds areas, the team found that huge savings could be made in training costs for new personnel by stabilizing the workforce and avoiding the former high rates of employee transfers; similarly, previous high overhead charges could be cut by having the necessary services performed within the department. These and other projected savings added up to more than $3 ½ million, and consequently the recommended changes were made and the department was not closed. Management was so happy with the results that it extended the cost study team mechanism to other departments, with annual savings that reached 40% for some departments.

Another example in a health-care setting was a long series of studies aimed at helping ex-mental hospital patients avoid the frequent problems of poor community adjustment and recidivism back to the hospital (Fairweather, Sanders, & Tornatzky, 1974). Five years of research showed that these problems could be greatly alleviated, and patient-care costs could be sharply reduced, if patients were discharged to a carefully planned and supervised **community lodge**—a kind of halfway house which required group living, remunerative work, and self-government. After further corroborative studies, the researchers launched a nationwide *dissemination study*, targeted at all 263 mental hospitals in the United States and aimed at inducing many of them to adopt similar forms of community lodges for posthospital care.

This dissemination study first developed detailed manuals explaining how to set up and run such lodges. Then, in a randomized experimental design, the researchers used several persuasion methods and made contacts with personnel from several different disciplines in the hospitals. In the final phase of the study, *implementation*, 25 matched pairs of hospitals were assigned to either a written-instruction condition or to consultation visits by change agents who helped the local staff in initial planning and later trouble-shooting of the new lodge program. The final results showed that dissemination of innovations such as the lodge concept is a difficult and obstacle-laden process. Essential conditions for success were found to be (a) a group of dedicated people (from any discipline) working together toward the goal and providing mutual support, and (b) active assistance and consultation from an outside change agent (Fairweather et al., 1974; also see Bauman, Stein, & Ireys, 1991).

Twenty-five years after the first community lodge was formed, the concept had persisted and was operating successfully in 32 different programs in the U.S. However, that number was less than 15% of the number of mental hospitals that could potentially benefit from

such a program. This fact underlines the difficulties and resistances that can plague new approaches, even when they are supported by strong empirical research findings (Fairweather, 1980; Mavis & Fergus, 1985).

An Outstanding Example— Preventing AIDS

A recent example of action research has built on many of the lessons of the Fairweather et al. findings, and applied them to the current crucial health problem of preventing the spread of AIDS (Fishbein et al., 1996). We will briefly describe key aspects of the AIDS Community Demonstration Projects (ACDP), sponsored by the Centers for Disease Control and Prevention (CDC). This was a four-year five-city program "using community volunteers to deliver a theory-based intervention designed to increase consistent condom use or consistent bleach use in a number of ethnically diverse, traditionally hard-to-reach, high-risk populations" (Fishbein et al., 1996, p. 178). These populations included men who had sex with men, injecting drug users and their female partners, and female prostitutes, in sections of Dallas, Denver, Long Beach, New York City, and Seattle.

The ACDP research began before 1990 with intensive consultation between CDC staff and outside experts to design a community-level intervention that would be used in all the cities, with specified adaptations to fit local populations and conditions. The intervention was based on widely used theories of behavioral change: the health belief model (Rosenstock, 1974), the theory of reasoned action (Fishbein & Ajzen, 1975), and Bandura's (1986) social cognitive theory. The research plan further specified that formative research would be done in the target communities before implementing the intervention, that a central part of the intervention would be distribution of "small media" materials (e.g., pamphlets, flyers) in the communities along with condoms and bleach kits, and that uniform summative evaluation procedures would be followed in all the project cities.

The intervention was designed to urge individuals from the high HIV-risk groups to move progressively

Photograph courtesy of George Fairweather. Reprinted by permission.

Box 16-1

GEORGE FAIRWEATHER, EXPERIMENTAL ACTION RESEARCHER

One of the founders of the field of community psychology, George Fairweather was born in Oregon in 1921 and graduated from Iowa State University. After completing his M.A. and Ph.D. in psychology and sociology at the University of Illinois in 1953, he held several research positions at VA hospitals, culminating in ten years spent as chief of a social-clinical research unit at the VA Hospital in Palo Alto, California, and as an adjunct faculty member at Stanford. In 1967 he moved to Portland State University, and in 1969 he settled at Michigan State University as a professor and Director of the Ecological Psychology Program, which focused on training students to carry out experimental action research in organizational and community settings.

Fairweather is best known for the research described in this chapter—the community lodge program, conducted while he was at Palo Alto, and the subsequent nationwide research project to disseminate its findings. Among his eight books and many articles, he has also written texts on applied social research entitled *Methods for Experimental Social Innovation* and *Experimental Methods for Social Policy Research.* His concern about social problems and public policy issues is displayed in his book *Social Change: The Challenge to Survival* and in his later research on change processes in universities.

through five stages of change specified in the transtheoretical model of behavior change (Prochaska, DiClemente, & Norcross, 1992). These stages are: (1) **precontemplation**, where they have no thought or intention of adopting a health protective behavior (e.g., using condoms); (2) **contemplation**, where they form an intention to adopt the behavior sometime in the future; (3) **preparation**, where the intended adoption date is imminent, and exploratory or trial attempts may be made; (4) **action**, where the new behavior is adopted; and (5) **maintenance**, where it becomes a routine part of life—(note the similarity of these stages to the stages of becoming a smoker, discussed in Chapter 12). The intervention used a variety of social modeling stimuli to encourage this process of change, such as brief stories about local community members who were also making such changes, and reinforcement of steps in the desired direction.

Six months of *formative research* in each city determined, through wide-ranging interviews and observations, the geographic areas where high HIV-risk individuals gathered, what specific risk behaviors were most common, and which local people were "gatekeepers" who were trusted by the high-risk individuals and could provide access to them. In addition, in each city, the project outreach workers recruited peer group members and other community people, who would later deliver the intervention. These network members were kept involved by provision of small incentives, recognition for their activities, and frequent meetings and parties at the project's storefront headquarters. During this period, also, the "small media" intervention materials were developed to address the specific attitudes and circumstances of the target populations.

With these materials developed, one area in each city was randomly chosen as an intervention area and a comparable area was designated as an untreated control area—a geographically-based quasi-experimental design. Of course, target group individuals who were found in a given area could not be limited to remaining there (as in a randomized experimental design), and it was possible that some individuals might move from the intervention area to the comparison area, or vice versa, thus causing some diffusion of the treatment. The intervention was delivered by the recruited network members, who had been carefully trained to encourage acceptance of and attention to the distributed materials and to reinforce community members' attempts to change their target high-risk behaviors. The various small media materials that they distributed included community newsletters and even baseball cards, giving basic AIDS information and notices of community events, and all telling factual role-model stories of local peers who were trying to change their risky behaviors and how they overcame obstacles in the process. Most of the stories in a given city were targeted at the stage in the behavior change model that was typical for most of the members of that commu-

nity—for example, moving from the contemplation to the preparation stage. The goal of the intervention was to saturate the selected community area with AIDS risk-prevention information.

Before the implementation of the intervention, two waves of a *baseline survey* of eligible community individuals were conducted from February through June 1991. Then, from July 1991 through May 1992, the *start-up* phase of the intervention was conducted, including three waves of data collection. The next phase, *early implementation*, lasted from June 1992 through August 1993, with three more waves of data collection. It was followed by the *full implementation* phase and two more waves of data collection during the following year. In each of these survey waves, trained interviewers went, at times when community residents were normally present, to a randomly determined location in the treatment or comparison community, and randomly selected respondents there to be interviewed with a standard protocol. This "brief street interview" (BSI) determined respondents' eligibility (based on their having had sexual intercourse and/or shared drug injection equipment in the last 30 days), and asked them about their consistency of using condoms and/or using bleach on needles. Other questions determined their relevant attitudes, perception of local norms, feelings of efficacy, exposure to AIDS information, exposure to the project intervention materials or network members during the last three months, and so on. The interviews were entirely anonymous, and respondents were given small amounts of cash or food vouchers for participating. During the early implementation phase, a longer interview schedule was added, and about 80% of respondents completed it as well as the BSI.

From this description, you can see that the interviews obtained a cross-sectional sample of eligible people who happened to be in that location on the interview occasions. To avoid counting the same individuals more than once within a phase, respondents were eliminated if they matched a previous interview on gender, ethnicity, and place and date of birth. However, in successive phases, the same individuals might or might not be repeat respondents. The data were averaged within a phase and plotted to compare changes across phases of the project. The key dependent variables were respondents' stages of change on consistent condom use for vaginal intercourse with (a) their main partner, (b) other partners, and (c) consistent use of bleach to clean injection needles. These dependent variables were all statistically adjusted to control for sample differences in gender, ethnicity, and age.

Only preliminary results of this research, prior to the full implementation phase, are currently available. As an example of the findings, we will display here the data (consolidated across all cities) for *use of condoms with other (nonmain) partners* (see Figure 16-1, which

is based on over 6000 respondents). The figure shows that, for the baseline period and the start-up period, respondents in the intervention areas and the comparison areas were almost identical, and that both areas increased a bit after the baseline phase. Other data showed that the percentage of respondents in the intervention areas who were classified as exposed to the intervention ranged from only 1% to 17% for different cities during the start-up phase, so it is not surprising that the intervention areas did not change more than the comparison areas.

In the early implementation phase, the rate of expo-

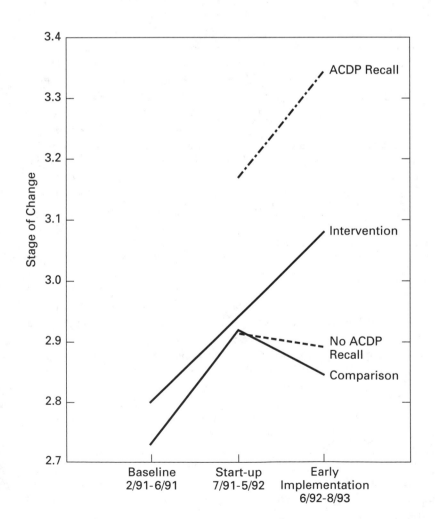

FIGURE 16-1   Mean stage-of-change values on consistent condom use for vaginal sex with other (nonmain) partners ($N = 6184$). (Source: Fishbein, M., et al. (1996). Using a theory-based community intervention to reduce AIDS risk behaviors: The CDC's AIDS Community Demonstration Projects. In S. Oskamp and S. Thompson (Eds.), *Understanding and predicting HIV risk behavior: Safer sex and drug use* (pp. 177–206). Copyright © 1996 by Sage Publications. Reprinted with permission of Sage Publications, Inc.

sure increased markedly and ranged from 21% to 68% for different cities. The figure shows two crucial comparisons for the early implementation phase. First, the two solid lines show that the whole group of respondents in the intervention areas continued to increase on the stage-of-change scale, whereas those in the comparison areas dropped a bit. The amount of change across time in the intervention areas was significantly higher than that for the comparison areas ($p < .03$). Second, two dotted lines are shown—separate plots for respondents in the intervention area who did or did not report any recall of exposure to the intervention. These lines show a dramatic difference, with the exposed respondents being about one-half of a stage-of-change higher than the unexposed respondents ($p < .0001$). Thus, the results indicate that substantial proportions of people in the intervention areas saw or heard the intervention information about AIDS risk, and that those who did were quite likely to increase in their intentions to use condoms with their nonmain sexual partners (remember that these respondents were hard-to-reach street people, including prostitutes and injection drug users). Other results showed that attitudes, norms, and efficacy were all significantly correlated with intentions to use condoms (the rs ranged from .55 to .74 for condom use with main partner)—Fishbein et al. (1996).

Limitations. These results are quite impressive, but there were limitations and questions about the data as well. First, of course, all the data came from self-reports, so the usual questions about their validity and reliability are applicable. Second, notice that the average level in Figure 16-1 was only around 3.0, which means the preparation stage—i.e., getting ready to try using condoms—*not* using them regularly (which would be stage 4.0 or higher). Even the intervention-recall group was well below stage 3.5, so there was still a long way to go before these respondents would be avoiding high HIV-risk behavior altogether. Furthermore, these data were for vaginal sex with *nonmain* partners, and the data for vaginal sex with the main partner showed a much lower level of intention to use condoms (a score around 2.0, or the contemplation stage) and less of a difference from the comparison

group. (The data for the variable of consistent bleach use were rather similar to those shown in Figure 16-1.)

Thus, these research findings are hopeful in showing that hard-to-reach, high-risk community populations *can* be contacted and interviewed through sustained and intensive efforts, and their risk behaviors can be modified. The stages-of-change model is helpful in showing that behavior changes take time and often occur in small steps, and the research demonstrates that community-level interventions can be mounted successfully. But the findings are challenging in showing how much more attitude and behavior change will be needed to move people fully into safe health practices.

Common Problems in Doing Action Research

As illustrated by the above examples, an essential preliminary step in doing action research is obtaining access to the target organization or population and earning the trust of its members. The next step, which is often a critical stumbling block, is negotiating any administrative agreements necessary to carry out the research. The researchers may have to acquire the power to assign participants randomly to experimental conditions, obtain funding, sign contracts for necessary services and supplies, obtain legal advice on procedures and safeguards, and persuade administrators or local authorities not to interfere in ways that would damage the value of the findings (such as changing procedures, reassigning or laying off personnel, or reducing financial support). Finally, a wide range of measures and a longitudinal design are usually required to study processes of change, which are of central interest (cf. Fairweather, 1979).

In order to obtain the necessary cooperation from administrators and from a large research team, all the main personnel should be involved in the planning and continuing decision making. Ideally, this should be done in a democratic manner so that everyone's ideas will be heard and included in the plan; yet at the same time it is necessary to avoid unproductive sidetracks and design changes that would decrease validity. This process demands researchers who are flexible but firm, who can communicate honestly and effectively with all participants, and who will work ethically, keeping the welfare of participants and the benefit of society uppermost in mind. The goals of action research can be achieved only by a true collaborative partnership between the researchers, responsible authorities, and the clients (Fairweather, 1979).

An even more fundamental problem in doing social research is that some social problems may be so persistent and intractable that they are essentially insoluble (Sarason, 1978). For instance, problems like poverty and mental illness may persist in somewhat varying forms and require continuing attacks, rather than being soluble in any final sense. This notion is contrary to the assumptions of most scientific thought, and scientists consequently tend to find intractable social problems particularly frustrating. This outlook may be overly pessimistic, for certainly there are some social problems for which at least partial solutions have been demonstrated (such as various diseases, illiteracy, and intergroup conflict). However, this view illustrates that scientists who want to have some impact on social problems may not be able to limit themselves to the role of expert or even collaborator. They may have to consider the other, "less scientific" roles of using advocacy or even coercive tactics, to which we turn next.

SERVING IN PUBLIC OFFICE

A relatively unusual form of activism which can advance social change is for social scientists to serve in public office. Depending on the office and the characteristics of the officeholder, this can involve any or all of the activist roles: expert, collaborative, advocacy, or coercive. Though most high elective offices in the United States are held by lawyers, social scientists are not unknown in governmental circles, and of course many citizens from all walks of life serve in local government and community affairs.

In Chapter 1 we mentioned John Gardner, who reached the highest U.S. political office yet held by a psychologist as Secretary of Health, Education, and Welfare, and later founded the advocacy organization Common Cause. Another influential psychologist was

Richard Atkinson, who was head of the National Science Foundation during the Carter administration. It is also possible to have a great deal of influence by working behind the scenes as a legislative staff member; a notable example is psychologist Patrick DeLeon, the executive assistant to U.S. Senator Daniel Inouye (Sobel, 1979; Vincent, 1990). On the state and local levels, occasional psychologists have served in state legislatures or been elected as mayors of various cities (e.g., Sullivan et al., 1995).

INFLUENCING LEGISLATION AND PUBLIC POLICY

Social scientists who are not in public office can still try to produce social change and reform by influencing public policy. Typically, they adopt an **advocacy role**—speaking and working for particular reforms (Foster, 1980). Advocates trying to change a social condition often aim their efforts not at the problem itself, but at mobilizing legislators, courts, or disadvantaged groups to take action directed toward reform. Because influencing public policy is the main topic of the next chapter, we will mention only a few brief examples here. One way to influence public policy is to consult with legislators as they develop proposed laws and programs (e.g., Lee et al., 1994). Another way is to offer expert testimony when bills are being considered by legislative committees. Of course, the classic way of influencing prospective legislation is by lobbying, as has been done with increasing effectiveness in recent years by the American Psychological Association and the American Psychological Society (cf. Melton, 1995; Vincent, 1990). However, all of these advocacy approaches suffer from the potential danger of role conflict: They may serve the interests of psychology or of groups of psychologists, but fail to serve or even actually damage the broader public interest.

On the practical level, there are useful books on the hows, whos, wheres, and whens of lobbying, designed for citizens who want to influence legislation (Alderson & Sentman, 1979). There are also more comprehensive manuals for citizen action aimed at affecting many other specific areas of public policy in the style pioneered by Ralph Nader (e.g., Ross, 1973). For instance, among many other topics, Ross describes ways to launch consumer campaigns to obtain lower prices on prescription drugs, or employment campaigns to achieve more jobs for women or minorities in the broadcasting industry.

ORGANIZING AND AGITATING

We come now to the final form of activism for social scientists, the **coercive role.** In contrast to the previous approaches, which made use of *consensus* tactics to build general public agreement, organizing and agitating frequently rely on *conflict* as a tactic. The conflict-arousing activities of **agitators** often diverge sharply from those of **reformers**—individuals who generally try to work within the norms of the system in their efforts to change it. However, both groups follow essentially the same five-stage process of developing their campaigns: (1) community analysis (of needs and resources), (2) design and initiation of a project, (3) implementation of action steps, (4) program maintenance and consolidation, (5) dissemination of results and reassessment (Bracht & Kingsbury, 1990). Community organization as a professional area had its heyday in the 1960s and declined somewhat during the subsequent decades (Reisch & Wenocur, 1986). However, recent years have seen the emergence of many diverse examples of **grassroots organizing**—a form of advocacy which originates with local community members and aims to empower them toward achieving locally determined collective goals (cf. Pilisuk et al., 1996; Wittig & Bettencourt, 1996).

Though conflict and agitation have a negative public image, it is nevertheless important to be familiar with these tactics and to understand their strengths and limitations in achieving social change. Therefore, it is unfortunate that very little systematic research attention has been directed at them. To quote Morton Deutsch, one of the foremost researchers in the area of social conflict resolution,

> Where I have functioned as a . . . consultant to those in low power, I [have been] struck by how little of what I have said is well-grounded in systematic research or theory. As social scientists we have rarely directed our attention to the defensiveness and resistance of the strong and powerful in the face of the need for social change. We have not considered what strategies and tactics are available to low power groups and which of these are likely to lead to a productive rather than destructive process of conflict resolution. (1969, p. 40)

A Renowned Community Organizer

Since there is little research evidence on conflict and coercive tactics for social change, we will rely here primarily on experiential reports from those who have used these tactics and written about their experiences. Among these, one of the most colorful and influential figures was Saul Alinsky (see Box 16-2). Drawing on more than 30 years of personal involvement as a community organizer, he wrote a book titled *Rules for Radicals: A Practical Primer for Realistic Radicals* (Alinsky, 1971), which he characterized as follows:

> *The Prince* was written by Machiavelli for the Haves on how to hold power. *Rules for Radicals* is written for the Have-Nots on how to take it away. (p. 3)

Alinsky had graduate training in sociology, but his tactics were largely self-taught and innovative ways of applying psychological principles of social influence. He believed in appealing to the self-interest of all parties in a conflict, and his tactics were designed to convince the opposition that it was in their best interest to grant the demands of Alinsky's community groups. Alinsky wrote about "revolution" and often appeared eager to shock his readers and listeners as a way of getting them to think more deeply about the nature of our social system. However, by "revolution" he did not mean armed insurrection or the use of violence. He was a "radical" in the sense that the word means "attacking the *root* of a problem." And he was committed to working within the system even while he was challenging the power and perquisites of the establishment.

Alinsky stressed that conflict and coercive tactics are used only after consensus and collaborative approaches have been thoroughly tried and have failed. Even then, conflict tactics should be used in combination with other, milder advocacy strategies, to provide variety and impact, and to emphasize the seriousness of one's cause. Alinsky and his organizing team were usually called into community problem areas only when all customary avenues of redress were blocked or fruitless.

Photograph courtesy of AP/Wide World Photos. Reprinted by permission.

Box 16-2

SAUL ALINSKY, PROFESSIONAL ORGANIZER AND AGITATOR

Saul Alinsky was the best-known community organizer of his generation. Born in Chicago in 1909, he became familiar with its streets and slums in his youth. He took graduate courses in sociology at the University of Chicago, was employed for a time at Joliet State Prison, and found neighborhood organization approaches useful in working with Chicago youth gangs. He next assisted John L. Lewis, the president of the United Mine Workers Union, during the early years of the establishment of the CIO. He greatly admired Lewis's organizing skills and later wrote a biography of him.

Alinsky's first major community organization project was behind the stockyards in Chicago, a vicious slum area about which Upton Sinclair had written in his book, *The Jungle*. In 1940 Alinsky founded the Industrial Areas Foundation, through which he and his staff members took on organizing jobs in many cities across the country. His famous organizing efforts included the Woodlawn Organization in the Black ghetto near the University of Chicago; FIGHT (Freedom, In-

tegration, God, Honor, Today) in the Black area of Rochester, New York; BUILD in Buffalo, New York; the Chelsea Community Council in a multiethnic area of New York City; and organizations in White, Puerto Rican, and Hispanic areas of several other cities.

During breaks in his organizing efforts, some of them spent in jail for his activities, Alinsky wrote several books about community organizing. The best known of them are *Reveille for Radicals* (1946) and *Rules for Radicals* (1971). These became highly influential texts for other organizers, and Alinsky later set up a training institute for community action workers. Many of his typical tactics are described in this chapter. Though a self-described "radical," Alinsky rejected Marxism and espoused a highly pragmatic democratic philosophy, the goal of which was "to promote the general welfare." Alinsky died in 1972, but his work continues through the Industrial Areas Foundation and the many organizers whom he influenced.

An extensive study of eight of Alinsky's most representative community organizing campaigns has corroborated Alinsky's typical use of less-conflictive techniques before resorting to more extreme tactics. In

500 action episodes, this study found 117 cooperative episodes, 219 positive campaign actions (conventional advocacy), 78 negative campaign actions (designed to embarrass or inconvenience the target), 83 incidents of

"contention" (more conflictive, but not challenging the legitimacy of the opposition group's existence), and only 3 incidents of full-scale "conflict" that tried to put the opposition group out of business (Lancourt, 1979, pp. 58–59).

Alinsky's Conflict Tactics

Though Alinsky often used cooperative or advocacy tactics, we will concentrate here on his conflict tactics because they are more colorful and less known to conventional psychologists. In his last book, Alinsky (1971) stated 13 rules for power tactics, which we will reproduce here with a bit of explanation when necessary.[1]

1. "Power is not only what you have but what the enemy thinks you have." Alinsky suggested that if you have developed a large mass-organization in your community, you can parade it visibly to impress the opposition; if your organization is small, you can still make a lot of noise; and "if your organization is too tiny even for noise, stink up the place." You have to start from where you are and use whatever you've got.

2. "Never go outside the experience of your people." By this, Alinsky meant that tactics should always be something your members are familiar and comfortable with.

3. "Wherever possible go outside of the experience of the enemy." By doing something unexpected and foreign to their experience, you can produce confusion, fear, and retreat. An example from the Civil War was Sherman's marching through Georgia instead of fighting a conventional battle against the Confederate armies.

4. "Make the enemy live up to their own book of rules. You can kill them with this, for they can no more obey their own rules than the Christian church can live up to Christianity."

5. "Ridicule is man's most potent weapon. It is almost impossible to counter-attack ridicule. Also it infuriates the opposition, who then react to your advantage."

6. "A good tactic is one that your people enjoy. If your people are not having a ball doing it, there is something very wrong with the tactic."

7. "A tactic that drags on too long becomes a drag."

8. "Keep the pressure on, with different tactics and actions, and utilize all events of the period for your purpose."

9. "The threat is usually more terrifying than the thing itself."

10. "The major premise for tactics is the development of operations that will maintain a constant pressure upon the opposition. It is this unceasing pressure that results in the reactions from the opposition that are essential for the success of the campaign." And your side's actions are in turn responses to the opposition's reactions.

11. "If you push a negative hard and deep enough it will break through into its counterside." By this, Alinsky meant that every positive feature of a strategy has some negatives or disadvantages, and vice versa. If you examine the disadvantages of your situation very closely, you may be able to turn them into advantages. For instance, if your organization has no money, you may use the bodies of your members as a source of power; their lack of jobs will make them available for mass demonstrations. Similarly, you can turn the orderly procedures of a bureaucracy into a tool against it by having your members clog its offices, filling out multitudes of forms.

12. "The price of a successful attack is a constructive alternative." You have to know what you want and be ready with a proposal or a plan whenever the opposition gives in to your pressure.

13. "Pick the target, freeze it, personalize it, and polarize it." Freezing the target means singling out who is to blame for a given problem and not letting them get off the hook. Personalizing means picking out a particular person or persons who are responsible (such as the mayor, or the officers of a corporation), not an anonymous organization. Polarizing it means to get people to line up strongly against your target, acting as if it were 100% bad.

A particularly pungent example of how to apply these rules was suggested by Alinsky when he was helping African Americans in The Woodlawn Organi-

[1]Reprinted by permission from pp. 126–130 in Saul D. Alinsky, *Rules for Radicals*. Copyright © 1971 by Random House, Inc.

zation negotiate with Chicago authorities. Some commitments by city hall were not being honored, and the frequently effective threat to vote for someone else was not effective at this time because it was in the middle of the 1964 Johnson-Goldwater presidential campaign, and Blacks saw no alternative to supporting Johnson. Consequently, organizers needed some other way to keep the pressure on city hall. The target chosen was Chicago's O'Hare Airport, the world's busiest airport. The method proposed was to tie up all of O'Hare's toilet facilities by busing loads of Woodlawn residents to the airport and having them occupy every stall, remaining there reading a magazine or newspaper, and thus preventing travelers from satisfying their bodily needs—what Alinsky called a "shit-in." Scouts were sent to the airport to count the number of toilets and urinals, and Woodlawn Organization leaders began fantasizing how this strategy would get worldwide publicity and mortify the Chicago city authorities. Alinsky reports that the plans for this tactic were "leaked" to informers, who quickly told city hall, and the simple threat was all that was necessary.

> Within forty-eight hours the Woodlawn Organization found itself in conference with the authorities who said that they were certainly going to live up to their commitments and they could never understand where anyone got the idea that a promise made by Chicago's City Hall would not be observed. At no point, then or since, has there ever been any open mention of the threat of the O'Hare tactic. Very few of the members of the Woodlawn Organization knew how close they were to writing history. (Alinsky, 1971, pp. 143–144)

This example clearly illustrates many of Alinsky's principles. Using toilets in public facilities was a familiar experience to Alinsky's followers, but having all the toilets in a whole airport permanently occupied was far beyond the experience of the authorities, and they had no procedures for handling such a situation. The Woodlawn residents would have enjoyed creating such a spectacle, and the result would have held the Chicago authorities up to international ridicule. This continued pressure was necessary to ensure the city's living up to commitments previously won by other pressure tactics. City hall knew that Alinsky's group had the power to carry out their tactic, and consequently only the hint of

a threat to do it was enough to gain the authorities' renewed cooperation.

Outcomes of Alinsky's Organizing

How successful are such tactics? It is difficult to give a single answer because the results have varied so much in different campaigns with differing external conditions. In more than 30 years of organizing, Alinsky either founded or consulted on a regular basis with 14 major community organizations in many cities. Each had its own grievances, goals, and priorities, around which Alinsky and his staff built the organization. In a general sense all the goals involved reducing neighborhood deterioration through a process of citizen participation and community control. The most frequent target areas for improvements were in the quality of housing, schools, and prospects for employment. Other goals of some of the organizations included improvement of welfare services, city services, police and fire protection, consumer problems, small business opportunities, and various neighborhood service programs (Finks, 1984; Lancourt, 1979).

These community campaigns achieved many of their specific goals, though it was often necessary to refight the same or similar battles to maintain the gains over time. Some of the success stories included The Woodlawn Organization's planning and building a 500-apartment development of low-income housing, complete operation of a ghetto-area grade school in Buffalo, and a campaign against the Kodak Co. in Rochester, New York, that won commitments for over 1000 new jobs for minorities in one year. Other goals were never reached, or abandoned as too difficult, but since each organization had a series of goals, there were usually enough successes to keep the group functioning. Indeed, a setback often led to more cohesion and dedication from the members. Even where there seem to have been few objective achievements, it is quite possible that the neighborhoods would be even worse off now if Alinsky and the organization had never been there.

In addition to the objective successes and failures, there were important subjective benefits from all the organizations. A central achievement was the pattern of members becoming socialized into the political process, becoming involved in local issues, developing a more positive self-image, and replacing their former apathy with hope (Finks, 1984; Lancourt, 1979). In today's terminology, this was a program of *empowerment*, based on a foundation of citizen participation in community affairs (Horwitt, 1989). The development of a corps of indigenous minority leaders with experience and skills in community organization was also a crucial outcome (Reitzes & Reitzes, 1986).

In terms of their long-term impact, some of Alinsky's organizations declined after some battles were won or when the issues changed. However, many of them adapted to change and continued as active forces in their communities in Chicago, Rochester, Buffalo, and other cities, some for as long as 40 years. The Woodlawn Organization, for instance, ran a complex set of community service programs with a staff of nearly 300 and an annual budget of $5 million. However, probably the most important national impact of Alinsky's organizations was in providing an influential model for other citizen action programs and a training ground for scores of community organizers who went on to work in other action programs—individuals like Cesar Chavez, who later founded the United Farm Workers union (Lancourt, 1979). Many current community organizers draw heavily on Alinsky's methods (e.g., Reitzes & Reitzes, 1986), and there are many testimonials to their success, though there is little direct research evidence on the subject.

Research Evidence on Confrontation

It is impossible to do tightly controlled research on community action campaigns because each campaign meets different circumstances and evolves as it develops. Therefore, most of the literature on community organization consists of anecdotal accounts and case studies of particular community campaigns. For instance, detailed descriptions of various peace action campaigns are offered by Marullo and Lofland (1990). Useful handbooks giving advice on each step in the process have been provided by Taber et al. (1972) and Zander (1990). There are also volumes containing examples of how-to-do-it information drawn from a wide

variety of topics of citizen campaigns (e.g., Meyers & Rinard, 1972; Ross, 1973), and scholarly analyses of the principles and potential of nonviolent action campaigns by community groups have been presented by Kelman (1968) and Zander (1990).

Despite the lack of direct research evidence, some findings from laboratory and field experiments may plausibly be extrapolated to the community level. On the basis of such data, Deutsch (1969) summarized the dangers in some confrontational influence methods that are likely to create resistance and alienation in members of opposing groups. These counterproductive methods include: (a) illegitimate methods that violate the other's social norms and values, (b) negative sanctions such as punishments and threats, (c) positive rewards or negative sanctions that are inappropriate in kind to the other's behavior (for example, payment for freely given cooperation may decrease later cooperative behavior), (d) rewards or sanctions that are excessive in size (these tend to be resisted as bribery or coercion). Many of these counterproductive effects could be derived from Brehm's (1966) theory of reactance. By contrast, Deutsch outlined a variety of positive, friendly, and collaborative techniques that are likely to induce cooperation from other groups.

Aren't these research findings in direct contradiction to many of Alinsky's techniques? Well, yes, it must be admitted that they are. And if so, aren't Alinsky's conflict techniques likely to create more resistance rather than less? Again the answer would seem to be yes, but the external situations under which Alinsky usually operated tended to require and validate his conflict tactics. First, he would normally advise using cooperation as long as it was effective, but he was typically called in only when cooperation had broken down or failed to gain any concessions. Thus, a conflict situation already existed. Second, many of his tactics were aimed at strengthening his own group's cohesiveness and dedication, rather than being designed primarily for their effect on the opposition. They might in fact increase the opposition's resistance somewhat, but if his own group's determination increased more, that would represent a net gain in power. Third, Alinsky's tactics were designed to demonstrate his group's power and convince the opposition that they would have to make concessions no matter how they felt about it. In other words, with an intransigent opposition, users of conflict tactics often have little to lose; and a convincing display of power and determination may gain much by forcing the other side to change its tactics. Finally, as soon as Alinsky saw a willingness to negotiate or make concessions from the opposition, he was ready to switch to collaborative tactics; thus he rewarded the other side's cooperative behavior (Finke, 1984)

Many current activist groups have adopted some of Alinsky's confrontational and polarizing tactics. One of the most successful of these has been Greenpeace, which specializes in direct action campaigns on environmental and health issues. In a recent example, publicity generated by Greenpeace prevented the Shell Oil Company from dumping an abandoned North Sea oil platform holding 130 tons of toxic waste into the deep ocean. Techniques used included nonviolent occupation of the abandoned platform, flying journalists in to observe and photograph the tugs pulling the platform, and mobilizing political and diplomatic support in eight other nations to boycott Shell products and pressure the English government to revoke the permit it had granted for dumping the platform. After several days of this confrontation, Shell admitted that its revenues were being decimated, and it agreed not to dump the rig in the ocean (*Greenpeace*, 1995).

EFFECTS OF PRESSURE GROUPS

All of our discussion of activism has been implicitly or explicitly assuming that it can be an effective technique, and there is much evidence to support this view. Many analysts have stressed that our political system is heavily influenced by the actions of pressure groups (e.g., Knoke, 1990; M. Smith, 1990). Some have even claimed groups to be so dominant in our system that the political and social views of any individual are irrelevant unless they are registered through group pressures (Goldner, 1971). Though this is probably an overstatement, it emphasizes how important group pressures are in our system because of their potential political effects. Anecdotal political lore stresses the same point, as in the following quotation:

It is not enough just to elect your candidates. You must keep the pressure on. . . . Keep in mind Franklin D. Roosevelt's response to a reform delegation, "Okay, you've convinced me. Now go out and bring pressure on me!" Action comes from keeping the heat on. (Alinsky, 1971, p. xxiii)

People often ask what they, as single individuals, can do to encourage social change. The answer is simple—*join an organization*! Better still, you can join several organizations that take public stands on social issues and work to support their positions (for instance, a political party, a civil rights group, or a single-issue organization working on a topic such as abortion or handgun control). It is true that individuals may occasionally influence their representatives through a friendly contact or a thoughtful letter, but the real political power in our pluralistic system lies in groups that are willing to organize and work to reach their goals (e.g., Zigler & Muenchow, 1984). As an experienced change agent wrote,

Whatever your role—company manager . . . college dean, missionary or society hostess—if you need more power to act, your aim must be to build (or change) an appropriate organization to provide it for you. (Peabody, 1971, p. 523)

Research has shown that the electorate has become more issue-oriented and sophisticated about the process of political influence (Nie, Verba, & Petrocik, 1979). As a consequence, we have seen an increase in contentious politics and conflict between sharply opposing viewpoints, as in the issue of abortion. A political scientist has pointed out that contending political groups

utilize the very model that U.S. society has made the test for political participation—namely, articulating interests in a legal manner, and withholding political support if necessary to achieve such interest. (Horowitz, 1977, p. 11)

As a result of these trends, citizens who do not register their opinions through an organized pressure group will have little influence on contemporary political or social events. By contrast, taking part in group plans and activities can increase one's sense of personal efficacy (Bandura, 1977a) and reduce feelings of social alienation.

CITIZEN PARTICIPATION
IN GOVERNMENT DECISIONS

Citizen participation in governmental decisions that affect their lives is a basic principle of democracy. However, the concept of citizen participation can mean very different things to different people. Disagreements often arise about which citizens should be involved, with how much responsibility, and in which kinds of decisions.

Far too often, in our country as well as other democracies, participation has been an unrealized ideal, with only a small "elite" group actually being involved. This lack of involvement in decisions that affected their lives has been especially true for the poor and for minority group members. As part of the reform movements of the 1960s, there were widespread attempts to change that situation and make citizen participation more of a reality. In this effort many different methods of participation were proposed and used. They ranged from needs assessments and other surveys to determine the desires and problems of affected groups, through public hearings on proposed new programs, and citizen advisory boards without any decision-making power, to complete control over local programs by the citizens who were affected.

Recent History

According to an historical review by Langton (1981), an early precedent for citizen involvement occurred in 1954, when Congress passed a law requiring citizen participation in local planning for federally funded programs in the field of urban renewal (that is, tearing down and rebuilding city neighborhoods). However, the citizens involved there were usually blue-ribbon advisory panels of civic leaders, businessmen, and officers of city-wide organizations—not representatives of the neighborhoods that would be affected by the urban renewal projects.

In 1964, the Economic Opportunity Act took a bold further step by requiring "maximum feasible participation of members of groups and areas served" in the Economic Opportunity and Community Action Pro-

grams. This meant citizens from local neighborhoods, who were usually minority group members and not "civic leaders." Later the law was amplified to require that at least one-third of the members of the board of directors of each community action agency had to be local citizens. This gave local citizens a major voice in planning and implementation of projects, not just an advisory role. However, controversy quickly developed regarding how much control over community projects could be exercised by the project's board of directors as opposed to the elected city officials. In 1967 this issue was resolved by Congress's adoption of an amendment to the Economic Opportunity Act, returning much of the control to elected officials. In many cities this city hall control had the effect of perpetuating the existing inadequate services and substandard conditions in poverty neighborhoods (Hallman, 1973).

A further vehicle for citizen involvement was created in 1970 by a law requiring that *environmental impact reports* be filed before the start of major real estate development and construction projects. The main method of participation in this process was through public hearings, but such hearings were typically not very effective methods of achieving citizen involvement in policy decisions (Cole & Caputo, 1984). By 1978, there was a long list of specific citizen participation procedures that were required in 155 different federal grant programs accounting for over 80% of federal grant money (Langton, 1981).

Rationale and Definitions

Among the touchy issues not resolved in any of these laws were: exactly how the group of affected citizens should be defined, how board member elections were to be held, what type and degree of board participation in decision making was required, and what powers were held by the elected board. Different proponents presented a variety of different rationales for citizen participation, ranging from a necessary check and balance on government power to a tool for eliciting new ideas and solutions for problems (Aleshire, 1970). Citizen participation was also seen as a means of developing indigenous leadership in the community, a way of placating aggrieved parties, or a technique for delaying or avoiding difficult decisions. The goals of citizen participation were variously stated as: decentralization of government, building public consent for the proposed programs, providing a form of therapy for alienated minority groups, ensuring equal protection for formerly powerless groups, providing employment for local citizens, redistribution of power and resources, and development of a constituency for the federal agency or the current administration (Fox, 1971). These multiple goals inevitably conflicted, and there were many bitter battles in local cities and in Washington, DC over procedures for planning and implementing projects—in short, over who would get the power and the money.

Thus, no single definition of **citizen participation** was ever accepted, and each local organization developed its own procedures for assuring that the requirement was met. The four main features most often included were: membership of the poor on boards, employment of the poor in projects, community meetings, and elections of board members (Lazar, 1971). Arnstein (1971) outlined a hierarchy of levels of "participation" according to the amount of actual citizen power (see Figure 16-2). At the bottom are public relations or therapeutic approaches, which substitute for real participation; in the middle are several degrees of token involvement, which allow citizens to have some influence in return for their support of public projects; and at the top are various arrangements that allow some real citizen power to negotiate, decide policies, or manage public programs. Arnstein declared that most socalled citizen participation is limited to the lower levels, allowing authorities to say that the public was consulted, without essentially changing the programs proposed.

Difficulties in Achieving Citizen Participation

The many varied arrangements for so-called citizen participation suggest some of the difficulties in bringing the concept into actual operation (DeSario & Langton, 1987; Fisher, 1994; "Symposium," 1987). Arnstein (1972) used the phrase "maximum feasible

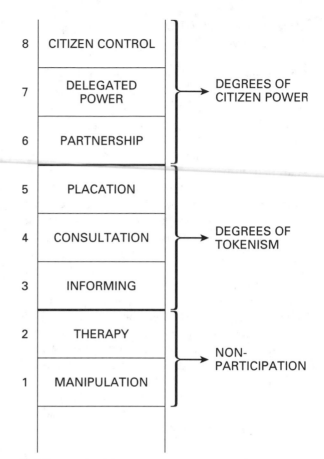

FIGURE 16-2   Eight rungs on the ladder of citizen participation. (Source: Arnstein, 1971, p. 70. Reprinted by permission.)

manipulation" in criticizing Philadelphia city officials who took over a Model Cities Program in the northern area of the city. In the end the citizen leaders in the area were bitterly disillusioned, feeling that they had been systematically deprived of all control over the community programs which they themselves had proposed and developed.

In an Oakland, California, Model Cities Program, a happier result was reached, but only after the same long process of conflict and intensive negotiation at every step (May, 1973). The citizens' planning committee insisted that they must be able to govern the features of any new urban programs in their area of the city, not just advise the city officials nor just cast votes in the decision process. In the end, a partnership of shared sovereignty was established, in which either the city or the citizens' planning committee could veto the plans for any project.

A number of authors have pointed out ways in which the process of citizen participation did not live up to the hopes of its proponents (e.g., Frederickson, 1973; Lazar, 1971). In the first place, in many cities neither individuals nor community groups rushed in to participate. Poverty areas often lack a structure of existing community groups, and their residents are frequently inexperienced in organizing; alienated; or lacking in self-confidence about their education, verbal or reasoning skills, or interaction with middle-class individuals. Second, residents who did come forward were not necessarily representative of the community, often being spokespersons for various special interests, such as churches and businesses. Thus, community meetings were apt to be poorly attended and dominated by a few verbal and atypical individuals.

Other problems in the citizen participation process stemmed from the fact that various community factions often had widely differing viewpoints about priorities and plans. Consequently, meetings were apt to be very long, slow to reach conclusions, easily sidetracked onto peripheral or irrelevant issues, and full of conflict and confusion. When poverty area residents were elected to planning boards, they often had to fight to get their community's views heard, and those with perspectives that might have provided needed balance or correction were likely to be ostracized, frustrated, or pushed into nonparticipation. Also, city officials and technical staff members frequently treated the citizen boards as rubber stamps or debating societies, so that they had no real decision-making power (Aleshire, 1970; Lazar, 1971).

Employment of the poor in community projects—another major goal of community participation—also had unexpected drawbacks. Some employees were ill-prepared in skills or work habits, while others got in trouble with crime or drugs and brought bad publicity to their projects. When frustrated by slow progress in getting programs planned and funded, many new staff members became discouraged and quit trying, or else

lost their effectiveness due to excessive anger and militancy. Finally, it is a sad fact that most of the newly created jobs were dead ends because they weren't in the regular city job hierarchy, and some were obviously make-work positions. Thus, the employees' frustration and anger at the lack of training, mobility, or advancement were reasonable and understandable reactions to a very unfortunate job situation (Lazar, 1971).

Many of these difficulties in the implementation of citizen participation provide examples of the general principle, which has been extensively documented by Sieber (1981), that social interventions can often have harmful effects quite contradictory to those intended by their proponents. This is a danger which change agents as well as public authorities must constantly guard against in their efforts to improve our community life. Research on community participation projects has begun to identify the factors producing various types of benefits and costs (e.g., Florin & Wandersman, 1990). Just as Alinsky (1971) proclaimed, studies have confirmed that people who are involved in community activities and organizations feel more empowered and less alienated than those who are not involved (Zimmerman, in press; Zimmerman & Rappaport, 1988).

TRAINING ACTIVISTS

Training activists is clearly an important and demanding job, but relatively little is known about how to do it. Saul Alinsky did informal education of organizers for many years, and late in his career he set up a formal training institute with regular courses and field experience requirements. Yet he confessed that knowing how to develop other organizers was still a mystery to him. Though he had trained a number of outstanding activists such as Cesar Chavez, he described his overall educational record as "unpromising," with more failures than successes (Alinsky, 1971). Alinsky's educational guidelines focused more on the characteristics that an organizer should have than on how they could be developed. He stated that the ideal organizer should be curious, irreverent, and imaginative, should possess a sense of humor, at least a blurred vision of a better world to which their work is contributing, an organized personality, strong self-confidence, a sense of political relativity, and finally, should be an excellent communicator and a "well-integrated political schizoid," able to polarize issues in extreme terms or to negotiate compromises pragmatically, as the occasion demands (1971, p. 78). A tall order!

How can change agents be trained? The group dynamics movement and community psychology have given attention to this question, though community psychologists have often lamented that there is insufficient training in community intervention methods (e.g., Heller, 1990). Several collections of articles offer examples of the work of change agents and action researchers (Alderfer, 1993; Elden & Chisholm, 1993; Mizrahi & Morrison, 1993; Whyte, 1991). Many of these examples focus more on settings in corporations or government agencies than on community action campaigns, and consequently the activities described tend to be more structured and supportive of the organization's major goals than is true in "revolutionary" community organizing such as Alinsky's.

There are many divergent models for training change agents (Doyle, Wilcox, & Reppucci, 1983). Some of the most practical training materials emphasize the importance of skills in working with groups (Guthrie & Miller, 1981). Havelock (1972) developed a complete manual for the design and conduct of training programs for change agents; although it was aimed mainly at work in educational settings, most of the material is applicable to other fields as well. Finally, the *American Journal of Community Psychology* and other similar periodicals provide valuable sources of ideas and case examples concerning community action issues and strategies.

SUMMARY

Social activism is an unfamiliar role for psychologists and one on which there is little research evidence. Kurt Lewin was one of its first proponents within social psychology, and his followers in the group dynamics movement are still among the most dedicated change agents. One classification of change agent behaviors lists four kinds of activist roles: expert, collaborative, advocacy, and coercive.

In the expert role, psychologists may conduct research for social change, as illustrated in the study of racial discrimination in New York restaurants by Selltiz. There are many ways this can be done, but the expert approach will only be successful if the responsible authorities feel a need for change and possess the capability and motivation to perform the required new behaviors.

Action research, in which social action and empirical research are integrally combined, places the social scientist in a collaborative role. It is illustrated by Fairweather's attempts to disseminate the concept of the community lodge for ex-mental patients to the staffs of hospitals around the United States, and by Fishbein et al.'s community interventions to reduce AIDS risk behaviors. Key steps in action research are gaining entry into the organization or the community, negotiating the necessary operational agreements, planning for the use of multiple measures and a longitudinal design, and involving all personnel in planning the research.

Serving in public office is another, relatively unusual, form of activism. Increasingly common, however, are cases where social scientists try to influence public policy, using an advocacy approach. This can be done by consulting work for legislators, by giving expert testimony, or by lobbying.

Organizing and agitating, the most intense forms of activism, often involve a coercive role, in which social conflict is encouraged in order to reach certain valued ends. This strategy is illustrated by Saul Alinsky's colorful and often effective combination of confrontation tactics with collaborative and advocacy approaches. Some of Alinsky's community organizations have persisted for 40 years or more, providing influential models for citizen action programs and training grounds for community organizers. Though confrontation tactics run counter to many research findings on successful conflict resolution, they can be effective when dealing with an intransigent opposition.

Our political system is heavily influenced by the actions of pressure groups, whereas individuals acting alone can rarely exert any influence. Therefore, more knowledge is needed on how best to train community organizers. Because poor people and racial minorities were so unlikely to have a say in public programs which affected their lives, requirements for citizen participation in governmental decision making were instituted in the 1960s. However, the concept meant very different things to different people, and there have been many difficulties in putting it into effect.

SUGGESTED READINGS

Alinsky, S. D. (1971). *Rules for radicals: A practical primer for realistic radicals.* New York: Random House.—A highly entertaining book, giving a master organizer's philosophy, tactical rules about community action, and samples of how he handled actual organizing situations.

Ross, D. K. (1973). *A public citizen's action manual.* New York: Grossman.—A how-to manual with many examples of citizen action programs in the areas of consumer protection, health care, equal opportunity, tax action, and making government more responsive.

Whyte, W. F. (Ed.). (1991). *Participatory action research.* Newbury Park, CA: Sage.—Chapters present fascinating examples of action research, in both industrial and agricultural settings.

Wittig, M. A., & Bettencourt, B. A. (Eds.). (1996). Social psychological perspectives on grassroots organizing [Special issue]. *Journal of Social Issues, 52*(1), 1–220.—An interesting collection of research articles on the processes and effects of organizing that stems from community members themselves.

CHAPTER 17

Influencing Public Policy

Behavioral sciences . . . are an essential and increasingly relevant instrument of modern government.

—National Research Council (1968, p. 17)

THE POLICY SCIENCES

Throughout this book we have discussed the application of social psychology in understanding and solving social problems. We have illustrated a variety of areas of application including health, education, work life, advertising, the environment, the legal system, and diversity issues. In this final chapter, we will examine the social sciences' role in influencing public policy, and more generally, the concept of **policy science.**

The policy scientist is an intermediary who helps to link knowledge and action, a mediator and integrator between the scientific research community and policy decision makers. This role involves both knowledge of the process of policy formation and implementation, and use of scientific knowledge in attempts to influence this process (Lasswell, 1970). This is by nature an interdisciplinary, problem-oriented enterprise—one that can be contributed to by all the social sciences, from anthropology through psychology and sociology to economics, political science, philosophy, and law (Nagel, 1995). One view of the policy scientist's task is to "speak truth to power"—the description originally given by Rexford Tugwell of his role in President Franklin D. Roosevelt's circle of advisors (Wildavsky, 1979).

Attempts to apply social science in this way began long before the term *policy sciences* was coined. In the 1700s and 1800s, social scientists in England, France, and Germany did pioneering studies of conditions in prisons, hospitals, factories, and slums, with the goal of social amelioration and reform (Weiss, 1978). Many similar efforts were launched during the great depression and the international upheavals of the 1930s; in our complex modern era, policy research has increased still more.

There is widespread agreement that this applied role for the social sciences is important and helpful (Kipnis, 1994). For instance, consider this quotation from an official report of the National Science Foundation (1969):

At those levels in the federal government where major policy is made, the social sciences should be deeply involved. Policies for handling the nation's most pressing issues and problems—whether they relate to the cities, pollution, inflation, or supersonic transport—must rest not only on knowledge drawn from the physical and biological sciences, but also on the best available knowledge about human individual and social behavior. Many of our most urgent domestic policy issues, indeed, are more closely related to the social sciences than to the other sciences. (pp. xiii–xiv)

Congress has probably done more to emphasize the need for social science knowledge than any other body. In 1970 it expanded the role of the General Accounting Office (GAO) in doing cost-benefit analyses of federal programs and assisting in congressional supervisory functions. In the next four years it created the Congressional Research Service (CRS), the Office of Technology Assessment (OTA—unfortunately disbanded in 1995), and the Congressional Budget Office (CBO)—all to provide it with various kinds of research-based information essential for policy analysis. Much of this information comes from economists, but the other social sciences also have important roles to play (Morin, 1993; Weiss, 1992).

What do social psychologists have to contribute to this policy analysis process? Of course one answer is their research skills and use of quantitative methods (Kipnis, 1994). A related point is their frequent emphasis on experimental approaches to research, quite different from the typical research approaches of many other social sciences. Another answer is their psychological approach—attending to the subjective feelings and actual behavior of individuals, as opposed to the common assumption of economists and political scientists that people gather information objectively, make decisions rationally, and act consistently (McConahay, 1980). Finally, some psychologists have pioneered in the area of public affairs psychology, addressed specifically to policy makers and applied to issues of policy formation and implementation (Brayfield & Lipsey, 1976; Goodstein & Sandler, 1978).

RESEARCH FOR PUBLIC POLICY

The amount of money devoted to research and development (R&D) in the United States is enormous. In 1995 approximately $70 billion was spent by the federal government on R&D. This money went primarily to private industry (45%), with lesser amounts going to federal laboratories (25%), academia (17%), and other independent organizations (13%). Of course, most of these funds were devoted to the physical sciences—defense 55%, medical research 16%, and space exploration 11% (National Academy of Sciences, 1995; National Science Foundation, 1995). The social and behavioral sciences received only a small fraction of the total—about 5% of all R&D funding according to a recent estimate by the National Science Foundation (Miller, 1991). Nevertheless, 5% of $70 billion is $3.5 billion—a substantial amount of federal funding. Private industry, private institutions, and state and local governments also fund social research and development at approximately the same level as the federal government (i.e., $3.5 billion). Thus, the total U.S. expenditure for applied social research in 1995 was estimated to be $7 billion dollars per year, though perhaps half of that R&D total went to development projects rather than true research.

The history of systematic government-supported social R&D in the United States began with establishment of the Federal Bureau of Ethnology in 1881, though there were occasional earlier examples, as in some of the studies made by the Lewis and Clark Expedition in 1804–1806 (Lynn, 1978). Federal funding for social research increased sharply during the depression of the 1930s, and in World War II the government employed social scientists to help with innumerable aspects of the war effort—homefront morale, efficient production, analyzing enemy propaganda, training servicemen, and so on. An important example was the social research on desegregation in the U.S. Army during and after World War II, which has been summarized by Lazarsfeld and Reitz (1975, pp. 148–152).

Another sharp increase in federal support for social research occurred during the late 1960s and early 1970s, stimulated by the urban riots of that period and the resulting "war on poverty." A huge and influential study from that period was the Coleman Report on the effects of segregated versus nonsegregated education, discussed in Chapter 8 (Coleman et al., 1966). Since then there has been a whole series of innovative social research programs and even some large-scale true experiments in areas such as education, housing, welfare, criminal justice, and energy use (Friedlander & Burtless, 1995; Hausman & Wise, 1985). This type of research is an essential feature of the "experimenting society" advocated by Donald Campbell (1969, 1988). A list of some of the major studies in eight areas of social experimentation is presented in Table 17-1.

Some of these studies have been truly monumental and long-term in scope. For instance, the Experimental Housing Allowance Program, sponsored by the U.S. Department of Housing and Urban Development, included three subsidiary experiments, which lasted seven years and cost about $350 million to conduct (Friedman & Weinberg, 1983; Greenberg & Robins, 1985). Other very important and expensive studies were the Negative Income Tax Experiments, originally begun by the Office of Economic Opportunity (Heclo & Rein, 1980). A major justification for these costly experiments is that, by trying out proposed government programs with a limited sample in a circumscribed area, they can avoid colossal mistakes and provide data on the effectiveness of programs that would cost more than 100 times as much as the research if they were implemented across the whole country. Table 17-2 gives details of some of the largest social experiments ever conducted. In a later section of this chapter we will discuss the results from several of these and other large-scale social experiments.

What is the value of these huge experiments? The most persuasive answer is that every dollar spent on research is returned later in greater savings. For example, a cost-benefit analysis of the Perry Preschool Project—a predecessor of the Head Start program—found that for every dollar spent on the preschool intervention program, a $7 savings to society was seen after 20 years—due to less welfare use, less crime, lower expenditures on education, and increased employment rates (Schweinhart, Barnes, & Weikart, 1993). Other examples of the cost-effectiveness of applied social re-

TABLE 17-1   Partial List of Major Social Innovations and Experiments

In Education	*In Housing*
Title I Allocation Experiment	Experimental Housing Allowance Program
Head Start Planned Variation	Urban Homesteading
Follow Through Planned Variation	
Educational Voucher	*In Health Care System Planning*
Emergency School Assistance Program	Health Insurance Experiment
Performance Contracting	Prospective Reimbursement
Experimental School	
	In Criminal Justice
In Child Care	Defendant Diversion
National Day Care Experiment	Kansas City Preventive Patrol Experiment
Income and Employment	*In Energy*
Supported Work Experiments	Solar Heating
Negative Income Tax Experiments	Subsidized Home Insulation
Work Incentive Program	
Youth Employment Incentive Pilot	*In Transportation*
Program	Energy Efficiency Labeling
Minnesota Work Equity Program	Services and Methods Demonstration Programs

Source: page 168 in Abt, C. C., Social science in the contract research firm. In R. F. Kidd & M. J. Saks (Eds.), *Advances in applied social psychology* (Vol. 1). Hillsdale, N.J.: Erlbaum, 1980. Reprinted by permission.

search include the Department of Health, Education, and Welfare's maternal and child health study, which resulted in decreased infant mortality, and the Manhattan bail bond experiment, which led to reforms that saved about $50 million per year in detention costs (Abt, 1980). In general, social programs that spend more money on applied research produce more beneficial effects. One estimate is that the return is roughly $100 in benefits for every applied social research dollar spent (Kiesler, 1980).

Despite their value, research findings are not the only determinant of public policy decisions—far from it! A model of the many factors that affect decision-making processes within an agency or an organization has been offered by Davis (1973). These include the participants' abilities, values, information, obligations, and resistances, and factors of timing, circumstances, and the expected yield or benefit from a policy. All these factors interact in the process by which organizational decisions are reached and actions taken. Thus, any one of them, or a combination, can scuttle an action that would seem to be indicated by the other factors. A frequent example is that research findings em-

phasize the expected yield or information requirements of a proposed policy, while decision makers may be more swayed by other aspects such as values, circumstances, or resistances. For instance, the U.S. Commission on Obscenity and Pornography was influenced by the expected policy effects or yield in its recommendations not to censor or limit the availability of allegedly pornographic materials to adult citizens. In contrast, President Nixon was sensitive to the value and resistance aspects of the issue, and he repudiated the commission's research-based recommendations as "morally bankrupt" (*Los Angeles Times*, 1970).

Thus, even thoughtful use of valid research evidence will not necessarily result in adoption of a policy that the research findings favor (Lazarsfeld & Reitz, 1975; Webber, 1992).

DOES PUBLIC OPINION AFFECT GOVERNMENT DECISIONS?

A related question is: To what extent is *mass public opinion* (a particular type of research evidence) incorporated into public policy? Of course the answer to this

TABLE 17-2 The Major Social Experiments

Experiment	Date of Field Work	Final Report Date	Nature of Treatment	Response Measured	Number of Participants	Research and Administrative Costs (1983 dollars)	Total Costs (1983 dollars)
1. New Jersey Income Maintenance Experiment	1968–72	1974	NIT	Head-spouse-family labor supply	1216 families	$15.4 million	$22.2 million
2. Rural Negative Income Tax Experiment	1970–72	1976	NIT	Head-spouse-family labor supply	809 families	$9.5 million	$15.6 million
3. Gary Income Maintenance Experiment	1971–74	—	NIT plus day care	Head-spouse-family labor supply, use of day care	1780 families	$33.0 million	$45.2 million
4. Seattle-Denver Income Maintenance	1971–78	1983	NIT plus employment counseling and educational vouchers	Head-spouse-family labor supply, marital stability, earnings capacity	4784 families	$97.8 million	$132.7 million
5. Education Performance Contracting	1970–71	1972	Cash payment as incentive for academic performance	Educational improvement of junior high students	19,399 students[1]	n.a.	$14.3 million
6. National Health Insurance	1974–81	n.a.	Different fee-for-service health insurance plans with alternative coinsurance rates and deductibles plus a prepaid group health insurance plan	Demand for health care and change in health status	2823 families	$94.4 million	$115.0 million

7. Housing Allowances[2]	1973–77	1980	Cash housing allowance	Use of allowance; effect on quality, supply, and costs of housing; administrative feasibility	—[3]	$160.4 million	$352.2 million
8. National Supported Work Project	1975–79	1980	Temporary Public Services Employment (PSE), work discipline, and group support	Administrative costs, effects on antisocial behavior and earnings	6606 individuals	$16.9 million[4]	$126.8 million
9. Employment Opportunity Pilot Project (EOPP)[5]	1979–81	1982	PSE preceded by required job search and training (if necessary)	Effect on welfare caseload, private sector labor market, use of program, administrative costs, and feasibility	Open to all heads of households on public assistance	n.a.	$246.0 million
10. Electricity Time-of-Use Pricing (15 Experiments)	1975–	1979–	Time-of-use electricity price schedules	Alterations in electricity use levels and patterns of residential consumers	n.a.	n.a.	≈$50.0 million

1. The number of students remaining in the program the entire school year. The initial sample comprised 24,000 students split evenly between control and experimental groups.
2. There were three different housing allowance experiments during the 1970s. They have been grouped together here for brevity.
3. One of the housing allowance experiments was open enrollment while the other two involved random selection.
4. Research only.
5. The EOPP was ended long before completion.

Source: Haveman, R. H. Social experimentation and social experimentation. *Journal of Human Resources, 21*(4), 586–605. Copyright 1986. Reprinted with permission of The University of Wisconsin Press.

question will vary in different countries, and we will confine our discussion to evidence from the United States, which is by far the most heavily researched political system.

A central principle of democracy is that government derives its legitimacy from the "consent of the governed," and therefore that public policy should generally follow the will of the people. Even politicians who view their role as leading the public usually realize that they can't get too far out in front of the people and still retain a following. Thus, most democratic leaders are vitally interested in the state of public opinion. Starting in the 1930s, scientific public opinion polling has given political leaders an invaluable tool for determining "the will of the people" quickly and accurately. Before polling was developed, the only sources of information on public opinion available to politicians were highly biased ones, such as newspaper editorials, letters from a few involved (and often self-seeking) citizens, or discussion with their own (highly atypical) circle of friends.

How well do our government's actions actually follow public opinion? Some important evidence on this question was provided by Miller and Stokes (1963). Studying a sample of 116 U.S. congressmen, they obtained data on the attitudes, perceptions, and roll call votes of each legislator; and they compared these variables with the attitudes of a randomly selected sample of constituents from the legislator's own district. Their findings showed not just a single pattern of relationships, but several different patterns that were typical of different sorts of issues.

Direct effects of public opinion on government actions were found for some issues, the most notable of which were civil rights bills in the 1960s. On these issues the congressmen generally perceived their constituents' attitudes correctly, and they usually voted in accord with them, no matter what their own attitudes might be (Miller & Stokes, 1963).

Lack of effects of public opinion on government action has frequently occurred on some kinds of issues. For instance, Congress blocked Medicare legislation for many years in the 1960s and still continues its inaction on national health insurance, even though both of these programs have had strong public approval (Childs, 1965; Jacobs, 1993). More recently, congres-

sional support for aid to the Nicaraguan Contra rebels lasted from 1981 to 1987, despite the lack of public support. Studies found no consistent relationship between public opinion in congressional districts and voting by members of Congress on support for the Nicaraguan rebels (LeoGrande, 1993; LeoGrande & Brenner, 1993).

Reverse effects have also been found—that is, instances where public policy influenced public opinion (Aronson, 1995; Childs, 1965). An excellent example was the change in racial attitudes, and subsequent reduction in prejudice, following the 1954 ruling of the Supreme Court requiring integrated public schools. It is unlikely that such changes would have occurred without a change in public policy. Another case where policy changed public opinion was the strong public acceptance of President Nixon's initiation of friendly contact with mainland China, despite the long and intense history of U.S. public disapproval of China's communist regime.

Two Illustrative Studies

Broader comparisons of public opinion with public policy actions have also been conducted. In this section, we will describe two such studies, both of which found a fairly strong relationship between public opinion and public policy. Monroe (1978) studied all the U.S. public issues between 1960 and 1974 for which there were poll data on citizens' policy preferences *and* a clear subsequent federal action. There were 248 nonrepeated cases of such issues—26 cases involving preferred levels of federal spending for a particular purpose, and 222 cases involving support for specific programs without mention of spending levels. Each case was classified as to whether the majority public preference (either favoring or opposing the proposed program) was consistent with the subsequent federal policy action. The cases were also classified by general policy areas and according to the *salience* of the particular problem they addressed (that is, the public's degree of concern about that problem at the time). Table 17-3 shows the results of this analysis for the 222 nonspending cases, and Monroe reported that the pattern for the 26 spending issues was similar.

TABLE 17-3 Consistency Between Public Opinion and Public Policy Outcomes

Classification	Percent Consistent	N
All Nonspending Cases	64%	222
By Policy Area		
Social welfare	57	35
Economic and labor	61	36
Defense	43	14
Foreign policy	92	24
Energy and environment	79	14
Civil rights and liberties	67	24
Reform	44	30
Vietnam	71	28
Miscellaneous	76	17
By Salience		
More salient	70	110
Less salient	59	112

Source: Monroe (1978, p. 545). Reprinted by permission.

The overall results of Monroe's study demonstrated that federal policy actions were consistent with public preferences in 64% of the cases. This indicates that the public policy process does respond to public opinion, but in a far from perfect way. The lowest consistency (i.e., policy more often contrary to public opinion than consistent with it) was found in the areas of defense (only 43% agreement) and reforms to the political system (44%). For most of these issues the policy effects were not very salient to the public—for example, topics like community bomb shelters, a volunteer army, abandoning the electoral college, and mandatory retirement for judges. In contrast, the consistency was considerably higher (70%) for more salient issues, and it was highest for the areas of foreign policy (92%) and energy and environmental issues (79%). Both foreign policy and environmental issues were areas where policy changes were highly visible and salient to the public (including topics such as the Korean War, nuclear testing, and the Arab oil embargo). Thus, it is clear that in certain areas, particularly for issues that are salient and visible, government actions do tend to follow public opinion.

A more recent examination of the relationship between public opinion and public policy found an even stronger relationship. Erikson, Wright, and McIver (1993) examined the relationship between liberal-conservative ideology and liberal-conservative policies at the state level. An index of liberal state policies was created by examining state policies on education, Medicaid, Aid to Families with Dependent Children (AFDC), consumer protection, criminal justice laws, legalized gambling, the Equal Rights Amendment, and tax progressivity. Public opinion in each state was assessed by combining the results from 122 CBS surveys. Both indices were found to be extremely stable between 1976 and 1988. The resulting relationship between public opinion and public policy is shown in Figure 17-1. The statistical correlation between these two measures was $r = .82$, which accounted for about 64% of the variance in the overall policy stance of the 50 states. In sum, at the state level, the correspondence between public opinion and policy was impressively high.

The results from both of these studies show a fairly strong relationship between public opinion and public policy, despite some exceptions. However, the conclusion that public opinion *causes* public policy, and not the reverse, is more tenuous. Although several authors have made a strong case for such a causal connection (e.g., Erikson et al., 1993), we have seen above that in some instances public opinion can be changed by public policy, instead of vice versa.

WAYS OF USING POLICY-RELEVANT RESEARCH

Beyond simply registering public opinion, how can research findings be used in the public policy process? There are many ways in which policy-relevant research can be useful. Its utilization could be *direct*, as when the findings from a study are used in developing a new policy. However, this type of effect rarely occurs, and most often the research-policy link is *indirect*. Various levels of indirect use include using research findings in policy debates, discussion of the findings by people influential in the policy process, and research studies that help to define a problem (Lynn, 1978; Webber, 1992).

A convenient classification of the types of use that can be made of social research in the policy arena has

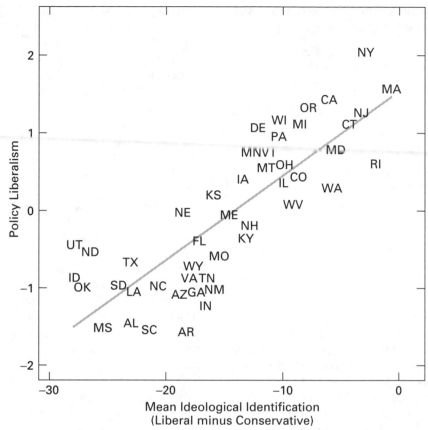

FIGURE 17-1   The relationship of public opinion liberalism to public policy liberalism across the 50 states. (Source: Erickson, Robert S., Wright, Gerald C., and McIver, John P. *Statehouse democracy.* New York: Cambridge University Press.)

been offered by Carol Weiss (1978). Here is her list of eight different types of use for social research.

1. Problem Solving. This is a direct, instrumental application of research. A problem is defined; information is needed to specify a desirable solution; research is commissioned, or existing research findings are gathered to provide the needed information; and a solution is found.

2. Knowledge-Driven Use. This is also an instrumental use of research, but in this case the research findings come first and point to an opportunity that can be grasped. This is more common in the physical sciences than in social research. The process begins with new ba-

sic research knowledge (for example, about hormones); applied research follows (to demonstrate their contraceptive effect); then development of a product (the pill); and finally use of the product in social situations.

3. Interaction of Research with Other Forces. In this model, policies result from the interaction of research findings with other factors, such as political pressures, technologies, and personal experiences of decision makers. As opposed to the linear processes above, this is generally a disorderly sequence of events and forces, where timing, circumstances, and chance all play a role in the final outcome.

4. Research Use for Conceptualization. This has often been called the **enlightenment function** of research (Weiss, 1977a). In it, concepts from social research are used in thinking about policy issues, defining the policy agenda, sensitizing policy makers to new issues, or redefining the nature of social problems. This is generally a cumulative process, not the result of a single study, and it may have diffuse effects on many issues rather than a clearly denotable effect on a specific policy decision. One important aspect of this type of use is identifying a set of facts as a social issue (for instance, illegal immigration, domestic violence, or safety factors in automobile design), and moving the issue onto the political agenda as a problem to be solved—a process often referred to as decision preparation or **agenda-setting**.

5. Research as Political Ammunition. This may be viewed as a less desirable or even an illegitimate use of research, but it is a very common one. In it, parties on one or more sides of a political issue cite, search for, or even commission research specifically to support their viewpoint (Maier, 1991). Congressional committee hearings, for example, are often "stacked" with witnesses who are advocates of one side of an issue (Scott & Shore, 1979). If both or several sides of a political issue have their own policy analysts to advocate their preferred solutions, this approach strongly resembles the adversary principle of the English and American legal tradition (Foster, 1980).

6. Research Use for Manipulation. Some social research findings can potentially be used to manipulate or control other people without their consent. Examples include police interrogation, some forms of advertising, and brainwashing. Such uses of research raise serious ethical and value questions. For instance, whose goals should take precedence—the policy maker's, the social scientist's, the general public's, or those of the person being manipulated?

7. Self-Serving Uses. These may be exploited by either policy makers or researchers. Policy makers may find research helpful in delaying action or avoiding the responsibility for decisions—commissioning or circulating a research report may be a substitute for action. Officials may also use research to win recognition for a successful program or bask in reflected glory from prestigious researchers, to denigrate an opponent, or to advance their own reputation. Researchers in turn may use research findings to gain financial support, fame, or influence for themselves or their institutions.

8. Research as a Language of Discourse. Even more dilute than the conceptualization use of research, this involves the pervasive presence and use of some concepts, terms, and principles from the social sciences in the discourse and thinking of people in public life. For instance, concepts like self-esteem, reinforcement, battered woman's syndrome, and cultural differences may provide an intellectual background and help to color the actions of policy makers.

EMPIRICAL STUDIES OF RESEARCH UTILIZATION

With this conceptual background, let's now examine data on how policy makers *actually do* use research results, as shown by empirical studies. Only a few such studies have been done, and they have added greatly to our knowledge of the realities of policy making, as differentiated from the speculative descriptions and theoretical prescriptions previously available (Beyer & Trice, 1982; Nilsson & Sunesson, 1993). Perhaps the best-known of these studies is one by Nathan Caplan and his associates, which we will discuss in some detail.

Caplan's Study of Federal Decision Makers

Caplan, Morrison, and Stambaugh (1975) studied 204 high-level officeholders in the executive branch of the federal government. During 1973–1974, professional interviewers conducted 90-minute face-to-face interviews with the respondents, who were chosen from the entire range of major cabinet departments, not just those primarily concerned with social problems or social programs. Of the respondents, 15% were at the deputy undersecretary to assistant secretary rank (high political appointees); 27% were directors of institutes, commissions, or other units, or serving in the Executive Office of the President; 33% were deputy or assistant directors, bureau or division chiefs, or upper-level administrators; and 25% were at somewhat lower levels, but experienced and knowledgeable about social science utilization.

Photograph courtesy of Carol H. Weiss. Reprinted by permission.

Box 17-1

CAROL H. WEISS, POLICY RESEARCH EXPERT

Internationally known as an authority on evaluation research and on policy research, Carol Weiss began her studies in government at Cornell University and later shifted to sociology, receiving her Ph.D. from Columbia. After working as a researcher in the Bureau of Applied Social Research at Columbia from 1965 to 1978, she moved to Harvard, where she remains as a professor in the Graduate School of Education.

Weiss's 1972 textbook on evaluation research was a pacesetter in the field, selling over 100,000 copies in ten years and being translated into German and Spanish. Her many other volumes in policy research include *Making Bureaucracies Work*, *Using Social Research in Public Policy Making*, and *Organizations for Policy Analysis.* Her earliest research was done with members of the Domestic Peace Corps and with

low-income groups, but later she studied members of American elites. Her writings include many methodological articles on survey research, interviewing, and evaluation research, as well as substantive papers on many policy issues. Her 1977 paper on the enlightenment function of social science research was an important contribution to the topic of this chapter.

In addition to her research and writing, Weiss has served as a consultant to more than 30 government agencies, civic groups, and private organizations and been a member of editorial boards of 16 professional journals. She has served as president of the Policy Studies Organization, and she was honored with the 1980 Myrdal Award for Science by the Evaluation Research Society.

These executives were asked detailed questions about their awareness of relevant social science information, their self-reported use of it, their evaluation of various kinds of social science data (other than economic research, which was largely excluded from the study), and particularly their interest in social indicators that would measure the quality of American life.

Overall Results. The 204 respondents reported 575 instances of social science use in relation to policy issues, only about one-fifth of which were duplicated mentions of the same facts by two respondents. These 575 instances of social science utilization constituted the main subject matter of the study. At the highest level of utilization, 13% of the respondents described five or more examples of social science knowledge use with good supporting evidence; 61% gave two to four examples of use with good evidence; 17% gave fewer examples or weaker supporting evidence; and 9% were unable to describe any instances. Of the 575 instances of use, 26% involved psychological or social psychological research; 20% involved sociological knowledge; while 7% stemmed from political science, 6% from education and training, and 6% from anthropology. The remaining 35% involved interdisciplinary knowledge and research. Two particularly interesting sets of findings were the kinds of research methods and policy areas most frequently involved in these instances of knowledge use, as shown in Table 17-4.

Most Useful Research Methods. About one-third of the instances of use reported by the executives were from secondary sources such as staff summaries or reports from outside consultants, where it was impossible to classify the research methodologies involved. The remaining 385 cases, involving primary data sources, are classified in Table 17-4. They show that program evaluations were the single most frequent category of useful research. The next three most common categories were survey research, demographic research, and social statistics, which made up 41% of the cases. None of the other methods (not even cost-benefit analysis) approached these in frequency of use.

TABLE 17-4   Distribution of Knowledge Use by Research Methodologies and Policy Areas

Research Methodologies	Percentage of Instances of Use[a]	Policy Area[b]	Percentage of Instances of Use[a]
Program evaluation	20%	Organizational management	11%
Survey research	18	Education	8
Demographic research	13	Health	8
Social statistics	10	Crime	7
Field experimentation	9	Communications	7
Cost-benefit analysis	8	Public opinion management	7
Organizational analysis	6	Welfare	7
Laboratory experimentation	4	Military	6
Participant observation	4	Employment	6
Clinical case histories	4	Other	6
Psychological testing	3	Civil rights and minority affairs	5
Experimental games and simulations	1	Environment	4
	100	Housing	4
		Transportation	4
		International relations	3
		Research methodology	3
		Consumer affairs	2
		Recreation	2
			100

[a]Based on 385 primary data sources.

[b]Energy as a decision-making area is conspicuously absent because it was just emerging as a major policy area when the survey was being conducted. References by respondents to energy matters were coded under such categories as Public opinion management, International relations, Transportation, and Environment.

Source: Adapted from Caplan, Morrison, & Stambaugh (1975, pp. 5 & 11). Reprinted by permission.

Policy Areas. The policy areas involved in the instances of social science research use were even more varied than the methods used. The most common single category, organizational management, referred to operational problems of running a government agency or department. In addition, many of the instances coded under the second most common category, education, also pertained to internal government issues, such as training of employees, rather than to broader issues of public policy; and the same was true for some of the cases coded in other categories. Thus, it appears that in the executive branch, "the predominant purpose of knowledge utilization is to improve bureaucratic efficiency" (Caplan, 1976, p. 192).

Research Sponsorship. Another crucial finding dealt with the sponsorship of the research used by these policy-makers. Of the two-thirds of knowledge-use instances involving primary sources of information, the funding sources for the research could be identified in 218 cases. These funding sources showed the following dramatic pattern:

Funded by using agency (conducted in-house)	51%
Funded by using agency (extramural research)	35%
Funded by another governmental agency	8%
Funded by nongovernmental agency	6%

Of course, these cases omit the majority of instances where secondary sources of research information were used or where no funding source could be identified. Still, the 86% of these cases that were funded by the using agency clearly demonstrate that government executives strongly tend to use research developed by their own agency, particularly studies done in-house. Indeed, in nearly 80% of the instances cited, the knowledge used had been gathered at the specific request of the policy maker who reported the instance (Caplan, 1976).

"Soft" Knowledge Versus "Hard" Knowledge. The sources of information used by these government officials included government reports, staff documents, and professional journals, as might be expected; but just as often they included newspapers, books, and magazines that were not explicitly research oriented. The officials less frequently cited TV or radio as sources of specific information, and, surprisingly, they seldom mentioned computerized knowledge retrieval systems except for the Congressional Research Service, which was praised by its users. Thus, these government executives were highly eclectic in their use of varied sources of information relevant to their jobs. Caplan reported that their most common use of social science was in the form of "soft" knowledge—qualitative and conceptual, stated in lay language, and not research-based. This soft-knowledge utilization pattern corresponds closely to Weiss's (1977a) description of the enlightenment function of social science, mentioned earlier.

However, the officials' use of soft knowledge should not be seen as deprecating the value of social research. Indeed, 85% of these executives agreed that the social sciences can contribute a great deal to the formation of intelligent government policy, and 87% said that the government should make the fullest possible use of social science. Caplan and his colleagues concluded that these high-level government officials did not need to be sold on the value of social research knowledge. When asked to rank the particular values of social science inputs in their own work, the executives gave the following overall ranking (Caplan et al., 1975, p. 22):

1. Sensitizing policy makers to social needs (the highest rank)
2. Evaluation of ongoing programs
3. Structuring alternative policies
4. Implementation of programs
5. Justification of policy decisions
6. Providing a basis for choosing among policy alternatives

Factors that Influence the Amount of Knowledge Use. Why is social science knowledge not used more widely? Using the interview data, Caplan tested three theoretical explanations:

- **Knowledge-specific theory** posits that low rates of utilization are due to the character of social science knowledge, the research methods used, or the limitations and prejudices of social researchers.
- **Two-communities theory** argues that low utilization is due to the large gap between knowledge producers and policy makers, who live and work in separate worlds having very different values, rewards, languages, and conceptual schemes.

- **Policy-maker-constraint theory** emphasizes that policy makers operate under such demands of timing, relevance, and political feasibility that research findings can rarely be helpful to them.

Caplan's tests of these theoretical views concluded that the two-communities theory accounted for more than twice as much of the variance in the interview responses of the government executives as the other two theories combined. For instance, the officials generally agreed that there was a gap between policy makers and social scientists in mutual understanding and interaction, and that their mutual mistrust was a factor in the underuse of social research. This finding led the authors to suggest that utilization could be improved by bridging the gap with **linking agents**—go-betweens who specialize in tying together scientific inputs and policy considerations.

Beyond this finding, Caplan and his colleagues also delineated factors that make social knowledge utilization more likely (Caplan, 1977). In brief, research findings are more likely to be used when (a) they are not counterintuitive, (b) they are objective in the sense of stemming from a strong database and a good research design, and (c) their implications for action are politically feasible.

Conclusion. Summing up his findings on the use of social science knowledge in national policy decisions, Caplan (1976, p. 193) concluded:

> Many of these instances of utilization involved strategically important applications of policy-related social science and would suggest reasons for modest satisfaction rather than the despair and cynicism so prevalent in the literature on social science utilization and public policy. Over half the instances of use involved matters of considerable individual and social consequence that affect sizable segments of the population or the nation as a whole.

IMPACT OF MAJOR POLICY RESEARCH STUDIES

Early in this chapter we mentioned several of the most extensive social experiments and best-known policy research studies. Now, in the light of the above findings on the utilization of social science knowledge in general, we will briefly summarize the impact of some of these major studies.

Social Experimentation on Welfare Programs

Nowhere has social experimentation been more prominent than in the area of welfare reform. Beginning in the late nineteenth century, programs of charity for the poor were implemented at the state and local levels, and in 1935 such support was federally funded through the Social Security Act (Schram, 1995). Since 1935 the purpose of welfare has changed. Early programs were intended to allow single mothers to focus on child care, and to keep women from competing with men in the labor force. More recent programs have been designed to encourage welfare recipients to work and become financially independent (Norris & Thompson, 1995).

Until 1996, welfare in the U.S. was largely administered through the federal Aid to Families with Dependent Children (AFDC) program, which provided cash allowances for children who had lost the support of a parent who was absent, deceased, incapacitated, or unemployed. States had flexibility in determining the monthly level of support, and the amounts varied widely from state to state (Norris & Thompson, 1995). AFDC recipients automatically qualified for other entitlements like food stamps and Medicaid. In 1992, 13.6 million Americans received money from the AFDC program at a cost of $22.2 billion.

Earlier welfare programs were based solely on the notions of policy makers, and were not driven by social science evidence. However, social science data have played an increasingly important role in redesigning and improving the programs.

Negative Income Tax Experiments. As the first of the major social experiments, the Negative Income Tax (NIT) experiments had a powerful influence on subsequent policy research efforts. The New Jersey-Pennsylvania NIT experiment was initiated by the Office of Economic Opportunity in 1967 to study the effectiveness of an income security system having two main features: a guaranteed annual income below which no participating family would be allowed to fall (any shortfall would be made up by government payments—the negative tax concept), and a reduced, graduated tax on the first block of income above the guaranteed level, intended to provide an incentive to family members to work and increase the total family income. The major political question involved in the NIT concept was whether a guaranteed income would constitute a work *dis*incentive, keeping family members out of the labor force and the family on welfare, contrary to the aims of the program. In general, the study concluded that there was no substantial evidence of such a work disincentive (Greenberg & Robins, 1985; Heclo & Rein, 1980).

However, despite the careful scientific conduct and admirable administrative procedures of the NIT experiment, research analysts have raised criticisms about some of its design features and about the possible effects of some coincidental historical events, both of which render its conclusions somewhat doubtful (Rossi & Lyall, 1976). The original New Jersey study was later expanded to rural Iowa and North Carolina, and to Gary, Seattle, and Denver. But even before the first experimental results were in, the study had a major impact on federal policies. The 1967 welfare reforms adopted the essential principle of a negative tax for mothers receiving AFDC welfare payments, and the NIT experiment quickly demonstrated that such programs could be administered without excessive intrusion into recipients' lives. When the Nixon administration took office in 1969, it developed a welfare proposal called the Family Assistance Plan (FAP) which incorporated the NIT principles of a guaranteed income combined with a graduated tax as a work incentive. Though Congress refused to pass the FAP, the NIT experiment data were frequently cited in the subsequent debates. Instead, Congress extended the experimental studies by authorizing $400 million for further income maintenance experiments, continuing for another five years. In addition, during the Nixon administration, some of the NIT principles were incorporated into two major social programs that Congress did pass: the food stamp program, and the Social Security program of assistance to the aged, blind, and disabled (Heclo & Rein, 1980; Rossi & Lyall, 1976).

Further Experiments with Welfare Reform. In 1981 the Omnibus Budgeting Reconciliation Act

(OBRA) provided states increased flexibility in developing welfare programs. This produced a proliferation of state programs and several large-scale social experiments. These state-level programs were designed to accomplish two related goals. First, the reform programs attempted to increase the earnings of people who received AFDC, and subsequently to reduce the amount of AFDC cash each participant received. With this in mind, many states implemented so-called **workfare** programs to help people get off welfare and return to work. We will briefly review the results from four such experimental programs implemented in Virginia, Arkansas, Maryland, and California, and reported by Friedlander and Burtless (1995).

Participants in the experiments were applicants for AFDC. The applicants were randomly assigned to either an experimental or a control condition. Control participants received the AFDC benefits normally provided in their area. Experimental recipients were required to participate in an additional program or risk reductions in AFDC benefits. The experimental interventions in the "workfare" programs were:

- Virginia: help in conducting a job search, and three months of unpaid work assignments intended to provide the recipient with work experience.
- Arkansas: job search help with some 3-month unpaid work assignments.
- Baltimore, Maryland: initial skills assessment with some choice in the job search process, along with either unpaid work assignments or education/training.
- San Diego, California: assisted job search, three months of unpaid work assignments, followed by some education/training.

Sample sizes were 3150 for Virginia, 1127 for Arkansas, 2757 for Baltimore, and 3211 for San Diego. Data were obtained from each participant quarterly for two years, at which time the experiment was discontinued. However, data were still collected for three years after the experiment was discontinued.

Results from the five years of data are summarized in Figure 17-2. The figure shows the program's impact in terms of increased earnings, reduced AFDC payments, and the net program cost for each of the four welfare experiments. The dollar figures for earnings impact are the average difference between the experimental and control groups over the 5-year period.

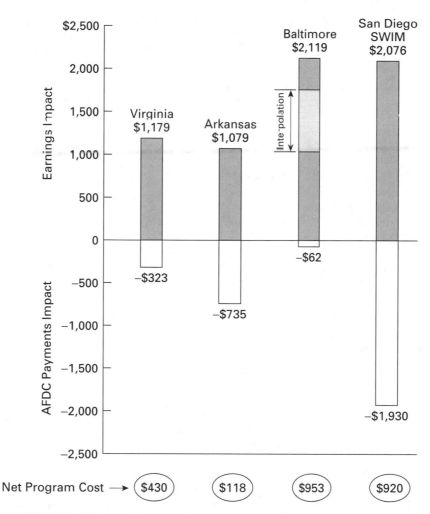

FIGURE 17-2   Observed impacts of "workfare" programs on participants' earnings and AFDC payments in four experimental programs. (Source: Friedlander & Burtless, 1995, p. 11.)

Thus, the average experimental participant in Virginia earned $1179 more than the average control participant over the 5-year period. The earnings impacts for the four studies ranged from about $1100 to about $2100. A similar procedure was used to calculate the AFDC payments impact, where the average amount of AFDC received by the control group was subtracted from the average amount for the experimental group. Thus, participants in the Virginia experiment received $323 less over the 5-year period than control participants. These savings ranged from about $60 to about $1900. Figure 17-2 also shows the net cost (i.e., cost of the services provided per individual) for each program participant over the 2-year experimental period. (The interpolation shown for the Baltimore program was due to a period when no data were collected, so that the impact assessment was based on estimates from the previous year.)

By the late 1980s the early results from these experiments were available, and in 1988 the Family Support Act was passed, providing support for the Job Opportunity and Basic Skills Training program (JOBS).

The JOBS program was patterned after the earlier "workfare" programs and provided federal funding for education, training, and assisted job searches for AFDC applicants whose youngest child was at least three years old. In addition, the JOBS program provided payments for child care—a much-needed addition (Phillips, 1991).

1996 Welfare Reform. The most recent change in U.S. welfare policy was the welfare reform bill signed into law by President Clinton in 1996 (Katz, 1996; Stanfield, 1996). This reform ended the guarantee of federal money to all eligible mothers and children, and it was estimated to save $54 billion by 2002. Some of the core elements of the program include:

- Welfare is funded through block grants to states, which allow for greater flexibility in administering the program at the state level.
- Adults who receive welfare benefits are required to begin work within two years, with some exceptions (e.g., single mothers with children under the age of one year).
- There is a maximum lifetime eligibility of five years for all welfare benefits.
- Only U.S. citizens are eligible for welfare benefits.

This legislation represents the largest overhaul of the welfare system in 61 years—but will it work? Clearly the intent of these changes is to motivate people to return to work. However, the changes were not based on the findings of empirical research, and predicting the exact effects of these changes is hazardous. Several key questions are salient: Are there enough jobs available at levels appropriate for the skills of ex-welfare recipients? If they get such jobs, can workers live and pay child-care and other expenses on the income from them? And what will happen to the families of indigent individuals who are unable to find work; will there be a "safety net" to keep them from homelessness and starvation?

Experimental Housing Allowance Program

The Experimental Housing Allowance Program (EHAP) was the largest and most costly of the federal social experiments, and its genesis was another of the major results of the NIT experiment. The 1968 Housing Act had markedly increased federal subsidies for *construction* of low- and moderate-cost housing, but by 1970 many problems had surfaced—in particular, rampant increases in total subsidy costs, low-quality construction, and escalating vacancies and foreclosures. In the 1970 Congressional debates on housing, a dramatically new plan was proposed: making housing assistance payments *directly to needy families* in order to allow them to occupy adequate housing, until their income rose to the point where assistance was no longer needed. However, no one knew exactly what the effects of such a plan would be on client reactions, rent levels, availability and quality of housing, or on such controversial issues as residential racial segregation. Congress was unwilling to pass a full-scale new housing program without more deliberation and better evidence, and consequently in the 1970 Housing Act it took the unusual step of directing the Department of Housing and Urban Development (HUD) to conduct a housing allowance experiment, following the general model of the NIT (Field, 1980; Friedman & Weinberg, 1985).

General planning, research design, and negotiation of the huge contracts involved took several years, and the enrollment of families and collection of data finally began in 1973. The study was scheduled to last as long as seven years and was located in 12 different cities, where nearly 40,000 families applied for the allowances. There were three separate experiments, concentrating respectively on recipient behavior, economic impacts in terms of housing supply (quality, availability, and costs), and alternative administrative procedures. Just as with NIT, before the experimental results were in, the federal administration had proposed a new housing policy, which incorporated many of the housing allowance features. In this case Congress passed the plan in the 1974 Housing and Community Development Act. Thus, the experimental findings did not lead to the enacted policy, but the smooth ongoing operation of the experimental programs was a powerful argument in the congressional debate (Field, 1980; Friedman & Weinberg, 1983, 1985).

Throughout the 1980s, reports on EHAP results were still appearing, but many policy-relevant findings had been clear long before that. Surprisingly, only about half of the eligible families who were contacted decided to participate in the program, despite its financial benefits to them. Thus, a similar nationwide program would probably cost only about half as much as expected, but would also benefit far fewer families than intended. Though the program allowed recipient families to move to better housing, most people chose not to leave, but to stay and upgrade their current residences. And in doing so, most people spent only a minority of their allowance on improving their housing quality, using the greater part of the funds on other budget items (Abt, 1980). These kinds of findings have figured prominently in subsequent housing programs and debates.

Studies of Other Policy Issues

Experimental research pertinent to public policy can be found regarding many other social issues (see Aiken & Kehrer, 1985). One continuing area for social experimentation has been early childhood interventions—programs designed to help children from disadvantaged backgrounds succeed in school. By far the most well-known example in this area is **Head Start**, a part-day program that provides education, health, and social services to children from low-income families (Zigler & Styfco, 1994). Support for the Head Start program was based on several social experiments conducted during the early 1960s, such as the Perry Preschool Project (Schweinhart et al., 1986; Schweinhart & Weikart, 1989). As we discussed in Chapter 8, evaluations of Head Start have found significant positive effects of the program, and in fiscal year 1994, the program received approximately $7.7 billion in federal funding. Since 1965, Head Start has served more than 13 million American children (Zigler, Styfco, & Gilman, 1993).

Other areas of policy-relevant research include:

- Gun control (Toch & Lizotte, 1992)
- Effects of pornography (Linz, Malamuth, & Beckett, 1992; Zillmann, 1992)
- Child care (Phillips, 1991; Phillips & Zigler, 1987)
- HIV prevention (Kelly et al., 1993; Weisse et al., 1990)
- Effects of prison confinement (Bonta & Gendreau, 1992; Paulus & Dzindolet, 1992)
- Homelessness (Jahiel, 1992; Yep, 1992)

- Drunk driving (Ross, 1992)
- Health care reform (Frank & VandenBos, 1994)

This partial list of topics demonstrates the broad range of policies to which social psychological research has been applied.

Failures of Social Research to Influence Policy

Despite the success of numerous social experiments, many cases can be found where relevant social research has not been used to influence public policy (Pallak, 1990). Since the late 1960s several blue-ribbon scientific study groups have been assembled to report on the relationship of public policy to knowledge from the behavioral and social sciences, and all have agreed that the amount and quality of research utilization has been disappointing. Two prominent cases where research has failed to produce commensurate public policy are the effects of pornography and gun control.

Public Policy and Pornography. The 1970 Presidential Commission on Obscenity and Pornography provided social scientists an opportunity to summarize the research evidence for policy makers. With a $2 million budget and two years to summarize the available social science evidence, the commission concluded that exposure to most forms of pornography did not cause changes in attitudes toward women, nor increase sexually violent tendencies. However, the commission was sharply criticized by knowledgeable inside observers for completely ignoring available research findings, citing inadequate and unconvincing research, and selectively mentioning research that fit their viewpoints and disregarding inconsistent data (Reuter, 1979; Wilson, 1978; Zillmann, 1992).

Another chance to summarize research on the effects of pornography came with the 1986 Attorney General's Commission on Pornography, which assembled evidence over the course of one year at a cost of $400,000 (Zillmann, 1992). This commission concluded that sexually violent (as opposed to only violent or only sexual) pornography causes negative changes in attitudes, perceptions, and in some cases an increase in aggression toward women. However, the policy recommendations made by the commission were to strengthen *local* obscenity laws—laws allowed by a 1973 ruling of the Supreme Court which stated that each community has the right to establish its own standard of obscenity, and that communities can use this standard to regulate the distribution of sexually explicit material (Linz, Malamuth, & Beckett, 1992). Thus, although some pornography has clearly harmful effects, nothing was done federally to address it (see Linz et al., 1992 for several instances of local policy regarding pornography).

Public Policy and Gun Control. The final report from the National Commission on the Causes and Prevention of Violence (1964) summarized research evidence on the effects of guns in the United States. The commission concluded:

> After extensive study we find that the availability of guns contributes substantially to violence in American society. . . . Our studies have convinced us that the heart of any effective national firearm policy for the United States must be to reduce the availability of the firearm that contributes to the most violence. This means restricting licensing of the handgun. . . . Reducing the availability of the handgun will reduce firearm violence. (pp. 169–188)

The report went on to outline explicit strategies to reduce the availability of handguns, including strict licensing procedures and a prohibition against selling "junk guns." Despite the research evidence and the strong conclusions reached by the commission, the President and Congress did little to reduce the availability of handguns (Toch & Lizotte, 1992). As described in Chapter 1, the major reason for this inaction was the extensive lobbying and campaign contributions of the National Rifle Association and other organizations opposed to any form of gun registration or control. These organizations prevailed despite the longtime favorability of a large majority of the U.S. population toward restrictive gun control laws (Moore & Newport, 1994).

REASONS RESEARCH MAY BE UNDERUTILIZED

What are the major reasons for the frequent underutilization of research knowledge? The obstacles to its use can be classified as problems in (a) research formula-

tion, (b) research results, (c) interpretation of research results, and (d) application of research to policy issues (Weiss, 1978).

Problems in Research Formulation

Problems in research formulation stem primarily from the "two communities" contrast in goals and standards between researchers and policy makers. Aspects of this contrast include the typical mind-set, training, and rewards of these two groups, the questions of interest, and the type of knowledge sought from research (Hedges & Waddington, 1993; Scott & Shore, 1979). As a result, a study that is well-designed from a scientific and theoretical standpoint may ask questions, or use measures or methods, which make it irrelevant or useless from a policy perspective. Policy makers are generally much less interested than social scientists in basic variables of social structure (such as class, race, or occupation), but more interested in variables that can be manipulated through administrative programs with relatively speedy and short-term effects.

Problems in Research Results

One of the greatest problems of research findings is timeliness. Research takes time, but policy issues often arise unexpectedly or come suddenly to a head, requiring urgent action without waiting for research results (as occurred in the NIT and EHAP experiments described above). Another problem is inconclusiveness. Senator Edmund Muskie found this problem so frustrating that he called for some "one-armed scientists" who would not testify "on one hand . . . but on the other hand" (Jones, 1976).

Even where research results are clear-cut, they may not support the findings of other studies. In fact, a common pattern is that additional research in an area yields only increasing complexity and higher order interactions instead of replicating simpler main effects. This outcome is satisfying from the standpoint of advancing scientific knowledge, but highly upsetting to the policy maker who wants practical advice on a concrete issue. Examples of this increasing complexity of findings may be seen in the areas of school desegregation and the Head Start program described in Chapter 8, as well as in the evaluation research of the D.A.R.E. campaign discussed in Chapter 7.

A recent advance in this area has been the use of meta-analytic review techniques. As described in Chapter 7, meta-analysis provides a quantitative technique through which dozens or hundreds of studies on a topic can be synthesized. In many cases, the conclusions reached through meta-analysis are stronger than those reached through less systematic reviews. Although disputes about the results do arise, meta-analysis provides a tool that scientists can use to help synthesize a large body of research, and ultimately to make clear and accurate policy recommendations (Mann, 1994).

Problems in Interpreting Research Results

A frequently mentioned aspect of the "two-communities" problem is difficulty of communication between researchers and policy makers—largely due to use of jargon, statistics, and different concepts and vocabularies (Nilsson & Sunesson, 1993). These communication problems may lead members of the two groups to quite different interpretations of a particular set of findings. For example, in fields such as education, medical care, or psychotherapy,

> An apparent finding of "no differences" may take on unfortunate significance to the policy-maker who lusts after cost-effectiveness evidence. (Parloff, 1979, p. 305)

Another aspect of the gap between the two groups is the scientist's common caution in interpreting data and reluctance to extrapolate from research results in answer to the decision maker's questions. A third typical difference is disagreement on some of the philosophical assumptions that would be invoked in interpreting empirical data. For instance, a social scientist might see people's poverty as largely the result of environmental forces and cultural patterns in a society, whereas an individualistically oriented policy maker might see it as due to personal failings or inadequacies. Counterintuitive findings can also present interpretive problems; no matter how well supported, they may be rejected by officials who are convinced of their own understanding of the world.

Finally, a general limitation of all findings is that they apply only to situations where other key variables are similar or identical to those in the research setting. The similarity of these other variables can only be estimated, and it may change between the time the research is done and its application in the future (Weiss, 1978). Thus, the processes of deciding about research applicability and deriving policy recommendations are always open to challenge.

Problems in Applying Research to Policy Issues

Applying research to policy issues may be difficult even if good research is done and reasonable interpretations are made. The first obstacle is the flood of information that inundates decision makers, particularly government administrators and legislators, and may prevent their attention to research (Dreyfus, 1977; Melton, 1995). Dissemination of research findings is often haphazard because it is nobody's main job. Also, issues change during the course of research (as illustrated in the NIT and EHAP experiments), so the findings may not bear on the current policy issues. Even if the researcher gains the policy maker's attention, any suggested policy recommendations stem from the researcher's values and notions of feasibility as well as from the findings; and thus they may be rejected due to conflicting values or feasibility estimates (Weiss, 1978).

Other application problems arise from the nature of the political system. Decision making is often diffuse and fragmented, and it sometimes seems that no one is in charge—a situation that has been termed a **policy vacuum** (Corwin & Louis, 1982). Frequent shifts in top-level personnel and responsibilities may change an agency's receptivity to research findings. Leaders of almost all organizations try to maintain the stability and traditions of the system; thus, changes are usually resisted, and research that recommends changes is threatening to many well-entrenched members of the organization. Furthermore, policy making is usually incremental, with options being gradually narrowed down by steps and choices that are often imperceptible to outside observers (Bevan, 1980; Scott & Shore, 1979).

A major reason for failure to use research findings is that policy makers have their own constituencies, priorities, and reward systems, all of which have more call on their attention than do social scientists bearing new knowledge. If research findings fit an official's needs, they may be used as political ammunition; if not, they are more likely to be ignored or disputed. In some cases, politicians can block potentially useful studies from being conducted through denying funding. Such was the case with the sexual behavior survey described in Chapter 3, and a similar study of adolescent sexuality (Gardner & Wilcox, 1993).

A final phase in applying research to policy issues, even after the passage of legislation, is *implementing* that legislation through government regulations and enforcement. Many social scientists are unaware that this process may require extensive further battles and sustained pressure (House, 1982; Stone, 1980). Costain (1978) has graphically illustrated such conflict in describing the 3-year-long fight to implement the Title IX provisions (prohibiting sex discrimination in education) of the 1972 Education Amendments Act.

PREPARING FOR THE FUTURE

How can social scientists become more effective in influencing public policy in the future? Pallak (1990) has suggested two possible paths through which social scientists can influence public policy: translation and testimony. *Translating* knowledge into policy involves drawing policy implications from research, making contact with people in the public policy arena (they are unlikely to take the initiative to seek out researchers), and recognizing who will endorse one's policy recommendations. In short, one must make the research knowledge understandable, available, and palatable to decision makers. One way that this translation of research findings is accomplished is through gaining coverage in media stories. However, in talking to reporters, scientists have to be careful to communicate their actual findings clearly and not to be misquoted, misinterpreted, or led into unfounded speculation (Martin, 1996).

The second path for influencing public policy is through *testimony*. Congressional testimony allows

scientists an ideal opportunity to summarize research findings for policy makers. However, several psychologists who have participated in these sessions have lamented their ineffectiveness (Zigler, 1993). Melton (1995) described the testimony process as one in which

> complex issues are reduced to five-minute lectures. Attendance by committee members usually is poor (television cameras being the primary stimulus for exceptions to the rule), and the information and opinions presented are largely preordained by the choice of witness by majority and minority staff members to support positions that their employers have already taken. (p. 767)

An alternative to the formal process of testifying before Congress is "congressional briefings." In these sessions, congressional staffers and an occasional congressperson attend invited discussion sessions organized around a unifying theme and featuring presentations by leading researchers in the area. For example, efforts have been made to influence U.S. child and family policy through several yearly briefings, and Melton (1995) described the sessions as an effective strategy for making research findings widely available:

> Attendance typically is standing room only, and the proportion of the audience that consists of senior committee staff continues to grow. Congressional staff frequently contact presenters for additional information, and few leave before the 90-minute session ends—a level of attention that is rare among busy congressional staff. (p. 768)

Ethical Issues

The topic of influencing public policy inevitably raises questions of values and ethics. What goals will applied social scientists try to accomplish, and in whose interests will they work? A frequent tendency of psychologists, who generally study or work with individuals, is to blame the disadvantaged for their own troubles, rather than focusing on structural problems in society such as poverty, racial discrimination, and unemployment. Earlier in this chapter and in Chapter 16 we have pointed out that social researchers have typically served the status quo and the establishment, and sometimes their activities have repressed desirable social change or had destructive consequences.

Even where social scientists avoid these problems, in trying to influence public policy they will inevitably be caught in a conflict of interest. No group in the political arena can completely escape the tendency to advance its own cause, partially at the expense of other groups. Psychology's lobbying activity is by no means immune from this tendency to promote the interests of the profession in some situations where they might conflict with the general public interest. In addition, it is important to note that even well-intentioned social reforms and interventions can often produce unexpected harmful effects, such as welfare programs that leave their clients more disadvantaged and dependent than before (Bermant, Kelman, & Warwick, 1978; Lindblom, 1990; Sieber, 1981).

There is no simple answer to these questions, but an important starting place is for applied social scientists to be aware of them. The ethical code of the APA (1992) stresses the importance of serving the public interest above the interests of other individuals or groups. The most important guideline, in trying to influence public policy, is that social scientists must be constantly vigilant to ensure that their efforts genuinely do "promote the general welfare."

SUMMARY

When the social sciences are applied to public policy issues, they may be termed the policy sciences. Use of social science findings has increased greatly in recent decades, with applications being made to problems of housing, welfare, education, public health, the legal system, foreign policy, and industry. Yet some of these uses have been criticized as misguided or inadequate, and many authorities have concluded that the degree of utilization of social research in policy decisions has been disappointing.

Policy decisions necessarily involve many interacting factors in addition to research findings. The use of research findings may be direct and instrumental in solving a problem, or it may take many less direct forms—conceptualization of a situation, use for political ammunition, or use for self-serving ends such as avoiding or delaying decisions. One of the most important studies of the way policy makers actually use

social research findings was Nathan Caplan and his colleagues' study of over 200 high-level federal executives. Its findings gave general support to the "two-communities" viewpoint that utilization of research findings is impeded by the gap in values, rewards, and conceptual schemes between social scientists and policy makers.

Among several extensive social policy experiments, the Negative Income Tax experiments and the Experimental Housing Allowance Program have had a marked impact, as have more recent experiments with welfare reform. Many other policy research studies have also been influential in areas such as HIV prevention, early childhood education, criminal justice, and health care.

The findings of many authors show that there are obstacles to research utilization at every stage, from research formulation through research results, interpretation of the results, and application of findings to policy issues. Nevertheless, despite these many obstacles, social science research has gained increasing influence in public policy decisions in recent decades. Whether through research, policy advice, or lobbying, the goal of applied social scientists should be to help solve the problems of society and improve the quality of people's lives.

SUGGESTED READINGS

Aiken, L., & Kehrer, B. (Eds.). (1985). *Evaluation studies review annual* (Vol. 10). Beverly Hills, CA: Sage.—Contains summaries of many social experiments on a wide range of topics, including health care, education, income maintenance, housing, transportation, and criminal justice.

Bermant, G., Kelman, H. C., & Warwick, D. P. (Eds.). (1978). *The ethics of social intervention*. Washington, DC: Hemisphere.—Presents vital ethical guidelines for applied social scientists working on many kinds of public affairs issues.

Friedlander, D., & Burtless, G. (1995). *Five years after: The long-term effects of welfare-to-work programs*. New York: Russell Sage Foundation.—An excellent example of social experimentation on a key policy issue.

Hausman, J., & Wise, D. (Eds.). (1985). *Social experimentation*. Chicago: University of Chicago Press.—This volume provides a thorough overview of several multimillion dollar social experiments conducted between 1965 and 1980.

Melton, G. (1995). Bringing psychology to Capitol Hill: Briefings on child and family policy. *American Psychologist, 50,* 766–770.—A good example of one path by which psychologists can influence public policy.

Weiss, C. H. (Ed.). (1992). *Organizations for policy analysis: Helping government think.* Newbury Park, CA: Sage.—Chapters were written by officers of various organizations that provide information to policy makers. They describe the boundaries, responsibilities, and procedures of external think tanks, executive government units, and legislative units.

References

Aaker, D. A. (1982). Deceptive advertising. In D. A. Aaker & G. S. Day (Eds.), *Consumerism: Search for the consumer interest* (4th ed., pp. 239–248). New York: Free Press.

Aaker, D. A., & Day, G. S. (1982). A guide to consumerism. In D. A. Aaker & G. S. Day (Eds.), *Consumerism: Search for the consumer interest* (4th ed., pp. 2–20). New York: Free Press.

Abelson, R. P., & Zimbardo, P. G. (1970). *Canvassing for peace: A manual for volunteers.* Ann Arbor, MI: Society for the Psychological Study of Social Issues.

Abraham, C., Sheeran, P., Spears, R., & Abrams, D. (1992). Health beliefs and promotion of HIV-preventive intentions among teenagers: A Scottish perspective. *Health Psychology, 11,* 363–370.

Abrams, S. (1989). *The complete polygraph handbook.* Lexington, MA: Lexington.

Abramson, J. (1994). *We, the jury: The jury system and the ideal of democracy.* New York: Basic Books.

Abramson, P. R., & Hayashi, H. (1984). Pornography in Japan: Cross-cultural and theoretical considerations. In N. M. Malamuth & E. Donnerstein (Eds.), *Pornography and sexual aggression* (pp. 173–183). Orlando, FL: Academic Press.

Abt, C. C. (1980). Social science in the contract research firm. In R. F. Kidd & M. J. Saks (Eds.), *Advances in applied social psychology* (Vol. 1, pp. 167–176). Hillsdale, NJ: Erlbaum.

Ackerman, P. L., & Humphreys, L. G. (1990). Individual differences theory in industrial and organizational psychology. In M. D. Dunnette & L. M. Hough (Eds.), *Handbook of industrial & organizational psychology* (2nd ed., Vol. 1, pp. 223–282). Palo Alto, CA: Consulting Psychologists Press.

Ackoff, R. L., & Emshoff, J. R. (1975). Advertising research at Anheuser-Busch, Inc. *Sloan Management Review, 16,* 1–15.

Adams, P. G., & Slocum, J. W. (1971). Work group and employee satisfaction. *Personnel Administration, 34,* 37–43.

Adler, N., & Mathews, K. A. (1994). Health and psychology: Why do some people get sick and some stay well? *Annual Review of Psychology, 45,* 229–259.

Adler, R. (1994). The Clean Water Act: Has it worked? *EPA Journal, 20,* 10–15.

Adler, R. P., Friedlander, B. Z., Lesser, G. S., Meringoff, L., Robertson, T. S., Rossiter, J. R., & Ward, S. (1977). *Research on the effects of television advertising on children.* Washington, DC: U.S. Government Printing Office.

Adorno, T. W., Frenkel-Brunswik, E., Levinson, D. J., & Sanford, R. N. (1950). *The authoritarian personality.* New York: Harper.

Advertising Age. (1965, July 19). Curtis conference on advertising for children brings heated exchanges. P. 41.

Advertising Age. (1992, January 20). Freberg: Humor's no laughing matter. P. 52.

Agho, A., Mueller, C., & Price, J. (1993). Determinants of employee satisfaction: An empirical test of a causal model. *Human Relations, 46,* 1007–1027.

Ahammer, I. M., & Murray, J. P. (1979). Kindness in the kindergarten: The relative influence of role playing and prosocial television in facilitating altruism. *International Journal of Behavior Development, 2,* 133–157.

Aiken, L., & Kehrer, B. (Eds.). (1985). *Evaluation studies review annual* (Vol. 10). Beverly Hills, CA: Sage.

Ajzen, I. (1987). Attitudes, traits, and actions: Dispositional prediction of behavior in personality and social psychology. In L. Berkowitz (Ed.), *Advances in experimental social psychology* (Vol. 20, pp. 1–63). San Diego, CA: Academic Press.

Ajzen, I. (1988). *Attitudes, personality, and behavior.* Chicago: Dorsey.

Ajzen, I. (1991). The theory of planned behavior. *Organizational Behavior and Human Decision Processes, 50,* 179–211.

Ajzen, I., & Fishbein, M. (1980). *Understanding attitudes and predicting social behavior.* Englewood Cliffs, NJ: Prentice-Hall.

Alderfer, C. P. (1976). Change processes in organizations. In M. D. Dunnette (Ed.), *Handbook of industrial and organizational psychology.* Chicago: Rand McNally.

Alderfer, C. P. (Ed.). (1993). Emerging developments in action research [Special issue]. *Journal of Applied Behavioral Science, 29,* 389–492.

Alderson, G., & Sentman, E. (1979). *How you can influence Congress: The complete handbook for the citizen lobbyist.* New York: Dutton.

Aleshire, R. M. (1970). Planning and citizen participation: Costs, benefits and approaches. *Urban Affairs Quarterly, 5,* 69–393.

Alexander, K. L., & Entwisle, D. R. (1988). Achievement in the first 2 years of school: Patterns and processes. *Monographs of the Society for Research in Child Development, 53,* 1–157.

Alinsky, S. (1946). *Reveille for radicals.* Chicago: University of Chicago Press.

Alinsky, S. D. (1971). *Rules for radicals: A practical primer for realistic radicals.* New York: Random House.

Allport, F. H., et al. (1953). The effects of segregation and the consequences of desegregation: A social science statement. *Minnesota Law Review, 37,* 429–440.

Allport, G. W. (1954). *The nature of prejudice.* Reading, MA: Addison-Wesley.

Alsop, R. (1989, October 18). Brand loyalty is rarely blind loyalty. *Wall Street Journal,* p. B8.

Altemeyer, B. (1988). *Enemies of freedom: Understanding right-wing authoritarianism.* San Francisco: Jossey-Bass.

American Council on Education. (1990). *Minorities in higher education.* Washington, DC: Office of Minority Concerns.

American Demographics. (1989, August). Here's what happened. Pp. 19–21.

American Psychological Association. (1982). *Ethical principles in the conduct of research with human participants* (rev. ed.). Washington, DC: Author.

American Psychological Association. (1992). Ethical principles of psychologists and code of conduct. *American Psychologist, 47,* 1597–1611.

Amir, Y. (1976). The role of intergroup contact in change of prejudice and ethnic relations. In P. A. Katz (Ed.), *Towards the elimination of racism* (pp. 245–308). New York: Pergamon.

Amirkhan, J. (1990). Applying attribution to the study of stress and coping. In S. Graham & V. S. Folkes (Eds.), *Attribution theory: Applications to achievement, mental health, and interpersonal conflict* (pp. 79–102). Hillsdale, NJ: Erlbaum.

Anastasi, A. (1979). *Fields of applied psychology* (2nd ed.). New York: McGraw-Hill.

Andison, F. S. (1977). TV violence and viewer aggression: A cumulation of study results, 1956–1976. *Public Opinion Quarterly, 41,* 314–331.

Andreasen, M. (1994). Patterns of family life and television consumption from 1945 to the 1990s. In D. Zillmann, J. Bryant, & A. Huston (Eds.), *Media, children, and the family: Social scientific, psychodynamic, and clinical perspectives* (pp. 19–36). Hillsdale, NJ: Erlbaum.

Andrews, F. M. (Ed.). (1986). *Research on the quality of life.* Ann Arbor: Institute for Social Research, University of Michigan.

Andrews, F. M. (1991). Stability and change in levels and structure of subjective well-being: USA 1972 and 1988. *Social Indicators Research, 25,* 1–30.

Andrews, F. M., & Withey, S. B. (1976). *Social indicators of well-being: Americans' perceptions of life quality.* New York: Plenum.

Andrews, J. C., & Shimp, T. A. (1990). Effects of involvement, argument strength, and source characteristics on central and peripheral processing of advertising. *Psychology & Marketing, 7,* 195–214.

Aniskiewicz, R. E., & Wysong, E. E. (1990). Evaluating DARE: Drug education and the multiple meanings of success. *Policy Studies Review, 9,* 727–747.

Antill, J. K., & Cotton, S. (1988). Factors affecting the division of labor in households. *Sex Roles, 18,* 531–553.

Archer, D., & Gartner, R. (1987). *Violence and crime in cross-national perspective.* New Haven, CT: Yale University Press.

Argyle, M. (1987). *The psychology of happiness.* London, England: Methuen.

Argyle, M. (1988). *Bodily communication* (2nd ed.). London, England: Methuen.

Argyle, M. (1989). *The social psychology of work* (2nd ed.). New York: Penguin.

Armstrong, G. M., & Brucks, M. (1988). Dealing with children's advertising. *Journal of Public Policy & Marketing, 7,* 98–113.

Arnstein, S. R. (1971). Eight rungs on the ladder of citizen participation. In E. S. Cahn & B. A. Passett (Eds.), *Citizen participation: Effecting community change.* New York: Praeger.

Arnstein, S. R. (1972). Maximum feasible manipulation. *Public Administration Review, 32,* 377–390.

Aronson, E. (1992). Stateways can change folkways. In R. Baird & S. Rosenbaum (Eds.), *Bigotry, prejudice, and hatred* (pp. 185–202). New York: Prometheus.

Aronson, E. (1995). *The social animal* (5th ed.). New York: Freeman.

Aronson, E., Blaney, N., Stephan, C., Sikes, J., & Snapp, M. (1978). *The jigsaw classroom.* Beverly Hills, CA: Sage.

Aronson, E., Brewer, M., & Carlsmith, J. M. (1985). Experimentation in social psychology. In G. Lindzey & E. Aronson (Eds.), *The handbook of social psychology* (3rd ed., Vol. 1, pp. 441–486). New York: Random House.

Aronson, E., & Gonzales, M. H. (1990). Alternative social influence processes applied to energy conservation. In J. Edwards, R. S. Tindale, L. Heath, & E. J. Posavac (Eds.), *Social influence processes and prevention* (pp. 301–325). New York: Plenum.

Aronson, E., & Osherow, N. (1980). Cooperation, prosocial behavior, and academic performance: Experiments in the desegregated classroom. In L. Bickman (Ed.), *Applied social psychology annual* (Vol. 1, pp. 163–196). Beverly Hills, CA: Sage.

Arvey, R. D., Carter, G. W., & Buerkley, D. K. (1991). Job satisfaction: Dispositional and situational influences. In C. L. Cooper & I. J. Robertson (Eds.), *International review of industrial and organizational psychology* (pp. 359–383). Chichester, England: Wiley.

Asch, S. E. (1958). Effects of group pressure upon modification and distortion of judgments. In E. E. Maccoby, T. M. Newcomb, & E. L. Hartley (Eds.), *Readings in social psychology* (3rd ed.). New York: Holt.

Assmus, G., Farley, J. U., & Lehmann, D. R. (1984). How advertising affects sales: Meta-analysis of econometric results. *Journal of Marketing Research, 21,* 65–74.

Atkin, C. K. (1980). Effects of television advertising on children. In E. L. Palmer & A. Dorr (Eds.), *Children and the faces of television: Teaching, violence, selling* (pp. 287–305). New York: Academic Press.

Atkin, C. K., Bowen, L., Nayman, O. B., & Sheinkopf, K. G. (1973). Quality versus quantity in televised political ads. *Public Opinion Quarterly, 37,* 209–224.

Atkin, C. K., & Gantz, W. (1978). Television news and political socialization. *Public Opinion Quarterly, 42,* 183–198.

Atkinson, J. W. (1977). Motivation for achievement. In T. Blass (Ed.), *Personality variables in social behavior.* Hillsdale, NJ: Erlbaum.

Attorney General's Commission on Pornography. (1986). *Final report.* Washington, DC: U.S. Government Printing Office.

Aune, R. K., & Basil, M. (1994). A relational obligations approach to the foot-in-the-mouth effect. *Journal of Applied Social Psychology, 24,* 546–556.

Austin, J., Hatfield, D., Grindle, A., & Bailey, J. (1993). Increasing recycling in office environments: The effects of specific informative cues. *Journal of Applied Behavioral Analysis, 26,* 247–253.

Azar, B. (1994). Psychologists are leaders in research on smoking: Policy-makers rely on psychology's findings. *APA Monitor, 25*(7), 30–32.

Babad, E. (1993). Pygmalion—25 years after interpersonal expectations in the classroom. In P. Blanck (Ed.), *Interpersonal expectations: Theory, research, and application* (pp. 125–153). Paris, France: Cambridge University Press.

Babad, E., Inbar, J., & Rosenthal, R. (1982). Pygmalion, Galatea, and the Golem: Investigators of biased and unbiased teachers. *Journal of Educational Psychology, 74,* 459–474.

Back, K. W. (1972). *Beyond words: The story of sensitivity training and the encounter movement.* New York: Russell Sage Foundation.

Backer, T., & Rogers, E. (Eds.). (1993). *Organizational aspects of health communication campaigns: What works?* Newbury Park, CA: Sage.

Baker, N. L. (1989). *Sexual harassment and job satisfaction in traditional and nontraditional industrial occupations.* Unpublished doctoral dissertation, California School of Professional Psychology, Los Angeles.

Bales, R. F. (1958). Task roles and social roles in problem-solving groups. In E. E. Maccoby, T. M. Newcomb, & E. L. Hartley (Eds.), *Readings in social psychology* (3rd ed., pp. 437–447). New York: Holt, Rinehart & Winston.

Ball, S., & Bogatz, G. A. (1970). *The first year of Sesame Street: An evaluation.* Princeton, NJ: Educational Testing Service.

Ball-Rokeach, S. J., Rokeach, M., & Grube, J. W. (1984). *The great American values test: Influencing behavior and belief through television.* New York: Free Press.

Ballard, S. C., Brosz, A. R., & Parker, L. B. (1980). Social science and social policy: Roles of the applied researcher. *Policy Studies Journal, 8,* 951–957.

Ballew v. Georgia, 435 U.S. 223 (1978).

Bandura, A. (1977). *Social learning theory.* Englewood Cliffs, NJ: Prentice-Hall.

Bandura, A. (1977a). Self-efficacy: Toward a unifying theory of behavioral change. *Psychological Review, 84,* 191–215.

Bandura, A. (1985). *Social foundations of thought and action.* Englewood Cliffs, NJ: Prentice-Hall.

Bandura, A. (1986). *Social foundations of thought and action: A social cognitive theory.* Englewood Cliffs, NJ: Prentice-Hall.

Bandura, A. (1995). Exercise of personal and collective efficacy in changing society. In A. Bandura (Ed.), *Self-efficacy in changing societies* (pp. 1–45). New York: Cambridge University Press.

Bandura, A. (1997). *Self-efficacy: The exercise of control.* New York: Freeman.

Bandura, A., Ross, D., & Ross, S. A. (1963). Imitation of film-mediated aggressive models. *Journal of Abnormal and Social Psychology, 66,* 3–11.

Baran, S. J., Chase, L. J., & Courtright, J. A. (1979). Television drama as a facilitator of prosocial behavior: "The Waltons." *Journal of Broadcasting, 23,* 277–285.

Barcus, F. E. (1980). The nature of television advertising to children. In E. L. Palmer & A. Dorr (Eds.), *Children and the faces of television: Teaching, violence, selling* (pp. 273–285). New York: Academic Press.

Barker, R. (1987). Prospecting in environmental psychology: Oskaloosa revisited. In D. Stokols & I. Altman (Eds.), *Handbook of environmental psychology* (Vol. 2, pp. 1413–1432). New York: Wiley.

Barker, R. (1989). Settings of a professional lifetime. *Journal of Personality and Social Psychology, 37,* 2137–2157.

Barnett, W. S. (1985). The Perry Preschool Program and its long-term effects: A benefit-cost analysis. *High/Scope Early Childhood Policy Papers.* Ypsilanti, MI: High/Scope Educational Research Foundation.

Barnett, W. S. (1992). Benefits of compensatory preschool education. *Journal of Human Resources, 27,* 279–312.

Baron, L., & Straus, M. A. (1989). *Four theories of rape in American society: A state-level analysis.* New Haven, CT: Yale University Press.

Baron, R., & Kenny, D. (1986). The moderator-mediator variable distinction in social psychological research: Conceptual, strategic, and statistical considerations. *Journal of Personality and Social Psychology, 51,* 1173–1182.

Baron, R. H., Tom, D. Y., & Cooper, H. M. (1985). Social class, race and teacher expectations. In J. Dusek (Ed.), *Teacher expectations* (pp. 251–270). Hillsdale, NJ: Erlbaum.

Barr, I. K. (1983). Physicians' views of patients in prepaid group practice: Reasons for visits to HMOs. *Journal of Health and Social Behavior, 24,* 244–255.

Bartlett, R. (1994). Evaluating environmental policy success and failure. In N. Vig & M. Kraft (Eds.), *Environmental policy in the 1990s* (2nd ed., pp. 167–188). Washington, DC: CQ Press.

Bartol, C., & Bartol, A. (1994). *Psychology and law: Research and applications* (2nd ed.). Pacific Grove, CA: Brooks/Cole.

Bass, B. M., Shackleton, V. J., & Rosenstein, E. (1979). Industrial democracy and participative management: What's the difference? *International Review of Applied Psychology, 28,* 81–92.

Bateman, T. S., & Organ, D. W. (1983). Job satisfaction and the good soldier: The relationship between affect and employee "citizenship." *Academy of Management Journal, 26,* 587–595.

Bauer, R. A., & Greyser, S. A. (1968). *Advertising in America: The consumer view.* Boston: Graduate School of Business Administration, Harvard University.

Baum, A., Fleming, R., & Singer, J. E. (1982). Stress at Three Mile Island: Applying psychological impact analysis. In L. Bickman (Ed.), *Applied social psychology annual* (Vol. 3, pp. 217–248). Beverly Hills, CA: Sage.

Baum, A., & Paulus, P. B. (1987). Crowding. In D. Stokols & I. Altman (Eds.), *Handbook of environmental psychology* (Vol. 1, pp. 533–570). New York: Wiley.

Bauman, L. J., Stein, R. E. K., & Ireys, H. T. (1991). Reinventing fidelity: The transfer of social technology among settings. *American Journal of Community Psychology, 19,* 619–639.

Baumrind, D. (1985). Research using intentional deception: Ethical issues revisited. *American Psychologist, 40,* 165–174.

Bechtel, R. B., Achelpohl, C., & Akers, A. (1972). Correlates between observed behavior and questionnaire responses on television viewing. In E. A. Rubinstein, G. A. Comstock, & J. P. Murray (Eds.), *Television and social behavior (Vol. 4). Television in day-to-day life: Patterns of use* (pp. 274–344). Washington, DC: U.S. Government Printing Office.

Becker, L. J., & Seligman, C. (1978). Reducing air conditioning waste by signalling that it is cool outside. *Personality and Social Psychology Bulletin, 4,* 412–415.

Beckett, K. (1994). Setting the public agenda: "Street crime" and drug use in American politics. *Social Problems, 41,* 425–447.

Beelmann, A., Pfingsten, U., & Losel, F. (1994). Effects of training social competence in children: A meta-analysis of recent evaluation studies. *Journal of Clinical Child Psychology, 23,* 260–271.

Been, V. (1995). Market forces, not racist practices, may affect the siting of locally undesirable land uses. In J. Petrikin (Ed.), *Environmental justice* (pp. 10–23). San Diego, CA: Greenhaven.

Bell, J. (1994). Managing evaluation projects step by step. In J. Wholey, H. Hatry, & K. Newcomer (Eds.), *Handbook of practical program evaluation* (pp. 510–533). San Francisco: Jossey-Bass.

Bell, P., Greene, T., Baum, A., & Fisher, J. (1997). *Environmental psychology* (4th ed.). Fort Worth, TX: Harcourt Brace Jovanovich.

Belson, W. (1978). *Television violence and the adolescent boy.* Westmead, England: Saxon House, Teakfield.

Bennett, E. (1955). Discussion, decision, commitment, and consensus in "group decision." *Human Relations, 8,* 251–274.

Bercovitch, J., & Rubin, J. Z. (Eds.). (1992). *Mediation in international relations: Multiple approaches to conflict management.* New York: St. Martin's.

Berkowitz, L., Fraser, C., Treasure, F. P., & Cochran, S. (1987). Pay, equity, job gratifications, and comparisons in pay satisfaction. *Journal of Applied Psychology, 72,* 544–551.

Berkun, M. M., Bialek, H. M., Kern, R. P., & Yagi, K. (1962). Experimental studies of psychological stress in man. *Psychological Monographs, 76* (15, Whole No. 534).

Bermant, G., Kelman, H. C., & Warwick, D. P. (Eds.). (1978). *The ethics of social intervention.* Washington, DC: Hemisphere.

Berrueta-Clement, J. R., Schweinhart, L., Barnett, W., Epstein, A., & Weikart, D. (1984). *Changed lives: The effects of the Perry Preschool Program on youths through age 19.* Ypsilanti, MI: High/Scope Educational Research Foundation.

Berry, G. L., & Asamen, J. K. (1993). *Children and television: Images in a changing sociocultural world.* Thousand Oaks, CA: Sage.

Berry, L., & Houston, J. (1993). *Psychology at work: An introduction to industrial and organizational psychology.* Madison, WI: Brown & Benchmark.

Berry, T. (1988). *The dream of the earth.* San Francisco: Sierra Club.

Bersoff, D. N. (1987). Social science data and the Supreme Court: *Lockhart* as a case in point. *American Psychologist, 42,* 52–58.

Bersoff, D. N. (Ed.). (1995). *Ethical conflicts in psychology.* Washington, DC: American Psychological Association.

Bersoff, D. N., & Ogden, D. W. (1987). In the Supreme Court of the United States: *Lockhart v. McCree. American Psychologist, 42,* 59–68.

Best, A. (1981). *When consumers complain.* New York: Columbia University Press

Best, A., & Andreasen, A. R. (1976). *Talking back to business: Voiced and unvoiced consumer complaints.* Washington, DC: Center for Study of Responsive Law.

Best, J. A., Bass, F., & Owen, L. E. (1977). Mode of service delivery in a smoking cessation programme for public health. *Canadian Journal of Public Health, 68,* 469–473.

Betancourt, H., & Lopez, S. R. (1993). The study of culture, ethnicity, and race in American psychology. *American Psychologist, 48,* 629–637.

Betz, N. E., & Fitzgerald, L. E. (1987). *The career psychology of women.* New York: Academic Press.

Bevan, W. (1980). On getting in bed with a lion. *American Psychologist, 35,* 779–789.

Beyer, J. M., & Trice, H. M. (1982). The utilization process: A conceptual framework and synthesis of empirical findings. *Administrative Science Quarterly, 27,* 591–622.

Bickman, L. (1981). Some distinctions between basic and applied approaches. In L. Bickman (Ed.), *Applied social psychology annual* (Vol. 2, pp. 23–44). Beverly Hills, CA: Sage.

Bickman, L., & Henchy, T. (Eds.). (1972). *Beyond the laboratory: Field research in social psychology.* New York: McGraw-Hill.

Biddle, B. J. (1979). *Role theory: Expectations, identities, and behaviors.* New York: Academic Press.

Blackwell, J. (1990). Current issues affecting Blacks and Hispanics in the educational pipeline. In G. Thomas (Ed.), *U.S. race relations in the 1980s and 1990s: Challenges and alternatives* (pp. 35–52). New York: Hemisphere.

Blanck, P. (Ed.). (1993). *Interpersonal expectations: Theory, research, and application.* New York: Cambridge University Press.

Blaney, N. T., Stephan, C., Rosenfield, D., Aronson, E., & Sikes, J. (1977). Interdependence in the classroom: A field study. *Journal of Educational Psychology, 69,* 139–146.

Block, J. H. (1973). Conceptions of sex role: Some cross-cultural and longitudinal perspectives. *American Psychologist, 28,* 512–526.

Bobko, P. (1990). Multivariate correlational analysis. In M. D. Dunnette & L. M. Hough (Eds.), *Handbook of industrial & organizational psychology* (2nd ed., Vol. 1, pp. 637–686). Palo Alto, CA: Consulting Psychologists Press.

Boerner, C., & Chilton, K. (1994). The folly of demand-side recycling. *Environment, 36,* 6–33.

Bogatz, G. A., & Ball, S. (1971). *The second year of Sesame Street: A continuing evaluation* (2 vols.). Princeton, NJ: Educational Testing Service.

Boggiano, A. K., Barrett, M., Weiher, A. W., McClelland, G. H.,

& Lusk, C. M. (1987). Use of the maximal-operant principle to motivate children's intrinsic interest. *Journal of Personality and Social Psychology, 53,* 866–879.

Bohm, R. M. (1991). American death penalty opinion, 1936–1986: A critical examination of the Gallup polls. In R. M. Bohm (Ed.), *The death penalty in America: Current research* (pp. 122–136). Cincinnati: Anderson.

Boldero, J. (1995). The prediction of household recycling of newspapers: The role of attitudes, intentions, and situational factors. *Journal of Applied Social Psychology, 25,* 440–62.

Bolger, N., DeLongis, A., Kessler, R. C., & Schilling, E. A. (1989). Effects of daily stress on negative mood. *Journal of Personality and Social Psychology, 57,* 808–818.

Bond, C. F., DiCandia, C. G., & MacKinnon, J. R. (1988). Responses to violence in a psychiatric setting: The role of patient's race. *Personality and Social Psychology Bulletin, 14,* 448–458.

Bond, M. H., & Smith, P. B. (1996). Cross-cultural social and organizational psychology. *Annual Review of Psychology, 47,* 205–235.

Bond, R., & Smith, P. (1996). Culture and conformity: A meta-analysis of studies using Asch's line judgment task. *Psychological Bulletin, 119,* 111–137.

Bonta, J., & Gendreau, P. (1992). Coping with prison. In P. Suedfeld & P. Tetlock (Eds.), *Psychology and social policy* (pp. 343–354). New York: Hemisphere.

Boone, L. E., & Kurtz, D. L. (1992). *Contemporary marketing* (7th ed.). Fort Worth, TX: Dryden.

Booth-Kewley, S., & Friedman, H. S. (1987). Psychological predictors of heart disease: A quantitative review. *Psychological Bulletin, 101,* 343–362.

Borden, D. F. (1980). *Leader-boss stress, personality, job satisfaction, and performance: Another look at the interrelationship of some old constructs in the modern large bureaucracy.* Unpublished doctoral dissertation, University of Washington, Seattle.

Borgatta, E. F. (1968). Some notes on the history of tobacco use. In E. F. Borgatta & R. R. Evans (Eds.), *Smoking, health, and behavior* (pp. 3–11). Chicago: Aldine.

Boruch, R. F. (1996). *Randomized experiments for planning and evaluation: A practical guide.* Thousand Oaks, CA: Sage.

Bosso, C. (1994). After the movement: Environmental activism in the 1990s. In N. Vig & M. Kraft (Eds.), *Environmental policy in the 1990s.* Washington, DC: CQ Press.

Bothwell, R. K., Brigham, J. C., & Malpass, R. S. (1989). Cross-racial identification. *Personality and Social Psychology Bulletin, 15,* 19–25.

Bothwell, R. K., Deffenbacher, K. A., & Brigham, J. C. (1987). Correlation of eyewitness accuracy and confidence: Optimality hypothesis revisited. *Journal of Applied Psychology, 72,* 691–695.

Boulding, E. (1966). *The image: Knowledge in life and society.* Ann Arbor: University of Michigan Press.

Bowers, W. J. (1988). The effect of executions is brutalization, not deterrence. In K. C. Haas & J. A. Inciardi (Eds.), *Challenging capital punishment* (pp. 49–89). Newbury Park, CA: Sage.

Boykin, A. W. (1994). Harvesting talent and culture: African-American children and educational reform. In R. Rossi (Ed.), *Schools and students at risk* (pp. 116–138). New York: Teachers College Press.

Bracht, N., & Kingsbury, L. (1990). Community organization principles in health promotion: A five-stage model. In N. Bracht (Ed.), *Health promotion at the community level* (pp. 66–88). Newbury Park, CA: Sage.

Bradburn, N. M., & Sudman, S. (1988). *Polls and surveys: Understanding what they tell us.* San Francisco: Jossey-Bass.

Braddock, J. H., II. (1985). School desegregation and Black assimilation. *Journal of Social Issues, 41*(3), 9–22.

Brainerd, C., & Ornstein, P. (1991). Children's memory for witnessed events: The developmental backdrop. In J. Doris (Ed.), *The suggestibility of children's recollections: Implications for eyewitness testimony* (pp. 10–20). Washington, DC: American Psychological Association.

Bramel, D., & Friend, R. (1987). The work group and its vicissitudes in social and industrial psychology. *Journal of Applied Behavioral Science, 23,* 233–253.

Brayfield, A. H., & Crockett, W. H. (1955). Employee attitudes and employee performance. *Psychological Bulletin, 52,* 396–424.

Brayfield, A. H., & Lipsey, M. W. (1976). Public affairs psychology. In P. J. Woods (Ed.), *Career opportunities for psychologists: Expanding and emerging areas.* Washington, DC: American Psychological Association.

Brehm, J. W. (1966). *A theory of psychological reactance.* New York: Academic Press.

Brehm, J. W., & Cohen, A. R. (1962). *Explorations in cognitive dissonance.* New York: Wiley.

Brennan, M., & Brennan, R. E. (1988). *Strange language: Child victims under cross examination.* Wagga Wagga, NSW, Australia: Riverina Murray Institute of Higher Education.

Bretl, D. J., & Cantor, J. (1988). The portrayal of men and women in U.S. television commercials: A recent content analysis and trends over 15 years. *Sex Roles, 18,* 595–609.

Brewer, M. B. (1986). The role of ethnocentrism in intergroup conflict. In S. Worchel & W. G. Austin (Eds.), *Psychology of intergroup relations* (2nd ed., pp. 88–102). Chicago: Nelson-Hall.

Brewer, M. B., & Miller, N. (1984). Beyond the contact hypothesis: Theoretical perspectives on desegregation. In N. Miller & M. B. Brewer (Eds.), *Groups in contact: The psychology of desegregation* (pp. 281–302). Orlando, FL: Academic Press.

Brief, A., Butcher, A., & Roberson, L. (1995). Cookies, disposition, and job attitudes: The effect of positive mood-inducing events and negative affectivity on job satisfaction in a field experiment. *Organizational and Behavioral Human Decision Processes, 62,* 55–62.

Brigham, J. C. (1971). Ethnic stereotypes. *Psychological Bulletin, 76,* 15–38.

Brigham, J. C. (1990). Target person distinctiveness and attractiveness as moderator variables of the confidence-accuracy relationship in eyewitness identifications. *Basic and Applied Social Psychology, 11,* 101–115.

Brinberg, D., & Cummings, V. (1983). Purchasing generic prescription drugs: An analysis using two behavioral intention models. *Advances in Consumer Research, 11,* 229–234.

Brinberg, D., & Durand, J. (1983). Eating at fast-food restaurants: An analysis using two behavioral intention models. *Journal of Applied Social Psychology, 13,* 459–472.

Brinkerhoff, D. B., & Booth, A. (1984). Gender, dominance, and stress. *Journal of Social and Biological Structures, 7,* 159–177.

Brobeck, S. (1991). Economic deregulation and the least affluent: Consumer protection strategies. *Journal of Social Issues, 47*(1), 169–191.

Brooke, P. P., & Price, J. L. (1989). The determinants of employee absenteeism: An empirical test of a causal model. *Journal of Occupational Psychology, 62,* 1–19.

Brophy, J. (1983). Research on the self-fulfilling prophecy and teacher expectations. *Journal of Educational Psychology, 76,* 236–247.

Brophy, J. (1985). Teacher-student interactions. In J. Dusek (Ed.), *Teacher expectations* (pp. 303–328). Hillsdale, NJ: Erlbaum.

Brown v. Board of Education of Topeka, Kansas, 347 U.S. 483 (1954).

Brown, J., Childers, K., & Waszak, C. (1990). Television and adolescent sexuality. Conference: Teens and television. *Journal of Adolescent Health Care, 11,* 62–70.

Brown, K. A., & Huber, V. L. (1992). Lowering the floors and raising ceilings: A longitudinal assessment of the effects of an earnings-at-risk plan on pay satisfaction. *Personnel Psychology, 45,* 279–311.

Brown, L. R. (1981). *Building a sustainable society.* New York: Norton.

Brown, L. R., et al. (1994). *State of the world 1994.* New York: Norton.

Brown, L. R., et al. (1995). *State of the world 1995.* New York: Norton.

Brown, S. P., & Stayman, D. M. (1992). Antecedents and consequences of attitude toward the ad: A meta-analysis. *Journal of Consumer Research, 19,* 34–51.

Brownell, K. D., & Rodin, J. (1994). The dieting maelstrom: Is it possible and advisable to lose weight? *American Psychologist, 49,* 781–791.

Brownell, K. D., & Wadden, T. A. (1992). Etiology and treatment of obesity: Understanding a serious, prevalent, refractory disorder. *Journal of Consulting and Clinical Psychology, 60,* 505–517.

Browner, E. (1993). Environmental tobacco smoke: EPA's report. *EPA Journal, 19,* 18–19.

Bruce, W., & Blackburn, J. W. (1992). *Balancing job satisfaction and performance.* Westport, CT: Quorum.

Bruvold, W. H. (1993). A meta-analysis of adolescent smoking cessation programs. *American Journal of Public Health, 83,* 872–880.

Bryan, J. H., & Schwartz, T. (1971). Effects of film material upon children's behavior. *Psychological Bulletin, 75,* 50–59.

Bryant, J., & Zillmann, D. (Eds.). (1994). *Media effects: Advances in theory and research.* Hillsdale, NJ: Erlbaum.

Buchko, A. (1992). Employee ownership, attitudes, and turnover: An empirical assessment. *Human Relations, 45,* 711–733.

Buerkel-Rothfuss, N. L., & Mayes, S. (1981). Soap opera viewing: The cultivation effect. *Journal of Communication, 31*(3), 108–115.

Bull, R., & Gibson-Robinson, E. (1981). The influences of eye-gaze, style of dress, and locality on the amounts of money donated to a charity. *Human Relations, 34,* 895–905.

Bureau of Justice Statistics. (1990). *Criminal victimization in the United States, 1988: A national crime survey report.* Washington, DC: U.S. Department of Justice.

Bureau of Justice Statistics. (1992). *Criminal victimization in the United States: 1973–90 trends.* Washington, DC: U.S. Department of Justice.

Bureau of Justice Statistics. (1994). *Criminal victimization in the United States, 1992* (NCJ-145125). Washington, DC: Author.

Burke, M. C., & Edell, J. A. (1989). The impact of feelings on ad-based affect and cognition. *Journal of Marketing Research, 26,* 69–83.

Burn, S. M. (1996). *The social psychology of gender.* New York: McGraw-Hill.

Burt, M. (1980). Cultural myths and supports for rape. *Journal of Personality and Social Psychology, 38,* 217–230.

Bush, K., & Raban, A. (1990). Quality circles: How effective are they in improving employee performance and attitudes? *Psychology: A Journal of Human Behavior, 27,* 11–17.

Bushell, D., Jr. (1978). An engineering approach to the elementary classroom: The behavior analysis Follow-Through project. In A. C. Catania & T. A. Brigham (Eds.), *Handbook of applied behavior analysis: Social and instructional processes* (pp. 525–563). New York: Irvington.

Butler, D., & Geis, F. L. (1990). Nonverbal affect responses to male and female leaders: Implications for leadership evaluations. *Journal of Personality and Social Psychology, 58,* 48–59.

Butler, M., & Paisley, W. (Eds.). (1980). *Women and the mass media: Sourcebook for research and action.* New York: Human Sciences Press.

Buunk, B. P., & Van Yperen, N. W. (1991). Referential comparisons, relational comparisons, and exchange orientation: Their relation to marital satisfaction. *Personality and Social Psychology Bulletin, 17,* 709–717.

Bylsma, W., & Major, B. (1994). Social comparisons and contentment: Exploring the psychological costs of the gender wage gap. *Psychology of Women Quarterly, 18,* 241–249.

Byrne, D., & Lamberth, J. (1970). The effect of erotic stimuli on sex arousal, evaluative responses, and subsequent behavior. In *Technical report of the Commission on Obscenity and Pornography* (Vol. 8). Washington, DC: U.S. Government Printing Office.

Cacioppo, J. T., & Petty, R. E. (1979). Effects of message repetition and position on cognitive responses, recall, and persuasion. *Journal of Personality and Social Psychology, 37,* 97–109.

Cacioppo, J. T., & Petty, R. E. (1981). Social psychological procedures for cognitive response assessment: The thought-listing technique. In T. V. Merluzzi, C. R. Glass, & M. Genest (Eds.), *Cognitive assessment.* New York: Guilford.

Calder, B. J., Phillips, L. W., & Tybout, A. M. (1981). Designing research for application. *Journal of Consumer Research, 8,* 197–207.

Califano, J. (1994). Revealing the link between campaign financing and deaths caused by tobacco. *Journal of the American Medical Association, 272,* 1217–1218.

California Integrated Waste Management Board. (1995). *Meeting solid waste diversion mandates: A state report to the legislature.* Sacramento: Author.

Cameron, C. (1977). Sex-role attitudes. In S. Oskamp, *Attitudes and opinions* (pp. 339–359). Englewood Cliffs, NJ: Prentice-Hall.

Campbell, A. (1981). *The sense of well-being in America: Recent patterns and trends.* New York: McGraw-Hill.

Campbell, A., Converse, P. E., & Rodgers, W. L. (1976). *The quality of American life: Perceptions, evaluations, and satisfactions.* New York: Russell Sage Foundation.

Campbell, B. A. (1981). Race-of-interviewer effects among southern adolescents. *Public Opinion Quarterly, 45,* 231–244.

Campbell, C. P. (1995). *Race, myth and the news.* Thousand Oaks, CA: Sage.

Campbell, D. T. (1969). Reforms as experiments. *American Psychologist, 24,* 409–429.

Campbell, D. T. (1979). "Degrees of freedom" and the case study. In T. D. Cook & C. S. Reichardt (Eds.), *Qualitative and quantitative methods in evaluation research* (pp. 49–67). Beverly Hills, CA: Sage.

Campbell, D. T. (1988). *Methodology and epistemology for social science.* Chicago: University of Chicago Press.

Campbell, D. T. (1988). The experimenting society. In D. Campbell & S. Overman (Eds.), *Methodology and epistemology for social science: Selected papers* (pp. 290–314). Chicago: University of Chicago Press.

Campbell, D. T., & Erlebacher, A. E. (1970). How regression artifacts in quasi-experimental evaluations can mistakenly make compensatory education look harmful. In J. Hellmuth (Ed.), *Compensatory education: A national debate* (Vol. 3). *Disadvantaged child.* New York: Brunner/Mazel.

Campbell, D. T., & Fiske, D. W. (1959). Convergent and discriminant validation by the multitrait multimethod matrix. *Psychological Bulletin, 56,* 81–105.

Campbell, D. T., & Stanley, J. C. (1966). *Experimental and quasi-experimental designs for research.* Chicago: Rand McNally.

Campbell, J. D., & Fairey, P. J. (1989). Informational and normative routes to conformity: The effect of faction size as a function of norm extremity and attention to the stimulus. *Journal of Personality and Social Psychology, 57,* 457–468.

Campbell, J. P. (1990). Modeling the performance prediction problem in industrial and organizational psychology. In M. D. Dunnette & L. M. Hough (Eds.), *Handbook of Industrial & Organizational Psychology* (2nd ed., Vol. 1, pp. 687–732). Palo Alto, CA: Consulting Psychologists Press.

Campion, M., & McClelland, C. (1991). Interdisciplinary examination of the costs and benefits of enlarged jobs: A job design quasi-experiment. *Journal of Applied Psychology, 76,* 186–198.

Cannings, K., & Montmarquette, C. (1991). Managerial momentum: A simultaneous model of the career progress of male and female managers. *Industrial and Labor Relations Review, 44,* 212–228.

Cantor, J. (1994). Fright reactions to the mass media. In J. Bryant & D. Zillmann (Eds.), *Media effects: Advances in theory and research* (pp. 213–245). Hillsdale, NJ: Erlbaum.

Cantor, M., & Cantor, J. (1992). *Prime-time television: Content and control* (2nd ed.). Newbury Park, CA: Sage.

Caplan, N. A. (1976). Social research and national policy: What gets used, by whom, for what purposes, and with what effect? *International Social Science Journal, 28,* 187–194.

Caplan, N. A. (1977). A minimal set of conditions necessary for the utilization of social science knowledge in policy formulation at the national level. In C. H. Weiss (Ed.), *Using social research in public policy making.* Lexington, MA: Lexington.

Caplan, N. A., Morrison, A., & Stambaugh, R. J. (1975). *The use of social science knowledge in policy decisions at the national level: A report to respondents.* Ann Arbor: Institute for Social Research, University of Michigan.

Caplan, N. A., & Nelson, S. D. (1973). On being useful: The nature and consequences of psychological research on social problems. *American Psychologist, 28,* 199–211.

Caplow, T. (1982, October/November). Decades of public opinion: Comparing NORC and Middletown data. *Public Opinion, 5(5),* 30–31.

Carlson, J. (1994). Multimodal treatment for smoking cessation. In J. Lewis (Ed.), *Addictions: Concepts and strategies for treatment* (pp. 113–122). Gaithersburg, MD: Aspen.

Carmelli, D., Swan, G. E., Robinette, D., & Fabsitz, R. (1992). Genetic influence on smoking—A study of male twins. *New England Journal of Medicine, 327,* 829–833.

Carmody, T. P., & Matarazzo, J. D. (1991). Health psychology. In M. Hersen, A. Kazdin, & A. Bellack (Eds.), *The clinical psychology handbook* (2nd ed., pp. 695–723). New York: Pergamon.

Carroll, J. S. (Ed.). (1990). *Applied social psychology and organizational settings.* Hillsdale, NJ: Erlbaum.

Carroll, J., & Johnson, E. (1990). *Decision research: A field guide.* Newbury Park, CA: Sage.

Carter, R. (1994). Maximizing the use of evaluation results. In J. Wholey, H. Hatry, & K. Newcomer (Eds.), *Handbook of practical program evaluation* (pp. 576–589). San Francisco: Jossey-Bass.

Cater, D., & Strickland, S. (1975). *TV violence and the child: The evolution and fate of the Surgeon General's Report.* New York: Russell Sage Foundation.

Caudle, S. (1994). Using qualitative approaches. In J. Wholey, H. Hatry, & K. Newcomer (Eds.), *Handbook of practical program evaluation* (pp. 69–95). San Francisco: Jossey-Bass.

Ceci, S. J. (1994). Cognitive and social factors in children's testimony. In B. Sales & G. VandenBos (Eds.), *Psychology in* legislation and litigation: APA master lectures. Washington, DC: American Psychological Association.

Ceci, S., & Bruck, M. (1995). *Jeopardy in the courtroom: A scientific analysis of children's testimony*. Washington DC: American Psychological Association.

Celsi, R. L., & Olson, J. C. (1988). The role of involvement in attention and comprehension processes. *Journal of Consumer Research, 15,* 210–224.

Centers for Disease Control. (1991). Weapon carrying among high school students. *Journal of the American Medical Association, 266,* 2342.

Centers for Disease Control. (1992). Tobacco, alcohol, and other drug use among high school students—United States, 1991. *Morbidity and Mortality Weekly Report, 41,* 698–703.

Chaffee, S. H., Jackson-Beeck, M., Durall, J., & Wilson, D. (1977). Mass communication in political communication. In S. A. Renshon (Ed.), *Handbook of political socialization: Theory and research* (pp. 223–258). New York: Free Press.

Chaiken, S. (1987). The heuristic model of persuasion. In M. P. Zanna, J. M. Olson, & C. P. Herman (Eds.), *Social influence: The Ontario symposium* (Vol. 5, pp. 3–39). Hillsdale, NJ: Erlbaum.

Chance, J., & Goldstein, A. (1996). The other-race effect and eyewitness identification. In S. Sporer, R. Malpass, & G. Koehnken (Eds.), *Psychological issues in eyewitness identification* (pp. 153–176). Mahwah, NJ: Erlbaum.

Chandler, W. U. (1988). Smoking epidemic widens: Smoking rates rise sharply in the developing world while they decline in the West. *World Watch, 1*(1), 39–40.

Chattopadhyay, A., & Basu, K. (1990). Humor in advertising: The moderating role of prior brand evaluation. *Journal of Marketing Research, 27,* 466–476.

Chattopadhyay, A., & Nedungadi, P. (1992). Does attitude toward the ad endure? The moderating effects of attention and delay. *Journal of Consumer Research, 19,* 26–33.

Chavez, D. (1985). Perpetuation of gender inequality: A context analysis of comic strips. *Sex Roles, 13,* 93–102.

Chelimsky, E. (1994). Making evaluation units effective. In J. Wholey, H. Hatry, & K. Newcomer (Eds.), *Handbook of practical program evaluation* (pp. 493–509). San Francisco: Jossey-Bass.

Chemers, M. M., Oskamp, S., & Costanzo, M. A. (1995). *Diversity in organizations: New perspectives for a changing workplace.* Thousand Oaks, CA: Sage.

Chemers, M. M., & Skrzypek, G. J. (1972). Experimental test of the contingency model of leadership effectiveness. *Journal of Personality and Social Psychology, 24,* 172–177.

Chen, H. (1990). *Theory-driven evaluations.* Newbury Park, CA: Sage.

Cherns, A. (1987). Principles of sociotechnical design revisited. *Human Relations, 4,* 153–162.

Chesler, M. A., Kalmuss, D. S., & Sanders, J. (1983). Methods of presenting scientific evidence in court: Panels versus party witnessing in school desegregation cases. *Sociological Methods and Research, 11,* 443–468.

Childs, H. L. (1965). *Public opinion: Nature, formation and role.* Princeton, NJ: Van Nostrand.

Chilton, K., & Lis, J. (1992). *Recycling for recycling's sake.* St. Louis, MO: Washington University, Center for the Study of American Business.

Chipman, S. F., & Wilson, D. M. (1985). Understanding mathematics course enrollment and mathematics achievement: A synthesis of the research. In S. F. Chipman, L. R. Brush, & D. M. Wilson (Eds.), *Women and mathematics: Balancing the equation* (pp. 275–328). Hillsdale, NJ: Erlbaum.

Choate, R. B. (1980). The politics of change. In E. L. Palmer & A. Dorr (Eds.), *Children and the faces of television: Teaching, violence, selling* (pp. 323–338). New York: Academic Press.

Chow, S. L. (1988). Significance tests or effect size? *Psychological Bulletin, 103,* 105–110.

Christensen, L. (1977). The negative subject: Myth, reality, or a prior experimental experience effect? *Journal of Personality and Social Psychology, 35,* 392–400.

Christensen, L. (1988). Deception in psychological research: When is its use justified? *Personality and Social Psychology Bulletin, 14,* 664–675.

Christie, R. (1976). Probability v. precedence: The social psychology of jury selection. In G. Bermant, C. Nemeth, & N. Vidmar (Eds.), *Psychology and the law: Research frontiers.* Lexington, MA: Lexington.

Cialdini, R. B. (1980). Full-cycle social psychology. In L. Bickman (Ed.), *Applied social psychology annual* (Vol. 1, pp. 21–47). Beverly Hills, CA: Sage.

Cialdini, R. B. (1993). *Influence: Science and practice* (3rd ed.). New York: HarperCollins.

Cialdini, R. B., Petty, R. E., & Cacioppo, J. T. (1981). Attitude and attitude change. *Annual Review of Psychology, 32,* 357–404.

Cialdini, R. B., & Schroeder, D. A. (1976). Increasing compliance by legitimizing paltry contributions: When even a penny helps. *Journal of Personality and Social Psychology, 34,* 599–604.

Cialdini, R. B., Trost, M., & Newsom, J. (1995). Preference for consistency: The development of a valid measure and the discovery of surprising behavioral implications. *Journal of Personality and Social Psychology, 69,* 318–328.

Cialdini, R. B., Vincent, J. E., Lewis, S. K., Catalan, J., Wheeler, D., & Darby, B. L. (1975). A reciprocal concessions procedure for inducing compliance: The door-in-the-face technique. *Journal of Personality and Social Psychology, 31,* 206–215.

Cicirelli, V. G., et al. (1969). *The impact of Head Start: An evaluation of the effects of Head Start on children's cognitive and affective development.* Athens: Ohio University & Westinghouse Learning Corporation.

Cimons, M. (1997, April 26). U.S. judge OKs FDA's power to regulate tobacco. *Los Angeles Times,* pp. A1, A12.

Clark, C. C. (1969). Television and social controls: Some observations on the portrayal of ethnic minorities. *Television Quarterly, 8,* 18–22.

Clark, D. G., & Blankenburg, W. B. (1972). Trends in violent content in selected mass media. In G. A. Comstock & E. A. Rubinstein (Eds.), *Television and social behavior* (Vol. 1, pp. 188–243). Washington, DC: U.S. Government Printing Office.

Clark, K. B., & Clark, M. P. (1947). Racial identification and preference in Negro children. In T. M. Newcomb & T. L. Hartley (Eds.), *Readings in social psychology* (pp. 169–178). New York: Holt.

Clark, M. S., & Mills, J. (1993). The difference between communal and exchange relationships: What it is and is not. *Personality and Social Psychology Bulletin, 19,* 684–691.

Clarke, J. (1994). Pieces of the puzzle: The jigsaw method. In S. Sharan (Ed.), *Handbook of cooperative learning methods* (pp. 34–50). Westport, CT: Greenwood.

Clayton, O., Jr. (Ed.). (1996). *An American dilemma revisited: Race relations in a changing world.* New York: Russell Sage Foundation.

Clayton, R. R., Cattarello, A., Day, L. E., & Walden, K. P. (1991). Persuasive communication and drug abuse prevention: An evaluation of the DARE program. In L. Donohew, H. Sypher, & W. Bukoski (Eds.), *Persuasive communication and drug abuse prevention* (pp. 295–313). Hillsdale, NJ: Erlbaum.

Clayton, S. D., & Crosby, F. J. (1992). *Justice, gender, and affirmative action.* Ann Arbor: University of Michigan Press.

Cleveland, J., Murphy, K., & Williams, R. (1989). Multiple uses of performance appraisal: Prevalence and correlations. *Journal of Applied Psychology, 74,* 130–135.

Cline, V. B., Croft, R. G., & Courrier, S. (1973). Desensitization of children to television violence. *Journal of Personality and Social Psychology, 27,* 360–365.

Coates, B., Pusser, H. B., & Goodman, I. (1976). The influence of "Sesame Street" and "Mister Rogers' Neighborhood" on children's social behavior in the preschool. *Child Development, 47,* 138–144.

Coch, L., & French, J. R. P., Jr. (1948). Overcoming resistance to change. *Human Relations, 1,* 512–532.

Cohen, B. C. (1963). *The press and foreign policy.* Princeton, NJ: Princeton University Press.

Cohen, D. (1980). The FTC's advertising substantiation program. *Journal of Marketing, 44,* 26–35.

Cohen, D. K. (1974). The equity package: Cities, families and schools. *Society, 12,* 34–40.

Cohen, J. (1992). A power primer. *Psychological Bulletin, 112,* 155–159.

Cohen, J. B., & Chakravarti, D. (1990). Consumer psychology. *Annual Review of Psychology, 41,* 243–288.

Cohen, S., Evans, G. W., Krantz, D. S., & Stokols, D. (1980). Physiological, motivational, and cognitive effects of aircraft noise on children: Moving from the laboratory to the field. *American Psychologist, 35,* 231–243.

Cohen, S., Evans, G. W., Stokols, D., & Krantz, D. S. (1986). *Behavior, health, and environmental stress.* New York: Plenum.

Cohen, S., Glass, D. C., & Phillips, S. (1979). Environment and health. In H. E. Freeman, S. Levine, & L. G. Reeder (Eds.), *Handbook of medical sociology* (pp. 134–149). Englewood Cliffs, NJ: Prentice-Hall.

Cohen, S., Tyrrell, D. A., & Smith, A. P. (1993). Negative life events, perceived stress, negative affect, and susceptibility to the common cold. *Journal of Personality and Social Psychology, 64,* 131–140.

Cohen, S., & Weinstein, N. (1982). Nonauditory effects of noise on behavior and health. In G. W. Evans (Ed.), *Environmental stress* (pp. 45–74). New York: Cambridge University Press.

Cohn, D. (1992, March 1). Per-can fees catch on as area's trash mounts. *Washington Post,* p. 1.

Cole, R. L., & Caputo, D. A. (1984). The public hearing as an effective citizen participation mechanism: A case study of the General Revenue Sharing Program. *American Political Science Review, 78,* 404–416.

Coleman, J. S. (1975). Racial segregation in the schools: New research with new policy implications. *Phi Delta Kappan, 57,* 75–78.

Coleman, J. S., Campbell, E. Q., Hobson, C. J., McPartland, J., Mood, A. M., Weinfeld, F. D., & York, R. L. (1966). *Equality of educational opportunity.* Washington, DC: U.S. Government Printing Office.

Colgrove v. Battin, 413 U.S. 149 (1973).

Collins, W. A. (1973). Effect of temporal separation between motivation, aggression and consequences: A developmental study. *Developmental Psychology, 8,* 215–221.

Collins, W. A., & Getz, S. K. (1976). Children's social responses following modeled reactions to provocation: Prosocial effects of a television drama. *Journal of Personality, 44,* 488–500.

Collins, W. A., & Zimmerman, S. A. (1975). Convergent and divergent social cues: Effects of televised aggression on children. *Communication Research, 2,* 331–346.

Columbia Broadcasting System. (1977). *Communicating with children through television: Studies of messages and other impressions conveyed by five children's programs.* New York: Author.

Comer, J. (1980). *School power.* New York: Free Press.

Commoner, B. (1990). *Making peace with the planet.* New York: Pantheon.

Comstock, G. (1985). Television and film violence. In S. Apter & A. Goldstein (Eds.), *Youth violence: Programs and prospects.* New York: Pergamon.

Comstock, G. (1991). *Television in America* (2nd ed.). Newbury Park, CA: Sage.

Comstock, G. (1993). The medium and the society: The role of television in American life. In G. Berry & J. Asamen (Eds.), *Children and television: Images in a changing sociocultural world* (pp. 117–131). Newbury Park, CA: Sage.

Comstock, G., Chaffee, S., Katzman, N., McCombs, M., & Roberts, D. (1978). *Television and human behavior.* New York: Columbia University Press.

Comstock, G., & Rubinstein, E. A. (Eds.). (1972). *Television and social behavior.* Washington, DC: U.S. Government Printing Office.

Congressional Digest. (1993, December). *Violence on television: Pros and cons.* Washington, DC: Author.

Conklin, J. E. (1975). *The impact of crime.* New York: Macmillan.

Conover, P. J., & Feldman, S. (1989). Candidate perception in an ambiguous world: Campaigns, cues and inference processes. *American Journal of Political Science, 33,* 912–939.

Conrad, K., Flay, B. R., & Hill, D. (1992). Why children start smoking cigarettes: Predictors of onset. *British Journal of Addiction, 102,* 689–701.

Cook, S. W. (1979). Social science and school desegregation: Did we mislead the Supreme Court? *Personality and Social Psychology Bulletin, 5,* 420–437.

Cook, S. W., & Berrenberg, J. L. (1981). Approaches to encouraging conservation behavior: A review and conceptual framework. *Journal of Social Issues, 37*(2), 73–107.

Cook, T. D. (1991). Clarifying the warrant for generalized causal inferences in quasi-experimentation. In M. McLaughlin & D. C. Phillips (Eds.), *Evaluation and education: At quarter century* (pp. 115–144). Chicago: University of Chicago Press.

Cook, T. D., & Campbell, D. T. (1979). *Quasi-experimentation: Design & analysis issues for field settings.* Chicago: Rand McNally.

Cook, T. D., Campbell, D. T., & Perrachio, L. (1990). Quasi experimentation. In M. D. Dunnette & L. M. Hough (Eds.), *Handbook of industrial and organizational psychology* (2nd ed., Vol. 1, pp. 491–576). Palo Alto, CA: Consulting Psychologists Press.

Cook, T. D., & Flay, B. R. (1978). The persistence of experimentally induced attitude change. In L. Berkowitz (Ed.), *Advances in experimental social psychology* (Vol. 11, pp. 1–57). New York: Academic Press.

Cook, T. D., Leviton, L. C., & Shadish, W. R. (1985). Program evaluation. In G. Lindzey & E. Aronson (Eds.), *The handbook of social psychology* (3rd ed., Vol. 1, pp. 699–777). New York: Random House.

Cook, T. D., & Shadish, W. R. (1994). Social experiments: Some developments over the past fifteen years. *Annual Review of Psychology, 45,* 545–580.

Cooley, C. H. (1956). *Human nature and the social order.* New York: Free Press.

Cooper, C. L., & Marshall, J. (1976). Occupational sources of stress: A review of the literature relating to coronary heart disease and mental ill health. *British Journal of Occupational Psychology, 49,* 11–28.

Cooper, H. (1993). In search of a social fact. A commentary on the study of interpersonal expectations. In P. Blanck (Ed.), *Interpersonal expectations: Theory, research, and application* (pp. 218–226). Paris, France: Cambridge University Press.

Cooper, H., & Hedges, L. V. (1994). *The handbook of research synthesis.* New York: Russell Sage Foundation.

Coovert, M., Penner, L., & MacCallum, R. (1990). Covariance structure modeling in personality and social psychological research: An introduction. In C. Hendrick & M. Clark (Eds.), *Research methods in personality and social psychology* (pp. 185–216). Newbury Park, CA: Sage.

Copple, C., Cline, M., & Smith, A. (1987). *Paths to the future: Long-term effects of Head Start in the Philadelphia School District.* Washington, DC: U.S. Department of Health and Human Services.

Cordes, C. (1982a, August). NAS gives behavioral research a boost: Study calls the benefits "significant and lasting." *APA Monitor, 13*(8), 40–41.

Cordes, C. (1982b, September). One more challenge: Clinical psychologist manages GM plant. *APA Monitor, 13*(9), 3.

Corr, C., Nabe, C., & Corr, D. (1994). *Death and dying, life and living.* Pacific Grove, CA: Brooks/Cole.

Corwin, R. G., & Louis, K. S. (1982). Organizational barriers to the utilization of research. *Administrative Science Quarterly, 27,* 623–640.

Costain, A. N. (1978). Eliminating sex discrimination in education: Lobbying for implementation of Title IX. *Policy Studies Journal, 7,* 189–195.

Costanzo, M., & Costanzo, S. (1994). The death penalty: Public opinions, legal decisions, and juror perspectives. In M. Costanzo & S. Oskamp (Eds.), *Violence and the law* (pp. 246–272). Thousand Oaks, CA: Sage.

Costley, C. L. (1988). Meta-analysis of involvement research. *Advances in Consumer Research, 15,* 554–563.

Cotton, J. L. (1993). *Employee involvement: Methods for improving performance and work attitudes.* Newbury Park, CA: Sage.

Cotton, J. L., & Tuttle, J. (1986). Employee turnover: A meta-analysis and review with implications for research. *Academy of Management Review, 11,* 55–70.

Court, J. H. (1984). Sex and violence: A ripple effect. In N. M. Malamuth & E. Donnerstein (Eds.), *Pornography and sexual aggression* (pp. 143–172). Orlando, FL: Academic Press.

Courtney, A. E., & Whipple, T. W. (1983). *Sex stereotyping in advertising.* Lexington, MA: Lexington.

Covello, V., & Mumpower, J. (1995). Risk analysis and risk management: An historical perspective. In S. Cutter (Ed.), *Environmental risks and hazards* (pp. 33–54). Englewood Cliffs, NJ: Prentice Hall.

Cowan, C. L., Thompson, W. C., & Ellsworth, P. C. (1984). The effects of death qualification on jurors' predisposition to convict and on the quality of deliberation. *Law and Human Behavior, 8,* 53–80.

Cox, T. (1985). Repetitive work: Occupational stress and health. In C. L. Cooper & M. J. Smith (Eds.), *Job stress and blue collar work* (pp. 85–111). Chichester, England: Wiley.

Coyle, S. L., Boruch, R. F., & Turner, C. F. (Eds.). (1991). *Evaluating AIDS prevention programs.* Washington, DC: National Academy Press.

Craig, J. M., & Sherif, C. W. (1986). The effectiveness of men and women in problem solving groups as a function of group gender composition. *Sex Roles, 14,* 453–466.

Craig, R. L. (1987). *Training and development handbook: A guide to human resource development* (3rd ed.). New York: McGraw-Hill.

Craig, R. S. (1992). The effects of television day part on gender portrayals in television commercials: A content analysis. *Sex Roles, 26,* 197–211.

Craik, K. H., & Feimer, N. R. (1987). Environmental assessment. In D. Stokols & I. Altman (Eds.), *Handbook of environmental psychology* (Vol. 1, pp. 891–918). New York: Wiley.

Crain, R. L., & Mahard, R. E. (1978). Desegregation and Black achievement: A review of the research. *Law and Contemporary Problems, 42*(3), 17–56.

Crain, R. L., & McPartland, J. (1984). A long-term view of desegregation: Some recent studies of graduates as adults. *Phi Delta Kappan, 66,* 259–264.

Cramer, D. (1993). Tenure, commitment, and satisfaction of college graduates in an engineering firm. *Journal of Social Psychology, 133,* 791–796.

Crandall, C. S., Priesler, J. J., & Aussprung, J. (1992). Measuring life event stress in the lives of college students: The Undergraduate Stress Questionnaire (USQ). *Journal of Behavioral Medicine, 15,* 627–662.

Creer, R. N., Gray, R. M., & Treshow, M. (1970). Differential responses to air pollution as an environmental health problem. *Journal of the Air Pollution Control Association, 20,* 814–818.

Crocker, J., & Major, B. (1989). Social stigma and self-esteem: The self-protective properties of stigma. *Psychological Review, 96,* 608–630.

Crocker, J., & Schwartz, I. (1985). Prejudice and ingroup favoritism in a minimal intergroup situation: Effects of self-esteem. *Personality and Social Psychology Bulletin, 11,* 379–386.

Cronbach, L. J. (1957). The two disciplines of scientific psychology. *American Psychologist, 12,* 671–684.

Cronbach, L. J. (1982). *Designing evaluations of educational and social programs.* San Francisco: Jossey-Bass.

Cronbach, L. J., et al. (1980). *Toward reform of program evaluation: Aims, methods, and institutional arrangements.* San Francisco: Jossey-Bass.

Crosby, F. (1976). A model of egoistical relative deprivation. *Psychological Review, 83,* 85–113.

Crosby, F. (1982). *Relative deprivation and working women.* New York: Oxford University Press.

Cross, D., & Warr, P. (1971). Work-group composition as a factor in productivity. *Industrial Relations Journal, 2,* 3–13.

Crowne, D. P., & Marlowe, D. (1964). *The approval motive: Studies in evaluative dependence.* New York: Wiley.

Crull, P. (1980). The impact of sexual harassment on the job: A profile of the experiences of 92 women. In D. A. Neugarten & J. M. Shafritz (Eds.), *Sexuality in organizations* (pp. 67–71). Oak Park, IL: Moore.

Cutler, B. L., & Penrod, S. D. (1989). Forensically relevant moderators of the relation between eyewitness identification accuracy and confidence. *Journal of Applied Psychology, 74,* 650–652.

Cutler, B. L., & Penrod, S. D. (1995). *Mistaken identification: The eyewitness, psychology, and the law.* New York: Cambridge University Press.

Cutler, B. L., Penrod, S. D., & Martens, T. K. (1987). The reliability of eyewitness identification: The role of system and estimator variables. *Law and Human Behavior, 11,* 223–258.

Cutlip, S. C. (1954). Content and flow of AP news—From trunk to TTS to reader. *Journalism Quarterly, 31,* 434–446.

Dake, K. (1992). Myths of nature: Culture and the social construction of risk. *Journal of Social Issues, 48*(4), 21–37.

Daschle, T. A., Cohen, R. J., & Rice, C. L. (1993). Health care reform: Single-payer models. *American Psychologist, 48,* 265–269.

D'Atri, D. A., & Ostfeld, A. (1975). Crowding: Its effects on the elevation of blood pressure in a prison setting. *Preventive Medicine, 4,* 550–566.

David, H. (1994). Reproductive rights and reproductive behavior. *American Psychologist, 49,* 343–349.

Davidson, E. S., Yasuna, A., & Tower, A. (1979). The effects of television cartoons on sex-role stereotyping in young girls. *Child Development, 50,* 597–600.

Davies, G. (1996). Children's identification evidence. In S. Sporer, R. Malpass, & G. Koehnken (Eds.), *Psychological issues in eyewitness identification* (pp. 233–258). Mahwah, NJ: Erlbaum.

Davis, H. R. (1973). Innovation and change. In S. Feldman (Ed.), *Administration in mental health.* Springfield, IL: Thomas.

Davis, J. H., Bray, R. M., & Holt, R. W. (1977). The empirical study of decision processes in juries: A critical review. In J. L. Tapp & F. J. Levine (Eds.), *Law, justice, and the individual in society: Psychological and legal issues* (pp. 326–361). New York: Holt, Rinehart & Winston.

Davis, J. H., Laughlin, P. R., & Komorita, S. S. (1976). The social psychology of small groups: Cooperative and mixed-motive interaction. *Annual Review of Psychology, 27,* 501–541.

Dawkins, M. (1994). Long-term effects of school desegregation on African Americans: Evidence from the National Survey of Black Americans. *Negro Educational Review, 45,* 4–15.

Dawson, P. A., & Zinser, J. E. (1971). Broadcast expenditures and electoral outcomes in the 1970 congressional elections. *Public Opinion Quarterly, 35,* 398–402.

Day, G. S. (1982). Assessing the effects of information disclosure requirements. In D. A. Aaker & G. S. Day (Eds.), *Consumerism: Search for the consumer interest* (4th ed., pp. 152–167). New York: Free Press.

Day, J. (1995). *The vanishing vision: The inside story of public television.* Berkeley: University of California Press.

DeAngelis, T. (1994). Psychologists' expertise is often essential in court. *APA Monitor, 25*(6), 1, 29.

de La Garza, R. O., Falcon, A., Garcia, F. C., & Garcia, J. A. (1992). Hispanic Americans in the mainstream of U.S. politics. *The Public Perspective, 3*(5), 10–22.

de Vries, S., & Pettigrew, T. F. (1994). A comparative perspective on affirmative action: *Positieve aktie* in the Netherlands. *Basic and Applied Social Psychology, 15,* 179–199.

Deaux, K., & Kite, M. (1993). Gender stereotypes. In F. L. Denmark & M. A. Paludi (Eds.), *Psychology of women: A handbook of issues and theories* (pp. 107–139). Westport, CT: Greenwood.

Deaux, K., & Lewis, L. L. (1984). The structure of gender stereotypes: Interrelationships among components and gender labels. *Journal of Personality and Social Psychology, 46,* 991–1004.

Deci, E. L., & Ryan, R. M. (1980). The empirical exploration of intrinsic motivational processes. In L. Berkowitz (Ed.), *Advances in experimental social psychology* (Vol. 13, pp. 40–80). New York: Academic Press.

Deffenbacher, J., Lynch, R., Oetting, E., & Kemper, C. (1996). Anger reduction in early adolescents. *Journal of Counseling Psychology, 43,* 149–157.

DeJong, W. (1979). An examination of self-perception mediation of the foot-in-the-door effect. *Journal of Personality and Social Psychology, 37,* 2221–2239.

DeJong, W. (1986). Project D.A.R.E.: Teaching kids to say "no" to drugs and alcohol. In *Schools without drugs: The challenge.* Washington, DC: U.S. Department of Education.

DeJong, W. (1987). A short term evaluation of Project D.A.R.E.: Preliminary indications of effectiveness. *Journal of Drug Education, 17,* 279–294.

DeLeon, P. H., O'Keefe, A. M., vandenBos, G. R., & Kraut, A. G. (1982). How to influence public policy: A blueprint for activism. *American Psychologist, 37,* 476–485.

Dennis, M. L., Soderstrom, E. J., Koncinski, W. S., & Cavanaugh, B. (1990). Effective dissemination of energy-relevant information: Applying social psychology and evaluation research. *American Psychologist, 45,* 1109–1117.

DePaulo, B. M. (1992). Nonverbal behavior and self-presentation. *Psychological Bulletin, 111,* 203–243.

DePaulo, B. M., & Pfeiffer, R. L. (1986). On-the-job experience and skill at detecting deception. *Journal of Applied Social Psychology, 16,* 249–267.

DePaulo, B. M., Stone, J. I., & Lassiter, G. D. (1985). Deceiving and detecting deceit. In B. R. Schlenker (Ed.), *The self and social life* (pp. 323–370). New York: McGraw-Hill.

Derksen, L., & Gartrell, J. (1993). The social context of recycling. *American Sociological Review, 58,* 434–442.

DeSario, J., & Langton, S. (Eds.). (1987). *Citizen participation in public decision making.* Westport, CT: Greenwood.

Deslauriers, B., & Everett, P. (1977). Effects of intermittent and continuous token reinforcement on bus ridership. *Journal of Applied Psychology, 62,* 369–375.

Deutsch, M. (1969). Conflicts: Productive and destructive. *Journal of Social Issues, 25*(1), 7–41.

Deutsch, M. (1975). Introduction. In M. Deutsch & H. A. Hornstein (Eds.), *Applying social psychology: Implications for research, practice, and training* (pp. 1–12). Hillsdale, NJ: Erlbaum.

Deutsch, M. (1980). Socially relevant research: Comments on "applied" versus "basic" research. In R. F. Kidd & M. J. Saks (Eds.), *Advances in applied social psychology* (Vol. 1). Hillsdale, NJ: Erlbaum.

Deutscher, M., & Chein, I. (1948). The psychological effects of enforced segregation: A survey of social science opinion. *Journal of Psychology, 26,* 259–287.

Devall, B., & Sessions, G. (1985). *Deep ecology: Living as if nature mattered.* Salt Lake City: Peregrine Smith.

Deveny, K. (1992, October 15). Displays pay off for grocery marketers. *Wall Street Journal,* p. B1.

DeVillar, R. (1994). The rhetoric and practice of cultural diversity in U.S. schools: Socialization, resocialization, and quality schooling. In R. DeVillar, C. Faltis, & J. Cummins (Eds.), *Cultural diversity in schools: From rhetoric to practice* (pp. 25–56). New York: State University of New York Press.

Devine, P. G. (1989). Stereotypes and prejudice: Their automatic and controlled components. *Journal of Personality and Social Psychology, 56,* 5–18.

Devine, P. G., Monteith, M. J., Zuwerink, J. R., & Elliot, A. J. (1991). Prejudice with and without compunction. *Journal of Personality and Social Psychology, 60,* 817–830.

Devlin, P. (1976, April 26). *Report to the Secretary of State for the House Department of the Departmental Committee on Evidence of Identification in Criminal Cases, House of Commons.* London: Her Majesty's Stationery Office. (Cited in Saks & Hastie, 1978.)

Diamond, S. S. (1974). A jury experiment reanalyzed. *University of Michigan Journal of Law Reform, 7,* 520–532.

Dickerson, C. A., Thibodeau, R., Aronson, E., & Miller, D. (1992). Using cognitive dissonance to encourage water conservation. *Journal of Applied Social Psychology, 22,* 841–854.

Diener, E., & DeFour, D. (1978). Does television violence enhance program popularity? *Journal of Personality and Social Psychology, 36,* 333–341.

Diener, E., & Diener, C. (1996). Most people are happy. *Psychological Science, 7,* 181–185.

Dieter, R. C. (1993). *Millions misspent: What politicians don't say about the high costs of the death penalty.* Washington, DC: Death Penalty Information Center.

Diges, M., Rubio, M., & Rodriguez, M. (1992). Eyewitness memory and time of day. In F. Lösel, D. Bender, & T. Bliesener (Eds.), *Psychology and law: International perspectives* (pp. 317–320). Berlin: de Gruyter.

Dillard, J. (1991). The current status of research on sequential-request compliance techniques. Special issue: Meta-analysis in personality and social psychology. *Personality and Social Psychology Bulletin, 17,* 283–288.

Dillehay, R. C., & Nietzel, M. T. (1980). Constructing a science of jury behavior. In L. Wheeler (Ed.), *Review of personality and social psychology* (Vol. 1, pp. 246–264). Beverly Hills, CA: Sage.

Dillman, D. A. (1978). *Mail and telephone surveys: The total design method.* New York: Wiley.

Dillman, D. A. (1991). The design and administration of mail surveys. *Annual Review of Sociology, 17,* 225–249.

Dion, K. L. (1985). Sex, gender, and groups. In V. E. O'Leary, R. K. Unger, & B. S. Wallston (Eds.), *Women, gender, and social psychology* (pp. 293–347). Hillsdale, NJ: Erlbaum.

DiSilvestro, R. (1991). There is an environmental crisis. In N. Bernards (Ed.) *The environmental crisis: Opposing viewpoints.* San Diego, CA: Greenhaven.

Dollard, J., & Miller, N. E. (1950). *Personality and psychotherapy: An analysis in terms of learning, thinking, and culture.* New York: McGraw-Hill.

Dominick, J. R. (1973). Crime and law enforcement on prime-time television. *Public Opinion Quarterly, 37,* 241–250.

Dominick, J. R., & Greenberg, B. S. (1970). Three seasons of Blacks on television. *Journal of Advertising Research, 10*(2), 21–27.

Domjan, M. (1993). *The principles of learning and behavior* (3rd ed.). Pacific Grove, CA: Brooks/Cole.

Donaldson, S. I. (1995). Peer influence on adolescent drug use: A perspective from the trenches of experimental evaluation research. *American Psychologist, 50,* 801–802.

Donaldson, S. I., Graham, J. W., & Hansen, W. B. (1994). Testing the generalizability of intervening mechanism theories: Understanding the effects of adolescent drug use prevention interventions. *Journal of Behavioral Medicine, 17,* 195–216.

Donaldson, S. I., Graham, J. W., Piccinin, A. M., & Hansen, W. B. (1995). Resistance-skills training and onset of alcohol use: Evidence for beneficial and potentially harmful effects in public schools and in private Catholic schools. *Health Psychology, 14,* 291–300.

Donnerstein, E., Donnerstein, M., & Barrett, G. (1976). Where is the facilitation of media violence: The effects of nonexposure and placement of anger arousal. *Journal of Research in Personality, 10,* 386–398.

Donnerstein, E., & Linz, D. (1994). Sexual violence in the mass media. In M. Costanzo & S. Oskamp (Eds.), *Violence and the law* (pp. 9–36). Thousand Oaks, CA: Sage.

Donnerstein, E., Linz, D., & Penrod, S. (1987). *The question of pornography: Research findings and policy implications.* New York: Free Press.

Doob, A. N. (1982). The role of the mass media in creating exaggerated levels of fear of being the victim of a violent crime. In P. Stringer (Ed.), *Confronting social issues: Some applications of social psychology* (Vol. 1). London: Academic Press.

Doob, A. N., & Macdonald, G. E. (1979). Television viewing and fear of victimization: Is the relationship causal? *Journal of Personality and Social Psychology, 37,* 170–179.

Doob, L. (1935). *Propaganda, its psychology and technique.* New York: Holt.

Dorans, N. J., & Livingston, S. A. (1987). Male-female differences in SAT-verbal ability among students of high SAT-mathematical ability. *Journal of Educational Measurement, 24,* 65–71.

Dorken, H. (1981). Coming of age legislatively: In 21 steps. *American Psychologist, 36,* 165–173.

Dorr, A. (1986). *Television and children: A special medium for a special audience.* Beverly Hills, CA: Sage.

Dorr, A., Graves, S. B., & Phelps, E. (1980). Television literacy for young children. *Journal of Communication, 30,* 71–83.

Dougherty, T., Turban, D., & Callender, J. (1994). Confirming first impressions in the employment interview: A field study of interviewer behavior. *Journal of Applied Psychology, 79,* 659–665.

Douglas, S. J. (1995). *Where the girls are: Growing up female with the mass media.* New York: Times Books.

Dovidio, J., & Gaertner, S. (1991). Changes in the expression and assessment of racial prejudice. In H. Knopke, R. Norrell, & R. Rogers (Eds.), *Opening doors: Perspectives on race relations in contemporary America* (pp. 119–148). Tuscaloosa: University of Alabama Press.

Downing, M. (1974). Heroine of the daytime serial. *Journal of Communication, 24*(2), 130–137.

Doyle, J. B., Wilcox, B. L., & Reppucci, N. D. (1983). Training for social and community change. In E. Seidman (Ed.), *Handbook of social intervention* (pp. 615–638). Beverly Hills, CA: Sage.

Dressel, P. L., Carter, V., & Balachandran, A. (1995). Second-order victim-blaming. *Journal of Sociology & Social Welfare, 22,* 107–123.

Dreyden, J. I., & Gallagher, S. A. (1989). The effects of time and direction changes on the SAT performance of academically talented adolescents. *Journal for the Education of the Gifted, 12,* 187–204.

Dreyfus, D. A. (1977). The limitations of policy research in congressional decision making. In C. H. Weiss (Ed.), *Using social research in public policy making.* Lexington, MA: Lexington.

Droge, C. (1989). Shaping the route to attitude change: Central versus peripheral processing through comparative versus noncomparative advertising. *Journal of Marketing Research, 26,* 193–204.

Dukes, R., Ullman, J., & Stein, J. (1995). An evaluation of D.A.R.E. using a Solomon four-group design with latent variables. *Evaluation Review, 19,* 409–435.

Dukes, R., Ullman, J., & Stein, J. (1996). Three-year follow-up of drug abuse resistance education (DARE). *Evaluation Review, 20,* 49–66.

DuMelle, F. (1993). Laws protecting nonsmokers. *EPA Journal, 9,* 21–22.

Dunbar-Jacob, J., Dwyer, K., & Dunning, E. J. (1991). Compliance with antihypertensive regimen: A review of the research in the 1980s. *Annals of Behavioral Medicine, 13,* 31–39.

Duncan, G. (1994). Families and neighbors as sources of disadvantage in the schooling decisions of White and Black adolescents. *American Journal of Education, 103,* 20–53.

Dunlap, R. E. (1991). Trends in public opinion toward environmental issues: 1965–1990. *Society and Natural Resources, 4,* 285–312.

Dunlap, R. E., Gallup, G., & Gallup, A. (1993). Global environmental concern: Results from an international pubic opinion survey. *Environment, 35,* 7–15, 33–39.

Dunlap, R. E., & Scarce, R. (1991). The polls and poll trends: Environmental problems and protection. *Public Opinion Quarterly, 55,* 651–672.

Dunlap, R. E., & Van Liere, K. D. (1978). The "new environmental paradigm:" A proposed measuring instrument and preliminary results. *Jounal of Environmental Education, 9*(4), 10–19.

Dunnette, M. D., & Hough, L. M. (Eds.). (1990–1994). *Handbook of industrial & organizational psychology* (2nd ed., Vols. 1–4). Palo Alto, CA: Consulting Psychologists Press.

Durkin, K. (1985). Television and sex-role acquisition: I. Content. *British Journal of Social Psychology, 24,* 101–113.

Dussere, S. (1976). *The effects of television advertising on children's eating habits.* Unpublished doctoral dissertation, University of Massachusetts at Amherst.

Dwyer, W. O., & Leeming, F. C. (1995). *Earth's eleventh hour: Environmental readings from the Washington Post.* Boston: Allyn & Bacon.

Eagly, A. H. (1987). *Sex differences in social behavior: A social role interpretation.* Hillsdale, NJ: Erlbaum.

Eagly, A. H. (1995). The science and politics of comparing women and men. *American Psychologist, 50,* 145–158.

Eagly, A. H., & Carli, L. L. (1981). Sex of researchers and sex-typed communications as determinants of sex differences in influenceability: A meta-analysis of social influence studies. *Psychological Bulletin, 90,* 1–20.

Eagly, A. H., & Chaiken, S. (1993). *The psychology of attitudes.* Fort Worth, TX: Harcourt Brace Jovanovich.

Eagly, A. H., & Johnson, B. T. (1990). Gender and leadership style: A meta-analysis. *Psychological Bulletin, 108,* 233–256.

Eagly, A. H., & Karau, S. J. (1991). Gender and the emergence of leaders: A meta-analysis. *Journal of Personality and Social Psychology, 60,* 685–710.

Eagly, A. H., Karau, S. J., & Makhijani, M. G. (1995). Gender and the effectiveness of leaders: A meta-analysis. *Psychological Bulletin, 117,* 125–145.

Earn, B. M., & Kroger, R. O. (1976). The subject in psychological experiments: Effects of experimentally induced subject roles on laboratory performance. *Personality and Social Psychology Bulletin, 2,* 466–469.

Easterbrook, G. (1991). The environment is improving. In N. Bernards (Ed.), *The environmental crisis: Opposing viewpoints.* San Diego, CA: Greenhaven.

Ebbesen, E. B., & Konecni, V. J. (1982). An analysis of the bail system. In V. J. Konecni & E. B. Ebbesen (Eds.), *The criminal justice system: A social psychological analysis.* San Francisco: Freeman.

Eberhardt, J. L., & Fiske, S. T. (1996). Motivating individuals to change: What is a target to do? In C. N. Macrae, C. Stangor, & M. Hewstone (Eds.), *Stereotypes and stereotyping* (pp. 369–415). New York: Guilford.

Eccles, A., Marshall, W. L., & Barbaree, H. E. (1988). The vulnerability of erectile measures to repeated assessments. *Behavior Research and Therapy, 26,* 179–183.

Eccles, J. S. (1989). Bringing young women to math and science. In M. Crawford & M. Gentry (Eds.), *Gender and thought: Psychological perspectives* (pp. 36–58). New York: Springer.

Eccles, J. S., Jacobs, J. E., Harold, R. D., Yoon, K. S., Arbreton, A., & Freedman-Dorn, C. (1993). Parents and gender-role socialization during the middle childhood and adolescent years. In S. Oskamp & M. Costanzo (Eds.), *Gender issues in contemporary society* (pp. 59–83). Newbury Park, CA: Sage.

Eckberg, D., & Blocker, T. (1989). Varieties of religious involvement and environmental concerns: Testing the Lynn White thesis. *Journal of the Scientific Study of Religion, 28,* 73–80.

Edell, J. A., & Burke, M. C. (1987). The power of feelings in understanding advertising effects. *Journal of Consumer Research, 14,* 421–433.

Edelman, M. W. (1973). Southern school desegregation, 1954–1973: A judicial-political overview. *Annals of the American Academy of Political and Social Science, 407,* 32–42.

Edney, J. J. (1980). The commons problem: Alternative perspectives. *American Psychologist, 35,* 131–150.

Edwards, J., Tindale, R. S., Heath, L., & Posavac, E. (Eds.). (1990). *Social influence processes and prevention.* New York: Plenum.

Ehrlich, P. R., & Ehrlich, A. H. (1991). *Healing the planet.* New York: Addison-Wesley.

Ekman, P. (1992). *Telling lies: Clues to deceit in the marketplace, politics, and marriage.* New York: Norton.

Elaad, E. (1990). Detection of guilty knowledge in real-life criminal investigations. *Journal of Applied Psychology, 75,* 521–529.

Elden, M., & Chisholm, R. F. (Eds.). (1993). Emerging varieties of action research [Special issue]. *Human Relations, 46,* 121–298.

Elliot, R. (1991). Social science data and the APA: The *Lockhart* brief as a case in point. *Law and Human Behavior, 15,* 423–437.

Elliott, C. H., & Denney, D. R. (1978). A multiple component treatment approach to smoking reduction. *Journal of Consulting and Clinical Psychology, 46,* 1300–1339.

Elliott, R., & Vasta, R. (1970). The modeling of sharing: Effects associated with vicarious reinforcement, symbolization, age and generalization. *Journal of Experimental Child Psychology, 10,* 8–15.

Ellis, E. (1983). A review of empirical rape research: Victim reactions and response to treatment. *Clinical Psychology Review, 3,* 473–490.

Ellis, G. T., & Sekyra, F. (1972). The effect of aggressive cartoons on the behavior of first grade children. *Journal of Psychology, 81,* 37–43.

Ellis, P., & Gaskell, G. (1978). *A review of social research on the individual energy consumer.* Unpublished manuscript, London School of Economics and Political Science.

Ellison, C. G., & Powers, D. A. (1994). The contact hypothesis and racial attitudes among Black Americans. *Social Science Quarterly, 75,* 385–400.

Elms, A. C. (1982). Keeping deception honest: Justifying conditions for social scientific research stratagems. In T. L. Beauchamp, R. R. Faden, R. J. Wallace, Jr., & L. R. Walters (Eds.), *Ethical issues in social science research* (pp. 232–245). Baltimore: Johns Hopkins University Press.

Engel, J. F., Blackwell, R. D., & Miniard, P. W. (1993). *Consumer behavior* (8th ed.). Fort Worth, TX: Dryden.

Engel, J. F., Warshaw, M. R., & Kinnear, T. C. (1994). *Promotional strategy: Managing the marketing communications process.* Burr Ridge, IL: Irwin.

England, P., & McCreary, L. (1987). Gender inequality in paid employment. In B. B. Hess & M. M. Ferree (Eds.), *Analyzing gender: A handbook of social science research* (pp. 286–320). Newbury Park, CA: Sage.

Ennett, S., Tobler, N., Ringwalt, C., & Flewelling, R. (1994). How effective is Drug Abuse Resistance Education? A meta-analysis of project DARE outcome evaluations. *American Journal of Public Health, 84,* 1394–1401.

Environmental Defense Fund. (1995, May). Global climate data show return of warming trend. *EDF Letter, 26*(3), 1, 8.

Equal Employment Opportunity Commission. (1980). Guidelines on discrimination because of sex. *Federal Register, 45,* 74676–74677.

Erikson, R., Wright, G., & McIver, J. (1993). *Statehouse democracy.* New York: Cambridge University Press.

Eron, L. D., Gentry, J. H., & Schlegel, P. (Eds.). (1994). *Reason to hope: A psychosocial perspective on violence and youth.* Washington, DC: American Psychological Association.

Eron, L. D., & Huesmann, L. R. (1980, September). *Integrating field and laboratory investigations of televised violence and aggression.* Paper presented at American Psychological Association meeting, Montreal.

Eron, L. D., & Huesmann, L. R. (1984). The control of aggressive behavior by changes in attitudes, values, and the conditions of learning. In R. J. Blanchard & D. C. Blanchard (Eds.), *Advances in the study of aggression* (pp. 139–171). New York: Academic Press.

Eron, L. D., Huesmann, L. R., Lefkowitz, M. M., & Walder, L. O. (1972). Does television violence cause aggression? *American Psychologist, 27,* 253–263.

Etzioni, A. (1969). *The semi-professions and their organization: Teachers, nurses, social workers.* New York: Free Press.

Evans, G. W., & Cohen, S. (1987). Environmental stress. In D. Stokols & I. Altman (Eds.), *Handbook of environmental psychology* (Vol. 1, pp. 571–610). New York: Wiley.

Evans, R. I., Hansen, W. B., & Mittelmark, M. B. (1977). Increasing the validity of self-reports of smoking behavior in children. *Journal of Applied Psychology, 62,* 521–523.

Everett, P., & Watson, B. (1987). Psychological contributions to transportation. In D. Stokols & I. Altman (Eds.), *Handbook of Environmental psychology* (Vol. 2, pp. 987–1008). New York: Wiley.

Eysenck, H. J. (1990). Biological dimensions of personality. In L. S. Pervin (Ed.), *Handbook of personality theory and research* (pp. 244–276). New York: Guilford.

Eysenck, H. J., & Nias, D. K. B. (1978). *Sex, violence and the media.* London: Morris Temple Smith.

Fairweather, G. W. (1979). Experimental development and dissemination of an alternative to psychiatric hospitalization: Scientific methods for social change. In R. F. Munoz, L. R. Snowden, & J. G. Kelly (Eds.), *Social and psychological research in community settings.* San Francisco: Jossey-Bass.

Fairweather, G. W. (1980). *The Fairweather lodge: A twenty-five year retrospective.* San Francisco: Jossey-Bass.

Fairweather, G. W., Sanders, D. H., & Tornatzky, L. G. (1974). *Creating change in mental health organizations.* New York: Pergamon.

Farkas, A., & Tetrick, L. (1989). A three-wave longitudinal analysis of the causal ordering of satisfaction and commitment on turnover decisions. *Journal of Applied Psychology, 74,* 855–868.

Farley, R., & Frey, W. (1994). Changes in the segregation of Whites from Blacks during the 1980s: Small steps toward a more racially integrated society. *American Sociological Review, 59,* 23–45.

Farley, R., Steeh, C., Krysan, M., Jackson, T., & Reeves, K. (1994). Stereotypes and segregation: Neighborhoods in the Detroit area. *American Journal of Sociology, 100,* 750–780.

Farquhar, J. W., Fortmann, S. P., Flora, J. A., Taylor, C. B., Haskell, W. L., Williams, P. T., Maccoby, N., & Wood, P. D. (1990). Effects of communitywide education on cardiovascular disease risk factors. *Journal of the American Medical Association, 264,* 359–365.

Farr, J. L., & Seaver, W. B. (1975). Stress and discomfort in psychological research: Subject perceptions of experimental procedures. *American Psychologist, 30,* 770–773.

Fazio, R. H. (1986). How do attitudes guide behavior? In R. M. Sorrentino & E. T. Higgins (Eds.), *The handbook of motivation and cognition: Foundations of social behavior* (pp. 204–243). New York: Guilford.

Fazio, R. H., Powell, M. C., & Williams, C. J. (1989). The role of attitude accessibility in the attitude-to-behavior process. *Journal of Consumer Research, 16,* 280–288.

Feagin, J. R. (1980). School desegregation: A political-economic perspective. In W. G. Stephan & J. R. Feagin (Eds.), *School desegregation: Past, present, and future* (pp. 25–50). New York: Plenum.

Federal Glass Ceiling Commission. (1995, November). *A solid investment: Making full use of the nation's human capital.* Washington, DC: Author.

Federal Trade Commission. (1981, October 30). Listerine corrective ads change consumer awareness of product's effectiveness. *FTC News Summary,* pp. 1–2.

Feeny, D., Berkes, F., McCay, B., & Acheson, J. (1990). The tragedy of the commons: Twenty-two years later. *Human Ecology, 18,* 1–19.

Feild, H. S., & Barnett, N. J. (1978). Simulated jury trials: Students vs. "real" people as jurors. *Journal of Social Psychology, 104,* 287–293.

Ferratt, T. W., & Starke, F. A. (1977). Satisfaction, motivation, and productivity: The complex connection. In J. L. Gray & F. A. Starke (Eds.), *Readings in organizational behavior: Concepts and applications.* Columbus, OH: Merrill.

Feshbach, S., & Singer, R. D. (1971). *Television and aggression: An experimental field study.* San Francisco: Jossey-Bass.

Festinger, L. (1954). A theory of social comparison processes. *Human Relations, 7,* 117–140.

Festinger, L. (1957). *A theory of cognitive dissonance.* Stanford, CA: Stanford University Press.

Fetterman, D. M., Kaftarian, S. J., & Wandersman, A. (1996). *Empowerment evaluation: Knowledge and tools for self-assessment and accountability.* Thousand Oaks, CA: Sage.

Fiedler, F. E. (1954). Assumed similarity measures as predictors of team effectiveness. *Journal of Abnormal and Social Psychology, 49,* 381–388.

Fiedler, F. E. (1955). The influence of leader-keyman relations on combat crew effectiveness. *Journal of Abnormal and Social Psychology, 51,* 227–235.

Fiedler, F. E. (1964). A contingency model of leadership effectiveness. In L. Berkowitz (Ed.), *Advances in experimental social psychology* (Vol. 1, pp. 150–190). New York: Academic Press.

Fiedler, F. E. (1966). The effect of leadership and cultural heterogeneity on group performance: A test of the contingency model. *Journal of Experimental Social Psychology, 2,* 237–264.

Fiedler, F. E. (1967). *A theory of leadership effectiveness.* New York: McGraw-Hill.

Fiedler, F. E. (1978). The contingency model and the dynamics of the leadership process. In L. Berkowitz (Ed.), *Advances in experimental social psychology* (Vol. 11, pp. 59–112). New York: Academic Press.

Fiedler, F. E. (1993). The leadership situation and the black box in contingency theories. In M. Chemers & R. Ayman (Eds.), *Leadership theory and research: Perspectives and directions* (pp. 1–28). San Diego, CA: Academic Press.

Fiedler, F. E. (1995). Cognitive resources and leadership performance. *Applied Psychology: An International Review, 44,* 5–28.

Fiedler, F. E. & Garcia, J. E. (1987). *New approaches to effective leadership: Cognitive resources and organizational performance.* New York: Wiley.

Fiedler, F. E., & House, R. J. (1988). Leadership theory and research. A report of progress. In C. L. Cooper & I. T. Robertson (Eds.), *International review of industrial and organizational psychology* (pp. 73–91). Chichester, England: Wiley.

Fiedler, F. E., & House, R. J. (1994). Leadership theory research: A report of progress. In C. L. Cooper & I. T. Robertson (Eds.), *Key reviews in managerial psychology: Concepts and research for practice* (pp. 97–116). Chichester, England: Wiley.

Fiedler, F. E., & Link, T. G. (1994). Leader intelligence, interpersonal stress and task performance. In R. J. Sternberg & R. K. Wagner (Eds.), *Mind in context: Interactionist perspectives on human intelligence* (pp. 152–167. Cambridge, England: Cambridge University Press.

Fiedler, F. E., & Mahar, L. (1979). The effectiveness of contingency model training: A review of the validation of Leader Match. *Personnel Psychology, 32,* 45–62.

Field, C. G. (1980). Social testing for United States housing policy: The Experimental Housing Allowance Program. In Organisation for Economic Co-operation and Development, *The utilisation of the social sciences in policy making in the United States: Case studies.* Paris: OECD.

Fields, C. M. (1981, February 2). Much research with human subjects freed from close scrutiny by panels. *Chronicle of Higher Education,* pp. 1, 16.

Fierman, J. (1990, July 30). Why women still don't hit the top. *Fortune,* pp. 83–93.

Fife, B. L. (1992). *Desegregation in American schools: Comparative intervention strategies.* New York: Praeger.

Final Report of the Surgeon General's Commission on Pornography. (1986). Nashville, TN: Rutledge Hill.

Finckenauer, J. O. (1978). Crime as a national political issue: 1964–76. *Crime and Delinquency, 24,* 13–27.

Fingerhut, L. A., & Kleinman, J. C. (1990). International and interstate comparisons of homicide among young males. *Journal of the American Medical Association, 263,* 3292–3295.

Finks, P. D. (1984). *The radical vision of Saul Alinsky.* New York: Paulist Press.

Finney, J. W., & Moos, R. H. (1992). The long-term course of treated alcoholism, II: Predictors and correlates of 10-year functioning and mortality. *Journal of Studies on Alcoholism, 53,* 142–153.

Fiore, M. C., Newcomb, P., & McBride, P. (1993). Natural history and epidemiology of tobacco use and addiction. In C. T. Orleans & J. Slade (Eds.), *Nicotine addiction: Principles and management* (pp. 89–104). New York: Oxford University Press.

Fiore, M. C., Novotny, T. E., Pierce, J. P., Giovino, G. A.,

Hatziandreu, E. J., Newcomb, P., Surawicz, T. S., & Davis, R. M. (1990). Methods used to quit smoking in the United States: Do cessation programs help? *Journal of the American Medical Association, 263,* 2760–2765.

Fish, J. M. (1995). Why psychologists should learn some anthropology. *American Psychologist, 50,* 44–45.

Fishbein, M., & Ajzen, I. (1975). *Belief, attitude, intention, and behavior: An introduction to theory and research.* Reading, MA: Addison-Wesley.

Fishbein, M., et al. (1996). Using a theory-based community intervention to reduce AIDS risk behaviors: The CDC's AIDS Community Demonstration Projects. In S. Oskamp & S. Thompson (Eds.), *Understanding and predicting HIV risk behavior: Safer sex and drug use* (pp. 177–206). Thousand Oaks, CA: Sage.

Fisher, E. B., Lichtenstein, E., & Haire-Joshu, D. (1993). Multiple determinants of tobacco use and cessation. In C. T. Orleans & J. Slade (Eds.), *Nicotine addiction: Principles and management* (pp. 59–88). New York: Oxford University Press.

Fisher, J. D., & Fisher, W. A. (1992). Changing AIDS-risk behavior. *Psychological Bulletin, 3,* 455–474.

Fisher, K. (1983, February). New NBC study downplays screen's impact on viewer. *APA Monitor, 14*(2), 8.

Fisher, R. (1994). *Let the people decide: Neighborhood organizing in America* (updated ed.). New York: Twayne.

Fisher, R., McCauley, M., & Geiselman, R. E. (1994). Improving eyewitness testimony with the cognitive interview. In D. Ross, J. D. Read, & M. Toglia (Eds.), *Adult eyewitness testimony: Current trends and developments* (pp. 245–272). New York: Cambridge University Press.

Fisher, R. J. (1982). The professional practice of applied social psychology: Identity, training, and certification. In L. Bickman (Ed.), *Applied social psychology annual* (Vol. 3, pp. 25–56). Beverly Hills, CA: Sage.

Fisher, R. J. (1993). Developing the field of interactive conflict resolution: Issues in training, funding, and institutionalization. *Political Psychology, 14,* 123–138.

Fiske, A. P. (1995). The cultural dimensions of psychological research: Method effects imply cultural mediation. In P. E. Shrout & S. T. Fiske (Eds.), *Personality research, methods, and theory: A festschrift honoring Donald W. Fiske* (pp. 271–294). Hillsdale, NJ: Erlbaum.

Fiske, S. T., & Glick, P. (1995). Ambivalence and stereotypes cause sexual harassment: A theory with implications for organizational change. *Journal of Social Issues, 51*(1), 97–115.

Fiske, S. T., & Stevens, L. E. (1993). What's so special about sex? Gender stereotyping and discrimination. In S. Oskamp & M. Costanzo (Eds.), *Gender issues in contemporary society* (pp. 173–196). Newbury Park, CA: Sage.

Fiss, O. M. (1979). School desegregation: The uncertain path of the law. In N. Mills (Ed.), *Busing U.S.A.* New York: Teachers College Press.

Fitzgerald, L. F. (1993). Sexual harassment: Violence against women in the workplace. *American Psychologist, 48,* 1070–1076.

Fitzgerald, L.F., Swan, S., & Fischer, K. (1995). Why didn't she just report him? The psychological and legal implications of women's responses to sexual harassment. *Journal of Social Issues, 51*(1), 117–138.

Flavin, C., & Tunali, O. (1996). *Climate of hope: New strategies for stabilizing the world's atmosphere.* Washington, DC: Worldwatch Institute.

Flay, B. R. (1993). Youth tobacco use: Risks, patterns, and control. In J. Slade & C. T. Orleans (Eds.), *Nicotine addiction: Principles and management* (pp. 365–384). New York: Oxford University Press.

Flor, H., Fydrich, T., & Turk, D. C. (1992). Efficacy of multidisciplinary pain treatment centers: A meta-analytic review. *Pain, 49,* 221–230.

Florin, P., & Wandersman, A. (1990). An introduction to citizen participation, voluntary organizations, and community development: Insights for empowerment through research. *American Journal of Community Psychology, 18,* 41–54.

Ford, R. N. (1969). *Motivation through the work itself.* New York: American Management Association.

Forge, K., & Phemister, S. (1987). The effects of prosocial cartoons on preschool children. *Child Study Journal, 17,* 83–88.

Forsyth, D. R. (1990). *Group dynamics* (2nd ed.). Pacific Grove, CA: Brooks/Cole.

Fortmann, S. P., Flora, J. A., Winkleby, M. A., Schooler, C., Taylor, C. B., & Farquhar, J. W. (1995). Community intervention trials: Reflections on the Stanford Five-City Project experience. *American Journal of Epidemiology, 142,* 576–586.

Fortmann, S. P., Taylor, C. B., Flora, J. A., & Jatulis, D. E. (1993). Changes in adult cigarette smoking prevalence after 5 years of community health education: The Stanford Five-City Project. *American Journal of Epidemiology, 137,* 82–96.

Fortmann, S. P., Winkleby, M. A., Flora, J. A., Haskell, W. L., & Taylor, C. B. (1990). Effects of long-term community health education on blood pressure and hypertension control. *American Journal of Epidemiology, 132,* 629–646.

Foster, J. B. (1995). The global policies of the U.S. are environmentally unjust. In J. Petrikin (Ed.), *Environmental justice* (pp. 100–107). San Diego, CA: Greenhaven.

Foster, J. L. (1980). An advocate role model for policy analysis. *Policy Studies Journal, 8,* 958–964.

Fowers, B. J., & Richardson, F. C. (1996). Why is multiculturalism good? *American Psychologist, 51,* 609–621.

Fowler, F. J., Jr. (1993). *Survey research methods* (2nd ed.). Thousand Oaks, CA: Sage.

Fowler, F. J., Jr., & Mangione, T. W. (1990). *Standardized survey interviewing: Minimizing interviewer-related error.* Newbury Park, CA: Sage.

Fowler, R. D. (1995). 1994 report of the Chief Executive Officer: The winds of change. *American Psychologist, 50,* 600–611.

Fox, D. M. (1971). Federal standards and regulations for participation. In E. S. Cahn & B. A. Passett (Eds.), *Citizen participation: Effecting community change.* New York: Praeger.

Foxall, G. R., & Goldsmith, R. E. (1994). *Consumer psychology for marketing.* London, England: Routledge.

Frank, R. E., & Greenberg, M. G. (1980). *The public's use of television: Who watches and why.* Beverly Hills, CA: Sage.

Frank, R. G., & VandenBos, G. R. (1994). Health care reform: The 1993–1994 evolution. *American Psychologist, 49,* 851–854.

Franzwa, H. (1974). Working women in fact and fiction. *Journal of Communication, 24,* 104–109.

Frazier, P. A., Candell, S., Arikian, N., & Tofteland, A. (1994). Rape survivors and the legal system. In M. Costanzo & S. Oskamp (Eds.), *Violence and the law* (pp. 135–158). Thousand Oaks, CA: Sage.

Frazier, P. A., Cochran, C. C., & Olson, A. M. (1995). Social science research on lay definitions of sexual harassment. *Journal of Social Issues, 51*(1), 21–37.

Frederickson, G. (1973). Epilogue. In G. Frederickson (Ed.), *Neighborhood control in the 1970s: Politics, administration, and citizen participation.* New York: Chandler.

Fredricks, A. J., & Dossett, D. L. (1983). Attitude-behavior relations: A comparison of the Fishbein-Ajzen and the Bentler-Speckart models. *Journal of Personality and Social Psychology, 45,* 501–512.

Freedman, J. L (1969). Role playing: Psychology by consensus. *Journal of Personality and Social Psychology, 13,* 107–114.

Freedman, J. L. (1975). *Crowding and behavior.* San Francisco: Freeman.

Freedman, J. L. (1984). Effects of television violence on aggression. *Psychological Bulletin, 96,* 227–246.

Freedman, J. L. (1988). Television violence and aggression: What the evidence shows. In S. Oskamp (Ed.), *Television as a social issue* (pp. 144–162). Newbury Park, CA: Sage.

Freedman, J. L., & Fraser, S. C. (1966). Compliance without pressure: The foot-in-the-door technique. *Journal of Personality and Social Psychology, 4,* 195–202.

Freeman, M. A. (1994). Economic incentives and environmental regulation. In N. Vig & M. Kraft (Eds.), *Environmental policy in the 1990s* (2nd ed., pp. 189–208). Washington, DC: CQ Press.

Frese, M. (1985). Stress at work and psychosomatic complaints: A causal interpretation. *Journal of Applied Psychology, 70,* 314–328.

Freudenheim, M. (1993, August 18). Many patients unhappy with H.M.O.'s. *New York Times,* 5, 16.

Freuh, T., & McGhee, P. E. (1975). Traditional sex role development and amount of time spent watching television. *Developmental Psychology, 11,* 109.

Frey, J. H. (1989). *Survey research by telephone* (2nd ed.). Newbury Park, CA: Sage.

Fried, S. B., Gumpper, D. C., & Allen, J. C. (1973). Ten years of social psychology: Is there a growing commitment to field research? *American Psychologist, 28,* 155–156.

Friedlander, D., & Burtless, G. (1995). *Five years after: The long-term effects of welfare-to-work programs.* New York: Russell Sage Foundation.

Friedman, J., & Weinberg, D. H. (Eds.). (1983). *The great housing experiment.* Beverly Hills, CA: Sage.

Friedman, J., & Weinberg, D. H. (1985). Experimental Housing Allowance Program: History and overview. In L. Aiken & B. Kehrer (Eds.), *Evaluation studies review annual* (Vol. 10, pp. 385–396). Beverly Hills, CA: Sage.

Friedman, M. (1991a). Consumer boycotts: A conceptual framework and research agenda. *Journal of Social Issues, 47*(1), 149–168.

Friedman, M. (Ed.). (1991b). Consumer protection issues. *Journal of Social Issues, 47*(1), 1–191.

Friedman, M. A., & Brownell, K. D. (1995). Psychological correlates of obesity: Moving to the next research generation. *Psychological Bulletin, 117,* 3–20.

Friedrich, L. K., & Stein, A. H. (1973). Aggressive and prosocial television programs and the natural behavior of preschool children. *Monographs of the Society for Research in Child Development, 38*(4, Serial No. 151).

Friedrich, L. K., & Stein, A. H. (1975). Prosocial television and young children: The effects of verbal labeling and role playing on learning and behavior. *Child Development, 46,* 27–38.

Friedrich-Cofer, L., & Huston, A. C. (1986). Television violence and aggression: The debate continues. *Psychological Bulletin, 100,* 364–371.

Friestad, M., & Thorson, E. (1986). Emotion-eliciting advertising: Effect on long term memory and judgment. *Advances in Consumer Research, 13,* 111–115.

Frieze, I. H., Bar-Tal, D., & Carroll, J. S. (Eds.). (1979). *New approaches to social problems: Applications of attribution theory.* San Francisco: Jossey-Bass.

Fry, P. (1992). Major social theories of aging and their implications for counseling concepts and practice: A critical review. *Counseling Psychology, 20,* 246–329.

Funkhouser, G. R. (1973). The issues of the sixties: An exploratory study in the dynamics of public opinion. *Public Opinion Quarterly, 37,* 62–75.

Gable, R. (1986). Social competence, coping skills, and youth crime: A pragmatic and theory-based approach. In S. Apter & A. Goldstein (Eds.), *Youth violence: Programs and perspectives* (pp. 160–177). New York: Pergamon.

Gaertner, S. L., & Dovidio, J. F. (1986). The aversive form of racism. In J. F. Dovidio & S. L. Gaertner (Eds.), *Prejudice, discrimination, and racism* (pp. 61–89). Orlando, FL: Harcourt Brace Jovanovich.

Gaertner, S. L., Rust, M. C., Dovidio, J. F., Bachman, B. A., Anastasio, P. A. (1994). The contact hypothesis: The role of a common ingroup identity on reducing intergroup bias. *Small Group Research, 25,* 224–249.

Gaines, S. O., Jr., & Reed, E. S. (1995). Prejudice: From Allport to DuBois. *American Psychologist, 50,* 96–103.

Galinsky, E., Bond, J. T., & Friedman, D. E. (1993). *The changing workforce: Highlights of the national study.* New York: Families and Work Institute.

Gallup, G. (1994). *The Gallup Poll: Public opinion 1993.* Wilmington, DE: Scholarly Resources.

Gallup, G. (1995). *The Gallup Poll: Public opinion 1994.* Wilmington, DE: Scholarly Resources.

Gallup, G. H., & Newport, F. (1991, June). Death penalty support remains strong. *Gallup Poll Monthly,* No. 309, 40–45.

Gallup Poll Monthly. (1992, March). Satisfaction with U.S. at a ten-year low. No. 318, pp. 47–50.

Gallup Poll Monthly. (1994, November). Gallup Poll accuracy record. No. 350, p. 53.

Gallup Poll Monthly. (1995, August). Preferred term: "Black" or "African-American." No. 359, p. 20.

Gamba, R., & Oskamp, S. (1994). Factors influencing community residents' participation in a commingled curbside recycling program. *Environment and Behavior, 26,* 587–612.

Gardner, G. T., & Stern, P. C. (1996). *Environmental problems and human behavior.* Boston: Allyn & Bacon.

Gardner, W., & Wilcox, B. (1993). Political intervention in scientific peer review. *American Psychologist, 48,* 972–983.

Geen, R. G., & Berkowitz, L. (1967). Some conditions facilitating the occurrence of aggression after the observation of violence. *Journal of Personality, 35,* 666–676.

Gelderloos, O. (1992). *Eco-theology: The Judeo-Christian tradition and the politics of ecological decision making.* Glasgow: Wild Goose.

Geller, E. S. (1981). The energy crisis and behavioral science: A conceptual framework for large scale intervention. In A. W. Childs & G. B. Melton (Eds.), *Rural psychology.* New York: Plenum.

Geller, E. S. (1989). Applied behavior analysis and social marketing: An integration to preserve the environment. *Journal of Social Issues, 45*(1), 17–36.

Geller, E. S., Paterson, L., & Talbott, E. (1982). A behavioral analysis of incentive prompts for motivating seat belt use. *Journal of Applied Behavioral Analysis, 15,* 403–415.

Gerard, H. (1983). School desegregation: The social science role. *American Psychologist, 38,* 869–878.

Gerbasi, K. C., Zuckerman, M., & Reis, H. T. (1977). Justice needs a new blindfold: A review of mock jury research. *Psychological Bulletin, 84,* 323–345.

Gerbner, G. (1993). *Women and minorities in television: A study in casting fate.* Philadelphia: Annenberg School for Communication, University of Pennsylvania.

Gerbner, G., Gross, L, Eleey, M., Jackson-Beeck, M., Jeffries-Fox, S., & Signorielli, N. (1977). The Gerbner violence profile—An analysis of the CBS report. *Journal of Broadcasting, 21,* 280–286.

Gerbner, G., Gross, L., Jackson-Beeck, M., Jeffries-Fox, S., & Signorielli, N. (1978). Cultural indicators: Violence profile no. 9. *Journal of Communication, 28*(3), 176–207.

Gerbner, G., Gross, L., Morgan, M., & Signorielli, N. (1980). The "mainstreaming" of America: Violence profile no. 11. *Journal of Communication, 30*(3), 10–29.

Gerbner, G., Gross, L., Morgan, M., & Signorielli, N. (1994). Growing up with television: The cultivation perspective. In J. Bryant & D. Zillmann (Eds.), *Media effects: Advances in theory and research* (pp. 17–42). Hillsdale, NJ: Erlbaum.

Gerbner, G., Morgan, M., & Signorielli, N. (1994). *Television violence profile no. 16: The turning point from research to action.* Philadelphia: Annenberg School for Communication, University of Pennsylvania.

Gerhart, B. (1990). Gender differences in current and starting salaries: The role of performance, college major, and job title. *Industrial and Labor Relations Review, 43,* 418–433.

Gerhart, B., & Milkovich, G. T. (1992). Employee compensation: Research and practice. In M. D. Dunnette & L. M. Hough (Eds.), *Handbook of industrial & organizational psy-*

chology (2nd ed., Vol. 3, pp. 481–569). Palo Alto, CA: Consulting Psychologists Press.

Getting ready for the V-chip. (1996, February 19). *New York Times,* p. A14.

Gibson, B. (Ed.). (1997). Social science perspectives on tobacco policy [Special issue]. *Journal of Social Issues, 53,* 3–192.

Gilbert, D. T., & Malone, P. S. (1995). The correspondence bias. *Psychological Bulletin, 117,* 21–38.

Glantz, S. A., Slade, J., Bero, L. A., Hanauer, P., & Barnes, D. E. (1996). *The cigarette papers.* Berkeley: University of California Press.

Glass, D. C., & Singer, J. E. (1972). *Urban stress: Experiments on noise and social stressors.* New York: Academic Press.

Glass, G. V., & Ellett, F. S., Jr. (1980). Evaluation research. *Annual Review of Psychology, 31,* 211–228.

Glick, P., Abbott, J. E., & Hotze, C. A. (1988). Keeping your distance: Group membership, personal space, and requests for small favors. *Journal of Applied Social Psychology, 18,* 315–330.

Glick, P., & Fiske, S. T. (1994, April). *The Ambivalent Sexism Inventory: Differentiating hostile and benevolent sexism.* Unpublished manuscript, Lawrence University.

Glynn, T. J. (1989). Essential elements of school-based smoking-prevention programs. *Journal of School Health, 59,* 181–188.

Goldberg, M. E. (1990). A quasi-experiment assessing the effectiveness of TV advertising directed to children. *Journal of Marketing Research, 27,* 445–454.

Goldberg, M. E., Gorn, G., & Gibson, W. (1978). TV messages for snack and breakfast foods: Do they influence children's preferences? *Journal of Consumer Research, 5,* 48–54.

Goldfarb, T. D. (1995). *Taking sides: Clashing views on controversial environmental issues.* New York: Dushkin.

Goldner, F. H. (1971). Public opinion and survey research: A poor mix. *Public Opinion Quarterly, 35,* 447–448.

Goldstein, A. (1986). Psychological skills training and the aggressive adolescent. In S. Apter & A. Goldstein (Eds.), *Youth violence: Programs and perspectives* (pp. 89–119). New York: Pergamon.

Goldstein, I. (1991). Training in work organizations. In M. D. Dunnette & L. M. Hough (Eds.), *Handbook of industrial & organizational psychology* (2nd ed., Vol. 2, pp. 507–619). Palo Alto, CA: Consulting Psychologists Press.

Golembiewski, R. T., & Proehl, C. W., Jr. (1978). A survey of the empirical literature on flexible work-hours: Character and consequences of a major innovation. *Academy of Management Review, 3,* 837–893.

Gonzales, M., Aronson, E., & Costanzo, M. (1988). Using social cognition and persuasion to promote energy conservation: A quasi-experiment. *Journal of Applied Social Psychology, 18,* 1049–1066.

Gonzalez, L. (1994). Effectiveness of bilingual education: A comparison of various approaches in an elementary school district. In R. DeVillar, C. Faltis, & J. Cummins (Eds.), *Cultural diversity in schools: From rhetoric to practice* (pp. 233–262). New York: State University of New York Press.

Good, T. L., & Findley, M. J. (1985). Sex role expectations and achievement. In Dusek (Ed.), *Teacher expectations* (pp. 271–302). Hillsdale, NJ: Erlbaum.

Goodman, G., Levine, M., Melton, G., & Ogden, D. (1991). Child witnesses and the confrontation clause. *Law and Human Behavior, 15,* 13–29.

Goodstein, L. D., & Sandler, I. (1978). Using psychology to promote human welfare: A conceptual analysis of the role of community psychology. *American Psychologist, 33,* 882–892.

Goodwin, J. (1995). *Research in psychology: Methods and design.* New York: Wiley.

Goodwin, L. (1971). On making social research relevant to public policy and national problem solving. *American Psychologist, 26,* 431–442.

Gore, A. (1992). *Earth in the balance: Ecology and the human spirit.* Boston: Houghton Mifflin.

Gorn, G. J., & Goldberg, M. E. (1980). Children's responses to repetitive television commercials. *Journal of Consumer Research, 6,* 421–424.

Gorn, G. J., & Goldberg, M. E. (1982). Behavioral evidence of the effects of televised food messages on children. *Journal of Consumer Research, 9,* 200–205.

Gorsuch, R. L. (1983). *Factor analysis* (2nd ed.). Hillsdale, NJ: Erlbaum.

Gorsuch, R. L., & Butler, M. C. (1976). Initial drug abuse: A review of predisposing social psychological factors. *Psychological Bulletin, 83,* 120–137.

Graber, J. M. (1980). *Conceptualization and measurement of quality of working life.* Unpublished doctoral dissertation, Claremont Graduate School.

Graen, G., Alvares, K., Orris, J. B., & Martelia, J. A. (1970). Contingency model of leadership effectiveness: Antecedent and evidential results. *Psychological Bulletin, 74,* 285–296.

Grams, W., & Rogers, R. (1990). Power and personality: Effects of Machiavellianism, need for approval, and motivation on use of influence tactics. *Journal of General Psychology, 117,* 71–82.

Gredler, M. E. (1996). *Program evaluation.* Englewood Cliffs, NJ: Prentice-Hall.

Greeley, A. (1993). Religion and attitudes towards the environment. *Journal for the Scientific Study of Religion, 32,* 19–28.

Green, B., Parham, L. A., Kleff, R., & Pilisuk, M. (Eds.). (1980). Old age: Environmental complexity and policy interventions. *Journal of Social Issues, 36*(2), 1–164.

Greenberg, B. S. (1974). British children and televised violence. *Public Opinion Quarterly, 38,* 531–547.

Greenberg, B. S. (1994). Content trends in media sex. In D. Zillmann, J. Bryant, & A. Huston (Eds.), *Media, children, and the family: Social scientific, psychodynamic, and clinical perspectives* (pp. 165–182). Hillsdale, NJ: Erlbaum.

Greenberg, B. S., & Brand, J. E. (1993). Cultural diversity on Saturday morning television. In G. Berry & J. Asamen (Eds.), *Children and television: Images in a changing sociocultural world* (pp. 132–142). Newbury Park, CA: Sage.

Greenberg, B. S., & Brand, J. E. (1994). Minorities and the mass media: 1970s to 1990s. In J. Bryant & D. Zillmann

(Eds.), *Media effects: Advances in theory and research* (pp. 273–314). Hillsdale, NJ: Erlbaum.

Greenberg, B. S., Brown, J. D., & Buerkel-Rothfuss, N. L. (1993). *Media, sex, and the adolescent.* Cresskill, NJ: Hampton Press.

Greenberg, B. S., & Gordon, T. F. (1972). Perceptions of violence in television programs: Critics and the public. In G. A. Comstock & E. A. Rubinstein (Eds.), *Television and social behavior* (Vol. 1, pp. 244–258). Washington, DC: U.S. Government Printing Office.

Greenberg, D., & Robins, P. (1985). The changing role of social experiments in policy analysis. In L. Aiken & B. Kehrer (Eds.), *Evaluation studies review annual* (Vol. 10, pp. 19–48). Beverly Hills, CA: Sage.

Greenberg, M., & Ruback, R. B. (1992). *After the crime: Victim decision making.* New York: Plenum.

Greenberg, R. A., Haley, N. J., Etzel, R. A., & Loda, F. A. (1984). Measuring the exposure of infants to tobacco smoke. *New England Journal of Medicine, 310,* 1075–1078.

Greenfield, P. M., Yut, E., Chung, M., Land, D., Kreider, H., Pantoja, M., & Horsley, K. (1993). The program-length commercial: A study of the effects of television/toy tie-ins on imaginative play. In G. Berry & J. Asamen (Eds.), *Children and television: Images in a changing sociocultural world* (pp. 38–52). Newbury Park, CA: Sage.

Greenpeace. (1995, July–September). North Sea victory over Shell. *4*(3), p. 1.

Greenwald, A. G., & Albert, R. D. (1968). Acceptance and recall of improvised arguments. *Journal of Personality and Social Psychology, 8,* 31–34.

Greenwald, J. (1996, April 1). Bitter ads to swallow. *Time,* pp. 48–49.

Greenwood, J. M., & McNamara, W. J. (1969). Leadership styles of structure and consideration and managerial effectiveness. *Personnel Psychology, 22,* 141–152.

Gribbon, J., & Gribbon, M. (1993). *The holes in the sky.* New York: Bantam.

Griffin v. County School Board of Prince Edward County, 377 U.S. 218 (1964).

Griffin, R. W. (1988). Consequences of quality circles in an industrial setting: A longitudinal assessment. *Academy of Management Journal, 31,* 338–358.

Griffin, R. W., Moorhead, G., Johnson, B. H., & Chonko, L. B. (1980). The empirical dimensionality of the job characteristics inventory. *Academy of Management Journal, 23,* 772–777.

Grofman, B. (1980). Jury decision making models and the Supreme Court: The jury cases from *Williams v. Florida* to *Ballew v. Georgia. Policy Studies Journal, 8,* 749–772.

Groves, R. M. (1990). Theories and methods of telephone surveys. *Annual Review of Sociology, 16,* 221–240.

Gruber, J. E., & Bjorn, L. (1982). Blue-collar blues: The sexual harassment of women autoworkers. *Work and Occupations, 9,* 271–298.

Gruneberg, M. M. (1979). *Understanding job satisfaction.* London: Macmillan.

Gruneberg, M. M., Startup, R., & Tapsfield, P. (1974). The effect of geographical factors on the job satisfaction of university teachers. *Vocational Aspects of Education, 26,* 25–29.

Grusec, J. E. (1973). Effects of co-observer evaluations on imitation: A developmental study. *Developmental Psychology, 8,* 141.

Grush, J. E. (1980). Impact of candidate expenditures, regionality, and prior outcomes on the 1976 Democratic presidential primaries. *Journal of Personality and Social Psychology, 38,* 337–347.

Guba, E. G., & Lincoln, Y. S. (1981). *Effective evaluation.* San Francisco: Jossey-Bass.

Gudjonsson, G. (1986). The relationship between interrogative suggestibility and acquiescence: Empirical findings and theoretical implications. *Personality and Individual Differences, 7,* 195–199.

Gueron, J. (1988). Work-welfare programs. In H. Bloom, D. Cordray, & R. Light (Eds.), *Lessons from selected program and policy areas* (pp. 7–28). San Francisco: Jossey-Bass.

Guerra, N. G., & Slaby, R. G. (1990). Cognitive mediators of aggression in adolescent offenders: II. Intervention. *Developmental Psychology, 26,* 269–277.

Guerra, N. G., Tolan, P., & Hammond, W. R. (1994). Prevention and treatment of adolescent violence. In L. D. Eron, J. H. Gentry, & P. Schlegel (Eds.), *Reason to hope: A psychosocial perspective on violence and youth* (pp. 383–404). Washington, DC: American Psychological Association.

Guilford, J. S. (1968). Smoking and health—Revisited. In E. F. Borgatta & R. R. Evans (Eds.), *Smoking, health, and behavior.* Chicago: Aldine.

Gupta, N., Jenkins, G. D., Jr., & Beehr, T. A. (1983). Employee gender, gender similarity, and supervisor-subordinate cross-evaluations. *Psychology of Women Quarterly, 8,* 174–184.

Gurman, E. (1994). Debriefing for all concerned: Ethical treatment of human subjects. *Psychological Science, 5,* 139.

Gutek, B. A. (1978). Strategies for studying client satisfaction. *Journal of Social Issues, 34*(4), 44–56.

Gutek, B. A. (1985). *Sex and the workplace.* San Francisco: Jossey-Bass.

Gutek, B. A. (1993). Responses to sexual harassment. In S. Oskamp & M. Costanzo (Eds.), *Gender issues in contemporary society* (pp. 197–216). Newbury Park, CA: Sage.

Gutek, B. A. (1995). How subjective is sexual harassment? An examination of rater effects. *Basic and Applied Social Psychology, 17,* 447–467.

Gutek, B. A., & Winter, S. J. (1992). Consistency of job satisfaction across situations: Fact or framing artifact? *Journal of Vocational Behavior, 41,* 61–78.

Guthrie, E., & Miller, W. S. (1981). *Making change: A guide to effectiveness in groups.* Minneapolis: Interpersonal Communication Programs.

Guttentag, M. (1971). Models and methods in evaluation research. *Journal for the Theory of Social Behaviour, 1,* 75–95.

Guttentag, M., & Struening, E. L. (Eds.). (1975). *Handbook of evaluation research* (2 vols.). Beverly Hills, CA: Sage.

Guzzardi, W., Jr. (1982). The mindless pursuit of safety. In D. A. Aaker & G. S. Day (Eds.), *Consumerism: Search for the consumer interest* (4th ed., pp. 363–375). New York: Free Press.

Guzzo, R. A., Jette, R. D., & Katzell, R. A. (1985). The effects of psychologically based intervention programs on worker productivity: A meta-analysis. *Personnel Psychology, 38,* 275–291.

Gwartney-Gibbs, P. A., Stockard, J., & Brohmer, S. (1983). Learning courtship violence: The influence of parents, peers, and personal experiences. *Family Relations, 36,* 276–282.

Gwynne, S. C. (1996, April 1). Undoing diversity: A bombshell court ruling curtails affirmative action. *Time,* p. 54.

Gyllenhammar, P. G. (1977). *People at work.* Reading, MA.: Addison-Wesley.

Hackett, R. D. (1989). Work attitudes and employee absenteeism: A synthesis of the literature. *Journal of Occupational Psychology, 62,* 235–248.

Hackett, R. D., & Guion, R. M. (1985). A reevaluation of the absenteeism-job satisfaction relationship. *Organizational Behavior and Human Decision Processes, 35,* 340–381.

(1989). Work attitudes and employee absenteeism: A synthesis of the literature. *Journal of Occupational Psychology, 62,* 235–248.

Hackman, J. R., & Lawler, E. E., III. (1971). Employee reactions to job characteristics. *Journal of Applied Psychology, 55,* 259–286. [Monograph]

Hackman, J. R., & Lee, M. D. (1979). *Redesigning work: A strategy for change.* Scarsdale, NY: Work in America Institute.

Hackman, J. R., Oldham, G., Janson, R., & Purdy, K. (1975). A new strategy for job enrichment. *California Management Review, 17,* 57–71.

Hadden, S. G. (1991). Regulating product risks through consumer information. *Journal of Social Issues, 47*(1), 93–105.

Hallman, H. W. (1973). The neighborhood as an organizational unit: A historical perspective. In G. Frederickson (Ed.), *Neighborhood control in the 1970s: Politics, administration, and citizen participation.* New York: Chandler.

Hallman, W., & Wandersman, A. (1992). Attribution of responsibility and individual and collective coping with environmental threats. *Journal of Social Issues, 48*(4), 101–118.

Halpin, A. W. (1966). *Theory and research in administration.* New York: Macmillan.

Hambacher, W. O. (1994). Expert witnessing: Guidelines and practical suggestions. *American Journal of Forensic Psychology, 12,* 17–35.

Hammond, E. C., & Horn, D. (1958). Smoking and death rates—Report on forty-four months of follow-up of 187,783 men. II. Death rates by cause. *Journal of the American Medical Association, 166,* 1294–1308.

Hammond, K. R., & Adelman, L. (1976). Science, values, and human judgment. *Science, 194,* 389–396.

Haney, C., Hurtado, A., & Vega, L. (1994). "Modern" death qualification: New data on its biasing effects. *Law and Human Behavior, 18,* 619–633.

Haney, W. (1993). Testing minorities. In L. Weis & M. Fine (Eds.), *Beyond silenced voices: Class, race, and gender in the United States.* New York: State University of New York Press.

Hanratty, M. A. (1969). *Imitation of film-mediated aggression against live and inanimate victims.* Unpublished master's thesis, Vanderbilt University.

Hansen, J. I. (1990). Interpretation of the Strong Interest Inventory. In C. E. Watkins, Jr. & V. Campbell (Eds.), *Testing in counseling practice* (pp. 177–209). Hillsdale, NJ: Erlbaum.

Hansen, J. I. (1994). The measurement of vocational interests. In M. G. Rumsey, C. B. Walker, & J. H. Harris (Eds.), *Personnel selection and classification* (pp. 393–416). Hillsdale, NJ: Erlbaum.

Hansen, W. B., Johnson, C. A., Flay, B. R., Graham, J. W., & Sobel, J. (1988). Affective and social influence approaches to the prevention of multiple substance abuse among seventh grade students: Results from Project SMART. *Preventive Medicine, 17,* 135–154.

Hardin, G. (1968). The tragedy of the commons. *Science, 162,* 1243–1248.

Hare, A. P., Blumberg, H., Davies, M., & Kent, M. V. (1994). *Small group research: A handbook.* Norwood, NJ: Ablex.

Harkins, S. G., & Petty, R. E. (1981). Effects of source magnification of cognitive effort on attitudes: An information processing view. *Journal of Personality and Social Psychology, 40,* 401–413.

Harmon, M. A. (1993). Reducing the risk of drug involvement among early adolescents: An evaluation of Drug Abuse Resistance Education. *Evaluation Review, 17,* 221–239.

Harris, M. (1993). Issues in studying the mediation of expectancy effects: A taxonomy of expectancy situations. In P. Blanck (Ed.), *Interpersonal expectations: Theory, research, and application* (pp. 350–378). Paris, France: Cambridge University Press.

Harris, M., & Rosenthal, R. (1985). Mediation of the interpersonal expectancy effect: 31 meta-analyses. *Psychological Bulletin, 97,* 363–386.

Harris, M., & Rosenthal, R. (1986). Four factors in the mediation of teacher expectancy effects. In R. Feldman (Ed.), *The social psychology of education: Current research and theory* (pp. 91–131). New York: Cambridge University Press.

Harris, R. (1994). The impact of sexually explicit media. In J. Bryant & D. Zillmann (Eds.), *Media effects: Advances in theory and research* (pp. 91–122). Hillsdale, NJ: Erlbaum.

Harvard Law Review. (1993). Pornography, equality, and a discrimination-free workplace: A comparative perspective. *106,* 1075–1092.

Harway, M. (1980). Sex bias in educational-vocational counseling. *Psychology of Women Quarterly, 4,* 412–423.

Hastie, R. (1993). Algebraic models of juror decision processes. In R. Hastie (Ed.), *Inside the juror: The psychology of juror decision making* (pp. 84–115). New York: Cambridge University Press.

Hatchett, S., & Schuman, H. (1975). White respondents and race-of-interviewer effects. *Public Opinion Quarterly, 39,* 523–528.

Hatfield, E. H., Traupmann, J., Sprecher, S., Utne, M., & Hay, J. (1985). Equity and intimate relationships: Recent research. In W. Ickes (Ed.), *Compatible and incompatible relationships.* New York: Springer-Verlag.

Hatry, H., Newcomer, K., & Wholey, J. (1994). Conclusions: Improving evaluation activities and results. In J. Wholey, H. Hatry, & K. Newcomer (Eds.), *Handbook of practical program evaluation* (pp. 590–602). San Francisco: Jossey-Bass.

Hausman, J., & Wise, D. (Eds.). (1985). *Social experimentation.* Chicago: University of Chicago Press.

Havelock, R. G. (1972). *Training for change agents: A guide to the design of training programs in education and other fields.* Ann Arbor: Institute for Social Research, University of Michigan.

Haveman, R. H. (1988). Social experimentation and Social Experimentation. *Journal of Human Resources, 21,* 586–605.

Hawkins, D. I., Best, R. J., & Coney, K. A. (1992). *Consumer behavior: Implications for marketing strategy* (5th ed.). Homewood, IL: Irwin.

Heaney, C. A., Israel, B. A., & House, J. S. (1994). Chronic job insecurity among automobile workers: Effects on job satisfaction and health. *Social Science and Medicine, 38,* 1431–1437.

Hearold, S. (1986). A synthesis of 1043 effects of television on social behavior. In G. Comstock (Ed.), *Public communication and behavior* (Vol. 1). Orlando, FL: Academic Press.

Hebbeler, K. (1985). An old and a new question on the effects of early education for children from low income families. *Educational Evaluation and Policy Analysis, 7,* 207–216.

Heckman, J. (1992). Randomization and social policy evaluation. In C. Manski & I. Garfinkel (Eds.), *Evaluating welfare and training programs* (pp. 201–230). Cambridge, MA: Harvard University Press.

Heclo, H., & Rein, M. (1980). Social science and negative income taxation. In Organisation for Economic Co-operation and Development, *The utilisation of the social sciences in policy making in the United States: Case studies.* Paris: OECD.

Hedges, L., & Waddington, T. (1993). From evidence to knowledge to policy: Research synthesis for policy formation. *Review of Educational Research, 63,* 345–352.

Heller, K. (1990). Social and community intervention. *Annual Review of Psychology, 41,* 141–168.

Helmreich, R. (1975). Applied social psychology: The unfulfilled promise. *Personality and Social Psychology Bulletin, 1,* 548–560.

Helson, H. (1964). *Adaptation-level theory: An experimental and systematic approach to behavior.* New York: Harper & Row.

Heneman, R. (1992). *Merit pay.* Reading, MA: Addison-Wesley.

Hennigan, K. M., Del Rosario, M. L., Heath, L., Cook, T. D., Wharton, J. D., & Calder, B. J. (1982). Impact of the introduction of television on crime in the United States: Empirical findings and theoretical implications. *Journal of Personality and Social Psychology, 52,* 461–477.

Hennigan, K. M., Flay, B. R., & Cook, T. D. (1980). "Give me the facts": Some suggestions for using social science knowledge in national policy-making. In R. F. Kidd & M. J. Saks (Eds.), *Advances in applied social psychology* (Vol. 1). Hillsdale, NJ: Erlbaum.

Herbert, T. B., & Dunkel-Schetter, C. (1992). Negative social reactions to victims: An overview of responses and their determinants. In L. Montada, S-H. Filipp, & M. J. Lerner (Eds.), *Life crises and experiences of loss in adulthood* (pp. 497–518). Hillsdale, NJ: Erlbaum.

Hermann, R. O. (1982). The consumer movement in historical perspective. In D. A. Aaker & G. S. Day (Eds.), *Consumerism: Search for the consumer interest* (4th ed., pp. 23–32). New York: Free Press.

Herrnstein, R. A., & Murray, C. (1994). *The bell curve.* New York: Grove.

Herzberg, F. (1966). *Work and the nature of man.* Cleveland: World.

Herzberg, F., Mausner, B., Peterson, R. O., & Capwell, D. F. (1957). *Job attitudes: Review of research and opinion.* Pittsburgh: Psychological Service of Pittsburgh.

Herzberg, F., Mausner, B., & Snyderman, B. B. (1959). *The motivation to work* (2nd ed.). New York: Wiley.

Hewstone, M. (1996). Contact and categorization: Social psychological interventions to change intergroup relations. In C. N. Macrae, C. Stangor, & M. Hewstone (Eds.), *Stereotypes and stereotyping* (pp. 323–368). New York: Guilford.

Hewstone, M., & Brown, R. (1986). Contact is not enough: An intergroup perspective on the "contact hypothesis." In M. Hewstone & R. Brown (Eds.), *Contact and conflict in intergroup encounters.* Oxford, England: Blackwell.

Higbee, K. L., & Wells, M. G. (1972). Some research trends in social psychology during the 1960s. *American Psychologist, 27,* 963–966.

Higgins, E. T., & Kruglanski, A. (Ed.) (1996). *Social psychology: Handbook of basic principles.* New York: Guilford.

Hill, R. P. (Ed.). (1996). *Marketing and consumer research in the public interest.* Thousand Oaks, CA: Sage.

Hiller, D. V., & Philliber, W. W. (1986). The division of labor in contemporary marriage: Expectations, perceptions, and performance. *Social Problems, 33,* 191–201.

Hilton, J., & von Hipple, W. (1996). Stereotypes. *Annual Review of Psychology, 47,* 237–271.

Himmelweit, H. T., Swift, B., & Jaeger, M. E. (1980). The audience as critic: A conceptual analysis of television entertainment. In P. H. Tannenbaum (Ed.), *The entertainment functions of television* (pp. 67–106). Hillsdale, NJ: Erlbaum.

Hines, M. (1990). Gonadal hormones and human cognitive development. In J. Balthazart (Ed.), *Hormones, brain and behavior in vertebrates: 1. Sexual differentiation, neuroanatomical aspects, neurotransmitters and neuropeptides* (pp. 51–63). Basel, Switzerland: Karger.

Hirayama, T. (1981). Non-smoking wives of heavy smokers have a higher risk of lung cancer: A study from Japan. *British Journal of Behavioral Medicine, 282,* 183–185.

Hite, S. (1976). *The Hite report: A nationwide study of female sexuality.* New York: Dell.

Hogan, R., Raskin, R., & Fazzini, D. (1990). The dark side of charisma. In K. E. Clark & M. B. Clark (Eds.), *Measures of leadership* (pp. 343–354). West Orange, NJ: Leadership Library of America.

Holder, H., Longabough, R., Miller, W. R., & Rubonis, A. V. (1991). The cost effectiveness of treatment for alcoholism: A first approximation. *Journal of Studies on Alcoholism, 52,* 517–540.

Hollander, E. P. (1979). Applied social psychology: Problems and prospects. *International Review of Applied Psychology, 28,* 93–100.

Hollander, E. P. (1985). Leadership and power. In G. Lindzey & E. Aronson (Eds.), *The handbook of social psychology* (3rd ed., Vol. 1, pp. 485–538). New York: Random House.

Hollander, E. P. (1993). Legitimacy, power, and influence: A perspective on relational features of leadership. In M. Chemers & R. Ayman (Eds.), *Leadership theory and research: Perspectives and directions* (pp. 29–48). San Diego, CA: Academic Press.

Homer, P. M. (1990). The mediating role of attitude toward the ad: Some additional evidence. *Journal of Marketing Research, 27,* 78–86.

Honts, C. R., & Perry, M. V. (1992). Polygraph admissibility: Changes and challenges. *Law and Human Behavior, 16,* 357–379.

Horner, M. S. (1972). Toward an understanding of achievement-related conflicts in women. *Journal of Social Issues, 28*(2), 157–174.

Horning, E. C., Horning, M. G., Carroll, D. I., Stillwell, R. N., & Dzidic, I. (1973). Nicotine in smokers, nonsmokers and room air. *Life Sciences, 13,* 1331–1346.

Hornstein, H. A. (1975). Social psychology as social intervention. In M. Deutsch & H. A. Hornstein (Eds.), *Applying social psychology: Implications for research, practice, and training* (pp. 211–234). Hillsdale, NJ: Erlbaum.

Horowitz, I. L. (1977). Social welfare, state power, and the limits to equity. In I. L. Horowitz (Ed.), *Equity, income, and policy: Comparative studies in three worlds of development.* New York: Praeger.

Horwitt, S. D. (1989). *Let them call me rebel: Saul Alinsky, his life and legacy.* New York: Knopf.

House, P. W. (1982). *The art of public policy analysis: The arena of regulations.* Beverly Hills, CA: Sage.

House, R. J., & Rizzo, J. R. (1972). Role conflict and ambiguity as critical variables in a model of organizational behavior. *Organizational Behavior and Human Performance, 7,* 467–505.

Hovland, C. I., Janis, I. L., & Kelley, H. H. (1953). *Communication and persuasion.* New Haven, CT: Yale University Press.

Howard, D. J., & Burnkrant, R. E. (1990). Question effects on information processing in advertising. *Psychology & Marketing, 7,* 27–46.

Howard, J. L., Reifler, C. B., & Liptzin, M. B. (1970). Effects of exposure to pornography. In *Technical report of the Commission on Obscenity and Pornography* (Vol. 8). Washington, DC: U.S. Government Printing Office.

Hoyle, R. H. (Ed.). (1995). *Structural equation modeling: Concepts, issues, and applications.* Thousand Oaks, CA: Sage.

Hoynes, W. (1994). *Public television for sale: Media, the market, and the public sphere.* Boulder, CO: Westview.

Hraba, J., & Grant, G. B. (1970). Black is beautiful: A reexamination of racial preference and identification. *Journal of Personality and Social Psychology, 16,* 398–402.

Huesmann, L. R. (1986). The effect of film and television violence among children. In S. J. Katz & P. Vesin (Eds.), *Children and the media* (pp. 101–128). Paris: Centre International de l'Enfance.

Huesmann, L. R., & Eron, L. D. (Eds.). (1986). *Television and the aggressive child: A cross-national comparison.* Hillsdale, NJ: Erlbaum.

Huesmann, L. R., Eron, L. D., Klein, R., Brice, P., & Fischer, P. (1983). Mitigating the imitation of aggressive behaviors by changing children's attitudes about media violence. *Journal of Personality and Social Psychology, 44,* 899–910.

Huesmann, L. R., Eron, L. D., Lefkowitz, M. M., & Walder, L. O. (1973). Television violence and aggression: The causal effect remains. *American Psychologist, 28,* 617–620.

Huesmann, L. R., Eron, L. D., Lefkowitz, M. M., & Walder, L. O. (1984). Stability of aggression over time and generations. *Developmental Psychology, 20,* 1120–1134.

Huesmann, L. R., & Miller, L. S. (1994). Long-term effects of repeated exposure to media violence in childhood. In L. Huesmann (Ed.), *Aggressive behavior: Current perspectives* (pp. 153–186). New York: Plenum.

Hughes, M. (1980). The fruits of cultivation analysis: A reexamination of some effects of television watching. *Public Opinion Quarterly, 44,* 287–302.

Hugick, L. (1991, August). American unhappiness with health care contrasts with Canadian contentment. *Gallup Poll Monthly,* No. 311, pp. 2–3.

Hume, S. (1992, October 5). Coupon use jumps 10% as distribution soars. *Advertising Age,* pp. 3, 42.

Hunt, H. K. (1991). Consumer satisfaction, dissatisfaction, and complaining behavior. *Journal of Social Issues, 47*(1), 107–117.

Hurtado, S. (1994). Graduate school racial climates and academic self-concept among minority graduate students in the 1970s. *American Journal of Education, 102,* 330–351.

Huston, A. C., Watkins, B., & Kunkel, D. (1989). Public policy and children's television. *American Psychologist, 44,* 424–433.

Huston, A. C., Zillmann, D., & Bryant, J. (1994). Media influence, public policy, and the family. In D. Zillmann, J. Bryant, & A. Huston (Eds.), *Media, children, and the family: Social scientific, psychodynamic, and clinical perspectives* (pp. 3–18). Hillsdale, NJ: Erlbaum.

Hyde, J. S., Fennema, E., & Lamon, S. J. (1990). Gender differences in mathematics performance: A meta-analysis. *Psychological Bulletin, 107,* 139–155.

Iaffaldano, M. T., & Muchinsky, P. M. (1985). Job satisfaction and job performance: A meta-analysis. *Psychological Bulletin, 97,* 251–273.

Idson, T. L., & Price, H. F. (1992). An analysis of wage differentials by gender and ethnicity in the public sector. *Review of Black Political Economy, 20,* 75–97.

Ikard, F. F., Green, D. E., & Horn, D. (1969). A scale to differentiate between types of smoking as related to management of affect. *International Journal of the Addictions, 4,* 649–659.

Index to International Public Opinion. (1995). Westport, CT: Survey Research Consultants International.

Industrial Democracy in Europe. (1993). *Industrial democracy in Europe revisited.* Oxford, England: Oxford University Press.

Ingham, G. K. (1970). *Size of industrial organization and worker behaviour.* Cambridge, England: Cambridge University Press.

Inglehart, R. (1990). *Culture shift in advanced industrial society.* Princeton, NJ: Princeton University Press.

Ingram, L. (1990). An overview of the desegregation meta-analyses. In K. Wachter & M. Straf (Eds.), *The future of meta-analysis* (pp. 61–70). New York: Russell Sage Foundation.

Inman, J. J., McAlister, L., & Hoyer, W. D. (1990). Promotion signal: Proxy for a price cut? *Journal of Consumer Research, 17,* 74–81.

Insel, P. M., & Lindgren, H. C. (1978). *Too close for comfort: The psychology of crowding.* Englewood Cliffs, NJ: Prentice-Hall.

Isaac, S., & Michael, W. (1995). *Handbook in research and evaluation.* San Diego, CA: Edits.

Isen, A. M., & Noonberg, A. (1979). The effects of photographs of the handicapped on donation to charity: When a thousand words may be too much. *Journal of Applied Social Psychology, 9,* 426–431.

Islam, R. M., & Hewstone, M. (1993). Dimensions of contact as predictors of intergroup anxiety, perceived outgroup variability, and outgroup attitude: An integrative model. *Personality and Social Psychology Bulletin, 19,* 700–710.

Itzhaky, H. (1993). Role stress and job satisfaction in nonprofessional female human service workers in Israel. *Social Development Issues, 15,* 38–49.

Iyengar, S., & Kinder, D. R. (1987). *News that matters: Agenda-setting and priming in a television age.* Chicago: University of Chicago Press.

Jacklin, C. N., & Maccoby, E. E. (1978). Social behavior at 33 months in same-sex and mixed-sex dyads. *Child Development, 49,* 557–569.

Jackson, L. (1989). Relative deprivation and the gender wage gap. *Journal of Social Issues, 45*(4), 117–133.

Jacobs, L. (1993). *The health of nations: Public opinion and the making of American and British health policy.* Ithaca, NY: Cornell University Press.

Jacobs, R. S. (1992). *Leader experience and stress: The use of stress management training to improve performance.* Unpublished doctoral dissertation, University of Washington, Seattle.

Jacobson, J. L. (1992, September). *Gender bias: Roadblock to sustainable development* (Worldwatch Paper 110). Washington, DC: Worldwatch Institute.

Jacoby, J., & Hoyer, W. D. (1989). The comprehension/miscomprehension of print communication. *Journal of Consumer Research, 15,* 434–443.

Jahiel, R. (1992). *Homelessness: A prevention-oriented approach.* Baltimore: Johns Hopkins University Press.

Jalbert, N. L., & Getting, J. (1992). Racial and gender issues in facial recognition. In F. Lösel, D. Bender, & T. Bliesener (Eds.), *Psychology and law: International perspectives* (pp. 309–316). Berlin: de Gruyter.

Jamal, M. (1990). Relationship of job stress and type-A behavior to employees' job satisfaction, organizational commitment, psychosomatic health problems, and turnover motivation. *Human Relations, 43,* 727–738.

Janus, S. S., & Janus, C. L. (1993). *The Janus report on sexual behavior.* New York: Wiley.

Jarvik, M. E. (1973). Further observations on nicotine as the reinforcing agent in smoking. In W. L. Dunn, Jr. (Ed.), *Smoking behavior: Motives and incentives* (pp. 33–50). Washington, DC: Winston.

Jeffery, R. W., Hellerstedt, W. L., & Schmid, T. L. (1990). Correspondence programs for smoking cessation and weight control: A comparison of two strategies in the Minnesota Heart Health Program. *Health Psychology, 9,* 585–598.

Jemmott, J. B., & Jones, J. N. (1993). Social psychology and AIDS among ethnic minorities: Risk behaviors and strategies for changing them. In J. Pryor & G. Reeder (Eds.), *The social psychology of HIV infection* (pp. 183–244). Hillsdale, NJ: Erlbaum.

Jensen, A. R. (1969). How much can we boost IQ and scholastic achievement? *Harvard Educational Review, 39,* 1–123.

Jensen, S. (1991, January/February). Pornography does make women sex objects. *Utne Reader,* p. 13.

Jessup, H. R. (1990). New roles in team leadership. *Training and Development Journal, 44,* 79–83.

Johnson v. Louisiana, 406 U.S. 356 (1972).

Johnson, D. W., & Johnson, R. T. (1989). *Cooperation and competition: Theory and research.* Edina, MN: Interaction Books.

Johnson, D. W., & Johnson, R. T. (1994). Cooperative learning in the culturally diverse classroom. In R. DeVillar, C. Faltis, & J. Cummins (Eds.), *Cultural diversity in schools* (pp. 57–74). New York: State University of New York Press.

Johnson, D. W., & Johnson, R. T. (1995). Social interdependence: Cooperative learning in education. In B. B. Bunker & J. Z. Rubin (Eds.), *Conflict, cooperation, and justice: Essays inspired by the work of Morton Deutsch* (pp. 205–251). San Francisco: Jossey-Bass.

Johnson, D. W., & Johnson, R. T. (1996). *Conflict resolution and peer mediation programs in elementary and secondary schools: A review of the research.* Unpublished manuscript, University of Minnesota.

Johnson, D. W., Johnson, R., Mitchell, J., Cotten, B., Harris, D., & Louison, S. (1996). Effectiveness of conflict managers in an inner-city elementary school. *Journal of Educational Research, 89,* 280–285.

Johnson, F. (1988). Encounter group therapy. In S. Long (Ed.), *Six group therapies* (pp. 115–158). New York: Plenum.

Johnson, M. K., Hashtroudi, S., & Lindsay, D. S. (1993). Source monitoring. *Psychological Bulletin, 114,* 3–28.

Johnson, T. W., & Stinson, J. E. (1975). Role ambiguity, role conflict, and satisfaction: Moderating effects of individual differences. *Journal of Applied Psychology, 60,* 329–333.

Johnston, J., & Davidson, T. (1980). *The persistence of effects—A supplement to "An evaluation of 'Freestyle': A television series to reduce sex role stereotypes."* Ann Arbor: Institute for Social Research, University of Michigan.

Jonah, B. A., Dawson, N. E., & Smith, G. A. (1982). Effects of a selective traffic enforcement program on seat belt usage. *Journal of Applied Psychology, 67*, 89–96.

Jones, C. O. (1976). Policy analysis: Academic utility for practical rhetoric. *Policy Studies Journal, 4*, 281–286.

Jones, E. E. (1979). The rocky road from acts to dispositions. *American Psychologist, 34*, 107–117.

Jones, E. E., & Davis, K. E. (1965). From acts to dispositions: The attribution process in person perception. In L. Berkowitz (Ed.), *Advances in experimental social psychology* (Vol. 2, pp. 219–266). New York: Academic Press.

Jones, E. E., Flammer, A., Grob, A., Luthi, R., Rubin, J., & Fletcher, G. (1989). Attribution theory. In J. Forgas & M. Innes (Eds.), *Recent advances in social psychology: An international perspective* (pp. 63–125). Amsterdam: North-Holland.

Jones, E. E., Kanouse, D. E., Kelley, H. H., Nisbett, E. E., Valins, S., & Weiner, B. (1971). *Attribution: Perceiving the causes of behavior.* Morristown, NJ: General Learning Press.

Jones, E. E., & Sigall, H. (1971). The bogus pipeline: A new paradigm for measuring affect and attitude. *Psychological Bulletin, 76*, 349–364.

Josephson, W. D. (1987). Television violence and children's aggression: Testing the priming, social script, and disinhibition prediction. *Journal of Personality and Social Psychology, 54*, 778–788.

Judd, C. M., & Park, B. (1993). Definition and assessment of ac curacy in social stereotypes. *Psychological Review, 100*, 109–128.

Judge, T. A., Boudreau, J., & Bretz, R. (1994). Job and life attitudes of male executives. *Journal of Applied Psychology, 79*, 767–782.

Judge, T. A., & Watanabe, S. (1993). Another look at the job satisfaction-life satisfaction relationship. *Journal of Applied Psychology, 78*, 938–949.

Juhnke, R., Vought, C., Pyszczynski, T. A., Dane, F. C., Losure, B. D., & Wrightsman, L. S. (1979). Effects of presentation mode upon mock jurors' reactions to a trial. *Personality and Social Psychology Bulletin, 5*, 36–39.

Jussim, L. (1986). Self-fulfilling prophecies: A theoretical and integrative review. *Psychological Review, 93*, 429–445.

Jussim, L. (1989). Teacher expectations: Self-fulfilling prophecies, perceptual biases, and accuracy. *Journal of Personality and Social Psychology, 57*, 469–480.

Jussim, L. (1993). Accuracy of interpersonal expectations: A reflection construction analysis of current and classic research. *Journal of Personality, 61*, 637–668.

Kagehiro, D. K., & Laufer, W. S. (Eds.). (1992). *Handbook of psychology and law.* New York: Springer-Verlag.

Kahn, H., & Cooper, C. (1990). Mental health, job satisfaction, alcohol intake and occupational stress among dealers in financial markets. *Stress and Medicine, 6*, 285–298.

Kahn, R. L., & Byosiere, P. (1992). Stress in organizations. In M. D. Dunnette & L. M. Hough (Eds.), *Handbook of industrial & organizational psychology* (2nd ed., Vol. 2, pp. 571–650). Palo Alto, CA: Consulting Psychologists Press.

Kahneman, D., & Miller, D. (1986). Norm theory: Comparing reality to its alternatives. *Psychological Review, 93*, 136–153.

Kairys, D., Schulman, J., & Harring, S. (Eds.). (1975). *The jury system: New methods for reducing prejudice.* Philadelphia: National Lawyers Guild.

Kalven, H., Jr., & Zeisel, H. (1966). *The American jury.* Chicago: University of Chicago Press.

Kalwani, M. U., Yim, C. K., Rinne, J. J., & Sugita, Y. (1990). A price expectations model of customer brand choice. *Journal of Marketing Research, 27*, 251–262.

Kanagy, C. L., & Willits, F. K. (1993). A "greening" of religion? Some evidence from a Pennsylvania sample. *Social Science Quarterly, 74*, 674–683.

Kane, E. W., & Macaulay, L. J. (1993). Interviewer gender and gender attitudes. *Public Opinion Quarterly, 57*, 1–28.

Karau, S. J., & Williams, K. D. (1993). Social loafing: A meta-analytic review and theoretical integration. *Journal of Personality and Social Psychology, 65*, 681–706.

Karp, S. A. (1977). Psychological differentiation. In T. Blass (Ed.), *Personality variables in social behavior.* Hillsdale, NJ: Erlbaum.

Kasl, S. V. (1973). Mental health and work environment: An examination of the evidence. *Journal of Occupational Medicine, 15*, 509–518.

Kassin, S. M., Ellsworth, P. C., & Smith, V. L. (1989). The "general acceptance" of psychological research on eyewitness testimony: A comparison of experts and prospective jurors. *Journal of Applied Social Psychology, 22*, 1241–1249.

Katz, D. (1974). Factors affecting social change: A social-psychological interpretation. *Journal of Social Issues, 30*(3), 159–180.

Katz, D., & Braly, K. (1933). Racial stereotypes of one hundred college students. *Journal of Abnormal and Social Psychology, 28*, 280–290.

Katz, D., & Kahn, R. L. (1978). *The social psychology of organizations* (2nd ed.). New York: Wiley.

Katz, E. (1971). Platforms and windows: Broadcasting's role in election campaigns. *Journalism Quarterly, 48*, 304–314.

Katz, E. (1980). On conceptualizing media effects. In T. MacCormak (Ed.), *Communications studies: Decade of dissent.* Greenwich, CT: JAI Press.

Katz, E., Gurevitch, M., & Haas, H. (1973). On the use of the mass media for important things. *American Sociological Review, 38*, 164–181.

Katz, J. (1996). Provisions of the welfare bill. *Congressional Quarterly, 54*, 2192–2196.

Katz, P. A., & Taylor, D. A. (Eds.). (1988). *Eliminating racism: Profiles in controversy.* New York: Plenum.

Katzell, R. A., Yankelovich, D., Fein, M., Ornati, O., & Nash, A. (1975). *Work, productivity, and job satisfaction: An evaluation of policy-related research.* New York: Psychological Corporation.

Katzman, N. I. (1972). Television soap operas: What's been going on anyway? *Public Opinion Quarterly, 36*, 200–212.

Kee, J. E. (1994). Benefit-cost analysis in program evaluation. In J. Wholey, H. Hatry, & K. Newcomer (Eds.), *Handbook of practical program evaluation* (pp. 456–488). San Francisco: Jossey-Bass.

Kelder, G. E., Jr., & Daynard, R. A. (1997). Judicial approaches to tobacco control: The third wave of tobacco litigation as a tobacco control mechanism. *Journal of Social Issues, 53,* 169–186.

Kelley, H. H. (1967). Attribution theory in social psychology. In D. Levine (Ed.), *Nebraska symposium on motivation* (Vol. 15, pp. 192–238). Lincoln: University of Nebraska Press.

Kelley, H. H., & Michela, J. L. (1980). Attribution theory and research. *Annual Review of Psychology, 31,* 457–501.

Kelley, H. H., & Thibaut, J. W. (1978). *Interpersonal relations: A theory of interdependence.* New York: Wiley.

Kelly, J., Murphy, D., Sikkema, K., & Kalichman, S. (1993). Psychological interventions to prevent HIV infection are urgently needed. *American Psychologist, 48,* 1023–1034.

Kelman, H. C. (1958). Compliance, identification, and internalization: Three processes of attitude change. *Journal of Conflict Resolution, 2,* 51–60.

Kelman, H. C. (1967). Human use of human subjects: The problem of deception in social psychological experiments. *Psychological Bulletin, 67,* 1–11.

Kelman, H. C. (1968). The relevance of nonviolent action. In H. C. Kelman, *A time to speak: On human values and social research.* San Francisco: Jossey-Bass.

Kelman, H. C. (1977). Privacy and research with human beings. *Journal of Social Issues 33*(3), 169–195.

Kelman, H. C. (1995). Contributions of an unofficial conflict resolution effort to the Israeli-Palestinian breakthrough. *Negotiation Journal, 11,* 33–41.

Kelman, H. C., & Warwick, D. P. (1978). The ethics of social intervention: Goals, means, and consequences. In G. Bermant, H. C. Kelman, & D. P. Warwick (Eds.). *The ethics of social intervention.* Washington, DC: Hemisphere.

Kempton, W., Boster, J., & Hartley, J. (1995). *Environmental values in American culture.* Cambridge, MA: MIT Press.

Kempton, W., Darley, J., & Stern, P. (1992). Psychological research for new energy problems. *American Psychologist, 47,* 1213–1223.

Kennedy, E. M. (1993). The Head Start Transition Project: Head Start goes to elementary school. In E. Zigler & S. Styfco (Eds.), *Head Start and beyond: A national plan for extended childhood intervention* (pp. 97–110). New Haven, CT: Yale University Press.

Keppel, G. (1991). *Design and analysis: A researcher's handbook* (3rd ed.). Englewood Cliffs, NJ: Prentice Hall.

Kerr, N. L. (1989). Illusions of efficacy: The effects of group size on perceived efficacy in social dilemmas. *Journal of Experimental Social Psychology, 25,* 287–313.

Kerr, N. L. (1993). Stochastic models of juror decision making. In R. Hastie (Ed.), *Inside the juror: The psychology of juror decision making* (pp. 116–135). New York: Cambridge University Press.

Kerr, N. L., Atkin, R. S., Stasser, G., Meek, D., Holt, R. W., & Davis, J. H. (1976). Guilt beyond a reasonable doubt: Effects of concept definition and assigned decision rule on the judg-

ments of mock jurors. *Journal of Personality and Social Psychology, 34,* 282–294.

Kerr, N. L., & MacCoun, R. (1987). The effect of jury size and polling method on the process and product of jury deliberation. In L. Wrightsman, S. Kassin, & C. Willis (Eds.), *In the jury box: Controversies in the courtroom* (pp. 209–234). Newbury Park, CA: Sage.

Kerr, N. L., Nerenz, D., & Herrick, D. (1979). Role playing and the study of jury behavior. *Sociological Methods and Research, 7,* 337–355.

Kershaw, D., & Fair, J. (1976). *The New Jersey income-maintenance experiment* (Vol. 1). New York: Academic Press.

Kessler, D. A., Witt, A. M., Barnett, P. S., Zeller, M. R., Natanblut, S. L., Wilkenfeld, J. P., Lorraine, C. C., Thompson, L. J., & Schultz, W. B. (1996). The Food and Drug Administration's regulation of tobacco products. *New England Journal of Medicine, 335,* 988–994.

Khaleque, A., Hossain, M., & Hoque, M. E. (1992). Job satisfaction, mental health, fatigue and performance of industrial workers. *Psychological Studies, 37,* 136–141.

Khator, R. (1993). Recycling: A policy dilemma for American states? *Policy Studies Journal, 21,* 210–226.

Kidder, L. H., & Cohn, E. S. (1979). Public views of crime and crime prevention. In I. H. Frieze, D. Bar-Tal, & J. S. Carroll (Eds.), *New approaches to social problems: Applications of attribution theory.* San Francisco: Jossey-Bass.

Kiesler, C. A. (1980). Psychology and public policy. In L. Bickman (Ed.), *Applied social psychology annual* (Vol. 1, pp. 49–67). Beverly Hills, CA: Sage.

Kilbourne, B. K. (1989). A cross-cultural investigation of the foot-in-the-door compliance induction procedure. *Journal of Cross-Cultural Psychology, 20,* 3–38.

Kimball, M. M. (1989). A new perspective on women's math achievement. *Psychological Bulletin, 105,* 198–214.

Kimmel, A. J. (1988). *Ethics and values in applied social research.* Newbury Park, CA: Sage.

Kinder, D. R., & Sears, D. O. (1981). Prejudice and politics: Symbolic racism versus racial threats to the good life. *Journal of Personality and Social Psychology, 40,* 414–431.

Kinsey, A. C., Pomeroy, W. B., & Martin, C. E. (1948). *Sexual behavior in the human male.* Philadelphia: Saunders.

Kinsey, A. C., Pomeroy, W. B., Martin, C. E., & Gebhard, P. H. (1953). *Sexual behavior in the human female.* Philadelphia: Saunders.

Kipnis, D. (1994). Accounting for the use of behavior technologies in social psychology. *American Psychologist, 49,* 165–172.

Kleck, G. (1991). *Point blank: Guns and violence in America.* Chicago: Aldine.

Klein, S., & Mowrer, R. (Eds.). (1989). *Contemporary learning theories: Pavlovian conditioning and the status of traditional learning theory.* Hillsdale, NJ: Erlbaum.

Kleinpenning, G., & Hagendoorn, L. (1993). Forms of racism and the cumulative dimension of ethnic attitudes. *Social Psychology Quarterly, 56,* 21–36.

Klitzner, M., Gruenewald, P., Bamberger, E., & Rossiter, C.

(1994). A quasi-experimental evaluation of Students Against Driving Drunk. *American Journal of Drug and Alcohol Abuse, 20,* 57–74.

Knoff, H., & Batsche, G. (1995). Project ACHIEVE: Analyzing a school reform process for at-risk and underachieving students. *School Psychology Review, 24,* 579–603.

Knoke, D. (1990). *Organizing for collective action: The political economies of associations.* New York: Aldine de Gruyter.

Knopf, R. C. (1987). Human behavior, cognition, and affect in the natural environment. In D. Stokols & I. Altman (Eds.), *Handbook of environmental psychology* (Vol. 1, pp. 783–825). New York: Wiley.

Knowles, J. H. (1977). The responsibility of the individual. In J. H. Knowles (Ed.), *Doing better and feeling worse.* New York: Norton.

Koeppel, D. (1991, January 1). RJR charged with violating Canadian tobacco law. *Marketing Week,* p. 6.

Koeske, G. F., Kirk, S. A., & Koeske, R. D. (1993). Coping with job stress: Which strategies work best? *Journal of Occupational and Organizational Psychology, 66,* 319–335.

Kolbe, R., & LaVoie, J. (1981). Sex-role stereotyping in preschool children's picture books. *Social Psychology Quarterly, 44,* 369–374.

Konecni, V. J., & Ebbesen, E. B. (1992). Methodological issues in research on legal decision making with special reference to experimental simulations. In F. Losel, D. Bender, & T. Bliesener (Eds.), *Psychology and law: International perspectives* (pp. 413–423). Berlin: de Gruyter.

Koop, C. E. (1988). Preface. In *The health consequences of smoking: Nicotine addiction: A report of the Surgeon General, 1988* (pp. iii–vii). Rockville, MD: U.S. Department of Health and Human Services.

Koss, M. P. (1990). The women's mental health research agenda: Violence against women. *American Psychologist, 45,* 374–380.

Koss, M. P. (1993). Rape: Scope, impact, interventions, and public policy responses. *American Psychologist, 48,* 1062–1069.

Koss, M. P., Gidycz, C. A., & Wisniewski, N. (1987). The scope of rape: Incidence and prevalence of sexual aggression and victimization in a national sample of higher education students. *Journal of Consulting and Clinical Psychology, 55,* 162–170.

Kovac, J. (1986). Productivity gainsharing: A Scanlon overview. *Psychology: A Quarterly Journal of Human Behavior, 23,* 24–31.

Kraus, S. (Ed.). (1979). *The great debates: Carter vs. Ford, 1976.* Bloomington: Indiana University Press.

Kraut, R. E., & McConahay, J. B. (1973). How being interviewed affects voting: An experiment. *Public Opinion Quarterly, 37,* 398–406.

Kremen, B. (1973, September 3). Lordstown—Searching for a better way of work. *New York Times,* Section 3, pp. 1, 4.

Kubler-Ross, E. (1969). *On death and dying.* New York: Macmillan.

Kunkel, D. (1993). *Policy and the future of children's television.*

In G. Berry & J. Asamen (Eds.), *Children and television: Images in a changing sociocultural world* (pp. 273–290). Newbury Park, CA: Sage.

Kunkel, D., & Roberts, D. (1991). Young minds and marketplace values: Issues in children's television advertising. *Journal of Social Issues, 47*(1), 57–72.

Ladd, E. C., Jr., & Lipset, S. M. (1975, October 20). Academics: America's most politically liberal stratum. *Chronicle of Higher Education,* pp. 1–2.

Lana, R. C. (1969). Pretest sensitization. In R. Rosenthal & R. L. Rosnow (Eds.), *Artifact in behavioral research.* New York: Academic Press.

Lance, E., LaPointe, J., & Stewart, A. (1994). A test of the context dependency of three causal models of halo rater error. *Journal of Applied Psychology, 79,* 332–340.

Lancourt, J. E. (1979). *Confront or concede: The Alinsky citizen-action organizations.* Lexington, MA: Lexington.

Lando, H. (1993). Formal quit smoking treatments. In C. T. Orleans & J. Slade (Eds.), *Nicotine addiction: Principles and management* (pp. 221–244). New York: Oxford University Press.

Landrine, H., Klonoff, E. A., Alcaraz, R., Scott, J., & Wilkins, P. (1995). Multiple variables in discrimination. In B. Lott & D. Maluso (Eds.), *The social psychology of interpersonal discrimination* (pp. 183–224). New York: Guilford.

Landy, D., & Aronson, E. (1969). The influence of the character of the criminal and his victim on the decisions of simulated jurors. *Journal of Experimental Social Psychology, 5,* 141–152.

Landy, F. J., Shankster, L. J., & Kohler, S. S. (1994). Personnel selection and placement. *Annual Review of Psychology, 45,* 261–296.

Lang, J. (1987). *Creating architectural theory: The role of the behavioral sciences in environmental design.* New York: Van Nostrand Reinhold.

Langton, S. (1981). The evolution of federal citizen involvement policy. *Policy Studies Review, 1,* 369–378.

Lasswell, H. D. (1970). The emerging conception of the policy sciences. *Policy Sciences, 1,* 3–14.

Latane, B., & Darley, J. M. (1970). *The unresponsive bystander: Why doesn't he help?* New York: Appleton-Century-Crofts.

Latkin, C., Mandell, W., Vlahov, D., Oziemkowska, M., & Celentano, D. (1996). The long-term outcome of a personal network-oriented HIV prevention intervention for injection drug users: The SAFE project. *American Journal of Community Psychology, 24,* 341–364.

Laumann, E. O., Gagnon, J. H., Michael, R. T., & Michaels, S. (1994). *The social organization of sexuality: Sexual practices in the United States.* Chicago: University of Chicago Press.

Lawler, E. E., III. (1981). *Pay and organizational development.* Reading, MA.: Addison-Wesley.

Lawler, E. E., III. (1982). Strategies for improving the quality of work life. *American Psychologist, 37,* 486–493.

Lawler, E. E., III. (1990). *Strategic pay: Aligning organizational strategies and pay systems.* San Francisco: Jossey-Bass.

Lawler, E. E., III. (1992). *The ultimate advantage: Creating the high involvement organization.* San Francisco: Jossey-Bass.

Lawler, E. E., & Mohrman, S. A. (1985, September). Quality circles after the fad. *Harvard Business Review,* 87–95.

Lazar, I. (1971). Which citizens to participate in what? In E. S. Cahn & B. A. Passett (Eds.), *Citizen participation: Effecting community change.* New York: Praeger.

Lazarsfeld, P. F., & Reitz, J. G. (1975). *An introduction to applied sociology.* New York: Elsevier.

Lazarus, R. S., & Folkman, S. (1984). Coping and adaptation. In W. D. Gentry (Ed.), *The handbook of behavioral medicine* (pp. 282–325). New York: Guilford.

Lee, J. A., DeLeon, P. H., Wedding, D., & Nordal, K. (1994). Psychologists' role in influencing Congress: The process and the players. *Professional Psychology—Research & Practice, 25,* 9–15.

Leeming, F., Dwyer, W., Porter, B., & Cobern, M. (1993). Outcome research in environmental education: A critical review. *Journal of Environmental Education, 24,* 8–21.

Lefkowitz, M. M., Eron, L. D., Walder, L. O., & Huesmann, L. R. (1977). *Growing up to be violent.* New York: Pergamon.

Leippe, M. R., Manion, A. P., & Romanczyk, A. (1992). Eyewitness persuasion: How and how well do fact finders judge the accuracy of adults' and children's memory reports? *Journal of Personality and Social Psychology, 63,* 181–197.

Lenart, S. (1994). *Shaping political attitudes: The impact of interpersonal communication and mass media.* Thousand Oaks, CA: Sage.

LeoGrande, W. (1993). Did the public matter? The impact of opinion on congressional support for Ronald Reagan's Nicaragua policy. In R. Sobel (Ed.), *Public opinion in U.S. foreign policy* (pp. 167–190). Lanham, MD: Rowman & Littlefield.

LeoGrande, W., & Brenner, P. (1993). The House divided: Ideological polarization over aid to the Nicaragua Contras. *Legislative Studies Quarterly, 18,* 105–123.

Leonard, J. (1983). Can your organization support quality circles? *Training and Development Journal, 37,* 67–72.

Lepore, S. J., & Sesco, B. (1994). Distorting children's reports and interpretations of events through suggestion. *Applied Psychology, 79,* 108–120.

Lepper, M. R., & Greene, D. (Eds.). (1978). *The hidden costs of reward.* Hillsdale, NJ: Erlbaum.

Leventhal, H. (1980). Applied social psychological research: The salvation of substantive social psychological theory. In R. F. Kidd & M. J. Saks (Eds.), *Advances in applied social psychology* (Vol. 1). Hillsdale, NJ: Erlbaum.

Leventhal, H., & Avis, N. (1976). Pleasure, addiction, and habit: Factors in verbal report on factors in smoking behavior. *Journal of Abnormal Psychology, 85,* 478–488.

Leventhal, H., & Cleary, P. D. (1980). The smoking problem: A review of the research and theory in behavioral risk modification. *Psychological Bulletin, 88,* 370–405.

Leventhal, H., & Everhart, D. (1979). Emotion, pain, and physical illness. In C. E. Izard (Ed.), *Emotion and psychopathology.* New York: Plenum.

Leventhal, H., Fleming, R., & Glynn, K. (1988). A cognitive-developmental approach to smoking intervention. In S. Maes, C. D. Spielberger, P. B. Defares, & I. G. Sarason (Eds.), *Topics in health psychology: Proceedings of the first annual expert conference on health psychology* (pp. 79–105). New York: Wiley.

Levin, J., & McDevitt, J. (1993). *Hate crimes: The rising tide of bigotry and bloodshed.* New York: Plenum.

Levine, B. L. (1986). The tragedy of the commons and the comedy of community: The commons in history. *Journal of Community Psychology, 14,* 81–99.

Levine, M., Toro, P. A., & Perkins, D. V. (1993). Social and community interventions. *Annual Review of Psychology, 44,* 525–558.

Levy, S. M. (1990). Psychosocial risk factors and cancer progression: Mediating pathways linking behavior and disease. In K. D. Craig & S. M. Weis (Eds.), *Health enhancement, disease prevention, and early intervention: Biobehavioral perspectives* (pp. 348–369). New York: Springer.

Levy, S. M., Herberman, R. B., Maluish, A. M., Achlien, B., & Lippman, M. (1985). Prognostic risk assessment in primary breast cancer by behavioral and immunological parameters. *Health Psychology, 4,* 99–113.

Levy-Leboyer, C. (1988). Success and failure in applying psychology. *American Psychologist, 43,* 779–785.

Lewin, K. (1935). *A dynamic theory of personality.* New York: McGraw-Hill.

Lewin, K. (1947). Group decision and social change. In T. M. Newcomb & E. L. Hartley (Eds.), *Readings in social psychology* (pp. 330–344). New York: Holt.

Lewin, K. (1948). *Resolving social conflicts.* New York: Harper.

Lewin, K. (1951). *Field theory in social science* (D. Cartwright, Ed.). New York: Harper. (Originally published, 1944.)

Lewin, K., Lippitt, R., & White, R. K. (1939). Patterns of aggressive behavior in experimentally created "social climates." *Journal of Social Psychology, 10,* 271–299.

Lewis, H., Sperry, L., & Carlson, J. (1993). *Health counseling.* Pacific Grove, CA: Brooks/Cole.

Lewis, J. (1994). Treating people with alcohol problems. In J. Lewis (Ed.), *Addictions: Concepts and strategies for treatment* (pp. 47–58). Gaithersburg, MD: Aspen.

Lewis, P. (1993, May 23). New U.N. index measures nations' quality of life. *New York Times,* p. L14.

Leyens, J. P., Parke, R. D., Camino, L., & Berkowitz, L. (1975). Effects of movie violence on aggression in a field setting as a function of group dominance and cohesion. *Journal of Personality and Social Psychology, 32,* 346–360.

Lichtenstein, D. R., Bloch, P. H., & Black, W. C. (1988). Correlates of price acceptability. *Journal of Consumer Research, 15,* 243–252.

Lichtenstein, D. R., & Burton, S. (1989). The relationship between perceived and objective price-quality. *Journal of Marketing Research, 26,* 429–443.

Lichtenstein, E., & Glasgow, R. E. (1992). Smoking cessation: What have we learned over the past decade? *Journal of Consulting and Clinical Psychology, 60,* 518–527.

Lichtenstein, E., & Hollis, J. (1992). Patient referral to smoking cessation program: Who follows through? *Journal of Family Practice, 24,* 739–744.

Liebert, D. E., Sprafkin, J. N., Liebert, R. M., & Rubinstein, E. A. (1977). Effects of television commercial disclaimers on the product expectations of children. *Journal of Communication, 27*(1), 118–124.

Liebert, R. M., & Schwartzberg, N. S. (1977). Effects of mass media. *Annual Review of Psychology, 28,* 141–173.

Liebert, R. M., & Sprafkin, J. N. (1988). *The early window: Effects of television on children and youth* (3rd ed.). New York: Pergamon.

Liebert, R. M., Sprafkin, J. N., & Poulos, R. W. (1975). Selling cooperation to children. *Proceedings of the 20th annual conference of the Advertising Research Foundation.* New York: Advertising Research Foundation.

Likert, R. (1961). *New patterns of management.* New York: McGraw-Hill.

Lin, N., & Ensel, W. (1989). Life stress and health: Stressors and resources. *American Sociological Review, 54,* 383–399.

Lindblom, C. (1990). *Inquiry and change: The troubled attempt to understand and shape society.* New Haven, CT: Yale University Press.

Lindgren, J. R., & Taub, N. (1988). *The law of sex discrimination.* New York: West.

Lindsay, R. C. L. (1994a). Biased lineups: Where do they come from? In D. Ross, J. Read, & M. Toglia (Eds.), *Adult eyewitness testimony: Current trends and developments* (pp. 182–200). New York: Cambridge University Press.

Lindsay, R. C. L. (1994b). Expectations of eyewitness performance: Jurors' verdicts do not follow from their beliefs. In D. Ross, J. Read, & M. Toglia (Eds.), *Adult eyewitness testimony: Current trends and developments* (pp. 362–384). New York: Cambridge University Press.

Lingsweiler, V. M., Crowter, J. H., & Stephens, M. A. P. (1987). Emotional reactivity and eating in binge eating and obesity. *Journal of Behavioral Medicine, 10,* 287–300.

Link, T. G. (1992). *Stress management training: An extension of cognitive resources theory.* Unpublished doctoral dissertation, University of Washington, Seattle.

Linn, N., Vining, J., & Feeley, P. A. (1994). Toward a sustainable society: Waste minimization through environmentally conscious consuming. *Journal of Applied Social Psychology, 24,* 550–1572.

Linz, D., Malamuth, N., & Beckett, K. (1992). Civil liberties and research on the effects of pornography. In P. Suedfeld & P. Tetlock (Eds.), *Psychology and social policy* (pp. 149–164). New York: Hemisphere.

Lipman, J. (1991, August 22). Volvo, Scali settle with FTC. *Wall Street Journal,* p. B3.

Lippmann, W. (1922). *Public opinion.* New York: Macmillan.

Lipsey, M. W. (1974). Research and relevance: A survey of graduate students and faculty in psychology. *American Psychologist, 29,* 541–553.

Lipsey, M. W. (1977). Attitudes toward the environment and pollution. In S. Oskamp, *Attitudes and opinions* (pp. 360–379). Englewood Cliffs, NJ: Prentice-Hall.

Lipsey, M. W. (1988). Practice and malpractice in evaluation research. *Evaluation Practice, 9,* 5–24.

Lipsey, M. W. (1990). *Design sensitivity: Statistical power for experimental research.* Newbury Park, CA: Sage.

Lipsey, M. W., Crosse, S., Dunke, J., Pollard, J., & Stobart, G. (1985). Evaluation: The state of the art and the sorry state of the science. In D. Cordray (Ed.), *Utilizing prior research in evaluation planning* (pp. 7–28). San Francisco: Jossey-Bass.

Lipsey, M. W., & Wilson, D. B. (1993). The efficacy of psychological, educational, and behavioral treatment: Confirmation from meta-analysis. *American Psychologist, 48,* 1181–1209.

Lipsitz, A., Brake, G., Vincent, E., & Winters, M. (1993). Another round for the brewers: Television ads and children's alcohol expectancies. *Journal of Applied Social Psychology, 23,* 439–450.

Lipsitz, A., Kallmeyer, K., Ferguson, M., & Abas, A. (1989). Counting on blood donors: Increasing the impact of reminder calls. *Journal of Applied Social Psychology, 19,* 1057–1067.

Lipton, J. P. (1977). On the psychology of eyewitness testimony. *Journal of Applied Psychology, 62,* 90–95.

Lipton, J. P. (1996). Legal aspects of eyewitness testimony. In S. Sporer, R. Malpass, & G. Koehnken (Eds.), *Psychological issues in eyewitness identification* (pp. 7–22). Mahwah, NJ: Erlbaum.

Locke, E. A. (1976). The nature and causes of job satisfaction. In M. D. Dunnette (Ed.), *Handbook of industrial and organizational psychology.* Chicago: Rand McNally.

Locke, E. A., & Latham, G. P. (1990). Work motivation and satisfaction: Light at the end of the tunnel. *Psychological Science, 1,* 240–246.

Lockhart v. McCree, 54 U.S.L.W. 4449 (1986).

Loeb, M. (1979, December 17). Ideas from a matchmaker. *Time,* p. 72.

Loftus, E. F. (1975). Leading questions and the eyewitness report. *Cognitive Psychology, 7,* 560–572.

Loftus, E. F. (1983). Silence is not golden. *American Psychologist, 38,* 564–572.

Loftus, E. F. (1986). Ten years in the life of an expert witness. *Law and Human Behavior, 10,* 241–263.

Loftus, E. F. (1991). Resolving legal questions with psychological data. *American Psychologist, 46,* 1046–1048.

Loftus, E. F., & Hoffman, H. G. (1989). Misinformation and memory: The creation of new memories. *Journal of Experimental Psychology: General, 118,* 100–104.

Loftus, E. F., & Ketcham, K. (1991). *Witness for the defense: The accused, the eyewitness, and the expert who puts memory on trial.* New York: St. Martin's.

Loftus, E. F., Loftus, G. R., & Messo, J. (1987). Some facts about "weapon focus." *Law and Human Behavior, 11,* 55–62.

Loftus, E. F., & Monahan, J. (1980). Trial by data: Psychological research as legal evidence. *American Psychologist, 35,* 270–283.

Loftus, E. F., & Zanni, G. (1975). Eyewitness testimony: The influence of the wording of a question. *Bulletin of the Psychonomic Society, 5,* 86–88.

Long, R. J. (1988). Factors affecting managerial desires for various types of employee participation in decision making. *Applied Psychology: An International Review, 23,* 726–737.

Longino, H. (1980). What is pornography? In L. Lederer (Ed.), *Take back the night: Women on pornography.* New York: Morrow.

Lonsway, K. A., & Fitzgerald, L. F. (1995). Attitudinal antecedents of rape myth acceptance: A theoretical and empirical reexamination. *Journal of Personality and Social Psychology, 68,* 704–711.

Loo, C., Fong, K. T., & Iwamasa, G. (1988). Ethnicity and cultural diversity: An analysis of work published in community psychology journals, 1965–1985. *Journal of Community Psychology, 16,* 332–349.

Los Angeles Times. (1970, October 16). Nixon repudiates U.S. commission's obscenity report.

Loscocco, K., & Spitze, G. (1991). The organizational context of women's and men's pay satisfaction. *Social Science Quarterly, 72,* 3–19.

Lösel, F. (1992). Psychology and law: Overtures, crescendos, and reprises. In F. Lösel, D. Bender, & T. Bliesener (Eds.), *Psychology and law: International perspectives* (pp. 3–21). Berlin: de Gruyter.

Lösel, F., Bender, D., & Bliesener, T. (Eds.). (1992). *Psychology and law: International perspectives.* Berlin: de Gruyter.

Lott, B. (1985). The devaluation of women's competence. *Journal of Social Issues, 41*(4), 43–60.

Lott, B. (1995). Distancing from women: Interpersonal sexist discrimination. In B. Lott & D. Maluso (Eds.), *The social psychology of interpersonal discrimination* (pp. 12–49). New York: Guilford.

Lott, B., & Maluso, D. (Eds.). (1995). *The social psychology of interpersonal discrimination.* New York: Guilford.

Lovelace, V. (1990). *Sesame Street* as a continuing experiment. *Educational Technology Research and Development, 38,* 17–24.

Lowe, R. H., & Wittig, M. A. (Eds.). (1989). Approaching pay equity through comparable worth [Special issue]. *Journal of Social Issues, 45*(4), 1–246.

Lowman, R. P. (1980). Psychologists testify before NSF. *Personality and Social Psychology Bulletin, 6,* 160–162.

Lucas, W. A., & Possner, K. B. (1975). *Television news and local awareness: A retrospective look.* Santa Monica, CA: Rand Corporation.

Lucker, G. W., Rosenfield, D., Sikes, J., & Aronson, E. (1977). Performance in the interdependent classroom: A field study. *American Educational Research Journal, 13,* 115–123.

Lumsden, M., & Wolfe, R. (1996). Evolution of the problem-solving workshop: An introduction to social-psychological approaches to conflict resolution. *Peace and Conflict: Journal of Peace Psychology, 2,* 37–67.

Luus, C. A. E., & Wells, G. (1994). Eyewitness identification and confidence. In D. Ross, J. Read, & M. Toglia (Eds.), *Adult eyewitness testimony: Current trends and developments* (pp. 348–361). New York: Cambridge University Press.

Luyben, P. D., & Bailey, J. (1979). Newspaper recycling: The effects of rewards and proximity of containers. *Environment and Behavior, 11,* 539–557.

Lynn, L. E., Jr. (Ed.). (1978). *Knowledge and policy: The uncertain connection* (Study Project on Social Research and Development, Vol. 5). Washington, DC: National Academy of Sciences.

Lyons, J., Anderson, R., & Larson, D. (1994). A systematic review of the effects of aggressive and nonaggressive pornography. In D. Zillmann, J. Bryant, & A. Huston (Eds.), *Media, children, and the family: Social scientific, psychodynamic, and clinical perspectives* (pp. 271–310). Hillsdale, NJ: Erlbaum.

Macaulay, J. E. (1992). *Group performance: The effects of stress and experience on leader use of fluid and crystallized intelligence.* Unpublished doctoral dissertation, University of Washington, Seattle.

Maccoby, E. E. (1988). Gender as a social category. *Developmental Psychology, 24,* 755–765.

Maccoby, E. E. (1990). Gender and relationships: A developmental account. *American Psychologist, 45,* 513–520.

Maccoby, E. E., & Jacklin, C. N. (1974). *The psychology of sex differences.* Stanford, CA: Stanford University Press.

Maccoby, E. E., & Jacklin, C. N. (1987). Gender segregation in childhood. In H. W. Reese (Ed.), *Advances in child development and behavior* (Vol. 20, pp. 239–288). New York: Academic Press.

MacInnis, D. J., & Park, C. W. (1991). The differential role of characteristics of music on high- and low-involvement consumers' processing of ads. *Journal of Consumer Research, 18,* 161–173.

Macrae, C. N., Stangor, C., & Hewstone, M. (Eds.). (1996). *Stereotypes and stereotyping.* New York: Guilford.

Maes, S., Spielberger, C. D., Defares, P. B., & Sarason, I. G. (Eds.). (1988). *Topics in health psychology.* New York: Wiley.

Mahard, R., & Crain, R. (1983). Research on minority achievement in desegregated schools. In C. Rossell & W. Hawley (Eds.), *The consequences of school desegregation* (pp. 103–125). Philadelphia: Temple University Press.

Maier, M. (1991). *The data game: Controversies in social science statistics.* New York: Sharpe.

Major, B. (1987). Gender, justice, and the psychology of entitlement. In P. Shaver & C. Hendrick (Eds.), *Sex and gender: Review of personality and social psychology 7* (pp. 124–148). Newbury Park, CA: Sage.

Major, B., Feinstein, J., & Crocker, J. (1994). Attributional ambiguity of affirmative action. *Basic and Applied Social Psychology, 15,* 113–141.

Makepeace, J. M. (1986). Gender differences in courtship violence victimization. *Family Relations, 35,* 383–388.

Malamuth, N. M., & Check, J. V. (1981). The effects of mass media exposure on acceptance of violence against women: A field experiment. *Journal of Research in Personality, 15,* 436–446.

Malpass, R. S., & Devine, P. G. (1981). Eyewitness identification: Lineup instructions and the absence of the offender. *Journal of Applied Psychology, 66,* 482–489.

Maluso, D. (1995). Shaking hands with a clenched fist: Interpersonal racism. In B. Lott & D. Maluso (Eds.), *The social psychology of interpersonal discrimination* (pp. 50–79). New York: Guilford.

Mangione, T. W., & Quinn, R. P. (1975). Job satisfaction, counterproductive behavior, and drug use at work. *Journal of Applied Psychology, 60,* 114–116.

Mann, C. C. (1994). Can meta-analysis make policy? *Science, 266,* 960–962.

Manne, S. L., Sabbioni, M., Bovbjerg, D. H., Jacobsen, P. B., Taylor, K. L., & Redd, W. H. (1994). Coping with chemotherapy for breast cancer. *Journal of Behavioral Medicine, 17,* 41–56.

Manski, C., & Garfinkel, I. (Eds.). (1992). *Evaluating welfare and training programs.* Cambridge, MA: Harvard University Press.

Marini, M. M. (1989). Sex differences in earnings in the United States. *Annual Review of Sociology, 15,* 343–380.

Mark, M. M., Cook, T. D., & Diamond, S. S. (1976). Fourteen years of social psychology: A growing commitment to field experimentation. *Personality and Social Psychology Bulletin, 2,* 154–157.

Mark, M. M., Sanna, L. J., & Shotland, R. L. (1992). Time series methods in applied social research. In F. Bryant et al. (Eds.), *Methodological issues in applied social psychology* (pp. 111–133). New York: Plenum.

Marquis, K. H., Marshall, J., & Oskamp, S. (1972). Testimony validity as a function of question form, atmosphere, and item difficulty. *Journal of Applied Social Psychology, 2,* 167–186.

Marsh, H., Chessor, D., Craven, R., & Roche, L. (1995). The effects of gifted and talented programs on academic self-concept: The big fish strikes again. *American Educational Research Journal, 32,* 285–319.

Martell, R. F., Lane, D. M., & Emrich, C. (1996). Male-female differences: A computer simulation. *American Psychologist, 51,* 157–158.

Martichuski, D. K., & Bell, P. A. (1991). Reward, punishment, and moral suasion in a commons dilemma. *Journal of Applied Social Psychology, 21,* 1356–1369.

Martin, S. (1996). Do's and don'ts for interviewing with the media. *APA Monitor, 27*(10), 35.

Marullo, S., & Lofland, J. (1990). *Peace action in the eighties: Social science perspectives.* New Brunswick, NJ: Rutgers University Press.

Marx, G. T. (1970). Racism and race relations. In M. Wertheimer (Ed.), *Confrontation: Psychology and the problems of today* (pp. 100–102). Glenview, IL: Scott, Foresman.

Maslow, A. H. (1970). *Motivation and personality* (2nd ed.) New York: Harper & Row.

Masters, W. H., & Johnson, V. E. (1966). *Human sexual response.* Boston: Little, Brown.

Matlin, M. W. (1987). *The psychology of women.* New York: Holt, Rinehart & Winston.

Mausner, B., & Platt, E. S. (1971). *Smoking: A behavioral analysis.* New York: Pergamon.

Mavis, B. E., & Fergus, E. O. (1985, August). *Survival in the '80s of the community lodge program.* Paper presented at American Psychological Association meeting, Los Angeles.

May, J. V. (1973). Two model cities: Negotiations in Oakland. In G. Frederickson (Ed.), *Neighborhood control in the 1970s: Politics, administration, and citizen participation.* New York: Chandler.

Mayer, W. G. (1993). Trends in media usage. *Public Opinion Quarterly, 57,* 593–611.

Mayo, C., & La France, M. (1980). Toward an applicable social psychology. In R. F. Kidd & M. J. Saks (Eds.), *Advances in applied social psychology* (Vol. 1). Hillsdale, NJ: Erlbaum.

Mayo, E. (1933). *The human problems of an industrial civilization.* New York: Macmillan.

McAlister, A., Puska, P., Kosketa, K., Pallonen, U., & Maccoby, N. (1980). Mass communication and community organization for public health education. *American Psychologist, 35,* 375–379.

McAndrew, F. T. (1993). *Environmental psychology.* Pacific Grove, CA: Brooks/Cole.

McAneny, L. (1993). The Gallup poll on crime: Most Americans again see crime on the rise. *Gallup Poll Monthly,* No. 339, 18–27.

McAneny, L. (1994, August). Ethnic minorities view the media's view of *them. Gallup Poll Monthly,* No. 347, pp. 31–41.

McAneny, L., & Saad, L. (1994, May). America's public schools: Still separate? Still unequal? *Gallup Poll Monthly,* No. 344, pp. 23–29.

McCarthy, E. D., Langner, T. S., Gersten, J. C., Eisenberg, J. G., & Orzeck, L. (1975). Violence and behavior disorders. *Journal of Communication, 25*(4), 71–85.

McClelland, D. C. (1961). *The achieving society.* Princeton, NJ: Van Nostrand.

McClelland, D. C. (1971). *Motivational trends in society.* Morristown, NJ: General Learning Press.

McClelland, D. C. (1978). Managing motivation to expand human freedom. *American Psychologist, 33,* 201–210.

McClelland, D. C. (1993). Intelligence is not the best predictor of job performance. *Current Directions in Psychological Science, 2,* 5–6.

McClelland, D. C., & Franz, C. E. (1992). Motivational and other sources of work accomplishments in mid-life: A longitudinal study. *Journal of Personality, 60,* 679–707.

McClelland, D. C., Koestner, R., & Weinberger, J. (1989). How do self-attributed and implicit motives differ? *Psychological Review, 96,* 690–702.

McClelland, D. C., & Winter, D. G. (1969). *Motivating economic achievement.* New York: Free Press.

McCombs, M. (1994). News influence on our pictures of the world. In J. Bryant & D. Zillmann (Eds.), *Media effects: Advances in theory and research* (pp. 1–16). Hillsdale, NJ: Erlbaum.

McConahay, J. B. (1980). Basic and applied social psychology and its contribution to public policy science. In R. F. Kidd & M. J. Saks (Eds.), *Advances in applied social psychology* (Vol. 1). Hillsdale, NJ: Erlbaum.

McConahay, J. B. (1986). Modern racism, ambivalence, and the Modern Racism Scale. In J. F. Dovidio & S. L. Gaertner (Eds.), *Prejudice, discrimination, and racism* (pp. 91–125). Orlando, FL: Harcourt Brace Jovanovich.

McConahay, J. B., Hardee, B. B., & Batts, V. (1981). Has racism declined in America? It depends on who is asking and what is asked. *Journal of Conflict Resolution, 25,* 563–579.

McConville, M., & Mirsky, C. (1995). Guilty plea courts: A social disciplinary model of criminal justice. *Social Problems, 42,* 216–234.

McDaniel, M., Whetzel, D., Schmidt, F., & Maurer, S. (1994). The validity of employment interviews: A comprehensive review and meta-analysis. *Journal of Applied Psychology, 79,* 599–616.

McFadden, A. C., Marsh, G. E., Price, B. J., & Hwang, Y. (1992). A study of race and gender bias in the punishment of school children. *Education and Treatment of Children, 15,* 140–146.

McGough, L. (1994). *Child witness: Fragile voices in the American legal system.* New York: Yale University Press.

McGrath, J. E. (1980). Social science, social action, and the Journal of Social Issues. *Journal of Social Issues, 36*(4), 109–124.

McGregor, D. (1960). *The human side of enterprise.* New York: McGraw-Hill.

McGuire, W. J. (1968). Personality and attitude change: An information-processing theory. In A. G. Greenwald, T. C. Brock, & T. M. Ostrom (Eds.), *Psychological foundations of attitudes* (pp. 171–196). New York: Academic Press.

McGuire, W. J. (1969). The nature of attitudes and attitude change. In G. Lindzey & E. Aronson (Eds.), *The handbook of social psychology* (2nd ed., Vol. 3, pp. 136–314). Reading, MA: Addison-Wesley.

McGuire, W. J. (1973). The yin and yang of progress in social psychology: Seven koan. *Journal of Personality and Social Psychology, 26,* 446–456.

McGuire, W. J. (1985). Attitudes and attitude change. In G. Lindzey & E. Aronson (Eds.), *The handbook of social psychology* (3rd ed., Vol. 2, pp. 233–346). New York: Random House.

McGuire, W. J. (1986). The myth of massive media impact: Savagings and salvagings. In G. Comstock (Ed.), *Public communication and behavior* (Vol. 1, pp. 173–257). Orlando, FL: Academic Press.

McGuire, W. J. (1992). Possible excuses for claiming massive media effects despite the weak evidence. In S. Rothman (Ed.), *The mass media in liberal democratic societies* (pp. 121–146). New York: Paragon House.

McIntyre, J. J., & Teevan, J. J., Jr. (1972). Television violence and deviant behavior. In G. A. Comstock & E. A. Rubinstein (Eds.), *Television and social behavior (Vol. 3): Television and adolescent aggressiveness* (pp. 383–435). Washington, DC: U.S. Government Printing Office.

McKenzie-Mohr, D. (1996). *Promoting a sustainable future: An introduction to community-based social marketing.* Ottawa, Canada: National Roundtable on the Environment and the Economy.

McKenzie-Mohr, D., & Zanna, M. P. (1990). Treating women as sexual objects: Look to the (gender schematic) male who has viewed pornography. *Personality and Social Psychology Bulletin, 16,* 296–308.

McKey, R. H., Condelli, L., Ganson, H., Barrett, B., McConkey, C., & Plantz, M. (1985). *The impact of Head Start on children, family, and communities: Final report of the Head Start Evaluation, Synthesis and Utilization Project* (DHHS Pub. No. OHDS 85–31193). Washington, DC: U.S. Government Printing Office.

McKusick, L., Coates, T. J., Morin, S. F., Pollack, L., & Hoff, C. (1990). Longitudinal predictors of reductions in unprotected anal intercourse among gay men in San Francisco: The AIDS Behavioral Research Project. *American Journal of Public Health, 80,* 978–983.

McLaughlin, M. W. (1975). *Evaluation and reform. The Elementary and Secondary Education Act of 1965/Title 1.* Cambridge, MA: Ballinger.

McLeod, J. M., Atkin, C. K., & Chaffee, S. H. (1972). Adolescents, parents and television use: Self-report and other-report measures from the Wisconsin sample. In G. A. Comstock & E. A. Rubinstein (Eds.), *Television and social behavior (Vol. 3): Television and adolescent aggressiveness* (pp. 239–313). Washington. DC: U.S. Government Printing Office.

McLeod, J. M., Kosicki, G., & McLeod, D. (1994). The expanding boundaries of political communication effects. In J. Bryant & D. Zillmann (Eds.), *Media effects: Advances in theory and research* (pp. 123–162). Hillsdale, NJ: Erlbaum.

McMorrow, M. J., & Foxx, R. M. (1983). Nicotine's role in smoking: An analysis of nicotine regulation. *Psychological Bulletin, 93,* 302–327.

McNett, I. (1981, August). Psychologists in medical settings: The academic scene. *APA Monitor, 12,* 66–68.

McPartland, J. (1969). The relative influence of school and of classroom desegregation on the academic achievement of ninth grade Negro students. *Journal of Social Issues, 25,* 93–102.

McShane, S. L. (1984). Job satisfaction and absenteeism: A meta-analytic reexamination. *Canadian Journal of Administration Sciences, 1,* 68–77.

Meadows, D. H., Meadows, D. L., & Randers, J. (1992). *Beyond the limits.* Post Mills, VT: Chelsea Green.

Megargee, E. I. (1969). Influence of sex roles on the manifestation of leadership. *Journal of Applied Psychology, 53,* 377–382.

Meier, P. (1972). The biggest public health experiment ever: The 1954 field trial of the Salk poliomyelitis vaccine. In J. M. Tanur et al. (Eds.), *Statistics: A guide to the unknown.* San Francisco: Holden-Day.

Mejta, C., Naylor, C., & Maslar, E. M. (1994). Drug abuse treatment: Approaches and effectiveness. In J. Lewis (Ed.), *Addictions: Concepts and strategies for treatment* (pp. 59–82). Gaithersburg, MD: Aspen.

Melamed, S., Ben-Avi, I., Luz, J., & Green, M. (1995). Objective and subjective work monotony: Effects on job satisfaction, psychological distress, and absenteeism in blue-collar workers. *Journal of Applied Psychology, 80,* 29–42.

Melton, G. B. (1995). Bringing psychology to Capitol Hill: Briefings on child and family policy. *American Psychologist, 50,* 766–770.

Meltzer, L. (1972). *Applied, applicable, appealing, and appalling social psychology.* Unpublished manuscript, Cornell University, Ithaca.

Merchant, C. (1992). *Radical ecology. The search for a livable world.* New York: Routledge.

Merson, M. H. (1993). Slowing the spread of HIV: Agenda for the 1990's. *Science, 260,* 1266–1268.

Messaris, P. (1996). *Visual persuasion: The role of images in advertising.* Thousand Oaks, CA: Sage.

Metalsky, G., Laird, R., Heck, P., & Joiner, T. (1995). Attribution theory: Clinical applications. In W. O'Donohue & L. Krasner (Eds.), *Theories of behavior therapy: Exploring behavior change* (pp. 385–413). Washington, DC: American Psychological Association.

Meyer, T. P. (1972). Effects of viewing justified and unjustified real film violence on aggressive behavior. *Journal of Personality and Social Psychology, 23,* 21–29.

Meyers, W., & Rinard, P. (1972). *Making activism work.* New York: Gordon & Breach.

Meza, L. (1982). *What is salient trial information to actual juror judgment?* Unpublished doctoral dissertation, Claremont Graduate School, Claremont, CA.

Michael, R. T., Gagnon, J. H., Laumann, E. O., & Kolata, G. (1994). *Sex in America: A definitive study.* Boston: Little, Brown.

Miller, C., & Schuster, M. (1987). A decade's experience with the Scanlon plan: A case study. *Journal of Occupational Behavior, 8,* 167–173.

Miller, D. (1991). *Handbook of research design and social measurement* (5th ed.). Newbury Park, CA: Sage.

Miller, G., Bender, D., Florence, T., & Nicholson, H. (1974). Real versus reel: What's the verdict? *Journal of Communication, 24,* 99–111.

Miller, G. A. (1969). Psychology as a means of promoting human welfare. *American Psychologist, 24,* 1063–1075.

Miller, G. T., Jr. (1990). *Living in the environment* (6th ed.). Belmont, CA: Wadsworth.

Miller, M. M., & Reeves, B. (1976). Linking dramatic TV content to children's occupational sex-role stereotypes. *Journal of Broadcasting, 20,* 35–50.

Miller, P. V. (1995). They said it couldn't be done: The National Health and Social Life Survey. *Public Opinion Quarterly, 59,* 404–419.

Miller, W. E., & Stokes, D. E. (1963). Constituency influence in Congress. *American Political Science Review, 57,* 45–56.

Milliken v. Bradley, 418 U.S. 717 (1974).

Millman, J., Samet, S., Shaw, S., & Braden, M. (1990). The dissemination of psychological research. *American Psychologist, 45,* 668–689.

Mills, J. (1976). A procedure for explaining experiments involving deception. *Personality and Social Psychology Bulletin, 2,* 3–13.

Mills, N. (Ed.). (1979). *Busing U.S.A.* New York: Teachers College Press.

Miniard, P. W., Batla, S., & Rose, R. L. (1990). On the formation and relationship of ad and brand attitudes: An experimental and causal analysis. *Journal of Marketing Research, 27,* 290–303.

Miniard, P. W., & Cohen, J. B. (1981). An examination of the Fishbein-Ajzen behavioral intentions model's concepts and measures. *Journal of Experimental Social Psychology, 17,* 309–339.

Minton, J. H. (1975). The impact of Sesame Street on readiness. *Sociology of Education, 48,* 141–151.

Mirvis, P. H., & Seashore, S. E. (1979). Being ethical in organizational research. *American Psychologist, 34,* 766–780.

Mitra, A., Jenkins, D., & Gupta, N. (1992). A meta-analytic review of the relationship between absence and turnover. *Journal of Applied Psychology, 77,* 879–889.

Mizrahi, T., & Morrison, J. (Eds.). (1993). *Community organization and social administration: Advances, trends, and emerging principles.* New York: Haworth.

Mobley, W. H., Griffeth, R. W., Hand, H. H., & Meglino, B. M. (1979). Review and conceptual analysis of the employee turnover process. *Psychological Bulletin, 86,* 493–522.

Moffitt, R. (1992). Evaluation methods for program entry effects. In C. Manski & I. Garfinkel (Eds.), *Evaluating welfare and training programs* (pp. 231–252). Cambridge, MA: Harvard University Press.

Mohai, P., & Bryant, B. (1992). Environmental racism: Reviewing the evidence. In B. Bryant & P. Mohai (Eds.), *Race and the incidence of environmental hazards.* Boulder, CO: Westview.

Moles, O. C. (1976). The Social Science Information Service. *Policy Studies Journal, 5,* 228–234.

Monahan, J. (Ed.). (1980). *Who is the client? The ethics of psychological intervention in the criminal justice system.* Washington, DC: American Psychological Association.

Monahan, J., & Loftus, E. (1982). The psychology of law. *Annual Review of Psychology, 33,* 441–475.

Monahan, J., & Walker, L. (1994). *Social science in law: Cases and materials* (3rd ed.). Westbury: State University of New York Foundation.

Monroe, A. D. (1978). Public opinion as a factor in public policy formation. *Policy Studies Journal, 6,* 542–548.

Montagu, A. (1951). *Statement on race.* New York: Schuman.

Moore, D. W. (1995, March). Americans today are dubious about affirmative action. *Gallup Poll Monthly,* No. 354, pp. 36–38.

Moore, D. W. (1995, June). Americans firmly support the death penalty. *Gallup Poll Monthly,* No. 357, pp. 23–25.

Moore, D. W., & Gallup, A. (1993, September). Are women more sexist than men? *Gallup Poll Monthly,* No. 336, pp. 20–21.

Moore, D. W., & Newport, F. (1994, January). Public strongly favors stricter gun control laws. *Gallup Poll Monthly,* No. 340, pp. 18–24.

Moos, R. H., & Finney, J. W. (1983). The expanding scope of alcoholism treatment evaluation. *American Psychologist, 38,* 1036–1044.

Moran, G., Cutler, B., & De-Lisa, A. (1994). Attitudes toward tort reform, scientific jury selection, and juror bias: Verdict inclination in criminal and civil trials. *Law and Psychology Review, 18,* 309–328.

Morin, A. (1993). *Science, policy, and politics.* Englewood Cliffs, NJ: Prentice-Hall.

Morris, M. D. (1979). *Measuring the condition of the world's poor: The Physical Quality of Life Index.* Washington, DC: Overseas Development Council.

Morris, W. N., Marshall, H. M., & Miller, R. S. (1973). The effect of vicarious punishment on prosocial behavior in children. *Journal of Experimental Child Psychology, 15,* 222–236.

Moskowitz, D. S., Suh, E. J., & Desaulniers, J. (1994). Situational influences on gender differences in agency and communion. *Journal of Personality and Social Psychology, 66,* 753–761.

Moston, S., & Engelberg, T. (1992). The effects of social support on children's eyewitness testimony. *Applied Cognitive Psychology, 6,* 61–76.

Mottaz, C. (1988). Work satisfaction among hospital nurses. *Hospital and Health Services Administration, 33,* 57–74.

Muehling, D. D., Stoltman, J. J., & Grossbart, S. (1990). The impact of comparative advertising on levels of message involvement. *Journal of Advertising, 19,* 41–50.

Mullen, B., & Johnson, C. (1990). *The psychology of consumer behavior.* Hillsdale, NJ: Erlbaum.

Munsterberg, H. (1908). *On the witness stand.* New York: McClure.

Murnighan, K. (Ed.). (1993). *Social psychology in organizations: Advances in theory and research.* Englewood Cliffs, NJ: Prentice-Hall.

Murphy, S. E., Blyth, D., & Fiedler, F. E. (1992). Cognitive resources theory and the utilization of the leader's and group member's technical competence. *Leadership Quarterly, 3,* 237–255.

Murray, B. (1995). Gender gap in math scores is closing. *APA Monitor, 26*(11), 43.

Murray, D. M., & Perry, C. L. (1987). The measurement of substance abuse use among adolescents: When is the "bogus pipeline" method needed? *Addictive Behaviors, 12,* 225–233.

Murray, J. P., & Kippax, S. (1979). From the early window to the late night show: International trends in the study of television's impact on children and adults. In L. Berkowitz (Ed.), *Advances in experimental social psychology* (Vol. 12, pp. 253–320). New York: Academic Press.

Murray, T. H. (1982). Ethics, power, and applied social psychology. In L. Bickman (Ed.), *Applied social psychology annual* (Vol. 3, pp. 75–95). Beverly Hills, CA: Sage.

Murrell, A. J., Dietz-Uhler, B. L., Dovidio, J. F., Gaertner, S. L., & Drout, C. (1994). Aversive racism and resistance to affirmative action: Perceptions of justice are not necessarily color blind. *Basic and Applied Social Psychology, 15,* 71–86.

Myers, D. G., & Diener, E. (1995). Who is happy? *Psychological Science, 6,* 10–19.

Myers, J. E., Poidevant, J. M., & Dean, L. A. (1991). Groups for older persons and their caregivers: A review of the literature. *Journal for Specialists in Group Work, 16,* 197–205.

Myrdal, G. (1944). *An American dilemma: The Negro problem and modern democracy.* New York: Harper.

Nacoste, R. B. (1994). If empowerment is the goal . . . : Affirmative action and social interaction. *Basic and Applied Social Psychology, 15,* 87–112.

Nadel, M. V. (1971). *The politics of consumer protection.* Indianapolis: Bobbs-Merrill.

Nader, R. (1973). Introduction. In D. K. Ross, *A public citizen's action manual.* New York: Grossman.

Nadler, D. A., & Lawler, E. E., III. (1983). Quality of working life: Perspectives and directions. *Organizational Dynamics, 11,* 20–30.

Naess, A. (1989). *Ecology, community, and lifestyle: An outline of an ecosophy.* Cambridge, England: Cambridge University Press.

Nagel, S. (1995). *Research in law and policy studies.* Greenwich, CT: JAI Press.

Narby, D. J., Cutler, B. L., & Penrod, S. D. (1996). The effects of witness, target, and situational factors on eyewitness identification. In S. Sporer, R. Malpass, & G. Koehnken (Eds.), *Psychological issues in eyewitness identification* (pp. 21–52). Mahwah, NJ: Erlbaum.

Nas, T. F. (1996). *Cost-benefit analysis: Theory and application.* Thousand Oaks, CA: Sage.

Nash, J. M. (1997, May 5). Addiction. *Time,* pp. 68–76.

National Academy of Sciences. (1995). *Allocating federal funds for science and technology.* Washington, DC: National Academy Press.

National Broadcasting Company, Social Research Department. (1976). *Public television.* New York: Author.

National Center for Employee Ownership. (1993). *Employee ownership reader.* Oakland, CA: Author.

National Center for Health Statistics. (1993). *Health, United States, 1992.* Hyattsville, MD: U.S. Public Health Service.

National Center for Health Statistics. (1995). *Health, United States, 1994.* Hyattsville, MD: U.S. Public Health Service.

National Commission on the Causes and Prevention of Violence. (1964). *To establish justice, to insure domestic tranquility: Final report.* Washington, DC: U.S. Government Printing Office.

National Institute of Mental Health. (1982). *Television and behavior: Ten years of scientific progress and implications for the eighties.* Washington, DC: U.S. Government Printing Office.

National Science Foundation. (1969). *Knowledge into action: Improving the nation's use of the social sciences* (Report of the Special Commission on the Social Sciences of the National Science Board). Washington, DC: Author.

National Science Foundation. (1995). *Federal funds for research and development annual.* Washington, DC: Government Printing Office.

Needleman, L. D., & Geller, E. S. (1992). Comparing interventions to motivate work-site collection of home-generated recyclables. *American Journal of Community Psychology, 20,* 775–787.

Neisser, U., et al. (1996). Intelligence: Knowns and unknowns. *American Psychologist, 51,* 77–101.

Nemeth, C. (1987). Interactions between jurors as a function of majority vs. unanimity decision rules. In L. Wrightsman, S. Kassin, & C. Willis (Eds.), *In the jury box: Controversies in the courtroom* (pp. 235–255). Newbury Park, CA: Sage.

Nettles, M. T. (1988). *Toward undergraduate student equality in American higher education.* New York: Greenwood.

Neuberg, S., & Newsom, J. (1993). Personal need for structure:

Individual differences in the desire for simple structure. *Journal of Personality and Social Psychology, 65,* 113–131.

Neuman, G. A., Edwards, J. E., & Raju, N. (1989). Organizational development interventions: A meta-analysis of their effects on satisfaction and other attitudes. *Personnel Psychology, 42,* 461–489.

Neuman, S. (1991). *Literacy in the television age: The myth of the TV effect.* Norwood, NJ: Ablex.

Newell, C. E., Rosenfeld, P., & Culbertson, A. L. (1995). Sexual harassment experiences and equal opportunity perceptions of Navy women. *Sex Roles, 32,* 159–168.

Newman, D. L., & Brown, R. D. (1996). *Applied ethics for program evaluation.* Thousand Oaks, CA: Sage.

Newsome, M., & Pillari, V. (1991). Job satisfaction and the worker-supervisor relationship. *Clinical Supervisor, 9,* 119–129.

Newspaper Advertising Bureau. (1980). *Children and newspapers: Changing patterns of readership and their effects.* New York: Author.

Nicks, S. D., Korn, J. H., & Mainieri, T. (in press). The rise and fall of deception in social psychology and personality research, 1921 to 1994. *Ethics and Behavior.*

Nie, N. H., Verba, S., & Petrocik, J. R. (1979). *The changing American voter* (enlarged ed.). Cambridge, MA: Harvard University Press.

Niemi, R. G., Mueller, J., & Smith, T. W. (1989). *Trends in public opinion: A compendium of survey data.* New York: Greenwood.

Nilsson, K., & Sunesson, S. (1993). Strategy and tactics: Utilization of research in three policy sector contexts. *Journal of Applied Behavioral Science, 29,* 366–383.

Nixon, W. (1995). The air down here. In T. D. Goldfarb (Ed.), *Taking sides: Clashing views on controversial environmental issues* (pp. 146–150). New York: Dushkin.

Noelle-Neumann, E. (1984). *The spiral of silence: Public opinion—Our social skin.* Chicago: University of Chicago Press.

Noelle-Neumann, E. (1992). The contribution of spiral of silence theory to an understanding of mass media. In S. Rothman (Ed.), *The mass media in liberal democratic societies* (pp. 75–84). New York: Paragon House.

Nord, W. R. (1977). Job satisfaction reconsidered. *American Psychologist, 32,* 1026–1035.

Norman, J. (1995). America's verdict on affirmative action is decidedly mixed. *The Public Perspective, 6*(4), 49–52.

Norris, F., & Thompson, M. (1995). Applying community psychology to the prevention of trauma and traumatic life events. In J. Freedy & S. Hobfoll (Eds.), *Traumatic stress: From theory to practice* (pp. 49–71). New York: Plenum.

Novotny, T. E., Romano, R. A., Davis, R. M., & Mills, S. L. (1992). The public health practice of tobacco control: Lessons learned and directions for the states in the 1990s. *Annual Review of Public Health, 13,* 287–318.

Nyquist, L. V., & Spence, J. T. (1986). Effects of dispositional dominance and sex role expectations on leadership behaviors. *Journal of Personality and Social Psychology, 50,* 87–93.

Oakland, T. (1994). Issues of importance to the membership of the American Psychological Association: Implications for planning. *American Psychologist, 49,* 879–886.

O'Brien, T., & Zoumbaris, S. (1993). Consumption behaviors hinge on financial self-interest. *American Psychologist, 48,* 1091–1092.

O'Carroll, P. W., Loftin, C., Waller, J. B., Jr., McDowall, D., Bukoff, A., Scott, R. O., Mercy, J. A., & Wiersema, B. (1991). Preventing homicide: An evaluation of the efficacy of a Detroit gun ordinance. *American Journal of Public Health, 81,* 576–581.

O'Donnell, M. P., & Harris, J. S. (Eds.). (1994). *Health promotion in the workplace* (2nd ed.). Albany, NY: Delmar.

Ogbu, J. U. (1978). *Minority education and caste: The American system in cross-cultural perspective.* New York: Academic Press.

Ogbu, J. U. (1990). Racial stratification and education. In G. Thomas (Ed.), *U.S. race relations in the 1980s and 1990s: Challenges and alternatives* (pp. 3–34). New York: Hemisphere.

Olczak, P., Kaplan, M., & Penrod, S. (1991). Attorney's lay psychology and its effectiveness in selecting jurors: Three empirical studies. *Journal of Social Behavior and Personality, 6,* 431–452.

Olmstead, R. E., & Bentler, P. M. (1992). Structural equation modeling: A new friend? In F. B. Bryant, J. Edwards, S. Tindale, E. Posavac, L. Heath, E. Henderson, & Y. Suarez-Balcazar (Eds.), *Methodological issues in applied social psychology: Social psychological applications to social issues* (pp. 135–158). New York: Plenum.

Olson, J. M., Herman, C. P., & Zanna, M. P. (Eds.). (1986). *Relative deprivation and social comparison: The Ontario symposium* (Vol. 4). Hillsdale, NJ: Erlbaum.

Olson, J. M., & Zanna, M. P. (1993). Attitudes and attitude change. *Annual Review of Psychology, 44,* 117–154.

Olson, R. L. (Ed.). (1991). *Mending the earth: A world for our grandchildren.* Berkeley, CA: North Atlantic.

Olson, R. L. (1995). Sustainability as a social vision. *Journal of Social Issues, 51*(4), 15–35.

Olzak, S., Shanahan, S., & West, E. (1994). School desegregation, interracial exposure, and antibusing activity in contemporary urban America. *American Journal of Sociology, 100,* 196–241.

O'Neill, J. (1985). The persistence of pay differentials: Human capital theory. In L. Larwood, B. A. Gutek, & A. H. Stromberg (Eds.), *Women and work: An annual review* (Vol. 1, pp. 50–75). Beverly Hills, CA: Sage.

Ophuls, W. (1977). *Ecology and the politics of scarcity.* San Francisco: Freeman.

Opotow, S. (1990). Moral exclusion and injustice: An introduction. *Journal of Social Issues, 46*(1), 1–20.

Orazem, P. F., & Matilla, J. P. (1989). A study of structural change in public sector earnings under comparable worth: The Iowa case. In R. Michael, H. Hartmann, & B. O'Farrell (Eds.), *Pay equity: Empirical inquiries.* Washington, DC: National Academy Press.

Orbell, J. M., van de Kragt, A. J. C., & Dawes, R. M. (1988). Explaining discussion-induced cooperation. *Journal of Personality and Social Psychology, 54,* 811–819.

Organ, D. W. (1988). A restatement of the satisfaction-performance hypothesis. *Journal of Management, 14,* 547–557.

Orleans, C. T., Glynn, T., Manley, M., & Slade, J. (1993). Minimal-contact quit smoking strategies for medical settings. In C. T. Orleans & J. Slade (Eds.), *Nicotine addiction: Principles and management* (pp. 181–220). New York: Oxford University Press.

Orne, M. T. (1969). Demand characteristics and the concept of quasi-controls. In R. Rosenthal & R. L. Rosnow (Eds.), *Artifact in behavioral research* (pp. 143–179). New York: Academic Press.

Orpen, C., & Nonnici, J. (1990). The causes and consequences of pay satisfaction: A test of Lawler's model. *Psychology: A Journal of Human Behavior, 27,* 27–29.

Oskamp, S. (1991). *Attitudes and opinions* (2nd ed.). Englewood Cliffs, NJ: Prentice Hall.

Oskamp, S. (1995a). Applying social psychology to avoid ecological disaster. *Journal of Social Issues, 51*(4), 217–239.

Oskamp, S. (1995b). Resource conservation and recycling: Behavior and policy. *Journal of Social Issues, 51*(4), 157–177.

Oskamp, S., Harrington, M., Edwards, T., Sherwood, P. L., Okuda, S. M., & Swanson, D. L. (1991). Factors influencing household recycling behavior. *Environment and Behavior, 23,* 494–519.

Oskamp, S., Kaufman, K., & Wolterbeek, L. A. (1996). Gender role portrayals in preschool picture books. *Journal of Social Behavior and Personality, 11*(5), 27–39.

Oskamp, S., & Thompson, S. C. (Eds.). (1996). *Understanding and preventing HIV risk behavior: Safer sex and drug use.* Thousand Oaks, CA: Sage.

Ottaway, R. N. (1983). The change agent: A taxonomy in relation to the change process. *Human Relations, 36,* 361–392.

Packard, T. (1989). Participation in decision making, performance, and job satisfaction in a social work bureaucracy. *Administration in Social Work, 13,* 59–73.

Paik, H., & Comstock, G. (1994). The effects of television violence on anti-social behavior: A meta-analysis. *Communication Research, 21,* 516–546.

Palardy, M. J. (1992). "Tall" school organizations: A negative factor in teacher/principal empowerment. *Journal of Instructional Psychology, 19,* 185–187.

Pallak, M. S. (1990). Public policy and applied social psychology: Bridging the gap. In J. Edwards, R. S. Tindale, L. Heath, & E. Posavac (Eds.), *Social influence: Processes and prevention* (pp. 327–338). New York: Plenum.

Pallak, M. S., Cook, D. A., & Sullivan, J. J. (1980). Commitment and energy conservation. In L. Bickman (Ed.), *Applied social psychology annual* (Vol. 1, pp. 235–253). Beverly Hills, CA: Sage.

Pallak, M. S., & Cummings, W. (1976). Commitment and voluntary energy conservation. *Personality and Social Psychology Bulletin, 2,* 27–30.

Palmore, E. (1969). Predicting longevity: A follow-up controlling for age. *The Gerontologist, 9,* 247–250.

Paludi, M. A. (1984). Psychometric properties and underlying assumptions of four objective measures of fear of success. *Sex Roles, 10,* 765–781.

Parke, R. D., Berkowitz, L., Leyens, J. P., West, S. G., & Sebastian, I. J. (1977). Some effects of violent and nonviolent movies on the behavior of juvenile delinquents. In L. Berkowitz (Ed.), *Advances in experimental social psychology* (Vol. 10, pp. 135–172). New York: Academic Press.

Parker, E. B. (1963). The effects of television on public library circulation. *Public Opinion Quarterly, 27,* 578–589.

Parloff, M. B. (1978). Can psychotherapy research guide the policymaker? A little knowledge may be a dangerous thing. *American Psychologist, 34,* 296–306.

Parsons, M. (1974). What happened at Hawthorne? *Science, 183,* 922–932.

Parsons, M. (1992). Hawthorne: An early OBM experiment. *Journal of Organizational Behavior Management, 12,* 27–43.

Parsons, T. (1955). Family structure and the socialization of the child. In T. Parsons & R. F. Bales (Eds.), *Family, socialization, and interaction process.* Glencoe, IL: Free Press.

Pascarella, E., Smart, J., Ethington, C., & Nettles, M. (1987). The influence of college on self-concept: A consideration of race and gender differences. *American Educational Research Journal, 24,* 49–77.

Pasmore, W., Francis, C., Haldeman, J., & Shani, A. (1982). Sociotechnical systems: A North American reflection on empirical studies in the seventies. *Human Relations, 12,* 1179–1204.

Patchen, M. (1982). *Black-White contact in schools: Its social and academic effects.* West Lafayette, IN: Purdue University Press.

Patten, T. H., Jr. (1988). *Fair pay: The managerial challenge of comparable job worth and job evaluation.* San Francisco: Jossey-Bass.

Patterson, T. E., & McClure, R. D. (1976). *The unseeing eye: The myth of television power in national elections.* New York: Putnam.

Patton, M. Q. (1986). *Utilization-focused evaluation* (2nd ed.). Newbury Park, CA: Sage.

Patton, M. Q. (1990). *Qualitative evaluation and research methods.* Newbury Park, CA: Sage.

Patton, M. Q., Grimes, P. S., Guthrie, K. M., Brennan, N. J., French, B. D., & Blyth, D. A. (1977). In search of impact: An analysis of the utilization of federal health evaluation research. In C. H. Weiss (Ed.), *Using social research in public policy making.* Lexington, MA: Lexington.

Paulson, F. L. (1974). Teaching cooperation on television: An evaluation of Sesame Street social goals programs. *Audio-Visual Communication Review, 22,* 229–246.

Paulus, P. B., & Dzindolet, M. (1992). The effects of prison confinement. In P. Suedfeld & P. Tetlock (Eds.), *Psychology and social policy* (pp. 327–341). New York: Hemisphere.

Paulus, P. B., McCain, G., & Cox, V. C. (1978). Death rates, psychiatric commitments, blood pressure, and perceived crowding as a function of institutional crowding. *Environmental Psychology and Nonverbal Behavior, 3,* 107–116.

Payne, S. L. (1951). *The art of asking questions.* Princeton, NJ: Princeton University Press.

Payton-Miyazaki, M., & Brayfield, A. H. (1976). The good job and the good life. In A. Biderman & T. Drury (Eds.), *Measuring work quality for social reporting.* Beverly Hills, CA: Sage.

Peabody, G. L. (1971). Power, Alinsky, and other thoughts. In H. A. Hornstein, B. B. Bunker, W. W. Burke, M. Gindes, & R. J. Lewicki (Eds.), *Social intervention: A behavioral science approach.* New York: Free Press.

Pearson, C. A. L. (1992). Autonomous workgroups: An evaluation at an industrial site. *Human Relations, 9,* 905–936.

Pechmann, C., & Stewart, D. W. (1990). The effects of comparative advertising on attention, memory, and purchase intentions. *Journal of Consumer Research, 17,* 180–191.

Pennington, N., & Hastie, R. (1990). Practical implications of psychological research on juror decision making. *Personality and Social Psychology Bulletin, 16,* 90–105.

Penrod, S., & Cutler, B. L. (1987). Assessing the competence of juries. In I. B. Weiner & A. K. Hess (Eds.), *Handbook of forensic psychology* (pp. 293–318). New York: Wiley.

Penrod, S., Fulero, S., & Cutler, B. (1995). Expert psychological testimony on eyewitness reliability before and after *Daubert:* The state of the law and the science. *Behavioral Sciences and the Law, 13,* 229–259.

Perez, S., Eliseo, J., Marin, B., & Marin, G. (1993). A comprehensive smoking cessation program for the San Francisco Bay area Latino community: Programa Latino para dejar de fumar. *American Journal of Health Promotion, 7,* 430–442.

Perse, E. M., & Rubin, A. M. (1990). Chronic loneliness and television use. *Journal of Broadcasting and Electronic Media, 34,* 37–53.

Peters, L., Hartke, D., & Pohlmann, J. (1985). Fiedler's contingency theory of leadership: An application of the meta-analysis procedures of Schmidt and Hunter. *Psychological Bulletin, 97,* 274–285.

Peterson, C., Buchanan, G. M., & Seligman, M. (1995). Explanatory style: History and evolution of the field. In G. M. Buchanan & M. Seligman (Eds.), *Explanatory style* (pp. 1–20). Hillsdale, NJ: Erlbaum.

Petrikin, J. (Ed.). (1995). *Environmental justice.* San Diego, CA: Greenhaven.

Pettigrew, T. F. (1967). Social evaluation theory: Convergences and applications. In D. Levine (Ed.), *Nebraska symposium on motivation, 1967.* Lincoln: University of Nebraska Press.

Pettigrew, T. F. (1975). The racial integration of the schools. In T. F. Pettigrew (Ed.), *Racial discrimination in the United States* (pp. 224–239). New York: Harper & Row.

Pettigrew, T. F. (1991). Advancing racial justice. In H. Knopke, R. Norrell, & R. Rogers (Eds.), *Opening doors: Perspectives on race relations in contemporary America* (pp. 165–178). Tuscaloosa: University of Alabama Press.

Pettigrew, T. F. (1994, October). *The deprovincialization hypothesis: Generalized intergroup contact effects on prejudice.* Paper presented at Society of Experimental Social Psychology meeting, Lake Tahoe, CA.

Pettigrew, T. F. (1995). *Generalized intergroup contact effects on prejudice.* Unpublished manuscript, University of California at Santa Cruz.

Pettigrew, T. F., & Meertens, R. W. (1995). Subtle and blatant prejudice in western Europe. *European Journal of Social Psychology, 25,* 57–75.

Pettigrew, T. F., Useem, E. L., Normand, C., & Smith, M. S. (1973). Busing: A review of "the evidence." *The Public Interest, 30,* 88–118.

Petty, R. E., & Cacioppo, J. T. (1979). Issue involvement can increase or decrease persuasion by enhancing message-relevant cognitive responses. *Journal of Personality and Social Psychology, 37,* 1915–1926.

Petty, R. E., & Cacioppo, J. T. (1981). *Attitudes and persuasion: Classic and contemporary approaches.* Dubuque, IA: Brown.

Petty, R. E., & Cacioppo, J. T. (1986). *Communication and persuasion: Central and peripheral routes to attitude change.* New York: Springer-Verlag.

Petty, R. E., Ostrom, T. M., & Brock, T. C. (Eds.). (1981). *Cognitive responses in persuasion.* Hillsdale, NJ: Erlbaum.

Petty, R. E., & Priester, J. R. (1994). Mass media attitude change: Implications of the elaboration likelihood model of persuasion. In J. Bryant & D. Zillmann (Eds.), *Media effects: Advances in theory and research* (pp. 91–122). Hillsdale, NJ: Erlbaum.

Petty, R. E., Priester, J. R., & Wegener, D. T. (in press). Cognitive processes in attitude change. In R. S. Wyer & T. K. Srull (Eds.), *Handbook of social cognition* (2nd ed., pp. 69–142). Hillsdale, NJ: Erlbaum.

Pfister, G. (1975). Outcomes of laboratory training for police officers. *Journal of Social Issues, 31*(1), 115–121.

Phillips, D. (1991). With a little help: Children in poverty and child care. In A. Huston (Ed.), *Children in poverty: Child development and public policy* (pp. 158–189). New York: Cambridge University Press.

Phillips, D., & Zigler, E. (1987). The checkered history of federal child care regulation. In E. Rothkopf (Ed.), *Review of research in education* (Vol. 14, pp. 3–42). Washington, DC: American Educational Research Association.

Pierce, C. H., & Risley, T. R. (1974). Recreation as a reinforcer: Increasing membership and decreasing disruptions in an urban recreation center. *Journal of Applied Behavior Analysis, 7,* 403–411.

Pierce, J., Newstrom, J., Dunham, R., & Barber, A. (1989). *Alternate work schedules.* Boston: Allyn & Bacon.

Pilisuk, M., McAlister, J., & Rothman, J. (1996). Coming together for action: The challenge of contemporary grassroots community organizing. *Journal of Social Issues, 52*(1), 15–37.

Pimentel, D., Harman, R., Pacenza, M., Pacarsky, J., & Pimentel, M. (1994). Natural resources and an optimum human population. *Population and Environment, 15,* 347–369.

Pingree, S., & Hawkins, R. P. (1980). Children and media. In M. Butler & W. Paisley (Eds.), *Women and the mass media: Sourcebook for research and action* (pp. 279–299). New York: Human Sciences Press.

Platt, J. (1973). Social traps. *American Psychologist, 28,* 641–651.

Podell, S., & Archer, D. (1994). Do legal changes matter? The case of gun control laws. In M. Costanzo & S. Oskamp (Eds.), *Violence and the law* (pp. 37–60). Thousand Oaks, CA: Sage.

Pomerleau, O. F. (1979). Behavioral factors in the establishment, maintenance, and cessation of smoking. In *Smoking and health: A report of the Surgeon General.* Washington, DC: U.S. Department of Health, Education, and Welfare.

Pomerleau, O. F., Adkins, D. M., & Pertschuk, M. (1978). Predictors of outcome and recidivism in smoking-cessation treatment. *Addictive Behaviors, 3,* 65–70.

Pomerleau, O. F., & Pomerleau, C. S. (1984). Neuroregulators and the reinforcement of smoking: Towards a biobehavioral explanation. *Neuroscience and Biobehavioral Reviews, 8,* 503–513.

Pomerleau, O. F., & Pomerleau, C. S. (1989). A biobehavioral perspective on smoking. In T. Ney & A. Gale (Eds.), *Smoking and human behavior* (pp. 69–93). New York: Wiley.

Pontieri, F. E., Tanda, G., Orzi, F., & Di Chiara, G. (1996). Effects of nicotine on the nucleus accumbens and similarity to those of addictive drugs. *Nature, 382,* 255–257.

Porter, L. W., & Lawler, E. E., III. (1968). *Managerial attitudes and performance.* Homewood, IL: Irwin.

Portney, P. (1990). Air pollution policy. In P. Portney (Ed.), *Public policies for environmental protection.* Washington, DC: CQ Press.

Posavac, E. J. (1992). Communicating applied social psychology to users: A challenge and an art. In F. B. Bryant, J. Edwards, R. S. Tindale, E. J. Posavac, L. Heath, E. Henderson, & Y. Suarez-Balcazar (Eds.), *Methodological issues in applied social psychology* (pp. 269–294). New York: Plenum.

Posavac, E. J., & Carey, R. (1989). *Program evaluation: Methods and case studies* (3rd ed.). Englewood Cliffs, NJ: Prentice-Hall.

Potter, E. H., III, & Fiedler, F. E. (1981). The utilization of staff member intelligence and experience under high and low stress. *Academy of Management Journal, 24,* 361–376.

Pratkanis, A. R., Greenwald, A. G., Leippe, M. R., & Baumgardner, M. H. (1988). In search of reliable persuasion effects: III. The sleeper effect is dead. Long live the sleeper effect. *Journal of Personality and Social Psychology, 54,* 203–218.

Pratto, F., Sidanius, J., Stallworth, L. M., & Malle, B. F. (1994). Social dominance orientation: A personality variable predicting social and political attitudes. *Journal of Personality and Social Psychology, 67,* 741–763.

President's Commission on Law Enforcement and the Administration of Justice. (1967). *The challenge of crime in a free society: A report.* Washington, DC: U.S. Government Printing Office.

Prilleltensky, I. (1990). Enhancing the social ethics of psychology: Toward a psychology at the service of social change. *Canadian Psychology, 31,* 310–319.

Prochaska, J. O., DiClemente, C. C., & Norcross, J. C. (1992). In search of how people change: Applications to addictive behaviors. *American Psychologist, 47,* 1102–1114.

Prochaska, J. O., DiClemente, C. C., Velicer, W., & Rossi, J. S.

(1993). Standardized, individualized, interactive, and personalized self-help programs for smoking cessation. *Health Psychology, 12,* 399–405.

Proshansky, H. M. (1987). The field of environmental psychology: Securing its future. In D. Stokols & I. Altman (Eds.), *Handbook of environmental psychology* (Vol. 2, pp. 1467–1488). New York: Wiley.

Proshansky, H. M. (1990). The pursuit of understanding: An intellectual history. In I. Altman & K. Christensen (Eds.), *Environment and behavior studies. Emergence of intellectual traditions* (pp. 9–30). New York: Plenum.

Prothrow-Stith, D., & Weissman, M. (1991). *Deadly consequences: How violence is destroying our teenage population and a plan to begin solving the problem.* New York: HarperCollins.

Pryor, J. B., & McKinney, K. (Eds.). (1995). Research advances in sexual harassment [Special issue]. *Basic and Applied Social Psychology, 17,* 421–611.

Quartstein, V. A., McAfee, B., & Glassman, M. (1992). The situational occurrences theory of job satisfaction. *Human Relations, 45,* 859–873.

Quinn, R. P., & Staines, G. L. (1979). *The 1977 Quality of Employment Survey: Descriptive statistics, with comparison data from the 1969–70 and the 1972–73 surveys.* Ann Arbor: Institute for Social Research, University of Michigan.

Rafaeli, A. (1989). When clerks meet customers: A test of variables related to emotional expression on the job. *Journal of Applied Psychology, 74,* 385–393.

Ragins, B. R., & Cotton, J. (1991). Easier said than done: Gender differences in perceived barriers to gaining a mentor. *Academy of Management Journal, 34,* 939–951.

Rains, J. C., Penzien, D. B., & Jamison, R. A. (1992). A structured approach to the management of chronic pain. In L. Vandecreek, S. Knapp, & T. L. Jackson (Eds.), *Innovations in clinical practice: A source book* (pp. 521–539). Sarasota, FL: Professional Resource Press.

Ralston, D. (1989). The benefits of flextime: Real or imagined? *Journal of Organizational Behavior, 10,* 369–373.

Ramirez, J. D. (1986). Comparing structured English immersion and bilingual education: First-year results of a national study. *American Journal of Education, 56,* 122–148.

Rattner, A. (1988). Convicted but innocent: Wrongful conviction and the criminal justice system. *Law and Human Behavior, 12,* 283–293.

Ray, D. L., & Guzzo, L. (1990). *Trashing the planet.* Washington, DC: Regnery Gateway.

Read, J. D. (1994). Understanding bystander misidentifications: The role of familiarity and contextual knowledge. In D. Ross, J. Read, & M. Toglia (Eds.), *Adult eyewitness testimony: Current trends and developments* (pp. 56–79). New York: Cambridge University Press.

Ree, M. J., Earles, J. A., & Teachout, M. S. (1994). Predicting job performance: Not much more than *g. Journal of Applied Psychology, 79,* 518–524.

Reed, S. K. (1994). Pornography addiction and compulsive sexual behavior. In D. Zillmann, J. Bryant, & A. Huston (Eds.),

Media, children, and the family: Social scientific, psychodynamic, and clinical perspectives (pp. 249–269). Hillsdale, NJ: Erlbaum.

Reed, T. E. (1969). Caucasian genes in American Negroes. *Science, 165,* 762–768.

Reichel, D. A., & Geller, E. S. (1981). Applications of behavioral analysis for conserving transportation energy. In A. Baum & J. E. Singer (Eds.), *Advances in environmental psychology (Vol. 3). Energy: Psychological perspectives.* Hillsdale, NJ: Erlbaum.

Reif, J. S., Dunn, K., Ogilvie, G. K., & Harris, C. K. (1992). Passive smoking and canine lung cancer risk. *American Journal of Epidemiology, 125,* 234–239.

Reisch, M., & Wenocur, S. (1986). The future of community organization in social work: Social activism and the politics of profession building. *Social Service Review, 60,* 70–93.

Reitzes, D. C., & Reitzes, D. C. (1986). Alinsky in the 1980s: Two contemporary Chicago community organizations. *Sociological Quarterly, 28,* 265–283.

Reno, R. R., Cialdini, R. B., & Kallgren, C. A. (1993). The transsituational influence of social norms. *Journal of Personality and Social Psychology, 64,* 104–112.

Repace, J. (1993). Tobacco smoke pollution. In C. T. Orleans & J. Slade (Eds.), *Nicotine addiction: Principles and management* (pp. 129–144). New York: Oxford University Press.

Reskin, B. (1993). Sex segregation in the workplace. *Annual Review of Sociology, 19,* 241–270.

Rethans, A. J., Swasy, J. L., & Marks, L. J. (1986). Effects of television commercial repetition, receiver knowledge, and commercial length: A test of the two-factor model. *Journal of Marketing Research, 23,* 50–61.

Reuter, P. (1979). Easy sport: Research and relevance. *Journal of Social Issues, 35*(3), 166–182.

Rhoodie, E. M. (1989). *Discrimination against women: A global survey.* Jefferson, NC: McFarland.

Rice, B. (1980, August). The unreality of prime-time crime. *Psychology Today,* pp. 26, 78.

Rich, F. (1996, February 28). The V-chip G-string. *New York Times,* p. A17.

Richins, M. L. (1991). Social comparison and the ideal images of advertising. *Journal of Consumer Research, 18,* 71–83.

Richmond, R. L., Harris, K., & de Almeida, N. (1994). The transdermal nicotine patch: Results of a randomized placebo-controlled study. *Medical Journal of Australia, 161,* 130–135.

Riley, G. F., Potosky, A. L., Lubitz, J. D., & Brown, M. L. (1994). Stage of concern at diagnosis for medicare HMO and fee-for-service enrollees. *American Journal of Public Health, 84,* 1598–1604.

Ring, K. (1967). Experimental social psychology: Some sober questions about frivolous values. *Journal of Experimental Social Psychology, 3,* 113–123.

Rist, R. C. (1980). On the future of school desegregation: A new American dilemma? In W. G. Stephan & J. R. Feagin (Eds.), *School desegregation: Past, present, and future* (p. 117–132). New York: Plenum.

Rivlin, A. M. (1973). Social experiments: The promise and the problem. *Brookings Bulletin, 10*(3), 6–9.

Roberts, D. F., & Bachen, C. M. (1981). Mass communication effects. *Annual Review of Psychology, 32,* 307–356.

Robinson, J. P. (1988). Who's doing the housework? *American Demographics, 10*(12), 24–28, 63.

Robinson, J. P., & Bachman, J. G. (1972). Television viewing habits and aggression. In G. A. Comstock & E. A. Rubinstein (Eds.), *Television and social behavior (Vol. 3): Television and adolescent aggressiveness* (pp. 372–382). Washington, DC: U.S. Government Printing Office.

Rodin, J., Bohm, L. C., & Wack, J. T. (1982). Control, coping, and aging: Models for research and intervention. In L. Bickman (Ed.), *Applied social psychology annual* (Vol. 3, pp. 153–180). Beverly Hills, CA: Sage.

Rodin, J., & Ickovics, J. R. (1990). Women's health: Review and research agenda as we approach the 21st century. *American Psychologist, 45,* 1018–1034.

Rodin, J., & Salovey, P. (1989). Health psychology. *Annual Review of Psychology, 40,* 533–579.

Rodriguez, J. (1990). Childhood injuries in the United States. *American Journal of Diseases of Childhood, 144,* 627–646.

Roethlisberger, F. J., & Dickson, W. J. (1939). *Management and the worker.* Cambridge, MA: Harvard University Press.

Rog, D. (1994). Constructing natural experiments. In J. Wholey, H. Hatry, & K. Newcomer (Eds.), *Handbook of practical program evaluation* (pp. 119–132). San Francisco: Jossey-Bass.

Rogers, E. M. (1993). Diffusion and re-invention of Project D.A.R.E. In T. Backer & E. Rogers (Eds.), *Organizational aspects of health communication campaigns: What works?* (pp. 139–162). Newbury Park, CA: Sage.

Rogers, T. F. (1976). Interviews by telephone and in person: Quality of responses and field performance. *Public Opinion Quarterly, 40,* 51–65.

Rokeach, M. (1971). Long-range experimental modification of values, attitudes, and behavior. *American Psychologist, 26,* 453–459.

Rokeach, M. (1973). *The nature of human values.* New York: Free Press.

Rokeach, M. (1979). Value theory and communication research. In D. Nimmo (Ed.), *Communication yearbook* (Vol. 3, pp. 7–28). New Brunswick, NJ: Transaction Books.

Romano, P., Bloom, J., & Syme, L. (1991). Smoking, social support, and hassles in an urban African-American community. *American Journal of Public Health, 81,* 1415–1422.

Romzek, B. (1991). Balancing work and nonwork obligations. In C. Ban & N. Riccucci (Eds.), *Public personnel management: Current concerns, future challenges.* White Plains, NY: Longman.

Rosa, E. A., & Dunlap, R. E. (1994). The polls—Poll trends. Nuclear power: Three decades of public opinion. *Public Opinion Quarterly, 58,* 295–325.

Roscoe, B., & Benaske, N. (1985). Courtship violence experienced by abused wives: Similarities in patterns of abuse. *Family Relations, 34,* 419–424.

Rosen, B., & Jerdee, T. H. (1978). Perceived sex differences in managerially relevant characteristics. *Sex Roles, 4,* 837–843.

Rosen, C., & Young, K. (Eds.). (1991). *Understanding employee ownership.* Ithaca, NY: Institute of Labor Relations.

Rosenbaum, W. (1991). *Environmental politics and policy* (2nd ed.). Washington, DC: CQ Press.

Rosenberg, M. (1986). Self-esteem research: A phenomenological corrective. In J. Prager, D. Longshore, & M. Seeman (Eds.), *School desegregation research: New approaches to situational analyses* (pp. 175–193). New York: Plenum.

Rosenberg, M. J. (1969). The conditions and consequences of evaluation apprehension. In R. Rosenthal & R. L. Rosnow (Eds.), *Artifact in behavioral research* (pp. 279–349). New York: Academic Press.

Rosenstock, I. M. (1974). The health belief model and preventive health behavior. *Health Education Monographs, 2,* 354–385.

Rosenthal, R. (1969). Interpersonal expectations: Effects of the experimenter's hypothesis. In R. Rosenthal & R. L. Rosnow (Eds.), *Artifact in behavioral research* (pp. 181–277). New York: Academic Press.

Rosenthal, R. (1973). The mediation of Pygmalion effects: A four-factor "theory." *Papua New Guinea Journal of Education, 9,* 1–12.

Rosenthal, R. (1976). *Experimenter effects in behavioral research.* New York: Irvington.

Rosenthal, R. (1985). From unconscious experimenter bias to teacher expectancy effects. In J. Dusek (Ed.), *Teacher expectations* (pp. 27–65). Hillsdale, NJ: Erlbaum.

Rosenthal, R. (1991). *Meta-analytic procedures for social research* (2nd ed.). Newbury Park, CA: Sage.

Rosenthal, R. (1994). On being one's own case study: Experimenter effects in behavioral research—30 years later. In W. Shadish & S. Fuller (Eds.), *The social psychology of science* (pp. 214–229). New York: Guilford.

Rosenthal, R., & Jacobson, D. (1968). *Pygmalion in the classroom.* New York: Holt, Rinehart & Winston.

Rosenthal, R., & Rubin, D. (1978). Interpersonal expectancy effects: The first 345 studies. *Behavioral and Brain Sciences, 1,* 377–415.

Rosnow, R. L., & Rosenthal, R. (1996). *Beginning behavioral research: A conceptual primer* (2nd ed.). Englewood Cliffs, NJ: Prentice-Hall.

Ross, A., & Grant, M. (1994). *Experimental and nonexperimental designs in social psychology.* Madison, WI: Brown & Benchmark.

Ross, A. S., & White, S. (1987). Shoplifting, impaired driving, and refusing the breathalyzer: On seeing one's name in a public place. *Evaluation Review, 11,* 254–260.

Ross, C., & Reskin, B. (1992). Education, control at work, and job satisfaction. *Social Science Research, 21,* 134–148.

Ross, D., Read, J. D., & Toglia, M. (Eds.). (1994). *Adult eyewitness testimony: Current trends and developments.* New York: Cambridge University Press.

Ross, D. K. (1973). *A public citizen's action manual.* New York: Grossman.

Ross, H. L. (Ed.) (1992). *Confronting drunk driving: Social policy for saving lives.* New Haven, CT: Yale University press.

Ross, H. L., Campbell, D. T., & Glass, G. V. (1970). Determining the social effects of a legal reform: The British "breathalyser" crackdown of 1967. *American Behavioral Scientist, 13,* 493–509.

Ross, L. (1977). The intuitive psychologist and his shortcomings: Distortions in the attribution process. In L. Berkowitz (Ed.), *Advances in experimental social psychology* (Vol. 10, pp. 174–221). New York: Academic Press.

Ross, L., Lepper, M. R., & Hubbard, M. (1975). Perseverance in self-perception and social perception: Biased attributional processes in the debriefing paradigm. *Journal of Personality and Social Psychology, 32,* 880–892.

Ross, S. I., & Jackson, J. M. (1991). Teachers' expectations for Black males' and Black females' academic achievement. *Personality and Social Psychology Bulletin, 17,* 78–82.

Rossell, C. (1983). Desegregation plans, racial isolation, White flight, and community response. In C. Rossell & W. Hawley (Eds.), *The consequences of school desegregation* (pp. 13–57). Philadelphia, PA: Temple University Press.

Rossell, C. (1990). *The carrot or the stick for school desegregation policy: Magnet schools or forced busing.* Philadelphia: Temple University Press.

Rossell, C., & Hawley, W. (1983). Introduction: Desegregation and change. In C. Rossell & W. Hawley (Eds.), *The consequences of school desegregation* (pp. 3–12). Philadelphia: Temple University Press.

Rossi, P. H., & Freeman, H. E. (1993). *Evaluation: A systematic approach* (5th ed.). Newbury Park, CA: Sage.

Rossi, P. H., & Lyall, K. C. (1976). *Reforming public welfare: A critique of the negative income tax experiment.* New York: Russell Sage Foundation.

Rossiter, J. R., & Robinson, T. S. (1974). Children's TV commercials: Testing the defenses. *Journal of Communication, 24*(4), 137–144.

Roth, S., Dye, E., & Lebowitz, L. (1988). Group therapy for sexual-assault victims. *Psychotherapy, 25,* 82–93.

Roth, S., Wayland, K., & Woolsey, M. (1990). Victimization history and victim-assailant relationship as factors in recovery from sexual assault. *Journal of Traumatic Stress, 3,* 169–180.

Rothman, S., Lichter, S., & Lichter, L. (1992). Television's America. In S. Rothman (Ed.), *The mass media in liberal democratic societies* (pp. 221–266). New York: Paragon House.

Rowley, D. J., Rosse, J. G., & Harvey, O. J. (1992). The effects of belief systems on the job-related satisfaction of managers and subordinates. *Journal of Applied Social Psychology, 22,* 212–231.

Ruback, R. B., Carr, T. S., & Hopper, C. H. (1986). Perceived control in prison: Its relation to reported crowding, stress, and symptoms. *Journal of Applied Social Psychology, 16,* 375–386.

Rubin, A. M. (1994). Media uses and effects: A uses-and-gratifications perspective. In J. Bryant & D. Zillmann (Eds.), *Media effects: Advances in theory and research* (pp. 417–436). Hillsdale, NJ: Erlbaum.

Rubin, A. M., & Bantz, C. R. (1989). Uses and gratifications of videocassette recorders. In J. Salvaggio & J. Bryant (Eds.), *Media use in the information age: Emerging patterns of adoption and consumer use* (pp. 181–195). Hillsdale, NJ: Erlbaum.

Rubinstein, E. (1983). Television and behavior: Research conclusions of the 1982 NIMH report and their policy implications. *American Psychologist, 38,* 820–825.

Rushton, J. P. (1979). Effects of prosocial television and film material on the behavior of viewers. In L. Berkowitz (Ed.), *Advances in experimental social psychology* (Vol. 12, pp. 321–351). New York: Academic Press.

Russell, M. A. H., Wilson, C., Taylor, C., & Baker, C. D. (1979). Effect of general practitioners' advice against smoking. *British Medical Journal, 2,* 231–235.

Rutman, L. (1977). Formative research and program evaluability. In L. Rutman (Ed.), *Evaluation research methods: A basic guide* (pp. 57–71). Beverly Hills, CA: Sage.

Ryan, N. (1976, June 5). Family viewing time: Has it passed the test? *TV Guide,* pp. 5–10.

Rychtarik, R. G., Foy, D. W., Scott, T., Lokey, L., & Prue, D. M. (1987). Five-six year follow-up of broad-spectrum behavioral treatment of alcoholism: Effects of training controlled drinking skills. *Journal of Consulting and Clinical Psychology, 55,* 106–108.

Saegert, S., & Winkel, G. H. (1990). Environmental psychology. *Annual Review of Psychology, 41,* 441–477.

Saks, M. J. (1974). Ignorance of science is no excuse. *Trial, 10,* 18–20.

Saks, M. J. (1977). *Jury verdicts: The role of group size and social decision rule.* Lexington, MA: Lexington.

Saks, M. J. (1978, August). *High-impact applied social psychology.* Paper presented at American Psychological Association meeting, Toronto.

Saks, M. J., & Hastie, R. (1978). *Social psychology in court.* New York: Van Nostrand Reinhold.

Salber, E. J., Freeman, H. E., & Abelin, T. (1968). Needed research on smoking: Lessons from the Newton study. In E. F. Borgatta & R. R. Evans (Eds.), *Smoking, health, and behavior.* Chicago: Aldine.

Salcedo, J., Jr. (1954). Views and comments on the Report on Rice Enrichment in the Philippines. In *Food and Agriculture Organization of the United Nations* (Report No. 12). Rome: United Nations.

Sales, S. M., & House, J. (1971). Job dissatisfaction as a possible risk factor in coronary heart disease. *Journal of Chronic Diseases, 23,* 861–873.

Salleh, A. (1992). The ecofeminism/deep ecology debate. A reply to patriarchal reason. *Environmental Ethics, 14,* 195–216.

Sankar, A. (1994). Images of home death and the elderly patient: Romantic versus real. In D. Shenk & W. Achenbaum (Eds.), *Changing perceptions of aging and the aged* (pp. 105–114). New York: Springer.

Sarason, I. G., Sarason, B. R., Pierce, G. R., Shearin, E. N., et al. (1992). A social learning approach to increasing blood donations. *Journal of Applied Social Psychology, 21,* 896–918.

Sarason, S. B. (1978). The nature of problem solving in social action. *American Psychologist, 33,* 370–380.

Saretsky, G. (1972). The OEO P. C. experiment and the John Henry effect. *Phi Delta Kappan, 53,* 579–581.

Sata, L. S. (1975). Laboratory training for police officers. *Journal of Social Issues, 31*(1), 107–114.

Sauter, S. L., Murphy, L. R., & Hurrell, J. J., Jr. (1990). Prevention of work-related psychological disorders: A national strategy proposed by the National Institute for Occupational Safety and Health (NIOSH). *American Psychologist, 45,* 1146–1158.

Sawyer, A. G., & Howard, D. J. (1991). Effects of omitting conclusions in advertisements to involved and uninvolved audiences. *Journal of Marketing Research, 28,* 467–474.

Saxe, L. (1994). Detection of deception: Polygraph and integrity tests. *Current Directions in Psychological Science, 3,* 69–73.

Saywitz, K., Goodman, G. S., Nicholas, E., & Moan, S. F. (1991). Children's memories of a physical examination involving genital touch: Implications for reports of child sexual abuse. *Journal of Consulting and Clinical Psychology, 59,* 682–691.

Schachter, S. (1977). Nicotine regulation in heavy and light smokers. *Journal of Experimental Psychology: General, 106,* 5–12.

Schaller, M., Crandall, C., Stangor, C., & Neuberg, S. (1995). What kinds of social psychological experiments are of value to perform? A reply to Wallach and Wallach. *Journal of Personality and Social Psychology, 69,* 611–618.

Schifter, D. E., & Ajzen, I. (1985). Intention, perceived control, and weight loss: An application of the theory of planned behavior. *Journal of Personality and Social Psychology, 49,* 843–851.

Schlegel, R. P., d'Avernas, J. R., Zanna, M. P., & Manske, S. R. (1988). *Problem drinking: A problem for the theory of reasoned action?* Unpublished manuscript, University of Waterloo.

Schmahl, D. P., Lichtenstein, E., & Harris, D. E. (1972). Successful treatment of habitual smokers with warm, smoky air and rapid smoking. *Journal of Consulting and Clinical Psychology, 38,* 105–111.

Schmidt, F. L., Hunter, J. E., McKenzie, R. C., & Muldrow, T. W. (1979). Impact of valid selection procedures on workforce productivity. *Journal of Applied Psychology, 64,* 609–626.

Schmitt, N., & Borman, N. (Eds.). (1993). *Personnel selection in organizations.* San Francisco: Jossey-Bass.

Schneider, A. L. (1981). Methodological problems in victim surveys and their implications for research in victimology. *Journal of Criminal Law and Criminology, 72,* 818–838.

Schneider, J. (1990). Research, meta-analysis, and desegregation policy. In K. Wachter & M. Straf (Eds.), *The future of meta-analysis* (pp. 55–60). New York: Russell Sage Foundation.

Schofield, J. W. (1986). *Black-White contact in desegregated schools.* Pittsburgh: University of Pittsburgh, Learning Research and Development Center.

Schofield, J. W., & Sagar, H. A., (1977). Peer interaction patterns in an integrated middle school. *Sociometry, 40,* 130–138.

Schofield, J. W., & Sagar, H. A. (1983). Desegregation, school practices, and student race relations. In C. Rossell & W. Hawley (Eds.), *The consequences of school desegregation* (pp. 58–102). Philadelphia: Temple University Press.

Schonfeld & Associates. (1989, November 13). Ratios indicate hikes in ad levels. *Advertising Age,* p. 32.

Schonpflug, W. (1995). The noncharismatic leader—Vulnerable. *Applied Psychology: An International Review, 44,* 39–42.

Schram, S. (1995). *Words of welfare: The poverty of social science and the social science of poverty.* Minneapolis: University of Minnesota Press.

Schriesheim, C., & Klich, N. (1991). Fiedler's least preferred coworker (LPC) instrument: An investigation of its true bipolarity. *Educational and Psychological Measurement, 51,* 305–315.

Schuetz, S., & Sprafkin, J. (1979). Portrayal of prosocial and aggressive behaviors on children's TV commercials. *Journal of Broadcasting, 23,* 33–40.

Schuler, R. S. (1977). Role conflict and ambiguity as a function of the task-structure-technology interaction. *Organizational Behavior and Human Performance, 20,* 66–74.

Schulman, J., Shaver, P., Colman, R., Emrich, B., & Christie, R. (1987). Recipe for a jury. In L. Wrightsman, S. Kassin, & C. Willis (Eds.), *In the jury box: Controversies in the courtroom* (pp. 13–47). Newbury Park, CA: Sage.

Schultz, P. W. (in press). Changing behavior with normative feedback interventions: A field experiment on curbside recycling. *Basic and Applied Social Psychology.*

Schultz, P. W., & Butler, J. C. (1996). *Twenty-five years of applied social psychology.* Unpublished manuscript.

Schultz, P. W., & Oskamp, S. (1996). Effort as a moderator of the attitude-behavior relationship: General environmental concern and recycling. *Social Psychology Quarterly, 59,* 375–383.

Schultz, P. W., Oskamp, S., & Mainieri, T. (1995). Who recycles and when? A review of personal and situational factors. *Journal of Environmental Psychology, 15,* 105–121.

Schultz, P. W., & Schultz, L. A. (1996). Students and handguns: Attitudes, behaviors, and policies in an urban high school. *Proteus: A Journal of Ideas, 13,* 57–60.

Schulz, R., & Hanusa, B. H. (1978). Long-term effects of control and predictability-enhancing interventions: Findings and ethical issues. *Journal of Personality and Social Psychology, 36,* 1194–1201.

Schuman, H., & Hatchett, S. (1974). *Black racial attitudes: Trends and complexities.* Ann Arbor: Institute for Social Research, University of Michigan.

Schuman, H., & Kalton, G. (1985). Survey methods. In G. Lindzey & E. Aronson (Eds.), *Handbook of social psychology* (3rd ed., Vol. 1, pp. 635–697). New York: Random House.

Schuman, H., & Presser, S. (1981). *Questions and answers in attitude surveys: Experiments on question form, wording, and context.* New York: Academic Press.

Schuman, H., Singer, E., Donovan, R., & Selltiz, C. (1983). Discriminatory behavior in New York restaurants: 1950 and 1981. *Social Indicators Research, 13,* 69–83.

Schumann, D. W., Petty, R. E., & Clemons, D. S. (1990). Predicting the effectiveness of different strategies of advertising variation: A test of the repetition-variation hypothesis. *Journal of Consumer Research, 17,* 192–202.

Schumer, C. (1993, April 4). The gun lobby is on the run. *New York Times.*

Schwartz, J. L. (1987). *Review and evaluation of smoking cessation methods: The United States and Canada.* Washington, DC: U.S. Department of Health and Human Services, Public Health Service.

Schwartz, J. L., & Dubitzky, M. (1968). One-year follow-up results of a smoking cessation program. *Canadian Journal of Public Health, 59,* 161–165.

Schwartz, S. H. (1994). Are there universal aspects in the structure and contents of human values? *Journal of Social Issues, 50*(4), 19–45.

Schwarz, R. (1989). Participative decision making: Comparing union-management and management design incentive pay programs. *Group and Organizational Studies, 14,* 104–122.

Schwarzer, W. (1991). Reforming jury trials. *Federal Rules Decisions, 132,* 581–583.

Schwarzwald, J., Raz, M., & Zvibel, M. (1979). The applicability of the door-in-the-face technique when established behavioral customs exist. *Journal of Applied Social Psychology, 9,* 576–586.

Schweinhart, L. J., Barnes, H. V., & Weikart, D. P. (1993). *Significant benefits: The High/Scope Perry Preschool Study through age 27.* Ypsilanti, MI: High/Scope.

Schweinhart, L. J., & Weikart, D. P. (1989). The High/Scope Perry Preschool Study: Implications for early childhood care and education. *Prevention in Human Services, 7,* 109–132.

Schweinhart, L. J., Weikart, D. P., & Larner, M. B. (1986). Consequences of three preschool curriculum models through age 15. *Early Childhood Research Quarterly, 1,* 15–45.

Scott, C., Klein, D. M., & Bryant, J. (1990). Consumer response to humor in advertising: A series of field studies using behavioral observation. *Journal of Consumer Research, 16,* 498–501.

Scott, K. D., & Taylor, G. S. (1985). An examination of conflicting findings in the relationship between job satisfaction and absenteeism: A meta analysis. *Academy of Management Journal, 28,* 599–612.

Scott, L. M. (1990). Understanding jingles and needledrop: A rhetorical approach to music in advertising. *Journal of Consumer Research, 17,* 223–236.

Scott, R. A., & Shore, A. R. (1979). *Why sociology does not apply: A study of the use of sociology in public policy.* New York: Elsevier.

Scriven, M. (1973). Goal-free evaluation. In E. R. House (Ed.), *Social evaluation* (pp. 319–328). Berkeley, CA: McCutchan.

Scriven, M. (1991). Beyond formative and summative evaluation. In M. McLaughlin & D. C. Phillips (Eds.), *Evaluation and education: At quarter century* (pp. 19–64). Chicago: University of Chicago Press.

Sears, D. O. (1986). College sophomores in the laboratory: Influences of a narrow data base on social psychology's view of human nature. *Journal of Personality and Social Psychology, 51,* 515–530.

Sears, D. O., & Kosterman, R. (1994). Mass media and political persuasion. In T. C. Brock & S. Shavitt (Eds.), *Persuasion: Psychological insights and perspectives* (pp. 251–278). Needham Heights, MA: Allyn & Bacon.

Seashore, S. E. (1975). Defining and measuring the quality of working life. In L. E. Davis & A. B. Cherns (Eds.), *The quality of working life: Problems, prospects, and the state of the art* (Vol. 1). New York: Free Press.

Seaver, W. B. (1973). Effects of naturally induced teacher expectancies. *Journal of Personality and Social Psychology, 28,* 333–342.

Sechrest, L., & Figueredo, A. J. (1993). Program evaluation. *Annual Review of Psychology, 44,* 645–674.

Sechrest, L., Perrin, E., & Bunker, J. (1990). *Research methodology: Strengthening causal interpretations of nonexperimental data.* Rockville, MD: U.S. Department of Health and Human Services.

Sechrest, L., & Sidani, S. (1995). Quantitative and qualitative methods: Is there an alternative? *Evaluation and Program Planning, 18,* 77–87.

Segall, M. H., Berry, J. W., & Kagitcibasi, C. (Eds.). (1997). *Handbook of cross-cultural psychology: Social behavior and applications* (2nd ed., Vol. 3). Needham Heights, MA: Allyn & Bacon.

Seggar, J. F., Hafen, J. K., & Hannonen-Gladden, H. (1981). Television's portrayals of minorities and women in drama and comedy drama, 1971–80. *Journal of Broadcasting, 25,* 3.

Seggar, J. F., & Wheeler, P. (1973). World of work on TV: Ethnic and sex representation in TV drama. *Journal of Broadcasting, 17,* 201–214.

Seidman, E. (Ed.). (1983). *Handbook of social intervention.* Beverly Hills, CA: Sage.

Seligman, C., Becker, L. J., & Darley, J. M. (1981). Encouraging residential energy conservation through feedback. In A. Baum & J. E. Singer (Eds.), *Advances in environmental psychology (Vol. 3). Energy: Psychological perspectives.* Hillsdale, NJ: Erlbaum.

Seligman, M. E. P. (1991). *Learned optimism.* New York: Norton.

Selltiz, C. (1955). The use of survey methods in a citizens campaign against discrimination. *Human Organization, 14*(3), 19–25.

Sexton, D., & Haberman, P. (1974). Women in magazine advertisements. *Journal of Advertising Research, 14,* 41–46.

Shadish, W. R. (1993). Critical multiplism: A research strategy and its attendant tactics. *New Directions for Program Evaluation, 60,* 13–57.

Shadish, W. R., Cook, T. D., & Leviton, L. C. (1991). *Foundations of program evaluation.* Newbury Park, CA: Sage.

Shadish, W. R., Newman, D. L., Scheirer, M. A., & Wye, C. (Eds.). (1995). *Guiding principles for evaluators.* San Francisco: Jossey-Bass.

Shapiro, D., & Goldstein, L. B. (1982). Biobehavioral perspectives on hypertension. *Journal of Consulting and Clinical Psychology, 50,* 841–858.

Shapiro, P. N., & Penrod, S. D. (1986). Meta-analysis of facial identification studies. *Psychological Bulletin, 100,* 139–156.

Sharan, S. (Ed.). (1994). *Handbook of cooperative learning methods.* Westport, CT: Greenwood.

Shaw, M. E., & Costanzo, P. R. (1982). *Theories of social psychology* (2nd ed.). New York: McGraw-Hill.

Sheikh, A. A. (1978, September). *Television advertising to children: Controversy, research, and policy implications.* Paper presented at American Psychological Association meeting, Toronto.

Sheley, J., McGee, Z., & Wright, J. (1992). Gun-related violence in and around inner-city schools. *American Journal of Diseases of Childhood, 146,* 677–682.

Sheppard, B. H., Hartwick, J., & Warshaw, P. R. (1988). The theory of reasoned action: A meta-analysis of past research with recommendations for modifications and future research. *Journal of Consumer Research, 15,* 325–343.

Shepperd, J. A. (1993). Productivity loss in performance groups: A motivation analysis. *Psychological Bulletin, 113,* 67–81.

Sherif, M. (1936). *The psychology of social norms.* New York: Harper & Row.

Sherif, M., & Hovland, C. I. (1961). *Social judgment: Assimilation and contrast effects in communication and attitude change.* New Haven, CT: Yale University Press.

Shimp, T. A., & Kavas, A. (1984). The theory of reasoned action applied to coupon usage. *Journal of Consumer Research, 11,* 795–809.

Shippee, G. (1979). Experimental social innovation as an alternative to a pseudo-relevant social psychology. *Personality and Social Psychology Bulletin, 5,* 491–498.

Shireman, W. K. (1993). Solid waste: To recycle or to bury California? In T. Palmer (Ed.), *California's threatened environment: Restoring the dream* (pp. 170–181). Washington, DC: Island Press.

Shiva, V. (1989). *Staying alive: Women, ecology, and development.* London: Zed Books.

Shotland, R. L. (1989). A model of the causes of date rape in developing and close relationships. In C. Hendrick (Ed.), *Close relationships.* Newbury Park, CA: Sage.

Shweder, R. A., & Sullivan, M. A. (1993). Cultural psychology: Who needs it? *Annual Review of Psychology, 44,* 497–523.

Sieber, J. E. (1992). *Planning ethically responsible research: A guide for students and internal review boards.* Newbury Park, CA: Sage.

Sieber, J. E., Iannuzzo, R., & Rodriguez, B. (1995). Deception methods in psychology: Have they changed in 23 years? *Ethics and Behavior, 5,* 67–85.

Sieber, J. E., & Sorensen, J. L. (1992). Ethical issues in community-based research and intervention. In F. B. Bryant, J. Edwards, R. S. Tindale, E. J. Posavac, L. Heath, E. Henderson, & Y. Suarez-Balcazar (Eds.), *Methodological issues in applied social psychology* (pp. 43–63). New York: Plenum.

Sieber, S. D. (1981). *Fatal remedies: The ironies of social intervention.* New York: Plenum.

Sigelman, L., & Welch, S. (1993). The contact hypothesis revisited: Black-White interaction and positive racial attitudes. *Social Forces, 71,* 781–795.

Signorielli, N. (1989). Television and conceptions about sex roles: Maintaining conventionality and the status quo. *Sex Roles, 21,* 341–360.

Signorielli, N. (1993). Television, the portrayal of women, and children's attitudes. In G. Berry & J. Asamen (Eds.), *Children and television: Images in a changing sociocultural world* (pp. 229–242). Newbury Park, CA: Sage.

Silverman, I. (1977). Why social psychology fails. *Canadian Psychological Review, 18,* 353–358.

Silverman, L. T., Sprafkin, J. N., & Rubinstein, E. A. (1979). Physical contact and sexual behavior on prime-time TV. *Journal of Communication, 29,* 33–43.

Simmons, D., & Widmar, R. (1990). Motivations and barriers to recycling: Toward a strategy for public education. *Journal of Environmental Education, 22,* 13–18.

Simmons, I. G. (1991). *Earth, air, and water: Resources and environment in the late 20th century.* London: Edward Arnold.

Sinclair, R., Lee, T., & Johnson, T. E. (1995). The effect of social-comparison feedback on aggressive responses to erotic and aggressive films. *Journal of Applied Social Psychology, 25,* 818–837

Singer, D. G., Zuckerman, D. M., & Singer, J. L. (1980). Teaching elementary school children television viewing skills: An evaluation. *Journal of Communication, 30,* 84–93.

Sinowitz, B. E. (1973). School integration and the teacher. *Today's Education, 62,* 31–33.

Skedsvold, P. R., & Mann, T. L. (Eds.). (1996). Affirmative action [Special issue]. *Journal of Social Issues, 52*(4).

Skelly, G. U., & Lundstrom, W. J. (1981). Male sex roles in magazine advertising, 1959–1979. *Journal of Communication, 31*(4), 52–57.

Skinner, B. F. (1948). *Walden two.* New York: Macmillan.

Skinner, B. F. (1957). The experimental analysis of behavior. *American Scientist, 45,* 343–371.

Skinner, B. F. (1982, August). *Intellectual self-management in old age.* Paper presented at American Psychological Association meeting, Washington, DC.

Skogan, W. G. (Ed.). (1976). *Sample surveys of the victims of crime.* Cambridge, MA: Ballinger.

Slaby, R. G., & Guerra, N. G. (1988). Cognitive mediators of aggression in adolescent offenders: I. Assessment. *Developmental Psychology, 24,* 580–588.

Slaughter, D., & Kuehne, V. (1989). Improving Black education: Perspectives on parent involvement. In W. Smith & E. Chunn (Eds.), *Black education: A quest for equity and excellence* (pp. 59–75). New Brunswick, NJ: Transaction.

Slavin, R. E. (1992). When and why does cooperative learning increase achievement? Theoretical and empirical perspectives. In R. Hertz-Lazarowitz & N. Miller (Eds.), *Interaction in cooperative groups: The theoretical anatomy of group learning* (pp. 145–173). New York: Cambridge University Press.

Slavin, R. E., Karweit, N., & Wasik, B. (Eds.). (1994). *Preventing early school failure: Research, policy, practice.* Boston: Allyn & Bacon.

Slavin, R. E., & Madden, N. (1994). Pieces of the puzzle: The jigsaw method. In S. Sharan (Ed.), *Handbook of cooperative learning methods.* Westport, CT: Greenwood.

Slottje, D. J., Scully, G. W., Hirschberg, J. G., & Hayes, K. J. (1991). *Measuring the quality of life across countries: A multidimensional analysis.* Boulder, CO: Westview.

Slovenko, R. (1993). Expert testimony: Use and abuse. *Medicine and Law, 12,* 627–641.

Smith, B. M. (1967). The polygraph. *Scientific American, 216,* 25–31.

Smith, C. (1991). Sex and genre on prime time. *Journal of Homosexuality, 21,* 119–138.

Smith, M. B. (1975). Psychology and ethics. In E. C. Kennedy (Ed.), *Human rights and psychological research.* New York: Crowell.

Smith, M. B. (1976). Some perspectives on ethical/political issues in social science research. *Personality and Social Psychology Bulletin, 2,* 445–453.

Smith, M. B. (1978). Psychology and values. *Journal of Social Issues, 34*(4), 181–199.

Smith, M. J. (1990). Pluralism, reformed pluralism and neopluralism: The role of pressure groups in policy-making. *Political Studies, 38,* 302–322.

Smith, P. C. (1974). The development of a method of measuring job satisfaction: The Cornell studies. In E. A. Fleishman & A. R. Bass (Eds.), *Studies in personnel and industrial psychology* (3rd ed.). Homewood, IL: Dorsey.

Smith, R. A. (1991). The effects of visual and verbal advertising information on consumers' inferences. *Journal of Advertising, 20,* 13–23.

Smith, T. W. (1990). The sexual revolution? *Public Opinion Quarterly, 54,* 415–435.

Smolowe, J. (1997, June 30). Sorry, pardner. *Time,* pp. 24–29.

Snyder, M. (1993). Motivational foundations of behavioral confirmation. In M. P. Zanna (Ed.), *Advances in experimental social psychology* (Vol. 25, pp. 67–114). San Diego, CA: Academic Press.

Snyder, M., & Swann, W. B., Jr. (1978). Hypothesis-testing processes in social interaction. *Journal of Personality and Social Psychology, 36,* 1202–1212.

Snyder, R. (1992). Comparative advertising and brand evaluation: Toward developing a categorization approach. *Journal of Consumer Psychology, 1,* 15–30.

Sobel, J., & Stunkard, A. J. (1989). Socioeconomic status and obesity: A review of the literature. *Psychological Bulletin, 105,* 260–275.

Sobel, S. B. (1979). Nick Cummings reflects on psychology's future in public policy. *The Clinical Psychologist, 33*(1), 13–15.

Soliday, E., & Stanton, A. (1995). Deceived versus nondeceived participants' perceptions of scientific and applied psychology. *Ethics and Behavior, 5,* 87–104.

Solomon, J., & Rogers, A. (1997, March 31). Turning a new leaf: Liggett breaks ranks with 'big tobacco.' *Newsweek,* p. 50.

Sommers-Flanagan, R., Sommers-Flanagan, J., & Davis, B. (1993). What's happening on music television? A gender role content analysis. *Sex Roles, 28,* 745–753.

Sonnert, G., & Holton, G. (1995). *Gender differences in science careers: The project access study.* New Brunswick, NJ: Rutgers University Press.

Sonnichsen, R. C. (1994). Evaluators as change agents. In J. Wholey, H. Hatry, & K. Newcomer (Eds.), *Handbook of practical program evaluation* (pp. 534–548). San Francisco: Jossey-Bass.

Sorrentino, R., Bodocel, D. R., Gitta, M., Olson, J., & Hewitt, E. (1988). Uncertainty orientation and persuasion: Individual differences in the effects of personal relevance on social judgments. *Journal of Personality and Social Psychology, 55,* 357–371.

Special topic forum on ecologically sustainable organizations. (1995). *Academy of Management Review, 20,* 873–1089.

Spence, J. T., & Helmreich, R. L. (1983). Achievement-related motives and behaviors. In J. T. Spence (Ed.), *Achievement and achievement motives.* San Francisco: Freeman.

Spencer, S. J., Steele, C. M., & Quinn, D. (1996). *Stereotype threat and women's math performance.* Unpublished manuscript, Stanford University.

Sperry, L. (1994). Helping people control their weight: Research and practice. In J. Lewis (Ed.), *Addictions: Concepts and strategies for treatment* (pp. 83–98). Gaithersberg, MD: Aspen.

Sporer, S. L., Malpass, R., & Koehnken, G. (Eds.). (1996). *Psychological issues in eyewitness identification.* Mahwah, NJ: Erlbaum.

Sprafkin, J. N., Liebert, R. M., & Poulos, R. W. (1975). Effects of a prosocial televised example on children's helping. *Journal of Experimental Child Psychology, 20,* 119–126.

Sprafkin, J. N., & Rubinstein, E. A. (1979). Children's television viewing habits and prosocial behavior: A field correlational study. *Journal of Broadcasting, 23,* 265–276.

SRI International. (1989). Values and lifestyles program. In *Descriptive materials for the VALS 2 segmentation system.* Menlo Park, CA: Author.

St. John, N. H. (1975). *School desegregation: Outcomes for children.* New York: Wiley.

Stachnik, T. J. (1980). Priorities for psychology in medical education and health care delivery. *American Psychologist, 35,* 8–15.

Stack, S. (1993). Execution publicity and homicide in Georgia. *American Journal of Criminal Justice, 18,* 25–39.

Stanfield, R. (1996). This reform may not be the answer. *National Journal, 28,* 1664.

Stangor, C., & Lange, J. E. (1994). Mental representations of social groups: Advances in understanding stereotypes and stereotyping. In M. P. Zanna (Ed.), *Advances in experimental social psychology* (Vol. 26, pp. 357–416). San Diego, CA: Academic Press.

Staples, S. L. (1996). Human response to environmental noise: Psychological research and public policy. *American Psychologist, 51,* 143–150.

Statistical Abstract of the United States, 1995 (115th ed.). Washington, DC: U.S. Government Printing Office.

Staub, E. (1996). Cultural-societal roots of violence: The examples of genocidal violence and of contemporary youth vio-lence in the United States. *American Psychologist, 51,* 117–131.

Stauffer, J., Frost, R., & Rybolt, W. (1983). The attention factor in recalling network television news. *Journal of Communication, 33*(1), 29–37.

Staw, B. M., & Ross, J. (1985). Stability in the midst of change: A dispositional approach to job attitudes. *Journal of Applied Psychology, 70,* 469–480.

Steeh, C., & Krysan, M. (1996). Affirmative action and the public, 1970–1995. *Public Opinion Quarterly, 60,* 128–158.

Steele, C. M. (1996). *A burden of suspicion: How stereotypes shape the intellectual identities and performance of women and African-Americans.* Unpublished manuscript, Stanford University.

Steele, C. M., & Aronson, J. (1995). Stereotype threat and the intellectual test performance of African Americans. *Journal of Personality and Social Psychology, 69,* 797–811.

Steenland, S. (1990). Women and television in the 80s. *Television Quarterly, 24,* 53–60.

Steinberg, L., Blinde, P. L., & Chan, K. S. (1984). Dropping out among language minority youth. *Review of Educational Research, 54,* 113–132.

Stelbay, N. M. (1992). A meta-analytic review of the weapon focus effect. *Law and Human Behavior, 16,* 413–424.

Stephan, W. G. (1978). School desegregation: An evaluation of predictions made in *Brown v. Board of Education. Psychological Bulletin, 85,* 217–238.

Stephan, W. G. (1980). A brief historical overview of school desegregation. In W. G. Stephan & J. R. Feagin (Eds.), *School desegregation: Past, present, and future* (pp. 3–24). New York: Plenum.

Stephan, W. G. (1987). The contact hypothesis in intergroup relations. In C. Hendrick (Ed.), *Group processes and intergroup relations* (pp. 13–40). Beverly Hills, CA: Sage.

Stephan, W. G. (1991). School desegregation: Short-term and long-term effects. In H. Knopke, R. Norrell, & R. Rogers (Eds.), *Opening doors: Perspectives on race relations in contemporary America* (pp. 100–118). Tuscaloosa: University of Alabama Press.

Stephan, W. G. (1994, October). *Intergroup anxiety.* Paper presented at Society of Experimental Social Psychology meeting, Lake Tahoe, CA.

Stephan, W. G., & Stephan, C. W. (1985). Intergroup anxiety. *Journal of Social Issues, 41*(3), 157–175.

Stern, P. C. (1992). Psychological dimensions of global environmental change. *Annual Review of Psychology, 43,* 269–302.

Stern, P. C., & Dietz, T. (1994). The value basis of environmental concern. *Journal of Social Issues, 50*(3), 65–84.

Sternthal, B., & Craig, C. S. (1973). Humor in advertising. *Journal of Marketing, 37,* 12–18.

Steuer, F. B., Applefield, J. M., & Smith, R. (1971). Televised aggression and the interpersonal aggression of preschool children. *Journal of Experimental Child Psychology, 11,* 442–447.

Stevens, R., & Slavin, R. (1995). The cooperative elementary school: Effects on students' achievement, attitudes, and social relations. *American Educational Research Journal, 32,* 321–351.

Stockdale, M. S. (Ed.). (1996). *Sexual harassment in the workplace: Perspectives, frontiers, and response strategies.* Thousand Oaks, CA: Sage.

Stogdill, R. M. (1948). Personal factors associated with leadership: A survey of the literature. *Journal of Personality, 25,* 35–71.

Stokes, B. (1978). *Worker participation—Productivity and the quality of work life* (Worldwatch Paper 25). Washington, DC: Worldwatch Institute.

Stokols, D. (1995). The paradox of environmental psychology. *American Psychologist, 50,* 821–837.

Stone, A. A., Neal, J. M., & Schiffman, S. (1993). Daily assessment of stress and coping and their association with mood. *Annals of Behavioral Medicine, 15,* 8–16.

Stone, C. N. (1980). The implementation of social programs: Two perspectives. *Journal of Social Issues, 36*(4), 13–34.

Stone, W. F. (1993). Psychodynamics, cognitive functioning, or group orientation: Research and theory in the 1980s. In W. F. Stone, G. Lederer, & R. Christie (Eds.), *Strength and weakness: The authoritarian personality today* (pp. 159–181). New York: Springer-Verlag.

Strack, F., Argyle, M., & Schwarz, N. (Eds.). (1991). *Subjective well-being: An interdisciplinary perspective.* Oxford, England: Pergamon.

Strickland, B. R. (1977). Internal-external control of reinforcement. In T. Blass (Ed.), *Personality variables in social behavior.* Hillsdale, NJ: Erlbaum.

Strube, M., & Garcia, J. (1981). A meta-analytic investigation of Fiedler's contingency model of leadership effectiveness. *Psychological Bulletin, 90,* 307–321.

Stuckert, R. P. (1964). Race mixture: The African ancestry of White Americans. In P. B. Hammond (Ed.), *Physical anthropology and archaeology: Selected readings* (pp. 192–197). New York: Macmillan.

Suchman, E. (1972). Action for what? A critique of evaluative research. In C. H. Weiss (Ed.), *Evaluating action programs: Readings in social action and education* (pp. 52–84). Boston: Allyn & Bacon.

Sudman, S., & Bradburn, N. M. (1974). *Response effects in surveys: A review and synthesis.* Chicago: Aldine.

Sudman, S., & Bradburn, N. M. (1982). *Asking questions: A practical guide to questionnaire design.* San Francisco: Jossey-Bass.

Sudman, S., Bradburn, N. M., & Schwarz, N. (1996). *Thinking about answers: The application of cognitive processes to survey methodology.* San Francisco: Jossey-Bass.

Suedfeld, P., & Tetlock, P. (Eds.) (1992). *Psychology and social policy.* New York: Hemisphere.

Sullivan, M. J., McNamara, K. M., Ybarra, M., & Bulatao, E. Q. (1995). Psychologists as state legislators: Introduction to the special section. *Professional psychology—Research & practice, 26,* 445–448.

Sundstrom, E., Bell, P. A., Busby, P. L., & Asmus, C. (1996). Environmental psychology 1989–1994. *Annual Review of Psychology, 47,* 485–512.

Sundstrom, E., Town, J., Rice, R., Osborn, D., & Brill, M. (1994). Office noise, satisfaction, and performance. *Environment and Behavior, 26,* 195–222.

Surgeon General's Scientific Advisory Committee on Television and Social Behavior. (1972). *Television and growing up: The impact of televised violence* (Report to the Surgeon General, U.S. Public Health Service). Washington, DC: U.S. Government Printing Office.

Sussman, S., Dent, C., Burton, D., Stacy, A., & Flay, B. (1995). *Developing school-based tobacco use prevention and cessation programs.* Thousand Oaks, CA: Sage.

Swim, J. K. (1994). Perceived versus meta-analytic effect sizes: An assessment of the accuracy of gender stereotypes. *Journal of Personality and Social Psychology, 66,* 21–36.

Symposium on neighborhood policy and practice. (1987). *Policy Studies Journal, 16,* 263–392.

Szafran, R. (Ed.). (1994). *Social science research: A cross section of journal articles for discussion and evaluation.* Los Angeles: Pryczak.

Taber, M. A., Lathrope, D. E., Small, S. C., Rempe, N., Flynn, M., & Coyle, J. J. (1972). *Handbook for community professionals: An approach for planning and action.* Springfield, IL: Thomas.

Tajfel, H. (1970). Experiments in intergroup discrimination. *Scientific American, 223*(2), 96–102.

Tan, A. S. (1979). TV beauty ads and role expectations of adolescent female viewers. *Journalism Quarterly, 56,* 283–288.

Tanford, J. A. (1990). The law and psychology of jury instructions. *Nebraska Law Review, 69,* 71–111.

Tanford, J. A., & Cox, M. (1987). The effects of impeachment evidence and limiting instructions on individual and group decision making. *Law and Human Behavior, 12,* 477–497.

Tanke, E. D., & Tanke, T. J. (1979). Getting off a slippery slope: Social science in the judicial process. *American Psychologist, 34,* 1130–1138.

Tannenbaum, P. H. (Ed.). (1980). *The entertainment functions of television.* Hillsdale, NJ: Erlbaum.

Tapp, J. L. (1981). Psychologists and the law: Who needs whom? In L. Bickman (Ed.), *Applied social psychology annual* (Vol. 2, pp. 263–289). Beverly Hills, CA: Sage.

Taub, E., Crago, J. E., Burgio, L. D., Groomes, T. E., Cook, E. W., DeLuca, S. C., & Miller, N. E. (1994). An operant approach to rehabilitation medicine: Overcoming learned nonuse by shaping. *Journal of Experimental Analysis and Behavior, 61,* 281–293.

Taylor, B. R. (1991). *Affirmative action at work: Law, politics, and ethics.* Pittsburgh: University of Pittsburgh Press.

Taylor, D. A. (1996). A reconceptualization of qualified: The ultimate dilemma. *Basic and Applied Social Psychology, 18,* 15–30.

Taylor, D. M., & Moghaddam, F. M. (1994). *Theories of intergroup relations: International social psychological perspectives.* Westport, CT: Praeger.

Taylor, J. C. (1977). Job satisfaction and quality of working life: A reassessment. *Journal of Occupational Psychology, 50,* 243–252.

Taylor, M. C. (1994). Impact of affirmative action on beneficiary groups: Evidence from the 1990 General Social Survey. *Basic and Applied Social Psychology, 15,* 143–178.

Taylor, S. E. (1995). *Health psychology* (3rd Ed.). New York: McGraw-Hill.

Taylor, S. E., & Levin, S. (1976). *The psychological impact of breast cancer: Theory and research.* San Francisco: West Coast Cancer Foundation.

Tedesco, N. (1974). Patterns of prime time. *Journal of Communication, 24,* 119–124.

Tellis, G. J., & Gaeth, G. J. (1990). Best value, price-seeking, and price aversion: The impact of information and learning on consumer choices. *Journal of Marketing, 54,* 34–45.

Terkel, S. (1974). *Working: People talk about what they do all day and how they feel about what they do.* New York: Pantheon.

Tharenou, P. (1993). A test of reciprocal causality for absenteeism. *Journal of Organizational Behavior, 14,* 269–287.

Thierry, H. (1987). Payment by results systems: A review of research, 1945–1985. *Applied Psychology: An International Review, 36,* 91–108.

Thomas, M. H., Horton, R. W., Lippincott, E. C., & Drabman, R. S. (1977). Desensitization to portrayals of real-life aggression as a function of exposure to television violence. *Journal of Personality and Social Psychology, 35,* 450–458.

Thomas, R. R., Jr. (1995). A diversity framework. In M. M. Chemers, S. Oskamp, & M. A. Costanzo (Eds.), *Diversity in organizations: New perspectives for a changing workforce* (pp. 245–263). Thousand Oaks, CA: Sage.

Thompson, E. L. (1978). Smoking education programs 1960–1976. *American Journal of Public Health, 68,* 250–257.

Thompson, L., & Norris, D. (1995). Introduction: The politics of welfare reform. In D. Norris & L. Thompson (Eds.), *The politics of welfare reform* (pp. 1–18). Thousand Oaks, CA: Sage.

Thompson, M. M., Naccarato, M. E., & Parker, K. E. (1989, June). *Assessing cognitive need: The development of the Personal Need for Structure and Personal Fear of Invalidity scales.* Paper presented at Canadian Psychological Association meeting, Halifax, Nova Scotia.

Thompson, W. (1993). Research on jury decision making: The state of the science. In N. J. Castellan (Ed.), *Individual and group decision making: Current issues* (pp. 203–218). Hillsdale, NJ: Erlbaum.

Thousand, J., Villa, R., & Nevin, A. (Eds.). (1994). *Creativity and collaborative learning: A practical guide to empowering students and teachers.* Baltimore: Brookes.

Toch, H., & Lizotte, A. (1992). Research and policy: The case of gun control. In P. Suedfeld & P. Tetlock (Eds.), *Psychology and social policy* (pp. 223–240). New York: Hemisphere.

Tollestrup, P. A., Turtle, J., & Yuille, J. (1994). Actual victims and witnesses to robbery and fraud: An archival analysis. In D. Ross, J. Read, & M. Toglia (Eds.), *Adult eyewitness testimony: Current trends and developments* (pp. 144–162). New York: Cambridge University Press.

Tongas, P. N. (1979). The Kaiser-Permanente smoking control program: Its purpose and implications for an HMO. *Professional Psychology, 10,* 409–418.

Topf, M. (1989). Sensitivity to noise, personality hardiness, and noise-induced stress in critical care nurses. *Environment and Behavior, 21,* 717–733.

Tornatzky, L. G., Solomon, T., et al. (1982). Contributions of social science to innovation and productivity. *American Psychologist, 37,* 737–746.

Travers, C. J., & Cooper, C. L. (1993). Mental health, job satisfaction and occupational stress among UK teachers. *Work and Stress, 7,* 203–219.

Treisman, U. (1985). *A study of mathematics performance of Black students at the University of California, Berkeley.* Unpublished manuscript.

Triandis, H. C. (1977). *Interpersonal behavior.* Monterey, CA: Brooks/Cole.

Triandis, H. C. (1993). The contingency model in cross-cultural perspective. In M. Chemers & R. Ayman (Eds.), *Leadership theory and research: Perspectives and directions* (pp. 167–188). San Diego, CA: Academic Press.

Triandis, H. C. (1995). A theoretical framework for the study of diversity. In M. M. Chemers, S. Oskamp, & M. A. Costanzo (Eds.), *Diversity in organizations: New perspectives for a changing workforce* (pp. 11–36). Thousand Oaks, CA: Sage.

Triandis, H. C. (1996). The psychological measurement of cultural syndromes. *American Psychologist, 51,* 407–415.

Triandis, H. C., Kurowski, L. L., & Gelfand, M. J. (1994). Workplace diversity. In H. C. Triandis, M. D. Dunnette, & L. M. Hough (Eds.), *Handbook of industrial & organizational psychology* (2nd ed., Vol. 4, pp. 769–827). Palo Alto, CA: Consulting Psychologists Press.

Trist, E. L., & Bamforth, K. W. (1951). Some social and psychological consequences of the longwall method of coalgetting. *Human Relations, 4,* 3–38.

Tucker, M. E., & Grim, J. (Eds.). (1993). *Worldviews and ecology.* London, England: Bucknell University Press.

Turner, C. F., & Krauss, E. (1978). Fallible indicators of the subjective state of the nation. *American Psychologist, 33,* 456–470.

Turner, C. F., Lessler, J. T., & Gfroerer, J. C. (1992). *Survey measurement of drug use: Methodological studies.* Washington, DC: USDHHS.

Turner, M. E., & Pratkanis, A. R. (1994a). Affirmative action: Insights from social psychological and organizational research. *Basic and Applied Social Psychology, 15,* 1–11.

Turner, M. E., & Pratkanis, A. R. (1994b). Affirmative action as help: A review of recipient reactions to preferential selection and affirmative action. *Basic and Applied Social Psychology, 15,* 43–69.

Turner, M. E., & Pratkanis, A. R. (Eds.). (1994c). Social psychological perspectives on affirmative action [Special issue]. *Basic and Applied Social Psychology, 15,* 1–220.

Twentieth Century Fund. (1993). *The report of the Twentieth Century Fund task force on public television.* New York: Author.

Tybout, A. M., & Artz, N. (1994). Consumer psychology. *Annual Review of Psychology, 45,* 131–169.

Ulrich, R. S. (1986). Human responses to vegetation and landscapes. *Landscape and Urban Planning, 13,* 29–44.

Unger, R., & Crawford, M. (1992). *Women and gender: A feminist psychology*. Philadelphia: Temple University Press.

United Nations Conference on Environment and Development. (1992). *United States of America national report*. Washington, DC: Council on Environmental Quality.

United Nations Human Development Programme. (1993). *Human development report*. New York: Oxford University Press.

U.S. Bureau of the Census. (1994). *Statistical abstract of the United States 1994* (114th ed.). Washington, DC: Author.

U.S. Bureau of the Census. (1995). *Statistical abstract of the United States: 1995* (115th ed.). Washington, DC: Author.

U.S. Commission on Civil Rights. (1977). *Reviewing a decade of school desegregation, 1966–1975*. Washington, DC: U.S. Government Printing Office.

U.S. Commission on Civil Rights. (1987). *The new evidence on civil rights in school desegregation*. Washington, DC: U.S. Government Printing Office.

U.S. Commission on Obscenity and Pornography. (1970). *Report of the Commission on Obscenity and Pornography*. Washington, DC: U.S. Government Printing Office.

U.S. Department of Agriculture. (1995–96). *Agricultural statistics, 1995–96*. Washington, DC: U.S. Government Printing Office.

U.S. Department of Health and Human Services. (1989). *Reducing the health consequences of smoking: 25 years of progress. A report to the Surgeon General*. Washington DC: U.S. Government Printing Office.

U.S. Department of Health and Human Services. (1990). *Smoking and tobacco and health: A factbook*. Washington DC: U.S. Government Printing Office.

U.S. Department of Health and Human Services. (1991). *National household survey on drug abuse: Main findings of 1990* (Publication No. (ADM) 91–1788). Washington, DC: U.S. Government Printing Office.

U.S. Department of Health and Human Services. (1994). *Preventing tobacco use among young people: A report of the surgeon general*. Washington DC: U.S. Government Printing Office.

U.S. Department of Health and Human Services. (1996). *Trends in the well-being of America's children and youth: 1996*. Washington DC: U.S. Government Printing Office.

U.S. Department of Health, Education, and Welfare. (1964). *Smoking and health: Report of the Advisory Committee to the Surgeon General of the Public Health Service* (USPHS Publication No. 1103). Washington, DC: Author.

U.S. Department of Health, Education, and Welfare. (1971). *The institutional guide to DHEW policy on protection of human subjects* (DHEW Publication No. (NIH) 72–102). Washington, DC: U.S. Government Printing Office.

U.S. Department of Health, Education, and Welfare, Public Health Service. (1979). *Smoking and health: A report of the Surgeon General* (DHEW Publication No. (PHS) 79–50066). Washington, DC: Author.

U.S. Department of Justice. (1990). *Sourcebook of criminal justice statistics*. Washington DC: U.S. Government Printing Office.

U.S. Department of Justice. (1994). *Criminal victimization in the United States, 1992*. Washington, DC: Bureau of Justice.

U.S. Environmental Protection Agency. (1992, August). *The consumer's handbook for reducing solid waste* (EPA530-K-92–003). Washington, DC: Author.

U.S. Environmental Protection Agency. (1994). *Determinants of effectiveness for environmental certification and labeling programs* (EPA 742-R-94–001). Washington, DC: Author.

University of California, Santa Barbara, University of North Carolina, Chapel Hill, University of Texas, Austin, & University of Wisconsin, Madison. (1996). *National television violence study* (Vol. 1). Thousand Oaks, CA: Sage.

Unnikrishnan, N., & Bajpai, S. (1996). *The impact of television advertising on children*. Newbury Park, CA: Sage.

Van Houwelingen, J., & Van Raaij, F. (1989). The effect of goal-setting and daily electronic feedback on in-home energy use. *Journal of Consumer Research, 16*, 98–105.

Van Zelst, R. H. (1951). Worker popularity and job satisfaction. *Personnel Psychology, 4*, 405–412.

Vander Kolk, C. J. (1978). Physiological reactions of Black, Puerto Rican, and White students in suggested ethnic encounters. *Journal of Social Psychology, 104*, 107–114.

Vanderslice, V. J. (1995). Cooperation within a competitive context: Lessons from worker cooperatives. In B. B. Bunker & J. Z. Rubin (Eds.), *Conflict, cooperation, and justice: Essays inspired by the work of Morton Deutsch* (pp. 175–204). San Francisco: Jossey-Bass.

Varela, J. A. (1971). *Psychological solutions to social problems: An introduction to social technology*. New York: Academic Press.

Varela, J. A. (1977). Social technology. *American Psychologist, 32*, 914–923.

Vasterling, J., Jenkins, R. A., Tope, P. M., & Burish, T. G. (1993). Cognitive distraction and relaxation training for control of side effects due to cancer chemotherapy. *Journal of Behavioral Medicine, 16*, 65–80.

Vincent, T. A. (1990). A view from the hill: The human element in policy making on Capitol Hill. *American Psychologist, 45*, 61–64.

Vlek, C. A. J. (1995, August). *Technical versus socio-behavioral solutions to environmental problems: Psychology's unexploited potential*. Paper presented at American Psychological Association meeting, New York.

Vooijs, M., & Van der Voort, T. (1993). Learning about television violence: The impact of a critical viewing curriculum on children's attitudinal judgments of crime series. *Journal of Research and Development in Education, 26*, 133–142.

Vroom, V. H. (1964). *Work and motivation*. New York: Wiley.

Wager, J. T. (1995–1996). Double exposure. *Nucleus, 17*(4), 1–3, 12.

Wagner, E. S. (1992). *Sexual harassment in the workplace: How to prevent, investigate and resolve complaints in your organization*. New York: AMACOM.

Walker, L. (1984). *The battered woman syndrome*. New York: Springer.

Wall, T. D., Corbett, J. M., Martin, R., Clegg, C. W., & Jackson, P. R. (1990). Advanced manufacturing technology, work design, and performance: A change study. *Journal of Applied Psychology, 75,* 691–697.

Wall, T. D., Jackson, P. R., & Davids, K. (1992). Operator work design and robotics system performance: A serendipitous field study. *Journal of Applied Psychology, 77,* 353–362.

Wallach, L., & Wallach, M. (1994). Gergen versus the mainstream: Are hypotheses in social psychology subject to empirical test? *Journal of Personality and Social Psychology, 67,* 233–242.

Wallack, L., & Russell, S. (1991). Media advocacy and public education in the Community Intervention Trial to Reduce Heavy Smoking (COMMIT). [Special issue: Community intervention for smoking cessation: COMMIT]. *International Quarterly of Community Health Education, 11,* 205–222.

Walsh, M. (1993). Highway vehicle activity trends and their implications for global warming: The U.S. in an international context. In D. Greene & D. Santini (Eds.), *Transportation and global climate change* (pp. 1–48). Berkeley, CA: ACEEE Books.

Walster, E., Berscheid, E., & Walster, G. W. (1973). New directions in equity research. *Journal of Personality and Social Psychology, 25,* 151–176.

Walster, E., Walster, G. W., & Berscheid, E. (1978). *Equity: Theory and research.* Boston: Allyn & Bacon.

Walton, W. W. (1982). An evaluation of the Poison Prevention Packaging Act. *Pediatrics, 69,* 363–370.

Ward, S., & Wackman, D. (1972). Television advertising and intra-family influence: Children's purchase influence attempts and parental yielding. *Journal of Marketing Research, 9,* 316–319.

Ward, S., Wackman, D., & Wartella, E. (1977). *How children learn to buy: The development of consumer information processing skills.* Beverly Hills, CA: Sage.

Warner, K. (1993). The economics of tobacco. In C. T. Orleans & J. Slade (Eds.), *Nicotine addiction: Principles and management* (pp. 46–58). New York: Oxford University Press.

Warning from Washington: Violence on television is harmful to children. *Time* (1982, May 17).

Warr, P., & Wall, T. (1975). *Work and well being.* Harmondsworth, England: Penguin.

Wartella, E. (1980). Individual differences in children's responses to television advertising. In E. L. Palmer & A. Dorr (Eds.), *Children and the faces of television: Teaching, violence, selling* (pp. 307–322). New York: Academic Press.

Warwick, D. P. (1982). Types of harm in social research. In T. L. Beauchamp, R. R. Faden, R. J. Wallace, Jr., & L. R. Walters (Eds.), *Ethical issues in social science research* (pp. 101–124). Baltimore: Johns Hopkins University Press.

Wasting opportunities. (1990, December 22). *The Economist,* p. 14.

Waters, L. K., & Waters, C. W. (1972). An empirical test of five versions of the two-factor theory of job satisfaction. *Organizational Behavior and Human Performance, 7,* 18–24.

Watkins, T. L., Sprafkin, J., Gadow, K., & Sadetsky, I. (1988). Effects of a critical viewing skills curriculum on elementary school children's knowledge and attitudes about television. *Journal of Educational Research, 81,* 165–170.

Watson, D., & Slack, A. (1993). General factors of affective temperament and their relation to job satisfaction over time. *Organizational Behavior & Human Decision Processes, 54,* 181–202

Watson, T. (1989). Product labeling efforts are on the march worldwide. *Resource Recycling, 8,* 18–21.

Weaver, J. B., Masland, J. L., & Zillmann, D. (1984). Effects of erotica on young men's aesthetic perception of their female sexual partner. *Perceptual and Motor Skills, 58,* 929–930.

Weaver, K. F. (1981, February). America's thirst for imported oil: Our energy predicament. *National Geographic,* 2–23.

Webber, D. (1992). The distribution and use of knowledge in the policy process. In L. Aiken & B. Kehrer (Eds.), *Evaluation studies review annual* (Vol. 10, pp. 383–418). Beverly Hills, CA: Sage.

Weber, R. P. (1990). *Basic content analysis* (2nd ed.). Newbury Park, CA: Sage.

Weber, S. J., & Cook, T. D. (1972). Subject effects in laboratory research: An examination of subject roles, demand characteristics, and valid inference. *Psychological Bulletin, 77,* 273–295.

Weeks, M. F., & Moore, R. P. (1981). Ethnicity-of-interviewer effects on ethnic respondents. *Public Opinion Quarterly, 45,* 245–249.

Wegenaar, A. C., Maybee, R. G., & Sullivan, K. P. (1988). Mandatory seat belt laws in eight states: A time series evaluation. *Journal of Safety Research, 19,* 51–70.

Weigel, R. H., & Howes, P. W. (1985). Conceptions of racial prejudice. *Journal of Social Issues, 41*(3), 117–138.

Weigel, R. H., Loomis, J. W., & Soja, M. J. (1980). Race relations on prime time television. *Journal of Personality and Social Psychology, 39,* 884–893.

Weigel, R. H., & Pappas, J. J. (1981). Social science and the press: A case study and its implications. *American Psychologist, 36,* 480–487.

Weinberg, M. (1977). *Minority students: A research appraisal.* Washington, DC: National Institute of Education, Department of Health, Education, and Welfare.

Weinberger, M. G., & Campbell, L. (1990/1991). The use and impact of humor in radio advertising. *Journal of Advertising Research, 30,* 44–52.

Weiner, B. (1990). Searching for the roots of applied attribution theory. In S. Graham & V. S. Folkes (Eds.), *Attribution theory: Applications to achievement, mental health, and interpersonal conflict* (pp. 1–13). Hillsdale, NJ: Erlbaum.

Weiner, J. J., & Wright, F. E. (1973). Effects of undergoing arbitrary discrimination upon subsequent attitudes toward a minority group. *Journal of Applied Social Psychology, 3,* 94–102.

Weingardt, K., Toland, H. K., & Loftus, E. F. (1994). Reports of suggested memories: Do people truly believe them? In D. Ross, J. Read, & M. Toglia (Eds.), *Adult eyewitness testimony: Current trends and developments* (pp. 3–26). New York: Cambridge University Press.

Weinstein, H., & Levin, M. (1997, June 21). $368-billion tobacco accord: Deal with states would restrict marketing. *Los Angeles Times,* pp. A1, A12.

Weinstein, R. S., Madison, S., & Kuklinski, M. (1995). Raising expectations in schooling: Obstacles and opportunities for change. *American Educational Research Journal, 32,* 121–160.

Weinstein, R. S., Soule, C. R., Collins, F., Cone, J., Melhorn, M., & Simantocci, K. (1991). Expectations and high school change: Teacher-researcher collaboration to prevent school failure. *American Journal of Community Psychology, 19,* 333–402.

Weiss, C. H. (1977a). Research for policy's sake: The enlightenment function of social research. *Policy Analysis, 3,* 531–546.

Weiss, C. H. (Ed.). (1977b). *Using social research in public policy making.* Lexington, MA: Lexington.

Weiss, C. H. (1978). Improving the linkage between social research and public policy. In L. E. Lynn, Jr. (Ed.), *Knowledge and policy: The uncertain connection* (Study Project on Social Research and Development, Vol. 5). Washington, DC: National Academy of Sciences.

Weiss, C. H. (Ed.). (1992). *Organizations for policy analysis: Helping government think.* Newbury Park, CA: Sage.

Weiss, D. J., Dawis, R. V., England, G. W., & Lofquist, L. H. (1967). *Manual for the Minnesota Satisfaction Questionnaire* (Minnesota Studies in Vocational Rehabilitation: XXII). Minneapolis: University of Minnesota, Work Adjustment Project.

Weisse, C. S., Nesselhof-Kendall, S. E. A., Fleck-Kandath, C., & Baum, A. (1990). Psychosocial aspects of AIDS prevention among heterosexuals. In J. Edwards, R. S. Tindale, L. Heath, & E. Posavac (1990). *Social influence: Processes and prevention* (pp. 15–38). New York: Plenum.

Weitzman, L. G., Eifler, D., Hokada, E., & Ross, C. (1972). Sex-role socialization in picture books for preschool children. *American Journal of Sociology, 77,* 1125–1149.

Welch, F., & Light, A. (1987). *New evidence on school desegregation.* Washington, DC: U.S. Commission on Civil Rights.

Welch, R. L., Huston-Stein, A., Wright, J. C., & Plehal, R. (1979). Subtle sex-role cues in children's commercials. *Journal of Communication, 29*(3), 202–209.

Wells, G. L. (1993). What do we know about eyewitness identification? *American Psychologist, 48,* 553–571.

Wells, G. L., & Lindsay, R. C. L. (1980). On estimating the diagnosticity of eyewitness nonidentifications. *Psychological Bulletin, 88,* 776–784.

Wells, G. L., & Luus, C. A. E. (1990). Police lineups as experiments: Social methodology as a framework for properly conducted lineups. *Personality and Social Psychology Bulletin, 16,* 106–117.

Wells, W. D. (1973). *Television and aggression: Replication of an experimental field study.* Unpublished manuscript, Graduate School of Business, University of Chicago.

Wells, W. D. (1993). Discovery-oriented consumer research. *Journal of Consumer Research, 19,* 489–505.

Wener, R. E., & Keys, C. (1988). The effects of changes in jail population densities on crowding, sick call, and spatial behavior. *Journal of Applied Social Psychology, 18,* 852–866.

Wentland, E. J., & Smith, K. W. (1993). *Survey responses: An evaluation of their validity.* San Diego, CA: Academic Press.

Werner, P. D., & La Russa, G. W. (1985). Persistence and change in sex-role stereotypes. *Sex Roles, 12,* 1089–1100.

Weyant, J. M. (1984). Applying social psychology to induce charitable donations. *Journal of Applied Social Psychology, 14,* 441–447.

Weyant, J. M. (1994, April). *Application of the door-in-the-face technique in a telephone campaign for charitable donations.* Paper presented at Western Psychological Association meeting, Kona, HI.

Weyant, J. M., & Smith, S. L. (1987). Getting more by asking for less: The effects of request size on donations of charity. *Journal of Applied Social Psychology, 17,* 392–400.

Wheelan, S. A., Pepitone, E. A., & Abt, V. (Eds.). (1990). *Advances in field theory.* Newbury Park, CA: Sage.

Wheeler, C. G. (1993, October). 30 years beyond "I have a dream." *Gallup Poll Monthly,* No. 337, pp. 2–10.

White, J. W. (1983). Sex and gender issues in aggression research. In R. G. Geen & E. I. Donnerstein (Eds.), *Aggression: Theoretical and empirical reviews* (Vol. 2, pp. 1–26). New York: Academic Press.

White, J. W., & Koss, M. P. (1991). Courtship violence: Incidence in a national sample of higher education students. *Violence & Victims, 6,* 247–256.

White, L. (1967). The historical roots of our ecologic crisis. *Science, 155,* 1203–1207.

Whitney, E. (1993). Lynn White, ecotheology, and history. *Environmental Ethics, 15,* 151–169.

Wholey, J. (1994). Assessing the feasibility and likely usefulness of evaluation. In J. Wholey, H. Hatry, & K. Newcomer (Eds.), *Handbook of practical program evaluation* (pp. 15–39). San Francisco: Jossey-Bass.

Wholey, J., Hatry, H., & Newcomer, K. (Ed.) (1994). *Handbook of practical program evaluation.* San Francisco: Jossey-Bass.

Whyte, W. F. (Ed.). (1991). *Participatory action research.* Newbury Park, CA: Sage.

Whyte, W. F., Greenwood, D. J., & Lazes, P. (1991). Participatory action research: Through practice to science in social research. In W. F. Whyte (Ed.), *Participatory action research* (pp. 19–55). Newbury Park, CA: Sage.

Wichman, A. (1994). Occupational differences in involvement with ownership in an airline employee ownership program. *Human Relations, 47,* 829–846.

Wicker, A. W. (1979). *An introduction to ecological psychology.* Monterey, CA: Brooks/Cole.

Wicker, A. W. (1987). Behavior settings reconsidered: Temporal stages, resources, internal dynamics, context. In D. Stokols & I. Altman (Eds.), *Handbook of environmental psychology* (Vol. 1, pp. 613–653). New York: Wiley.

Wiegman, O., Kuttschreuter, M., & Baarda, B. (1992). A longitudinal study of the effects of television viewing on aggressive and prosocial behaviors. *British Journal of Social Psychology, 31,* 147–164.

Wildavsky, A. (1979). *Speaking truth to power: The art and craft of policy analysis.* Boston: Little, Brown.

Wilder, G. Z., & Powell, K. (1989). *Sex differences in test performance: A survey of the literature* (College Board Report No. 89–3). New York: College Entrance Examination Board.

Williams v. Florida, 399 U.S. 78 (1970).

Williams, J. A., Jr., Vernon, J. A., Williams, M. C., & Malecha, K. (1987). Sex role socialization in picture books: An update. *Social Science Quarterly, 68,* 148–156.

Williams, J. E., & Best, D. L. (1990). *Measuring sex stereotypes: A multination study.* Newbury Park, CA: Sage.

Williams, K. D., & Karau, S. J. (1991). Social loafing and social compensation: The effects of expectations of co-worker performance. *Journal of Personality and Social Psychology, 61,* 570–581.

Williams, T. G. (1982). *Consumer behavior: Fundamentals and strategies.* St. Paul, MN: West.

Willie, C. (1989). The intended and unintended benefits of school desegregation. In W. Smith & E. Chunn (Eds.), *Black education: A quest for equity and excellence* (pp. 127–135). New Brunswick, NJ: Transaction.

Willig, A. (1985). A meta-analysis of selected studies on the effectiveness of bilingual education. *Review of Educational Research, 55,* 269–317.

Wilson, B., Linz, D., Donnerstein, E., & Stipp, H. (1992). The impact of social issue television programming on attitudes toward rape. *Human Communication Research, 19,* 179–208.

Wilson, D. W., & Donnerstein, E. (1977). Guilty or not guilty? A look at the "simulated" jury paradigm. *Journal of Applied Social Psychology, 7,* 175–190.

Wilson, J. Q. (1978). Social science and public policy: A personal note. In L. E. Lynn, Jr. (Ed.), *Knowledge and policy: The uncertain connection* (Study Project on Social Research and Development, Vol. 5). Washington, DC: National Academy of Sciences.

Wilson, R., & Crouch, E. (1995). Risk assessment and comparisons: An introduction. In S. Cutter (Ed.), *Environmental risks and hazards* (pp. 236–243). Englewood Cliffs, NJ: Prentice-Hall.

Winett, R. A. (1973). Parameters of deposit contracts in the modification of smoking. *Psychological Record, 23,* 49–60.

Winett, R. A., & Neale, M. S. (1979). Psychological framework for energy conservation in buildings: Strategies, outcomes, directions. *Energy and Buildings, 2,* 101–116.

Winett, R. A., Neale, M. S., & Grier, H. C. (1979). Effects of self-monitoring and feedback on residential electricity consumption. *Journal of Applied Behavior Analysis, 12,* 173–184.

Winslow, R. W., Franzini, L. R., & Hwang, J. (1992). Perceived peer norms, casual sex, and AIDS risk prevention. *Journal of Applied Social Psychology, 22,* 1809–1827.

Winter, D. D. (1996). *Ecological psychology: Healing the split between planet and self.* New York: HarperCollins.

Winterton, J. (1994). Social and technological characteristics of coal-face work: A temporal and spatial analysis. *Human Relations, 47,* 89–118.

Witt, A. L., & Nye, L. G. (1992). Gender and the relationship between perceived fairness of pay or promotion and job satisfaction. *Journal of Applied Psychology, 77,* 910–917.

Wittenbraker, J., Gibbs, B. L., & Kahle, L. R. (1983). Seat belt attitudes, habits, and behaviors: An adaptive amendment to the Fishbein model. *Journal of Applied Social Psychology, 13,* 406–421.

Wittig, M. A. (1996, June). *Taking affirmative action in education and employment.* Presidential address to Society for the Psychological Study of Social Issues, Ann Arbor, MI.

Wittig, M. A., & Bettencourt, B. A. (Eds.). (1996). Social psychological perspectives on grassroots organizing [Special issue]. *Journal of Social Issues, 52*(1), 1–220.

Wittig, M. A., & Lowe, R. H. (1989). Comparable worth theory and policy. *Journal of Social Issues, 45*(4), 1–21.

Wollman, N. (Ed.). (1985). *Working for peace.* San Luis Obispo, CA. Impact.

Women on Words and Images. (1975). *Dick and Jane as victims: Sex stereotyping in children's readers.* Princeton, NJ: Author.

Wood, J., Nezworski, M. T., & Stejskal, W. (1996). The comprehensive system for the Rorschach: A critical examination. *Psychological Science, 7,* 3–10.

Wood, W., Wong, F. Y., & Chachere, J. G. (1991). Effects of media violence on viewers' aggression in unconstrained social interaction. *Psychological Bulletin, 109,* 371–383.

Woodruff, D. (1992, August 17). Saturn. *Business Week,* 52–55.

World almanac and book of facts, 1995. (1994). New York: Funk & Wagnalls.

World Commission on Environment and Development. (1987). *Our common future.* Oxford, England: Oxford University Press.

Wright, B., Bryant, P., & Bullard, R. (1995). Coping with poisons in cancer alley. In R. Bullard (Ed.), *Unequal protection* (pp. 110–129). San Francisco: Sierra Club.

Wright, I., Bengtsson, C., & Frankenberg, K. (1994). Aspects of psychological work environment and health among male and female white-collar and blue-collar workers in a big Swedish industry. *Journal of Organizational Behavior, 15,* 177–183.

Wrightsman, L. S. (1978). The American trial jury on trial: Empirical evidence and procedural modifications. *Journal of Social Issues, 34*(4), 137–164.

Wrightsman, L. S., Kassin, S. M., & Willis, C. (Eds.). (1987). *In the jury box: Controversies in the courtroom.* Newbury Park, CA: Sage.

Wyer, R., & Srull, T. (Eds.). (1994). *Handbook of social cognition* (Vol. 1). Hillsdale, NJ: Erlbaum.

Wyman, R. (Ed.). (1991). *Global climate change and life on earth.* New York: Routledge, Chapman, & Hall.

Yarmey, D. A. (1993). Stereotypes and recognition memory for faces and voices of good guys and bad guys. *Applied Cognitive Psychology, 7,* 419–431.

Yee, A. H., Fairchild, H. H., Weizmann, F., & Wyatt, G. E. (1993). Addressing psychology's problems with race. *American Psychologist, 48,* 1132–1140.

Yep, R. (1992). Advocating in the public arena. In C. Solomon & P. Jackson-Jobe (Eds.), *Helping homeless people: Unique challenges and solutions* (pp. 29–40). Alexandria, VA: American Association for Counseling and Development.

Yuille, J. C., & Tollestrup, P. (1992). A model of the diverse effects of emotion on eyewitness memory. In S. A. Christian (Ed.), *The handbook of emotion and memory* (pp. 201–215). Hillsdale, NJ: Erlbaum.

Yukl, G., & Van Fleet, D. (1992). Theory and research on leadership in organizations. In M. D. Dunnette & L. M. Hough

(Eds.), *Handbook of industrial & organizational psychology* (2nd ed., Vol. 3, pp. 147–197). Palo Alto, CA: Consulting Psychologists Press.

Zaccaro, S. J., Craig, B., & Quinn, J. (1991). Prior absenteeism, supervisory style, job satisfaction, and personal characteristics: An investigation of some mediated and moderated linkages to work absenteeism. *Organizational Behavior and Human Decision Processes, 50,* 24–44.

Zajonc, R. B., Wolosin, R. J., & Wolosin, M. A. (1972). Group risk taking under various group decision schemes. *Journal of Experimental Social Psychology, 8,* 16–30.

Zaller, J. R. (1987). Diffusion of political attitudes. *Journal of Personality and Social Psychology, 53,* 821–833.

Zander, A. (1990). *Effective social action by community groups.* San Francisco: Jossey-Bass.

Zeigler, H., & Huelshoff, M. (1980). Interest groups and public policy. *Policy Studies Journal, 9,* 439–448.

Zeisel, H. (1971). " . . . And then there were none": The diminution of the federal jury. *University of Chicago Law Review, 38,* 710–724.

Zeisel, H., & Diamond, S. S. (1974). "Convincing empirical evidence" on the six-member jury. *University of Chicago Law Review, 41,* 281–295.

Zeisel, H., & Diamond, S. S. (1978). The effect of peremptory challenges on the jury and verdict. *Stanford Law Review, 30,* 491–531.

Zerega, A. M. (1981). Transportation energy conservation policy: Implications for social science research. *Journal of Social Issues, 37*(2), 31–50.

Zhu, H. J., Milavsky, R., & Biswas, R. (1994). Do televised debates affect image perception more than issue knowledge? A study of the first 1992 presidential debate. *Human Communication Research, 20,* 302–333.

Zigler, E., & Muenchow, S. (1984). How to influence social policy affecting children and families. *American Psychologist, 39,* 415–420.

Zigler, E., & Muenchow, S. (1992). *Head Start: The inside story of America's most successful educational experiment.* New York: Basic Books.

Zigler, E., & Styfco, S. (Eds.). (1993). *Head Start and beyond: A national plan for extended childhood intervention.* New Haven, CT: Yale University Press.

Zigler, E., & Styfco, S. (1994). Head Start: Criticisms in a constructive context. *American Psychologist, 49,* 127–132.

Zigler, E., Styfco, S., & Gilman, E. (1993). The national Head Start program for disadvantaged preschoolers. In E. Zigler & S. Styfco (Eds.), *Head Start and beyond: A national plan for extended childhood intervention* (pp. 1–42). New Haven, CT: Yale University Press.

Zillmann, D. (1992). Pornography research, social advocacy, and public policy. In P. Suedfeld & P. Tetlock (Eds.), *Psychology and social policy* (pp. 165–189). New York: Hemisphere.

Zillmann, D., & Bryant, J. (1982). Pornography, sexual callousness, and the trivialization of rape. *Journal of Communication, 32,* 10–21.

Zillmann, D., & Bryant, J. (1984). Effects of massive exposure to pornography. In N. M. Malamuth & E. Donnerstein (Eds.), *Pornography and sexual aggression* (pp. 115–141). Orlando, FL: Academic Press.

Zillmann, D., & Bryant, J. (1988). Pornography's impact on sexual satisfaction. *Journal of Applied Social Psychology, 18,* 438–453.

Zimbardo, P. G. (1977). *Shyness.* Reading, MA: Addison-Wesley.

Zimmerman, M. A. (in press). Empowerment theory: Psychological, organizational, and community levels of analysis. In J. Rappaport & E. Seidman (Eds.), *Handbook of community psychology.* New York: Plenum.

Zimmerman, M. A., & Rappaport, J. (1988). Citizen participation, perceived control, and psychological empowerment. *Journal of Applied Social Psychology, 16,* 725–750.

Zube, E. H. (1991). Environmental assessment, cognition, and action: Research applications. In T. Garling & G. Evans (Eds.), *Environment, cognition, and action: An integrated approach* (pp. 96–108). New York: Oxford University Press.

Zuckerman, M. (1990). Some dubious premises in research and theory on racial differences. *American Psychologist, 45,* 1297–1303.

Zuckerman, M., Lazzaro, M. M., & Waldgeir, D. (1979). Undermining effects of the foot-in-the-door technique with extrinsic rewards. *Journal of Applied Social Psychology, 9,* 292–296.

Zuravin, S. J. (1986). Residential density and urban child maltreatment: An aggregate analysis. *Journal of Family Violence, 1,* 307–322.

Zuwerink, J. R., Devine, P. G., Monteith, M. J., & Cook, D. A. (1996). Prejudice toward Blacks: With and without compunction? *Basic and Applied Social Psychology, 18,* 131–150.

Name Index

Subject Index